A HISTORY
OF
THE CONCERTO

A HISTORY
OF
THE CONCERTO

Michael Thomas Roeder

AMADEUS PRESS
Reinhard G. Pauly, General Editor
Portland, Oregon

Copyright © 1994 by Amadeus Press
(an imprint of Timber Press, Inc.)
All rights reserved.
ISBN 0-931340-61-6
Printed in Hong Kong

AMADEUS PRESS
The Haseltine Building
133 S.W. Second Avenue, Suite 450
Portland, Oregon 97204-3527, U.S.A.

Library of Congress Cataloging-in-Publication Data

Roeder, Michael Thomas
    A history of the concerto / Michael Thomas Roeder.
        p.   cm.
    Includes bibliographical references and indexes.
    ISBN 0-931340-61-6
    1. Concerto. I. Title.
ML1263.R64   1994
784.2'3'09--dc20   92-41967
                                                                CIP
                                                                MN

CONTENTS

Part II THE CLASSICAL CONCERTO

LIST OF FIGURES

LIST OF ILLUSTRATIONS

To my mother

ACKNOWLEDGMENTS

I owe my deep gratitude to a number of people and to an institution for helping to make this book a reality.

I thank the University of Alberta for its support in this long-term project. Much of the time needed to write this book was made possible by a McCalla Research Professorship in 1982–83 and a study leave in 1989–90. The university also provided travel grants to work at the music libraries at the University of California at Berkeley and Santa Barbara. I also worked at home in our own university library and I thank our music librarian, James Whittle, for his expert help, which he so willingly provided. His assistant, Cedric Abday, also deserves my gratitude for his persistence in pursuing troublesome sources. I also thank my good friend, Robert Stangeland, for his many years of support while he served as chairman of our Department of Music.

Some have participated more directly in this project and to them I give my very special thanks. Several graduate students have assisted me over the years, helping in a variety of ways. Three, in particular, deserve special mention for their greater involvement: Jill Sanderson, Susan Bradley, and Michelle Bozynski.

I express my fondest thank you to my dear friend and colleague, Gerhard Krapf, who read the entire manuscript and offered numerous suggestions for improvements.

To the staff at Amadeus Press I offer my gratitude. Reinhard G. Pauly, general editor, provided stimulating comments and gently worded suggestions for changes in the manuscript, for which I am deeply indebted. Richard Abel proved a critical reader who helped to sharpen my use of the language. Eve Goodman offered expert editorial help and sound advice for the final polishing of the manuscript. All are to be thanked for their painstaking and sensitive approach.

I thank my students for their eagerness and stimulating interest in music and in my project.

And finally I thank the members of my family. My wonderful wife, Antoinette, has always provided encouragement and loving support. My daughter, Sasha, and son, Nick, have tolerated an often-preoccupied father all the while continuing to express their love in meaningful ways.

Without the help and support of those named and many other caring friends and family this book would never have seen the light of day.

Michael Thomas Roeder
Edmonton, Alberta, Canada

INTRODUCTION

The term *concerto* conjures up an image of a virtuoso instrumental soloist displaying magnificent technical and musical skills to the accompaniment of an orchestra. This is certainly an apt characterization of most concertos heard on today's orchestral programs. A typical example is the deservedly popular Concerto in A Minor for Piano and Orchestra by Robert Schumann. This image, however, does not suit all concertos. If we were to hear a concerto from Corelli's Op. 6 collection, we would rarely hear soloistic display, but would be captivated by the constant alternation in the amount and quality of sound. When listening to one of Mozart's piano concertos, we are not only excited by the scintillating piano parts, but find we are fascinated by the equally important role of the orchestra, which is playing much more than mere accompaniment.

Composers, throughout the more than 300-year history of the concerto, have attached the term to a rich variety of works. What underlying compositional principle is common to such diverse pieces as Vivaldi's *The Four Seasons*, Bach's Brandenburg Concertos, Beethoven's "Emperor" Concerto, Liszt's E-flat Major Piano Concerto, Berg's Violin Concerto, Bartók's Concerto for Orchestra, and Carter's Double Concerto for Harpsichord and Piano with Two Chamber Orchestras? What is a concerto?

It is obvious the concerto meant something different to each of these composers, but there are common and persistent characteristics. The most important is the contrast of sound achieved by dividing the performance group into two parts, normally the orchestra and soloist or group of soloists. This contrast typically involves a difference in the size of the two groups, and sometimes a difference in the type of sound or tone color, as in the case of a solo piano versus an orchestra. The contrast is often enhanced by the soloist's impressive and sometimes dazzling display silhouetted against the typically more conservative orchestral writing.

The relationship between the two groups is variable and has undergone fundamental changes throughout the history of the form. From its very origins in the sixteenth and seventeenth centuries, the concerto idea depended upon a split personality, for it conveyed at once the different meanings of contention and cooperation, both of which are found in the dualistic etymological roots of the word *concerto*. The Italian *concertare* means to join together or to agree, while the related Latin *concertare* means to fight or contend. This duality of cooperation and contention lies at the heart of the concerto principle. The great challenge faced by concerto composers through the centuries has been directly related to this dual nature, and the history of the concerto is very much the story, not only of the tension between contention and cooperation, but also of their changing relationship.

Our journey, then, takes us through a dynamic, evolving terrain where we will stop to explore major, well-known landmarks as well as lesser-known monuments and the works of lesser-known composers whose contributions were important to the changing character of the concerto. The book is comprehensive in its treatment of the concerto from its beginnings up to the present day, but it is not an exhaustive history with comments on all concertos ever written. The focus is on those works and composers whose contributions are of greater significance and interest in the overall story.

There are many pinnacles in the terrain that provide "mountain-top" experiences, and these will receive greater attention. For example, in Part I of this book, we will find among Vivaldi's tremendous output of concertos outstanding works that serve to define the new form in its earliest standardized state. These works illustrate the cumulative effects of a century of Italian composers' experimentation with the concerto principle. At the same time, this culmination led to new growth and the concerto fanned out across Europe. J. S. Bach's discovery of Vivaldi's concertos led to a complete transformation of the German composer's style, and yet he transformed the concerto by bringing to it elements more characteristic of his northern German background. The contrasts between the concertos of these two Baroque giants, Vivaldi and Bach, reveal the dynamic nature of the concerto form and its inherent malleability to suit differing needs in different places or in different times. To clearly reflect this diversity, the book has four large parts corresponding to the major historical-stylistic periods of Western music—Baroque, Classical, Romantic, and Twentieth Century—through which the concerto has evolved. Subdivisions often highlight geographical areas, reflecting strikingly different approaches to the concerto from one region to another.

The book may be read from cover to cover, but readers may also use the index to focus on specific concertos and their composers. Numerous musical examples illuminate important points in particular concertos. While some readers may want to study the more detailed analyses with scores in hand, this is not essential for an understanding of the text. Much of the repertory treated here is available on commercial recordings, making it easy for readers to experience the sound of this music. Important technical terms are defined as they occur in the text and appear in the index for easy access.

I hope this book will open the fascinating history of the concerto to readers of widely varying musical backgrounds. I invite the enthusiastic amateur and the inquisitive lover of music, as well as the serious student, the professional musician, and the musical scholar to join me on an exploratory journey that traverses several continents and spans more than three centuries.

Part I

THE BAROQUE CONCERTO

Chapter One

THE CONCERTO PRINCIPLE

One of the most striking and distinctive, but by no means exclusive, features of Baroque music is the principle of strong contrast and opposition of sonorities, often achieved through division of the performance medium into two or more groups. This principle, known as the *stile concertato,* originated in the late sixteenth century and took on greater significance throughout the seventeenth century, culminating in the development of a new instrumental form—the concerto—that capitalized specifically on this important Baroque principle of composition.

The desired contrast was usually achieved by pitting one body of musical sound against another. This simple effect could take on several guises: voice(s) against instrument(s); one group, perhaps brass, against another, perhaps strings; or a soloist or group of soloists against the larger ensemble. The goal was to achieve contrast in sonority, and the principal method of highlighting this contrast was a simple one involving the alternation of the sonority groups.

The use of musical forces in alternation has a very long history, but a group of late sixteenth- and early seventeenth-century Venetian composers in particular created some very dramatic works in which the antiphonal treatment, or the alternation of two or more performing forces, is the central compositional element. In fact, a formal architectural design encouraged the development of the concertato style in Venice, a leading musical center in sixteenth-century Europe. Here musical life centered around the Cathedral of St. Mark. The cathedral's spacious design, with a floor plan in the shape of a Greek cross with arms of equal length, permitted the placement of two organs on facing balconies and the arrangement of musicians in clearly differentiated locations. Accordingly, the Venetian composers began to place central importance on the elements of space and contrast, developing a new music in which contrast became the main form-building element.

These composers created polychoral music to be performed by two, three, or more vocal or instrumental choirs, separated in the space of the cathedral. Contrast could be intensified by giving each choir a unique sonority, through specific instrumental and vocal combinations. Antiphonal effects involving the alternation of the choirs were common, while the occasional combination of the choirs for massed effects further heightened the element of contrast. Composers focused on broad, bold effects, not nuances. The complexities of counterpoint were ill-suited to such music; a simple chordal texture allowed for greater exploitation of the spatial effects available from alternating or combining the performing forces.

The Fleming Adrian Willaert (c. 1490–1562) is considered the founder of the

Venetian school. Willaert was born in Flanders, moved to Rome in 1516, and was appointed *maestro di cappella* in St. Mark's Cathedral in 1527, where he remained until his death. Willaert exerted tremendous influence on composers of the later sixteenth century, particularly as a teacher. Although Willaert did not invent the *coro spezzato* (literally, broken choir) technique, he exploited it. His famous *Salmi spezzati* (publ. 1550) are double-choir settings of Psalms. Psalms, with their common construction of verses in which the second half of each is a paraphrase of the first, provided a natural text for many early double-choir compositions.

Willaert's pupil, Andrea Gabrieli (c. 1515–1586), a native of Venice, introduced the element of concertato to the polychoral construction and moved beyond the mere juxtaposition of essentially similar choirs. He enhanced the element of contrast through the use of various combinations of voices and instruments. While specific instruments are not indicated in the scores, the title pages of several works mention the use of instruments. Many instrumentalists were available at St. Mark's, and composers were encouraged to exploit to the utmost the sonorous possibilities of such performers.

The Venetian school of polychoral composition culminated in the work of Giovanni Gabrieli (c. 1557–1612), nephew and pupil of Andrea Gabrieli. The younger Gabrieli wrote music primarily for specific festive occasions in the church calendar, and it is here that the terms *concerto* and *symphony* first appeared as titles. Some of G. Gabrieli's most significant works are motet settings of parts of the liturgy used on Christmas and Easter. Some three dozen of these motets survive, the principal ones contained in three published collections: the *Concerti* (publ. 1587), the *Sacrae Symphoniae* Part I (publ. 1597), and the *Sacrae Symphoniae* Part II (publ. posthumously in 1615). However, the new musical terms, such as *concerto* and *symphony*, which appear in these collection titles, were often applied to music of diverse content and form before a more specific meaning came to be attached to them. It was to be another century before the term *concerto* was associated with a specific type of instrumental composition. Here, Gabrieli is calling attention to the new concertante style. Similarly, the term *symphonia* was probably used to point out the use of instruments, as opposed to purely vocal sacred works.

The texts most often set were the rejoicing Psalms used at Vespers, for which Gabrieli could call on a skilled choir and a variety of instrumentalists (mostly wind players), plus two organists and occasionally a third on a portable instrument. Even in his earlier works, such as "O Magnum Mysterium" from the *Concerti* of 1587, Gabrieli already displayed a complete mastery of the effects possible with a many-voiced choir. Later works trace the perfection of his polychoral style and seem amazingly modern.

His earliest published motets are described as "for singing and playing," although no specific instruments are indicated. Even though some works make no mention of instruments and all parts are supplied with words, it appears purely vocal performances were not typically presented. Gabrieli intensified the dramatic contrast between choirs, as compared with earlier polychoral music, in part by using instruments to establish and define the different sonorities. In his later works specific directions appear for the combinations of voices and instruments to be used, although not consistently.

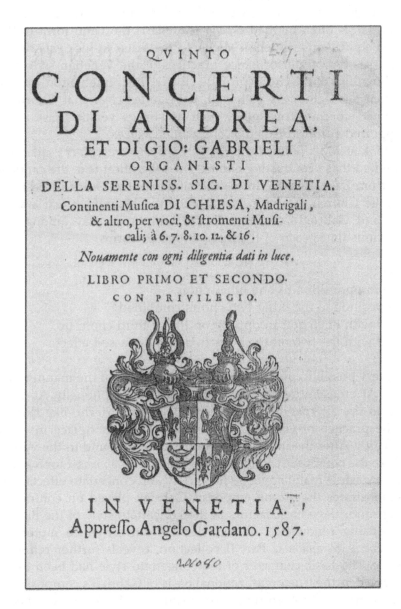

QVINTO

CONCERTI
DI ANDREA,

ET DI GIO: GABRIELI
ORGANISTI
DELLA SERENISS. SIG. DI VENETIA.

Continenti Mufica DI CHIESA, Madrigali,
& altro, per voci, & ftromenti Mufi-
cali; à 6. 7. 8. 10. 12. & 16.

Nouamente con ogni diligentia dati in luce.

LIBRO PRIMO ET SECONDO.
CON PRIVILEGIO.

IN VENETIA.
Appreffo Angelo Gardano. 1587.

The title page of the 1587 publication of *Concerti* by Andrea and Giovanni Gabrieli. This is a very early application of the term *concerto* to a type of composition. Venetian composers of the late sixteenth and early seventeenth centuries had developed an approach to composition that heavily relied upon the new *stile concertato,* in which various parts of the performing ensemble were pitted against one another to create striking contrasts. This practice eventually led to the independent instrumental concerto. (By permission of the British Library.)

Many of Gabrieli's motets and Magnificats were written for three groups, each with a distinct sonority. The first is typically a *coro grave* for four low voices, the second is a high *coro superiore*, while the third, in the standard soprano-alto-tenor-bass format, is often marked *capella* (capella is the Latin form of the more familiar Italian equivalent, cappella). Michael Praetorius, in his *Syntagma Musicum* of 1619, discusses typical performance practices of the Venetian style and notes that clef combinations of the choirs provide clues to instrumentation when it is not specified. When such clues are followed, it becomes clear that Gabrieli had in mind quite vivid contrasts of sound, such as strings versus brass and instrumentally supported voices versus unaccompanied voices.

A brief look at a Magnificat from the *Sacrae Symphoniae* Part I[1] illustrates how Gabrieli exploited these contrasting choirs. The Magnificat text, the canticle of the Virgin Mary from Luke 1:46–55, forms the climax of the Office of Vespers in the Roman Catholic Church. As with Psalm texts, the Magnificat text was chanted antiphonally, and Gabrieli's setting calls for antiphonal play among the three groups. At various times each of the three choirs performs:

- alone,
- alone in opposition to one other choir,
- in opposition to the other two choirs combined,
- united with one choir in opposition to the third choir, or
- united with the two other choirs in a grand massed effect.

Not only is every possible combination of groups used, but the manner of opposition is varied. At times entire phrases are performed antiphonally. At other times there is a rapid-fire alternation of short chordal ideas in echo-like fashion—this was a favorite practice of Gabrieli and it became commonplace in the mature Baroque concerto. After the intense antiphonal singing found in the verses of the Magnificat text, the composer combines the three choirs *en masse* for a grand finale in the Doxology, while maintaining some variety and concertato effects. This composition demonstrates the strong emphasis Gabrieli placed on contrast and the opposition of sonorities—basic factors in the concertato style of the Baroque.

The justifiably renowned "In ecclesiis," a fourteen-voice motet from the posthumous *Sacrae Symphoniae* Part II collection, reveals further refinements in Gabrieli's style. The basic character of the concertato style had been established, and it now served as the true organizational basis of Gabrieli's compositional technique. In this work, the by-then traditional features of Venetian polychoral music are utilized: the text is one of rejoicing, and the musical forces are divided into three vocal and instrumental choirs. The disposition of the choirs is markedly altered from that in the Magnificat just discussed. One choir, marked *capella*, has the usual soprano-alto-tenor-bass make-up and sings in a chordal style. But the second choir, specifically marked *voce*, sings significantly more virtuosic material accompanied by organ. The nature of the vocal writing in this choir seems to call for the use of solo voices. The third choir is exclusively instrumental, with an ensemble of three cornetti, a viola, and two trombones in the score. The instrumental choir supports the vocal forces at times or is at times independent, as in the sinfonia, providing contrast with the vocal choirs. The other new feature not found in the earlier Magnificat is the use of basso continuo,[2] played on the organ.

The different textures and sonorities which are achieved by the juxtapositions of these forces include:

Solo soprano supported by organ
Solo tenor supported by organ
Solo soprano with capella
Solo tenor with capella
Solo soprano and tenor with capella
The instrumental group alone
Solo alto and solo tenor with instrumental group
Solo alto and solo tenor with instrumental group and capella
Soprano and tenor duet
Instrumental group with capella and solo quartet

"In ecclesiis" also contains instances of the striking use of dissonance and chromaticism that came to characterize Gabrieli's later works, usually used in pursuit of word-painting or the musical depiction of certain words.

The heightened level of contrast in works such as "In ecclesiis" results in a highly sectional form, similar to the contemporary instrumental canzona, discussed below. Talented composers compensated for the resultant feeling of disorganization by creating a rondo-like structure; this relied on frequent refrains, such as the Alleluia refrain of "In ecclesiis," to impose a sense of unity. The piece is a remarkably sumptuous work, overwhelming in its opulence and display of colorful sonority.

Gabrieli's polychoral music represents the peak of an extended development, even though the application of the concertato principle and of the term *concerto* to sacred music was continued by German composers, especially G. Gabrieli's greatest disciple, Heinrich Schütz (1585–1672). However, in the domain of instrumental music, Gabrieli's contribution amounts to the genuine beginnings of a radically new direction.

Gabrieli's purely instrumental compositions, excluding those for organ, consist of eight called sonata and thirty-six called canzona. For Gabrieli the terms were practically interchangeable. The canzona or canzona da sonare (songs to be sounded) derived from instrumental transcriptions of songs, which had their prototype in the French chanson. The form is characteristically sectional with the repetition of some sections providing unity in the new abstract form. Some composers, such as Gabrieli, already dropped the canzona designation, using the term *sonata* to indicate the new instrumental form. Throughout the Baroque era, the sections grew and gained sufficient substance to split apart into separate movements, giving rise to the multimovement sonata of Corelli and later Baroque composers. The bulk of Gabrieli's abstract instrumental works are contained in two collections: two sonatas and fourteen canzonas in the *Sacrae Symphoniae* I (1597) while five sonatas and fifteen canzonas make up all of *Canzoni e Sonate* (publ. 1615). These works were probably designed for performance in St. Mark's Cathedral and share the same brilliance and splendor of the motets composed for the same space. As in the motets, the instruments are divided into choirs, and antiphonal exchanges among the choirs are the favored means of contrast. Some of the compositions from the 1615 collection exemplify a highly elaborate polychoral style. Sonata 19 is scored for fifteen instruments divided into four choirs while Sonata 20 requires twenty-two instrumentalists divided into five choirs.

These attractive and intriguing works stand at the very beginning of the history of the instrumental concerto. They are the essence of a sustained application of the concerto idea—contrast by way of cooperation and opposition of various groups of the performing forces.

In concluding this brief summary of Gabrieli's quite momentous accomplishments, we should note that his works display stylistic features which, although modified, are all strongly associated with the concerto proper of a century later. These elements are directly founded upon the concertato principle. Gabrieli's distinct fondness for homophonic texture creates the opportunity for a strong unity of sonority within a phrase, thereby offering the option of introducing contrast between one phrase and the next. Furthermore, the phrases are short, limiting the possibilities of imitative development. From an harmonic perspective, Gabrieli's works exhibit a noticeable tendency to rely on primary triads and cadential formulas, and on a rather regular harmonic rhythm which helps to build tension as climax points are reached. All these features are common to the late Baroque concerto and complement the ever-increasing fascination with the virtuoso solo performer. We have seen that the strong concentration on contrast resulted in a highly sectional, almost disarticulated, form in the Venetians' works. Gabrieli introduced a refrain-like structure to help create a sense of unity within the varied musical passages. The resultant structure foreshadows the later use by concerto composers of ritornello form, in which orchestral statements of recurring thematic material alternate with episodes devoted to soloistic display.

THE BAROQUE CONCERTO:
SYNTHESIS OF FUNDAMENTAL BAROQUE PRACTICES

From the initial steps taken by Gabrieli in his exploitation of the concertato principle, the instrumental concerto evolved to become the most important form of Baroque orchestral music. Before exploring the historical development of the concerto, we should consider how this form fully incorporated other fundamental Baroque practices in addition to the concertato principle. A second basic element of Baroque music is the use of the basso continuo. This new form of accompaniment permitted an increased independence of treble and bass, of solo and accompaniment, and possibly grew from an increased interest in polarity of treble and bass that came to characterize much Baroque music. This polarity is accentuated in the instrumental concerto where the solo instruments are typically in the treble range. The fundamental texture, with a firm, slower-moving bass and more florid treble, is synthesized as a basic ingredient in the concerto.

The basso continuo also reflected the new harmonic orientation of Baroque composers. Seventeenth-century composers experimented with a new major-minor tonal system that was widely adopted and extended, gradually displacing the older modal system. Tonality lent continuity, which in part modified the sectional quality of earlier instrumental works. Subsequently more modern works could be conceived on a larger scale with clearly defined movements united by means of tonality. Themes and chord progressions were designed to clarify keys, while the technique of sequence permitted the ready expansion of the musical material. The concerto provided a natural environment for the enlivening of sequences through the use of solo figuration, as we will see in numerous examples. Composers of concertos may have been the first to exploit the dramatic opposition of tonalities that became so important in the late eighteenth century. In short, the concerto composers quickly adopted the new Baroque tonal principle and depended heavily upon it as an element of formal design.

In addition to providing the grounds for the synthesis of these important Baroque musical practices, the concerto represents the climax of instrumental music in the Baroque era. As instrumental music gained in importance, performers not only perfected performance techniques but also made increasing demands on instrument makers for better, more responsive instruments. Composers became enthralled with the qualities and capabilities of instruments and so made increasing demands on performers. This cyclical relationship of performer–composer–instrument maker led to greater levels of competence in all of these related undertakings. Of all orchestral instruments of the late seventeenth century, the violin was the most important, and it and its bow underwent the most remarkable changes. The upsurgence of the new instrumental forms of the sonata and concerto and the development of the violin were directly related.

These numerous factors and musical characteristics converged in northern Italy where elaborate church services and the penchant for festivals created an environment conducive to the intense development of the brilliant new concerto form. By the eighteenth century the term *concerto* denoted an instrumental work of one of three types: the solo concerto for one soloist and orchestra, the concerto grosso for two or more soloists and orchestra, and the ripieno or orchestral concerto for undivided orchestra. The solo concerto quickly became the favored type, but the concerto grosso represented the earliest essays in the new form.

Chapter Two

THE EARLY CONCERTO GROSSO

ALESSANDRO STRADELLA

During the last third of the seventeenth century, Roman composers experimented with a type of instrumentation that became characteristic of the concerto grosso. Many vocal works composed in Rome in the 1660s and 1670s employed accompaniments composed for two groups of instruments opposed in a concertato style. A small group of solo instruments, commonly consisting of two violins and basso continuo (a texture developed in the contemporary trio sonata), was called the concertino (little ensemble), while the larger orchestral ensemble, usually composed in four parts, was called the concerto grosso (large ensemble). Later composers might also refer to the larger group as the ripieno (full) orchestra, because the parts were usually played by more than one player. Through most of the first century of the concerto's history, the term *tutti* (all) designated performance by the combined solo and orchestral groups.[1] Evidence for the use of concerto grosso instrumentation in the late 1660s exists, but the earliest surviving musical examples date from the 1670s.

Alessandro Stradella (c. 1643–1682), the composer of these examples, was one of the most significant composers of opera and oratorio of his generation in Italy. He was born in Rome and worked mainly there until 1677, later making shorter stays in Modena, Naples, Venice, Turin, and Genoa. It is possible he relocated so frequently in an effort to flee assassins, who eventually did murder him in the employ of a jealous Venetian whose mistress the composer had carried off.

About a dozen of Stradella's works composed in Rome in the 1670s use concerto grosso instrumentation. The serenata *Qual Prodigio é ch'io Miri* of about 1675 requires a concertino and concerto grosso, designated respectively in the opening sinfonia as *primo crocchio* (first group) and *secondo crocchio* (second group), the latter with parts doubled. In this serenata Stradella experimented with the dramatic possibilities of the new technique of instrumentation. In the solo arias the concerto grosso scoring heightens the contrast between vocal and instrumental sections. The concerto grosso plays during rests or short breathing places in the vocal parts, while the concertino provides a more delicate accompaniment for the voice. When the voice is a higher-pitched soprano or alto, the concertino material is kept comparatively simple so that the violins will not interfere with the vocal soloist. When the vocal soloist is a bass, however, the violins do not conflict with the voice part so are frequently given more difficult, virtuosic parts that are truly soloistic in nature. For example, in the bass aria "Basilisco allor" the concertino violin parts are clearly soloistic and very different from those of the concerto grosso.

Stradella also experimented with the technique of associating a particular concertino with a particular character, creating a sense of character delineation through instrumentation. For example, the character Dama in this same serenata is given a unique concertino which is the only accompaniment to her aria "Amor, amor sempre." In the following sinfonia and aria "Mio petto inerme," this concertino is juxtaposed against a larger group of instruments consisting of the earlier-mentioned first and second groups combined, which Stradella calls the *concerto de primo e secondo crocchio.*

The concerto grosso instrumentation technique may have developed to solve the problems of balance in Roman vocal compositions, as composers tried to find ways lightly to accompany the solo voice parts without forfeiting the use of a larger orchestra. Stradella successfully exploited the technique, enhancing the dramatic content of his vocal works. The sinfonias or overtures found at the beginnings of many of these works also made use of the concerto grosso instrumentation, leaving but a simple step to divorce the technique from dramatic vocal works and to use it in the independent instrumental sinfonia not associated with a vocal work. Three such works by Stradella survive.[2] One of these is possibly the first work to announce the concerto principle in its title: *Sinfonia a violini e bassi a concertino e concerto grosso distinti.* Another copy of this sinfonia carries the following title: *Sonata di viole cioè concerto grosso di viole concertino de due violini e leuto.* These incipient concertos were probably composed by Stradella in the 1670s and are the immediate forerunners to Corelli's Op. 6 set.[3]

ARCANGELO CORELLI

Arcangelo Corelli (1653–1713) was born in Fusignano near the important musical center of Bologna. We have conflicting reports as to when and with whom "Il Bolognese" first studied music, but it is certain that he resided from 1666 to 1670 in Bologna, where he studied with master violinists. He gained acceptance into the Accademia Filarmonica at the age of seventeen. Several sources cite visits to France and Germany that cannot be confirmed, but the composer clearly took up residence in Rome by 1675, when he played violin in the first performance of Stradella's *San Giovanni Battista,* an oratorio with the new mode of scoring for divided orchestra.

Corelli's principal appointment as first violinist and director of music to the newly appointed Cardinal Ottoboni came in 1689. Ottoboni, a great lover of music and a patron of Alessandro Scarlatti, regularly presented concerts in his magnificent palace. Corelli and Ottoboni became close friends so that the composer enjoyed a great sense of security. Corelli's fame spread as publication of his music brought it before a very large public. He was well regarded by musicians and was considered one of the greatest composers of his time. In recognition of his superb talent, he was admitted to the exclusive Accademia dei Arcadi in 1706.

Italians have traditionally shown a natural flair for vocal music, which may, in part, be explained by the fluidity, crispness, and magnificent sonority of the Italian language. In the late seventeenth and early eighteenth centuries the art of vocal composition and performance in the bel canto style reached a peak. Although Corelli did not contribute to the vocal music of his time, he did translate the expressive lyric qualities of the voice to the violin. Corelli emphasized graceful and smoothly flowing lines, demanding only modest technical skills of the instrumentalists. Fast runs, difficult double stops, or other elements of flashy violin writing were avoided. The more challenging upper range was also avoided, as he observed the common upper limit of the third position, while the instrument's lowest notes were only rarely used. In spite of these technical limitations and the obvious transfer of vocal qualities to the instrumental medium, Corelli's violin music is very idiomatic and coincides in time with the high point in the art of violin making in northern Italy, where he spent his formative years.

When a composer of Corelli's genius realizes his full capability at the time of a great many significant musical developments—in Corelli's case, the full understanding and exploitation of the concertato style, the emerging independence and importance of instrumental music, the pinnacle of violin making, the peaking of the bel canto style, and the maturation of the tonal system—his music is bound to summarize and define an epoch in the history of music. This is not to imply that Corelli's music is the greatest of its time; other composers, such as Giuseppe Torelli (1658–1709), also realized their mature potential at this point. Corelli's music does, however, reveal what William S. Newman, the sonata historian, calls a "remarkable sense of balance in the concentration and direction of his musical forces."[4] No element of a Corelli composition is treated flamboyantly; all are handled with moderation and create a marvelously cohesive entity. The compositional styles and techniques of the first century of Baroque music were successfully united and synthesized by Corelli in works that were, and still are, viewed as outstanding examples of the period.

Few Baroque composers were able to focus their attention so single-mindedly on one type of composition as could Corelli, and few could spend so much time in the meticulous polishing of their compositions. Indeed, few seventeenth- and eighteenth-century composers were so fortunate as to hold positions similar to Corelli's, which permitted him to concentrate his creative powers so extensively in one compositional field. Corelli's attention to every musical detail may be the reason for his small published output, but these works were of great significance. They were reprinted several times, indicating their popularity and importance during the period. They were issued in six sets:

Opus 1 Twelve Trio Sonatas (*Sonate da chiesa* or Church Sonatas, publ. 1681)

Opus 2 Eleven Trio Sonatas (*da camera* or Chamber Sonatas) and one chaconne (publ. 1685)

Opus 3 Twelve Trio Sonatas (*da chiesa*, publ. 1689)

Opus 4 Twelve Trio Sonatas (*da camera*, publ. 1695)

Opus 5   Twelve Solo Sonatas (six *da chiesa,* five *da camera,* and one set of
         variations on *Follia,* publ. 1700)
Opus 6   Twelve Concerti Grossi (publ. 1714)

Corelli's trio sonatas Opp. 1–4 are a monumental achievement in the history of Italian chamber music, for they consolidate, clarify, and, in a way, codify the musical achievements of the previous century. The solo sonatas and concerti grossi of Opp. 5 and 6 not only define past achievements but in a significant way serve as the springboard for new departures.

Corelli's Op. 6 set of concertos was published posthumously in 1714, despite evidence Corelli composed at least some of them as early as 1682 when the German composer Georg Muffat (1645–1704) reported having heard Corelli concertos in Rome. It is, of course, not possible to determine if the concertos of Op. 6 were those performed in 1682, but their many stylistically conservative features suggest an early date of composition. The Op. 6 works are probably among the earliest concerti grossi composed.

Corelli's concerti grossi grew out of his application of the concertato principle to the trio sonata, a genre he helped to perfect. The forms and textures of the concerti grossi were derived from the trio sonata. As in the Stradella examples discussed earlier, the concertino is played by two violins and basso continuo, providing a texture similar to that of the trio sonata, while the string orchestra or concerto grosso is divided into four parts consisting of first and second violins, violas, and basses. When the orchestra plays it usually doubles or reinforces the concertino, thereby producing a *chiaroscuro,* or shading, effect similar to the loud and soft alternation already present in the sonatas. As noted by Corelli on the title page, the orchestra is optional. Muffat, who left a detailed account of Corelli's concerto practices in his own set of concertos published as *Ausserlesene Instrumentalmusik* in 1701, recounted that Corelli's concertos could be played as trio sonatas by the concertino alone or with the optional addition of the orchestra. The bass parts for both groups are figured, suggesting the use of two keyboard instruments, if an orchestra is used, and the spatial separation of the groups.

When Corelli's concertos are performed with an orchestra, two levels of contrast are evident. The first is obviously that between the concertino and the orchestra. The second is found within the concertino, as in some chamber concertos when the first solo violin dominates, hinting at the future solo concerto.

When the concertino performs alone, parts are marked *solo;* when the concertino and ripieno sound together the score is marked *tutti* (all) at which point the violins of both groups and often the basses of both groups play identical material. Aside from the obvious contrast in dynamics and sonority thus created, the tutti sections often serve to underline cadences. There is normally no significant thematic difference between solo and tutti sections; most frequently the ensembles simply echo one another. In general, the contrasted sections are of very short duration. Although the orchestra often duplicates what the concertino is playing, this is not always the case. The concertino sometimes may be featured in a soloistic role to the accompaniment of the orchestra, as in the second Largo of Concerto No. 1.

Virtuosic, figurative displays, though limited, appear in the concertino.

Examples may be found in the following movements: the first Allegro, Concerto No. 5; first Allegro, Concerto No. 3; and final Allegro in Concerto No. 1, No. 3, and No. 8. These movements are all strongly dance oriented, while the more contrapuntal movements do not easily accommodate soloistic display. In spite of these examples, Corelli generally wrote little for virtuosic, soloistic display, but depended upon the simple contrasts of loud and soft or large and small ensembles.

Corelli largely standardized two formal trio sonata structures which served as the basis for his concerti grossi. They are the *sonata da chiesa,* church sonata, and *sonata da camera,* chamber sonata, which can be distinguished from one another, although features often cross from one type to the other. Typically, the church sonata is more polyphonic in texture and weightier in mood than the chamber sonata, which usually contains movements derived from dance patterns. In both forms the more complex movements tend to be near the beginning, while the simpler, lighter movements are placed at the end. The scoring of both types of trio sonatas is identical; two violins and basso continuo, but the continuo instruments were different. Most likely the figured bass was realized on an organ in the church sonatas, while on harpsichord in the chamber sonatas.

The concerti grossi of Op. 6 are divided into two groups. The first eight can be considered church concertos, although some diversity of movement schemes suggests the earlier canzona. Nevertheless, their overall scheme is similar to that of the church sonatas. The last four concertos of Op. 6 are grouped under the title *Preludii, Allemande, Gighe, Corrente, Sarabande, Gavotte e Minuetti Parte Seconda per camera* and correspond to the chamber sonatas.

The majority of the sonatas have all their movements in the same key. In those cases in which a movement is in a different key, it is usually in a slow tempo and occurs in the relative minor. However, in the concertos one movement is invariably in a contrasting key. Ten of the twelve concertos are in the major mode with the contrasting slow movement in the relative minor. This pattern of tonal design was to remain common in the concerto throughout the eighteenth century. The choice of keys—four in F major, three in D major, two in B-flat major, and one each in C minor and G minor—is typical of string music of the period, which was generally limited to key signatures with three flats or three sharps, most likely because of the accompanying keyboard instruments whose tuning temperaments did not accommodate more.

A closer examination of three Corelli concertos will help clarify the beginnings of the instrumental concerto as an independent genre.

Concerto Grosso da Chiesa in D Major, Op. 6, No. 1

The opening movement of this six-movement D major concerto consists of two main parts, superficially resembling the French overture: a Largo followed by an Allegro with several short Adagio interruptions. Unlike the slow movements opening the church trio sonatas, the slow sections opening the church concertos are more tentative—they seem more like slow introductions and have been conceived in orchestral, rather than chamber music, terms. The opening Largo of this concerto is scored for the entire ensemble in tutti fashion, eliminating any contrast between the concertino and orchestra.

The fermata on the rests separating the Largo from the Allegro section probably does not indicate a grand pause, but rather a cadenza. The practice of ornamenting cadences was common in Baroque music involving vocal or instrumental soloists. In this concerto, one of the soloists, probably the first violinist (Corelli in the original performance?), improvised a short, unaccompanied passage leading into the next section. Such a cadenza is usually concise—perhaps a mere flourish of notes—but it conveniently and dramatically introduces the soloists who appear alone at the beginning of the next section. Few contemporary documents shed any light on the exact nature of such an improvised cadenza, but one important early source is an edition of six of Corelli's Op. 5 solo church sonatas published by E. Roger of Amsterdam about 1710–15. This edition does not contain cadenzas as such, but the slow movements include an embellished variant that can provide some sense of the scope and style that would be appropriate in a short cadenza. Consider the cadence passage in mm. 6–7 of Ex. 2-1 from Op. 5. Longer, more involved, and flashier cadenzas were generally reserved for the solo concerto, but the art of improvisation was very much alive in the Baroque era, and opportunities for short, improvised, virtuoso display passages were probably offered in most concerti grossi as well. Lead-in cadenzas, those brief improvised passages that lead to true solo passages, are effective ways of introducing a soloist and were probably fairly common. Mozart even used them in some of his piano concertos a century later.

Ex. 2-1. Corelli, Op. 5, No. 3; Adagio, mm. 1–8 (Embellished variant).

The musical separation of the concertino from the tutti occurs as the Allegro begins, producing a startling effect, particularly in the large church in which the concerto was probably first performed. The sound of the two bands suddenly separates in space; when combined with the change of tempo, sonority, and texture, the result is breathtaking. In the course of the movement, the concertino is exposed alone three times, to be joined later each time by the ripieno. The cello of the solo group is given rapid sixteenth-note figures throughout the fast portions of the movement and provides an element of virtuosity not found in the other parts.

The sound of the violins moving in parallel thirds pervades the following Largo. The dominant homophonic texture (that is, a texture with clear melody and accompaniment, but in this case with a strong bass creating a clear polarity between the high and low parts) and the regularity of rhythm and phrasing (usually in eight measures) mark this as a dance-influenced movement. The broadening effect of the hemiola placed at the ends of phrases was common in triple-meter dances during the Baroque period. Hemiola occurs when accents cause two measures of $\frac{3}{4}$ to feel like one large measure of $\frac{3}{2}$ (Ex. 2-2). The concertino begins alone and states one complete phrase, exactly echoed by the tutti. The alternation of solo and tutti continues, governed by the phrase lengths. The final cadence links directly to the following Allegro section, which is scored tutti throughout. The first and second violins, however, alternate a sixteenth-note arpeggiation figure (Ex. 2-3) of the kind that was to become common in later Baroque concertos.

Ex. 2-2. Hemiola.   Ex. 2-3. Corelli, Op. 6, No. 1; Allegro, mm. 1–2.

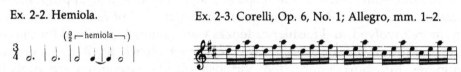

The subsequent Largo is the only movement set in a contrasting key—B minor, the relative minor. The concertino begins alone and is featured throughout the movement, the orchestra joining for only a few measures of tutti performance. For the rest the ripieno orchestra plays only an accompanying role. The solo violins alternate short motives in echolike fashion (Ex. 2-4) or join in duet passages emphasizing parallel thirds or chains of 2–3 suspensions, creating a characteristic Corellian sonority.

Ex. 2-4. Corelli, Op. 6, No. 1; Largo, mm. 1–4.

The Phrygian cadence concluding this movement is frequently found at the end of movements in the relative minor key. The final chord, the dominant, is approached by the subdominant chord in first inversion, resulting in the characteristic bass movement of a descending semitone from the minor sixth scale degree to the dominant. The cadence does not sound final, but acts as a transition to the next movement which, as usual, returns to the tonic key of the work. Many later Baroque composers used the Phrygian cadence in similar places. Curiously, the middle movement of Bach's Brandenburg Concerto No. 3 consists only of a Phrygian cadence, although, as will be noted later, it may have been the concluding cadence of an assumed cadenza.

Most of Corelli's church concertos contain one fast, fugal movement of which the following Allegro is typical. The movement is not a strict fugue, but makes use of the imitative contrapuntal texture characteristic of a fugue and concentrates on a single main subject as does a fugue. The movement is played tutti, with the exception of the concertino opening and a few solo measures in the middle. Fugal movements appear in a number of concertos in the early stages of the new form's development, but this feature faded as the truly virtuosic solo concerto took hold.

The gigue-like finale provides great contrast to the preceding movement. As is typical of Corelli's final movements, it offers the most room for virtuosic display, albeit of a restrained nature. A new texture is introduced to the work as the two solo violins rise out of the concertino to play without the accompaniment of the continuo. This surprising texture appears right at the movement's outset, as the two unaccompanied solo violins play triplet figuration. In the first half of the movement, the solo violins are handled in a duet fashion and often play in parallel thirds or exchange material every few bars in echolike fashion. In the last half of this movement, however, the first solo violin gains complete independence and a true solo concerto texture results. While the solo violinist performs figuration not previously used, a contrast of large and small sounds is maintained through a fluctuating accompaniment that shifts between second solo violin and the ripieno orchestra. Throughout the movement, the ripieno orchestra never plays the same material as the solo violins; this intensifies the aloofness and independence of the solo parts.

Concerto Grosso da Chiesa in G Minor, Op. 6, No. 8 ("Christmas Concerto")

The two concertos of Corelli that have enjoyed the greatest popularity with audiences in the past century are the only ones of the set in the minor mode. Concerto No. 3 in C minor is a highly engaging work with all movements in the minor mode (the slow movement in the contrasting key is in F minor). The other minor mode concerto is the famous "Christmas Concerto," No. 8 in the published set. It was identified in the published score by the inscription *Fatto per la notte di natale* (written for Christmas Eve) and contains a pastorale traditionally performed in church on that night. The account books kept by Ottoboni from 1689 until his death reveal that Corelli was paid for the composition of a concerto for Christmas in 1690,[5] which might be No. 8.

The quiet, flowing, lyrical pastorale came to be associated particularly with Christmastime in seventeenth-century Italy. The Christmas pastorale was intended to recall the Biblical shepherds who attended the birth of Jesus and is closely related to the strong tradition of rural Italian shepherds who came to town on Christmas morning to serenade images of Christ, which were set up along the roadsides, in imitation of the Biblical shepherds. The highly stylized pastoral movements of the Baroque composers still reveal musical characteristics associated with the simple music of the shepherds, who commonly played pipes or bagpipes. The drone of the bagpipe is imitated by long-held notes in the lower instruments and the simple, lyrical melodic lines of the *Pifferari* are imitated in the upper parts. The brightness of the major mode is stressed and melodies are often doubled in thirds and sixths. Trills often adorn melodies having a lilting dotted rhythm ($\sqrt{.}\sqrt{}\sqrt{}$), known as the siciliano rhythm, most often set in a moderately slow compound meter ($\frac{6}{8}$, $\frac{9}{8}$, or $\frac{12}{8}$).

These features, including the trills that were probably improvised, are found in Corelli's idyllic G major pastorale that brings Op. 6, No. 8 to a close. This is the earliest known pastorale to find its way into a concerto. The term *ad libitum* after the pastoral movement's title probably indicates the entire movement is optional; if it were omitted, the remainder of the concerto could serve a useful function outside the Christmas season.[6] It appears Corelli established the convention of providing the pastorale as an additional movement to a concerto grosso to be performed during Midnight Mass on Christmas Eve; Manfredini, Torelli, and Locatelli were followers of this convention. The instrumental pastorale was also incorporated into operas and oratorios to evoke a pastoral atmosphere; both Bach in the sinfonia opening Part II of the Christmas Oratorio and Handel in the "Pifa"—a corrupt German spelling of the Italian "Piva," the name given the bagpipe in northern Italy—in *Messiah* use it specifically to create the appropriate atmosphere for the announcement of Christ's birth to shepherds in the fields.

Concerto Grosso da Camera in F Major, Op. 6, No. 12

The last four concertos of Op. 6 are chamber concertos; as in two other published sets of Corelli's chamber works, the final work in this set is also a bit unusual. The last trio sonata in Op. 2 is a one-movement chaconne, and that of the Op. 5 solo sonatas is the famous set of variations on "La Follia," the most virtuosic number in the opus. The twelfth concerto in Op. 6 was in turn conceived as a showpiece for the first solo violin.

Op. 6, No. 12, like the other chamber concertos, includes a prelude and several stylized dances, although not all of the movements are given dance titles. The chamber concertos more frequently than the church concertos contain solo sections with material that is distinctive from the tutti sections, and the solo figuration is typically more virtuosic than that found in the church concertos. Such display was felt to be inappropriate in church concertos, and the homophonic texture that predominates in the chamber concertos was better suited to the writing of flashy figuration. The chamber concertos may also be later works and thus display a more advanced style than the church concertos.

In contrast to this general impression of increased emphasis on the soloists in the chamber concertos, some movements are scored tutti throughout (for example, the allemande of Concerto No. 10), and some movements trade identical phrases from solo to tutti (for example, the sarabande of Concerto No. 11).

No. 12, however, is the most soloistic in the group. From the outset of the prelude, the concertino is dramatically pitted against the ripieno orchestra. The short solo passages contain material different from the tutti sections, and the final solo is strikingly different from the previous two. Typical of the chamber works, the prelude is more contrapuntal than the succeeding dance movements.

The next movement, Allegro, was not given a dance title, but has distinct gavotte characteristics. From the movement's beginning, the first solo violin is given soloistic material accompanied only by the concertino instruments (Ex. 2-5). Throughout the movement, the first violin plays idiomatic figuration of the type that was to become commonplace in later Baroque concertos. The figuration is frequently dependent upon broken chord patterns. Two particular patterns are quite common. One involves a rapid oscillation between two chord tones (Ex. 2-6a), and the other includes rapid repetitions of one pitch before changing to the other chord tone (Ex. 2-6b). At times, as in Ex. 2-6b, one tone acts as a pivot point to other tones throughout an entire measure. A variation of this pattern occurs a few measures later (Ex. 2-7).

Ex. 2-5. Corelli, Op. 6, No. 12; Allegro, mm. 1–2.

Ex. 2-6a. Corelli, Op. 6, No. 12; Allegro, mm. 5–8.

Ex. 2-6b. Corelli, Op. 6, No. 12; Allegro, mm. 17–20.

Ex. 2-7. Corelli, Op. 6, No. 12; Allegro, mm. 25–28.

Setting such figuration in sixteenth-notes in fast common time soon became standard. This feature creates a relentless rhythmic drive; combined with sequences that are often intensified by dissonance, it packs a sense of urgency and emphatic thrust toward major cadence points. This rhythmic pattern was to become a major characteristic of Italian instrumental music, particularly in fast concerto movements. This is an important way in which Corelli prefigured the future development of the solo concerto.

Limited use of tutti scoring further illustrates the greater emphasis on the soloist in this movement. In most passages the ripieno does not stand alone but unites with the second violin and continuo of the concertino to provide a simple accompaniment for the solo work. Yet the soloist may be accompanied only by the concertino continuo, creating a delicate sparseness that was to characterize many later Italian solo concertos. The movement ends with a substantial tutti section, as do all of the movements in the Op. 6 concertos.

The following Adagio is not dancelike, so it provides a contrasting interlude or transition between two fast dances. This is the movement in the related key, D minor. The entire movement consists of throbbing eighth-note chords scored tutti and concludes with a Phrygian cadence on the dominant. It is quite possible one of the soloists improvised a melody to this chordal accompaniment.

Next a lively sarabande opens with four bars for the concertino. The remainder of the movement is scored tutti but features a striking change of texture and timbre after the double bar.

Final movements of all the chamber concertos are dances in fast triple or compound meter. Concertos Nos. 9 and 10 conclude with minuets marked *vivace* and are constructed in a minuet-and-trio fashion. Gigas are found at the ends of concertos 11 and 12. The giga of No. 12 is primarily a vehicle for the first solo violin, although the material is not extremely flashy. The accompaniment is effectively written to produce rapid changes between smaller and larger forces, and cadences are scored tutti. The final sixteen-measure passage is also tutti, featuring a rising scale figure in the solo cello line.

In these Op. 6 concerti grossi Corelli established many elements that were to become standard characteristics of the mature Baroque concerto style. Several of these features depended upon the newly established principles of tonality. As tonality came to be an increasingly significant factor, the relationship between melody and chord progression underwent a change. Melodies came to depend upon and be conditioned by the harmonic accompaniment, but the practice of writing continuo parts preserved a melodically oriented bass. The "plain harmony" that would be characteristic of the late eighteenth century was still tempered by the continuo which tended to preserve the horizontal element of the texture. The resultant texture is referred to as "continuo-homophony," a term coined by Manfred Bukofzer in an attempt to capture the "dualistic conception of the musical structure."[7] This new texture was particularly compatible with the concerto since emphasis is placed on the outer parts, thereby allowing the soloist to stand apart from the supporting material.

As composers moved toward tonality and continuo-homophony, they made increasing use of diatonic sequences, which help to create key-feeling. Sequences may easily involve patterns that are tailor-made for the writing of idiomatic, instrumental display passages because of their repetitious nature. In those passages in which Corelli placed greater emphasis on the soloist, such as the first Allegro of Concerto No. 12, patterns of figuration dominate the material. These patterns in themselves can become tiresome, but his casting them as diatonic sequences lends musical interest and direction because the tonal context can help achieve harmonic variety and a clear sense of destination. The simple device of the sequence was used by Corelli and later composers with great skill, sensitivity, and resourcefulness.

Through these devices and the consistent application of the concerto principle of contrast, Corelli established the basic techniques that remained constant in the Baroque concerto. In the arena of form, however, his basic reliance on the church and chamber sonatas as models is not a feature that found its way into the late Baroque concerto. In sum, Corelli's concerti grossi are carefully wrought compositions that repay serious listening with deep pleasure. His music is simple but sensuous, restrained yet vital. His concertos possess great intrinsic musical value and stand at the beginning of the long and rich history of the form.

THE EARLY SOLO CONCERTO

THE BOLOGNESE SCHOOL

While Stradella and Corelli were working out the principles of the concerto grosso in Rome, composers in Bologna took the first tentative steps toward the solo concerto. Bologna, home of the oldest and one of the most famous universities in Europe, supplied the intellectual and artistic environment that nurtured a unique musical development in the late seventeenth century. The enormous church of San Petronio had become the center of musical activities in Bologna; its size and its two opposing galleries for musicians encouraged the development of a polychoral style similar to Gabrieli's in the first two-thirds of the seventeenth century. Later, under the influence of Mauritio Cazzati (1620–1677), who was hired as *maestro di cappella* in 1657, there was a noticeable shift to independent instrumental music. Cazzati bolstered the church's musical forces by adding instrumental musicians, especially the highly skilled trumpet players from the Concerto Palatino, a group that often performed at the university and for public functions in the city.

Cazzati initiated the Bolognese "Trumpet Sonata" tradition (the earliest such works known are three by Cazzati included in his Op. 35, publ. in 1665), by employing the concertato principle of contrast to exploit the differing timbres of the trumpet and strings. Not only was the tone color of the trumpet different, but the material the valveless instrument could play was much more restricted than that of the strings. The trumpet, used primarily in its clarino, or high, register, was typically limited to triadic and scalar passages. Composers not only gave contrasting material to the trumpet and strings, but the breathing rests required by trumpet players compelled the composer to shift abruptly from the trumpet to the string sound, further augmenting the natural play of concertato effects. Trumpet parts were written for solo performance, while the string parts were doubled in orchestral fashion as in the true solo concerto that was soon to develop. Cazzati, and other composers of similar works, explored the idiomatic potential of the solo instrument and took into consideration the performing abilities of the various soloists.

Following Cazzati's lead, during the 1680s and 1690s Domenico Gabrielli (1651–1690) and his pupil, Giuseppe Maria Jacchini (c. 1663–1727), further explored these tentative beginnings of the solo concerto within the trumpet sonata idiom. Their works are all cast in the form of the Bolognese sonata with four to six movements in alternating slow and fast tempos. Both Gabrielli and Jacchini were talented cellists, so they often included solo passages for cello, allowing it to engage in imitative dialogues with the solo trumpet or to provide a lively obbligato accompaniment to the brass instrument.

GIUSEPPE TORELLI

As the concerto idea developed, composers made sharper distinctions between the solo part and the orchestra. Concomitantly, to maintain some overall sense of unity in their compositions, they refined the method of dealing with the formal organization of the conspicuously opposed forces. Giuseppe Torelli (1658–1709), the most important of the Bolognese composers, played a significant role in constructing the formal solution to this problem, one that was to endure throughout the Baroque era and beyond.

Torelli was born in Verona in 1658, moved to Bologna, and was elected to the prestigious Accademia Filarmonica in 1684. Two years later he was appointed to San Petronio where he played viola in the church orchestra until it was disbanded in 1695 for financial reasons. He then traveled first to work in Ansbach, Germany, and then in Vienna before returning to Bologna in 1701 to join a new church orchestra. He died there in 1709, highly regarded by his contemporaries.

Torelli was probably the most prolific and famous of the Bolognese composers. His earliest works, Opp. 1–4 (publ. 1686–1688), which follow the church or chamber sonata format, are for strings. In the 1690s Torelli turned his attention to the trumpet sonata, perhaps inspired by the excellent trumpet player Giovanni Pellegrino Brandi. Torelli wrote several trumpet sonatas that were not published, probably because there was little demand for such works outside of Bologna, but that have survived in manuscript form. In these works the concerto texture is evident, particularly the contrast between solo and orchestra (the presence of multiple string parts indicates orchestral, rather than chamber-style, performance). Contrast is intensified by the repetition of the orchestra's thematic material as opposed to the trumpet's greater reliance on patterns of figuration. As is the case in other Bolognese trumpet sonatas, one of the slow movements is usually in a key other than the tonic. This precluded the use of the valveless trumpet, which could not play the required pitches. In such movements the Bolognese composers often explored more adventuresome harmonies, at times highlighting a solo string instrument. Torelli frequently used either a single violin or two for which he wrote impressive virtuosic passages, foreshadowing his later solo concertos.

Works in the Bolognese "alla tromba" (in the manner of a trumpet) style are characterized by repeated note patterns, triadic melodic figures, and homophonic texture. As Torelli's interest shifted in his later works to the violin as solo instrument, he adapted these elements to the string concerto. These stylistic characteristics became embedded in the concerto style and are strongly associated with the later writing of Albinoni and Vivaldi, for example.

In Torelli's Op. 5, *Sinfonie a 3 e concerti a 4* (publ. 1692), a clear distinction in style is made between the sinfonias and concertos. The latter lack the tutti-solo contrast we might expect in concertos, but as ripieno or orchestral works they exhibit elements of what was coming to be known as the concerto style. The sinfonias, on the other hand, are orchestral works with greater contrapuntal texture.

Torelli's next publication, *Concerti musicali*, Op. 6 (publ. 1698), contains three works each with one or more passages marked *solo*. The historically important preface explains that these passages should be played by one violin per part, while tutti passages should be performed by up to three or four players per part. These instructions are probably the first of their kind in print, predating Muffat's similar remarks of 1701. Torelli assigns very different musical material to the tutti and solo groups, and on occasion features only one violin.

Bolognese composers were moving from the trumpet sonata tradition toward the solo concerto within the orchestral concerto at roughly the same time that Corelli was foreshadowing the solo concerto within the concerto grosso in Rome. The Bolognese Torelli also introduced two important formal features that were to remain strongly associated with the concerto during the following century. Both features are borrowed from the world of opera and first appear in Torelli's Op. 6 set of concertos.

One of the new formal features is the sequence of three movements in the order fast-slow-fast. This appears to have come from the Italian opera overture, known as the sinfonia, which was typically cast in three movements, or large sections, in a fast-slow-fast order. The other new formal feature affected the design of individual movements, especially the opening fast movements. The model from the world of opera was the aria, the concerto's closest vocal counterpart. In an aria a solo voice singing a text is set against the orchestra. Opera composers developed a successful form for juxtaposing these two strongly contrasting forces without causing interference or confusion. In most seventeenth-century opera arias, the voice is accompanied by continuo only and the strophes are separated by independent orchestral passages based on a recurring theme called a ritornello (the diminutive form of *ritorno*, return). In the later seventeenth and early eighteenth centuries bits of the ritornello were increasingly used between phrases of the strophe and even to accompany the voice part. Ritornello form, ideal for the juxtaposition of a solo instrument and orchestra, was transplanted into the concerto from opera. Ritornello form is discussed more fully in Chapter 4.

In Torelli's Op. 6 concertos, ritornello form is used in only a tentative way. Portions of the ritornello alternate with episodes of nonthematic material. The opening material is modulatory, which limits its use as an integral ritornello. The sixth concerto of the set illustrates this and other tentative characteristics. Every new section, including those in which the soloists participate, begins with a tutti statement of the opening motive. Each of the two solo sections continues this initial motive, but in different ways, creating some semblance of thematic differentiation between tutti and solo as Figure 1 suggests.

Motives	a–b	a–c	a–d	a–e	a–b′	a′
Performer	Tutti	T–Solo	T–S	T–T	T	T

T = Tutti; S = Solo

Figure 1. Early concerto ritornello form, Torelli: Op. 6, No. 6

Torelli's final contribution to the concerto is found in the twelve works for strings published posthumously as Op. 8 (there is no known Op. 7) under the title *Concerti grossi con pastorale per il Santissimo Natale* (publ. 1709). In spite of the published title, only the first six concertos are concerti grossi; the remainder are solo concertos. Individual works are not dated, but some may predate sets of solo concertos published by Albinoni and Jacchini in 1700 and 1701. Op. 8 is a major document in the early history of the concerto, for the set quite clearly employs elements typical of late Baroque concerto style.

Most of the Op. 8 concertos use the three-movement fast-slow-fast scheme. Middle movements employ three sections—slow-fast-slow—a common pattern taken over from the late Bolognese trumpet sonatas. Characteristically, the middle fast portion contains the greatest amount of virtuosic material found in the concerto while its framing slow sections frequently feature the violin soloist in richly embellished parts. The overall plan stresses an allegro tempo, widely favored by concerto composers.[1]

In addition to establishing the three-movement concerto structure, the concertos of Op. 8 more consistently exploit the principle of contrast between solo and tutti sections. What had been hinted at in Corelli's Op. 6, especially in No. 12, is firmly established in Torelli's Op. 8. The solo passages consist of lively, idiomatic figuration that is often highly diversified, while the tutti passages contain material of a solid, incisive thematic character. The method of construction and the clear distinction between solo and tutti passages place a brilliant spotlight on the soloist or soloists. Soloists are no longer employed merely to create an effective change of scoring; their presence becomes the most striking element in the music while the virtuosic display places the soloists on a level distinctly different from that of the ripieno orchestra.

The form had evolved to something like a stage setting for the instrumental superstar equivalent to the opera stage for the virtuoso singer. Supporting the increased prominence of the solo sections and the inherent distinction between solo and tutti sections were further refinements in the construction of the allegro movements that paved the way to the mature ritornello design.

The first six concerti grossi of Op. 8 feature a concertino of two violins. The fast movements approach mature ritornello design, although the frequent and rapid shifts between solo and tutti sections prevent a full realization of the ritornello form here. Fugal openings, a carryover from the older church sonata, are still characteristically used. Concertos No. 1 and No. 2 are unusual in that they open with the two soloists alluding to the fugal texture normally reserved for the tutti. Within the solo sections of Op. 8, the two soloists frequently echo one another or play in parallel thirds. When both are present they are often unaccompanied. At times, particularly in the middle movements, one or the other of the soloists is given longer solo passages, hinting at the solo concerto to come.

Concerto No. 6 in G minor is a Christmas concerto in the same tonality as Corelli's. The pastorale is placed near the beginning, following a short Grave introduction that establishes a serious mood through the use of suspensions reminiscent of Corelli's introductory slow movements.

The six solo concertos of Op. 8, quite possibly written later than its concerti grossi, possess features of a more advanced ritornello form. Most of the outside movements contain three or four major tutti sections consisting of ritornello material. All of these movements begin with tutti statements and most conclude with identical tutti statements when the opening tuttis close in the tonic. Solo sections consistently contain nonthematic figuration, another example of Torelli's role in crystallizing various elements into stylistic features of the mature concerto. The single soloist is usually accompanied only by the continuo instruments, although Torelli sometimes uses the orchestra to interject motives derived from the ritornello, maintaining the thematic dichotomy between soloist and orchestra. The middle movements of these concertos are modeled on those of the Bolognese sonata, with a brilliant allegro for the soloists with continuo accompaniment framed by adagio sections, also dominated by the soloist. Occasionally Torelli creates a tutti-solo contrast by using the ritornello form. The slow sections are very lyrical and dramatic. Final movements are strongly dancelike and most are in triple meter.

Torelli advanced the concerto from its roots in the Bolognese trumpet sonata and the Roman concerto grosso to its initial state as a solo concerto in its broad outlines and many minor details. His successive publications show the gradual evolution of the new form and the creation of stylistic principles that were to underlie the future Baroque concerto. At this time Rome and Bologna were the major musical centers of late seventeenth-century Italy, but shortly after the turn of the century Venice once again took the spotlight.

TOMASO ALBINONI

We have seen Venice as the home not only of the early concertato style but also of a burgeoning interest in instrumental music. Venice remained a brilliant center of music into the eighteenth century and was the setting for the next significant contributions to the concerto, in the works of Tomaso Albinoni (1671–1751) and Antonio Vivaldi (1676–1741).

St. Mark's continued, in this last period of the city's splendor, as an important musical center, but the focus of musical attention soon shifted to the theaters of Venice. The theater of San Cassiano, Europe's first public opera house, opened in Venice in 1637. Increased demand for public entertainment subsequently encouraged the construction of several more opera houses and theaters. By 1700 Venice could claim fourteen theaters, seven of which mounted opera exclusively and three of which staged opera occasionally. Venice clearly enjoyed an intense theater life, for at times as many as ten different operas might be performed simultaneously.

Extensive concert performances were also presented in the four large *ospedali*. These *ospedali* were charitable institutions dedicated to looking after the sick or providing care and education for illegitimate children and orphans. Music became one of the chief subjects taught. As a consequence many of the pupils became virtuoso performers, their presence sparking an enormous outpouring of instrumental music near the beginning of the eighteenth century. As the place of virtuosic display grew in the affections of the audiences, the concerto, particularly the solo concerto, came into its own as the instrumental equivalent of opera. By consolidating and building upon Torelli's achievements, the Venetian composers made the concerto an extraordinarily viable form with clearly identifiable features.

The basic characteristics of the Venetian concerto were stated, refined, and elaborated in the concertos of Albinoni and Vivaldi. Their concertos display the strong influence of Venetian opera, which may account for those features that distinguish them from the Bolognese and Roman concertos, which were more influenced by church music.

The Venetian concerto consists of three long movements; a slow movement is flanked by two fast movements. One tempo is maintained throughout the slow movement, unlike the adagio-allegro-adagio complex characterizing the Bolognese form. As noted earlier, the fast-slow-fast movement plan was probably derived from the fledgling opera sinfonia. The first movements, sometimes the last movements, and occasionally the middle movements of Venetian concertos employ ritornello form, derived directly from opera arias. While the ritornello themes are built of simple, easily remembered motives, the contrasting solo material is virtuosic, only occasionally recalling the ritornello. The slow movements often suggest operatic arias with their intense lyricism and expressivity. While solo string instruments were favored, the Venetians increasingly explored the use of solo wind instruments.

Tomaso Albinoni was born of a wealthy family in 1671 in Venice and died there in 1751. Little is known of his early years, but Remo Giazotto, author of a comprehensive account of the composer,[2] believes Legrenzi was his teacher. Since Albinoni did not depend on music for a livelihood, he referred to himself as *musico di violino dilettante veneto.* (Dilettante had no pejorative connotations in those days, simply denoting one who made music for pleasure, not as a means of earning a living.) In his first publication following his father's death in 1709, he identified himself merely as *musico di violino*—a freelance violinist. Albinoni never held a music position.

Albinoni's creative undertakings were equally divided between writing operatic and instrumental music. He left fifty-seven extant stage works, ninety-seven sonatas (including *balletti*), sixty concertos, and a handful of works in other forms. He was apparently well respected during his lifetime. J. J. Quantz, writing only a generation later, singled out Albinoni and Vivaldi as the most important composers of concertos after Torelli.[3] Subjected to unjust criticism and subsequent neglect, Albinoni's music passed into oblivion after his death, until revived by Bach scholars. The knowledge that Bach had used some of Albinoni's fugue subjects as the main ideas in his music led students of Bach to an intense investigation of Albinoni's music. While Bach's use of Albinoni's themes gave the Italian composer some degree of respectability and credibility, scholars have turned only relatively recently to the study of Albinoni and his instrumental music for its own sake. Unfortunately, Albinoni's operas, together with dozens of other Venetian operas of the time, remain virtually unknown.

In publishing his instrumental works, Albinoni alternated sonatas and concertos. While the sonatas are conservative, showing the influence of Corelli, the concertos are more progressive, particularly in their homophonic texture, increased call for virtuosic performance, incisive thematic statements, and occasional harmonic daring.

Albinoni was the first Venetian to publish concertos; although his innovations were modest, they were important, contributing more directly to the succeeding development of the concerto than did the works of his Bolognese or Roman predecessors. We may never know the extent of his influence, but the professional polish, originality, and high overall quality of his concertos are such that one can well imagine they must have exerted an enormous effect on his contemporaries. Vivaldi, four years younger, must surely have known Albinoni's work and must quite surely have been influenced by it.

Of Albinoni's ten publications, Nos. 2, 5, 7, 9, and 10 contain concertos. The collection *Sinfonie e concerti a cinque*, Op. 2, was published in 1700, the first publication of any Venetian concertos. The set brings to mind Torelli's Op. 5 of 1692; Albinoni alternates six sonatas with six orchestral concertos and distinguishes between the two types largely by way of style: the concertos are homophonic, while the sonatas are polyphonic. Unlike Torelli's Op. 5 concertos, Albinoni's are always in three movements: he was the first to employ, consistently, the fast-slow-fast plan. The texture is also more homophonic than that of Torelli's Op. 5.

A solo violin appears in very brief independent passages in Albinoni's next set of concertos, Op. 5 (publ. 1707), also entitled *Concerti a cinque*. The unusual five-part scoring—principally for three violins, viola, and continuo, or for two violins, two violas, and continuo, indicated by the *a cinque* in the title—became a hallmark of Albinoni's concertos. He also created an unusual structure for his opening movements that can best be described as a three-part form with ritornello features. The first part is an opening statement of distinctive motivic material that closes in the tonic, enabling its use as a cohesive unit at the conclusion of the movement.

The second is a large central portion of the movement typically launched with a statement of the opening motto in the tonic that is immediately repeated in the dominant. This simple form of sequence became a stereotypical feature in Albinoni's first movements and a source of irritation to many modern listeners. Figuration then follows with additional statements of the motto before the middle section closes in the subdominant key.

The third part, in the tonic, is the reprise of the entire opening statement. The reprise is introduced by a short link moving from the subdominant to the tonic, or a statement of the motto in the submediant, or a simple hiatus. A coda, occasionally containing new material, normally concludes the movement. The first movement of Concerto No. 8, in Op. 5, provides a good example of this three-part form. It contains abrupt switches to the dominant in the second part while the following figuration is primarily given over to the orchestral violins, although the solo violin intrudes briefly with a new figure.

Albinoni never abandoned this three-part form in its basic outline, even though other aspects of his style evolved as the *style galant* made its impact. (This term referred to the emerging light and elegant music of the early Classical period.) His creation of a consistently strong and clear relationship between parts one and three of this form was an important step in establishing a framework for the solo material, but it was also limiting and static. Vivaldi moved beyond this simple three-part structure to a more elaborate and flexible ritornello form, capable of encompassing greater dramatic breadth.

The slow movements of Albinoni's early concertos show more variety, although they are often in the relative minor, and are often short and homophonic, with a few suspensions. And they typically conclude with a Phrygian cadence on the dominant of the new key. The middle movement of Op. 5, No. 10, is a good example. The Adagio of No. 5 provides a hint of the highly impassioned slow movements to come. It is the work of an opera composer—the soloist is featured in two short passages of instrumental recitative.

The final movements of the Op. 5 concertos are all fugal, with short solo sections, and retain conservative characteristics more common in the polyphonic textures of his sonatas. Typically, Albinoni's fugal movements possess a striking rhythmic vitality.

Albinoni's next two sets of concertos, Op. 7 and Op. 9, were published in Amsterdam in 1715 and 1722. They follow identical organizational schemes of four orchestral concertos, four solo oboe concertos, and four concertos for two oboes. The first matter of note in the orchestral concertos is the disappearance of any use of the church sonata form and the wholesale acceptance of the practices developed in connection with the newer opera sinfonia. The serious fugal quality of the final movements has been replaced by the lighter air of the sinfonia finale, several even written in $\frac{3}{8}$ meter and in binary form, a two-part form common in Baroque dance movements. Only one of the Op. 7 orchestral concertos contains any short solo violin passages, while all four in Op. 9 require a violin soloist.

Albinoni's inclusion of concertos for one and two solo oboes was highly unusual for an Italian composer; these oboe concertos may in fact be the first published by an Italian. The oboe had been perfected in mid-seventeenth-century France and found its way into a few Italian orchestras by late in the century, but any precedent for using a single oboe must have been limited at the best. Because of the instrument's trumpet-like timbre, early composers for the oboe tended to give it trumpet-like parts, but once it was firmly established in orchestras, the oboe was usually expected to function like a violin and often doubled violin parts. It only gained an independent place in the late eighteenth century. Despite the oboe's association with the violin, Albinoni wrote the oboe parts in the four solo oboe concertos in the style of the bel canto vocal idiom with which he was familiar, obviously preferring the vocal stepwise movement and small leaps rather than the arpeggiated violin style.

Features borrowed from vocal arias also led to slight modifications to Albinoni's three-part first-movement form. In particular, the popular motto opening for an aria was paralleled in the oboe concertos. In this form, the initial ritornello is usually followed by the soloist with a paraphrase of the opening motto, which is cut short by the return of the orchestral ritornello. The soloist then repeats the opening motto and continues with patterns of figuration without interruption. The mutual use of the opening motto by soloist and tutti helps to integrate the opposed forces. The ritornello often contains several distinct motives; these the composer exploits to heighten the contrast between the forces by subsequently giving one motive to the soloist and another to the orchestra. For example, in Op. 7, No. 6, the first two oboe entries are based on mm. 1–4 of the opening statement, while the tutti statements are based on mm. 5–7. At the end of the movement, the two separated motives of the ritornello are recombined as a total unit. This procedure points very strongly toward the Vivaldi ritornello design. In Albinoni's later Op. 9 oboe concertos, the ritornello statements are expanded even further by the addition of more motives.

The orchestration in the oboe concertos is often one of their most attractive elements. This is particularly true of slow movements of the solo concertos in which the oboe is often pitted against the first violins in dialogue, or a richly scored string orchestra accompanies a lyrical melody in the solo instrument. When a dialogue between oboes and strings occurs in the double concertos, the texture is luxuriant.

The slow movements of Op. 9 have gained in expressive power over the earlier works. Concluding movements of the oboe concertos are often dancelike, structured similarly to the opening movements.

The final volume of Albinoni's concertos, Op. 10, was discovered in 1968 by Michael Talbot, who established the date of publication close to 1735. Albinoni's most intense outpouring of operas occurred during the time between Opp. 9 and 10. The concertos of Op. 10 display features of the newer *style galant,* such as grace notes, triplets, and other embellishing gestures. Concertos Nos. 1, 5, 7, 9, and 11 have no solo parts. Nos. 2, 3, and 4 contain short solo passages for the principal violin as well as for other instruments, and in Nos. 6, 8, and 12 the principal violinist is featured in extended solo passages. Nos. 8 and 12 are the most virtuosic of the set. The solo violinist is given a particular place of honor in No. 12, reminding us of the tradition dating back to Corelli of placing the most spectacular works in the final positions in each published set.

Albinoni's music, though still relatively little known today, is gradually receiving greater attention both in research and in performance. Albinoni's contributions to the development of the concerto were important. He may well have been the first composer to infuse the concerto with striking musical effects and practices developed for opera, instilling a dramatic quality into the instrumental form. Albinoni's instrumental music has an ingratiating style that is most appealing to listeners; a melodic and orchestral warmth often sets it apart from the music of his Venetian contemporary, Vivaldi.

ANTONIO VIVALDI AND THE MATURE BAROQUE CONCERTO

Antonio Vivaldi (1678–1741) was born and educated in Venice, becoming one of that city's leading composers. Vivaldi received his musical training under Legrenzi at St. Mark's where his father played violin in the orchestra. Vivaldi was subsequently trained for the priesthood and ordained in 1703, but was relieved of liturgical duties in 1705, probably due to ill health.

From 1704 to 1740 Vivaldi was employed at the Seminario Musicale dell' Ospedale della Pietà (Musical Seminary of the Hospital of Mercy) where he served as teacher of violin, conductor, composer, and general superintendent of music. During frequent leaves of absence, however, he seems to have concentrated on composing and conducting operas in Venice as well as in other Italian cities and nearby parts of Europe. After one of his longest absences, 1718–1723, he entered into a new agreement with the Pietà, which called for him to compose two new concertos per month with the assurance that there would be three to four rehearsals for each performance.

Virtually all of Vivaldi's instrumental and sacred vocal music was composed for the Pietà, which was a home for illegitimate and orphaned girls. Music was one of the chief subjects taught, with performances given every Sunday and holiday, usually at the Vespers service. Reports by contemporary visitors document the impressive skills of these girls, almost all under the age of twenty. Apparently the performers were placed behind a grillwork to hide them from view, since females were usually denied any role in the church service. The glorious sound of the music was desired, however.

The working conditions at the Pietà had much to do with Vivaldi's success. He was able to call upon practically unlimited musical resources. The young musicians were well trained and had an enthusiasm for new music composed especially for their performance. The musicians were of differing skills and experience, however, so he regularly wrote music adapted to these varied abilities. For the less capable musicians he composed the ripieno concertos and sinfonias, but for the more skilled he wrote the many solo concertos. His extended, demanding solo works, particularly for the violin, were probably designed for his most gifted students or for himself.

Vivaldi's contract called for a constant supply of new music. Forced to compose rapidly, he relied heavily on repetition, which gave his music a predictable quality. His manuscripts reveal special forms of musical abbreviation devised to indicate commonly repeated elements, thus reducing the time spent actually writing out each work. Yet he was never discouraged from experimenting. Thanks to the Pietà, Vivaldi was able to realize to the fullest his abilities as a composer of instrumental music. Although Vivaldi was also a prolific composer of successful vocal music, his fame today rests primarily on a small portion of his more than 500 concertos.

THE CONCERTOS: TYPES AND CHOICES OF INSTRUMENTS

About two-thirds of Vivaldi's concertos are for a single solo instrument. The violin was favored, with almost 230 concertos for it preserved in their entirety. Surprisingly, the bassoon is featured next most frequently in close to forty works; despite the fact that the early eighteenth-century instrument had only two keys, the composer made daunting technical demands on the performer. The cello is the solo instrument in twenty-eight solo concertos, the oboe in twenty, and the flute in fifteen (including the six of Op. 10, probably the first published concertos for the instrument). In addition, there are solo concertos for viola d'amore, recorder (including flautino, a high-pitched sopranino recorder), and mandolin.

Of the approximately forty concertos for two soloists, twenty-five feature two violins. There are also double concertos for trumpets, for horns, and for mandolins. A few of the double concertos feature unlike instruments such as violin and oboe, violin and cello, and the exotic combination of viola d'amore and lute (RV 540).[1]

About a half-dozen works call for three or four violins and two dozen for various combinations of three or more diverse solo instruments, such as RV 577 for violin, two oboes, two flutes, and bassoon; or RV 568 for violin, two oboes, two horns, and bassoon. Some very unusual instruments appear in these concertos. For example, there are timpani (RV 562a); *trombon da caccia*, possibly a trombone, although the identity of the instrument is uncertain (RV 574); *claren*, probably the newly developing clarinet, although some think the term indicates *clarini*, or high trumpet parts (RV 556); *salmoè*, possibly chalumeaux, a relative of the clarinet (RV 558), and theorbos (RV 558).

Vivaldi viewed the contemporary keyboard instruments, harpsichord and organ, as primarily continuo instruments. There is some evidence that two continuo instruments were required to perform in the concertos, as might have been the case in Corelli's concerti grossi mentioned earlier. However, a few concertos feature keyboard instruments in the true solo group, and several have slow movements intended as vehicles for the improvising skill of the continuo player. Of the latter category, one of the most famous of his concertos, *L'autunno* (Autumn, RV 293) provides a good example. Here the special instruction *il cembalo arpeggio* is written above the part, indicating the harpsichordist should improvise in an arpeggiated fashion. RV 555 includes two harpsichords in a massive solo ensemble; the harpsichords are also featured in short solo passages. The organ is treated as both a continuo and concertante instrument in four concertos.

In the works for two soloists, the two voices are usually treated as equals. In those with diverse groupings of solo instruments, the wind instruments appear in pairs (except for bassoon) and play solo sections as pairs. The principal violinist often emerges as the dominant soloist in the works with diverse soloists. He rarely scored for the soloists in the Roman concerto grosso tradition, that is, with a solo group of two violins and basso continuo, and the composer avoided the title concerto grosso as well as solo concerto.

Vivaldi wrote sixty-three three-movement works primarily for a four-part orchestra with no dominant solo instrument. These works were variously called sinfonia, concerto, or concerto ripieno. They contain elements in common with concertos, but tend to be simpler, less brilliant, generally of smaller dimensions, and often indistinguishable from his opera sinfonias. There are also five concertos involving soloists and two string orchestras juxtaposed in an antiphonal manner similar to the tradition in St. Mark's. Approximately twenty chamber concertos use the united soloists in place of the ripieno orchestra; Bach was to follow this example in his Third Brandenburg Concerto.

THE PUBLISHED CONCERTOS

Vivaldi published nine collections of concertos:

Opus 3   *L'estro armonico* (Harmonic Caprice). Amsterdam: E. Roger, c. 1711–12. Twelve concertos for one, two, and four violins, some with violoncello obbligato.

Opus 4   *La stravaganza.* Amsterdam: E. Roger, c. 1712–15. Twelve concertos for solo violin.

Opus 6   *VI Concerti a 5 stromenti.* Amsterdam: J. Roger, c. 1716–17. Six concertos for solo violin.

Opus 7   *Concerti a 5 stromenti.* Amsterdam: J. Roger, c. 1716–17. Ten concertos for solo violin and two for solo oboe.

Opus 8   *Il cimento dell'armonia e dell'invenzione concerti a 4 e 5* (The Encounter of Harmony and Imagination). Amsterdam: Le Cène, c. 1725. Twelve concertos for solo violin (two are alternatively for oboe).

Opus 9   *La cetra concerti* (The Lyre). Amsterdam: Le Cène, 1727. Eleven concertos for solo violin and one for two violins.

Opus 10   *VI Concerti.* Amsterdam: Le Cène, c. 1729–30. Six concertos for solo flute (some are reworkings of earlier works for other instruments).

Opus 11   *6 Concerti.* Amsterdam, Le Cène, c. 1729–30. Five concertos for solo violin and one for solo oboe (that a reworking of Op. 9, No. 3).

Opus 12   *6 Concerti.* Amsterdam: Le Cène, c. 1729–30. Five concertos for solo violin and one ripieno concerto.

The eighty-four concertos making up these published collections represent less than one-fifth of Vivaldi's contribution to the genre, but they provide a solid foundation for study since the publications can be dated with some certainty and so record the stylistic changes between earlier and later works. These collections were published in two major periods, the late 1710s and the late 1720s, which together with stylistic analysis of manuscript concertos suggests Vivaldi concentrated his concerto writing in these two periods. The following observations are largely based on a study of these published concertos, in part because they are best known today.

GENERAL FEATURES

Vivaldi's central position in the history of the Baroque concerto is analogous to that of Corelli in the history of the sonata. Vivaldi's massive concerto output represents the culmination of past developments and crystallizes the form and practice of the Baroque concerto. Although these concertos serve as the measure of the mature Baroque concerto, they are amazingly varied. Vivaldi obviously viewed the new genre as quite elastic; while his concertos share characteristics, each work by the Red Priest has its own artistic integrity.

Vivaldi followed in the footsteps of Torelli and Albinoni in most of their external and internal plans of organization. Vivaldi was not a great innovator, but compared with the concertos of his predecessors, his works seem more carefully planned and the structures more clearly defined. In addition, the dramatic tension between solo and tutti often only hinted at earlier comes to full fruition in the concertos of this great Venetian, who was, not surprisingly, a very successful opera composer. Together with this dramatic intensity, the most distinctive qualities of Vivaldi's concerto style are impelling rhythmic vitality, varied texture, and relatively spontaneous-sounding melodic ideas.

SEQUENCE OF MOVEMENTS

Most of Vivaldi's concertos are in the three-movement, fast-slow-fast scheme. A rather large proportion, about one-third, of initial movements is in the minor mode, and a distinct fondness for middle movements in the minor mode is evident in about two-thirds of the concertos. The relationship of keys between movements is fairly flexible, with about one-third of the slow movements in the same key as the outer movements; slightly less frequently the relative major or minor is selected, and in still fewer cases the dominant or subdominant is used. E minor is a particular favorite for highly expressive slow movements.

RITORNELLO FORM

Most of the opening movements are in ritornello form, which Torelli earlier had introduced tentatively to the concerto. Ritornello form was developed as a convention in opera arias as an excellent means of highlighting the vocal soloist and of providing unity through the use of recurrent thematic material in the orchestra. The basic design involves an alternation of sections for orchestra alone and those featuring solo voice with orchestral accompaniment. The form was adapted to the instrumental concerto, commonly for the first movement.

Ritornello form is similar to rondo form in that it employs periodic returns of some thematic material separated by contrasting episodes. In the rondo, the theme usually returns in the tonic key, whereas in ritornello form the theme returns in different keys, except for the first and last appearances which define the tonic. In the concerto, the principle of thematic recurrence is combined with the then-recently inaugurated but little developed principle of key relationships. The result is a dynamic form possessing both thematic unity and tonal variety. The ritornello passages are normally marked by tonal stability, whereas the solo sections are tonally unstable, modulating from one period of stability to another. The tutti statements of the ritornello provide the structural pillars supporting the soloistic decorations in the movement. The ritornello is usually stated at least four times, separated by solo episodes. The initial and final ritornellos are usually in the tonic, while the second is usually in the dominant or relative minor. The essential features of ritornello form are distilled in Figure 2.

Section	Key	Motives
Ritornello 1 (Tutti)	I	a b c d e c′ e
Solo 1	I–V (III, if minor)	Figuration
Ritornello 2 (Tutti)	V (III, if minor)	a b d e
Solo 2	Modulatory (x x)	Figuration
Ritornello 3 (Tutti)	Various keys, although VI fairly common	a c d
Solo 3	VI–I	Figuration
Ritornello 4 (Tutti)	I	a b c d e c′ e

Roman numerals are conventionally used to indicate a position within a home key. Thus, I stands for the tonic, V for the dominant, III for the mediant or relative major, and VI for the submediant or relative minor. The letter x indicates a broad fluctuation of keys and lack of tonal stability.

Figure 2. Concerto ritornello form

The Ritornello or Tutti Sections

The ritornello, typically played by the tutti, contains the vigorous, decisive thematic material of the movement. The initial ritornello clearly and resolutely defines the tonic key through the use of simple, precise motives that are most often triadic or scalar or a combination of the two. These motives are separable; that is, each can be presented and can stand by itself without destroying the coherence of the entire ritornello. The motives are used like building blocks, a form of construction which stands midway between the Baroque technique of spinning out one long theme and the Classical practice of developing independent themes.

The opening ritornello of Vivaldi's Op. 3, No. 8, RV 522, is a good example. It is made up of several separate and identifiable motives as indicated by the letters a through e in Ex. 4-1. The composer selects from these motives to construct the internal ritornellos, which are only infrequently restatements of the entire ritornello.

Ex. 4-1. Vivaldi, Op. 3, No. 8, RV 522; I. Allegro, mm. 1–16.

The opening ritornello can usually be divided into three sections; the opening phrase, the midsection, and the tail-motive. Of these the first and last are the most important. The opening phrase (a in Ex. 4-1) commonly gives a strong and clearly identifiable character to the entire movement, and by virtue of its strong character is often used by the tutti between solo episodes.

The opening phrases from various concertos presented in Ex. 4-2 are quite typical. They use scales and triadic material and often emphasize notes of the tonic triad through repetition. The basic materials are the same, but each is given a unique shape and rhythmic design.

Ex. 4-2. Vivaldi. Opening ritornello motives.

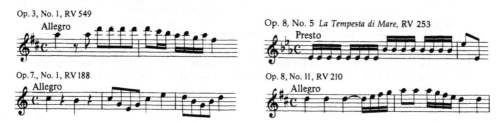

The scoring of the first tutti section is variable, although it is largely homophonic. Only a few are polyphonic—some are fugal, a holdover from earlier decades. Still others present unison statements of a strongly rhythmic nature. Due to the strong reliance on triads and scales in the melodic ideas, the harmony is necessarily often stark and occasionally monotonous. Rarely, one of the motives in the ritornello introduces the parallel tonic mode, particularly if the work is in the major mode. Intense rhythmic drive provides an element of tension that is otherwise missing in the harmonic material.

The major ritornello portions of the movement provide the harmonic ground plan. They are the structural pillars of the movement between which the solo sections are placed. At times portions of the ritornello may even be extracted for use in accompanimental passages, thus bringing a greater sense of unity to the work. Within the major solo sections collisions frequently occur between solo and tutti when short passages of one or two measures of tutti suddenly appear.

The Solo Sections

The soloists in Vivaldi's concertos have more significant roles than in those of his predecessors. Vivaldi's solo instruments play highly decorative passages, lightly accompanied, making for marked contrast with the thematic tutti sections. This opposition augments the dramatic role of the soloist.

The demands made on the soloists far surpass those made by earlier concerto composers. This is of particular note in the violin concertos. Vivaldi probably made a larger contribution to the violin repertoire than did any other single composer in the history of the instrument. The published concertos provide a healthy sampling of that massive body of work. The published works include fifty-three for solo violin, five for two violins (two with cello obbligato), four for four violins (three with cello obbligato), three specifically for oboe, and two other solo violin concertos marked for alternative use by the oboe.

VIOLIN TECHNIQUE

With Francesco Maria Veracini (1690–c. 1750), Franceso Geminiani (1687–1762), Pietro Locatelli (1693–1764), and Giuseppe Tartini (1692–1770), Vivaldi played a leading role in the development of violin technique of the period. As compared with Corelli and Torelli, Vivaldi expanded violin technique by exploiting a greater variety of arpeggiated figures, producing some striking sonorities; by calling for extended positions up through the eighth and possibly beyond according to some contemporary accounts; and by introducing a wider set of bowing requirements. These included staccato (the playing of several detached notes with one stroke of the bow), *spiccato* (the playing of detached notes by dropping the bow on the string and lifting it after each note), *détaché* (the use of single, vigorous bow strokes for individual notes, creating a slight articulation or detachment between notes), and *bariolage* (a coloristic effect involving the rapid vacillation between open and stopped strings).

Vivaldi seldom used multiple stops, and in those few cases they are usually limited to double stops. At times double stops are used for a special effect or to evoke a specific atmosphere, as in the horn-like motives of *La Caccia* (Op. 8, No. 10, RV 362) or in the trumpet-like fanfare passages of several concertos.

Some of the solo violin sections are exceedingly demanding, probably intended for performance by the gifted composer himself. The fingering sometimes given by the composer demonstrates an advanced and highly sophisticated left-hand technique. Although the violin is treated in a brilliant, virtuosic fashion, the parts remain highly idiomatic.

RELATIONSHIP OF SOLO AND TUTTI

Usually there is little or no thematic relationship between the solo and tutti sections, but that is not always the case. Some solo sections are thematically related to the tutti; some may open in a related way only to become decorative; some begin with figuration but return to the ritornello material; and some even introduce a new theme. All of these alternatives are occasionally employed within a single movement, but in those cases in which thematic material is correlated in a single movement it commonly occurs in the opening and closing solo sections. Vivaldi sometimes begins the concerto with a solo section, in which case the soloist usually states the important thematic material. Sometimes Vivaldi has the soloist dramatically interrupt the final ritornello.

THE CADENZA

Coupled with the rise in popularity of virtuoso performance was the increased importance of improvised embellishment. The speed of the outer movements precluded much ornamentation except in improvised cadenzas. The cadenza, an unaccompanied solo passage in which a prominent cadence near the end of the movement is embellished, grew in size and importance during this period, and Vivaldi played a greater or lesser role in its expansion. Quantz even implied that Vivaldi was among the first to use the unaccompanied terminal cadenza in an Allegro movement.[2] Cadenzas were commonly improvised, but some were composed and written down. Nine "longish cadenzas" by Vivaldi do exist.[3] Some are quite simple, with a succession of arpeggiated chords over a dominant pedal point followed by a short section built of modulating sequences leading to the final trill. Some of the more complex examples involve thematic quotations from all three movements.[4] The cadenza was usually inserted before the final recurrence of the ritornello, as an embellishment of the dominant to tonic cadence at that point. The cadenza's length was probably determined by the often-cited rule of the time: that it be limited to what could be sung or played in one breath. Although that practical consideration did not constrain string or keyboard players, it probably served as a convenient guide.

THE SLOW MIDDLE MOVEMENT

Prior to Albinoni and Vivaldi, the concerto middle movement was short and often viewed as a transitional section between the weightier outer movements. Drawing upon the more dramatic music of opera, these Venetian composers intensified the slow movement, sometimes creating the sense that it is the high point of a work. In contrast with the fast movements, the slow middle movement is not generally in ritornello form. No standard form was devised, but many middle movements are built on long cantabile, or songlike, lines in the manner of an adagio operatic aria. The ripieno orchestra is entirely silent in some slow movements, leaving the field to the soloist accompanied by basso continuo throughout (see Op. 8, No. 5, RV 519). Slightly more common are those middle movements in which the cantabile solo is framed by tutti passages at the beginning and end (see Op. 3, No. 11, RV 565). Others make use of the motto entrance of the solo discussed earlier in connection with Albinoni (see Op. 3, No. 3, RV 310). Among the most appealing, but infrequently encountered, of Vivaldi's slow movements are those built on a basso ostinato or ground bass (see Op. 3, No. 8, RV 522). Vivaldi's musical sensitivity is displayed not only in the lyrical solo melodies of the slow movements but in the nuances of dynamic shading and often delicate orchestration. Performers in the eighteenth century continued and expanded the tradition of improvising embellishments for slow movements. Their ornamentation enlivened and transformed the apparently static melodies that were written in their parts.

THE FINALE

Final movements are similar in construction to the opening movements, but in comparison are lighter and more playful. They move very quickly and are generally the shortest of the three movements. A great many are set in triple meter and have a dance quality reminiscent of the final movement of the chamber sonata and of the closing movement of the developing sinfonia. A minuet character occurs in some, particularly those involving woodwind solo instruments. Tutti sections are quite light in texture with an emphasis on three-part homophonic writing.

THE EARLY CONCERTOS

Vivaldi's earliest published concertos clearly indicate the composer's awareness of the formal and technical achievements of Torelli and Albinoni. In addition to discerning the more modern features associated with the work of these two, we can also readily identify qualities recalling Corelli's Op. 6. The mixture of old and new in the Op. 3 works suggests they were composed over a fairly extended period of time, some possibly dating from as early as 1700.

Of the early published sets with concertos (Opp. 3, 4, 6, and 7), Op. 3 is the most interesting and one of the most influential musical publications of the early eighteenth century.[5] Its fanciful title, *L'estro armonico* (Harmonic Caprice), is well suited to the set, which contains concertos printed in a sequence that best shows off their variety. All feature the violin as solo instrument, while solo cello is used as an obbligato instrument in five of the twelve. Four concertos call for one solo violin (Nos. 3, 6, 9, and 12); two for two solo violins (Nos. 5 and 8); two for two solo violins with cello obbligato (Nos. 2 and 11); one for four violins (No. 4); and three for four violins with cello obbligato (Nos. 1, 7, and 10). All are scored for an

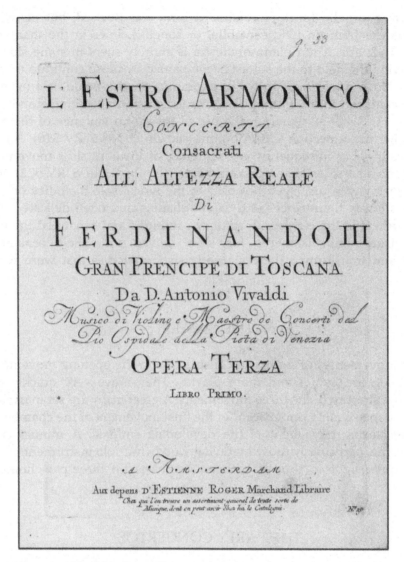

The title page of Vivaldi's Op. 3. This set of twelve concertos, given the fanciful title *L'Estro Armonico* (Harmonic Caprice), was published in Amsterdam in c. 1711–12 by E. Roger. It became widely known and exerted a great influence throughout Europe, but most particularly on J. S. Bach who made keyboard arrangements of half the set in approximately 1713–14. Bach's contact with the Italian concerto had a monumental impact on his musical style and informed his own outstanding contributions to the concerto. (By permission of the British Library.)

eight-part orchestra consisting of four violins, two violas (a distinctly Venetian characteristic), cello, and continuo. The doubling of parts is frequent; for example, third and fourth violins double the second violin in the solo violin concertos, and the viola parts are scored in unison throughout most of the works.

The least modern concertos in the set (Nos. 2, 4, and 7) preserve elements of the Corellian church concerto. They are built on a plan of four or five movements with an opening slow movement and at least one other additional slow movement between the two main allegro movements. Another Corellian feature is the Roman concerto grosso scoring with the addition of the cello to the concertino in several cases, a feature also noted in some Bolognese works. The role of the soloists, even in these more conservative works, however, is more in keeping with then-current practice. They are given more genuinely soloistic parts, far removed from the earlier concerto grosso tradition. To be sure, there remain conservative passages for the solo instruments, but these more nearly approximate the Torelli model, rather than the work of Corelli, as, for example, in passages where two solo violins play together in thirds or echo each other.

In the concertos for one solo violin, we seem to enter the more contemporaneous Venetian world of Albinoni's music. These works depend upon the new dramatic concept of the soloist's role. This concept even spills over into the works for more than one soloist. In the latter Vivaldi tends to feature the soloists individually and in succession, yet commonly placing greater emphasis on the first solo violinist. In Op. 3 the composer is obviously working toward highlighting individual soloists. We have here the embryonic form of the gradual century-long development of the solo-dominated concertos characteristic of the hero-worshipping Romantic age. Salient characteristics of two contrasting concertos from Op. 3 are discussed below.

Concerto for Four Violins and Cello Obbligato in B Minor, Op. 3, No. 10, RV 580

This concerto follows the by-then accepted three-movement plan, despite some organizational features in individual movements which point toward an early date of composition. The opening movement contains elements of the ritornello plan, but the ritornello itself lacks the cohesiveness of later works. The complete motivic independence of solo and tutti, save for the opening four measures, also suggests a relatively early date of composition. As in the more mature examples of ritornello form, however, the main solo sections function as modulatory passages between tonally stable tutti sections.

In a not very common gesture, Vivaldi opens the work with two solo violins introducing the major motives (a and b in Ex. 4-3) of the ritornello, to the accompaniment of a solo viola on a simply articulated tonic pedal point. Throughout the opening movement the soloists dominate, appearing in nearly twice as many measures as the tutti and standing out dramatically. The four solo violins are used in various combinations, but never do all four play within a solo passage at the same time, and only once and for a brief passage do three play together. Generally they appear in pairs or singly. The first violin is the most important, appearing first and most frequently. It dominates the first main solo section and carries the most significant parts most of the time. The other solo instruments follow in order of importance, the second violin controlling the second main solo section. In the final

Ex. 4-3. Vivaldi, Op. 3, No. 10; I. Allegro, mm. 1–2.

and longest solo section (mm. 72–97), all the soloists, including the cellist, appear, but not all at the same time. This solo section provides the climax of the movement with its intense exploration of motive a in diminution, its insistent and characteristic Vivaldian rhythmic drive, and most importantly its kaleidoscopic textural changes.

The great variety of textures in solo sections is one of the most appealing qualities of Vivaldi's concertos. In general, the reduction in the number of parts lightens the texture; accompaniments range from the simplest and most common with only one line for continuo or ripieno violins or violas, to denser ones involving other soloists in more active roles—the obbligato cellist in this case. When soloists are used in pairs, they usually double in thirds or sixths or engage in a game of catch by tossing short motives back and forth.

The second movement, centering in the tonic key of B minor, is multisectional in the older style. The central portion, a Larghetto in $\frac{3}{4}$ time, reveals the composer's fascination with arpeggiated figuration on the violin. Vivaldi's continued exploration and exploitation of the idiomatic possibilities of the violin led him to employ a seemingly inexhaustible array of arpeggiated patterns; in this movement four different patterns are stated simultaneously, creating an interesting display of contrasting sonorities (Ex. 4-4).

Ex. 4-4. Vivaldi, Op. 3, No. 10; II. Larghetto, mm. 1–2.

In passages of extended arpeggiation the composer frequently resorted to a common Baroque shorthand method of notation in which only the chords are shown, leaving the style of arpeggiation to the performer's discretion. An arpeggiated pattern is sometimes written out in the first measure of such a passage to serve as a guide for the realization of the following chords. In the case of this Larghetto, Vivaldi gives verbal directions for the solo first violin, *arpeggio battuto di biscrome,* indicating the beat should be divided into 32nd-notes. Gian Francesco Malipiero (1882–1973), who headed the Istituto Italiano Antonio Vivaldi and edited much of the composer's music, provided a realization in the collected edition (Ex. 4-5). Others are possible, of course, and one modern edition even gives a

Ex. 4-5. Vivaldi, Op. 3, No. 10; II. Larghetto, m. 1.

realization in sixteenth-notes, departing from the original printed edition of E. Roger. Clearly Vivaldi viewed the first violin part here as a solo line, and so its greater animation and intended improvisational character allow it to stand apart from the other solo instruments.

This movement lacks the lyrical solo line so typical of many of Vivaldi's slow movements. It is framed by two dramatic Largo sections in which miniature solos emerge from the tutti chordal passages, reminding us of accompanied recitative found in operas of the time. The adagio measure with its single held chord, separating the Larghetto from the final Largo, was probably intended as a place for a small cadenza.

The finale, an Allegro in ⅝ time, is dancelike and follows a clear ritornello plan. Again the first violin dominates, although each solo instrument is given a place on the stage.

Concerto for Two Violins in A Minor, Op. 3, No. 8, RV 522

A well-defined ritornello (Ex. 4-1) and its subsequent use in the first movement of Op. 3, No. 8, mark this work as more advanced than Op. 3, No. 10. The three bold hammer-strokes (marked x in Ex. 4-1) and subsequent rushing scale constitute a typical opening gesture. The work's tonality, meter, and tempo are made clear from the outset, and the strong rhythmic articulation of the various motives gives the common building blocks character and definition. The solo sections focus on new figuration or on the simple neighboring-note motive b of the ritornello. Frequently one of the solo violins plays sequences of the b motive while the other plays new patterns of figuration. As in several of the concertos for two like instruments, the parts are often reversed so that each soloist has an opportunity to play each figure and to create the sense of lively discussion.

In comparison with the first movement of the B Minor Concerto, Op. 3, No. 10, the A Minor Concerto seems more strongly unified because of the development of ritornello motive b within several of the solo sections. Although both soloists normally play during the solo passages, the first violin part is consistently more virtuosic, with six solo measures (mm. 30–36) to itself.

The Larghetto e spiritoso second movement in D minor presents a cantabile melody in the solo instruments with expressive decorated chains of suspensions (Ex. 4-6). The solo portion is framed by a unison tutti statement of a passacaglia-like theme; this theme serves as the basis of the delicately scored accompaniment of unison third and fourth violins and violas throughout the movement. The term passacaglia normally refers to a set of continuous variations occurring over a repeating bass theme of four to eight measures' duration.

Ex. 4-6. Vivaldi, Op. 3, No. 8; II. Larghetto e spiritoso, mm. 13–15.

The final movement is in the typical fast triple meter and makes use of less complex thematic material than the first movement. The customary figuration for violins pervades the solo passages, with improvised arpeggiation dominating in two substantial sections for the first violin. The most striking feature is the surprising introduction of a warm, cantabile theme in the second violin in the midst of the rapid stylized figuration (Ex. 4-7). The sudden and dramatic introduction of such an engaging melody is a strongly appealing element in this concerto and a technique which Vivaldi successfully uses in numerous other works.

Ex. 4-7. Vivaldi, Op. 3, No. 8; III. Allegro, mm. 87–90.

The solo passages in the four solo concertos of Op. 3 tend to involve more expansive and more virtuosic flourishes, yet in the opening movements there is also greater development of ritornello material. For example, the first movement of Op. 3, No. 6, RV 356, begins with a strong ritornello in the tutti. In the first two solo sections the solo violin develops the first two ritornello motives as well as introducing figuration. The middle movements of the solo concertos are especially notable for their long cantabile solo lines often richly ornamented, as in Op. 3, No. 6. Here the soft, sustained chords of the high string accompaniment enhance the lyrical D-minor melody.

Op. 4, with the intriguing title *La stravaganza* (c. 1712–15), still contains some evidence of an older tradition. Even though all the concertos in this set are solo concertos, an additional solo violin emerges from the ripieno in five of the concertos, responding to the main soloist in several solo sections. This allusion to the older concerto grosso tradition is even more pronounced in the four-movement Op. 4, No. 7, in which a solo cello is also added to solo sections.

In the remainder of Op. 4 and in the concertos contained in Opp. 6 and 7, Vivaldi left the older characteristics behind; in general, however, they lack the sparkling creativity found in many of the Op. 3 concertos. All are true solo concertos, two for oboe and the remainder for violin. The soloist is given neither exceedingly demanding nor imaginative parts, and, indeed, an almost mechanical reliance on sequential figuration, arpeggiation, and bariolage mars several fast movements. Only a few provide genuinely splendid solo parts, as for example Op. 4, No. 5, with its difficult double stops. Vivaldi approached slow movements with much greater flexibility, giving the soloist beautiful lyrical lines and considerable freedom for improvised decoration. Accompaniments to the lyrical solo parts show great care, and their varied delicacy demonstrates Vivaldi's concern for orchestral coloration.

THE LATE CONCERTOS

The most interesting concertos from Vivaldi's second publishing period are those of Op. 8 (publ. 1725). These differ from the earlier concertos in two important respects. Several of the newer works are more or less programmatic, either in a specifically or vaguely descriptive way. Secondly, the technical demands made of the soloist exceed those of the earlier works. In fact, the concertos of Op. 8 are truly brilliant masterpieces of which several have entered the standard repertoire for violinists and Baroque chamber orchestras.

The solo parts, which Vivaldi may have intended for himself, are longer and require greater stamina than those of the earlier concertos. The upper range is extended, and the tessitura of several passages remains in the higher ranges. Other evidence of intentionally flashy writing includes wide-ranging arpeggiated patterns and special effects such as double stops combined with bariolage. The brilliant solo parts require of the violinist supreme technical skill, great vivacity, and sensitivity, particularly in the emotional slow movements.

Twenty-eight of Vivaldi's concertos bear programmatic titles, of which seven appear in Op. 8. The opus has the magnificent and mysterious title *Il cimento dell'armonia e dell'invenzione* (The Encounter of Harmony and Invention). Of course, the intriguing idea indicated by the title of a Vivaldi work does not necessarily have a significant impact on its formal layout, although some of the thematic material can be seen as programmatic. In some cases the thematic material might have prompted the composer to give the work its fanciful name.

Op. 8, No. 5, RV 253, is entitled *La Tempesta di Mare* (The Tempest at Sea); the turbulent material of the first movement may suggest a storm at sea, but the traditional concerto structure remains intact. *La Caccia* (The Hunt), Op. 8, No. 10, RV 362, opens with a hunting horn fanfare while the fugal entry of the second violins suggests a chase. In addition, the solo violin part contains several measures of double stops involving open intervals, suggesting the sounds of a pair of natural horns. The sixth concerto in the set, RV 180, has the title *Il Piacere* (The Amusement) and is a fairly light, entertaining work in C major. Obviously in these three cases, knowing the titles does not necessarily enhance appreciation of the music.

This is not the case in the first four concertos of Op. 8, which together comprise *The Four Seasons*, Vivaldi's most famous composition. Although these four concertos can be enjoyed without knowledge of the program, much of the pleasure in listening to them arises out of following the way in which the composer embodied in music the sense of the four sonnets he is believed to have written.

In the preface of Op. 8, directed to the dedicatee, the Count of Morzin, Vivaldi writes:

> I beg of you not to be surprised if among these few and feeble concertos your Highness should find the Four Seasons which, with your noble bounty, Your Highness has for so long regarded with indulgence. But may you believe that I have found them worthy of appearing in print, because with the sonnets not only are they enhanced by a completely clear interpretation, but so are all the things which are expressed in them.

From this we learn the concertos had been performed before publication.

The sonnets were published along with the concertos, but it cannot be determined whether the sonnets originally served as the basis of the compositions or whether the composer added the sonnets for the publication later. Sections of the poetry were marked off by letters in the left-hand margin as in the following translation of "Summer":

Summer

A Under burning heat of Summer's sun
   Droops man and cow and scorched tree.
B Now calls the cuckoo joined soon
C By song of turtledove and finch.
D Sweet zephyr's airs are sorrowfully turned
   By brusque, contending northern winds.
E Then shepherds cry in dread of barren morrow
   Brought by tempests' flailing might.
F His weary body knows no rest
   In feat of lightning bolt, of thunderclap,
   Assailed by furious swarms of countless flies.
G Alas, he knows his fate full well.
   The howling storm, the pelting hail, sweep down
   To crush to earth the waving corn.

The letters and their accompanying lines are also quoted directly in the musical score to establish the close correspondence of the music and the poetry. In addition, subtitles, such as "The Enervating Heat" at the opening of *The Summer Concerto,* are given for each section of the score.

The concertos of *The Four Seasons* successfully accommodate the expression of the program within normal concerto theory and practice. A ritornello theme sets the general mood; within the formal concerto framework and backed by the general mood of the ritornello, the solo violin performs the more highly descriptive passages.

Spring. In the bright, E-major opening movement of *La primavera* (Op. 8, No. 1, RV 269), a joyous song welcoming the new season serves as the ritornello frame for the "Song of the Birds" with its unmistakable bird calls in the main solo violin as well as in the two solo orchestral violins. A "Murmuring Fountain" and a storm of "Thunder" (and lightning) precede the movement's closing in the tranquil repeat of the "Song of the Birds" ritornello. The solo violin, with its warmly lyrical theme, represents "The Sleeping Goatherd" in the middle movement to an accompaniment of gently rocking violins, whose parts are identified as "The Rustling of the Leaves and Plants." The two repeated notes on the violas represent the shepherd's dog barking. The final movement, the "Danza Pastorale," creates the atmosphere suggested by the closing lines of the sonnet. It recalls the pastorale tradition we saw in Corelli's "Christmas Concerto."

Summer. *L'estate* (Op. 8, No. 2, RV 315) begins in G minor with a tutti representation of "The Enervating Heat." The solo violin represents the cuckoo, the turtledove, and the goldfinch in the B and C sections of the sonnet quoted earlier. Sweet zephyr winds succeeded by the ever strengthening "various winds" and "Boreal Wind" comprise the D section. After brief allusions to the languishing opening, the solo violin plays "The Peasant's Plaint" of section E. The movement closes with an agitated passage representing the tempests. The G-minor Adagio movement corresponds to section F of the sonnet and continues the description of the shepherd's lamentable condition. The accompaniment alternates between material marked "Flies and Horseflies" and "Thunder." Section G of the sonnet is depicted in the final movement, entitled "Summer's Impetuous Climate."

Autumn. *L'autunno* (Op. 8, No. 3, RV 293) opens with a happy F-major movement, "Dancing and Singing of the Peasants," over the lines:

> With dance and song the peasants hail
> The happy time of harvest's fruits.

The tutti theme is in the style of an authentic peasant dance (Ex. 4-8). The soloist repeats this theme in double stops, and the orchestra concludes the opening section. In the next section, "The Drunkard," the solo violin is given a wild succession of broken chords, triplet figures, and scales in an exceedingly wide range to depict the exuberant state of inebriation. Snatches of the tutti dance theme punctuate this long solo, picturing for the listener the peasant's merrymaking. The ritornello peasant dance returns in G minor, moving to D minor. The drunkard returns with his characteristically wild gestures (Ex. 4-9); after another tutti dance section a quiet Larghetto depicts the "Drunkard Sleeping" as "they end their joy with slumber deep." The movement closes with the boisterous ritornello marked allegro assai, rather than allegro as in the beginning.

Ex. 4-8. Vivaldi, *Autumn*, Op. 8, No. 3; I. Allegro, mm. 1–3.

Ex. 4-9. Vivaldi, *Autumn*, Op. 8, No. 3; I. Allegro, mm. 67–77.

In the D-minor slow movement all have finally succumbed to sleep. The title of the section is "The Drunken Ones Sleep," and the sonnet reads:

> Now one by one they've left their sport.
> The Season's mild and temperate clime
> Brings peace and restful sleep to all.

The strings, muted, play sustained tones while the harpsichordist is instructed to improvise arpeggiated figures. The music is quite similar to a Largo portion of the concerto *La Notte* (The Night, Op. 10, No. 2, RV 439).

The finale, "The Hunt," is similar in structure to the first movement, with a ritornello (Ex. 4-10) of rustic simplicity and strength:

> At dawn's first light the hunters come
> With horn and hound and hunting gun.

Ex. 4-10. Vivaldi, *Autumn*, Op. 8, No. 3; III. Allegro, mm. 1–4.

In the section headed "Guns and Hounds," the ripieno strings simulate gun shots and baying, while the soloist represents the prey with frenzied runs and arpeggios. Each twist and turn in the solo part portrays an effort to escape, but the orchestra pursues its victim with the ritornello hunt theme until the prey, "fatigued and wounded, falls and dies." The tutti hunting theme closes the movement in true ritornello form.

Winter. *L'inverno* (Op. 8, No. 4, RV 297) is a fantastic winterscape painted by the tonal master; the music is the servant of the detailed program. Repeated F-minor eighth-note chords establish the bleakness of the scene, while the soloist is the whistling of the "terrible wind." The "running and stamping of feet because of the cold" (Ex. 4-11a) and chattering of teeth (Ex. 4-11b) are clearly depicted.

Ex. 4-11a. Vivaldi, *Winter*, Op. 8, No. 4; I. Allegro non molto, mm. 22–23.

Ex. 4-11b. Vivaldi, *Winter*, Op. 8, No. 4; I. Allegro non molto, m. 47.

The Largo movement portrays the pleasant feeling shared by those at the fireside, now sheltered from the cold and wet. The pizzicato violin accompaniment to the aria-like solo represents rain throughout.

The finale opens with a "Walking on Ice" section depicting the alternately slow and hurried, frightened and confident treading on ice, complete with a fall and cracking of the ice. In the last section, "The Sirocco," a wind "howls round each bolted door." The final words over the violin part, "such is winter, yet it has its joys," provide some comfort even though the howling tempest continues to the end.

Vivaldi's concertos of the late 1720s refine and adjust to the basic concerto form which he had helped to standardize. Some reveal the influence of the newer *style galant* in much the same way that Albinoni's later works do. The *style galant* is especially evident in the use of graces, triplets, short trills, and other embellishing figures (see, for example, the Largo of Op. 9, No. 2, RV 345). A movement toward vocally conceived solo parts along the lines of coloratura singing, and away from the clearly violinistic type of figuration, is evident in some late works, especially in his last published concertos of Op. 12. Nevertheless, virtuoso violin traits are retained, as can be seen in the tricky double stops and extended cadenza of Op. 11, No. 5, RV 202, or the dramatic opening with triple-stopped chords of Op. 11, No. 4, RV 308. The flute is introduced as a solo instrument in the six works of Op. 10, five of which are reworkings of earlier chamber concertos.

Vivaldi's concertos range from those written in a conservative Corellian style to those pointing to the symphonic style of the late eighteenth century. The dramatic conception of the soloist's role, the clear and flexible forms, the rhythmic and instrumental vitality of the fast movements, the intense lyricism and delicate scoring of the operatic slow movements, the exploration of motivic development, the use of winds, and some fondness for programmatic content all combine to make Vivaldi's concertos some of the most significant and influential compositions of the late Baroque era.

GEORGE FRIDERIC HANDEL

Handel, the cosmopolitan, was born in Halle, Germany, in 1685. In his youth he became an accomplished organist and violinist, but wishing to pursue opera composition he went to the cultural metropolis of Hamburg, the site of Germany's first opera company and one of the most important centers of opera in Europe. He remained there from 1703 to 1706. His continuing interest in opera then led him to the major opera centers of Italy—Rome, Florence, Naples, and Venice—during the years 1706 to mid-1710. In the course of his Italian sojourn he was not only exposed to the music of great Italian composers but also came to meet and know Alessandro and Domenico Scarlatti, Pasquini, Marcello, Lotti, Gasparini, Steffani, and Corelli.

These experiences so decisively influenced his musical thinking that his mature compositional style was largely formed by the time he left Italy. For a short time in 1710 Handel was composer at the Court of the Elector of Hanover. In the fall of that year Handel traveled to London where he enjoyed a sensational success with his opera *Rinaldo*. After a short interval in Hanover, the composer returned in 1712 to London where he remained for the rest of his life. He became a naturalized British subject in 1726 and has come to be regarded by the English as one of their foremost composers.

A fascinating aspect of Handel's music is its basis in several national styles—German, French, and Italian. The coexistence of these distinct and disparate styles in individual pieces greatly adds to their appeal. Yet however cosmopolitan the springs of his musical inspiration, the Italian style remained dominant, so that the English viewed him as a representative of genuine Italian music.

In Rome and Venice, Handel witnessed the startling and rapid development of the concerto and acquired a lasting taste for larger orchestral sounds. Even before his trip to Italy, Handel might have known Torelli's Op. 6, *Concerti musicali*, for it was published in Germany in 1698, and Torelli was resident, for a time, in Ansbach, not far from Handel's home in Halle. Finally established in London, Handel could still refer directly to Italian instrumental models, for several Italian violinists lived there or made extensive visits to London. For example, the great violinist Geminiani, a pupil of Corelli, had settled in England, and the Italian violinist and composer Veracini spent several months and years there, thanks to his warm reception by the English. In addition, numerous Italian concertos were beginning to circulate in printed form in the early decades of the eighteenth century; Handel must surely have been aware of them.

While Handel's concertos exhibit a broad acquaintance with the work of many Italian composers, the dominating influence is clearly that of Corelli. It is easy to imagine Handel's attraction to Corelli's restrained, idiomatic, yet almost bel canto use of the violin and the resultant bright, sensuous sound. Vivaldi's brilliant virtuoso and strongly instrumental style had far less appeal to Handel.

Despite the manifest influence of Corelli and the Roman concerto grosso tradition, Handel's concertos are highly personal works of art. They mix old and new traditions in a delightful blend of such diverse musical elements as the *sonata da chiesa*, French overture, French, English, and Italian dances, aria, duet, accompanied recitative, fugue, and theme and variations. The appealing qualities of Handel's style—the tuneful melodic material, the fresh rhythms (often dotted, showing a French influence), the transparent texture, and the dramatic juxtapositions—further enhance his concertos.

Handel's concertos include four published sets and several individual works. The earliest known example, the serenata *Il Trionfo del Tempo e del Disinganno* (The Triumph of Time and Truth), dates from his stay in Rome in 1707. The concerto grosso technique of scoring receives some important attention, and the overture resembles a one-movement concerto grosso for oboes, trumpets, and strings.

THE CONCERTOS OF OP. 3 AND OP. 6

In 1734 Walsh published Handel's Op. 3, containing six concerti grossi that have come to be known by the misleading title, "The Oboe Concertos." A pair of oboes is specified together with strings, but the oboes are not the featured soloists. Bassoon, recorders, flute, harp, and small organ also appear in these richly scored works. The concertos of Op. 3 seem to have been hastily put together; many movements are reworkings of earlier pieces. Chrysander, the great nineteenth-century Handel scholar, even claimed that No. 3 dates from Handel's Hanover stay of 1711–12. Inevitably, the later Op. 6, when compared to Op. 3, is found to be finer. Nevertheless, there are numerous attractive movements in the earlier set with its colorful and pleasing scoring.

The Twelve Grand Concertos, published in 1739 by Walsh as Op. 6, rank among the greatest achievements of Baroque orchestral music. They were composed in a few weeks in the fall of 1739 probably to be performed between acts of Handel's oratorios and operas, as was the case with his organ concertos.

The conservative features of these pieces bear a fundamental likeness to those of Corelli's concerti grossi, which were composed forty years earlier. The concertino retains the texture of the trio sonata with its two violins of equal importance and basso continuo. The solo episodes are typically short and thematically identical to the tutti sections; the focus is on the contrast between solo and orchestral textures, not on soloistic display. Handel's Op. 6 concerti grossi are dignified and reserved like Corelli's; the sober, but sensuous, slow movements particularly recall the Corelli model.

The church concerto appears to have served as the formal model for these concertos, although the overall organization of each work is quite flexible. Three of the concertos have four movements; eight have five movements, and one has six. The slow-fast-slow-fast church scheme with one fugal movement provides the basic plan which is often expanded by the addition of a dance movement.

No regular or predictable alternation between solo and tutti is evident, and in some movements, such as the Andante of Concerto No. 3 in E Minor, or the opening Larghetto of Concerto No. 4 in A Minor, the concertino is never given a solo passage. Concerto No. 7 in B-flat Major is tutti throughout. As mentioned earlier, the solo passages seldom differ thematically or stylistically from the tutti passages. Exceptions to this practice can be found in the final Allegro of Concerto No. 11 in A Major and the Allegro fourth movement of Concerto No. 6 in G Minor which employ solo passages of decorative figuration. The Allegro second movement of Concerto No. 3 in E Minor is a rare exception reminding us that these works are really contemporary with Vivaldi, not Corelli.

Concerto No. 5 in D Major, a favorite of eighteenth-century music historian Charles Burney, is one of the lighter, yet one of the most extraordinary in the group. The first movement, a full-scale French overture, opens with a simple but typically gracious French gesture on solo violin expressed over a two-octave range (Ex. 5-1). The remaining slow portion of the French overture consists of a stately tutti built on the motive introduced by the solo employing rapidly descending scale fragments. The fugal portion of the French overture opens with typical Handelian rhythmic momentum (Ex. 5-2) and features the concertino in short passages. The Presto and second Allegro movements are symphonic in conception—the rhythmic drive of the Presto resembles that of a scherzo(!) while the busy string writing of the Allegro foreshadows a common technique found in an early symphonic movement. The dignified and more conservative Largo is placed between these modern movements. With its expressive suspensions and sustained tones, it could easily be mistaken for a movement by Corelli. The Minuet, marked *un poco larghetto* and scored tutti throughout, has been a favorite of Handel admirers for centuries. Its tuneful melody, the clarity of phrase structure and texture, and the fact that it is a theme with two variations are all modern features pointing toward the music of the Classical period.

Ex. 5-1. Handel, Op. 6, No. 5; I. Largo, mm. 1–3.

Ex. 5-2. Handel, Op. 6, No. 5; II. Allegro, mm. 1–3.

Concerto No. 6 in G Minor is one of the most frequently performed today. The first movement, Larghetto e affettuoso, is long and dramatic with frequent juxtapositions of tutti and concertino, strong dynamic contrasts, and effective pauses. The fugal Allegro, tutti throughout, is based on a most unusual chromatic subject (Ex. 5-3). The gentle Musette, with its bagpipe-inspired drones, is constructed in a rondo fashion and features short antiphonal sections between concertino and ripieno or between tutti first violins and tutti second violins, as in several of Corelli's concerto movements. In the powerful Allegro that follows, the jagged contour, energetic rhythm, and Vivaldi-like solo material for first violin provide strong contrast to the serene Musette. The final Allegro in $\frac{3}{8}$ time is one of Handel's most delightfully light pieces. The texture is reduced to three parts with unison violins playing a catchy dance tune to the simple eighth-note accompaniment of violas, basses, and continuo. The clarity and simplicity, along with the quick triplet figures, derive from the French tradition which Handel so greatly admired.

Ex. 5-3. Handel, Op. 6, No. 6; II. Allegro, ma non troppo, mm. 1–3.

THE ORGAN CONCERTOS

Handel may have originated the genre of the organ concerto for his own use as intermezzo in his equally original genre, the English oratorio. The idea would have occurred quite naturally to such a great keyboard artist, since an instrument and orchestra were readily available at such times. It is apparent that he improvised much of his solo material, for the printed works frequently carry the direction *ad libitum,* and the solo parts are usually quite sketchy. The printed solo passages should only be thought of as a skeletal framework for what the composer actually played. Several contemporary writers remarked on Handel's skill as an organist and often made note of his exceptional improvisational gifts.

Op. 4, the first collection of organ concertos entitled *Six Concertos for the Harpsichord or Organ,* was published by Walsh in 1738. These concertos are certainly suitable for harpsichord performance; the modest English organ Handel played had only one manual and no pedal board. This small organ was well suited to accompanying a chorus and was played by Handel during performances of his oratorios. Handel is known to have been interested in the relatively new swell pedal, which may have been incorporated into both the organ and harpsichord he played. The less well-known adaptation to the harpsichord was peculiar to England and functioned much the same way as did the swell mechanism on the organ. On the harpsichord it was a mechanical device that either opened or closed a portion of the lid and/or louvers installed directly over the string case.

Although Handel must have known the polyphonic church music designed by northern German composers for their glorious organs, he never composed anything for such an instrument or in such a manner. Handel's organ music is relaxed, light, and transparent, reflecting his Italian leanings. The organ concertos are pleasant concert music unlike the serious, overwhelming style of the German organ masters which was never conceived as light entertainment. The two-part setting of Handel's organ passages often relies on the style of figuration characteristic of violin concertos of the period. The texture may require filling in and embellishing, but the homophonic idiom must remain.

The Op. 4 concertos are modest examples of intimate chamber music. Five of the six are in four movements, generally following the *sonata da camera* plan but employing some contrapuntal elements. Only the fourth concerto has a fugal movement, the finale, and the autograph manuscript includes a concluding choral alleluia revealing a connection to the oratorio *Il Trionfo del Tempo.*

Many historians have noted that Handel anticipated several characteristics of the Classical style, suggesting that this modernism must have been what kept his music alive at a time when J. S. Bach's had passed into oblivion. Rather than to infer Handel's anticipation of upcoming tendencies, it is wiser to acknowledge that he was keenly aware of new trends, particularly those developing in Italy, and that he drew upon them while maintaining a basically conservative stance. One of the more striking modern features in the organ concertos is the occasional use of contrasting themes to highlight changes of key or mode in a movement, tentatively pointing toward a characteristic feature of sonata-allegro form of the later eighteenth century. For example, after the second ritornello passage in the Allegro second movement of Op. 4, No. 1, the solo organ presents a strongly contrasting theme in the tonic minor.

In 1740 Walsh issued six more organ concertos without opus number. These concertos are arrangements of other Handel works. Only the first two arrangements were made by Handel and employ a ripieno orchestra, while the remaining four were made by Walsh's assistants and are simply reductions for organ. Five of these six were arrangements of the previously issued Op. 6, *Twelve Grand Concertos,* and were obviously published by Walsh to exploit an eager public. Although these later arrangements are not highly regarded and are rarely performed, they do demonstrate the organ's ability to function like the concertino.

The Op. 7 set of six organ concertos was published posthumously in 1760 by Walsh. These late works, dating from 1740 to 1751, are on a larger scale than those of Op. 4; they employ more counterpoint and exhibit greater variety and freedom of style. They demand a great deal of improvisation throughout—indeed the entire slow middle movement must be improvised for the second, fourth, and sixth concertos. The trend toward the inclusion of dual themes and the tonal plan of the Classical sonata form is more evident as well.

Movements in variation form and binary form occur frequently in the works of Opp. 4 and 7, for both provide natural opportunities for improvisation, especially in the repeated parts. The only concerto requiring an organ with a pedal is Op. 6, No. 1; its passacaglia-like variations in the first movement provide an excellent opportunity for fancy footwork.

Concertos not contained within published sets include three for solo oboe, one for violin, the C Major Concerto in *Alexander's Feast* (1736), calling for a trio sonata solo group, and three concertos "a due cori."

Handel used the concerto in still another way. Concerto grosso scoring and concerto instrumental style clearly informed his dramatic vocal music. Handel frequently employed concerto grosso orchestration in his vocal works, following Stradella's lead. The tutti, comprising both concertino and ripieno, usually plays the overture—frequently in concertante style—and ritornellos in the arias, while the concertino accompanies the solo voices. Handel was one of the great orchestrators of the Baroque era, and his subtle use of the orchestra owes much to the concerto as developed by his predecessors.

Chapter Six

THE CONCERTO IN GERMANY

The emergence of national musical styles became clearly evident in the Baroque era, and German music of the Baroque period exhibits several fairly distinctive qualities—a strongly contrapuntal texture, a sophisticated harmonic idiom, and a sense of color. German musicians were particularly receptive to outside musical influences as well, quite easily assimilating and appropriating elements of Italian and French styles. From the Italians, with their love of song, the German composers took the dramatic use of solo voice and eventually participated in the transference of qualities associated with the vocal idiom to instruments. From the French, with their love of ballet, the German composers acquired the elegant dance rhythms and the French interest in rich orchestral textures. German composers forged a unique and original Baroque style from the synthesis of these foreign elements with those from their own tradition.

Numerous musicians throughout the seventeenth and eighteenth centuries were involved in transmitting foreign styles to Germany. Many Italian musicians came to live and work in Germany but continued to compose and perform music as they had known it in their homeland. Italy, in turn, with its many flourishing operatic institutions and centers of violin making and playing, drew hosts of German musicians to its soil. They returned home with strongly formed impressions of the southern style. The plan of the Italian sonata was adopted by the Germans but their fondness for counterpoint and greater contrasts in sound colors led them to modify and adapt it to suit the national taste of the northern audiences. For example, to incorporate greater color contrast, German composers might substitute a gamba for the traditional second violin in the trio sonata. Texture was also changed to satisfy the Germans' appetite for counterpoint. For example, Ignaz Franz Biber (1644–1704) experimented extensively with *scordatura*, or unusual tuning of the violin's strings, to facilitate the playing of multiple stops, often suggesting a more polyphonic texture in his solo violin sonatas. The most extreme examples of this German penchant for the art of polyphony is to be found in J. S. Bach's writing for the solo string instrument in his unaccompanied sonatas for violin. The Italians, on the other hand, had tended to treat the instrument as an extension of the voice.

While German composers were to appropriate the Italian concerto as an important form of orchestral music, they had, prior to the development of the concerto, already created a new type of orchestral suite. The suite of dances had become the major vessel for German orchestral music by the end of the seventeenth century, and so was the form which most readily accommodated elements of the imported concerto grosso. Thus it is within the suite that the first elements of the Italian concerto style can be detected.

The suite had a long history in Germany, but by the mid-seventeenth century the patterns of French dance music as contained in the French suite made their way into the German suite. Near the end of the seventeenth century the French influence on German orchestral music became more pronounced, particularly in the south, where pupils of the archetypal French composer, Lully, composed suites "in the French manner." Many of these suites open with a French overture, and the word *Ouverture,* that appeared over the first movement was often used to designate the entire work. Georg Muffat (1653–1704) was one of the first German composers to publish a collection of suites in the Lullian manner and was also the first to introduce the Corellian concerto grosso to Germany.

Muffat considered himself German and lived out his life in several German cities. Yet his place of birth (Mégère in the principality of Savoy in southeastern France close to Italy and Switzerland) coupled with family background (his father was of Scottish ancestry and his mother of French) probably kindled his enthusiasm for the blending of various national musical styles. As a student, he spent six years mastering the French style in Paris under Lully and several of the master's followers. In 1678 Muffat was appointed organist at the Cathedral of Salzburg. He was granted a leave in 1682 to study in Rome where he came to know Corelli and became acquainted with the concerto grosso. This Italian journey deeply affected the young composer and markedly altered his musical style. In 1690 Muffat was appointed organist to the Bishop of Passau and in 1695 was made Kapellmeister, remaining in Passau until his death in 1704.

As we have seen in Chapter 2, Muffat wrote an important and detailed commentary to elucidate the principles and practices governing Corelli's concertos. Muffat extended the same principles and practices to the French suite in two important publications. The first, *Armonico Tributo* (1682), was issued in Salzburg in honor of the 1100th anniversary of the founding of the Archbishopric of Salzburg and was dedicated to Archbishop Max Gandolf who had underwritten Muffat's trip to Italy.

The five compositions making up this harmonic tribute to Italian music present clear evidence of Muffat's early efforts to incorporate concerto grosso elements in the French suite. The works are scored for a five-part orchestra consisting of two violins, two violas, and violone (and continuo harpsichord), in imitation of the French practice. In the preface, the composer advises that the works may be played with one instrument per part or by full orchestra throughout. Muffat offers a still more interesting option by suggesting the orchestra may be split into two contrasting groups—a concertino of two violins, violoncello, or viola da gamba, and a concerto grosso consisting of full orchestra. Muffat explains that the letters printed in the parts, S for solo or concertino; T for tutti or concerto grosso, designate passages to be played by the contrasting groups if this option is exercised. Such concertato passages are found in almost every movement.

The formal plan of the works, which the composer calls sonatas, is a curious hybrid of church sonata, chamber sonata, and French suite. Four of the five compositions open with movements marked *Sonata,* but no plan of construction standard to these movements is evident. They are rather a tentative mixture of French overture, clearly apparent in Sonatas 1 and 3, and the patchwork movements found in some of Corelli's Op. 6 concerti grossi. Some of the Grave opening sections are chordal, as in the French overture (for example, No. 3), while others are linear and contain the suspensions so typical of Corelli's opening slow sections (for example, No. 2). Muffat used the movement title Sonata to indicate an introductory movement, as is made clear in the quadrilingual titles given to the first movements of the Suites in his *Florilegium* set where he uses the French *Ouverture*, the Latin *Exordium* or *Praeludium*, the German *Vorspiel* or *Eingang*, and the Italian *Introduzione* or *Sonata* interchangeably.

Following the initial movement, faster dance movements usually alternate with slower, non-dance sections, but in no consistent pattern. In general, the dance movements have strong French traits while the non-dance sections appear to have been modeled after the music of Corelli. The dances, including those not of French origin, such as the Balletto, are filled with dotted rhythms that Muffat carried over from the French style. The style of ornamentation reflects the composers French training, too, as he uses a small *t* to indicate the notes to be ornamented, but not the specific ornament to be played. The five-part scoring is also typically French, although the choice of instruments for each part more closely follows German tradition. The concerto grosso option is, of course, Italian.

Muffat's manner of juxtaposing and contrasting the concertino and concerto grosso inevitably brings to mind Corelli's Op. 6; only occasionally does the musical material in the two groups differ. The virtual equality of the two violins, their frequent crossing of parts, the use of suspensions, and the limited technical demands also derive from Corelli's practice. On the other hand the generally full texture, the occasional use of chromaticism, and the basic outlines of the suite derive from the German tradition.

In 1707 Muffat published his last collection under the title *Ausserlesene Instrumentalmusik: 12 Concerti grossi* (Selected Instrumental Music: 12 Concerti Grossi). Several of these works are based on pieces from the composer's 1682 collection while others were completed prior to 1690. If this group had been issued in 1695, when Muffat first initiated this publication, it would have contained the earliest works published bearing the name concerto grosso.

In reworking the earlier sonatas (concertos Nos. 5, 4, 2, and 11 are based respectively on sonatas 1, 2, 3, and 4; Sonata No. 5 is the basis for parts of concertos 10 and 12), Muffat changed the number and order of movements, and, most importantly, made the concerto element more explicit by providing a true concerto grosso scoring. As with Corelli's concerti grossi, a continuo is assigned to both the concertino and ripieno groups.

Most of the twelve concertos share a similar structure, with their movements in the following order:

    I. Sonata
   II. A dance—Ballo, Corrento, Sarabande, Allemande, or Aria
  III. Grave
  IV. A dance—typically a newer one, such as Gavotte, Giga, or Minuet, although Arias or Sarabandes do appear
   V. A dance—usually from the French Ballet, such as a Giga, a Rondeau, Borea, or Minuet

In comparison with his earlier sonatas, these works have fewer Italian-style slow interludes, and the movements are longer. A further departure is found in a reduction in the number of solo-tutti contrasts, while at the same time the first violin is given greater exposure, as in some of Corelli's concertos. With their strong juxtaposition of styles, the earlier set clearly displays the work of a composer thoroughly trained in the French style who had discovered the Italian style. By contrast the later concertos represent a stronger fusion or synthesis of a variety of styles. The works of *Ausserlesene Instrumentalmusik* are truly a blending of suite and concerto and can be viewed as either suites with strong concertante elements or as concertos with pronounced features of the suite.

Muffat probably introduced the concerto to Germany, but it is difficult to trace any direct influence of his work, except in the music of one of his colleagues in Passau, Benedikt Anton Aufschnaiter (1665–1742). The two principal sets of orchestral pieces by Aufschnaiter parallel the two sets by Muffat just discussed. In 1695 Aufschnaiter published *Concors discordia* (The Concord of Discord), a set of eight orchestral suites with concertino sections, and in 1703 the *Dulcis Fidium Harmonia Symphoniis ecclesiasticis concinnata* (Sweet String Harmony Adapted to Church Symphonies). In the later collection two violins are called for in the concertino, and this small group is more frequently set in contrast with the orchestra than in Muffat's *Ausserlesene Instrumentalmusik*.

Muffat failed to set in motion a great German trend of concerto composition, but his intimate knowledge of the musical styles of Europe, revealed both in his music and in his important discussions of musical practices in the prefaces to his published works, must have made a sufficient impact to prepare German composers for what was to follow. His concertos, easy and graceful early attempts to synthesize French, Italian, and German styles, paved the way for the culminating works of J. S. Bach and others. Through Muffat, the plan and practices of Corelli's concertos had been introduced, but the great, almost overwhelming, influence of the Italian concerto was not to be decisively felt until the works of Torelli, Albinoni, and Vivaldi began to circulate around 1710. And when the concerto form truly began to take hold in Germany, Vivaldi's concertos provided the basic model not just for Bach but for his contemporaries as well.

Chapter Seven

JOHANN SEBASTIAN BACH

Johann Sebastian Bach (1685–1750) produced superb and lasting contributions to all of the great forms of Baroque music except for opera. While he wrote few concertos, they are of monumental significance. Bach produced his music to meet the needs of a particular situation, as did his contemporaries. Thus the works of this period, including Bach's, reflect the requirements of the different employers composers served. For example, most of Bach's organ works derive from the early part of his career when he was primarily employed as an organist, despite the fact that he maintained an interest in organ music throughout his life. Similarly, his concertos were composed at specific points in his career when such instrumental music was required by his position. His concertos are the work of that period when he was music director at the court of the Prince of Cöthen (1717–23) and again when he was especially involved with the Collegium Musicum (1729–37; 1739–41) in Leipzig.

Bach learned his craft by copying and studying the scores of other composers, then writing in imitation of their styles. In this way he assimilated many diverse styles; accordingly, the influence of various composers can be detected at different points in his career. His earliest compositions document the impact of the northern German composers of organ music, especially Buxtehude, Lübeck, and Böhm. The organ works from Bach's early appointments at Arnstadt (1703–07) and Mühlhausen (1707–08) are characteristically rhapsodic and exuberant with a strong emotional quality, reflecting this influence.

Accounts of Bach's having been introduced to the Italian concerto by his distant cousin J. G. Walther (1684–1748)—the great lexicographer whose *Musicalisches Lexicon* (1732) was the first major music dictionary in German and the first in any language to include both terms and biographies—remain uncorroborated. Circumstantial evidence now seems to indicate that the Duke of Weimar's young nephew, Prince Johann Ernst, may have been responsible for bringing the Italian concerto style to the attention of Bach and possibly to Walther at the same time. Whatever the avenue of Bach's acquaintance, it is clear that it was not until Bach took up the position of court organist at Weimar (1708–17) that he came into direct contact with Italian instrumental music.

Prince Johann Ernst was a great music enthusiast and his interests clearly influenced the artistic endeavors at his uncle's courts. The Prince traveled extensively and so became acquainted with musical developments throughout Europe. He in turn brought this knowledge to Weimar in the form of purchased scores and parts. He spent some time in Utrecht and Amsterdam in 1713, and we know the

Prince was unstinting in his expenditures to acquire the latest compositions then available in Amsterdam, a center of eighteenth-century music publishing. Bills for binding, copying, and shelving music at the Weimar court in June 1713 suggest the Prince returned with a veritable trove of musical treasures. While we cannot be certain that he acquired Vivaldi's recently published Opp. 3 and 4 concertos, he might well have. It is also possible that on his return the Prince urged Bach (and Walther) to make keyboard transcriptions of the Italian concertos similar to those the Prince had heard by the blind organist J. J. de Graaf while in the Netherlands. Whatever the actual course of affairs, the Italian concerto swept through Weimar and elicited an immediate response from Bach, whose works of around 1713–14 show striking stylistic changes directly related to the Italian concerto.

The impact of the Italian concerto on Bach was enormous and lasting. He learned the style in his usual manner of copying scores, then assimilated and combined it with his own contrapuntal north German style. The result is a synthesis of Italian and German traits into what we now think of as the Bach style. As was noted earlier, German composers were peculiarly receptive to practices developed elsewhere, which they integrated into their national style to create in turn a newly synthesized style. Bach's artistic accomplishments are certainly the apogee of this proclivity for synthesis in the German Baroque.

Bach's introduction to the concerto brought fundamental changes to his music. On the most obvious level, the principle of tutti-solo contrast, coupled with a formal and tonal scheme, invaded virtually all of Bach's musical output. At a less obvious, but perhaps more important, level, Bach learned the art of clarity and conciseness that characterizes the compelling Italian melodic style. Bach's fondness for the Italian melodic style is evidenced by his use of themes by Corelli, Legrenzi, and Albinoni as subjects for several fugues. He was probably attracted by their strong character and their extraordinary potential for contrapuntal writing. A new incisive rhythmic quality, greater reliance on motivic unity, and a clearer and stronger harmonic foundation also appear in Bach's music of this period, certainly a direct result of his assimilation of the Italian concerto style.

It is no mere coincidence that the works identified as marking the advent of Bach's compositional maturity date from his exposure to Italian music—specifically the Italian concerto. The discovery of Italian instrumental music was undoubtedly one of the most significant events in Bach's creative life.

THE KEYBOARD TRANSCRIPTIONS

Bach's earliest works in the concerto form are solo keyboard transcriptions and arrangements of violin concertos by Vivaldi and others. He wrote these in Weimar soon after he was introduced to the concerto. Six are written for organ (BWV 592–597) and sixteen for harpsichord (BWV 972–987). The original models include nine by Vivaldi (see endnote 5, Chapter 4, for details), five by Johann Ernst, and one each by A. Marcello and Telemann, while four remain unknown.[1]

These arrangements not only represent Bach's learning process but also reveal the blending of elements of Italian and German styles. The originals were adopted, adapted, and transformed into something new and different. While the violin, with its voice-like qualities, had become the instrument of the south, the keyboard instruments, with their capacity for multivoiced counterpoint, became the instruments of the north. Bach's transcriptions demonstrate not only the German fondness for the keyboard but Bach's extraordinary skill in adapting the idiom of the violin to the keyboard.

Although Bach made no radical changes in musical substance, he did alter details of the originals to make them more suitable for the keyboard. His general procedure was to transpose the violin works down one tone in order to accommodate the violin's upper reach on the keyboard. The right hand of the keyboard player is given the solo part, while the left hand—or, in some of the organ transcriptions, the pedal—is given a more lively and idiomatic version of the bass line. The harmony is often realized through broken chord patterns. The tutti-solo contrasts of the concerto are imitated through changes of manual, which are carefully detailed. Bach adds ornamentation to the slow movements for which no decoration is indicated in the original sources since ornamentation would have been improvised by the Italian performers. Other alterations—such as the intensification of the inner parts, the introduction of counterpoint and points of imitation, the addition of pedal points, the enriching of harmony, and the use of important motives in the bass—while related to the keyboard medium were not necessitated by it. These alterations grew out of Bach's German musical heritage and tend to make his transcriptions more complex than the original works.

All are the products of a German keyboard composer who had recently discovered the Italian concerto style. They typically appear more Germanic than Italianate, as Bach superimposed German polyphony on the Italian structure of the originals. Eventually, once Bach incorporated elements of the concerto style into his own compositions, he integrated the German and Italian styles in a more complete fashion. This merger formed the basis of his mature compositional style.

Bach's opportunities for writing instrumental music appear to have been limited in Weimar, for no original concertos survive from that period of his life. Some of his contemporary keyboard music, however, does reveal his exposure to the concerto. The Toccata in G Major for Clavier (BWV 916) is constructed along the lines of the concerto's three-movement form, and the first movement strongly resembles the style of his Vivaldi arrangements. A tutti is repeated in various keys between which modulating solo passages serve as links. A lyrical Adagio reflects the simplicity of the Italian models while the final movement is fugal. The organ Toccata in C Major (BWV 564) has similar features, and the organ Pastorale (BWV 590) reveals the master's introduction to the Christmas Pastorale that had found its way into so many Italian concertos.

THE VIOLIN CONCERTOS

In 1717 Bach accepted the position of Kapellmeister and Director of Chamber Music to the Prince of Cöthen. For the first time in his career, the composer had no responsibility for the writing of sacred music; instead he was expected to concentrate on the creation of instrumental music for the court's elaborate array of eighteen musicians. Bach remained in this position until 1723, creating an amazingly splendid collection of instrumental music including his first original concertos.

Although some scholars maintain that parts of the Brandenburg Concertos may date back to the earlier Weimar years, it seems more likely that Bach's earliest concertos were written for the violin, following his Italian models. Only three concertos for violin, two for solo, and one for two instruments survive from the Cöthen period, but others were no doubt written. Indeed it is believed most of the later harpsichord concertos are based on violin concertos of the Cöthen period, many of which were since lost.

The solo concertos, probably composed for the Cöthen court's star violinist, Josephus Spiess, are clearly inspired by Vivaldi. The emphasis on the strong melodic lines, the cantilenas (lyrical, non-virtuosic melodies) over an ostinato bass in the slow movements, the clear use of ritornello form, and the use of a four-part string orchestra with continuo all point to Vivaldi. But masterfully integrated with Vivaldi's style is Bach's passion for counterpoint and motivic elaboration, transforming the Vivaldi violin concerto.

The vitality of motivic and contrapuntal play alters the relationship between solo and tutti in a striking way. The simple juxtaposition of solo and tutti characterizing the Italian concerto becomes more complex and interconnected as the ritornello material penetrates the solo sections. The result is a richer texture than that typical of Vivaldi's concertos. Bach also introduced a more varied and adventuresome harmonic idiom. He gave careful attention to all details of the composition, even writing out the ornamentation thereby creating well thought-out works, in contrast with Vivaldi's, which, in spite of their greater reliance on stereotyped formulas, seem to communicate a greater sense of spontaneity.

Bach's two solo violin concertos of c. 1720 are widely acknowledged to be masterworks in the concerto repertoire and, likely due to their deeply moving slow movements, are extraordinarily popular with both performers and audiences.

The opening movement of the A Minor Violin Concerto (BWV 1041) is characterized by extensive development of motivic material contained within the ritornello. The development may take place within the ripieno as it accompanies the soloist or in the solo as it adopts ritornello motives for patterns of figuration. Although such a procedure can be found in the concertos of Vivaldi, it is more characteristic of Bach's. The ritornello plan is clear, but because of Bach's propensity to intertwine the tutti and solo both may be combined in any given section of the ritornello design. Furthermore, Bach was reluctant to reduce the number of parts in the ripieno accompaniments as had Vivaldi. With a few striking exceptions, all of the orchestral instruments participate throughout.

The concerto opens with a ritornello built on several motives in the Venetian manner (Ex. 7-1). But the stamp of the German composer is clear in the complex texture resulting from the activity and independence of the inner and lower parts. The opening phrase (a in Ex. 7-1) is a major component of the tutti sections, and its head also appears in accompaniments to solo passages, as in the first solo section (Ex. 7-2). This motive repeats in the ripieno instruments to mark off two major formal divisions—the shift to the relative major in m. 52 and the return to the tonic in m. 123—while the solo part continues its active figuration, illustrating the strength of the interpenetration of solo and tutti (Ex. 7-3).

Ex. 7-1. J. S. Bach, Violin Concerto in A Minor, BWV 1041; I. [Allegro], mm. 1–24.

Ex. 7-2. J. S. Bach, Violin Concerto in A Minor, BWV 1041; I. [Allegro], mm. 32–39.

Ex. 7-3. J. S. Bach, Violin Concerto in A Minor, BWV 1041; I. [Allegro], mm. 50–56.

Another passage demonstrating the interconnectedness and yet independence of solo and tutti occurs twice in the movement (mm. 59–68 and mm. 146–155). Here two-measure accompanied solos serve to link the united solo-tutti sequential statements of ritornello motive c (Ex. 7-4).

Ex. 7-4. J. S. Bach, Violin Concerto in A Minor, BWV 1041; I. [Allegro], mm. 59–66.

Bach's ability to integrate the solo and tutti while maintaining the necessary independence of the solo is perhaps best illustrated by the solo instrument's first entry. The ear is fully attentive to the solo violin whose entry is made more dramatic through the use of new material that sounds like a second theme. On closer examination, however, we see that the master used bits of the opening ritornello to fashion the new theme and its accompaniment. The neighboring-tone motive comes from the ritornello motive b while the upward leap of the fourth matches the head of phrase a. This upward leap is expanded in the following sequences and is echoed by the orchestra (Ex. 7-5). As the solo trails off into unrelated scale-wise figuration, the accompaniment's references to the head-

Ex. 7-5. J. S. Bach, Violin Concerto in A Minor, BWV 1041; I. [Allegro], mm. 24–28.

⌐ neighboring-tone motive of phrase b
⌒ upward leap from phrase a

motive become stronger (see Ex. 7-2). The b motive later becomes an important basis for sequential figuration in the solo part.

Not only are the solo and tutti well integrated, but the solo sections relate strongly to one another. The solo's entry in the dominant (m. 84) is identical to its tonic opening, transposed. In addition to the frequent use of the b motive, a purely soloistic motive (see Ex. 7-6) appears in two different solo sections. The concluding tutti-solo complex (mm. 146–end) is the same as that found in the first half of the movement (mm. 59–84), but transposed.

Ex. 7-6. J. S. Bach, Violin Concerto in A Minor, BWV 1041; I. [Allegro], mm. 43–45.

The Andante in C, the relative major, is one of the characteristic cantilenas Bach wrote for the violin concerto middle movements. An ostinato, or repetitious, bass pattern appearing in variants and in several keys provides the foundation for the richly ornamented and highly fluid solo part with its preponderance of sixteenth-note triplets. The inner parts are reduced to playing on-the-beat chords so that the listener's attention is focused on the moving outside parts, for active counterpoint would detract from the beautiful violin melody. The basis of such a violin-dominated, lyrical slow movement is found in the concertos of the Venetian composers, Albinoni and Vivaldi, but the richness of Bach's musical language, such as the extensive use of chromaticism, intensifies the expressive quality of such a movement.

The final movement, Allegro assai in $\frac{9}{8}$, may be less exuberant than the E Major Concerto's finale, but its driving dancelike rhythmic propulsion and brilliant solo writing are unquestionably exciting. Bach incorporates formal contrapuntal elements in the ritornello, which is designed like a fugal exposition. The soloist's entry, with a new theme and much leaner textural accompaniment, provides a strong contrast to the ritornello. The flashy arpeggios, extensive use of bariolage, and pause for a cadenza reveal Bach's sense of the concerto as a work for the virtuoso. As in Corelli's earlier concertos, the final, dancelike movements of the concerto form opened the way to greater displays of virtuosity. In Bach's concertos the element of virtuosity is always balanced by profundity of musical substance.

The E Major Concerto (BWV 1042), of a brighter disposition than the A Minor Concerto, opens with the tonic chord in ascending form set in the Vivaldian three hammer-stroke style (Ex. 7-7). This three-note motive is a germ idea, appearing frequently throughout the movement. It is heard especially in the orchestra as an accompaniment to the violinist's figuration, sometimes imitatively treated, thereby creating that motivic unity so important to Bach. The opening measure of the solo part is interesting for the way in which the soloist enunciates the three notes while the ripieno violins simultaneously play the second measure of the ritornello theme (Ex. 7-8).

Ex. 7-7. J. S. Bach, Violin Concerto in E Major, BWV 1042; I. Allegro, m. 1.

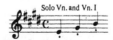

Ex. 7-8. J. S. Bach, Violin Concerto in E Major, BWV 1042; I. Allegro, m. 12.

The first movement is in da capo form, following the popular aria form of the day. The middle section, which opens in C-sharp minor and closes in G-sharp minor, further develops ritornello motives, especially the three hammer-strokes. The upper orchestral instruments also introduce new lyrical material in a lush contrapuntal setting as a backdrop for more typical violinistic figuration (see mm. 57–69). Later (mm. 82–95) the scoring becomes particularly dense as the orchestra restates the opening bars in E, F-sharp, and C-sharp, to the accompaniment of the very active solo violin. In another passage (mm. 95–101) the soloist, using double stops, not a common practice by Bach, contrapuntally develops the ritornello motive b to the accompaniment of the a motive in the bass. The exact repeat of the opening fifty-two measures is prefaced by a cadenza-like passage for solo violin ending in an unusually expressive Adagio passage.

The Adagio movement, in $\frac{3}{4}$ time in the relative minor (C-sharp), is similar to the slow movement of the A Minor Concerto. A fascinating ground bass (Ex. 7-9) frames and underpins the expressive solo violin part, which dominates in spite of the active accompaniment assigned the ripieno violins.

Ex. 7-9. J. S. Bach, Violin Concerto in E Major, BWV 1042; II. Adagio, mm. 1–6.

The finale—a fast $\frac{3}{8}$ dancelike movement in rondo form—provides a superb contrast to the flowing, operatic style of the previous movement. The ritornello, sixteen measures long, returns unchanged four times. The solo sections, each also sixteen measures long (the last one is two times sixteen measures), grow in intensity. The first two make use of continuous running sixteenth-notes, the third introduces double stops, and the culminating fourth solo section makes use of 32nd-notes and a more varied accompaniment. The movement has a tremendous sense of forward momentum launched by the upward thrust of the initial four measures (Ex. 7-10).

Ex. 7-10. J. S. Bach, Violin Concerto in E Major, BWV 1042; III. Allegro assai, mm. 1–4.

The Double Violin Concerto in D Minor (BWV 1043, c. 1718) was particularly popular in the nineteenth century and remains so today. The opening movement, with its fugal exposition, resembles some of Torelli's concertos in which the first statement of the fugue subject is accompanied, but this treatment is unusual in Bach's concertos. While the main theme may have been inspired by Torelli, the contrasting countersubject (Ex. 7-11) is certainly Bachian. The internal and final tuttis are limited to the main theme in four-measure blocks. The soloists, however, introduce strong thematic contrast by presenting two additional themes—one at the beginning of the first solo (Ex. 7-12) and the other at the opening of the second. The third and final solo section includes material from the two earlier solos, with a major recapitulation of the final part of solo 1 and tutti 2, transposed, intact, at the end of the movement.

Ex. 7-11. J. S. Bach, Double Violin Concerto in D Minor, BWV 1043; I. Vivace, mm. 5–8.

Ex. 7-12. J. S. Bach, Double Violin Concerto in D Minor, BWV 1043; I. Vivace, mm. 21–25.

With two soloists at his disposal, Bach's contrapuntal prowess comes to the fore in the solo sections. Canonic entries, as at the beginning of the first solo, and invertible counterpoint appear regularly in the Double Concerto. The latter technique is especially characteristic since it allows both soloists to play active and equal roles, as they exchange lines. A sample of Bach's use of invertible counterpoint is given in Ex. 7-13. With two active soloists, Bach limits the orchestral accompaniment to simpler material than was the case in the solo violin concertos. At times, only continuo accompanies, and when the orchestra appears it usually remains in the background with sustained chords. The occasional interjections of the head-motive and a six-measure passage based on another unobtrusive motive stay out of the way of the soloists.

Ex. 7-13. J. S. Bach, Double Violin Concerto in D Minor, BWV 1043; I. Vivace, mm. 32–33.

As in the solo concertos, the middle movement, a pastoral F-major Largo ma non tanto in $\frac{12}{8}$ time, is dominated by the soloists who provide moving, intertwining cantilenas. The exchange of parts using invertible counterpoint and chains of decorated suspensions are highly characteristic. The final Allegro, in $\frac{3}{4}$, not $\frac{3}{8}$

time, is stormier than the strongly dancelike finales of the two solo violin concertos. The soloists begin the movement imitatively to a motivic accompaniment recalling a similar orchestral motive in the first movement (compare mm. 63–68 of movement I). More thematic variety is provided than in the previous two movements, and an ascending sixteenth-note triplet motive gives a strong rhythmic drive.

A fragment of a Concerto in D Major (BWV 1045) for solo violin with an orchestra consisting of strings, oboes, trumpets, and timpani is preserved in Bach's hand. It may have been intended as an instrumental introduction to a now-lost cantata. Karl Geiringer believes the work is not up to the quality of Bach's other compositions, and suggests it may have been the work of an unknown composer copied by Bach.[2]

THE BRANDENBURG CONCERTOS

Bach dedicated his collection, *Six Concerts avec plusieurs instruments*, to the Margrave of Brandenburg in the spring of 1721, just a few days after the composer's thirty-sixth birthday. Bach must have met Margrave Christian Ludwig on a trip to Berlin to purchase a new harpsichord for the Cöthen court in 1718 or early 1719. The Margrave evidently commissioned some works by Bach, who eventually selected these half-dozen, which are now some of the best-known and best-loved concertos in the musical world. Interestingly, the varied instrumental requirements made the concertos unusable by Margrave Ludwig, for he had only meager orchestral resources and thus probably could not have performed the Brandenburg Concertos in Berlin. The works seem instead to have been designed for the rather large and illustrious group of musicians assembled at the court of Prince Leopold at Cöthen. If it is true that these concertos were written for the Cöthen orchestra, it can be assumed they were completed between 1717 and 1721.

Heinrich Besseler, in an article[3] published in 1955, assigned the six concertos, together with an earlier version of No. 1, BWV 1046a, that probably served as a three-movement introductory sinfonia to Cantata No. 208, to three groups on the basis of their styles, estimating their dates of composition as follows:

c. 1718   No. 3, No. 6, and the early version of No. 1
c. 1719   No. 2, No. 4, and third movement of No. 1 not in the
          earlier version
c. 1720   No. 5

Although Bach scholars have accepted the general outlines of this chronological ordering, some have argued that the earliest could be backdated to the Weimar period, possibly as early as 1713. Even if this were true, it seems reasonable to assume Bach revised the works prior to presenting them to the Margrave. Nos. 3 and 6 are placed early because of their homogeneous string texture, and because Nos. 1, 3, and 6 also share closer structural and motivic ties to Italian models. These earlier concertos are solely orchestral concertos with no specific concertino. Nos. 2 and 4, with their heterogeneous instrumentation, point to a later period, and the more sophisticated use of the harpsichord as a solo instrument places No. 5 still later.

The Brandenburg Concertos hold a special place in any study of music history, for they are some of the most significant and most inspired concertos of the Baroque or any other era. These great works reflect the splendor of the Cöthen court, while Bach's decision to group such highly varied pieces together, even though they were never designed to be performed as a cycle, probably grows out of his concern with creating great cycles of didactic works. Bach's position in Cöthen called for him to teach music, which clearly satisfied his pedagogical inclinations evident in these and several other important works from this period. For example, his son Wilhelm Friedemann turned nine years old in 1720, whereupon the composer undertook the composition of his *Clavier-Büchlein* (Little Clavier Book). This manual begins with an explanation of notes and clefs, ornaments, and short pieces for clavier. Included were eleven preludes destined for use in the great didactic cycle, *The Well-Tempered Clavier*, Book I, which Bach published in 1722. The two- and three-part inventions and sinfonias also date from this period.

The Brandenburg Concertos may also have served a didactic purpose, for they are virtually a great compendium of concerto practices, pointing out an array of ways suitable to achieving musical contrast. Three of the Brandenburgs are orchestral concertos while three are concerti grossi. A systematic reduction in the obvious means of contrast is evident from one orchestral concerto to the next. No. 1 is richly scored for winds and strings, No. 3 is scored for strings only in three groups, and No. 6 requires still more limited resources of low strings only, essentially divided into two groups. The concerti grossi, scored for string ripieno and varied concertinos of three or four players, are arranged in order of increasing concentration on a single soloist. In No. 2 each of the highly contrasted instruments making up the concertino plays an important role, although the brilliant tone of the high trumpet tends to dominate. The solo violin of Concerto No. 4 is supported by its concertino companions, two recorders. In No. 5 the harpsichord takes a significant step forward on its path to becoming a major concerto solo instrument, while the roles of flute and violin, the other members of the concertino, are reduced to less brilliant parts.

Even though the six concertos were not composed as a group and were not intended to form a unified cycle, the order of the six concertos displays a strong sense of symmetry and balance. The First Concerto, with the largest and most festive orchestra, is balanced by the last, with the smallest and most somber chamber ensemble. If the six works are divided into two groups of three, Nos. 1–3 and 4–6, interesting parallels become evident. In each group two concertos calling for both winds and strings are followed by one with strings only. The concertos of the first group require instruments capable of producing a greater volume of sound than those of the second group. The first group calls for horns, trumpet, (three) oboes, and bassoon in the winds, none of which appears in the concertos of the second group, which use the quieter recorders and flute. The concerto employing the stronger string instruments—violins, violas, and cellos—is placed after those using stronger winds; similarly, the one with the gentler strings of lower pitch—violas, viole da gamba, and solo cello—follows those with the gentler winds.

In addition to the marked use of counterpoint and thematic or motivic development already noted in Bach's violin concertos, the scoring of these works reflects the composer's German heritage in other ways. Their imaginative instrumentation, particularly of the concertino groups, similar to those found in concertos by Bach contemporaries Telemann and Graupner, illustrates a typical German fondness for wind instruments, that may relate to the long-standing tradition of the *Stadtpfeifer* (town pipers).[4] It is true Vivaldi had composed a few concertos for winds, but the wind instrument, usually bassoon, oboe, or flute, tends to appear as the only soloist. Less often Vivaldi used the winds in like pairs as the concertino or as part of a larger group of soloists. Bach, on the other hand, sought to highlight the contrast available within the concertino by using unlike instruments.

German composers throughout the Baroque period had a greater interest in a more varied and colorful orchestra than did the Italians. Italian composers used the orchestra to support bel canto lines of opera singers, so a more colorful orchestra would have encroached upon the main focus of the music. German composers, on the other hand, often used differing orchestral colors to help define and highlight the important independent lines in the contrapuntal fabric they wove. The Brandenburg Concertos can be seen, then, as Bach's greatest synthesis of the Italian and German styles. The two are beautifully intertwined and amalgamated to form the mature Bach style.

Brandenburg Concerto No. 1 in F Major, BWV 1046

This is the most unorthodox of Bach's concertos; the unusual features probably stem from its early history. An earlier version of this work, mentioned in the beginning of this discussion, is preserved as a sinfonia (BWV 1046a). It is scored for horns, oboes, and strings and is in the typical three-movement sinfonia design of fast-slow-minuet, but with two trios. Johannes Krey, in an article in the Heinrich Besseler *Festschrift*,[5] presented a comparative study of this and the later Brandenburg version, concluding that the earlier version was written as an overture to Cantata No. 208, performed at Weissenfels in 1716. He further believes it was later rewritten for the court orchestra at Dresden, which Bach visited in the late summer of 1717. Krey notes the modern Italian concerto had become fashionable at the Dresden court and suggests Bach modified the work with this local performance in mind. A solo part for the now-obsolete violino piccolo (a small violin, in this case tuned a minor third higher than the standard instrument) was written for the French-born Konzertmeister, Volumier, and tutti-solo contrasts were added. A typical concerto third movement was composed to replace the sinfonia's minuet finale, which was not really removed but retained as an additional movement following the newly composed third movement. According to Krey, the unusual polonaise (a term designating a piece in the Polish style) may have been included as an additional dance in the final movement in honor of Augustus I, Elector of Saxony, who was also King of Poland. It is known Polish music was frequently performed at his Dresden court.

Of all the Brandenburgs, this concerto calls for the most colorful orchestra.[6] Bach divided his resources into three choirs that are strikingly contrasted throughout the work:

- two horns;
- three oboes and one bassoon; and
- strings in six parts (solo violino piccolo, first and second violins, viola, cello, and bass).

The most unusual instrument, the violino piccolo, plays a prominent solo role. The current obsolescence of this instrument probably accounts for the relatively few modern performances of this work. When performed today on modern instruments, the violino piccolo part is usually played on a standard violin, resulting in a loss of contrast in sonority originally intended.

The boisterous first movement (lacking a tempo marking, but understood to be Allegro according to tradition and style) is scored for the entire orchestra, which plays the ritornello sections. The texture lightens in the solo sections as the three component choirs are pitted against one another. In the first solo section (beginning in m. 13) the three choirs essentially begin together, but after a measure and a half the pair of horns is given a one-beat solo accompanied by basses and continuo. From that point on, the hunting horns gain some prominence in this movement. Certainly their tone and the richness of their active parts, written in the tradition of clarino trumpet parts, lend them an air of importance. Each subsequent solo section begins with the horns stating a sequential motive (Ex. 7-14), or a derivative of it, in thirds, echoed by two oboes in thirds or sixths and violins in thirds or sixths, with the violino piccolo doubling the first violin line. In one short passage (mm. 53–56) the echoes of the horn parts are compressed in time, and the oboe and violino piccolo parts are reduced to solo lines. This delicate web leads to the tonic and a major recapitulation of ritornello and solo sections combined (mm. 57–63 = mm. 13–18; mm. 63–72 = mm. 33–43, with more activity in the horns; and mm. 72–84 = mm. 1–13).

Ex. 7-14. J. S. Bach, Brandenburg Concerto No. 1 in F Major, BWV 1046; I. [Allegro], mm. 24–26.

The horns only abandon their florid lines in the opening and closing tuttis where their repeated triplets on notes of the tonic triad add to the rhythmic flow and texture.

The bulk of the movement's motivic material is developed from the opening theme. Both the alternating note motive beginning in the oboes and the triadic one of the strings are used (Ex. 7-15). A contrasting theme (Ex. 7-16) makes brief appearances.

Ex. 7-15. J. S. Bach, Brandenburg Concerto No. 1 in F Major, BWV 1046; I. [Allegro], m. 1.

Ex. 7-16. J. S. Bach, Brandenburg Concerto No. 1 in F Major, BWV 1046; I. [Allegro], m. 6.

The Adagio, in the relative key of D minor, is a lyric movement featuring a florid, flowing melody presented by solo oboe and violino piccolo, occasionally augmented by the bass instruments. The change of key and the quiet mood necessitate the omission of the horns. Canonic writing for the two solo instruments (beginning in m. 12 and m. 23, with reversed roles of leader and follower) and increased chromaticism in treble and bass voices intensify the expressive quality of the movement. A small oboe cadenza leads to the concluding unadorned quarter-note chords. Perhaps a soloist was expected to improvise embellishments during these final measures.

In the following gigue-like movement, which could have served as the concerto's finale, solos restricted to the violino piccolo, duets, and trios alternate with the brilliant ritornello. Most of the movement focuses on the ritornello's opening four-measure phrase that serves as the movement's main theme. The violino piccolo begins its first solo with this theme and plays it again following the unusual two-measure Adagio passage. Bach's fine art of motivic elaboration is at work as the one-measure motive at the beginning of the ritornello serves as the basis of most of the material played by the soloists and their supporting bass parts. The motive may appear as originally stated in the violins (Ex. 7-17) or be combined with the alternating sixteenths of the accompanying horns. One major exception to the concentrated use of this motive in the solo sections occurs in the contrasting lyric duet between violino piccolo and solo oboe in mm. 53–60, but even here the main motive is present in the bass. The intense forward drive resulting from the almost constant use of sixteenth-notes is interrupted only once, by that Adagio passage (mm. 82–83) featuring solo violino piccolo with string accompaniment. One wonders if the soloist here might have been expected to elaborate this Adagio with improvisation.

Ex. 7-17. J. S. Bach, Brandenburg Concerto No. 1 in F Major, BWV 1046; III. Allegro, mm. 1–3.

The minuet-dance complex of the earlier version was retained and expanded by Bach as the finale, thereby creating a hybrid of concerto and suite that is unique among his compositions. The use of dance-inspired finales was common in the concerto, but the use of the dance's binary form was not, nor was the alternation of dances as in this minuet-trio-minuet-polonaise-minuet-trio-minuet complex.

The graceful minuet, with its free imitation of the main theme between treble and bass instruments, alternates in rondo (or ritornello) fashion with other dances. All but the first trio, which is in the relative minor, are in the tonic key. The element of tutti-solo contrast exists between the minuet proper and the alternating dances. The minuet is scored for the full orchestra, the horns abandoning their florid style to play supporting, repeated notes in a pattern that was also heard at the conclusion of the previous movement in mm. 119, 120, and 123. Each of the other dances is scored for one of the three featured choirs. The trios are nothing more than new minuets, that is, minuets with different thematic material, scored for the traditional trio of wind instruments. Trio No. 1 is for two oboes and bassoon, Trio No. 2 is for two horns with a third line for the three oboes in unison, and the polonaise is for the strings minus the violino piccolo.

Brandenburg Concerto No. 2 in F Major, BWV 1047

This concerto grosso uses a concertino consisting of trumpet, recorder, oboe, and violin, and a ripieno string orchestra with continuo. The treble-dominated concertino and especially the sound of the valveless trumpet played in its upper (clarino) register create the bright quality of this concerto. The special appeal of the Baroque trumpet and its prominence in the work probably account for the great popularity of this concerto, but the intrinsic joy and exuberance of the outer movements and the pathos of the middle movement also contribute in this connection.

The Allegro first movement is in a tightly knit ritornello form. The ritornello, stated by the tutti, begins with an easily identifiable, strongly triadic initial idea (a) and continues with three other ideas (Ex. 7-18). Phrases a and c are related rhythmically and through the use of the tonic triad, while b and d are related through the use of sixteenth-note scalewise motion. The motives of b and d are also related to the active bass line that accompanies the first appearance of a. Motives of a and c are especially prominent in both tutti and solo passages.

Ex. 7-18. J. S. Bach, Brandenburg Concerto No. 2 in F Major, BWV 1047; I. [Allegro], mm. 1–8.

The solo sections not only make use of ritornello material, but also introduce and develop a theme and its countermelody associated exclusively with the solo group. This theme (Ex. 7-19) is first played at the opening of the first solo section by the solo violin with continuo accompaniment. Two-measure interjections by the tutti of its a motive separate subsequent entries of each remaining soloist (in the order of oboe, recorder, trumpet) with the new theme. Each of these solo statements is accompanied by the previous soloist; that is, the oboe is accompanied by violin, recorder by oboe, and trumpet by recorder. The use of the same material in each of the very different instrumental parts demonstrates the Baroque composer's greater concern for thematic unity than for the particular qualities of each instrument. For example, the line in the accompanying instruments seems to have been conceived for the violin, which can easily negotiate it with string crossings, but the same passage is awkward to execute on the other instruments.

Ex. 7-19. J. S. Bach, Brandenburg Concerto No. 2 in F Major, BWV 1047; I. [Allegro], mm. 9–10.

Although the trumpet is not formally introduced as a solo instrument until it plays the new theme in m. 21 (a variant of Ex. 7-19), the brass instrument's prominence has already been assured. It had been set apart from the very beginning when it accompanied the main theme by outlining the tonic triad and by climbing into its upper register to enunciate the dominant on repeated notes and in an ear-catching trill. And before its solo entry as well, the trumpet twice embellished the tutti's interpolations of a by playing in its upper register what had once been the florid bass line.

Probably because of the large concertino, Bach chose to keep the ripieno accompaniments relatively simple. When the soloists are involved in developing their own theme, only the continuo accompanies; when the concertino works with ritornello material, the strings supply either short chords separated by rests with a syncopated triadic line in the first violin (for example, mm. 50–55) or a soft repeated figure (for example, mm. 40–47). The ripieno here, unlike Bach's practice in other concertos, does not accompany the soloists with bits of the ritornello.

The use of some distinctive solo material creates a dramatic contrast between the two groups, a contrast enhanced by the frequent juxtaposition of tutti, with ritornello material, and solo. The opposition of forces is very powerful, leading Bach to balance their roles by frequently having the solo instruments share in announcing or developing the ritornello. This sense of combined opposition and integration is well illustrated in the final ritornello statement (mm. 102ff.), which is expanded through the insertion of a concertino development of the original mm. 5–8 (motives c and d) in mm. 107–114. The movement is propelled by a tremendous rhythmic drive that leads without pause to a full cadence in A minor just prior to this final ritornello statement.

The Andante, in D minor, is in the style of intimate chamber music. It is scored only for solo recorder, oboe, and violin with continuo support; the strings and solo trumpet (it cannot play in the new key) are silent. The three solo parts weave a contrapuntal fabric by means of free imitation, developing two motives (Ex. 7-20) and their variants. Both motives make use of the descending sigh motive, bracketed in Ex. 7-20, that is highlighted in mm. 34–36 and especially in mm. 44–57. In the latter passage, solo instruments are paired in the three different possible arrangements of flute and violin, oboe and violin, and flute and oboe, playing in contrasting echolike fashion as the sigh becomes the more poignant semitone interval (Ex. 7-21). Throughout the movement the basic insistent eighth-note motion provides a strong harmonic support.

Ex. 7-20. J. S. Bach, Brandenburg Concerto No. 2 in F Major, BWV 1047; II. Andante, mm. 2–5.

Ex. 7-21. J. S. Bach, Brandenburg Concerto No. 2 in F Major, BWV 1047; II. Andante, mm. 47–53.

The last movement is fugal, as are several of Bach's final concerto movements. It begins with the exposition in the solo instruments with continuo support. The trumpet starts; its bright sound, absent in movement II, and the joy of its theme provide a strong contrast to the slow movement. (Note the similarity of the trumpet's theme, Ex. 7-22, to the ritornello theme of movement I.) The trumpet makes the final statement of this theme at the very end of the work. The ripieno strings are often silent, for the contrapuntal interplay among the four soloists requires only continuo support. Even when the ripieno enters in m. 47 it merely acts as an expanded continuo to support the subsidiary theme presented in the solo instruments, as is true of its role throughout much of the movement.

Ex. 7-22. J. S. Bach, Brandenburg Concerto No. 2 in F Major, BWV 1047; III. Allegro assai, mm. 1–7.

Brandenburg Concerto No. 3 in G Major, BWV 1048

This more conservative concerto was dated c. 1718 by Besseler, and others believe it may go back to 1715 or earlier. It is an orchestral concerto for three choirs of strings (violins, violas, cellos), each in three parts, and continuo and double bass. In the original performances there was probably only one player per part, or eleven soloists altogether, counting two continuo players. No one instrument or group stands out markedly from the rest. Even though the concerto lacks the brilliant, often coloristic effects of the other concertos with more varied instrumentation, it is one of the most exciting of the Brandenburg Concertos. Kaleidoscopic changing textures replace the more obvious instrumental contrasts of the concerti grossi. This feature and the intensity of motivic concentration create strong forward momentum.

The theme of the first movement is one of the most concentrated and forward-thrusting of the concertos (Ex. 7-23). It provides practically all of the motivic material for the movement, the only exception being the new countersubject introduced by the first violin in mm. 78–81, following the only major break in the continuity of the movement. The initial three-note motive is developed most extensively in both thematic and accompanimental parts.

Ex. 7-23. J. S. Bach, Brandenburg Concerto No. 3 in G Major, BWV 1048; I. [Allegro moderato], mm. 1–8.

Although this concerto lacks a distinct concertino, various levels of contrast are important. The tutti sections are played by all the instruments, with each choir in unison, resulting in three-part harmony. Occasionally all parts join in forceful unison and doubled octave passages at cadence points (see mm. 7–8 and m. 57).

The choirs separate in the solo sections; each choir is then scored in three parts, and all nine solo string players are heard on independent parts. In these sections the main element of contrast is the difference of pitch. Timbre, such an important element of contrast in the Brandenburgs' concerti grossi, is less important in this work for like instruments.

On occasion, individual instruments within each choir receive miniature solo passages, usually echoing other choir members. These short solos are accompanied by another choir. For example, in mm. 10–11 the violins exchange a short motive to the accompaniment of the violas. In one unusual passage, the three solo violins are paired across choirs with the violas in an open and delicately filigreed texture, involving the ubiquitous three-note opening motive. This passage occurs first in mm. 97–99 and returns in mm. 119–121.

Bach's harmony is often complex and exciting; consider one truly unusual passage in this concerto. The chromatic alteration of the B to B-flat in m. 30 pulls us to the darker subdominant F from the acting tonic of C. This is a startling move, even after we have heard the passage several times.

We have noted, in the earlier discussion of Corelli's concertos, the common occurrence of an unusual "final" cadence in slow movements written in the relative minor key. Here, in Brandenburg Concerto No. 3, the Phrygian cadence, ending on the dominant of E minor, comprises the entire Adagio movement found in the written score. Although the concerto is often performed today with only these two adagio chords separating the fast outer movements, there seems little doubt that the cadence must have been intended to serve as a closing to an extemporized movement in E minor improvised by one or more of the soloists.[7] In some modern performances a slow movement in E minor from another work is inserted to fill the perceived void.

The finale is a gigue in the style of a virtuosic perpetuum mobile of swirling sixteenth-notes. The gigue was a strongly contrapuntal dance, and Bach characteristically begins each part of the binary form[8] with imitative entries of the theme. Bach does not, however, follow the common procedure of inverting the theme after the double bar; instead he inverts the order of the entries. All instruments participate in presenting the theme while the first violin and first viola enjoy a few additional passages of independent and more virtuosic material. And as is the case with many Baroque composers, Bach makes greater use of soloists and virtuosic display in the final dance-inspired movement of a concerto. In this concerto movement, not only do the first violin and first viola stand out briefly, but the entire movement is a marvel of collective virtuosity.

Brandenburg Concerto No. 4 in G Major, BWV 1049

In the Fourth Brandenburg Concerto, Bach placed a high-pitched concertino of two recorders[9] and violin against a string ripieno with continuo. Compared with the treatment of the solo instruments in the Second Concerto, also a concerto grosso, one solo part in the Fourth has gained an increased prominence. Here the violin dominates with material that is more demanding than that of either of the solo violin concertos.

The bright G major tonality, the sound of the recorders, and the lilting quality of the triple meter (most concerto first movements are in duple meter) all combine to create a cheerful pastoral mood in the first movement, the longest individual movement in all of Bach's concertos. The concerto begins with what is for Bach an unusually long and diverse ritornello played primarily by the concertino with simple ripieno accompaniment. The two principal motives of the ritornello are the opening arpeggio (a) in the recorders followed immediately by the contrasting descending motive (b) in parallel thirds (Ex. 7-24). The little three-note prefix in m. 4 gains in importance in some interesting syncopated passages (Ex. 7-25). A repeated-note figure of descending thirds first heard in m. 14 is also important.

Ex. 7-24. J. S. Bach, Brandenburg Concerto No. 4 in G Major, BWV 1049; I. Allegro, mm. 1–7.

Ex. 7-25. J. S. Bach, Brandenburg Concerto No. 4 in G Major, BWV 1049; I. Allegro, mm. 67–75.

The first solo section is begun by the solo violin, unaccompanied, with nonthematic figuration; a nonthematic solo entry is a rarity in Bach's concertos. It must have been used here to draw the listener's attention to the violinist as a soloist; previously it and the recorders had dominated the ritornello. The radically new texture and content of the solo passage dramatically set the violinist apart; the violinist is clearly the main attraction throughout the middle of the movement as it engages in dazzling flights of 32nd-notes (see mm. 187–208).

The middle movement, an Andante in E minor, is the only slow one of the set that makes use of the full orchestra. Bach takes advantage of the orchestra's presence by involving it with the concertino in short passages of dialogue reminiscent of Corelli's concerti grossi. The movement concludes with a Phrygian cadence, preceded by a brief written-out cadenza for the first recorder, an instrument that twice before in the movement had been singled out in unaccompanied flourishes (mm. 29 and 31).

The final Presto is a fugue on a subject first stated by the ripieno violas (Ex. 7-26). The next three entries are reserved for the strings. The pair of recorders then make their first appearance in the movement by stating the theme in unison. An interesting variation of the fugue subject is later stated by the recorders (Ex. 7-27—the circled notes in the example are new additions to the fugue subject). The solo sections that alternate with the fugal material are dominated by long demanding passages for the solo violin, often thinly accompanied; once again the final movement contains the most overtly virtuosic material.

Ex. 7-26. J. S. Bach, Brandenburg Concerto No. 4 in G Major, BWV 1049; III. Presto, mm. 1–4.

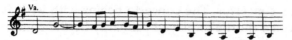

Ex. 7-27. J. S. Bach, Brandenburg Concerto No. 4 in G Major, BWV 1049; III. Presto, mm. 159–163.

Brandenburg Concerto No. 5 in D Major, BWV 1050

The Fifth Brandenburg Concerto represents the culmination of the trend toward increased emphasis on a single soloist, an emphasis merely suggested in the other concerti grossi in the set. Here the main solo part is the most demanding in any of Bach's concertos. Even though this is a concerto grosso, it paradoxically represents the apogee of the solo concerto as composed by Bach.

The concerto is scored for a concertino of solo flute (Bach specified the more modern transverse flute as distinct from the flûte à bec or recorder), solo violin, and harpsichord concertato. The orchestra includes parts for violin, viola, cello, and double bass. Traditionally the harpsichord's role as part of the concertino was to realize the harmonies in the continuo part. This role is largely abandoned here, except when the harpsichord still serves as an accompanying instrument. In its new role as a solo instrument, it not only matches the brilliance of the solo flute and violin, but exceeds it. The harpsichord dominates to such an extent that this concerto can quite correctly be viewed as the earliest known concerto for solo harpsichord. The unusual use of the keyboard instrument, the use of the modern flute, and other aspects of style have led scholars to place this concerto last among the Brandenburgs in order of composition. Perhaps the new harpsichord purchased in Berlin in 1719 inspired the composition of the work, which probably dates from the winter of 1720–21.

Bach took a leading role in freeing the harpsichord from its customary accompanying role in ensemble works. During his Cöthen years, he composed several sonatas for various individual instruments (violin, BWV 1014–1019; viola da gamba, BWV 1027–1029; and flute, BWV 1030, 1032) and harpsichord, in which the keyboard instrument is treated as an equal partner. In these pieces, the right hand of the keyboard part is often treated as a second treble instrument, while the left hand plays the continuo bass line, but in a typically active and motivically involved Bachian way.

Bach was a great synthesizer of Baroque trends. Yet in his brilliant use of the harpsichord as a solo instrument in the context of a larger ensemble, the great keyboard artist must be seen as the innovator and instigator of a new departure. Not only that, he created a new genre—the keyboard concerto—and Brandenburg Concerto No. 5 stands at the beginning of his explorations of this new direction.

The Fifth Brandenburg's D major opening Allegro is one of Bach's most dramatic instrumental movements. The nine-measure ritornello, heard in an exact repeat at the end of the movement and only partially in the interior, is stated by the tutti. In tutti sections of this work, the solo violin joins the ripieno violins, the solo flute is silent, and the harpsichord functions as a continuo instrument with only the left hand written out, but well figured. The essentially Vivaldian homophonic ritornello, propelled by an almost constant stream of sixteenth-notes, is divisible into three phrases (Ex. 7-28). Within the movement, the very short ritornello statements are confined to the first two phrases, separately or together. Ritornello material is also used by the ripieno in accompanying passages at times, but the harpsichord's presence in the solo group minimizes the need for elaborate orchestral support.

Ex. 7-28. J. S. Bach, Brandenburg Concerto No. 5 in D Major, BWV 1050; I. Allegro, mm. 1–9.

The entry of the soloists is particularly striking as the harpsichord's new role is made apparent from the outset. It accompanies the new, imitative theme of the flute and violin with a busier, more elaborate version of that same theme, doubling the other parts in thirds (Ex. 7-29). The sixteenth-note triplets introduced by the harpsichord in m. 2 of the solo section are taken over as a motive to be echoed back and forth between the other solo instruments. Closer inspection reveals this motive embellishes an inverted version of the soloist's opening four-note descending motive. The four-note scalewise motive, whether decorated or not, remains the exclusive property of the solo group. Similarly, the repeated-note motive of the ritornello is associated only with the ripieno instruments.

Ex. 7-29. J. S. Bach, Brandenburg Concerto No. 5 in D Major, BWV 1050; I. Allegro, mm. 9–10.

As the movement unfolds, the bravura writing for the harpsichord, probably first played by the composer, increases, culminating in the overwhelmingly virtuosic display in the sixty-five-measure unaccompanied cadenza—an unprecedented and boldly innovative gesture. The cadenza is essentially figurative, but the soloist's four-note scale motive is also used (Ex. 7-30a and b). To render indelible our memory of this impressive passage, Bach follows it immediately with the closing ritornello in its complete form.

Ex. 7-30. J. S. Bach, Brandenburg Concerto No. 5 in D Major, BWV 1050; I. Allegro: (a.) mm. 153–157; (b.) mm. 182–183.

The scoring and basic sentiment of the gentle B minor Affetuoso, perhaps the most famous movement to have such an appellation, bring to mind the slow movement of the Second Brandenburg. As in that work, the orchestra is silent; only the solo flute, violin, and harpsichord contrapuntally and caressingly manipulate the movement's two important motives. The first (Ex. 7-31) is heard at the beginning in the violin, imitated by the flute; the second (Ex. 7-32) is introduced later by the harpsichord. Both motives are also used in inverted form (Ex. 7-33). As seen in Example 7–33, the second motive is often used to answer the first. Throughout most of the movement, the trio creates a four-part texture, the outcome of treating the keyboard player's right- and left-hand parts independently. The main element of contrast in the movement obtains between the harpsichord and the other soloists.

Ex. 7-31. J. S. Bach, Brandenburg Concerto No. 5 in D Major, BWV 1050; II. Affettuoso, m. 1.

Ex. 7-32. J. S. Bach, Brandenburg Concerto No. 5 in D Major, BWV 1050; II. Affettuoso, mm. 6–7.

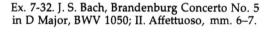

Ex. 7-33. J. S. Bach, Brandenburg Concerto No. 5 in D Major, BWV 1050; II. Affettuoso, m. 14.

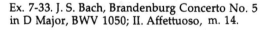

The Allegro in $\frac{2}{4}$, but sounding like $\frac{6}{8}$ because of the steady use of the gigue-like triplet rhythm, is another of Bach's fugal, dance-inspired movements. Here, as in Brandenburg Concerto No. 2, the concertino provides the fugal exposition in which the harpsichord makes two separate entries, one in each hand. More varied patterns of contrast between the solo group and orchestra occur in this movement than in the first movement, but the harpsichord dominates again with its scintillating passages of figuration. Numerous references are made throughout to the short fugue subject (Ex. 7-34), but the most interesting is a still lighter, songlike soloistic variant heard in the movement's B minor middle section (mm. 79ff). The movement's opening seventy-eight measures are brought back as a da capo ending announced by a sudden and unexpected move from B minor to D major (m. 233).

Ex. 7-34. J. S. Bach, Brandenburg Concerto No. 5
in D Major, BWV 1050; III. Allegro, mm. 1–3.

Brandenburg Concerto No. 6 in B-flat Major, BWV 1051

This orchestral concerto, with its archaic instrumentation and somber tone quality, is thought to be one of the earliest, if not the earliest, of the set, dating from 1718 or earlier. The use of strings only in the final concerto seems to balance the purely string sound of No. 3. The latter work used the modern violin, but No. 6 calls for a chamber group consisting of two violas, two viole da gamba, cello, and continuo (double bass and harpsichord)—seven musicians. The emphasis on lower strings, the use of the then-almost-obsolete viola da gamba and the key of B-flat, the greatest number of flats appearing in any Brandenburg concerto opening movement, all contribute to the somber quality found in this concerto.

The main contrast in the work emerges in the different levels of pitch within the lower register, in the timbre contrast between violas and viole da gamba, and in the greater amount of solo work given the violas and cello as compared with the simple viole da gamba parts. (Bach probably played one of the viola parts while his employer, Prince Leopold, played one of the simple viola da gamba parts.)

The first movement (Allegro, ¢) begins with a sixteen-measure ritornello, of which the first fifteen measures consist of a canon between the two violas. The closely following second viola begins after only an eighth rest, resulting in syncopation in its line against the leader (Ex. 7-35). The remainder of the orchestra provides a throbbing repeated-note accompaniment supporting the canon. The three-note, neighboring-tone motive at the beginning is frequently heard in the solo sections, even in the gambas in the accompaniment. The tonal areas in which the ritornello returns are a bit unusual, with the second statement in C minor rather than the more common F major, the dominant. This feature also contributes to the movement's more somber mood.

Ex. 7-35. J. S. Bach, Brandenburg Concerto No. 6 in B-flat Major, BWV 1051; I. Allegro, mm. 1–5.

The gambas remain silent in the slow movement which features the violas in a series of canonic duets. The final gigue-like movement, combining elements of ritornello, da capo, and rondo forms, places the violas and solo cello in the limelight. The content of the soloist's first passage seems to be patterns of figuration, but closer inspection reveals the patterns are really a decorative form of the movement's ritornello.

THE HARPSICHORD CONCERTOS

Bach's numerous harpsichord concertos date from his Leipzig years and are particularly associated with his term as director of the Leipzig University's Collegium Musicum. This voluntary association of professional musicians and university students was founded by Telemann in 1704. Bach was the Collegium's director from 1729 to 1737 and again from 1739 to 1741. He probably accepted this position not only to earn additional income, but also to associate with a group of instrumentalists with whom he was free to pursue his musical ideas, a freedom his work as Kantor of the Thomaskirche did not allow. Performances of the Collegium Musicum were scheduled at least weekly—on Wednesdays from 4 to 6 P.M. in the coffee-garden before the Grimmesches Thor in the summer, and on Fridays from 8 to 10 P.M. in Zimmermann's coffee house in the winter. The death in 1741 of the society's organizer and landlord, Gottfried Zimmermann, eventually brought an end to the Collegium's activities.

We have no evidence as to the exact content of the weekly programs, but it is generally thought that many of Bach's instrumental works from Weimar and Cöthen were performed. These must often have been in revised versions, as is indicated, for example, by the revised performance parts for the orchestral suites. The purchase of a new harpsichord in 1733, the increasing abilities of the composer's sons as harpsichordists, and their need for music to perform must have stimulated Bach to compose or arrange during this time the fourteen completed concertos involving the harpsichord as solo instrument. Most are thought to date from 1730 to 1736 and were probably played at concerts of the Collegium Musicum. It is quite possible the works written for more than one solo harpsichord were performed in the Bach home, since he owned several harpsichords (his estate included four large harpsichords and one small, plus several other instruments). Bach's sons Wilhelm Friedemann (1710–1784), Carl Philipp Emanuel (1714–1788), and Johann Gottfried Bernhard (1715–1739) likely participated in these multiple keyboard concertos along with Bach and possibly his student Johann Ludwig Krebs.

The keyboard[10] concertos include seven for one harpsichord (BWV 1052–1058), three for two harpsichords (BWV 1060–1062), two for three harpsichords (BWV 1063–1064), one for four (BWV 1065), and a Triple Concerto for Flute, Violin, and Harpsichord in A Minor (BWV 1044). Also dating from this period is the well-known Italian Concerto (BWV 971) for unaccompanied harpsichord.

Given Bach's fascination with counterpoint and his gifts as a keyboard performer, he came naturally to initiate the new form of the harpsichord concerto. Since the harpsichord traditionally had been viewed as a continuo or unaccompanied solo instrument, Bach had no direct models to follow as he had in the violin concertos. He therefore created his harpsichord concertos by applying the same principles of arrangement and transcription as in his solo keyboard arrangements of the Italian violin concertos made during his earlier Weimar years. Now, in Leipzig, Bach adapted and adopted earlier concertos for the violin or other instruments to the keyboard idiom. Bach's three surviving violin concertos and Brandenburg Concerto No. 4, which features the solo violin, formed the basis of four of the harpsichord concertos:

HARPSICHORD CONCERTO		=	ARRANGEMENT OF EARLIER CONCERTO
D Major for 1 Hpsd, BWV 1054		=	E Major Violin, BWV 1042
F Major for 1 Hpsd, BWV 1057		=	Brandenburg Concerto No. 4 in G Major, BWV 1049
G Minor for 1 Hpsd, BWV 1058		=	A Minor Violin, BWV 1041
C Minor for 2 Hpsds, BWV 1062		=	D Minor Double Violin, BWV 1043

The Concerto for Four Harpsichords in A Minor, BWV 1065, is an arrangement of the B Minor Concerto for Four Violins from Vivaldi's *L'estro armonico*, Op. 3, No. 10, RV 580.

Extensive studies of Bach's craft of keyboard transcription have shown that his method in these concertos was very similar to that of his Weimar transcriptions. The original is often transposed lower by a tone in order to accommodate the violin's then-traditional highest pitch E on the harpsichord, which extended only up to D. The right hand of the keyboard part takes over the solo part while the left hand assumes the role of a continuo bass part. Ornamentation is sometimes added to one or both parts.

The existence of the original versions of five of these harpsichord concertos and the lack of a consistently idiomatic harpsichord style have led scholars to believe that the remaining harpsichord concertos are also transcriptions or arrangements of earlier works no longer extant. By applying Bach's craft of transcription in reverse to some of the remaining harpsichord concertos, W. Fischer has reconstructed several of the presumed earlier versions.[11] Most of the originals are thought to have been violin concertos, although characteristics of some seem to point to other possibilities. For example, the A Major Harpsichord Concerto, BWV 1055, originally may have been intended for oboe d'amore, while the C Minor Concerto for Two Harpsichords, BWV 1060, is thought to have been based on a concerto for violin and oboe. The Concerto for Two Harpsichords in C Major, BWV 1061, displays a true keyboard idiom throughout, and, for that reason, is generally viewed as an original keyboard work.

During the period of the 1730s and, especially, the 1740s, Bach collected and revised earlier works, such as his Weimar organ chorales. In fact, all of the concertos for one harpsichord survive in the same autograph manuscript source dated 1735–44, later than their supposed date of composition. Two versions of the best known D Minor Harpsichord Concerto are included, revealing successive steps toward a more idiomatic harpsichord style. In the earlier version (BWV 1052a), the left hand functions very much as a continuo bass part, whereas in the later version (BWV 1052) soloistic figuration appears in the left as well as the right hand.

Bach's exploration of and initiation of the harpsichord concerto, roughly contemporary with Handel's organ concertos, prefigured developments that eventually led to the piano concerto of the late eighteenth and early nineteenth centuries. Two of Bach's sons, Carl Philipp Emanuel and Johann Christian, were to play major roles in advancing the movement started by the Baroque master. Thus the harpsichord concerto remained virtually the exclusive property of the Bach family until around 1750.

The D Minor Concerto, BWV 1052, is the best known of Bach's harpsichord concertos. He had earlier used the first movement as a sinfonia to Cantata No. 188, *Ich habe meine Zuversicht* (c. 1728), and the first and second movements as the sinfonia and first chorus of Cantata No. 146, *Wir müssen durch viel Trübsal* (1726–28). The cantata movements were probably adaptations of an earlier violin concerto, now lost.[12]

The first movement of the concerto opens with a powerful unison six-measure ritornello, the first motive of which recurs through much of the movement (Ex. 7-36). The solo material is thoroughly virtuosic and similar to the toccata-like figuration found in several solo keyboard works by Bach. Accompaniments are generally kept quite simple, often only pedal points, or little pieces of the ritornello may be used, but the elaborate contrapuntal richness of the Brandenburgs and violin concertos is absent in this movement. Two brief cadenzas are included.

Ex. 7-36. J. S. Bach, Harpsichord Concerto in D Minor, BWV 1052; I. Allegro, mm. 1–6.

The Adagio movement is in G minor; it is quite unusual for Bach to set the middle movement of a minor mode concerto in the minor as well. The quasi-ostinato bass and singing cantilena of the harpsichord's right-hand part (the left hand joins the continuo bass) remind the listener of the violin concertos' slow movements. The rich embellishments of the solo part have a strong improvisational quality.

The finale, an Allegro in $\frac{3}{4}$, is in ritornello form. In comparison with the first movement, there are more references to the ritornello throughout and the ♩♪♪♩ motive is quite prominent in solo and orchestral passages. Some of the solo passages consist of toccata-like figuration.

The F Minor Concerto, BWV 1056,[13] probably a transcription of a violin or oboe concerto, has a particularly beautiful Largo movement in A-flat. The flowing and highly ornamented, improvisatory right-hand harpsichord part is accompanied by pizzicato strings in patterns that substitute for the ostinato bass lines Bach commonly wrote in such movements. The fluidity of the solo line seems to require the warmth of tone and sustaining power of a string or wind instrument, and one can easily imagine it on a violin or oboe. The solo line dominates the entire movement and provides a good example of how, in Bach's slow movements, ornamentation is integrated into the whole (see Ex. 7-37). The ritornello of the opening movement makes an interesting use of triplets (Ex. 7-38), and triplets occur extensively in the solo episodes. The bass motive of the opening is also taken up by the harpsichord's left-hand part as an accompaniment to many triplet passages. The soloist's first appearance apart from the tutti consists of a charming one-beat echo of the triplet cadence of the first violin. The first major solo passage bursts forth in m. 15, before the ritornello has reached its cadence (in m. 20), providing the most unexpected and startling entry of a soloist in any Bach concerto. The final movement contains several playful two-note echo passages, reminiscent of the echo effects in the first movement.

Ex. 7-37. J. S. Bach, Harpsichord Concerto in F Minor, BWV 1056; II. Largo, mm. 1–6.

Ex. 7-38. J. S. Bach, Harpsichord Concerto in F Minor, BWV 1056; I. [Allegro], mm. 1–8.

The E Major Concerto, BWV 1053, is one of the largest and most brilliant of the solo harpsichord concertos. It may possibly be recast from a lost violin or oboe concerto. Its first movement, transposed to D, also served as the introduction to Cantata No. 169, in which the solo part is given to the organ. The powerful C-sharp minor siciliano movement is found as a solo aria in the same cantata, transposed to B minor, and the finale, with its da capo form and sudden shift from G-sharp minor to E major at the repeat, was used as a sinfonia to Cantata No. 49.

The outer movements of the Concerto for Harpsichord in A Major, BWV 1055, are some of Bach's most joyful concerto movements. They are separated by a strongly contrasting siciliano, marked Larghetto, in F-sharp minor, characterized by dramatic dialogue between strings and harpsichord and a chromatically moving bass line.

The harpsichord concertos for which we have Bach's original violin concertos are rarely performed, because the transcriptions are felt to be less successful than the originals. The keyboard version of the Fourth Brandenburg is a strong transcription, however, and is the only one of the harpsichord concertos to include instruments other than strings—the two recorders found in the original Brandenburg.

In the concertos for more than one harpsichord, the soloists easily dominate. Sometimes the harpsichord tone can be too overwhelming, as in Bach's arrangement of Vivaldi's Op. 3, No. 10, for four harpsichords and orchestra; in the two concertos for three harpsichords; and especially in the C Major Concerto for Two Harpsichords, BWV 1061. The latter concerto displays a more consistent idiomatic keyboard style than any other. Furthermore, the orchestra is silent in the middle movement, seldom used in the finale, and restrained in the first movement—all of which suggests that this concerto may be from an original work for harpsichords without accompaniment.

The Triple Concerto for Flute, Violin, and Harpsichord, the same solo group as in Brandenburg Concerto No. 5, in A Minor, BWV 1044, has its roots in several solo keyboard works by Bach. The outer movements are arrangements of the Prelude and Fugue in A Minor, BWV 897, while the middle movement is an arrangement of the Adagio e dolce of Organ Sonata No. 3, BWV 527.

Bach's popular Concerto in the Italian Style for harpsichord represents a penetration of the concerto principle and style into the world of unaccompanied keyboard music. It is one of the few works in which he actually specified the keyboard instrument. The work resembles Bach's Weimar keyboard transcriptions of violin concertos. Dynamic contrast creates the illusion of tutti and solo. Tuttis are played by both hands, *forte*, while solo melody is played on one manual with the other accompanying. Enhancing the tutti-solo contrast is the appearance of distinctive solo thematic material. The slow movement is another of Bach's cantilenas.

In spite of the immense historical importance of Bach's development of the harpsichord concerto and the wonderful musical moments therein, it is generally agreed that Bach's keyboard concertos are musically less satisfying than his concertos for other instruments or groups of instruments. This could be the result of the reduced role of the orchestra, perhaps in turn the consequence of a less competent body of instrumentalists; accordingly, a reduction in the use of counterpoint and in thematic development allowed a greater dominance of soloistic passage work.

Bach's crowning achievement in the concerto genre remains the Brandenburg Concertos. In these works, and to a substantial degree in the violin concertos as well, Bach created a style which maintained a constant and dramatic separation of the forces while keeping them musically tightly interconnected and integrated as a coherent whole. It is Bach's extraordinary skill with contrapuntal development that permitted him to balance effectively the dual elements of cooperation and contention. Bach had taken the simple juxtaposition of solo and tutti of the Italian concerto and transformed it into an infinitely more complex relationship, thereby increasing the tension of the whole.

Despite Bach's monumental contribution to the concerto, his influence on his contemporaries and on succeeding composers was limited. His style was viewed as old-fashioned before his death; only one of his concertos was published during his lifetime—the Concerto in the Italian Style for unaccompanied harpsichord in *Clavier Übung II*. Yet a few composers of the younger generation were deeply affected by Bach's experiments with the keyboard concerto—most notably Bach's sons, Carl Philipp Emanuel and Johann Christian.

Part II

THE CLASSICAL CONCERTO

Chapter Eight

THE EMERGENCE OF THE CLASSICAL CONCERTO

As the Baroque concerto culminated, in many respects, in the works of J. S. Bach, a younger generation of composers was already busy forging a new style that was to be known as Classical. This newer style reflected changing tastes and attitudes across Europe.

The public concert came into its own as the middle class rose to a position of greater cultural influence. Some of the new music was no longer designed primarily for the nobility, nor was it typically intended to overwhelm or edify its audience. Music of the Classical era was first and foremost designed to entertain and please its audience, an audience that valued clarity, elegance, and balanced proportions. The music was intended to meet the listener on his or her own ground; it was to be "natural," or free of technical complications.

This new style was characterized by greater simplicity, greater variety, and greater contrast than were typical of the Baroque style. Changes were introduced into most elements of the music. Melodies tended to become more tuneful and were divided into clear, compact, and usually well-balanced phrases. Harmonies were generally diatonic and straightforward, designed to give the music forward momentum within clear tonal structures. The element of dynamics, the relative volume of sound, came into greater play as composers began to explore a broader range of dynamic levels and more subtle or gradual changes from one level to another. The dominant texture became homophonic, and as inner parts of the texture took on more supportive harmonic roles, the need for and role of the basso continuo faded. But this pursuit of variety and contrast in melody, rhythm, dynamics, texture, and harmony led to that patchwork quality often found in early Classical works; later composers were able to master the challenge of achieving a balance between variety and unity, creating a paradoxical unity in variety. Composers developed new forms or modified old ones to help control contrast. The concerto, with its built-in principle of contrast, therefore, continued to be a form of great interest and utility.

The solo concerto became the preferred type, the concerto grosso gradually fading out of existence. Works were written virtually for each orchestral instrument in the solo role, although the violin remained the favorite. A growing interest in the cello as a solo instrument may be detected, but the repertory is small. The flute held its own through the Classical period, but interest in it as a solo instrument died in the Romantic era. Eventually a nonorchestral instrument—the harpsichord, and later, the newer pianoforte—became the most popular choice for several reasons:

- The sound of the keyboard instrument, particularly that of the hammered strings of the piano, contrasts strongly with that of the orchestra.
- It is the only instrument capable of matching the orchestra in range, textural complexity, and, in the case of the piano, fullness of sound.
- It is capable of accompanying itself; that is, it can play melody and provide its own harmonic support, and so could be used alone to create a striking contrast with the orchestra.

  The composers were often keyboard artists of great accomplishment and wrote concertos for their own use. The orchestra, which gradually expanded in size and more regularly included winds and percussion, was used by composers in extremely effective ways to counterbalance increasingly virtuosic solo writing.

The concerto continued in the three-movement format inherited from the Baroque, but the structures of individual movements were modified to suit the revised elements of the modern style. Classical composers developed a new instrumental form responding to the recently established focus on tonal organization, which offered fresh, dramatic possibilities for contrast. This form, usually called the sonata-allegro form, was especially common in the first movements of sonatas, symphonies, and chamber works. It gradually worked its way into the concerto's first movement where it was very effectively synthesized with the Baroque ritornello form. The resultant concerto-sonata form seemed to have, in the hands of a master concerto composer like Mozart, the potential for the perfect balance of soloistic and orchestral cooperation and contention. The development of this form and other elements of the emerging Classical concerto are explored in this chapter.

ITALY

Although Italian composers maintained an interest in the concerto during this period, they relinquished their leadership role to composers further north. Italian concerto composers, for the most part, continued to be performing violinists writing for their instrument.

Pietro Locatelli (1695–1764) was a leading performer-composer of the early portion of this transitional period. He was a pupil of Corelli in Italy, but spent most of his career centered in Amsterdam. He was one of the first in a line of composers of highly virtuosic music for the violin, making extensive use of double stops and scordatura. His training in the conservative Roman tradition can be seen in his twelve concerti grossi of Op. 1, published in Amsterdam in 1721, which are modeled after Corelli's Op. 6. Like the latter, Locatelli's Op. 1 contains eight church concertos, the eighth of which is his "Christmas Concerto," and four chamber concertos. His Op. 3, *L'arte del Violino* (1733), shows his command of the newer style of the Venetian composers. In these works he employed the lyrical bel canto style and made extensive use of the instrument's very high register. Each of the twelve concertos of Op. 3 has two caprices appended to both slow and fast movements. These are written-out cadenzas, demanding a high technical skill, and are representative of the most consistent use of the cadenza up to that time. Eighteen other concertos were published later (Op. 4 in 1735; Op. 7 in 1741; and Op. 9, now lost, in 1762). In Op. 7, No. 6, named *Il pianto d'Arianna*, an early example of instrumental recitative appears.

Leonardo Leo (1694–1744), a Neapolitan contemporary of Locatelli, was best known as a composer of music for church and theater. His contributions to the concerto, six cello concertos (five dated 1737–38) and one for four violins, are few in number, but interesting. They contain a curious mixture of conservative and progressive traits. Leo used the four-movement church-concerto plan of slow-fast-slow-fast long after the three-movement scheme had become standard, and three of the works have fast, fugal movements typical of the older form. Despite the use of these older elements, they rank among the very early examples of the solo concerto for cello and demonstrate Leo's deep understanding of the instrument's beautiful, singing tone. Four of the cello concertos' third movements are sicilianos that highlight the cello's rich sonority. The "singing allegro" style, a new expressive, lyrical melodic style of faster movements derived from vocal models, is especially evident in second movements. D. Green notes the form of the opening movements of four of Leo's cello concertos is strikingly similar to the later mature classical concerto-sonata form. Green further comments that Leo was the only Neapolitan composer interested in this design. Since Leo's music did not circulate beyond Naples, it is unlikely he exerted any influence on contemporary or succeeding composers.[1]

Giuseppe Tartini (1692–1770), the great violinist, theorist, and teacher, was the most important Italian composer of string music during this period. He established the famous School of Nations in Padua to which violinists from all over Europe flocked. Tartini's music is noted for its blending of virtuosity and lyricism and for the passionate quality of the slow movements. He made significant contributions to the development of violin technique, especially by bringing the bow and art of bowing close to modern practice. Very few of Tartini's approximately 135 concertos for violin are available in modern editions. M. Dounias has examined the works in manuscript, however, and placed them in chronological categories based on stylistic evidence. Dounias recognizes three periods: early, up to 1735; middle, 1735–50; late, 1750–70.[2] Throughout his lifetime, Tartini showed a general tendency to follow early Classic patterns.

Edwin J. Simon has pointed out that the concertos of the earliest period used five or six tuttis in opening movements, whereas the middle works had four or occasionally three, and the late works contained only three short tuttis.[3] This decrease in the number and importance of tutti sections relates directly to the proportionally increased importance of the soloist. In the late works the sonata-allegro form exerts a strong influence on the organization of first movements.

The figuration in the solo sections in Tartini's concertos of the middle period changes constantly. There is no relationship to the opening tutti, unless to its opening phrase, and in the case of subsequent solo sections there is normally no relationship to earlier ones in the movement. This practice is changed in the later concertos as solo sections take on features of sonata-allegro form. The first solo section is equivalent to a sonata-allegro exposition as suggested in Figure 3. This exposition, together with the opening tutti, is repeated just as in a sonata-allegro movement. The second solo section resembles the second part of a sonata-allegro form movement, incorporating development and recapitulation. This section, preceded and followed by tutti sections, is also repeated, as in the early examples of sonata-allegro form. The final tutti usually repeats the closing of the first tutti, while the second tutti usually begins with the head-motive in the dominant and ends with the final portion of Tutti 1 transposed to the dominant.

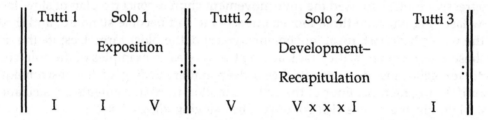

Figure 3. Early concerto-sonata form

The true ritornello design, in which the tutti sections serve as the structural pillars of the work, has been modified. In one of these newer movements, the composer seems first to have the sonata plan in mind, but then to have added tuttis to serve as opening and closing sections. The solo sections have become the important structural elements for which the tuttis simply provide a frame. In fact, several movements of concertos by a prolific pupil of Tartini, Michele Stratico (1721?–1782?), have solo sections that correspond closely to, or are even identical to, movements from his sonatas. The sonata movements probably were composed first and served as the basis for the concerto movements with their framing tutti sections.

Composers of this period clearly wanted to incorporate the dynamic sonata-allegro form into their concerto first movements. But this early attempt in Italy did not prove viable, for there were two strikes against it. First, the complete repeats of such large amounts of material led to a stagnant form, and, second, the orchestra's role had been too severely limited.

Pietro Nardini (1722–1793) was Tartini's most famous pupil, having come to study with the master for six years, beginning at age twelve. Leopold Mozart praised his playing of lyrical material, and his style of composition suited his tender manner of performance. His six violin concertos of Op. 1 (publ. c. 1765 in Amsterdam) are of moderate difficulty and in a strongly Baroque style, lacking thematic contrast.

Luigi Boccherini (1743–1805) was a prolific composer of chamber music whose interest in the concerto was clearly secondary. He did, however, compose eleven concertos for his own instrument, the cello, as well as a harpsichord concerto and another work featuring two violins. Four of the cello concertos (G. 477, G. 479–481,[4] publ. in Paris in 1770–71) bear a strong resemblance to the Baroque form but incorporate Classical melodic material. Another cello concerto of 1785 (G. 483) is less conservative. Unfortunately, the best known "Boccherini" Cello Concerto in B-flat is a concoction of Grützmacher, who published an arrangement in 1895. The outer movements combine a sonata (G. 565) and a concerto (G. 482) mixed in with the arranger's own harmonies and ornamentation. The slow movement is the Adagio of a still-different concerto (G. 480).

Boccherini did make extensive demands on the cellist in his authentic concertos, particularly requiring accuracy in the upper register, but his use of a cello of smaller size than the modern cello would have made such passages easier to negotiate. His works are generally valued for their lyrical melodic content and the rich, sometimes chromatic, harmonies.

MANNHEIM

During the second half of the eighteenth century, Mannheim became a major center of orchestral music, much of it composed by musicians of Bohemian descent. Mannheim's rise to importance was sudden, coinciding with its selection as electoral seat by Carl Philipp in 1720. His first court was in Breslau, and he brought many of his original band of Bohemian musicians with him as he moved first to Innsbruck, then to Heidelberg, before settling in Mannheim. Here he built one of the most impressive Baroque palaces in Germany and augmented the number of musicians in his employ. Few of the musicians were Italian; most were from Bohemia, Austria, or Bavaria, unlike the practice at other courts in Europe at that time.

Carl Philipp died in 1742 and was succeeded by Carl Theodor, who proved to be one of music's great patrons. He took a lively interest in music as an amateur and boosted the musical ranks at the court to ninety by 1778 when Mannheim's position as electoral seat came to an end. During the thirty-five years under Carl Theodor, music flourished in Mannheim, and the composers associated with the court formed what came to be known, even in the late eighteenth century, as the Mannheim school, connoting not an institution but a recognizable style of orchestral composition.

Johann Stamitz (1717–1757), the great violinist, served in Mannheim from 1741 or 1742 until his death in 1757. After becoming the orchestra's leader, he thoroughly trained his musicians, particularly the violinists, in the art of performance. The orchestra, noted for its discipline and polished technical facility, dazzled its audience by the precision of its attack, by its uniform bowing, and, most of all, by its effective executions of subtle and far-ranging dynamic variation.

The Mannheim school is best remembered for its contributions to the early history of the symphony, especially for the effective use of the brilliant orchestra in the Mannheim composers' symphonic works. Of the many composers active in Mannheim during its thirty-five-year peak period of activity, several made significant contributions to the symphony. Their contributions to the concerto, though less important, are of interest. The orchestra consisted of virtuosos on each instrument; inevitably the concerto found its way into the orchestra's repertory. Wind players as well as string players were highly talented; Mozart wrote music for a Mannheim flute player, an oboist, and a bassoonist. He also was definitely impressed by the orchestra's clarinetist.

Johann Stamitz started his career as a violin virtuoso. E. Wolf, in his study of Stamitz as a symphonist, remarks that the earliest known reference to him occurs in an advertisement for a concert in Frankfurt am Main in which the virtuoso was to perform alternately on violin, viola d'amore, cello, and double bass.[5] Stamitz wrote seventeen (three are now lost) concertos for violin, two for harpsichord, eleven for flute, and one each for oboe and clarinet, possibly the first for this single-reed instrument. Judging from their comparative conservatism, the concertos were probably composed early in his career, before his shift of interest to the symphony. Some exciting features associated with the symphonies—the effective dynamics and the vigorous rhythmic drive—do appear, however, in the concertos.

Carl Stamitz (1745–1801), Johann's son, was the most prolific of the Mannheim composers. His more than sixty concertos—including fifteen for violin, ten for clarinet, seven for flute, and seven for bassoon—are clear evidence that much of the Baroque had by this time been left behind. He adopted a pronounced homophonic style, consistently used contrasting themes, and presented new material in solo expositions. To the clarity of the Classical style, Carl Stamitz added an idiomatic treatment of the orchestra and striking dynamic effects characteristic of the Mannheim school. The first movements of his concertos are in ritornello form with three or four tuttis in various keys. The rondo, a Classical concerto feature, became the norm in his concerto final movements, while the slow movements were in a two-part form with a strong cantabile quality. He also composed thirty-eight symphonies concertantes, written as a result of his travels to Paris and London where this form was popular. This is a special form featuring more than one solo instrument, as will be seen below.

Other composers. The name of Mozart is associated with three other Mannheim musicians. Two were regular members of the orchestra singled out by Mozart as gifted composers of music, including concertos, for their own instruments—the flautist Johann B. Wendling (1723–1797), and the oboist Ludwig A. Lebrun (1752–1790). The other, Christian Cannabich (1731–1798), was the orchestra's leader during its greatest period and was admired by Mozart as the best director he knew. Cannabich focused his compositional energy on the symphony; he only composed five concertos: two for flute, one for keyboard instrument, one *Concerto alla pastorale a 8,* and a triple concerto for flute, oboe, and bassoon in the style of a symphonie concertante. He is noted for using the *galant* style, one of light melodic quality. Another important, but later, figure from Mannheim is Franz Danzi (1763–1826), who wrote several concertos for flute, bassoon, cello, and keyboard, and one for horn.

PARIS

Paris had become the center of French cultural life in the eighteenth century, and the Parisian love of drama and spectacle made the theater the epicenter of the city's cultural life. Variety in any entertainment was viewed as absolutely essential by the French; as a result dramatic scenes were regularly given over to the performance of airs, recitatives, choruses, and dances. Ballet received special attention with the result that orchestral music was given a more central role in the French theater of the seventeenth and eighteenth centuries than it had received in Italian opera. As a consequence, French opera typically contained numerous purely instrumental sections to accommodate dance scenes and even to accompany vocal numbers. The fuller texture of the typical five-part string writing developed by Lully contrasted strongly with the three-part texture common in Italian orchestral writing of the period. Jean-Philippe Rameau (1683–1764) later reduced the string texture to four parts, but added striking effects of orchestral color by the greater use of wind instruments. In short, the French composers writing to meet the needs of the theater developed a style of composing for full orchestra which provided the basis for public orchestral concerts emerging in Paris.

In 1725 a concert series was established to provide musical entertainment during those seasons of the church year, such as Lent, when theaters closed for religious reasons. The series, called the Concert Spirituel, was initially built around an offering of instrumental music and vocal music employing sacred Latin texts. But the orchestra soon became the mainstay of the concerts and as such the Concert Spirituel became the model for public orchestral concerts throughout Europe. In time, the increasingly popular Concert Spirituel extended its season to the point that the series rivaled the performances offered by the theaters.

These orchestral concerts attracted the attention of traveling virtuosos, so the concerto began to take on considerable importance in Paris. Visiting performers brought their own music so that the number of concertos written by French composers remained small until near the end of the century.

Jean-Marie Leclair "l'aîné" (1697–1764), the first important French composer of concertos, was a student of Somis in Turin, Italy, and may have studied with Locatelli in London or Amsterdam. He made his debut in 1728, performing his own sonatas and concertos written almost exclusively for the violin. He modified Italian sonata and concerto forms to accommodate French taste. As a result, frequent references to the French dance style can be found in the sonatas; slow movements of the concertos have an elegant and graceful French touch, while the fast movements bear a close resemblance to Vivaldi's style. The graces of the richly ornamented melodies are written out in the French manner, and the sometimes surprisingly chromatic harmonies are of French origin. The virtuosic complexity of the concertos have their origin neither in the French nor Italian tradition, but from the composer himself, who was noted for his brilliant violin playing. His twelve concertos, published in two sets (Op. 7, 1737 and Op. 10, 1745), demand regular use of high positions, frequent double stops (occasionally through entire movements), double trills, tremolo, and unusual bowing techniques. Leclair was the only significant French contributor to the Baroque concerto. Later Gallic composers all devoted themselves to composing in the newer Classical style.

Pierre Gaviniès (1728–1800) continued Leclair's brilliant approach to the violin concerto. Viotti, the culminating figure in the history of the French violin concerto, referred to Gaviniès as "the French Tartini," probably out of admiration for his outstanding abilities as violinist and teacher. From the age of forty on, he frequently played at the Concert Spirituel—the Mozart family heard him there during the 1763–64 season—and between 1773 and 1777 he was a director of the series, joined by Leduc and Gossec. When the Paris Conservatory opened in 1795, Gaviniès became professor of violin, a position he held until his death. His Op. 4 violin concertos (publ. 1764, the first French violin concertos to be published since Leclair's) contain virtuosic passages with double stops and flourishes. Solo sections of the concertos lack contrasting thematic material and consist mostly of patterns of figuration.

G. M. Giornovichi (c. 1740–1804) made a successful debut at the Concert Spirituel in 1773 and soon became a favorite of the Parisian audiences. His sixteen violin concertos are typical *galant* works—elegant, graceful, and simple, lacking in drama. Chappell White writes, "[Giornovichi] did much to stabilize certain typical aspects of the French violin concerto in the 1770s. He introduced the *romance*, which quickly became the most characteristic slow movement, and he established the rondo as the finale."[6] The romance is a slow movement of great lyricism usually written in a simple style, yet in these works often coupled with virtuosic demands.

François Devienne (1759–1803), who became professor of flute at the Paris Conservatory, is credited with breathing life into concertos for winds. Most French concertos were written for the violin, but a few featured other orchestral instruments, notably the flute. Devienne's sixteen flute concertos and four concertos for bassoon, another instrument he played, are typically graceful French works in which the soloist is given dazzling technical display.

Johann Schobert (c. 1735–1767) was the only French composer of harpsichord concertos to emerge in this early period, as the keyboard concerto was not greatly favored by the French. This may explain why Schobert developed a style more strongly associated with the Mannheim school. He wrote five concertos for harpsichord. His music was much admired by the youthful Mozart, who recast several of Schobert's sonata movements in concerto form.

The Symphonie Concertante

In the 1770s the French love of grand effects and of a melodious, yet flashy, style led to the development of a new musical genre, the symphonie concertante.[7] It resulted from a blending of elements associated with the solo concerto, the concerto grosso, and the symphony. Although the term literally means "concerted symphony," the works are closer to the concerto than to the symphony. In its simplest form, the symphonie concertante is an orchestral work featuring two or more soloists. It was certainly of French, particularly Parisian, origin, and the bulk of the symphonies concertantes were composed by Parisian composers of the

A poster advertising a Concert Spirituel. The Concert Spirituel, the first important series of public concerts in Europe, was founded in 1725 in Paris. Typical programs featured the orchestra, often with instrumental and vocal soloists, and the concerto came to figure prominently, as in this 1781 concert. In addition to the solo concerto, the Parisians had a distinct liking for works featuring more than one soloist, and the French created a new form, the symphonie concertante, by blending elements of the solo concerto, concerto grosso, and symphony. Also typical is the strong interest shown in solo wind instruments, as represented here by the oboe in a concerto and the bassoon in the symphonie concertante. (Photo: Bibl. Nat. Paris.)

1770s and '80s. The genre also enjoyed a degree of popularity in London, which often came under French musical influence, as well as a lesser degree of favor in Mannheim, as noted earlier.

These new works, involving two or more virtuoso soloists, were specifically designed to appeal to the Parisian taste, and so were largely performed at public concerts, such as the Concert Spirituel. They have the character of divertimentos—light and entertaining, never dramatic or profound. They are richly melodious, with a wealth of graceful tunes. The texture is light, never standing in the way of the melody. Rhythms are lively, and orchestration is varied and colorful. As compared to the symphony, the symphonie concertante is more relaxed and even-tempered. Barry S. Brook, an authority on French orchestral music of this period, has noted that the lightness of mood seems to require a consistent use of the major mode—only two or three, or 0.5 percent of all symphonies concertantes were composed in the minor mode, as compared to 2.5 percent of the Classical symphonies and about 50 percent of all concerti grossi.[8]

The earliest symphonies concertantes featured a pair of solo violins; later, pairs of winds or mixed strings became popular. Still later, a move toward using three or four soloists emerged, accompanied by a continuing increase in the winds. The first movements of some of the earliest works are in the Baroque ritornello form, eventually to be displaced by the Classical concerto-sonata form. The symphonic development of motives, so characteristic of the Classical period, is absent, however. The soloists are always in the forefront, the orchestra furnishing a light accompaniment, except during the first orchestral statement. The soloists are given the important thematic material; because each soloist presents the same thematic material (possibly varied) in turn, first movements tended to be lengthy. Impassioned slow movements were considered out of place in these divertimento-like works, so that most French composers simply omitted a slow movement. Finales are typically light-hearted rondos, though some theme-and-variations movements occur, but both forms provide ideal opportunities for soloistic display. A minuet-and-trio movement is occasionally used for a finale.

These characteristically brilliant and diverting two-movement works were highly successful, and some French composers specialized in their composition almost exclusively. One was Giuseppe Maria Cambini (1746–1825), who arrived in Paris in the early 1770s just as the new genre began to capture public attention. His charming, yet brilliant, style was eminently suited to the symphonie concertante of which he composed more than eighty, mostly for two violins, but also for combinations of winds and strings. Other important Parisian composers in the new genre were Devienne, François-Joseph Gossec (1734–1829), Ignaz Pleyel (1757–1831), and Jean-Baptiste Sébastien Bréval (1753–1823). The later composers often show the influence of the Mannheim school.

As the symphonie concertante gained in popularity, composers outside France showed more interest in it. Representative examples by Haydn and Mozart will be discussed later.

However, the increasing importance accorded the individual in the burgeoning middle class ethos of the nineteenth century and an associated hero worship brought an abrupt end to this short-lived phenomenon. Even in Paris, where such works continued to be composed until 1830, the impact of the symphony and of the solo concerto overwhelmed the national tradition.

The culminating figure of the French Classical school, G. B. Viotti (1755–1824), was also the founder of a new trend in the nineteenth-century violin concerto. His contributions will be discussed in Chapter 12, "The Virtuoso Concerto."

BERLIN

Dresden, Hamburg, and Berlin, at the court of Frederick the Great, were the major centers of musical activity in northern Germany. In general, the more northerly composers remained more conservative throughout the mid- to late eighteenth century than their southern counterparts. Thus, the Baroque style persisted longer in the north, which may explain the greater attention northern composers gave to the concerto as compared with the symphony. The strong keyboard tradition of the north also encouraged the further nurturing of the keyboard concerto initiated by J. S. Bach.

Truly notable progress in the development of the keyboard concerto emerged from the work of four important sons of J. S. Bach. Three were active in northern Germany; the other moved to Milan, then to London, and proved to be a direct link to Mozart and his culminating piano concertos.

Wilhelm Friedemann Bach (1710–1784) was the oldest of the four musical brothers, and for this reason he probably found it the most difficult to cast off the older Baroque style or to integrate it with the newer Classical style. His six concertos for harpsichord date from the years he spent as organist in Dresden, 1733–46, and are all in the Baroque style. He followed in his father's footsteps by writing a concerto for two harpsichords. Wilhelm Friedemann's style is noted for its strong reliance on counterpoint, rich melodies, and occasionally bold harmonic progressions.

Carl Philipp Emanuel Bach (1714–1788) was the most important of Bach's sons active in northern Germany. He was the foremost representative of the dramatically expressive *empfindsamer Stil*. The music of this newer "sensitive" or "sentimental" style of northern Germany is characterized by sigh motives, wide-ranging and often sudden dynamic changes, and chromaticism designed to express, more powerfully, deep emotional sentiment. Bach effectively used this style, with its intensity of expression and high degree of contrast, to blend elements of the old and new modes of musical expression. His most striking examples of the *empfindsamer Stil* are to be found in his solo keyboard works, particularly those intended for the very intimate clavichord, an instrument highly sensitive to the performer's touch. His concertos, on the other hand, adhere more closely to tradition, incorporating the unusual qualities of *Empfindsamkeit* only infrequently. In spite of what appears on the surface to be a conservative approach to the form, Emanuel Bach's fifty-two keyboard concertos are of great significance.

Building on his father's concept of the keyboard concerto as a derivative of the Italian violin concerto, Emanuel elevated the new genre to a position not only as an independent form but also as one of considerable importance among accepted forms. The solo parts become more idiomatic, leaving behind their dependence on the idiom of the violin. Emanuel even transcribed some of his keyboard concertos for other instruments, reversing the usual procedure of his father.

From the time of C. P. E. Bach's move to Berlin in 1738 to 1755, he composed twenty-five concertos for one harpsichord and one for two. Thereafter he paid only sporadic and less intense attention to the concerto. In the concertos of the early period, Bach worked within the established Baroque concerto form to create works of a truly contemporary scope. Adjustments to the old ritornello form are especially of interest.

It was customary for Bach, in using the ritornello form in fast movements, to rely on only four tutti and three solo sections. At times, as in the Harpsichord Concerto in D Minor, W. 23,[9] he includes five tutti sections. Much less frequently he uses only three tutti sections. He increased the scope of the initial ritornello by expanding the traditional motives of the Baroque form into longer themes. Clearly contrasting themes in the tonic are separated by a transitional section of a modulatory character, which winds its way back to the tonic. A concluding passage confirming the tonic key rounds off the ritornello. This form must have been reached through some experimentation, for in some of Bach's earliest concertos the modulatory section closes in the dominant or relative major, rather than returning to the tonic, and the remainder of the opening ritornello follows in the new key. This structure presented the problem of repeating the modulation in the first solo section, which begins in the tonic. To enhance the contrast between the solo and tutti sections, Bach preferred to wait for the solo section before making the dramatic change to the new key. A rapidly modulating section that refuses to establish clearly a single new key between the contrasting themes was found to provide the necessary coloration for the long tonic ritornello, without leading to an anticlimax at the solo entry.

The first movement of C. P. E. Bach's Harpsichord Concerto in D Minor, W. 23, provides a good example of an opening ritornello planned along the newer lines. The wide leaps and strong, dotted rhythms of the opening D minor theme are characteristic of the passionate, emotional quality of Bach's *Empfindsamkeit* (Ex. 8-1). The fifteen-measure modulatory section (mm. 11–25) introduces contrasting motives (Ex. 8-2) used sequentially, first moving away from the tonic and then returning to it by way of a dominant pedal. The final section of the ritornello (mm. 26–42) begins with a short motive (Ex. 8-3) related to m. 3. This motive is repeated and fragmented in a striking harmonic move to the submediant before a motive from the modulatory section pulls the music back to the tonic.

Ex. 8-1. C. P. E. Bach, Harpsichord Concerto in D Minor, W. 23; I. Allegro, mm. 1–10.

Ex. 8-2. C. P. E. Bach, Harpsichord Concerto in D Minor, W. 23; I. Allegro, mm. 11–25.

Ex. 8-3. C. P. E. Bach, Harpsichord Concerto in D Minor, W. 23; I. Allegro, mm. 26–27.

The first solo section of an Emanuel Bach concerto typically opens with a version of the first phrase or theme of the ritornello. For example, in the D Minor Concerto (mm. 44–53), this theme has been transformed to suit it to the solo idiom and to give it brilliance through the use of rapidly executed scales and other virtuosic devices. The orchestra usually joins in near the end of the phrase once the soloist's leading role has been established. There is an interesting give-and-take between the soloist and orchestra in W. 23 as they alternate in presenting elements of the dramatic first theme. This pattern of alternation continues into the repeat of the first bars of the modulatory section of the ritornello, but the soloist soon introduces new virtuosic figuration, accompanied by the orchestra. These new patterns of figuration are usually used sequentially to continue the modulation to a new key, rather than to return to the tonic (see mm. 54–78 in W. 23). It is interesting to note that Bach favored the subdominant minor as the contrasting key in the first solo section in his minor-mode movements, rather than the more common relative major. Thus, the solo section moves to G minor in the D Minor Concerto.

As the modulation is completed, the solo instrument takes on an even-more-dominant role as it introduces distinctive new material. In the later Classical concertos of J. C. Bach and Mozart, this new material is usually a strikingly different theme, often remaining the private property of the soloist throughout the remainder of the movement. C. P. E. Bach occasionally followed this practice, but more often intensified the contrast between solo and tutti by writing new idiomatic and virtuosic figuration for the soloist while leaving the orchestra with material taken from the ritornello (Ex. 8-4). In other words, Bach provided the soloist with an independent role without necessarily providing an independent theme. The solo section usually ends with a passage of unaccompanied bravura, as in W. 23 (mm. 87–97).

Ex. 8-4. C. P. E. Bach, Harpsichord Concerto in D Minor, W. 23; I. Allegro, mm. 83–84.

The second ritornello, in the new key (the dominant, if the movement is in the major mode), usually focuses on the opening of the ritornello and sometimes concludes with the ritornello's cadential section as in W. 23 (mm. 98–125).

Solo 2 typically begins as Solo 1 does, but in the new key. After a few measures of thematic material (only four in W. 23's first movement, mm. 126–129), new patterns of figuration are introduced, appearing in sequential modulatory passages. Initially these passages contrast strongly with the ritornello material—often the easily remembered first motive—that is briefly interjected by the orchestra (Ex. 8-5). The soloist and orchestra truly seem to be contesting for supremacy in these passages. But eventually, the soloist comes to dominate the work in the midportion of Solo 2 as it is given ever-more-impressive display material. The orchestra meanwhile comes to provide only harmonic support, which often still makes use of ritornello material (mm. 152–175).

Ex. 8-5. C. P. E. Bach, Harpsichord Concerto in D Minor, W. 23; I. Allegro, mm. 130–137.

In the final third of Solo 2 (mm. 175ff.) the tutti again becomes more assertive by first alternating, then uniting with, the soloist to develop thematic material. Typically, an unaccompanied solo passage leads to the concluding cadence of Solo 2 in a new key. (Bach uses the dominant minor in W. 23, his common choice for movements in the minor mode, whereas the new key at this point in a major-mode movement is usually the relative minor.)

The third tutti is the most flexible and shortest of the four tutti sections in the Classical concerto. In W. 23, the short Tutti 3 uses the musical material from the beginning and end of the ritornello, transposed to the key of A, the dominant minor (mm. 202–221). In addition to this practice, Emanuel Bach sometimes moves from the new key back to the tonic during the course of the third tutti.

The first movement of the D Minor Concerto, W. 23, contains five tutti and four solo sections. In such a case the third solo section is short, about half the length of Solo 1, and functions as a continuation of the figuration introduced in Solo 2, while the orchestra provides a simple, yet interesting accompaniment (mm. 221–242 in W. 23). In the final bars of Solo 3, the soloist returns to the tonic key. In the D Minor Concerto, this quiet passage follows a jolting orchestral recall of the opening idea in C major (mm. 241–242), its only appearance in major in the movement.

Tutti 4 of W. 23 restates the ritornello's opening eight measures in the tonic, initiating the recapitulation. The solo instrument breaks in, Solo 4, to close off the first theme with the same echo material used in Solo 1, and the solo and orchestra then unite to recapitulate Solo 1 with adjustments to retain the second half in the tonic.

The final tutti, as in W. 23, usually consists of the closing portion of the ritornello. It is preceded by a cadenza. The first movement of Bach's D Minor Concerto can be analyzed as in Figure 4.

Because of the shortness of the penultimate tutti section and the increased alternation of tutti and solo in the subsequent recapitulation of material from the initial solo section, these two sections, Tutti 4 and Solo 4 in Figure 4, are often welded into a single unit. This practice points to that of Mozart.

Section	Tutti 1	Solo 1		Tutti 2
Theme or material	A B C	A B D C virtuoso display (new figuration)		A C
Key	I	I IV		IV

Section	Solo 2 (concentration of virtuosity)	Tutti 3
Theme or material	A (Begins like Solo 1, continues with new figuration; orchestra supports with ritornello motives.)	A C
Key	movement to V	V

Section	Solo 3	Tutti 4 and Solo 4	Tutti 5
Theme or material	figuration light orch.	A B D E cadenza (Tutti 4 and Solo 4 integrated to form recapitulation.)	C
Key	to I	I	I

Figure 4. First-movement form, C. P. E. Bach, Concerto in D Minor

Jane Stevens, in her dissertation on C. P. E. Bach's keyboard concertos, notes the composer seemed especially concerned to incorporate a recapitulation in the ritornello design of the early concertos.[10] He experimented with various ways to include the recapitulation satisfactorily, but usually settled on the final solo section, whether the work contained three or four, as the place to do so. Leon Crickmore has observed that only in the movements containing five tutti sections does Bach begin the penultimate tutti in the tonic key.[11] Further, in such cases Bach also tends to initiate the recapitulation at this place, continuing it into the final solo section.

The slow movements of Emanuel Bach's early concertos are usually in ritornello form with four tutti sections. The composer quite typically focuses on the development of one four-measure phrase in these slower movements. The emphasis is on ornamentation and other expressive details which often give a strong improvisational quality to the solo sections. A cadenza precedes the final tutti. Final movements are constructed along lines of opening movements.

During the 1750s and '60s Bach came to pay greater attention to details of expression and less to the solution of formal problems.[12] Yet Stevens observes that the ritornellos during this period become less distinctly sectional and more of an integrated whole, and that the first solo sections depart little from the opening ritornello, except for the modulation to the second key.[13]

Bach seems to have lost interest in the keyboard concerto in his final years in Berlin. His attention shifted to a new musical form he appears to have invented, under the influence of the lighter style of music prevalent in Vienna and southern Germany. The new works, called sonatinas by Bach, are for keyboard and orchestra, but show little influence of the concerto. They are more like the divertimento of the south, in that they have three to eight movements, all in the same key, in binary form, and include wind instruments, unlike his earlier concertos. Bach's twelve *galant* sonatinas, composed between 1762 and 1764, lack the intense opposition of forces so characteristic of the concerto; instead the soloist and orchestra often double and complement one another.

After Bach's move to Hamburg in 1768, he composed eleven more keyboard concertos, including the Double Concerto for Harpsichord and Piano, W. 47 (1788). These pieces reflect work with the sonatinas in that the soloist and orchestra are used to make musical statements cooperatively. The orchestra rarely interjects or interrupts solo sections, and the solo never states any independent thematic material. And, as in the sonatinas, slow movements and final movements of these concertos are shorter and lighter in mood.

It may never be possible to demonstrate a direct link between Emanuel Bach's concertos and those of Mozart (or Beethoven, as some wish to do), but it can be said with certainty that the Berlin Bach profitably cultivated the new genre started by his father and, by virtue of his experimentation, developed an intensely exciting new concerto idiom.

Johann Christoph Friedrich Bach (1732–1795), Emanuel's brother, worked at the highly cultured small court at Bückeburg, which was strongly influenced by Italian music. Friedrich Bach composed five concertos for keyboard instruments— one around 1765 and the others between 1787 and 1792. The later works may have been intended for the pianoforte, since the composer had purchased one of the new instruments in 1778, when he visited his younger brother Christian in London. The earliest concerto clearly shows the influence of Emanuel, but his subsequent work in this form demonstrates an understanding of the Classical practices being formulated by Christian Bach and Mozart. For example, the final movements of Friedrich Bach's later concertos are all rondos in the Classical style.

VIENNA

Vienna was to become the home of an unusually rich musical tradition in the late eighteenth and into the nineteenth centuries. In addition to the great compositions of the well-known Viennese masters, valuable material can be found in the works of their predecessors and lesser-known contemporaries.

Georg Matthias Monn (1717–1750) occupies an important place not only in the history of the symphony (one of his symphonies, dated 1740, is the earliest dated four-movement symphony), but also in the Viennese Classical concerto. His concertos were probably the first composed in Vienna to contain clearly identifiable Classical elements, notably in the nature of the thematic material. He continued to use ritornello structure; as in the case of Emanuel Bach's practice, the second solo sections of the first movements are given a strongly modulatory function matching the tonally restless development portion of sonata-allegro form. Orchestral interjections and a lively give-and-take between orchestra and soloist characterize the solo sections. Monn composed seven harpsichord concertos, which are fairly idiomatic, and one well-respected Cello Concerto in G Minor, which makes good use of the instrument's low register. Arnold Schoenberg was so taken by the work that he edited it in 1911–12.

Georg Christoph Wagenseil (1715–1777), teacher of the imperial family at Schönbrunn, was a well-known keyboard performer and composer whose music was known by Mozart. His early works reveal the contrapuntal influence of J. J. Fux, but toward 1750 *galant* features dominate. Trills, triplets, short note values, and repetitions of short phrases, often turned to minor, are common. Equally characteristic are the thin accompaniment, usually consisting of two violins and bass, and the minuet finales possessing a divertimento quality. Most of his approximately sixty keyboard concertos were probably intended for the dilettante. Of special importance is Wagenseil's emphasis on an idiomatic keyboard style with a proliferation of broken chords, scales, arpeggios, broken octaves, trills, and turns. His Cello Concerto and Trombone Concerto are expressive works that repay study.

Carl Ditters von Dittersdorf (1739–1799) was a popular composer of a cheerful disposition who wrote in the prevailing *galant* style. He was a violin virtuoso and wrote approximately forty concertos, including eighteen for violin, five for harpsichord, five for viola, and four for oboe. In his mature concertos soloists are given new thematic material in the modulatory and second key areas of the first solo section. Dittersdorf's Harpsichord Concerto in A Major (c. 1775) is a characteristic work exhibiting some traits of the mature Viennese style.

Other composers. Josef Antonín Štěpán (1726–1797) and Johann Vanhal (1739–1813) were Czech composers active in Vienna. Both used native folk melodies in the lighter finales of their keyboard concertos. Štěpán anticipated important Romantic tendencies in his later concertos. For example, he used a large, expressive slow introduction in the minor key in which the soloist participates and created such extreme dominance of the solo instrument that the concerto begins to resemble an accompanied sonata.

Close relatives of Haydn and Mozart made minor contributions to the concerto. Michael Haydn (1737–1806), Joseph's younger brother, wrote a vital duo concertante for viola and organ or harpsichord and orchestra (c. 1761). Wolfgang Amadeus Mozart's father, Leopold (1719–1787), was active mainly in Salzburg where he wrote concertos mostly for wind instruments. It is curious that the man who wrote *Violinschule* (publ. 1756), a violin method book of such great importance, did not write any violin concertos.

LONDON

Although England produced no native composers of great distinction during the eighteenth century, London enjoyed a vigorous musical life, thanks to foreign musicians, mostly from Italy and Germany, who visited for extended periods or took up residence and established careers. The active concert life of London's theaters and "pleasure gardens" attracted many musicians, including those of the first rank such as Haydn and the young Mozart. Further, the flourishing music publishing industry of London made the music of composers from throughout Europe well-known in the British Isles.

Johann Christian Bach (1735–1782), the eleventh and last son of J. S. Bach, settled in London in 1762, becoming one of that city's most distinguished composers. He was born in Leipzig, and must have received his earliest training from his father. At fifteen, after his father's death in 1750, Christian moved to Berlin where he came under the care of his half-brother, Emanuel, who tutored the young man in composition and performance. The *Versuch über die wahre Art Das Clavier zu spielen* (Essay on the True Art of Playing Keyboard Instruments, parts I and II published in 1753 and 1762) might serve as a guide to some of the subject matter of these studies, for Emanuel published Part I while Christian was living with him in Berlin.

Of the compositions Johann Christian is known to have written while in Berlin, the most important are five keyboard concertos scored for an orchestra of two violins, violas, and bass. Stylistic features typical of Emanuel's *Empfindsamkeit* are quite evident in these early works, such as passages in recitative, an emphasis on the minor mode, and markings such as *adagio affettuoso con sordini*, indicating the unusual exploitation of muted strings and tenderly expressive playing. These traits disappear from Christian's later works. These concertos are in three movements, with the slow middle movement in a contrasting key. Yet it is in the opening movements that J. C. Bach substantially anticipated later Classical practice in the development of a new form.

The first movements of these early concertos are typically organized in seven sections, four tuttis and three solos. The first movement of the B-flat Major Concerto (c. 1752)[14] illustrates the common design, which is similar to that employed by C. P. E. Bach during this period. The soloist, however, in a marked departure from Emanuel's practice, enters with new material in Solo 1 and continues with other new material when the dominant key is reached. A tutti interjection of the opening idea is the only link to the ritornello in Solo 1. As in his brother's ritornello design, J. C. Bach's Solo 2 here begins as Solo 1 did, but then moves through modulatory, often sequential, harmonic progressions with various patterns of solo figuration. And, echoing C. P. E. Bach's experimentation with the concept of recapitulation, Solo 3 serves as a partial recapitulation. Here the soloist, in dialogue with orchestra, repeats the ritornello's opening theme in the tonic and then continues with material from the second half of Solo 1 transposed to the tonic. This integration of material from Tutti 1 and Solo 1 is a significant innovation which was commonly used in the later Classical period. This structure is analyzed in Figure 5.

Section	Tutti 1	Solo 1	
Formal Division	Ritornello 1	"Exposition"	
Material	A B C D E	F G A (tutti interjection of head-motive)	H J
Key	I	I	V

Section	Tutti 2	Solo 2
Formal Division	Ritornello 2	"Development"
Material	A C D E	F (figurative with orchestra on ritornello motives)
Key	V	V x x x (modulatory to) VI

Section	Tutti 3	Solo 2	
Formal Division	Ritornello 3	"Recapitulation"	
Material	A D	A (dialogue with orchestra)	H J
Key	VI I	I	

Section	Tutti 4
Formal Division	Ritornello 4
Material	A B C D E
Key	I

Figure 5. First-movement form, J. C. Bach: Concerto in B-flat Major (c. 1752)

With the exception of a short tutti interjection in Solo 1 and the dialogue at the beginning of Solo 3, the orchestra is very passive in these solo sections. But in Solo 2, the orchestra plays a more active role, often accompanying with ritornello material or engaging in a give-and-take with the soloist. The form tends to emphasize the contrast between the orchestra and the soloist through their alternation, except in Solo 2 which integrates the two forces more carefully. Especially notable is the almost complete separation of thematic content between forces, except at the beginning of Solo 3.

Most of the remainder of Christian Bach's concertos were written in London after his seven-year (1754–62) sojourn in Italy. His love of opera had brought him to Italy at the age of about twenty, where he became fully absorbed with the production of Italian vocal music, composing a great number of conservative works for the Roman Catholic church under the guidance of his famous teacher, Padre Martini (1706–1784). He also became eminently successful in the genre of *opera seria,* or Italian serious opera.

Bach's success as a composer of Italian opera brought him international fame, and in 1762 he was invited to serve as composer and director of operas for the King's Theatre in London. He remained in London until his death in 1782, save for absences in 1772 and 1776 to produce operas in Mannheim and in 1778 to prepare an opera in Paris.

In addition to his operatic work in London, Bach was engaged as a teacher, becoming the music master to the Queen. He was also active as a concert artist participating in a variety of performances including the famous Bach-Abel concerts beginning in 1765. These varied activities brought forth an amazing amount of music—about 400 works, of which two-thirds are instrumental.

During the London years, Bach published three important sets of keyboard concertos, each containing six works, at approximately seven-year intervals. These works document significant changes in the keyboard concerto, and although no writer would contend that Christian Bach initiated any notable number of these changes, his contributions are of considerable importance, especially in light of his relationship with Mozart.

It is highly probable that a considerable percentage of Bach's concertos were conceived with the amateur performer in mind, since they lack technically demanding and overtly virtuosic keyboard parts. Other factors seem to point to their design for domestic use as well. The very fact of their publication is an important clue—Bach clearly meant for them to be used in the home. All are scored for only two violins and cello, a chamber music combination readily available in many homes. Furthermore, four of each set of six concertos are in only two movements, a form popular in the less demanding music intended for the amateur.[15] The final movement in the two-movement concertos is usually a minuet in the early works and a rondo in the later ones. The three-movement works of each opus have a more ambitious tone about them; solo parts tend to be more demanding and the composer takes full advantage of the greater possibilities of contrast.

Op. 1 was dedicated to the Queen and published in 1763. Two of the concertos (Nos. 4 and 6, both in three movements) have first movements representative of a stage in the concerto form that may be an offshoot of developments made in the concertos of the Tartini school of the 1750s and '60s. The tutti and solo take turns in presenting the important parts of the sonata-allegro form, as in Op. 1, No. 6 (Figure 6). This design did not persist, probably because it was not expansive enough and because it did not offer adequate room for the dramatic opposition of forces. In short, the spirit of the concerto was absent.

In other works of Op. 1, Christian Bach continued to explore the concerto from another direction, that is, by introducing elements of the sonata form into the concerto, without impinging upon the essence of the concerto. The first movements are cast in the formal pattern later employed by Mozart, but on a smaller scale. In comparison with the earlier Berlin works, all tutti sections but the first are

Formal Division	Exposition				
Section	Tutti	Solo	Tutti	Solo	Tutti
Material	A transition	B	C	Figuration	Cadence : :
Key	I	V	V	V	V

Formal Division	Development		Recapitulation				
Section	Tutti	Solo	Tutti	Solo	Tutti	Solo	Tutti
Material	A	Figuration	A	B	C	Figuration	Cadence :
Key	V	x x x	I	I	I	I	I

Figure 6. First-movement form, J. C. Bach, Op. 1, No. 6 in D Major

reduced in size, whereas the solo sections have been expanded in size and given greater importance. Solo 1 now begins by restating the ritornello's opening theme, creating greater unity, while thematic contrast is reserved for a new key (ideas F and G). Tutti 3 is kept quite short and tends to merge with Solo 3; a long Tutti 3 would feel redundant both tonally and thematically, since Solo 3 is designed as a large recapitulation section in the tonic. Figure 7 shows the formal layout of such a movement.

Section	Tutti 1	Solo 1	Tutti 2
Formal Division	Ritornello 1	Exposition	Ritornello 2
Material	A B C D E	A B F G (figuration)	A E
Key	I	I V	V

Section	Solo 2	Tutti 3 & Solo 3		Tutti 2
Formal Division	Development	Recapitulation		Ritornello 3
Material	Figuration	A	A B G	E
Key	V x x x VI–I	I	I	I

Figure 7. Early concerto-sonata form, J. C. Bach

In the Op. 7 concertos, published in 1770, a few formal refinements to, or experiments with, this earlier plan are evident. The most obvious and important innovation is indicated by the title, which announces these works are for the harpsichord *or* the piano. Bach may have been the first to play the piano as a solo instrument at a public concert, doing so in England in 1768.[16] The new instrument quickly gained favor among amateurs, perhaps because it required less upkeep and fewer tunings than the harpsichord. The piano was also eminently desirable for musical reasons associated with the new mode of musical expression in the Classical period. With its vast musical and technical capacities, and a tone well set off from the orchestra, it is an ideal solo instrument for the concerto. The enthusiasm of the Classical composers and audiences for instrumental brilliance led to its rapid acceptance, which in turn increased the demands made upon the orchestra. The new instrument may have inspired Christian to write more active orchestra parts in the concertos of Opp. 7 and 13.

The first movement of Op. 7, No. 5, in E-flat Major[17] contains a number of Bach's formal refinements and changes which make it quite different from those of his earlier concertos. The solo sections have been further increased in size and importance, while the tuttis have shrunk. The tutti previously placed between Solos 2 and 3 (or between the development and recapitulation) has been omitted, a practice sometimes followed in mature Classical concertos as well. But the composer more commonly sets off the two major structural solo sections by inserting a tutti to manifest a clear contrast between the sections. The first solo section here is very much like Tutti 1, except that a new, contrasting, lyrical theme in the dominant key is introduced by the solo instrument (theme 4 in Figure 8). Such a contrasting lyrical theme is virtually a trademark of Mozart's piano concertos, so that the spirit of Bach's thematic contrast and use of the piano is very close to that of Mozart. The presentation of this new thematic material by the soloist without orchestral accompaniment not only reinforces the identity of the soloist, but also intensifies the contrast between the orchestra and solo. It must be noted again that only a keyboard instrument can successfully present such thematic material without orchestral support, for it is the only instrument able to accompany itself.

Following the pattern established in his earlier works and those of his brother, Emanuel, Christian Bach placed most of the virtuosic display in the theme-free, figuration-dominated Solo 2. In addition, the closing portion of Solo 1, its companion passage in the recapitulation of Solo 3, and the transition sections between thematic areas all contain virtuoso figuration. (Mozart used the same sections of the concerto-sonata form as the principal vehicles for virtuoso passages.) Throughout the movement, Bach gives the solo instrument a good balance of thematic and figurative material. As in most early Classical works, Bach places the major cadenza in the final measures of Solo 3. By contrast, later composers, including Mozart, interrupt the final ritornello with the cadenza, thereby giving it a more dramatic place, despite the fact that the cadenza serves no formal function at this place.

As in the Op. 1 concertos, Solo 3 is the equivalent of a recapitulation, although its makeup can be quite variable. The thematic material included may be taken from both Tutti 1 and Solo 1, but it seldom includes all thematic material contained in these earlier sections. In Op. 7, No. 5, the distinct theme (theme 4)

Section	Tutti 1				
Formal Division	Ritornello 1				
Material (Motive)	Theme 1 A B	Transition C D E F	Theme 2 G H	Theme 3 I	Closing theme J K
Key	I				

Section	Solo 1					
Formal Division	Exposition					
Material	Theme 1	Transition	Theme 4	Theme 2	Theme 3	Closing Cadenza theme
(Motive)	A´ B´	C´ D´ E´	L M N O (solo theme)	G H	I	J
Key	I		V			

Section	Tutti 2	Solo 2
Formal Division	Ritornello 2	Development
Material (Motive)	Theme 3 Closing theme I J	Various new figures in the solo, including one from the exposition. Figuration, more suitable for display, is preferred to thematic material. Concludes with space for cadenza.
Key	V	V x x x x V

Section	Solo 3 (Note no tutti between S2 and S3.)					
Formal Division	Recapitulation					
Material	Theme 1	Transition	(New solo figure–x)	Theme 2	Theme 3	Closing Cadenza theme
(Motive)	A´ B´	C´		G H	I	J
Key	I					

Section	Tutti 3
Formal Division	Ritornello 3 (identical to the end of R1)
Material (Motive)	Theme 3 Closing theme I J K
Key	I

Figure 8. First-movement form, J. C. Bach, Keyboard Concerto in E-flat Major,
Op. 7, No. 5

given the keyboard at the beginning of the dominant key in Solo 1 is omitted in the recapitulation, being replaced by new figuration at the corresponding point.

Op. 13, which appeared in 1777, does not contain the sort of major departures evidenced in previous works. A few minor changes are worth noting. These concertos are on a grander scale. The composer provides optional parts for pairs of oboes and horns, thus bolstering the orchestra if these instruments are available. Although the title indicates an option for the use of either the harpsichord or the piano, the latter was probably the preferred instrument. The solo parts are uniformly more demanding and all of the works include substantial bravura sections at the ends of Solo 1 and Solo 3, whereas only half of the concertos of Op. 7 do. The concerto-sonata plan of Op. 7 is continued, except that a very short Tutti 3 is reinstated between Solo 2 and Solo 3, serving to begin the recapitulation. This tutti section merges with the following solo recapitulation, which integrates the major themes of both the opening tutti and solo sections. The form, the multiplicity of thematic ideas, and the lyricism bring to mind the later concertos of Mozart.

Mozart greatly respected and enjoyed J. C. Bach's music—he performed it in concert as early as 1764, recommended it to his sister in 1774, used it in teaching, and surely had a hand in his father's endorsement of Bach's music in 1778. From their first meeting of 1764 in London when the boy of eight played duets sitting on Christian's knees, to their reunion in Paris in 1778, and finally to the day in 1782 when Mozart wrote to his father, "I suppose you have heard that the English Bach is dead? What a loss to the musical world,"[18] Mozart remained loyal to his friend.

The influence of Christian Bach's music on the younger composer is unmistakable. In addition to general stylistic similarities, Mozart's earliest concertos, composed when Mozart was nine, are arrangements of Bach's Op. 5 sonatas, while Christian's concertos must have served as models for Mozart's later concertos. Clearly Mozart's are closer to Bach's than to the works of the Viennese composers, such as Wagenseil, with which Mozart was surely familiar. In particular, the concerto-sonata form developed in Bach's concertos is very close to the approach used by Mozart. They share the multiplicity of themes, the graceful lyricism, and the clearly defined thematic dualism that enhances the contrast between soloist and orchestra. The development of this form was not the exclusive work of Bach, but he certainly was the first to couple its development with the nativity of the concerto for piano and orchestra.

Charles Burney, eighteenth-century music historian, noted that Bach seemed to have been the first composer who observed the "law of *contrast, as a principle.*" Although this assumption of Bach's priority is suspect, his concertos unquestioningly and amply exemplify this law and its relative success as a principle. Not only do they create contrast and opposition, but they do so while maintaining a sense of integrated and harmonious cooperation.

Bach's concertos are the interesting compositions of a highly gifted musician that document significant steps in the evolution of the keyboard concerto. Certainly Bach's concertos lack the greatness and intensity of Mozart's later works, but they lead directly to the towering achievements of Mozart.

Chapter Nine

WOLFGANG AMADEUS MOZART

Wolfgang Amadeus Mozart's (1756–1791) contributions to music include outstanding examples in all the forms and media common during his day, yet the mature operas and piano concertos of his Vienna period (1781–1791) are generally considered his greatest achievements. It is perhaps natural that a composer in whom such unfathomably rich and intense musical gifts were combined with such a creative innate sense of drama should excel in these two highly dramatic musical art forms, both of which must have challenged and stimulated him. By the age of twelve, Mozart had already composed two operas—one, an Italian *opera buffa, La finta semplice*; the other, a German *Singspiel, Bastien und Bastienne*—both attesting not only to his uncanny dramatic sense but also to his ready ability to write in two distinctly different contemporary operatic forms. Shortly before, he had created his first concerto-arrangements of keyboard sonatas movements by other composers and his first independent concerto (K. 47c for trumpet, now lost; see letter of Leopold Mozart, 12 November 1768).

Mozart's interest in the concerto persisted throughout the remainder of his life. He composed approximately forty completed concertos, as well as several individual concerto movements. Included are two complete, extant works for flute; one for clarinet; one for bassoon; three for horn; five for violin; and twenty-one for solo keyboard instrument. There are also concertos for flute and harp, for two pianos and for three pianos, a concertone or "large concerto" for two violins (also featuring solo oboe and cello), a symphonie concertante for violin and viola, and one for two flutes, two oboes, and two horns. Several of the independent concerto movements were written to replace movements in previously completed works. Several incomplete works also survive, including a long and fascinating fragment for keyboard instrument and violin (1778); a symphonie concertante for violin, viola, and cello; a concerto for oboe; two for horn; and one for basset horn, material from which he later used in the clarinet concerto.

Mozart's concertos are all of interest, but the mature piano concertos are of greatest importance. These are the fourteen written between February 1784 (K. 449 in E-flat) and January 1791 (K. 595 in B-flat). This body of work constitutes not only the high point of the eighteenth-century concerto, but a chief pinnacle of concerto writing throughout its entire history. Certainly the piano concertos hold a special place in the entire catalog of Mozart's music. They are informed by the same musical sensibilities as those of his symphonic and other instrumental music, but, in addition, provide a showcase for Mozart's dramatic genius sparked by that duality and contrast inherent in the concerto idiom.

While Mozart's genius as a composer of concertos is already evident in his earlier essays in the form, it only comes to full flower in the later works. His remarkable conception of the concerto emerges in the mature compositions principally in four ways:

First, with few exceptions, Mozart wrote the concertos for his own performance or for others possessing a musical and technical competence of a very high level. The great virtuosity required does much to account for the scintillating quality of the solo parts. No matter what the instrument, these brilliant solo parts are thoroughly idiomatic, confirming the composer's profound understanding of the instrument chosen—its strengths, its weaknesses, and, most of all, its character—much in the same way as he seemed so fully aware of the inner nature of his opera characters. The concertos are not, however, primarily vehicles for the virtuoso. That is to say, although the works are thoroughly virtuosic, the expressiveness of the music never suffers. Rarely is the passage work devoid of musical interest. As in Mozart's operas, virtuosity is used to enhance dramatic content and to move the action forward.

Second, the orchestra is never neglected in favor of the soloist, but rather is given a role equal in importance to that of the solo instrument. The orchestra regularly presents important thematic material, helps define formal divisions, and adds color, thanks especially to Mozart's bold use of the woodwind instruments. Mozart establishes a spirit of dramatic opposition between the solo instrument and orchestra, while at the same time he calls for a lively give-and-take and active cooperation of the forces. He successfully realized a subtle balance between contrast and cooperation, creating a tension which has rarely been equaled. The orchestra's role and style are truly as important and brilliant as those of the soloist.

Third, Mozart's unfailing sense of timing plays a major role in the dramatic placement of solo passages.

Fourth, Mozart combined his love of contrast with his superb creative melodic genius to produce, to a greater extent in the concertos than in any other of his works, an extraordinary richness of melodic material. He used his seemingly unlimited genius for the creation of melodic ideas to enhance the contrast between soloist and orchestra; consequently, the diversity of melodies, many of which are tunes or wonderfully lyrical themes, adds immensely to the appeal of these works. The abundance of melodic inspiration contrasts sharply with Haydn's more economic melodic style, as will be seen in the next chapter.

In addition to these four qualities, Mozart cultivated others common to his work in all musical forms. Especially noteworthy are the brilliant use of chromaticism, the luxuriant harmonic colorations and glorious modulations, the subtle and effective use of counterpoint, and a supreme understanding of musical form.

Mozart used and helped to perfect the concerto-sonata form common at the time. The formal features commonly found in Mozart's concerto opening movements are:

Tutti 1 (Ritornello 1). The opening ritornello is multithematic, with a clear first theme group, transition, a second theme group, often of more lyrical quality, and cadential material establishing the tonic. Although this section normally remains in the tonic area, excursions to contrasting keys may occur. The typically quiet ending of the ritornello creates a sense of expectancy, almost as though the orchestra is inviting the soloist to appear.[1]

Solo 1 (Exposition). The soloist usually enters with a brief flourish or lead-in cadenza before stating the ritornello's primary theme. The solo section then proceeds along the lines of a sonata-allegro exposition in which themes of the ritornello are restated. The soloist's first real bravura passage occurs in the transition, which carries the music to the dominant, occasionally introducing a minor key along the way. In the dominant (or relative major, if the movement is in a minor key) Mozart characteristically introduces a new theme in the solo instrument, which remains the exclusive or near exclusive property of the solo instrument—J. C. Bach's practice in his later concertos as noted earlier. Secondary thematic material from the ritornello is usually also reintroduced at this point in the new key. The closing section of the solo exposition is given over to bravura writing, usually concluding with a trill, which heralds the reentry of the orchestra with its brief central ritornello, made up of material from the opening ritornello.

Tutti 2 (Ritornello 2). The central ritornello normally remains in the dominant and serves to round off the solo exposition, although it may at times veer away to new keys and launch the development section.

Solo 2 (Development). The second solo section is equivalent to the Classical sonata-allegro form's development section, and is widely modulatory. This section is the main bravura portion of the movement, characterized by sequences of figuration or motivic material very often not heard earlier in the movement. Previously introduced thematic material may be vigorously developed as well. The orchestra is given a more lively role in this section; the dialogue between parts of the orchestra (usually the woodwinds in the piano concertos) and the soloist serves to integrate the two forces. A period of retransition over dominant harmony or a dominant pedal with closing trill in the solo instrument prepares the way for the reentry of the movement's opening thematic material in the tonic key.

Tutti 3 and Solo 3 (Ritornello 3 and Recapitulation). These two sections combine to form a recapitulation normally of all thematic material from the opening ritornello and solo exposition, often with some of the secondary material reordered. The orchestra usually opens the section, but the soloist quickly joins in. A concluding display section ends with a trill in the solo instrument.

Tutti 4 (Final Ritornello). This section, in the tonic, is usually short and forms the setting for a solo cadenza. The section prior to the cadenza is often characterized by greater animation (often through syncopation) and a louder dynamic level to set the stage for the unaccompanied cadenza. Figure 9 illustrates this first-movement structure.

Section	Orchestra (or Tutti)			
Formal Division	Ritornello 1			
Thematic Content	1st theme group A B C	Transition	2nd theme group D E	Closing theme group F G
Key	I			

Section	Solo 1			
Formal Division	Exposition			
Thematic Content	(Solo entry) 1st theme group A B	Transition figuration	2nd theme group X D E	Closing section: much virtuoso figuration
Key	I		V	

Section	Orchestra	Solo 2	
Formal Division	Ritornello 2	Development	
Thematic Content	often cl. th.	Main bravura section; much figuration	
Key	V	x x x	V

Section	Tutti 3—Solo 3 (usually begun by orchestra, soloist joins)			
Formal Division	Recapitulation			
Thematic Content	1st theme group A B C	Transition figuration	2nd theme group D E (X possible)	Closing section figuration (possibly F G)
Key	I			

Section	Tutti 4
Formal Division	Final Ritornello
Thematic Content	Short, interrupted by solo cadenza (after a I $\frac{6}{4}$ chord in orchestra). The soloist does not play after the cadenza.
Key	I

Figure 9. Mature concerto-sonata form typical of first movements

The second, slow movements are cast in a variety of forms. Common are the concerto-sonata form on a smaller scale; a simple sonata-allegro form, with little or no development; ternary form; theme and variations; and romanza in a rondo form.

The fast final movements usually employ a strong rondo element, often mixed with features of sonata-allegro form. Mozart developed a particularly complicated concerto-rondo form that combines the gaiety of the rondo with the intensity of sonata form. Many of its features resemble the concerto-sonata form and it may be seen as a special application of that form to the rondo. This form can be described in the following way:[2]

Refrain 1. The solo instrument usually begins the refrain, which recurs in the tonic key throughout the movement. It is usually characterized by a dancelike tunefulness, comprising distinguishable, independent elements like the ritornello, but with fewer thematic ideas. The orchestra normally concludes the refrain.

Episode 1. This section is constructed along the lines of a sonata-allegro form exposition, with a first theme in the tonic key. A transition leads to second and closing themes in the dominant key. Unlike the solo exposition of the concerto-sonata form, this section normally does not restate material from the movement's opening portion. This episode is one of the elements clearly distinguishing Mozart's concerto-rondo form from the ordinary rondo form. The soloist begins the episode with a new theme in the tonic, whereas in the ordinary rondo a modulating passage leads to a new theme in a new key at the episode's outset.

Refrain 2. The movement's main theme is usually first stated by the soloist followed by the orchestra in the tonic key, sometimes in a shortened version. On occasion the orchestra may initiate a harmonic movement away from the tonic, toward the new key of Episode 2.

Episode 2. Mozart sometimes employs the standard rondo procedure here by introducing a new theme in the solo instrument in a new key, the subdominant, or, in movements in minor, the submediant, as in the finale of the A Major Piano Concerto, K. 488. At other times, the second episode is given over to development, as in the finale of the D Minor Piano Concerto, K. 466. Occasionally, as in the finale of the Clarinet Concerto, K. 622, a new theme *and* development may be included.

Refrain 3. This section is frequently omitted as is the third ritornello in the concerto-sonata form. If it is present, a short version of the rondo theme is given in the tonic.

Episode 3. The material of Episode 1 is recapitulated here in the tonic key, but often in a shortened form. A cadenza may be placed after the closing theme.

Refrain 4. A short version of the refrain leads to a coda.

Figure 10 illustrates this form, which Mozart probably developed in part to increase the options for the introduction of more thematic material and in part to separate more clearly and widely the soloist and orchestra. This he accomplished by intensifying the thematic and tonal contrast as compared to those of the normal rondo.

A	B	A	C	B	A	Coda
Refrain 1	Episode 1	Refrain 2	Episode 2	Episode 3	Refrain 4	Coda
Main tune	Exposition	Tune	Develop-ment	Recap.	Tune	
I	I V	I	x x x V	I	I	I

Figure 10. Concerto-rondo form typical of third movements

We are now ready to explore some of the most exciting terrain that we will encounter on our historical trip through the development of the concerto. We will examine Mozart's concertos in chronological and instrumental groupings, in order to bring out clearly Mozart's maturing conception of the concerto.

THE EARLIEST CONCERTOS

The enormous musical gifts of the very young Mozart were immediately apparent to his father, Leopold, himself a talented violinist and composer. Leopold thereafter devoted himself to nurturing the gifts of his son, traveling to other musical centers of Europe considered essential to the education of the child genius. These journeys, often of substantial duration, exposed Mozart to the mid-eighteenth-century's diverse musical styles and deeply stimulated the mind of the youthful genius. The boy had been thoroughly and systematically trained by his father so each new musical impression could be turned to good use. Each encounter seemed to invoke a creative musical response that incorporated the fundamental significance of the music which the young Mozart had witnessed. At first he mainly imitated, but after a period devoted to assimilation, he eventually synthesized these diverse influences into what we now recognize as Mozart's personal style.

Mozart's travels began early in life. At the age of seven, early in June 1763, he and his family embarked on an extended journey which consumed the following three years to late November 1766. This journey included extended stays in Paris, London, and the Hague.

Bills advertising concerts by the Mozart family include concertos played by young Wolfgang, but seldom indicate the specific works performed. We do know, however, that for Maria Theresa in 1762, Mozart played a concerto by Wagenseil, who turned pages for the boy. There can be no doubt that Mozart heard and played numerous keyboard concertos by composers active in Paris and London. The principal keyboard concerto composers in Paris were Germans who had settled there—including Raupach, Honauer, and Schobert—while Johann Christian Bach was a leading figure in London's musical life.

Mozart's first compositional efforts with the concerto, mostly in the popular *galant* style, grew directly from his experiences on this long journey. With the assistance of his father, the child adapted and arranged several keyboard sonata movements by composers he had heard and studied on the trip. The arrangements involved adding or inserting orchestral ritornellos and accompaniments to the sonata movements, thereby converting them into concerto movements.

Alfred Einstein, a leading Mozart scholar, believed the earliest of these arrangements were those based on three sonatas from J. C. Bach's Op. 5 set. These three works (K. 107), calling for an orchestra of only two violins and bass, are dated by Einstein to the summer or fall of 1765, either immediately before or soon after Mozart left London.[3] The Mozarts arrived in London in April 1764 and remained there fifteen months, during which time Wolfgang developed a close relationship with the London Bach that lasted until the latter's death. We know that Mozart thrice visited the court where J. C. Bach was Music Master to Queen Charlotte, and Mozart at that time may even have played or studied Christian Bach's six keyboard concertos of Op. 1, which had been published shortly before in 1763. Certainly, much of Bach's concerto style and form can be seen in Mozart's later concertos, while two of Mozart's three early concertos are in two movements, a plan used by Bach in both his concertos and sonatas.

Shortly after returning to Salzburg in 1766, Mozart created four three-movement concertos by arranging various sonata movements of several German composers active in Paris.[4]

From 1770 to 1773, Mozart, then in his teens, made three extended trips to Italy, accompanied by his father. These trips gave Mozart an intimate contact with Italian opera which profoundly influenced the young man. Not only was he commissioned to write several dramatic works for Italian audiences, but he also composed a number of symphonies in the lighter Italian manner using the typical Italian three-movement form, rather than the four-movement scheme common in Austria. But since concertos for keyboard instruments were not popular among the Italians, Mozart composed none, nor did he compose any violin concertos during this period. This may seem surprising, in view of the continued popularity of the violin concerto in Italy. Whatever the reason, the composition of symphonies and dramatic works certainly provided Mozart with valuable experience in writing for the orchestra.

Mozart and his father returned to Salzburg from their last Italian journey in March 1773 only to travel to Vienna in July of that year, for Leopold, although relatively well to do, desired not only to improve his own status but to provide better prospects for his son as well. They remained in Vienna until October 1773, and, although no suitable position was found, Mozart's musical world was greatly expanded. He likely encountered Haydn's most recent experiments in the *Sturm und Drang* style, which, especially in the string quartets and symphonies of 1770–73, exhibit a new intensity through an exciting use of motivic development, counterpoint, dynamic contrasts, and fondness for the minor mode. Mozart composed six string quartets in Vienna (K. 168–173) at this time, which, in marked contrast to his earlier Milanese quartets, contain many identical features, particularly an intensity of thematic development and counterpoint as well as fugal finales in two of the quartets similar to those in Haydn's Op. 20 quartets. Within days of his return to Salzburg, Mozart completed his first symphony in a minor key, the "Little G Minor Symphony," (K. 183/173dB),[5] which also displays his grasp of the urgency and intensity of the new style. The seventeen-year-old composer's style had clearly been broadened, deepened, and intensified by his ten-week Viennese visit.

Shortly thereafter, in December 1773, Mozart completed his first original concerto, K. 175 in D major for keyboard instrument.[6] We do not know for what occasion or for what performer Mozart wrote this work, but it remained one of his
favorites and was well accepted by audiences in various places for the next several
years. He played it to great acclaim in Mannheim in 1777 and 1778 and in Vienna
in 1782 and 1783, at which time he used a new, lighter finale—the Rondo, K. 382,
which is actually a set of variations—in place of the original finale, which was on a
larger and more profound scale than the typical finale of the 1780s.

Although its mood differs from that of the "Little G Minor Symphony,"
fascinating congruities of style between the two works are evident. The concerto is
a highly original work, effectively scored for a large orchestra including trumpets
and timpani. The first movement, with its rhythmically incisive themes and limited
use of lyrical passages, stamps it as a work touched more by the *Sturm und Drang*
than by the *galant* style. The brief hints of lyricism include a new thematic idea
given the solo instrument upon reaching the dominant key in the solo exposition
(mm. 59ff.) and another new idea in the development (mm. 128ff.) The reflective
Andante ma un poco Adagio in G major is in concerto-sonata form with a brief
development section, during which the piano introduces a new idea over a
dominant pedal. Two cadenzas by Mozart for each of the first two movements
survive. The finale, more than the previous two movements, reveals the influence
of Mozart's Viennese stay. It is similar to his earlier experiments with fugal finales
in the string quartets, and it forecasts, near the movement's conclusion, the contrapuntal intensity of the "Jupiter" Symphony's finale, composed fifteen years
later. The concerto finale opens with a canon, the first notes of which are whole
notes. In the soloist's entry, Mozart enlivened the sustained notes with
embellishing eighth-notes, providing a striking contrast yet compelling unity at the
same time. At that entry, the orchestral strings play the same theme with the longer
notes (Ex. 9-1). Mozart's earliest original concerto is the equal of any concerto of
the time and hints at the greatness to come.

Ex. 9-1. Mozart, Piano Concerto in D Major, K. 175; III. Allegro, mm. 40–46.

Mozart's next concerto-style composition is the charming Concertone in C
Major (K. 190/186E) in the *galant* style featuring two violins with some solo writing
for oboe and cello as well, in the second and third movements. This work, completed on 31 May 1774,[7] for an unknown occasion, was given the unusual title
Concertone, which, as noted earlier, simply means large concerto, probably to
indicate it called for several soloists. It is close to the symphonie concertante style
of J. C. Bach, and incorporates a minuet finale as was the case in several of the

London Bach's lighter works. The solo parts are only slightly virtuosic; Mozart seemed more interested in coloristic effects, pairing solo instruments in unusual ways. Mozart composed ensemble cadenzas for the solo violins and oboe in the first movement and a larger one for oboe, violins, and cello in the second movement. The orchestra, with oboes, horns, trumpets, and strings, is handled in an equally colorful way. The scoring provides an early example of Mozart's frequent division of the viola section into two parts, the outcome of Mozart's particular fondness for the timbre of the alto string instrument, which he played himself. He tended to score for it more lavishly than did his contemporaries.

Only four days after completing the concertone, Mozart wrote his first (surviving) concerto for a wind instrument—the Concerto for Bassoon in B-flat Major, K. 191, dated 4 June 1774. The bassoon was not, nor is it now, an obvious choice for a solo instrument, but Mozart is believed to have written five concertos for the low-pitched double reed instrument of which only K. 191 survives. Mozart most likely first heard the bassoon as a solo instrument in Paris, where it appeared in several symphonies concertantes and the occasional concerto, while J. C. Bach composed two concertos for the bassoon, as well.

As with Mozart's other wind instrument concertos, K. 191 shows the composer's understanding of the character and limitations of the instrument. Here Mozart exploits the bassoon's special qualities—its staccato, its contrasts of registers, its comic and lugubrious voices, and its ability to sing a lyric melody in its middle register. The orchestra, consisting of two oboes, two horns, and strings, participates in a lively manner; rests, necessary for breathing in the solo part, are artfully used to juxtapose the soloist and orchestra.

The soloist's entry with a restatement of the main theme in the short opening Allegro also attests to Mozart's exquisite sense of the instrument's unique qualities. Whereas the violin in the original statement leaps upward only a minor seventh, the bassoon in its restatement leaps an octave and a minor seventh, thus providing the strongest kind of contrast of register (Ex. 9-2). Such leaps of great intervals, characteristic of much of Mozart's dramatic vocal music, appear repeatedly throughout the concerto, often side by side with lyrical passages. The bassoon's staccato quality is exploited in the soloist's transition to the second key. Interestingly Mozart does not state a new theme in the dominant key, but does give the bassoon a new counterpoint to accompany the violin's restatement of the second theme. In the recapitulation the parts are reversed, in effect giving the bassoon a new melody to play at that point.

Ex. 9-2. Mozart, Bassoon Concerto in B-flat Major, K. 191; I. Allegro, mm. 35–38.

The F major Andante ma adagio movement is one of Mozart's lovely "pathetic" movements of an arioso type, with throbbing strings contributing to the mood. The opening phrase (Ex. 9-3), one of Mozart's favorites, dates back to the eight-year-old composer's London sketch books. The same idea, with a bit of ornamentation, graces the opening of the slow movement of his next concerto, the B-flat Major Violin Concerto, K. 207, as well. A better known use of the phrase is found in the count's cavatina, which opens Act II of *The Marriage of Figaro* (1786).

Ex. 9-3. Mozart, Bassoon Concerto in B-flat Major, K. 191; II. Andante ma adagio, mm. 1–2.

The concluding movement of the Bassoon Concerto is a rondo in the style of a minuet, continuing Mozart's move away from the serious contrapuntal finale of the K. 175 Piano Concerto.

THE VIOLIN CONCERTOS

Mozart wrote no concertos for nearly eleven months after completing the Bassoon Concerto. During the summer of 1774 he was commissioned to write an *opera buffa* for the carnival season in Munich and subsequently completed several lighter works, including his earliest surviving piano sonatas (K. 279–283/189d-h), all closely following the model set by J. C. Bach. Returning to Salzburg, Mozart entered one of his most depressed periods, feeling that his opportunities there were limited and that his talent was stifled. In March and April, despite his depression, he completed a festival opera, *Il re pastore*, to a libretto by Metastasio, for a visit to Salzburg of Archduke Maximilian Franz.

In April 1775, something suddenly turned Mozart's attention to the concerto for violin, and over the next few months he composed all five of his works in this medium. The first was performed on the day of Franz's visit, 23 April 1775, and one wonders if perhaps the Archduke may have requested more. We simply do not know why the works were composed, nor do we know, in spite of what some have written, whether Mozart wrote them for his own performance or for Antonio Brunetti, the first violinist in the Salzburg court orchestra.

Mozart was not only an exceptional player of keyboard instruments, but a highly skilled violinist and violist as well, which is not surprising in light of the fact that his father was a great violin teacher of the day. Surprisingly, however, Mozart was evidently a self-taught violinist. One story, told by Leopold's friend Andreas Schachtner, related how the seven-year-old Wolfgang, having been given a violin but no instruction, one day joined in to sight-read string trios, amazing everyone, including his father. By the age of fourteen, Mozart had been appointed Konzertmeister of the Salzburg Court Orchestra. His letters record the admiration his violin playing evoked, while Leopold often remarked on his son's string-playing abilities. It is certainly possible that Mozart wrote the concertos for himself; he did play some of them in later years.

We do not know what stimulated Mozart to create these works, and neither can we point to any obvious models. He must have been exposed to the violin concerto in Italy, and the violin technique, based on a light, melodic style similar to that of the Italians, may have derived from his time spent there. But the violin concertos also contain elements of French brilliance, gracefulness, and the French-favored form of the closing rondeau, in addition to a penchant to incorporate folk music deriving from Austro-Hungarian tradition.

Mozart's violin concertos are not highly virtuosic works; the upper register is seldom called for and traditional virtuosic technical devices, such as the use of double stops, are almost totally absent. He seems to have concentrated on musical qualities, above all on melody, for each of the concertos contains an overwhelming abundance of melodic material.

The two earlier works, K. 207 in B-flat (14 April 1775) and K. 211 in D (14 June 1775) are constructed on a more modest scale than the later three. K. 216 in G (12 September 1775), K. 218 in D (October 1775), and K. 219 in A (20 December 1775) are not only spacious and more demanding, they are more personal; in them Mozart plumbs new depths of expression, especially in the introspective slow movements. It is small wonder these last three have captivated the attention of violinists and audiences the world over.

All these concertos are scored for the standard orchestra of two oboes, two horns, and strings, with the winds being given a more prominent role in the later works. Mozart also created in the last three a closer relationship between the orchestra and the solo instrument. This occurs despite the light accompaniment in many of the solo passages in all five concertos—the accompaniment is often reduced to the upper string instruments as was typical of so many Italian concertos of the period.

The violin concertos all follow the same basic pattern, with concerto-sonata first movements, arioso or cantilena slow movements in the dominant, and rondo finales (actually rondeau finales with clear couplets, following the French form). The first concerto provides the only exceptions; its slow movement is in the subdominant, and the original finale is in sonata form.

The G Major Concerto, K. 216, is one of the great works of Mozart's youth, the central movement of which equals the expressive peaks of much later compositions. The themes are elegant and abundant, but in comparison with the earlier violin concertos, Mozart works with the thematic material in a more extended fashion. The Allegro's main theme (Ex. 9-4) is taken from the third aria of the recently completed *Il re pastore*. Four other themes, the last of which derives from the world of *opera buffa*, are presented in the orchestral ritornello. As if this were not enough thematic material, the solo violin adds two more themes in the solo exposition and yet another in the development. In addition to the latter surprise, a brief passage of dramatic recitative occurs at the end of the development just before the cadenza.

Ex. 9-4. Mozart, Violin Concerto in G Major, K. 216; I. Allegro, mm. 1–4.

The D major Adagio is the core of this concerto; indeed it is so effective that it is occasionally played independently of the balance of the concerto. A cantilena for solo violin on one of Mozart's exquisite melodies (Ex. 9-5) is accompanied by muted strings, pizzicato basses, flutes (here replacing the oboes), and horns. The movement, with its triplets, sudden dynamic shifts, and harmonic subtleties, is in many respects similar to the highly expressive slow movement of the much later C Major Piano Concerto, K. 467.

Ex. 9-5. Mozart, Violin Concerto in G Major, K. 216; II. Adagio, mm. 1–2.

A rondeau, opening in $\frac{3}{8}$, closes the G Major Concerto; like that of K. 218, it contains a very extensive and diverse array of tempos and meters. It is, in addition, marked by a multiplicity of themes, including a charming one in the style of a pavane in the Andante ¢ in G minor (Ex. 9-6) and a folklike tune in the G major Allegretto section (Ex. 9-7). In the latter, oboes join the solo violin and lend the theme a country air.

Ex. 9-6. Mozart, Violin Concerto in G Major, K. 216; III. Rondeau, mm. 252–259.

Ex. 9-7. Mozart, Violin Concerto in G Major, K. 216; III. Rondeau, mm. 265–268.

The combination of dance and folk or exotic elements was to become a strong trait in many Romantic violin concerto finales and was repeated as a feature in Mozart's next two violin concertos. The finale of the D Major Concerto, K. 218, combines the French rondeau with an Italian gavotte and musette, whose tune has been identified as the "Danse de Strasbourg." The finale of the A Major Concerto, K. 219, incorporates a surprising central episode in A minor, making use of popular Janissary or Turkish elements. The characteristic Turkish march style depended heavily upon the use of Turkish percussion instruments, especially the bass drum, cymbals, and triangle (all of which appear in the famous Turkish march in the finale of Beethoven's Ninth Symphony) and strong, march-like rhythms, with an accented first beat. In the A Major Concerto Mozart does not use special percussion instruments, but imitates them through a preponderance of *fp* accents, the use of multiple grace notes in the basses, and sharp staccatos to evoke the Turkish march in the exotic duple-meter Allegro section which interrupts the movement's main minuet character.

In addition to the five complete violin concertos, Mozart also composed a few separate movements, most of which were intended to replace movements in the concertos. For example, in 1776 Mozart composed a new Adagio in E, K. 261, for Brunetti, who found the original middle movement of K. 219 "too studied." There are also some interesting violin concertos hidden within several of Mozart's serenades composed around the time of his devotion to the true violin concerto. In these works, Mozart often featured a solo instrument or group in two or three of the movements. Characteristically these movements (usually a fast and slow pair with the possible addition of the trio of the following minuet) are in a different key from the rest of the serenade. For example, the Serenade in D, K. 204/213a, composed in August 1775, contemporaneously with the violin concertos, contains a two-movement violin concerto in A. Other serenades with internal violin concertos are K. 185/167a (July–August 1773), K. 203/189b (August 1774, with a three-movement internal concerto), and the Haffner Serenade, K. 250/248b (June–July 1776).

Furthermore, in his devotion to string concertos, Mozart apparently did not neglect the cello. A now-lost autograph once housed in Paris was inscribed *Concerto per il Violoncello del Sig; Car. Amadeo Wolfgango Mozart nel Marzo 1775*. The opening six-measure theme is given in Köchel's thematic catalog (K. 206a).

THE PIANO CONCERTOS OF THE LATE 1770s

In January 1776, while still in Salzburg, Mozart shifted his attention to the piano concerto, writing three over the next three months. These three works are essentially *galant* in manner and, since they are relatively ordinary, are rarely played today. The three concertos are the intimate K. 238 in B-flat, K. 246 in C, composed for the amateur, Countess Antonia von Lützow, and the very light F Major Concerto for three keyboard soloists, K. 242, written for Countess Lodron of Salzburg and her two daughters who may have been pupils of Mozart. In spite of the overall slightness of the last work, its middle movement, one of only two slow movements in the piano concertos to be marked Adagio, is numbered among Mozart's more expressive movements.

The next several months were, in large part, a fallow period for Mozart. He had remained in Salzburg since March 1775, and his music during the end of this period, his longest stay in Salzburg, reflects the lack of external stimulus so important to Mozart's creative genius. Stimulation eventually came not from a journey to another musical center, but from the visit in December 1776 or January 1777 of a French virtuoso keyboard player, Mlle. Jeunehomme. The E-flat Concerto, K. 271, written in January 1777 for "Jenomy," as Mozart called her, is imaginative and bold. It is the most important work of this two-year period.

The unique composition comes as such a surprise that Einstein refers to K. 271 as Mozart's "Eroica."[8] It stands well apart from his earlier *galant* works and marks the first evidence of his mature music. The E-flat Concerto, completed in the month of the composer's twenty-first birthday, is more demanding, both technically and musically, than any of his earlier concertos. The movements are larger and more substantial, taking about twice as long to perform; the orchestra is given a more vital, symphonic role; and the relationship between the orchestra and solo instrument is more intimate, more closely interconnected, than in the earlier works.

Its unusual qualities become evident immediately upon the opening of the first movement, with the piano answering the orchestra in the second measure (Ex. 9-8). Despite this early entry of the solo instrument, there is no basic change in the movement's form, for after an immediate repeat of the orchestra's statement and piano's answer, the orchestra returns to play a standard opening ritornello. Nevertheless, Mozart establishes a new, more flexible relationship between the soloist and orchestra as the piano completes the first phrase initiated by the orchestra and pulls the music immediately away from the traditional unison triadic opening, giving the concerto a more personal feeling. The opening is unique to all of Mozart's work and anticipates Beethoven's bold use of the piano at the beginning of his Fourth and Fifth Concertos, a feature that was to become common in the nineteenth century.

Ex. 9-8. Mozart, Piano Concerto in E-flat Major, K. 271; I. Allegro, mm. 1–4.

As the movement unfolds, several instances of Mozart's new grasp of the dramatic potential of the concerto become evident. The soloist's reentry for the solo exposition occurs in an unexpected spot with unexpected new material. The orchestra had prepared for the soloist's entry with a loud cadential passage in mm. 50–52, but instead of presenting the soloist in m. 53, Mozart has the orchestra play a different and quiet cadential figure, introducing the piano in the midst of it with a sustained trill on B-flat. The orchestra now becomes silent, but the piano does not restate the opening theme, playing instead four measures of completely new material that never appears again. This is Mozart's first use of new material to introduce the solo exposition, a device he was to use in several later works. It is a dramatic device effectively setting the piano apart momentarily upon its first (normal) entry.

Mozart may have been inspired to resort to this device in K. 271 for two reasons: First, because the piano had already appeared as a partner in presenting the original statement of the main theme, something new was necessary to grab the listener's attention. Second, the orchestra-piano dialogue is retained for the first theme in the solo exposition; therefore, if it were to be repeated without some new introductory material, it would only sound like a repeat of the orchestral ritornello, not like the beginning of the first solo section.

Further thematic separation occurs as the piano presents a new lyric theme in the second key, but this happens only after the piano has already restated themes of the ritornello's second theme group in the new key. A new lyric flourish (mm. 82–83) in the solo instrument does, however, precede the second theme group.

While the thematic separation of the piano and orchestra brings greater drama to the work, the sharing of other thematic material creates a sense of fruitful cooperation intensifying the organic structure of the work, making it into a highly integrated whole. Examples of such sharing include the startling first theme, and the use of its initial chordal outline in the transition section of the solo exposition and in the development section. Traditionally, the introduction of new patterns of solo figuration would have been more characteristic in these places. Another passage based on a new spirit of cooperation occurs in the solo instrument's presentation of a part of the second theme group. The piano presents the theme while violins provide a simple contrapuntal line that easily could have been placed in the piano's left-hand part. As the theme is repeated in oboe and violin, the piano takes up the counterpoint in a more lively version. One last example of this sharing occurs in the recapitulation. Here the piano gives the chordal call, followed by the orchestra's response, reversing their original roles.

As these examples suggest, Mozart has unified the movement by an unusual blurring of some traditional dividing lines. The concluding measures of the movement further illustrate this approach. The piano sneaks back in after its cadenza, whereas traditionally the conclusion of the movement following the cadenza was played only by the orchestra.

Some of the features noted here are unique to K. 271, but the closer relationship between tutti and solo and the general integration of musical forces are qualities that surface again in Mozart's mature concertos written in his later Vienna years. A significant upgrading of the role of the wind instruments, which becomes such an important feature of the later piano concertos, is first observed here. The winds are not yet given the freedom and flair they come to enjoy in the later works (nor are there as many woodwinds as in later works), but Mozart has set off in that direction. At one point, the horns, revelling in their new role, even help the piano present a lyrical theme (mm. 217ff.).

The C minor Andantino is the first concerto slow movement written by Mozart in a minor key, and so is often thought of as a forerunner of the still more moving C minor Andante of the soon-to-be-composed Sinfonia Concertante for Violin and Viola. The Andantino is an intense, operatic movement. Its tutti opening is quite unusual: Muted first and second violins softly play a deeply felt theme in their lowest register, in canon with *fp* accented appoggiaturas (Ex. 9-9). Strong fluctuations in dynamics characterize the remainder of the tutti, which closes with a passage imitating recitative (Ex. 9-10). The piano's entry brings new, more elaborate material of an improvisatory nature layered on top of the orchestra's repeat of the opening canon, creating an unusually rich texture. The orchestra not only provides accompaniment, but is an equal partner with the solo instrument. A sudden modulation to the relative major, E-flat, brings a brighter mood as the piano plays a new theme, unaccompanied. This theme returns in the recapitulation in E-flat, before its second half returns to the tonic, C minor, dramatically altering its character. Twice in the movement, as well as in the cadenza Mozart wrote, the piano plays a dramatic recitative which is used as an extremely effective conclusion to the movement.

Ex. 9-9. Mozart, Piano Concerto in E-flat Major, K. 271; II. Andantino, mm. 1–7.

Ex. 9-10. Mozart, Piano Concerto in E-flat Major, K. 271; II. Andantino, mm. 13–16.

The finale is an extended seven-part rondo in Presto tempo, somewhat like the robust finales Beethoven was to write. It is much more serious and intense than the final movements of the violin concertos or the three earlier piano concertos, but Mozart was not yet ready to discard the common minuet completely, for the central episode is a songful Menuetto. Its graceful appearance, though, in the middle of all the hustle and bustle of the rest of the movement, comes as a complete shock. Cadenzas, written into the score, serve as transitions between major divisions of the movement, anticipating the functional use of the cadenza in some nineteenth-century concertos.

THE FLUTE CONCERTOS

Mozart's unhappiness in Salzburg reached its breaking point in 1777. In August Mozart requested a release from the archbishop's employ. Leopold felt he could not afford to give up his position, so he remained in Salzburg while Wolfgang, accompanied by his mother, left on 23 September 1777 to seek a better position elsewhere. After brief stops in Munich and Augsburg, where he met the piano maker J. A. Stein, whose instruments became Mozart's favorites, they arrived in Mannheim on 30 October. Mannheim, as we have seen, had become a major center of orchestral music as Mozart's letters to his father clearly reveal. The orchestra was noted not only for its size, but also for its brilliance, precision, and excellent wind section. The excellence of the wind players probably pricked Mozart's interest in the qualities and capabilities of the woodwind instruments. Even though Mozart had heard the clarinet earlier in Italy, it was in Mannheim that his lifelong attachment to the warm, sensuous sound of this relatively new orchestral instrument first developed.

While Mozart's effort to gain a position at the court failed, he decided to remain in Mannheim until the spring and do a little teaching to support himself and his mother. He quickly developed a friendly relationship with several of the leading Mannheim musicians, most notably the flautist J. B. Wendling. Wendling introduced Mozart to a Dutch amateur flute player who commissioned the composer to write three "easy" concertos and quartets for flute. In a letter of 10 December 1777 to his father, Mozart identified the flute player as "De Jean" (possibly a phonetic representation of de Jong). Later, on 14 February 1778, the composer complained that he felt "quite inhibited when I have to compose for an instrument which I cannot endure." This statement, which is difficult to reconcile with the beautiful music he wrote for the flute, may explain the reason for his procrastination in fulfilling this commission. It also would have been difficult for him to sustain an interest in writing for an amateur when surrounded by virtuosos. He did write, however, two concertos for flute (K. 313/285 and 314/285d) and two quartets (K. 285/285 and 285a/285a) for "de Jean" in early (probably February) 1778.

The Flute Concerto in G Major (K. 313) was written for the small orchestra—two oboes, two horns, and strings—to which he had been accustomed in Salzburg, but the texture of the orchestral writing is richer, perhaps reflecting the sound of the Mannheim ensemble. One wonders if the flute part is as easy as "de Jean" wished, for Mozart exploits the instrument's agility with many wide leaps and running scale passages. The majestic dotted rhythm of the first theme (Ex. 9-11) well fits the movement's title, Allegro maestoso, a rare marking for Mozart at this time. In the development the flute presents a new theme which illustrates both these characteristic leaps and running figures (Ex. 9-12). Adagio ma non troppo in D major opens with a solemn and unusual passage in octaves for horns and strings, with the violins and violas. The long, delicate, and richly embellished main theme, played by violins and oboes, follows. (The replacement of oboes by flutes in this movement is of uncertain authority and highly doubtful, since the contrast in timbre with the solo instrument would have been lost.) The personal, warm, romantic quality of this movement approaches that of the middle movement of the G Major Violin Concerto. For the finale, Mozart again relies on the rondo in minuet tempo with a central episode in a minor key. The solo part particularly sparkles in the rondo.

Ex. 9-11. Mozart, Flute Concerto in G Major, K. 313; I. Allegro maestoso, mm. 1–4.

Ex. 9-12. Mozart, Flute Concerto in G Major, K. 313; I. Allegro maestoso, mm. 107–111.

The Concerto for Flute in D Major, K. 314, is most likely a transcription by Mozart of his own earlier C Major Oboe Concerto, which had been composed in the summer of 1777 for Giuseppe Ferlendis, an oboist new to the Salzburg orchestra. This cannot be said for certain since the oboe concerto is lost, but Mozart's letters indicate he had the Ferlendis oboe concerto with him in Mannheim and, lacking any real interest in writing a new work for an amateur flute player, he may have finally resorted to making such a transcription. K. 314 is a much lighter work than K. 313 and has strong melodic and rhythmic references to the world of *opera buffa*. The soloist's entry in the Allegro aperto[9] is most stunning—it runs up the scale in a linking measure to a high sustained D, under which the orchestra restates the main theme. The triple-meter Andante ma non troppo in G is pleasant, never approaching the depth of the slow movement of K. 313. The final movement is one of the young Mozart's liveliest rondos.

One other work for flute and orchestra, the Andante in C, K. 315/285e, probably dates from this same period in Mannheim. There is no proof to support Einstein's claim that it was written at the request of "de Jean," who, presumably, desired a simpler replacement for the slow movement of K. 313. Such a thing is a possibility, of course, but if "de Jean" could handle the outer movements, he could certainly have played the original Adagio. Perhaps it was too profound a movement for "de Jean" (or someone else), who may have preferred a lighter movement. The Andante, however, is not to be taken lightly—its principal flute melody

(Ex. 9-13) is one of Mozart's most beautiful for the instrument, bringing to mind the flute passages written for Tamino in *The Magic Flute,* as he passes through his first trial by fire and water. The highly unusual five-chord opening on pizzicato strings in multiple stops returns five times, each differing slightly, to serve as points of articulation in the long, arioso-like flute part. At one particularly poignant juncture the strings enunciate this pizzicato passage beneath a sustained D in the flute as the music slips into G minor.

Ex. 9-13. Mozart, Andante for Flute, K. 315; mm. 3–10.

THE SYMPHONIES CONCERTANTES

Mozart had fallen in love with the sixteen-year-old Aloysia Weber while in Mannheim, postponing still longer his trip to Paris, in spite of a letter from his father in February ordering him to leave for Paris. In mid-March he and his mother finally departed for Paris, arriving there 23 March 1778. Mozart immediately began visiting one nobleman's house after another to earn money by giving lessons. One of his composition pupils, the daughter of Count Guines, played harp, and the count, a flute player, commissioned Mozart to write a concerto to feature the two of them. Mozart wrote his Concerto for Flute and Harp, K. 299/297c (April 1778), in the easy key of C major, making only modest demands on the amateurs, even though he had told his father, in a letter dated 14 May 1778, that the count played extremely well and the harpist was "magnifique." (He did note the girl had no talent as a composer.)

The work clearly shows the immediate impact of Paris. The solo instruments are favorites of the French, and the form Mozart adopted is the symphonie concertante, the first he had composed that is extant. The style is also that of light French salon music and, like his "Paris" Symphony, K. 297/300a, of the same period, it is full of melody. The symphonie concertante form encourages an abundance of unique themes, since each solo instrument must be given one or more themes entirely, or largely, its own. Mozart follows this practice as well as having the solo instruments repeat themes from the ritornello.

The Concerto for Flute and Harp is a thoroughly Mozartian piece of entertainment music. It is amazing how skillfully Mozart wrote for the unusual combination of instruments, one of them an instrument he had never previously used. The orchestra is the same as in his previous works (two oboes, two horns, and strings); additional winds would have detracted from the delicate sound of the solo instruments. The winds that do appear are rarely highlighted.

The opening Allegro is in concerto-sonata form with a very short development section. The soloists appear at the very opening to help present the broken-chord patterns so characteristic of French symphonic music. In the solo exposition the flute is responsible for presenting most of the thematic material while the harp supplies an active accompaniment consisting largely of arpeggio figurations.

The Mozart family in 1779. At this time Mozart composed two works for two soloists and orchestra. The extremely moving and profound Sinfonia Concertante for Violin and Viola, K. 364, may have been written for performance by Leopold on violin and Wolfgang on viola. The much lighter Concerto for Two Keyboard Instruments, K. 365, was probably to feature Mozart in a performance with his sister, Nannerl.

Because the harp can be used as an accompanying instrument, several short passages are written exclusively for the soloists without orchestral accompaniment. Not only are new themes presented by the solo instruments in the solo exposition, but two new themes are presented in the development section—the last stated first by the harp (mm. 150ff.).

The winds are silent in the Andantino, while the violas are divided throughout. The two soloists exchange musical ideas throughout the movement and the harp is given a variety of accompanimental figures. The finale is strongly influenced by French taste with its courtly gavotte-like theme, its use of orchestral winds as concertante partners to the flute and harp, its numerous themes, and its pronounced minor key episode.

In the same month Mozart composed the Flute and Harp Concerto, he completed a symphonie concertante requested by Jean Le Gros, director of the Concert Spirituel. According to Mozart's letter of 5 April 1778, he was going to compose a symphonie concertante "for flute, Wendling; oboe, Ramm; horn, Punto; and bassoon, Ritter." All but Punto were Mannheim musicians visiting Paris. Mozart completed the work by 20 April, but in a letter of 1 May Mozart notes Le Gros had not yet had the parts copied and feared something was wrong. Indeed, it was never performed and was probably lost.[10]

Mozart's search for a suitable court position in Paris or Versailles was proving fruitless, and he became increasingly unhappy in the city. He despised French music and French taste, despite the one great success he enjoyed with the lasting masterpiece, the "Paris" Symphony. His mother's death on 3 July added to Mozart's misery. The only bright spot in Mozart's Parisian stay seems to have been a visit with J. C. Bach, who had come to Paris to prepare an opera.

In late August 1778 Leopold wrote advising Wolfgang that the post of Konzertmeister (as Court Organist) was now available to him in Salzburg, so he left Paris on 26 September 1778 heading for home via Mannheim. He stayed in Mannheim a month visiting his favorite violinist, Ignaz Fränzl, then the leader of a newly formed group, the Académie des Amateurs. Fresh from his recent experience with the symphonie concertante, Mozart was inspired to begin a Concerto for Piano and Violin in D (K. Anh. 56/315f) for himself and Fränzl. Unfortunately, the death of the Elector led to the dissolution of the Académie, and Mozart never completed the work. A substantial fragment of the first movement exists (120 mm., with the first seventy-four in full score) which makes it obvious that Mozart's crea-

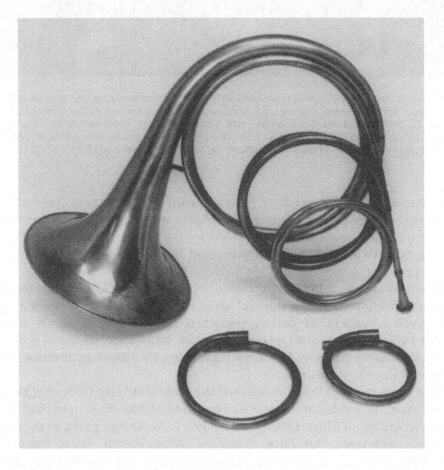

An eighteenth-century horn. The horn pictured here is the valveless horn whose basic pitch could be adjusted by changing the crook, a piece of tubing replaceable by others of differing lengths. But once a crook was selected, the rest was up to the horn player. Masterful players, such as Leutgeb, for whom Mozart wrote his horn concertos, could get around the limitations of the natural horn by means of accurate hand-stopping and careful embouchure and breath control that permitted a remarkably complete selection of pitches.

tive imagination was deeply involved. It is majestically scored for a typically large Mannheim orchestra of two flutes, two oboes, two horns, two trumpets, timpani, and strings; according to the Mozart scholar, Einstein, it must "be counted among the greatest losses of art that Mozart did not finish this work."[11]

Leopold, frustrated by his son's delay, urgently sought his return to Salzburg, but Mozart moved on to Munich where he stayed with the Webers (who had moved with Carl Theodor's court) from 25 December into mid-January. He was terribly disappointed to discover that Aloysia was not interested in him, so he returned to Salzburg around 15 January 1779, a very disappointed young man: He had gained no position, he had strained the relationship with his father and placed a great burden on the family finances, he had fallen in love and been hurt, his mother had died, and he returned to a city he disliked and an employer he hated.

He was appointed Court Organist, a post he occupied for two years without major incident. Shortly after his arrival home, the symphonie concertante, or concerto for more than one solo instrument, surfaced again. By the end of the summer of 1779 he had completed the Concerto for Two Keyboard Instruments in E-flat, K. 365/316a, and the very fine Sinfonia Concertante in E-flat for Violin and Viola, K. 364/320d.

K. 365, probably intended for Mozart and his sister, is a piece of joyful entertainment music in which the two keyboard instruments frequently echo one another or respond in a statement-and-answer dialogue. The orchestra, the standard Salzburg band with two bassoons added, is fairly subdued until the rondo finale. Mozart often played the work with Fräulein Aurnhammer in the early part of his stay in Vienna. For these performances he added clarinets, trumpets, and timpani. His cadenzas to the outer movements survive.

The Sinfonia Concertante for Violin and Viola is Mozart's last and greatest completed work in this form. Because no autograph manuscript survives and Mozart, at home while composing it, wrote no letters which might shed light on its composition, we know nothing of the circumstances which prompted the writing of this great piece. The date of composition is even conjectural, but it is believed to be 1779–80, with late summer 1779 the estimate of most scholars. Nothing is known of the intended performers, but they easily might have been Mozart and his father. Leopold was a talented violinist, and Mozart had increasingly turned his affection and attention to the viola. An unusual set of circumstances must have impelled Mozart to advance to these new compositional heights, for the work is not only full of references to what he had learned in Mannheim and Paris, but also demonstrates a vast growth in his musical thought related to a great enrichment of his personal life. In short, Mozart in the course of his journey had vastly expanded his musical horizons and had passed through a series of deeply moving personal events that did much to mature him.

Just as the E-flat Piano Concerto, K. 271, of 1777 marked the transition from youth to maturity, the Sinfonia Concertante for Violin and Viola can be considered the first full-fledged example of his mature period, ranking with the great works of his last decade in Vienna. We observed single movements of earlier works, such as the Adagio of the G Major Violin Concerto, K. 216, as profound expressions presaging the depth of his later works. Yet the entire Sinfonia Concertante for Violin and Viola can be seen in this way. It is conceived, both physically and emotionally, on a bigger, more profound scale, on a par with the great works still to come. Especially important to his new mode of expression is the replacement of the earlier *galant* style by a style with greater levels of contrast, one in which moods of triumph and majesty exist side by side with those of tragedy and sorrow.

The new style is characterized by the use of more varied and more subtle themes and a new and richer manner of handling the orchestra. So different is the sound of the orchestra that it is difficult to believe Mozart was writing for the same orchestra as in his earlier Salzburg works—two oboes, two horns, and strings. A particularly important change occurs in the scoring of the violas in two parts throughout. Further, Mozart notated the solo viola part in D in the Sinfonia Concertante so as to tune the instrument a semitone higher than normal in order to make the solo viola stand out more brilliantly than the orchestral violas.[12] In his unfinished symphonie concertante for violin, viola, and cello started at the same time,[13] Mozart called for tuning the solo viola a tone higher than normal.

The work contains an interesting blend of musical gestures that may be traced to influences in Mannheim, Paris, and Salzburg. From Mannheim, for example, come such gestures as the majestic opening and sustained orchestral crescendo, accompanied by rising trills over a pedal point, near the end of the first tutti (mm. 46ff.). The profusion of themes, especially the elaborate array in the solo exposition and development sections, is typically Parisian and strongly associated with the symphonie concertante form. The horn and oboe calls (Ex. 9-14) of the first and third movements are derived from the Salzburg serenade style.[14]

Ex. 9-14. Mozart, Sinfonia Concertante in E-flat Major, K. 364; I. Allegro maestoso, mm. 38–42.

Throughout the piece the soloists are treated as equals. Their equality is established by their extraordinary first entry in octaves on an unobtrusive sustained high E-flat while the orchestra continues to play; the effect is reminiscent of the opening of the solo section in the dynamic E-flat Piano Concerto, K. 271. In the first solo sections of the outer movements the violin is the first to present new themes, followed by the viola, but in the recapitulation sections the roles are reversed. In the slow movement the violin takes the lead, but the dialogue is so intimate the listener is only aware of the duet quality.

Of the many special moments in the first movement, one particularly deserves comment: The horn and oboe calls mentioned earlier (Ex. 9-14) in the opening ritornello recur in the recapitulation with an exquisite accompaniment, first in the solo viola, then in the solo violin (mm. 293–301).

The intensity and depth of feeling of the C minor Andante had been hinted at in the earlier Andantino in the same key of K. 271. The main theme (Ex. 9-15) is given out by orchestral violins over a throbbing accompaniment figure in the violas. This theme is then restated with embellishment by the solo violin and then by solo viola with still more embellishment. The second theme in E-flat (mm. 35ff.)

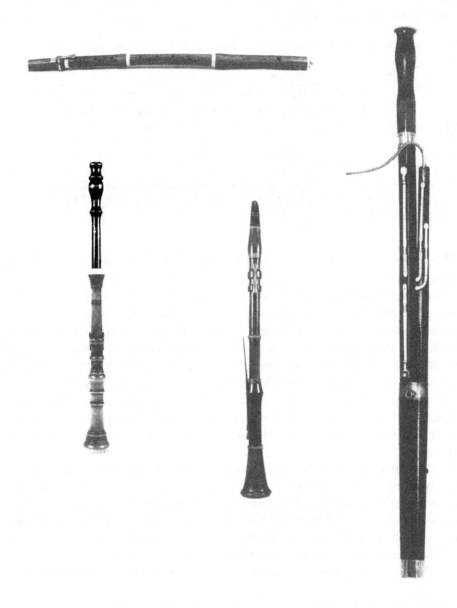

Eighteenth-century woodwind instruments. Most woodwind instruments of the eighteenth century had only a few keys, as is the case with the flute (top), oboe (left), clarinet (center), and bassoon (right) pictured here. Performers on modern instruments with many more keys are still challenged by Mozart's great writing for woodwind instruments, a fact that further intensifies our appreciation of the performers Mozart knew and admired. Mozart had a particularly keen awareness of the individual voices of the woodwind instruments and wrote supremely idiomatic parts for them, not only in the solo concertos for these instruments, but also as members of the orchestra in the great series of piano concertos from 1784 to 1786.

turns on canonic writing for the violins and violas. Mozart's cadenzas for movements I and II are not highly virtuosic; they concentrate on sustaining the mood and heightening the emotional tension.

Ex. 9-15. Mozart, Sinfonia Concertante in E-flat Major, K. 364; II. Andante, mm. 1–7.

The Presto finale is a concerto-rondo containing numerous well-defined themes. Here, as in the Concerto for Flute and Harp, the winds play a prominent role, with one concertante passage given exclusively to oboes and horns. One sudden harmonic shift should be noted: A strong cadence in C minor in m. 241 is followed by a one-measure rest and then a quick shift to G major; this, in turn, is followed by a one-measure rest and then an unprepared shift to A-flat major, in which the first theme of the first solo episode is repeated. The soloists' last fling is their most brilliant, as scale passages take them into their highest register.

In this, his last complete symphonie concertante, Mozart transcended the traditional light and playful mood of the French form. After he moved to Vienna he apparently made no further use of the form, for no such works, complete or fragmentary, exist.

In the summer of 1780, Mozart received an important commission for the composition of an *opera seria* (*Idomeneo*) for Munich. He remained in Munich until March 1781 when the archbishop demanded his return to Vienna to participate in the celebrations on the accession of Emperor Joseph II. Mozart arrived in Vienna on 16 March but so resented the servile manner in which he was treated that he sought and discovered the possibility of earning an independent living in Vienna. On 9 May 1781 Mozart requested a discharge from service to the Archbishop of Salzburg.

He initially moved in with his old friends the Webers, who were now in Vienna. Mozart's first love, Aloysia, had recently married, and Mozart was now attracted to her sister, Constanze, whom he married on 4 August 1782.

The years up to 1784 were marked by relative security thanks both to a decent income received from teaching and concertizing and a kind of freedom he had never before known, making these some of the happiest years of his life. His interest in the piano concerto was rekindled, and he composed a series of works that are his greatest achievement in instrumental music. Before focusing on these piano concertos, though, I turn momentarily to his concertos for horn, of which he composed several throughout the Vienna period.

THE HORN CONCERTOS

As with all his wind concertos, Mozart's music for horn and orchestra was composed for and inspired by a particular performer. Joseph Leutgeb (sometimes referred to as Ignaz Leutgeb or Leitgeb, c. 1745–1811) had served as a hornist in the Salzburg court orchestra from the early 1760s and became a friend of the Mozart family at least by 1763. This friendship lasted until the composer's death (Mozart mentions Leutgeb in his last letter), making it the longest lasting of Mozart's musical friendships. Leutgeb achieved a degree of fame as a soloist, making appearances in Vienna, Paris, and Milan. In Paris, in 1770, he played one of his own concertos (now lost) at the Concert Spirituel, where he was praised for his ability to "sing an adagio as perfectly as the most mellow, interesting and accurate voice."[15] In 1777 Leutgeb settled in Vienna, where he opened a cheesemonger's shop, for which some of the capital was borrowed from Leopold Mozart. He not only kept shop but continued to play, and Mozart must have been delighted to see his talented friend in Vienna.

Mozart seems to have composed all or part of six horn concertos during his Vienna period, from 1781 to 1791.[16] Three are known to have been composed for Leutgeb, and others may also have been intended for his friend, since no other horn player is mentioned in Mozart's letters. Of the six works, only three, K. 417, K. 447, and K. 495, all in E-flat, survive in a completed form. The other works are the frequently performed K. 412/386b in D, consisting of two movements, which Mozart may never have intended to be part of the same work, the Rondo in E-flat, K. 371 (probably part of an intended, but not completed, concerto), and a fragment of a concerto in E, K. 494a, which trails off in a solo section.

These compositions demonstrate that Mozart not only understood the limitations of the valveless horn, but also exploited these limitations to create works of unusual beauty. The horn of the eighteenth century was nothing more than a coil of slightly conical brass tubing with a mouthpiece, its diatonic range limited to the first fifteen notes of the overtone series. In a range in which nine of these notes occurred close together, in the highest of its three octaves, diatonic melodies of a penetrating power could be written for the instrument. After the middle of the century, experiments had shown that inserting a hand into the instrument's bell could lower the pitch up to one full tone, so that a skilled player, with sensitive ears, lips, and hand, could produce a series of pitches, in addition to those of the natural overtone series. Leutgeb was one of the earliest of the hornists skilled in playing in this manner; his performances in Paris in 1770 provided Parisians with their first opportunity to hear the stopped horn. Passages such as the D-flat melody from the development of K. 447's first movement (Ex. 9-16) could only have been executed by a skillful stopping of the bell. (Tones marked with * in the example require stopping.) Mozart's works even challenge the modern hornist with a valved instrument; they must have been formidable on the eighteenth-century instrument. Mozart's horn concertos obviously take into account Leutgeb's skills.

Ex. 9-16. Mozart, Horn Concerto in E-flat Major, K. 447; I. Allegro, mm. 85–92.

Aside from these special instances, there is little bravura writing in the concertos; instead, greater concentration is placed on the creation of "singing" themes for the horn and for the lyrically inclined Leutgeb. Themes, even when first presented by the orchestra, seem to have been created specifically for the horn; on the other hand, as with the first theme of K. 417, the solo instrument is given its own peculiar version of a previous tutti theme. Because the horn cannot perform figuration which moves through different keys, the usual practice in the development section of a typical concerto, Mozart gives the soloist new cantabile material while the orchestra is given figuration. Although the horn concertos follow the same basic plan as Mozart's other concertos, they are significantly shorter in consideration of the fatigue of the soloist's lips.

We do not know for certain if Mozart relied upon other composers' horn concertos as models for his own, but if so they might have been the popular works of Antonio Rosetti (also known as Rösler, c. 1750–1792). Rosetti used the same cantabile writing for the horn and the same general layout with romanza slow movements and ⅛ hunting-style finales featuring galloping themes.

Mozart's horn concertos are generally of a light quality with an air of good humor about them. Some of the autograph manuscripts even contain jocular remarks addressed to his hornist friend. For example, the following remarks occur over passages in the rondo of K. 412:

> Adagio (the orchestra is marked allegro) . . . For you, Mr. Ass . . . come on . . . quick . . . get on with it . . . like a good fellow . . . courage . . . You ass . . . oh, what a horrid noise . . . oh, dear [at a repeated F-sharp] . . . Oh, finish, please! Curse you . . . bravura as well? [over a short run] . . . You're done? Thank heaven . . . enough, enough.[17]

At the head of K. 417, Mozart inscribed: "Wolfgang Amadeus Mozart took pity on Leitgeb, ass, ox, and fool, at Vienna, 27 May, 1783."

K. 417 in E-flat is the first of Mozart's horn concertos surviving in its entirety. It is scored for oboes, ripieno horns, and strings, the winds appearing only in tutti sections, never in accompaniments. This is a strongly melodic and somewhat more spacious work than the others. K. 447 is the most unusual not only because clarinets and bassoons are used rather than oboes and horns, but also in its A-flat major Romanza, the main theme of which returns (also in A-flat), transformed, in the second episode of the rondo finale. Because the middle movement is in the subdominant, rather than the dominant, the notes available to the horn fall at different places in the scale, and Mozart took full advantage of the new melodic possibilities. The last of the horn concertos, K. 495, entered in Mozart's catalog as "for Leitgeb," is the most technically demanding, with its rapid runs, frequent use of stopped notes, and cantabile passages in the upper register.

THE EARLY VIENNESE PIANO CONCERTOS (1782–83)

Mozart composed seventeen concertos for piano and orchestra in his Vienna years. Becoming a star piano performer and thereby gaining the attention and favor of the Viennese audiences, he could attract more students as well as earn money from the concerts. So Mozart wrote his Viennese concertos largely for his own performances.

An early appearance took place in March 1782, when he played one of his favorite earlier concertos, the dynamic D Major, K. 175, from 1773. He realized before the concert, however, that for an audience not yet familiar with him and whose taste was on the conservative side, he would have to provide a new finale as a substitute for the bold, forward-looking, intensely contrapuntal original movement. The simple rondo-variations of the newly composed finale (K. 382) were cast in the well-understood minuet form. This, his first Viennese composition for piano and orchestra, set the tone for the next three concertos.

Late in 1782 Mozart announced his intention to compose three new piano concertos (K. 413–415) to be offered for sale by subscription, a common practice in Vienna at the time. He was fully aware that for the concertos to sell well, the solo parts would have to possess a brilliant sound yet not be very difficult to play. In addition, the works needed to be suitable for use in the home as well as in the concert hall. Because of the latter requirement the orchestra would have to be adaptable to the needs of a string quartet, or other equivalent instrumental groups. Even though winds are used in these three concertos, they are not essential since they virtually duplicate material found in the strings.

Mozart described these concertos in a 28 December 1782 letter to his father:

> These concertos are a happy medium between what is too easy and too diffi-
> cult; they are brilliant, pleasing to the ear, and natural, without being vapid.
> There are passages here and there from which connoisseurs alone can derive
> satisfaction; but these passages are written in such a way that the less learned
> cannot fail to be pleased, though without knowing why.[18]

Although Mozart's compositional technique and use of the keyboard in K. 413–415 are more advanced than in his Salzburg concertos, the style here retreats to the lighter quality of the concertos preceding the expansive K. 271 in E-flat of 1777, even to the point of reintroducing the *menuet en rondeau* type of finale in K. 413, the last of his concerto movements in minuet tempo.

K. 414 in A Major is the most interesting and appealing of the three. It overflows with the intimate, graceful lyricism so common to Mozart's works in that key and anticipates the mood of the great A Major Piano Concerto, K. 488. These qualities are apparent from the opening lyrical theme (Ex. 9-17), which is in such contrast to the more common fanfare or martial gestures used in the openings of his previous concertos. The expressive middle movement of K. 414, an Andante in D major, uses as its main theme a quotation from the overture to J. C. Bach's *La Calamità dei cuori* (1763, publ. 1770). Mozart may have included this theme in homage to his recently deceased friend; Bach's opera dates from the time of Wolfgang's childhood visit. The finale is a tune-filled Allegretto in concerto-rondo form.

Ex. 9-17. Mozart, Piano Concerto in A Major, K. 414; I. Allegro, mm. 1–4.

THE PIANO CONCERTOS OF 1784–86

Beginning in February 1784, Mozart focused his attention on composing for piano in orchestral and chamber settings, creating some of his most remarkable and highly esteemed works. Between February 1784 and March 1785 he composed eight piano concertos (K. 449, 450, 451, 453, 456, 459, 466, and 467). After an interruption of a few months, he then added four more (K. 482, 488, 491, 503) between December 1785 and December 1786. He also composed during this remarkable three-year period (1784–86) the two great piano quartets (K. 478 in G Minor of October 1785 and K. 493 in E-flat of June 1786) and the piano and woodwind quintet, K. 452 (of March 1784), each of which features the piano in a prominent role. The two final piano concertos date from February 1788 (K. 537) and January 1791 (K. 595). Taken as a group, Mozart's last fourteen piano concertos form a towering achievement in the entire history of the concerto.

By 1784 Mozart had come to terms with the Viennese public, realizing they possessed a more sophisticated taste than did his Salzburg audience. In the cosmopolitan world of Vienna, he had gained a sense of freedom, which revealed itself in the extraordinary synthesis of the diverse influences to which he had been exposed in his earlier years. Particularly notable are the incorporation of the art of counterpoint as a lively and central compositional technique, the heightened use of chromaticism, and the forsaking of all musical cliché. In these concertos, the relationship between the soloist and the orchestra is finally fully integrated; the increasing brilliance of the solo parts is paralleled by an increase in the size, importance, and richness of the orchestral role as the two become an organic whole. The woodwinds in particular acquire a new prominence as the foil for the piano parts.

In the piano concertos, which were central to his creative life over these three years, both Mozart's increased technical prowess and a deepening of the emotional content can be sensed, as well as the waning of interest in creating light, entertaining pieces. As a result of this increased emotional and musical substance as well as Mozart's increased expertise in handling the concerto's basic form, each concerto takes on a personality of its own. The richness of these masterworks is beyond description, and each has become the personal friend of untold numbers of music lovers.

It is significant that the Piano Concerto in E-flat Major, K. 449, the first of his group of great concertos, was the very first work to be entered in his thematic catalog, which he began on 9 February 1784 and kept until only a few weeks before his death. K. 449 marks a new beginning in Mozart's sense of concerto composition. But unlike the immediately following concertos, the solo part is not as brilliant since it was composed for Barbara Ployer, a pupil of Mozart. He noted in a letter of 26 May 1784 to his father, "the one in E♭ does not belong at all to the same category [as K. 450 and K. 451, which] . . . are bound to make the performer perspire."[19]

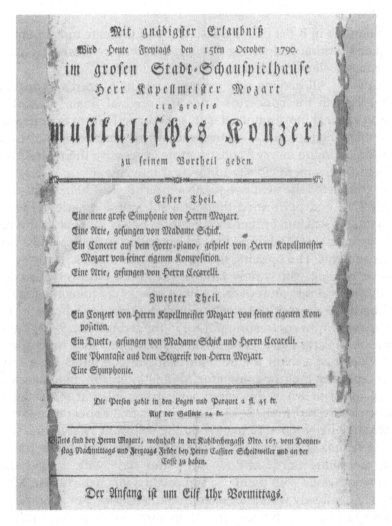

An admission ticket and poster advertising a Mozart concert in Vienna in October 1790. The poster indicates Mozart was to play two concertos, possibly K. 537 in D Major and K. 459 in F Major, which he played at the coronation of Leopold II in Frankfurt that month. Mozart composed fourteen piano concertos between February 1784 and January 1791. These works comprise a pinnacle in the history of the form. During this period, Mozart's fame as a keyboard artist and composer encouraged many to pay well to hear him play. These concerts were an important source of income for Mozart and also led to his acquiring new students.

Like the first movement of K. 414, the Allegro vivace of K. 449 displays a cornucopia of themes, but they are more varied in nature. The unusual tonal ambiguity of the opening (E-flat major or C minor, Ex. 9-18) sets the stage for a tonally restless movement, especially in the opening tutti. This ambiguity is further highlighted in the recapitulation by a striking modulation to C minor (m. 319). Mozart's cadenza refers to the C minor passage and cadential material from the opening tutti, which the soloist had not previously played.

Ex. 9-18. Mozart, Piano Concerto in E-flat Major, K. 449; I. Allegro vivace, mm. 1–4.

The Andantino in B-flat major is a simple and intimate movement, but thanks to its lush piano writing and strong flowing quality it evokes a strongly romantic mood. It combines elements of sonata and rondo form.

The finale, a $\frac{2}{4}$ Allegro ma non troppo, contains Mozart's strongest flirtation with counterpoint in the concertos since the original finale of K. 175. One of Mozart's most original movements, it is in sonata-rondo form, incorporating variations on the main theme when it returns and further variations on the main theme and its companion in the merry $\frac{6}{8}$ coda. A more aggressive theme in C minor (mm. 152ff.) links this movement closely to the first movement.

Mozart completed the next two piano concertos (K. 450 in B-flat and K. 451 in D) in March 1784 and performed them at a subscription series of well-attended Lenten concerts. A striking, brilliant virtuosity is newly evident in the piano parts, a brilliance which is matched in part by an expanded orchestra and a new role for the wind instruments. The opening thirteen measures of K. 450 advise the listener that Mozart is dealing with a new kind of orchestra. No previous concerto had opened with winds alone; moreover, a pair of bassoons[20] joins the familiar pairs of oboes and horns to present the richly chromatic opening phrase in thirds. This phrase is answered by a contrasting phrase in the strings (Ex. 9-19) offering a perfect example of Mozart's keen sense of the element of duality, here operating even within the context of a main theme. The dialogue continues for a few bars, the woodwinds repeating their opening idea, shifted interestingly to a new part of the beat (mm. 4–5). Even when the winds and strings play at the same time, their independence is stressed (mm. 8–13). The piano's first appearance gives clear evidence of Mozart's heightened demands on the soloist. A twelve-measure sparsely accompanied cadenza-like passage precedes the piano's presentation of the main theme, whose double thirds endow the piano style with a new sparkle. The coupling of woodwinds with piano, so important a characteristic in Mozart's later concertos, is here already well integrated into the texture. For example, a dialogue between strings and woodwinds, found in mm. 8–10 of the tutti, becomes a dialogue between piano and woodwinds when the passage is repeated in the solo exposition in mm. 78–80. Here the piano takes over the part originally played by the strings.

Ex. 9-19. Mozart, Piano Concerto in B-flat Major, K. 450; I. Allegro, mm. 1–4.

This concerto is one of Mozart's most obviously virtuosic works. The solo instrument is given many fewer themes than usual so more room is available for display work. Even when the orchestra is busy with thematic material, the piano remains brilliantly active; the places traditionally devoted to bravura writing—the transition and closing sections of the exposition and recapitulation and most of the development—are expanded with brilliant runs, broken octaves, and dazzling arpeggio patterns.

The meditative Andante in E-flat major is a set of two variations on a simple theme, with each half being varied on repeat, resulting in a set of double variations. This is Mozart's first use of variation form in the concertos, aside from the Rondo, K. 386. The $\frac{6}{8}$ hunting-style finale contains more display, including the crossing of the left hand over the right (see mm. 76–85 and 141–160), a visually exciting effect not often found in Mozart's keyboard music. The most effective surprise in the movement is also the quietest passage: the *pianissimo* repeated horn-call motive just before the end.

Mozart augments the orchestra of K. 451 by adding trumpets and timpani, instruments often associated with the brilliant key of D major. Here they enhance the martial character of the opening ritornello. The Andante, in G major, opens with a characteristically effective chromatic melody. It is in a romanza style using five-part rondo form. The second episode, which begins in E minor, moves to C major for the presentation of a new theme (Ex. 9-20, top staff), which, incidentally, Mozart's sister found too bare. To accommodate her concern, Mozart sent her an embellished version of the theme (Ex. 9-20, bottom staff). Such an example demonstrates the way in which Mozart embellished such simple themes, particularly in slow movements—a model modern performers can use to advantage. The concluding Allegro di molto is a $\frac{2}{4}$ dance presented in the rustic style more usually associated with Haydn. It follows the outlines of concerto-rondo form, with much of the second episode (after the introduction of a new theme in B minor) given over to development of a Haydnesque motive from the second theme of the first episode. A lengthy coda in $\frac{3}{8}$ time augments the rustic mood reminiscent of the way in which rustic Austrian dances were often paired, one in duple, one in triple meter.

Ex. 9-20. Mozart, Piano Concerto in D Major, K. 451; II. Andante, mm. 56–63, with embellished version by Mozart.

The opening pages of Mozart's own thematic catalog. In February 1784 Mozart began to keep track of his new compositions by notating their opening themes, titles, dates, and other data in a private thematic catalog. It is significant that each of the five first entries shown here features the piano as a brilliant solo instrument in the context of orchestral and chamber works. Furthermore, four of the five works are concertos, marking the beginning of the remarkable series of twelve composed over the next three years. (By permission of the British Library.)

Shortly after composing K. 451, Mozart completed a second concerto for Barbara Ployer—K. 453 in G Major (12 April 1784). G major is one of Mozart's favorite keys for the expression of intimate and lyrical ideas, and this concerto is unusually melodic. While the solo part calls for less virtuosic display than in K. 450 and 451, the music for the wind instruments—one flute, two oboes, two bassoons, and two horns—is more elaborate. As Mozart establishes a special relationship between the piano and the woodwinds, the woodwinds take on unusual importance, setting a trend for most of his later piano concertos. This relationship is created in two principal ways: first, the woodwinds provide interesting, motivically generated accompaniment for the piano display passage work; second, they are prominent in the sharing of lyrical thematic material with the piano, especially in the second key area of the solo exposition. As was to become his custom, Mozart has the solo piano present its new lyrical theme at the beginning of the second key area of the exposition, unaccompanied by the orchestra. Soon after its first appearance, the new theme is handed over to the woodwinds, which are then accompanied by the piano (mm. 110–125 and 139–152). The two forces are closely integrated, yet Mozart maintains a careful separation of their dramatic roles. The overall coordination leads to a remarkably intimate juxtaposition of the solo instrument with a most colorful part of the orchestra.

The $\frac{3}{4}$ Andante in C major is both lyrical and dramatic. Drama is created by sudden pauses, far-ranging modulations, and striking dynamic contrasts. One passage of unusually large leaps in the piano right-hand part (Ex. 9-21) suggests vocal leaps greater than an octave, so characteristic of Mozart's dramatic music. He could have intended these leaps to be filled in with improvised embellishments.

Ex. 9-21. Mozart, Piano Concerto in G Major, K. 453; II. Andante, mm. 39–41.

The Allegretto finale comprises five variations of which variations 2 through 5 are double variations, the piano varying the repeat of each strain, on a Papageno-like theme which Mozart's favorite pet starling could supposedly sing. The next-to-last variation, in minor, is singularly austere and archaic sounding with its syncopated phrasing and unusual doublings, as between bassoon and first violin in the second half. After a fascinating transition, full of suspensions, and a dramatic pause on the dominant, the helter-skelter presto coda of 175 measures, in the style of an *opera buffa* finale, brings the concerto to a happy conclusion. The main theme of the movement is reintroduced about halfway through the coda, virtually serving as another variation.

There is provision for a cadenza in each of the first two movements of K. 453, this being the last of Mozart's concertos to include a cadenza in the slow movement. Mozart wrote two cadenzas for each movement, and performers may choose between a more or less brilliant one for each.

Piano Concerto in B-flat Major, K. 456, was completed on 30 September 1784 for the twenty-five-year-old virtuoso pianist Maria Theresia von Paradis, who had been blind since childhood. The concerto was to have been performed in Paris, apparently prompting Mozart to provide elaborate wind parts and a sensuous piano part. The first movement, Allegro vivace, contains a mysterious-sounding episode in minor, first introduced in the ritornello. The slow movement is a set of variations and the finale is a $\frac{6}{8}$ hunting-style Allegro vivace with a multitude of themes.

The F Major Piano Concerto, K. 459, Mozart's last of 1784, is one of his most exhilarating and thematically concentrated, involving fugal writing in each movement. The first movement lacks the thematic diversity of the other 1784 concertos; in its place is an intense development of the opening theme (Ex. 9-22). This theme reappears frequently in fragmented form in the orchestra, as it accompanies virtuosic outbursts in the piano. The main theme even appears in a small fugato at the very point that the piano is usually expected to present a new lyrical theme (m. 106). The woodwinds eventually introduce the new second theme, which is then repeated in a varied form by the piano.

Ex. 9-22. Mozart, Piano Concerto in F Major, K. 459; I. Allegro, mm. 1–4.

The sensitive woodwind writing helps to establish the pastoral mood of the slow movement in $\frac{6}{8}$. There is an exquisite four-part canon for piano (with two parts), oboe, and bassoon at m. 104 and a short fugal section for woodwinds near the beginning. The very long Allegro assai finale combines the gaiety of a rondo with the seriousness of a fugue. The piano, as is so typical of Mozart's concerto rondo finales, opens the movement alone, with a *buffa* style theme (Ex. 9-23). A long fugal passage in the orchestra follows. Near the end of the movement, the two themes are combined in a great double fugue beginning in m. 289.

Ex. 9-23. Mozart, Piano Concerto in F Major, K. 459; III. Allegro assai, mm. 1–4.

The D Minor Concerto, K. 466, and C Major Concerto, K. 467 (February–March 1785), are the first example of several intriguing, contrasting pairs of works Mozart composed in like genre in his last years. It is as if the inspiration leading to the creation of the first work in the pair carried with it a counter idea which suggested that the composer create soon afterward another work in the same genre, but of a very different mood. The other most striking such pairs are the string quintets in C major, K. 515, and G minor, K. 516 (April–May 1787); the symphonies No. 40 in G minor, K. 550, and No. 41 in C major, K. 551 (July–August 1788); and the piano concertos in A major, K. 488, and C minor, K. 491 (March 1786).

The D Minor Concerto was the Mozart concerto most loved by the Romantics. The autograph manuscript was for some years in the possession of Johannes Brahms, who not only performed it but also wrote cadenzas for it. Beethoven, whose cadenzas are most often used today, did as well. This concerto was entered in Mozart's personal catalog on 10 February 1785. Leopold arrived for a visit on that very day and, in a letter to his daughter, not only praised the concerto but remarked that the copyist was busy preparing parts for performance the following day.

Only two of Mozart's concertos are in the minor mode; in general, few of his works are in minor, but those that are have extraordinarily powerful emotional connotations. With the key of D minor, Mozart entered a new, rich, intense musical world. It was to be the key of his unfinished Requiem Mass, and the co-key, with D major, of the opera *Don Giovanni,* which mixes comic and tragic elements; D minor is specifically used for the entrance of the Commendatore's statue in the finale of Act II, and it plays an important role in the overture and the duet following the death of the Commendatore. In the latter, D minor expresses not only the tragic but anger and vengeance as well, as in the Queen of the Night's famous aria "Der Hölle Rache" from *The Magic Flute,* and in parts of Count Almaviva's angry aria "Vedrò mentr'io sospiro" in *The Marriage of Figaro.*

The opening of the D Minor Concerto establishes a quiet but tense and highly energized mood. The tension of the minor mode is increased by the conflict between syncopations in high strings across the barline and thrusting motives in the basses that emphasize the downbeat, as well as by sudden harmonic shifts (Ex. 9-24). Tension mounts as the bass line and harmonic motion quicken and winds introduce a coloristic element. There is a shocking outburst in m. 16 with tremolo and spurts of the bass motive exchanged between basses and violins. All this vigorous activity comes to a halt on the dominant in m. 32; silence precedes a strongly contrasting, brief lyrical idea first offered in F major. This episode is a typically Mozartian passage involving rapid changes of texture and orchestral color (Ex. 9-25). Though the idea is quietly introduced, the rising sequences of its development rebuild the earlier tension. A return to D minor and the introduction of other compact motives follow. A calmer contrapuntal passage provides an inviting gesture to which the piano graciously responds as though coming from another musical world (Ex. 9-26).

Ex. 9-24. Mozart, Piano Concerto in D Minor, K. 466; I. Allegro, mm. 1–4.

Ex. 9-25. Mozart, Piano Concerto in D Minor, K. 466; I. Allegro, mm. 33–34.

Ex. 9-26. Mozart, Piano Concerto in D Minor, K. 466; I. Allegro, mm. 77–85.

This wonderfully different, powerfully lyrical piano song, accompanied by gentle thirds in the left-hand part of the piano in the treble clef, remains the exclusive property of the piano. This idea plays a major role in the development. Here the piano part is juxtaposed against the tense opening theme in the orchestra in a series of sequences moving through F major, G minor, and E-flat major. While flashes of virtuoso display occur between these two ideas, the second half of the development features greater pianistic display pitted against the strings with the thrusting motive of the opening bass line. This segment proceeds through F minor and G minor to the dominant, A major, in preparation for the return to the tonic.

The slow movement is entitled Romanza, but bears no specific tempo marking. Its B-flat major opening theme, first given to the solo piano, provides a striking contrast to the previous movement (Ex. 9-27). The Romanza is a five-part rondo (ABACA), with a surprising C section, in G minor, returning to the agitated mood that dominated the first movement. Mozart employs the very common thematic structure of aababa in the refrain (A), which offers the opportunity of an interesting distribution of the theme's parts between soloist and orchestra:

a	a	b	a	b	a
piano	orchestra	piano	piano	orchestra	orchestra

In performance, Mozart probably decorated the returns of the refrain (only the first part, aa, returns after the first episode) with improvised ornamentation. The coda begins with a startlingly beautiful passage for wind choir, followed by the piano with widely separated hand positions, anticipating piano textures more commonly associated with Beethoven.

Ex. 9-27. Mozart, Piano Concerto in D Minor, K. 466; II. Romanza, mm. 1–4.

The finale is unusual in that it is a rondo in the minor mode. Its main theme is powerful and thrusting (Ex. 9-28), not at all akin to the common dance tunes used in the typical rondo. Mozart eventually does introduce a jaunty, rondo-like theme in F major at the end of the first episode (B) of this concerto-rondo form (ABACB'A) movement (Ex. 9-29). This playful theme is not reached until m. 140, though, and it only comes after an agitated theme in F minor and a lengthy bravura solo passage. The C section of the rondo is a development based on the opening refrain and the lyric D minor theme from the beginning of the first episode. The tension of this minor-mode rondo movement and concerto is finally resolved in the rondo's long coda in D major. Here the jaunty closing theme of the first episode plays a major role, but its impact is heightened by the introduction of a new, amusing trumpet-and-horn figure that seems to come from the world of comic opera (Ex. 9-30). Once again the eighteenth-century fondness for a happy ending is evident.

Ex. 9-28. Mozart, Piano Concerto in D Minor, K. 466; III. Rondo: Allegro assai, mm. 1–5.

Ex. 9-29. Mozart, Piano Concerto in D Minor, K. 466; III. Rondo: Allegro assai, mm. 140–143.

Ex. 9-30. Mozart, Piano Concerto in D Minor, K. 466; III. Rondo: Allegro assai, mm. 402–403.

Mozart's next concerto, K. 467, is in the ceremonial key of C major. It is a very bright piece of music and numbers among Mozart's most demanding for the pianist. A rare somber moment in the concerto occurs in the solo exposition of the first movement when the piano introduces a theme in G minor, before presenting the true, lyrical second theme in major. This G minor theme is remarkably close to the first theme of Symphony No. 40 in G Minor, written three years later, but it never reappears in this concerto. The Andante is one of Mozart's most romantic-sounding movements, with a very fluid melody over continuous triplets. The muted strings and strong dissonances enhance the mood. The rondo finale is given a very active main theme in which the first full measure strongly pulls to the second measure (Ex. 9-31). The central episode is an exciting development section focused on the first six notes of the main theme.

Ex. 9-31. Mozart, Piano Concerto in C Major, K. 467; III. Allegro vivace assai, mm. 1–4.

Mozart's next three concertos are his only piano concertos calling for clarinets in the orchestra; this single-reed instrument adds a new, distinctly warm sound to the orchestra. Mozart wrote all three while he was at work on *The Marriage of Figaro*, December 1785 to March 1786. K. 482 is in E-flat, the key for some of Mozart's most significant Masonic music, including *The Magic Flute*. This concerto is large, its luxurious sound resulting from the extensive doubling of thirds and sixths in the woodwinds. Woodwinds are featured in little solos in the C minor middle movement, which also combines elements of variation with those of the rondo; the refrain is dealt with in variation terms upon its return. The finale is a hunting rondo in galloping $\frac{6}{8}$ time.

The A Major Piano Concerto, K. 488, shares a common lyrical thread with Mozart's other A major compositions, especially the Clarinet Quintet and Clarinet Concerto. The piano concerto's extraordinary lyricism is evident from the very first measure (Ex. 9-32).

Ex. 9-32. Mozart, Piano Concerto in A Major, K. 488; I. Allegro, mm. 1–4.

In the first movement, Mozart postponed the introduction of the new second theme until the second tutti section and permitted the orchestra to present it. This is unusual, for he customarily assigned the new theme to the piano during the solo exposition. This second theme dominates the development section that follows.

The Adagio is the only F-sharp minor movement in Mozart's music and is possibly his most romantic sounding. In the coda the piano is given widely spaced, sustained notes against a pizzicato background. This is a passage that leads the listener to wonder at its beautiful simplicity, and yet Mozart most likely decorated it in performance. However, graceful arabesques tastefully employed in such a passage merely transform its beauty without diminishing it. The rondo is most appealing with its wealth of lively melodic material, including some exciting passages for clarinets and bassoons.

K. 491 is Mozart's second and last concerto in a minor key, C. It includes the largest wind section of any Mozart concerto with clarinets in addition to, rather than as substitutes for, oboes, as in the two previous concertos. Although the dramatic content of Mozart's concertos is legendary, this is truly the most dramatic of all. The triple meter of the first movement clearly departs from any sense of the more common martial opening of so many of his concertos. The opening theme, in bare octaves, sets the tense mood with its jagged, dissonant leaps, descending sequences, and silences. The distinctive motivic content lends itself well to extensive development (Ex. 9-33).

Ex. 9-33. Mozart, Piano Concerto in C Minor, K. 491; I. Allegro, mm. 1–11.

Lyrical moments are introduced by the piano at its entry and in its later statement of the new second theme.

The Larghetto in E-flat is given a musical expression strongly reminiscent of the tender sadness of the Countess's cavatina "Porgi amor" in *The Marriage of Figaro*. Mozart deepens the luxuriant sonority associated with E-flat by the shifts to C minor, A-flat major, and F minor. He departed radically in this work from the rondo finale traditionally employed in his concertos. Here a set of variations ending in C minor concludes the work.

K. 503 was completed in early December 1786, in time for Mozart to use it in a concert he gave during the Advent season. This is another of his great virtuosic concertos in the majestic key of C major. C major also seems well-suited for the creation of strong contrapuntal effects, such as those in the "Jupiter" Symphony, and in the first movement of this concerto, which contains some very complex canonic writing as well. The concerto also contains exciting tonal shifts to keys related by thirds, relationships which had only recently come to be used with some regularity by Mozart and Haydn and were to color strongly the music of Beethoven and later Romantic composers.

THE LAST TWO PIANO CONCERTOS

Mozart's incredible series of twelve piano concertos created in a period of just over two years came to a close with K. 503. Mozart's popularity as a piano virtuoso with Viennese audiences began to fade, most likely accounting for his loss of interest in creating new piano concertos. More than a year elapsed before he was to complete his next, K. 537 in D Major, in February 1788. This concerto lacks the sparkle of the earlier works, particularly in the woodwind parts. Mozart performed this concerto, but not in Vienna, so he may have written it for an orchestra with less gifted wind players than he had grown accustomed to. The work received the nickname "Coronation" because it, together with K. 459, was performed at the coronation of Leopold II in Frankfurt in October 1790.

Mozart's last piano concerto is K. 595 in B-flat, completed in early January 1791, the year of his death. It has been often remarked that the late works of many great composers become increasingly introspective, so it is fascinating to observe the still-young Mozart, with every prospect of many years ahead of him, following the same path as if the end of his short life was somehow known to him. The B-flat Concerto possesses a remarkably intimate, personal, introspective quality, communicated not only by its smaller orchestra (there are no clarinets, trumpets, or timpani) but by its melodic content as well. The opening measure of murmuring orchestral accompaniment sets the mood prior to the statement of the first theme

(Ex. 9-34). The establishment of mood by means of introductory accompaniment became a common feature of Romantic music.

Ex. 9-34. Mozart, Piano Concerto in B-flat Major, K. 595; I. Allegro, mm. 1–5.

The Larghetto is in E-flat major, the key Mozart used for some of his most tender and melancholy melodies, such as at the opening of this movement. The finale is another ⅛ hunting rondo with a refrain similar to his contemporary song "Sehnsucht nach dem Frühlinge," ("Yearning for Spring," K. 596), which has the qualities of a folk song. The melody is suitably happy (Ex. 9-35). By including this song in this introspective final piano concerto, Mozart almost seems to be making a gesture comparable to those by Gustav Mahler in his programmatic symphonies. Was Mozart looking back to the spring of his youth or seeking an avenue which might lead out of the pain and anguish which now surrounded him?

Ex. 9-35. Mozart, Piano Concerto in B-flat Major, K. 595; III. Allegro, mm. 1–4.

THE CLARINET CONCERTO

Mozart's response to the rich and varied timbre of the clarinet, the newest addition to the orchestra's woodwind family, was profound. During his visit to Mannheim in 1777–78, he developed a deep interest in the instrument, but he lacked opportunities for its use. Only in his last years was the clarinet more readily available in Vienna and other major centers in the southern part of the German-speaking world, the instrument only gradually having worked its way into the orchestra as a regular member of the woodwind family.

Mozart's fondness for the instrument must have been related to its fine warm tone and its capability for unusual contrasts of timbre from range to range. Its lowest register, known as the chalumeau, after the single-reed ancestor of the clarinet, has a particularly rich, haunting, almost hollow tone quality. The few notes above the chalumeau form another distinctive range, often referred to as the throat register, with a thinner tone. The next higher range is the clarinet's sweetest and the one best suited to present lyrical ideas. The instrument's highest range is referred to as its clarino register, because the tone quality slightly resembles that of trumpets in their upper register. Mozart's writing for the clarinet demonstrates his remarkable understanding of the various tone colors inherent in the instrument, and he cast his scores to exploit fully this quality of contrast. He also took full advantage of its agility and strongly lyrical voice.

In those situations in which Mozart knew he could call upon the clarinet, his writing almost invariably takes on a different character; an unmistakable warmth permeates the texture. In his operas, he tended to reserve clarinets for use with special characters, particularly with those of society's upper levels. Although clarinets are called for in the opening numbers of *The Magic Flute,* it is not until the Prince, Tamino, sings of his love for Pamina that the single-reed instrument's voice stands out, significantly modifying the orchestral texture. He also used the instrument's tone color to enhance the portrayal of several female roles, including that of Donna Elvira in *Don Giovanni;* the clarinet's first appearance in the opera following the overture is to accompany Elvira's entrance.

It was not only the instrument but also a particularly gifted clarinetist who inspired Mozart's most important contributions to the clarinet literature. Anton Stadler (1753–1812) had resided in Vienna from about 1771 and was, like Mozart, a Freemason. They developed a close friendship in the late 1780s, and Mozart, although himself destitute, loaned his clarinetist friend money over the years, much of which was still owed to Mozart at his death. Stadler was a great clarinetist known for his virtuosic technique and expressive playing. As Mozart did with his horn-playing friend Leutgeb, the composer wrote several pieces for the clarinet to highlight Stadler's gifts. In addition to the Clarinet Concerto in A Major, K. 622, Mozart wrote the Clarinet Quintet in A Major, K. 581 (1789), and the Trio for Clarinet, Viola, and Piano in E-flat Major, K. 498 (1786), with Stadler in mind. Stadler also played the basset horn, a later relative of the clarinet with a lower range and very distinctive tone color, which Mozart called for in some of his most "spiritual" music, such as in the orchestral accompaniment for Sarastro and the march of priests in *The Magic Flute* and his Masonic Funeral Music, K. 477. In addition, he wrote obbligato parts for the instrument in two numbers in *La Clemenza di Tito* (1791) which were played by Stadler, who accompanied the Mozarts to Prague for performances of the opera.

Mozart began the Clarinet Concerto as a work for basset horn, possibly as early as October 1789, shortly after completion of the Clarinet Quintet. About 200 measures of this version of the work exist in autograph manuscript. It was begun in G major, but near the end Mozart shifted to A major, probably already having decided to recast it for the clarinet. He reworked what he had composed and continued on to complete the concerto in early October 1791, only two months before his death.

Mozart must have written the concerto for Stadler to perform on a "basset-clarinet," which Stadler had designed and specially constructed to extend its lower range by four semitones. Although Mozart's autograph manuscript of the Clarinet Concerto is lost, musical evidence has led scholars to conclude that the work as most often heard is based on an edition from 1801, the clarinet part for which was reworked to move those four lowest notes into the range of the normal clarinet in A. Such a recasting involves shifting those notes up an octave, which, of course, changes the contour of the musical line and register placement of the instrument, resulting in some unusual clarinet crossings of the violin parts. In most cases only isolated notes are affected, but in one place an entire nine-measure passage is shifted up an octave. The volume of the collected edition of Mozart's music (*Neue Mozart Ausgabe*) containing the Clarinet Concerto includes the traditional musical text as usually heard and a reconstruction of the text as it is believed Mozart originally wrote it. Some modern clarinetists have performed the work on reconstructed Stadler basset-clarinets with startlingly effective results. This best known of all clarinet concertos has thus come down in a distorted version, but in the only way it can be performed on the modern clarinet.

The Clarinet Concerto is scored for an orchestra of flutes, bassoons, horns, and strings, the cellos being freed somewhat from the contrabasses. Mozart must have considered the piercing tone of oboes inappropriate for this warm work, excluding them as well as keeping the remaining woodwinds on the quiet side, especially in solo passages, so as not to compete with the woodwind solo instrument. The emphasis on string accompaniment and the intimate nature of the music often bring to mind the earlier Clarinet Quintet. In the concerto score the clarinetist is expected to double the first violin part in most of the main tutti sections, reminding us of the origin of the term tutti to designate those portions of a movement played by the united forces. In modern performances, the clarinet is usually omitted from the large tutti sections.

The strings open the concerto with a quiet lyrical melody entirely characteristic of Mozart's later works in A major (Ex. 9-36). The solo instrument's expanded restatement of this theme at the outset of the solo exposition illustrates Mozart's thorough understanding of the clarinet, as he takes full advantage of its varied tone colors, decorating the theme with runs, arpeggios, and wide leaps. One surprising moment occurs near the beginning, when, after pausing on the dominant, Mozart restates the main theme in a quiet, imitative passage instead of introducing the expected contrasting theme (mm. 25ff.). When this passage recurs in the solo exposition, the violins continue imitatively while the clarinet accompanies with an Alberti-style bass figure in its low register (mm. 134–137)—a very colorful and effective use of the instrument. An unusual tutti passage in the development section involves a loud passage in octaves immediately followed by an eerily quiet repeat with additional new sighing motives in bassoon, violas, and cellos. This segment is first presented in F-sharp minor and then in E minor. There is no place for a cadenza in this movement.

Ex. 9-36. Mozart, Clarinet Concerto in A Major, K. 622; I. Allegro, mm. 1–4.

Mozart's mature expressions can depend upon the simplest of means, as in the second movement, in D major. It is in triple meter with a tempo indication of Adagio, a rare marking in Mozart's concertos. It is in ABA form. The A portion consists of two eight-measure sections, each first stated by the clarinet and then repeated by orchestra. The B section features the clarinet throughout in a more ornate melody. In the reprise of A, parallel thirds in flutes and bassoons render an extremely lush orchestral repeat of the second strain.

The final movement is an abundantly melodic rondo in $\frac{6}{8}$ time. It calls for the greatest clarinet virtuosity in the work. The opening phrase (Ex. 9-37) contains some intriguing staccato and slurred articulations, playfully varied when the phrase returns in this ABACBA concerto-rondo form. Important references to the parallel minor and dominant minor add an element of melancholy sadness to this otherwise dancelike movement.

Ex. 9-37. Mozart, Clarinet Concerto in A Major, K. 622; III. Rondo: Allegro, mm. 1–4.

MOZART'S ACHIEVEMENTS AS A COMPOSER OF CONCERTOS

The Clarinet Concerto, still regarded as the greatest of all clarinet concertos, was Mozart's last work in the concerto form and his last completed instrumental composition. It marked the end of a career of a composer whose musical gifts were remarkably well-suited to the writing of concertos. At least a dozen of his piano concertos must surely be judged as outstanding, the clarinet concerto is exceptional, the other wind concertos for flute, for bassoon, and for horn are not to be overlooked, the violin concertos are charming with some profound moments, and the remarkable Sinfonia Concertante for Violin and Viola is Mozart's magnificent contribution to the eighteenth century's last vestiges of the concerto grosso. In the concerto, Mozart's dramatic and musical genius was challenged by one of music's most difficult forms, a challenge to which he rose by creating works of lasting beauty and interest, of scintillating virtuosity and profound musical substance. The vivid orchestral parts and multiplicity and diversity of melodic content are like whipped cream added to an already delectable dessert.

Mozart's concertos exerted little influence on contemporaries or immediate followers. Beethoven's early piano concertos do show that he learned from Mozart, but the nineteenth-century Romantics were to move in new and different directions compelled by artistic and emotional objectives quite different from those of the eighteenth century.

One element of the Romantic mind did, however, lead some to find inspiration in the music of Mozart and his predecessors. That element was the Romantics' fascination with things remote in time or place. This urge to explore things remote extended to a fascination with earlier periods in the European experience. In music this spawned a serious study of music history; some composers, including Felix Mendelssohn (1809–1847) and Johannes Brahms (1833–1897), became deeply interested in the music of earlier times, often drawing direct inspiration and even specific musical techniques from their study. Brahms was one of the most important of the nineteenth-century composers of concertos to incorporate elements of Mozart's conception of the concerto with those of the nineteenth century. But before turning to Brahms and other nineteenth-century composers, we will explore the concertos of Mozart's greatest contemporary, Haydn.

Chapter Ten

FRANZ JOSEPH HAYDN

Franz Joseph Haydn (1732–1809), largely self-taught as a composer, entered the service of the wealthy and powerful Hungarian family, the Esterházys, in 1761, after a brief stint as music director in the chapel of Count von Morzin. Haydn retained his position with the Esterházys for the rest of his career as Prince Nicholas, a great enthusiast for music who succeeded his brother Paul Anton to the title in 1762, not only built a substantial orchestra and group of singers but encouraged Haydn to develop his compositional talents to their fullest as well.

Haydn, the father of the symphony and of the string quartet, had no great interest in the concerto. He was not a virtuoso performer and felt no compulsion to write showpieces for himself. Furthermore, his love of symphonic development— the extensive working out of a small amount of thematic or motivic material into a fairly substantial movement—was antithetical to the dramatic duality intrinsic to the concerto. Haydn did not possess Mozart's dramatic genius, which thrived on the contrast of elements; rather Haydn's music has a dramatic intensity of a very different sort, one emerging from the ingenious and extensive development of thematic material coupled with great rhythmic vitality.

Haydn's attention to the concerto was limited to a group of early works and a smaller group from the 1780s and '90s. Although some of these later works are of great interest and continue to be performed, most musicians and scholars agree that the quality of Haydn's concertos is not equal to that of his symphonies and string quartets.

Haydn's output of some thirty-five concertos, although fairly large, is only about a third as large as his symphonic output. He composed concertos for keyboard instruments, violin, hurdy-gurdy, baryton (a cello-like instrument played by Haydn's employer, Prince Nicholas Esterházy), cello, bass, flute, and trumpet. Many of these works are, however, lost, and of the few remaining, those for trumpet, cello, and the D Major Keyboard Concerto are of greatest interest.

THE KEYBOARD CONCERTOS

Haydn's earliest experiments with writing for solo instrument and ensemble are variously called concerto, concertino or divertimento, dating from the 1750s and '60s. It is often difficult to discover any significant difference between these early keyboard concertos and the divertimentos or concertinos, which are early examples of chamber music with keyboard obbligato. Examples include Hob.

XIV:C2,[1] a two-movement work in C major for harpsichord and small string ensemble consisting of first and second violins and basso, and Hob. XIV:12,[2] a three-movement work for the same combination of instruments. These divertimentos are essentially small-scale chamber works, but employing the concerto element of a solo keyboard player. The movements are in binary form, lacking both ritornello and independent tutti sections. The songlike middle movement so characteristic of the concerto is often replaced by a minuet.

Eleven of the concertos for keyboard instrument are thought to be authentic. The usual ambiguity about which keyboard instrument was intended—harpsichord or piano—is compounded in some cases by the organ as a possible choice. For example, Hob. XVIII:1 (c. 1756) is titled on the autograph score as a *Concerto per l'Organo,* but in Haydn's draft catalog as *per il clavicembalo.*[3] The solo parts in all cases are written on two staves and can be played equally well on organ, harpsichord, or piano.

In all but two of the concertos the solo parts require no technical virtuosity. They are charming works approximating the texture of chamber music. The solo part for the G Major Clavier Concerto, Hob. XVIII:4, is of moderate difficulty, calling for some technical skill. This concerto was published in Paris in 1784 with the indication it had been performed at the Concert Spirituel by Maria Theresia von Paradis, the blind Austrian pianist for whom Mozart had written his B-flat Concerto, K. 456. Haydn apparently entered the work in his catalog in the early 1770s,[4] but its superficial style, inconsistent with the intensity of his *Sturm und Drang* works of that time, suggests that it dates from an earlier period. Or, as the Haydn scholar Landon speculates, it might merely demonstrate that Haydn had a different conception of the concerto than he did of the symphony and string quartet, viewing the concerto as a more public form of art that required concessions to public taste.[5]

Haydn's last keyboard concerto, the popular D Major, Hob. XVIII:11, is the only one that can be compared with Mozart's piano concertos. It was published in 1784 and was probably composed close to that date. The great friendship between Haydn and Mozart probably began in that year,[6] after which the music of both composers shows some degree of mutual influence. For example, from Haydn, Mozart gained a deeper understanding of the art of motivic development, while from Mozart, Haydn probably engendered a greater appreciation for chromaticism and thematic contrast, both of which figure in Haydn's D Major Concerto.

The solo part is listed in the Breitkopf catalog of 1782–84 as for harpsichord, but Artaria published it in 1784 as *per il clavicembalo ò fortepiano.* Geiringer thinks it was probably intended for piano and Ripin believes some dynamic markings suggest the use of the piano. Landon thinks that either instrument is possible and points out that some passages work better on harpsichord, while others are more effective on piano.[7] The composer may not have cared which keyboard instrument played the part, as it was characteristic of the time to create, publish, and sell music with the widest possible use in mind.

The Vivace opening movement follows the by-then mature Classical concerto-sonata plan. The opening tutti contains several different thematic ideas, quite different from Haydn's more monothematic symphonic first movements. The use of some chromaticism adds a colorful dimension to the ritornello. The most important ideas are the opening theme (Ex. 10-1), especially the three notes of its second measure, and a sequential passage near the end of the ritornello (mm. 31ff.). The orchestra is used in a manner typical of Haydn's symphonic work: strings begin alone and winds join in later for a more lyrical idea (mm. 12ff.).

Ex. 10-1. Haydn, Keyboard Concerto in D Major, Hob. XVIII:11; I. Vivace, mm. 1–6.

The solo instrument repeats the opening ritornello with modifications, including little scale runs and grace notes, but introduces no new thematic material. Haydn, in his exposition sections, commonly uses thematic material from the opening tonality in the contrasting key area. Mozart, on the other hand, characteristically introduced a strongly contrasting, usually lyrical, and, in the piano concertos, often idiomatic piano theme at this point. Haydn preferred to expand his material and here lets us know that the three-note motive of the ritornello's second measure is being singled out for attention. Later this motive becomes the basis of much of the development section (mm. 113–174), where the motive is tossed from one orchestral instrument to another, always associated with the keyboard player's left hand, while the right hand provides figuration characteristic of concerto-sonata development sections. At m. 164 a five-note motive, which seems to grow out of the three-note one, is exchanged between keyboard and orchestra.

The A major middle movement, marked Un poco adagio, is one of Haydn's most beautiful slow movements and seems to be more greatly influenced by Mozart than are the other movements. The colorful writing for the winds, the important role played by chromaticism, the luxuriant melodic lines, and the fluidity of the solo part all bring to mind the younger composer. The most prominent motive (bracketed in Ex. 10-2) fits its context beautifully. The movement is in ABA form, with the final A richly embellished by the soloist.

Ex. 10-2. Haydn, Keyboard Concerto in D Major, Hob. XVIII:11; II. Un poco adagio, mm. 1–5.

The playful finale, on the other hand, is pure Haydn. It is marked Rondo all'Ungharese: Allegro assai ($\frac{2}{4}$) and opens with the soloist stating the main theme (Ex. 10-3), as is the case in many Classical concerto rondos. Early, in the first episode, the minor mode is introduced and the main theme is transformed through the use of biting, grace notes and new intervals into a theme with a strong Hungarian (gypsy) folk quality, a quality Haydn frequently enjoyed imitating. Enhancing this quality are the strong use of the minor mode (E minor in mm. 25ff., D minor in mm. 150ff., and B minor in mm. 214ff.), syncopation (mm. 160ff.), and the numerous repeated phrases. It is interesting to note that many Romantic concertos, especially for violin but also for piano, have finales depending upon explicit folk-dance qualities, especially those associated with gypsy fiddler music.

Ex. 10-3. Haydn, Keyboard Concerto in D Major, Hob. XVIII:11; III. Rondo all' Ungharese: Allegro assai, mm. 1–4.

THE STRING CONCERTOS

Haydn's three surviving violin concertos[8] were composed before 1770–71 and were all probably intended for a four-part string orchestra with basso continuo.[9] The G Major Violin Concerto, Hob. VIIa:4, is probably the earliest, judging by the comparatively limited technical requirements expected of the solo part, the fact that the soloist participates little in developing themes, and the frequent, short repeated phrases.

The C Major Concerto, Hob. VIIa:1, was entered c. 1765 in Haydn's draft catalog as "Concerto for Violino made for Luigi." Luigi is most certainly Luigi Tomasini, Haydn's concertmaster at the Esterházy court. The Italian violinist had been hired shortly after Haydn had been appointed Vice Kapellmeister to the Esterházy court in 1761. Tomasini had also been featured in several concertante passages of Symphonies Nos. 6, 7, and 8 (Le Matin, Le Midi, and Le Soir), which Haydn had composed to announce his new position. With these works the composer must have endeared himself not only to his employer but also to his musicians, by giving solos to most of them, including the bassist. These fascinating symphonies brilliantly blend symphony and concerto, with elements of suite and opera thrown in.

The C Major Violin Concerto is significantly more demanding and interesting than the G Major Concerto. The violinist's entry, with its double stops, brilliant arpeggios, fast runs, and the later use of its then-highest register announces the increased level of competence expected. The aria-like F major Adagio (molto) begins and ends with a dramatic throbbing crescendo over which the soloist has a rising scale passage in slower notes—probably offering an opportunity for improvised embellishment. It is easy to imagine Haydn writing this operatic movement inviting virtuosic display for his Italian violinist, just as he had the recitative and aria of Symphony No. 7. The solo part is varied and wide in range. The Presto, $\frac{3}{8}$, finale is typical of the early Classical period.

The A Major Violin Concerto, Hob. VIIa:3, known as the "Melk" Concerto, because the surviving parts are located in the Benedictine Monastery in Melk, may also have been composed for Tomasini. Its structure and style are similar to those of the C Major Concerto.

Both of Haydn's cello concertos are now part of the cellist's standard repertory and are the earliest cello concertos to be heard in the concert hall with any
regularity. In both cases, the solo parts are brilliant, often making use of the instrument's upper register, and dominate the work. The C Major Cello Concerto, Hob.
VIIb:1, dates from c. 1765 and was probably written for Joseph Franz Weigl, who
served as first cellist in the Esterházy orchestra at that time. As there is no separate
orchestral cello part, the soloist was to join in during the tutti sections, as in the
Baroque period. The orchestra includes pairs of oboes and horns in addition to
strings; the winds play only in the tutti sections of the fast movements and are
silent during the middle movement.

The exuberance often associated with C major during this period characterizes the opening motive with its many dotted notes (Ex. 10-4). The finale is also
high-spirited, but Haydn abandons the light $\frac{3}{8}$ movements so typical of his finales
at that time and writes a substantial Allegro molto in common time. The F major
Adagio, with its richly decorated melody, provides a strong contrast. Of particular
interest are the entries of the soloist in the second and third movements on long-
held notes while the orchestra is restating its opening material.

Ex. 10-4. Haydn, Cello Concerto in C Major, Hob. VIIb:1; I. Moderato, mm. 1–2.

The C Major Cello Concerto had been lost until 1961 when it was found in
the National Museum in Prague, but the D Major Cello Concerto, Hob. VIIb:2, had
been known for years in the overly elaborate orchestration made by the Belgian
François Gevaert in the late nineteenth century. Following the discovery of
Haydn's autograph score, the concerto is now usually performed in his original
orchestration with pairs of oboes and horns added to the string orchestra. The
winds occasionally accompany the soloist, and the oboes add their tone color to
the slow movement.

The D Major Concerto was thought to have been a work by Anton Kraft
(1749–1820), but the discovery of the autograph score proved it to be by Haydn. It
was probably composed in 1781 for Kraft who was then principal cellist in the
Esterházy orchestra.

The first movement is in the mature Classical concerto-sonata form. The
orchestra states the main themes—one in the tonic (Ex. 10-5), the other in the
dominant (Ex. 10-6)—which the cellist restates in the solo exposition without
adding any new thematic material. The expected figuration is added in the transition and following the dominant key theme. Virtuoso passage work also occurs in
the development section, and a cadenza is placed at the end of the recapitulation.

Ex. 10-5. Haydn, Cello Concerto in D Major, Hob. VIIb:2; I. Allegro moderato, mm. 1–2.

Ex. 10-6. Haydn, Cello Concerto in D Major, Hob. VIIb:2; I. Allegro moderato,
mm. 13–14.

The Adagio in A major begins with a motive also heard in the first measure of the first movement (Ex. 10-7), and the rondo finale in § is based on a folklike theme. The three episodes feature the soloist in bravura passages.

Ex. 10-7. Haydn, Cello Concerto in D Major, Hob. VIIb:2; I. Adagio, mm. 1–4.

In 1786–87 Haydn composed five sprightly concertos, Hob. VIIh:1–5, for two *lire organizzate*, a sort of hurdy-gurdy. This was the favorite instrument of King Ferdinand IV of Naples who had commissioned the works for himself and a companion. The pieces, scored for two violins, two violas, cello (possibly with bass doubling), two horns, and the two *lire*, are really more ensemble works than concertos. The *lire* parts, which resemble parts for woodwinds, hardly stand out above the orchestra.

In 1790 Haydn's employer Prince Nicholas died. His successor, Prince Nicholas II, cared less for music and so allowed Haydn to travel. It was during this time that Haydn made his well-known trips to London, for which he composed his last twelve symphonies as well as other works. The charming Symphonie Concertante in B-flat Major was composed during Haydn's first visit to London in early 1792 at the urging of Salomon, who had observed the great success of Pleyel's recent works of a similar kind. Haydn chose to feature four musicians, and gave Salomon, the violinist, a slightly more important role than the others on oboe, bassoon, and cello, particularly outshining them in the finale. The orchestra is of the same size as that called for in his first six London Symphonies, consisting of one flute, pairs of oboes, bassoons (but no clarinets, which were not added to the orchestra until the time of Haydn's second visit), horns, trumpets, timpani, and the usual string section. The work is in three movements, unlike the earlier Parisian symphonie concertante.

The opening Allegro begins in a quietly lyrical way with strings and flute, before the full orchestra enters *forte*. The soloists appear in brief snatches before the main tutti is completed. Thereafter the tutti enters for only short passages to mark off important structural divisions. In general, the soloists play as an ensemble (sometimes in opposing pairs in delightful question-and-answer passages) or separately, often playing the same thematic material. Haydn seemed little interested either in exploiting the idiomatic differences of the instruments or in creating a brilliant showpiece. Some features of the first movement are also characteristic of Haydn's London Symphonies. For example, there are dramatic pauses and sudden harmonic shifts, often involving keys a third apart, as in the move from F major to D-flat major in mm. 126–168. On the whole, however, the work is nothing more than charming entertainment music, which is true even of the cadenza Haydn supplied for the four soloists at the end of the opening movement.

The songlike Andante in F major begins with a violin and bassoon duet followed by one for oboe and cello. The string orchestra, without horns, trumpets, and timpani in the movement, provides a delicate pizzicato accompaniment repeated throughout the Andante. Each soloist is highlighted, but the violinist is assigned longer segments.

The wonderfully spirited finale, marked Allegro con spirito, begins with the full orchestra's aggressive statement in unison and octaves. This is twice interrupted by an Adagio recitative for the solo violin, reminiscent of the instrumental recitative Haydn wrote for Tomasini in Symphony No. 7, thirty years earlier. Ironically, this dramatic scene leads to one of Haydn's playful final movements with a rondo-like theme. This movement is alive with the composer's characteristic delight in playing upon the audience's expectations. The recitative is repeated one more time near the end of the movement. Although this work lacks the profundity of Haydn's late symphonies and the brilliance of his solo cello concertos or trumpet concerto, it is a shame that this charming piece of music is performed so little today.

THE TRUMPET CONCERTO

Haydn's last concerto[10] is the extremely popular Concerto for Trumpet in E-flat Major composed in 1796 for his friend, Anton Weidinger (1767–1852), a trumpeter in the court orchestra in Vienna. Curiously, this concerto suffered a fate similar to that of the Cello Concerto in C Major; the Trumpet Concerto was lost from Haydn's time until 1929 when an arrangement of the work for trumpet and piano was brought out, followed two years later by the original for trumpet and orchestra.

The Trumpet Concerto is thought by many to be Haydn's greatest concerto. The newly invented keyed trumpet for which Haydn wrote this piece must have played a significant role in spurring the sixty-three-year-old composer to such a peak of creativity. Before Weidinger invented the keyed trumpet about 1793, the brass instrument's usable notes were limited to those of the natural overtone series. Baroque trumpet players had become expert at playing in the instrument's extremely high range where the natural notes occur closer together so limited melodic shapes could be played. During the Classical era this high art had died out so that trumpets were used only in their middle and lower ranges to play fanfare or martial figures and to provide harmonic and rhythmic punctuation at important cadence points in orchestral music. Weidinger's invention involved covering and uncovering holes bored into the wall of the instrument with pads operated by five keys somewhat like those on a saxophone. This innovation enabled the player to execute successive semitones, or, in other words, to play all twelve chromatic pitches. The trumpet gained its new-found freedom and flexibility at a cost, however; the holes detracted from the instrument's formerly brilliant tone. In 1813 the invention of the valved trumpet restored the brilliance while retaining the dimension of chromatic pitch, leaving the keyed trumpet to fade into oblivion. Haydn's concerto, although written for the keyed trumpet, is performed on the valved trumpet today.

When listening to this familiar work, we should try to imagine the astonishment of audiences upon hearing the formerly restricted trumpet playing lyrical lines, often involving chromaticism in its middle and lower registers. Passages such as the transition of the Andante (Ex. 10-8) demonstrate the instrument's new capabilities. In another striking passage, in the approach to the recapitulation in the first movement (mm. 115–116), the trumpet is actually supplying a chromatic bass line with a low concert C-flat, a note never before possible on the instrument. Equally astounding was the fact that it could play in the key of A-flat, the key of the middle movement.

Ex. 10-8. Haydn, Trumpet Concerto in E-flat Major, Hob. VIIe:1; II. Andante, mm. 18–22.

The symphonic handling of the large orchestra (two flutes, two oboes, two bassoons, two horns, two ripieno trumpets, timpani, and strings) mark this as a typical late Haydn work. Aside from the overtures to the oratorios, the Trumpet Concerto was his last purely orchestral composition. It displays his consummate mastery of the medium; the orchestra's importance matches the soloist's vibrant style.

This revolutionary concerto is quite compact, perhaps out of regard for the problems of stamina experienced by brass players. The first movement, in concerto-sonata form, begins with the strings, supported at the outset by horns, softly stating the main theme (Ex. 10-9), a lyrical idea far removed from the traditional martial world of trumpet music. Soon, however, the winds enter and the full orchestra, *forte*, pronounces a typical fanfare figure (m. 8). The initial tutti is quite brief (only thirty-six measures) after which the soloist restates the opening theme in expanded form, quickly taking advantage of the instrument's new-found chromatic freedom (m. 47 and mm. 55ff.). The solo trumpet plays a moderately contrasting theme in the dominant (m. 60ff.). Interesting passages display the trumpet's virtuosity in the development section, where running scale figures culminate in a very high pitch (m. 110), and near the end of the movement. Here tricky leaps, triplet figures, and scales are amply separated by rests to give the brass player's lips respite. Provision is made for a cadenza within the final tutti, which Weidinger no doubt improvised or composed on his own.

Ex. 10-9. Haydn, Trumpet Concerto in E-flat Major, Hob. VIIe:1; I. Allegro, mm. 1–4.

The Andante in A-flat major evokes a quiet pastoral mood with its lilting dotted rhythms in $\frac{6}{8}$ time, short pedal points, and use of the flute. The trumpet is given tender lines in its middle register. The short movement is in ABA form, in which the middle section veers into C-flat major, the lowered mediant of the movement's tonic. This is another example of the shifts of a third that had become characteristic of Haydn's harmonic palette during the 1790s. The exceptional dissonance in the trumpet's chromatic line at this juncture is a high point in the concerto. A chromatic passage (mm. 30–32) shortly before the return of A is similar to a passage at a parallel place in the first movement, offering some sense of unity between the movements.

The third movement begins softly, as did the first movement, with only violins and violas playing the main theme of this sonata-rondo movement. But the music soon bursts forth into what is "without any question," according to Landon "one of the most fascinating, scintillating and formally brilliant rondos that Haydn ever composed."[11] The movement is filled with the sudden unexpected harmonic twists, dynamic contrasts, and changes of direction so characteristic of Haydn's rondos of the 1790s. The finale contains brilliant solo material with some especially demanding passages. These involve awkward octave leaps moving up the scale, preceded by a rapidly descending triadic figure (Ex. 10-10) and chains of trills (mm. 249ff.). After a pause, the *pianissimo* repeat of the main theme by the trumpet, with a delicate string accompaniment in C-flat, is a totally unexpected turn executed just before the final *fortissimo* rush to the end.

Ex. 10-10. Haydn, Trumpet Concerto in E-flat Major, Hob. VIIe:1; III. Allegro, mm. 204–214.

Although Haydn's contributions to the concerto probably were not of great significance overall in the development of the form, modern trumpeters and cellists would agree that their concerto repertory would be significantly diminished were it devoid of Haydn's works for these instruments. It is through these three compositions, most particularly the trumpet work, that Haydn will remain among the notable composers of concertos in the late eighteenth century.

Chapter Eleven

LUDWIG VAN BEETHOVEN

Ludwig van Beethoven (1770–1827), the musical giant who stood astride the century change, based his music on the classical models of the late eighteenth century. But he adapted and modified those models to suit his own aesthetic needs. Many of the new principles and stylistic practices introduced or developed by Beethoven came to characterize nineteenth-century Romantic music. The later nineteenth-century composers tended to view Beethoven both as their immediate musical predecessor and as a kind of spiritual leader. No important composer of that century was able, nor genuinely wished, to escape Beethoven's influence.

His concertos, all completed by 1809, represent important stages in the development of the form in the early Romantic period; in many ways, these works were the model for much of what became characteristic of the Romantic concerto. Beethoven expanded Mozart's Classical model to epic proportions so that the soloist dominated, often as the heroic center of attention.

Beethoven's completed, mature concertos include five for piano; one for piano, violin, and cello (the Triple Concerto); and one for violin. A solo piano is a prominent element in the Choral Fantasy, Op. 80. Before turning to these works, I would like to explore briefly some incomplete concertos that demonstrate the young composer's early dedication to and mastery of the concerto form.

BEETHOVEN'S EARLY CONCERTO EFFORTS

Beethoven, in his early (Bonn) years, had developed an enviable reputation as a gifted pianist. Upon moving to Vienna in November 1792, just before turning twenty-two, Beethoven was quickly recognized as not only a great virtuoso, but also an unrivaled improviser. It was inevitable that Beethoven was compared with Mozart. Mozart was noted for his lyrical and sensitive performances, while Beethoven was acknowledged as a stronger, more aggressive performer, yet one who remained capable of executing delicate effects. Beethoven's interest in such a very broad expressive range led him to demand even more of his pianos. He never relinquished his search for the ideal instrument, and indeed went so far as to encourage one piano maker to experiment with a variety of hammers and methods of attack. Beethoven especially sought greater resonance, richness of sound, and differentiation of tone color. He experimented with various pedal mechanisms and was one of the first composers to enter specific pedal practices in his scores, often resulting in a highly unusual blending of tones or other special effects.

The piano figures prominently in Beethoven's early works; it was natural for the young virtuoso to create concertos for his own use. Beethoven's earliest surviving concerto writing dates from 1784, before his fourteenth birthday. This is the E-flat Concerto for Piano, WoO4,[1] which survives only in an incomplete form. The orchestral tutti passages appear transcribed for piano in the surviving solo part, but there is now no way to determine what material the orchestra played during the solo passages. Although the work, lacking in formal integrity and thematic interest, is that of an immature composer, it does contain elements that were to emerge in a better developed form in later works. One element worthy of note is the appearance of brilliant keyboard figuration. Another more specific element of special interest is the use of the minor mode for the second episode in the rondo, a gesture that was to remain a striking feature of Beethoven's concerto rondos.

Two other concertos are thought to have been written by Beethoven prior to his move to Vienna. One, for oboe, is lost, although several themes survive on a sheet in the Beethoven Archives in Bonn.[2] The other, for violin, exists only as a fragment of a first movement in C major (WoO5).[3] This Allegro con brio fragment dates from approximately 1790 to 1792 and consists of the opening ritornello, solo exposition, second ritornello, and beginning of the development section. The opening ritornello, almost 100 measures long, contains strongly contrasting material, interesting and abrupt modulations, and a distinct second theme group in the dominant, before closing in the tonic with a repeat of the opening fanfare. The scope of this orchestral opening points toward the more "symphonic" nature of Beethoven's later concertos. His early understanding of the violin is revealed in the beauty of its lyrical passages in the very high register, similar to those in the later D Major Concerto, Op. 61.

One or both of the Romances for Violin and Orchestra (Op. 40 in F; Op. 50 in G—both published in 1802) may originally have been intended as a slow movement for this concerto.

PIANO CONCERTOS NOS. 1–3

The first three of the five piano concertos surviving in completed form come from Beethoven's early period (prior to 1802 or 1803) and clearly relate to his appearances as a virtuoso performer:

No. 2 in B-flat Major, Op. 19
    Possibly dating back to the Bonn period, c. 1785; reworked from
    1794 to mid-March 1795; rev. 1798; solo part rev. 1801.
No. 1 in C Major, Op. 15
    1795–96; completed 1798.
No. 3 in C Minor, Op. 37
    1800; final form in 1802.

The B-flat Concerto is the earliest but is misleadingly labeled No. 2 because it was published after the C Major Concerto.

Beethoven may have completed most of the work on the B-flat Concerto at the time of completion of his earliest published sonatas of Op. 2. He first performed the concerto on 29 March 1795 in Vienna. It was performed on several later occasions in Vienna, but a Prague concert in 1798 prompted Beethoven to make further revisions.

The B-flat Concerto follows Mozart's lead with respect to formal outlines, balance between soloist and orchestra, and the basic style of the piano writing. This concerto even shares the same key and scoring (no clarinets, trumpets, or timpani) with Mozart's last piano concerto, K. 595. Some strikingly different stylistic features are present, however, so that a careful listener is not likely to confuse Beethoven's concerto with that of Mozart. Unusual key relationships are especially telling. For example, the opening ritornello contains several abrupt and compelling changes of key from B-flat major through C major to B-flat minor before returning to B-flat major. A favorite key relationship of the composer occurs in the solo exposition when the soloist repeats the new second theme in the dominant, F major, following the orchestra's presentation of the theme, and then abruptly shifts down a major third to D-flat major (m. 149).

The improvisatory entry of the piano (in m. 90) with new material seems more formal and more substantial than the little lead-in cadenzas found in some Mozart concertos. Here the new material is substantial enough to play a role in the development section (mm. 213ff.). Some of the pianistic figuration, such as in mm. 161ff., seems more characteristic of the mature Beethoven than of Mozart. The rapid movement from register to register and the doubling of lines in octaves are pianistic devices associated with Beethoven, even though their early consistent use can be traced to M. Clementi. Other imprints of Beethoven are the frequent *sf* markings, the insistent repetition of a simple rhythmic figure in the development section, a few detailed pedal markings, the emphatic dominant preparation at the end of the development section, and the *ff* return of the tonic after a *pp* passage.

The Adagio in E-flat is filled with carefully thought-out ornamentation, paradoxically creating the feeling of an improvisation. The little "cadenza" near the end of the movement consists of a most unusual single line of broken phrases in the solo instrument in dialogue with the strings. The piano part here is a fascinating experiment of a highly expressive nature that points toward much later developments in Beethoven's piano writing. This little cadenza is marked *con gran espressione* and the first portion is to be played *senza sordino*. Beethoven probably used a knee lever to raise the dampers, allowing the tone to ring and blend in a mysterious way. The mood is dramatic and quietly intense.

Whereas the second movement, especially near its conclusion, has some of the mysterious aura of the nineteenth century, the rondo finale is clearly derived from eighteenth-century sensibilities. Its playful, tuneful nature is reminiscent of Mozart and Haydn. The piano writing is nothing short of brilliant with frequent broken octaves and double thirds. Characteristically, the second episode is in minor (mm. 126ff.). Here Beethoven intensifies the *sf* syncopations associated with the main theme (Ex. 11-1a and 1b).

Ex. 11-1. Beethoven, Piano Concerto No. 2 in B-flat Major, Op. 19; III. Rondo: Molto Allegro: (a.) mm. 1–4; (b.) mm. 126–129.

Another rondo from 1795, that in B-flat major, WoO6, may have been the original finale for this concerto. It contains an unusual E-flat major Andante episode in the center, which Beethoven may have felt disturbed the movement's flow.

At the time Beethoven published his early concertos, cadenzas were still expected to be improvised by the performer, so printed scores contained no written-out cadenzas. Beethoven later came to a different point of view, including cadenzas in his scores and even composing several cadenzas for his earlier concertos. The popular cadenza for the first movement of Op. 19 was composed in 1808 or 1809, a product of Beethoven's middle period (1802–16). Not only is this cadenza typical of Beethoven's later style, but it was written for a newer form of piano with a greater range in the upper register than had been the case before 1804. The substantial cadenza opens with a fugal setting of a variation of the concerto's fanfare opening and continues with other themes from the fast movement.

The C Major Concerto, Op. 15, of slightly later date than Op. 19, requires a larger orchestra calling for the addition of clarinets, trumpets, and timpani, the brass and drums long being associated with the ceremonial key of C major. The first theme (Ex. 11-2), typical of the ceremonial style, provides the rhythmic and melodic content for much of the movement. The contrasting second theme (Ex. 11-3) appears first in E-flat major, the lowered mediant. The solo exposition presents this theme in more complete form in the expected key of G major. Beethoven cleverly combines elements of these two themes in a third thematic section of the ritornello. Note, in Ex. 11-4, how the opening octave leap of the first theme is joined to the descending eighth-note scale of the second theme, the whole new combination being presented in canon between bassoon and oboe against the upward rising sixteenth-note scale from theme 1 in the violins. This combination of motives is also heard at the opening of all three of Beethoven's cadenzas for the movement.

Ex. 11-2. Beethoven, Piano Concerto No. 1 in C Major, Op. 15; I. Allegro con brio, mm. 1–4.

Ex. 11-3. Beethoven, Piano Concerto No. 1 in C Major, Op. 15; I. Allegro con brio, mm. 49–52.

Ex. 11-4. Beethoven, Piano Concerto No. 1 in C Major, Op. 15; I. Allegro con brio, mm. 72–74.

The three cadenzas are contemporary with that for the B-flat Concerto, and, like that one, all contain notes beyond the range of the older form of the instrument for which the concertos themselves were written. The first cadenza for the C Major Concerto has not survived in complete form. The second is short. The third is exceptionally long and includes references to all the movement's themes. Near the end of this cadenza Beethoven plays with the listener's expectations by introducing a trill on the supertonic that does not cadence on the tonic, but progresses to a statement of the closing theme in the dominant. The trill appears again, is highly embellished, and then disappears in a flood of virtuosic display, leaving the cadenza to conclude without the customary trill.

The Largo movement, in A-flat major, an example of a chromatically altered submediant relative to the work's tonic, has the intimacy of chamber music and features the cantabile lines of the clarinet in response to the piano's lyricism.

The brilliant rondo finale is marked Allegro scherzando. The modifying term is one Beethoven came to use to denote playfulness and, often, a rhythmic energy. The solo presentation of the rondo theme, following Mozart's example, is a perfect illustration of Beethoven's use of Classical models. The theme has the playful, even Haydnesque, character of the eighteenth century, but the piano's presentation, with frequent double thirds, demands a level of virtuosity not common in such eighteenth-century themes (Ex. 11-5). The central episode depends upon two alternating, strongly contrasting themes. The first is a sprightly little dance tune; the second is a legato, chromatic tune in a polyphonic setting.

Ex. 11-5. Beethoven, Piano Concerto No. 1 in C Major, Op. 15; III. Rondo: Allegro scherzando, mm. 1–10.

Three little cadenzas are composed into this humorous movement, the last followed by a very curious and effectively ironic two-measure adagio passage for oboes and horns. This little passage is quite similar to a somber cadenza for oboe in the opening movement of Beethoven's Symphony No. 5 in C Minor. The oboe was often used by Beethoven to present somber, often sad tunes, and in the concerto's rollicking finale the oboe passage is a shocking intrusion. The element of surprise is relieved by the rush to the final cadence at which time the listener realizes the composer has been pulling the listener's leg.

It is difficult to date Piano Concerto No. 3 in C Minor, Op. 37, precisely. Sketches appear in the same notebooks as those for the Third Piano Sonata and the Sextet for Winds, which Beethoven composed around 1796. The autograph score of the concerto bears the date 1800, but Kinsky concludes that the final form was not fixed until 1802.[4] Even then, the piano part was not written down until 1804, one year after the first performance on 5 April 1803, at the Theater an der Wien. Seyfried, Beethoven's page turner for that performance, related that the written solo part contained "almost nothing but empty leaves . . . a few Egyptian hieroglyphics wholly unintelligible to me. . . ."[5] Ries, who performed the work on 19 July 1804 with Beethoven conducting, reported that the piano part was never completely written out in the score, so Beethoven wrote the solo part on separate sheets for him. The work was published in Vienna in late summer 1804.

Beethoven composed the concerto at the peak of his performing career, when he was widely regarded as the foremost pianist and composer of piano music of the day. He used the piano in several seminal works in the few crucial years leading up to and following the famous Heiligenstadt Testament of October 1802. In this document, the composer expressed increasing despair over his progressive and incurable deafness, and in the musical works of that period he stretched the traditional Classical forms to meet the expressive needs of his expanded musical vision. A growing sense of isolation, humiliation, and anxiety nearly led him to suicide. But a countervailing devotion to music, indeed a sense of calling, restored perspective, giving his music a greater urgency and becoming this deaf person's most effective means of communication.

These turbulent times, of which the C Minor Piano Concerto marks the beginning, were characterized by intense creative fervor. Despite the concerto's crucial role as a turning point, it is essentially built on Classical principles, though somewhat expanded in scope. In the following few years, he experimented even more boldly, forcing traditional forms into shapes better suited to his intensely conceived objectives.

The C Minor Concerto, among the earliest concertos composed in the nineteenth century, contains some of the forceful vigor characteristic of Beethoven's middle period. The opening theme in C minor is typical of this period (Ex. 11-6). It is compact and made up of very simple materials, which are amenable to intense development while passing through various keys. Particularly important is motive b, which is fragmented in the orchestra and used as a soft accompaniment to dense scale passages and brilliant figuration in the solo instrument during the development and at the end of the solo exposition.

Ex. 11-6. Beethoven, Piano Concerto No. 3 in C Minor, Op. 37; I. Allegro con brio, mm. 1–4.

The orchestra's first presentation of the contrasting theme, in the relative major, E-flat, in the opening tutti, anticipates the actual key in which it will be presented in the solo exposition. This theme is an equally typical second theme of this period—lyrical and compact (Ex. 11-7).

Ex. 11-7. Beethoven, Piano Concerto No. 3 in C Minor, Op. 37; I. Allegro con brio, mm. 50–57.

The ritornello closes in the tonic, creating such a strong feeling of finality after the modulation for the second theme that the listener hardly expects the entry of the solo instrument. The sense of expectation had been undermined by the early appearance of the contrasting theme in the contrasting key during the ritornello. Beethoven never followed this practice again.

The soloist enters with three short, introductory scales which reappear in later reentries of the piano. The pianist's traditional bravura at the conclusion of the solo exposition closes with the expected trill, but over this the orchestra surprisingly states the closing theme as a somewhat mysteriously romantic horn call, in clarinets and horns.

The coda following the cadenza is most unusual, opening with a great sense of mystery. The listener has been led to expect the orchestra to enter loudly in C minor, but it enters *pianissimo* with the C major triad. Yet a further surprise is in store, for the piano continues leading the harmony to a secondary dominant-seventh chord built on C. The timpani, in one of its earliest important roles, plays motive b. The departure from tradition here is enormous, for in the eighteenth century the soloist rarely played after the cadenza; the one noteworthy earlier exception occurs in Mozart's great C Minor Piano Concerto, K. 491.

The Largo, one of Beethoven's most extensive and highly decorated slow movements, is in the remote key of E major, the raised mediant. The boisterous rondo-finale opens with a single G in the piano, providing some harmonic shock after the final E major triad of the Largo. Beethoven exploits the conflict between G-natural and G-sharp at several places in the movement. He also includes his typical rondo episode in minor, this time in fugato style based on the main theme in F minor (mm. 230ff.)

PIANO CONCERTO NO. 4 IN G MAJOR

Beethoven's Fourth and Fifth Piano Concertos are his finest achievements in the genre and introduce several of his innovations which were to exert a lasting impact on the nineteenth-century concerto. No. 4 in G major, a key of high lyrical connotations for Beethoven, must, in many ways, have been inspired by the newly developed Viennese six-octave piano. Not only did this instrument have an additional octave at the top of the range in contrast to Beethoven's earlier pianos, but the entire character of its sound was radically altered. Whereas only the top two and a half octaves were triple-strung on his earlier five-octave piano, every note was triple-strung on the new instrument. This created increased tension, requiring heavier construction. As a result the new instrument had a wider dynamic spectrum to which Beethoven responded by broadening his notated dynamic markings from *ff–pp* to *fff–ppp*. The *una corda* pedal controlled true one-string, two-string, and three-string striking of the hammers, resulting in remarkably different timbres that cannot be duplicated on today's instrument. The damper mechanism was worked by a pedal, thus permitting greater control than the knee lever on the older five-octave piano.

Beethoven was an eager student of piano-making techniques and regularly experimented with the newest models. The "Appassionata" Sonata, Op. 57, is the first of his piano works exploiting the characteristics of the new six-octave Viennese piano. The Fourth Piano Concerto, probably begun in early 1804 and completed in March 1806, followed shortly thereafter.[6] The first performance was given in March 1807 at the Palace of Prince Lobkowitz in Vienna, with Beethoven as soloist. On the same program the premiere performances of the composer's Fourth Symphony and the *Coriolan* Overture were also given—certainly one of the more significant concerts in the history of Western music.

The Fourth Concerto is not only the most lyrical and poetic, it is in many respects his most unusual. It is the first following the Heiligenstadt Testament of October 1802, which marked a turn to new directions. The G Major Concerto appeared in that highly productive and experimental period which saw the completion of the Fourth Symphony, the Violin Concerto, the quite original Op. 59 "Razumovsky" Quartets, and the Thirty-two Variations in C Minor for Piano. The powerful and radically different "Eroica" Symphony and "Appassionata" Sonata had been completed only a few years earlier. Throughout the early portion of this experimental period, the piano served as a major source of inspiration.

The opening of the Fourth Piano Concerto is at once startling, in the context of the history of the concerto, and tranquil. We are startled by the utterance of the first sound by the solo instrument, unaccompanied. The piano presents the gentle, opening, cantabile five-bar phrase, marked *p, dolce* (Ex. 11-8). Interestingly, the distinctive rhythm of the theme is identical to that of the opening theme of the Fifth Symphony. Sketches for the two works are found side by side in Beethoven's notebooks, but it is remarkable what different moods the two themes create, the result of the difference of mode, articulation, dynamics, orchestration, and interval structure.

Ex. 11-8. Beethoven, Piano Concerto No. 4 in G Major, Op. 58; I. Allegro moderato, mm. 1–5.

Beethoven completely isolates the soloist in this daring opening, creating a dramatic gesture of enormous consequences. But the composer did not yet discard his Classical heritage and still regarded the concerto as a form in which the soloist and orchestra share on equal footing. After the solo introduction of the theme, the orchestra presents a full-scale ritornello of sixty-seven measures, and the movement generally proceeds along the lines of the Classical formal scheme.

Beethoven's attention to detail, particularly of the tonal design and thematic content, however, is fascinating. Unusual modulations enliven the opening ritornello and create extensive surface interest, while the basic key of the tonic is never felt to be absent. Beethoven saves the functional modulation to the dominant for the solo exposition. The more striking examples of unusual tonal design in the first movement are:

- the orchestra's restatement of the opening theme at the beginning of the ritornello in the distant key of B major, a third away from the original statement by piano;

- the appearance of the second theme (Ex. 11-9) of the ritornello in A minor, after a sense of movement to B-flat, and the rapid movement of this theme through a variety of keys, eventually reaching the remote region of F-sharp major;

- the curious mixture of dominant-seventh harmony over a tonic pedal at the conclusion of the opening ritornello;

- the piano's early entry at the beginning of the development with a simple, but dramatic, statement of the basic rhythmic motive on F-natural, creating a sudden shift to D minor; and

- modulations to E-flat, B-flat, and F in the traditionally stable recapitulation.

Ex. 11-9. Beethoven, Piano Concerto No. 4 in G Major, Op. 58; I. Allegro moderato, mm. 29–32.

The writing for the solo instrument is clearly beyond the world of Mozart's concertos, for Beethoven not only introduces virtuoso effects rarely heard earlier, but also makes effective use of the new upper reach of the instrument. Two very interesting examples of the latter are coupled with two of the movement's most surprising moments. In the solo exposition, prior to the modulation to the dominant, the piano introduces a new theme in the unexpected key of B-flat major over sustained string harmony. This passage, marked *pp espressivo*, has a mysterious aura created by the wide spread between the right hand, playing high notes unavailable on the older instrument, and the left hand, playing triplet arpeggiated chords in the very lowest register (Ex. 11-10). The second passage making special use of the new high range occurs at the very end of the solo exposition where the traditional closing trill leads not to the expected second tutti, but to the solo instrument's ethereal transformation of the movement's third theme (mm. 170ff.). In both these instances the instrument's new upper notes intensify the mood.

Ex. 11-10. Beethoven, Piano Concerto No. 4 in G Major, Op. 58; I. Allegro moderato, mm. 105–106.

Another passage of special interest is the beginning of the recapitulation. Here the composer engages in one of his favorite techniques by transforming the original character of the piano's gentle opening into a bold statement involving full, *sf* chords and much sixteenth-note activity in the accompaniment.

Beethoven composed two cadenzas for this movement, probably for Archduke Rudolph, in 1809–10, at the same time he composed the cadenzas for his earlier concertos. The divergence in style so evident in the cadenzas for the earlier concertos is not noticeable here, in this case because of the close proximity of composition. The longer and more brilliant cadenza for the G Major Concerto is the more popular of the two. It is based on three of the movement's four themes and vacillates between ⁶⁄₈ and common time. Once again, as in the Third Concerto, the soloist continues through the coda with lavish ornamentation in a great crescendo to the final cadence.

The Andante con moto second movement is surely one of Beethoven's most unusual creations. It is in no set instrumental form and seems to have been conceived as a quasi-operatic scene. Frequent references are found in the literature to Tovey's qualified statement that Liszt interpreted this movement as recounting the legend of Orpheus, represented by the piano, taming the Furies, represented by the orchestra.[7] Some have accepted this undocumented statement, others have questioned it, but it remained for Owen Jander to discount the fact that Liszt had anything to do with it, for Beethoven himself clearly noted that he had the Orpheus-Euridice story in mind as he composed this movement.[8] Jander, in tracing the literary and musical sources influencing Beethoven's programmatic intentions here, points to Gluck's *Orfeo ed Euridice* (1762) and Friedrich August Kanne's (1778–1833) *Orpheus* as particularly important. Kanne was an eccentric composer, poet, physician, and theologian, known to have helped Beethoven with literary matters on several occasions[9] and whose opera was apparently composed contemporaneously with Beethoven's concerto.

The movement, in E minor, the submediant, focuses on the alternation of solo and tutti in short sections marked by extreme contrast. The orchestra, reduced to strings only, begins with a powerful statement of a rhythmically fidgety staccato figure in stark unisons and octaves in the lower register. The piano's molto cantabile response, in full chords, is as different as can be imagined: Its underlying fluid lyricism and gentleness are intensified by the *una corda* pedal, effective throughout the instrument's full range, up to m. 55. The exchanges between the soloist and orchestra occur with greater frequency until the strings are gradually tamed. Their intense octave passages give way to a few widely spaced pizzicato chords, accompanying, rather than opposing, the soloist. At this moment the full range of the piano is called upon as the left hand plays arpeggios deep in the bass while the right hand plays decorations, starting in the highest octave. The composer makes this passage even more effective by calling for the sustained use of the sostenuto pedal, further magnifying the difference between the solo instrument and the pizzicato accompaniment.

A miniature cadenza is composed into the solo part, beginning with the traditional tonic ⁶⁄₄ chord in m. 51. Here Beethoven makes unusual use of the shifting pedal to increase the volume and intensity of sound and to change the color of the piano sound by shifting from *una corda* to *due corde* and then on to *tre corde*. These shifts accompany a passionate increase of activity in the piano part, with the left hand crossing back and forth over the right hand, playing fragments of chromatic scales. The cadenza ends *diminuendo*, accompanied by a return to *due* and then *una corda*. The tamed strings return, arco and *ppp*. Only the cellos and double basses state a fragment of the original dotted figure, the upper strings playing only sustained notes. The solo and orchestral forces play in full cooperation in the final four measures, the strings having forsaken the powerful staccato character of their opening phrases, assuming a sustained, supportive, rather than a combative, role.

The rondo finale begins softly, without pause, in the strange key of C major, the subdominant. In a contemporary work, the first "Razumovsky" Quartet, Op. 59, No. 1, Beethoven similarly starts the finale in the "wrong" key. The gigantic 600-measure finale of the concerto is in the form ABACBA coda, along the lines of Mozart's rondo finales. The main theme (Ex. 11-11), organized in the common aa'ba" structure, is playful and rhythmic. The alternation of tutti and solo and changes of orchestration provide interest.

Ex. 11-11. Beethoven, Piano Concerto No. 4 in G Major, Op. 58; III. Rondo: Vivace, mm. 1–10.

The movement sparkles with virtuosic display in the piano, especially in transition sections; the C section, which serves as a development section; and coda. The distinctive lyrical theme of the first episode in D major is first presented by the piano, using its new high octave. Among the many interesting passages in the movement is an extraordinary transformation of the main theme beginning in m. 366 in the *divisi* violas (Ex. 11-12). The theme is stretched out, thereby losing its rhythmic vitality, yet the intervals and thematic contour are retained throughout. Beethoven left a choice of three very short cadenzas for this movement.

Ex. 11-12. Beethoven, Piano Concerto No. 4 in G Major, Op. 58; III. Rondo: Vivace, mm. 366–376.

PIANO CONCERTO NO. 5 IN E-FLAT MAJOR

Beethoven's Piano Concerto No. 5 in E-flat Major, Op. 73, is the composer's most ambitious and is the culmination of his work in this form. It was completed in 1809, the year of Napoleon's occupation of Vienna. The war may have delayed the work's first performance, but more likely Beethoven's deafness prevented him from performing, so he delayed its presentation until Czerny could present it in Vienna on 11 February 1812. There may have been a performance a few months earlier in Leipzig.

The "Emperor" Concerto (the nickname is not Beethoven's and the origin of the name is unknown) is in the key of E-flat major, the key Beethoven associated with the expression of heroic and noble sentiments. It contains march motives, strong melodies, and other "military" qualities, but lacks the shallow, bombastic virtuoso displays that had become popular among other composers of the period. To be sure, the solo part is exceptionally virtuosic, abounding in such techniques as broken octaves and staccato passages doubled in demanding octaves. But the virtuoso element is not shallow; Beethoven uses it as a dramatic technique to develop the musical material.

Many of the musical devices with which Beethoven experimented in the Fourth Concerto are found in the Fifth, but in a more developed form. The soloist steps boldly to the front at the very beginning; the age of the virtuoso concerto is upon us. The enormous first movement (582 measures of $\frac{4}{4}$ time, Allegro) begins with a decisive tonic chord in the full orchestra followed by a rhapsodic, improvisatory, cadenza-like passage for the soloist. The subdominant and dominant chords are equally decisively stated by the orchestra and embellished by the piano, leaving no doubt that this will be a work of heroic proportions calling for nothing short of a brilliant performance by the soloist. The dashing, iridescent style of this opening was to be imitated repeatedly by dozens of nineteenth-century concerto composers.

Immediately following the initial "cadenza" is a normal orchestral ritornello of approximately 100 measures. It presents the main material, comprised of five distinct themes, all handled along the lines of the traditional concerto-sonata form. The opening theme in E-flat major, itself made of three distinct rhythmic ideas (Ex. 11-13), is first presented by the violins in their low register accompanied by tremolando second violins and violas. Horns and lower strings reinforce motive c. This theme is made the focus of the development with motive c the most persistent element (see strings, mm. 294–303; winds and piano, mm. 304–311; and bassoon, mm. 314–333).

Ex. 11-13. Beethoven, Piano Concerto No. 5 in E-flat Major, Op. 73; I. Allegro, mm. 11–17.

The second subject undergoes several interesting variations throughout the movement, often changing from minor to major mode. It is first heard played by violins in a staccato version, *pianissimo*, in minor (mm. 41–48), then is immediately taken up by horns and presented in a legato major form (mm. 49–56, Ex. 11-14). In the solo exposition this theme is first heard in B minor in the solo instrument over a delicate pizzicato accompaniment. An ethereal enharmonic modulation to C-flat major, anticipating the key of the climax of the development, occurs before the orchestra gives out the theme, *forte*, as a march in B-flat major, the movement's dominant. The same sequence of events transpires in the recapitulation, but the keys involved are C-sharp minor, D-flat major, and E-flat major, and the latter, the movement's tonic, permits the use of trumpets and horns to enhance the martial character of the transformed theme.

Ex. 11-14. Beethoven, Piano Concerto No. 5 in E-flat Major, Op. 73; I. Allegro, mm. 49–56.

The reentry of the piano in preparation for the solo exposition is quite effective. The piano is reintroduced early with a rising chromatic scale passage over dominant harmony before the actual solo exposition begins, paralleling the early solo entry in the G Major Piano Concerto. This surprise reentry is also used to mark the beginning of the development, at which time the chromatic scale is doubled in both hands. Another extraordinary place in the movement occurs following the traditional tonic six-four-chord preparation for a cadenza. But instead of leaving room for an improvised cadenza, Beethoven composes directly into the score a substitute passage for the soloist. This passage incorporates the traditional trill on the supertonic, but the trill concludes in yet another surprise: The soloist, not the orchestra, provides the cadence and begins the substantial coda, which amounts to another recapitulation of the ritornello based on the second theme and succeeding material. As in Beethoven's earlier concertos, the piano is present to the end.

As is true of many nineteenth-century concertos, the slow movement is comparatively brief, since the tempo is not well-suited for virtuoso showmanship. The Adagio un poco mosso is in B major, the key of the first remote modulation in the first movement and the enharmonic equivalent of C-flat major, the emphasized key in the development section of the first movement. The Adagio is delicately scored, beginning with muted strings and avoiding strong contrasts of orchestral sound. The writing for the piano has a strongly improvisatory quality as the piano plays material based on the opening theme, often without clearly stating it. The movement has the overall effect of a set of variations.

A magical and compelling moment occurs at the end of the slow movement. Here Beethoven has composed one of his most dramatic links to a succeeding movement. All instruments reach B-natural, the tonic note of the movement, which then sinks a semitone to B-flat, the dominant of the final movement's tonic. Over this B-flat pedal in the horns, the piano in adagio tempo hints at the finale's rondo theme, before it bursts out in the allegro tempo of the finale.

The Allegro $\frac{6}{8}$ finale is another huge movement based on a powerful syncopated theme, first presented by the soloist, as usual (Ex. 11-15). Only one thematically contrasting episode appears, both times starting in the tonic and presented by the piano. The huge middle episode includes three false starts of the main theme in the keys of C, A-flat, and E major, an interesting sequence of lower thirds. Each of these false starts leads to a brilliant solo display. The principal return of the rondo theme in m. 328 is prepared by an echo of the final bars of the slow movement. Only here the piano plays the dominant pedal in trills, while the violins prefigure the theme. The coda includes a stirring passage of seventeen measures for piano and timpani alone.

Ex. 11-15. Beethoven, Piano Concerto No. 5 in E-flat Major, Op. 73; III. Rondo: Allegro, mm. 1–4.

In the years immediately following the completion of the "Emperor" Concerto in 1809, Beethoven wrote little for the piano. His last public appearance as pianist was in the same year. His deafness may well have been the reason he turned away from the instrument for a few years. But beginning in 1814 he again wrote intensively for the piano, completing his first sonata (Op. 90) since 1809 (Op. 81a). In the following year he tried his hand at another piano trio and piano concerto. Neither of these was completed—only fragments and sketches for a concerto in D major remain.[10] The mighty "Emperor" remained his last completed concerto.

THE VIOLIN CONCERTO

I have focused on the concerto for keyboard instruments, especially the piano, in tracing the history of the Classical concerto of the late eighteenth and early nineteenth centuries, in part because, in most of the musical centers of Europe, the violin had become the second favored instrument, although in some places, such as Paris, it still dominated. The differing natures of the piano and violin prompted composers to write concertos for each in contrasting ways. More specifically:

- The inherent contrast between the sound of the piano and that of the orchestra is absent in a violin concerto, which pits a principal orchestral instrument against the orchestra.

- To compensate for the difficulty of making the solo violin stand out from the orchestra, composers tend to place the solo violin part in its high registers, clearly separated in range from the orchestral violins. This also allows the solo violin more effectively to penetrate heavier accompaniments. Composers of piano concertos do not have this problem, and the piano can easily occupy the same tonal range as the orchestra.

- By the early 1800s piano makers had developed a powerful instrument capable of producing a very large volume of sound. The simple fact of its enhanced sound-making capacity allowed the piano to better compete with the orchestra. Orchestral accompaniments for solo violin passages generally require a thinner and lighter texture, while those for the more powerful piano can be denser and more complex.

- The violin, unable to accompany itself effectively except in the most unusual circumstances, is usually provided with an orchestral accompaniment. The piano, on the other hand, can accompany itself, permitting long and attractive solo passages without the assistance of the orchestra. Composers exploited this possibility in the presentation of new themes in the second key area of the solo exposition and in lively exchanges between the orchestra and piano in development sections. Obviously this form of writing allows composers to intensify the degree of contrast between orchestra and soloist in a piano concerto. This means of contrast is far less common in violin concertos.

These differences, all the result of idiomatic instrumental considerations, account for the composition of violin concertos which are, in general, less dramatic than those for the piano. In addition, greater emphasis is placed on the lyrical, songlike quality of the violin. Beethoven's D Major Violin Concerto, Op. 61, clearly illustrates those differences in comparison with his works for the piano in this form.

Beethoven sketched and completed the Violin Concerto in the second half of 1806, the same year as the G Major Piano Concerto. The young violinist Franz Clement, for whom Beethoven had composed the piece, was the leader of the Theater an der Wien orchestra. He had known Beethoven since he was a boy and had conducted the first performance of the "Eroica" Symphony. Clement was the soloist in the Violin Concerto's first performance, 23 December 1806. The performance was rough—there had been no rehearsal as the parts were not ready in time—which may account for the virtual oblivion into which the work passed for nearly thirty-five years before Pierre Baillot (1771–1842) revived it and gave it its first Paris performance on 23 March 1842. Joseph Joachim subsequently discovered the work and was responsible for establishing it in the standard repertory with his first performance in 1852. Joachim's cadenza for the first movement is favored by most violinists to this day.

Though Beethoven was a pianist, he had studied violin in his youth and had developed a clear understanding of the instrument's character and potential. This is evident in his early chamber works and in the substantial fragment of a Violin Concerto in C Major, WoO5, composed in the early 1790s. Furthermore, Beethoven was familiar with the playing of several of the leading figures in the French school of violin playing: Giovanni Battista Viotti (1755–1825) and his great disciples, all of whom Beethoven knew, Pierre Rode (1774–1830), Rodolphe Kreutzer (1766–1831) and Pierre Baillot. According to Boris Schwarz, the noted historian of violin music, Beethoven borrowed idiomatic features of French violin music, but transformed them from simple virtuosic display devices to embellishments of profound musical ideas.[11]

Schwarz cites several specific similarities between Beethoven's treatment of the violin in Op. 61 and his French models, but particularly stresses that the march-like character of movement I most closely links Beethoven to the French school. Indeed Beethoven used the characteristic march-like opening in other works, including the opening movement of the "Emperor" Concerto, as did other Viennese composers in their orchestral works as well. A more general trait possibly linking Beethoven to the French violin school is the practice of initiating the third movement of a concerto immediately, and without pause, on the completion of the second movement, as was noted in the discussion of Beethoven's Fourth and Fifth Piano Concertos. This practice also occurs in the Violin Concerto, Op. 61. But an obvious difference can also be noted: The slow movements of most French violin concertos of this period were both brief and little embellished. (Recall that the eighteenth-century French composers of symphonies concertantes often omitted slow movements altogether, since they were not well suited to the highly virtuosic goals or lighter character expected by French audiences.) Beethoven, on the other hand, lavished much attention on his slow movements, which typically are complex and profound; certainly that of the Violin Concerto is no exception.

In spite of the profound music Beethoven wrote for the violin, he never exceeded conventional violin technique, although, according to Schwarz, his writing for the instrument is comparatively unidiomatic.[12] Schwarz points out that Beethoven showed no interest in the various bold strokes then in common currency; he avoided, almost entirely, double stops, and did not exploit the (low) G string except in the finale's rondo theme and the coda statement of the first movement's lyrical second theme, preferring instead the (high) E string. In general, Beethoven made only modest demands on the soloist, and the more elaborate passages are rarely written for mere display, but rather as elaborations of material presented in the orchestra.

The opening movement of the Violin Concerto contains a wealth of thematic material, mostly of a lyrical nature with little contrast, as is the case with the opening movements of the Fourth Piano Concerto and Triple Concerto, both from this period. The themes of the Violin Concerto not only share a similar quality of lyricism, but the three most important (Ex. 11-16) also share a common rhythmic idea first presented in mm. 8–9 of the main theme (Ex. 11-16a).

Ex. 11-16. Beethoven, Violin Concerto, Op. 61; I. Allegro, ma non troppo: (a.) Theme 1. mm. 1–9; (b.) Theme 2. mm. 43–46; (c.) Theme 3. mm. 77–79.

Although the themes lack strong contrast from one to another, Beethoven introduces contrast *within* some thematic statements. For example, the stark five-quarter-note opening motive in the timpani provides contrast within the opening theme—first the drum motive alternates with lyric phrases in the woodwinds; subsequently, when violins take up the theme, the drum motive initiates an unexpected harmonic shift. It also serves as an accompaniment to the second theme (Ex. 11-16b), much as the outstanding rhythmic motive of the opening movement of the Fifth Symphony underlies that movement's second theme. Beethoven also introduces another level of contrast in the statement of the second theme, as it is immediately repeated in minor in the strings, after its first appearance in major in the winds.

Beethoven achieves thematic contrast later in the movement by resorting to thematic transformation as he brings some themes back in a stronger version. For example, the second theme's character is altered in the second ritornello, and the *dolce* first theme, with its gentle accompanying drum beat, becomes more strident when stated by the full orchestra at the beginning of the recapitulation.

In addition to these interesting features, the first movement has numerous striking moments, including:

- shocking harmonic shifts, exemplified by the strange introduction of the D-sharp in m. 10 or the sudden move to F major, after A major, at the beginning of the second ritornello;

- the thirteen-measure improvisatory entry of the soloist over a dominant pedal, following the full orchestral ritornello and preceding the solo exposition;

- the unusual treatment of important solo trills, which had traditionally indicated the conclusions of major solo sections (Beethoven often uses these trills to launch extraordinary extensions to solo sections, as at the end of the solo exposition; here the orchestra introduces the drum motive underneath the solo trill, and the trill moves chromatically upward to complex scale passages before the second ritornello explodes on the scene in the unexpected key of F major);

- the solo instrument's introduction of a new, tender idea in the development, to the accompaniment of horns sounding the drum motive (mm. 330ff.);

- the soloist appearance in the coda, following the cadenza, as in several of Beethoven's piano concertos. (Here the solo violin engages in a lovely duet with bassoon.)

The G major Larghetto of the Violin Concerto features a dialogue between the soloist and orchestra, made colorful through the exquisite use of clarinet, bassoon, horn, and muted strings. The movement, in essence a theme with four variations, remains centered in G major. A new theme in the same key is introduced, however, after the third variation, and a subsequent variation on this secondary theme occurs after the intervening variation on the original theme. Before the movement's end, muted horns play the distinctive opening motive, *ppp*, accompanied only by filigree of the solo violin—an innovative scoring detail that creates a strongly romantic feeling. A purposeful, angry-sounding, string recitative pulls the music to the dominant of D major and prepares for the soloist's improvised link to the final movement.

The finale is a rondo of standard design, ABACABA, with a substantial coda and Beethoven's typical minor-mode second episode. All the thematic material is simple and tuneful, while some of the transitional passages contain the most overtly virtuosic passages in the concerto, complete with double stops. The $\frac{6}{8}$ rondo theme presented by the solo violin in its lowest range, one of the few exposed uses of the G string, evokes the quality of a rollicking peasant dance, while the *delicatamente* repeat in the solo violin's upper register provides an element of humorous contrast. As in places in the first two movements, Beethoven treats cadential trills in an unusual manner. The trill at the conclusion of the improvised cadenza is written into the score and shifts chromatically to the very distant key of A-flat major for a statement of the first theme. Eventually D major is restored, and oboe and violin engage in a dialogue on the first theme, prior to the dazzling rush to the end.

From the first appearance of the Violin Concerto, pianists expressed interest in it, and Muzio Clementi finally succeeded, through his persistence, in convincing Beethoven to create a version for piano. It was completed in 1807 and was actually published prior to the original violin version. Beethoven did not alter the orchestral part in the new arrangement, but adjusted the solo part to the idiomatic requirements of the piano, in particular augmenting the use of the keyboard's lower register. Beethoven eventually composed cadenzas for the piano version; an innovative one for the first movement includes a part for timpani on the distinctive rhythm of the opening theme.

THE TRIPLE CONCERTO IN C MAJOR, OP. 56, AND THE CHORAL FANTASY, OP. 80

In 1803–04 Beethoven composed his Triple Concerto for violin, cello, and piano and orchestra, fusing the concerto with a popular medium of chamber music—the piano trio. It is probably the first of a number of works Beethoven wrote for Archduke Rudolph, then fifteen or sixteen years old. The soloists Beethoven had in mind were probably violinist Carl August Seidler, cellist Anton Kraft, and the Archduke as pianist. Kraft, the lead cellist of Haydn's Esterházy orchestra and a great virtuoso cellist of the time, was given not only the most prominent role but also the lead in all the solo sections. Many cellists regard the concerto as one of the most taxing works in the instrument's repertory.

The Triple Concerto is from one of Beethoven's most productive and highly experimental periods. In 1803 he completed the expansive "Kreutzer" Sonata, Op. 47, reflecting a different fusion of concerto and chamber music elements, in some ways like a double concerto for piano and violin without orchestra. The extremely different "Waldstein" Sonata is exactly contemporary with Op. 56, and Beethoven interrupted work on the most radical of the works of this period, the "Eroica" Symphony, to concentrate on the Triple Concerto. Unfortunately, the Triple Concerto does not equal its contemporaries in stature. Like those other works, the Triple Concerto is very long, but its length is its major drawback. Beethoven seems to have wanted to share the lyrical melodic material among the solo instruments, without developing his ideas in his normal fashion. The work is built upon statement and restatement, but the themes are not strong enough to hold the listener's attention throughout. The opening movement is particularly long and tedious, with more than a third of the development comprising literal repetitions of thematic material. The slow movement is short; further, as in Beethoven's subsequent solo concertos, the slow movement is linked directly to the finale.

Beethoven composed the Choral Fantasy in 1808 as a grand finale to the concert in which his fifth and sixth symphonies and the Piano Concerto No. 4 were first performed in public. The Choral Fantasy is a twenty-minute, single-movement work for orchestra, chorus, and solo piano. In some respects it is a light precursor of the monumental choral finale of the Ninth Symphony. Like that movement, the Choral Fantasy is largely a set of variations on a theme similar to the "Ode to Joy" theme. In both works, the chorus is used as a climactic resource, but in Op. 80 the choral part is generally slight. Only in several isolated moments does the chorus exhibit the power that the Ninth Symphony would summon.

The Choral Fantasy begins with solo piano in an improvisatory fantasia of three to four minutes' duration. Beethoven actually improvised this portion at the first performance—his last public performance as pianist. He did not provide the fantasia in written form until the following year.

BEETHOVEN'S CONTRIBUTIONS AND INFLUENCE

Beethoven began his writing for the concerto with the conception of proportion and balance characteristic of Mozart. As he gained familiarity with the form, he called for increasing levels of virtuosity in the solo parts, without diminishing the importance of the orchestra. Indeed, in many ways he also demanded more of the orchestra, so the concerto became quite symphonic in nature. Beethoven increasingly wished to cast the soloist as an heroic figure, and therefore introduced the soloist at the outset of the last two piano concertos. Despite this departure from tradition, he followed these innovative introductions with standard ritornello structures in the opening movements. In the slow movements, Beethoven followed the practice of his contemporaries by reducing their size in comparison with the outer movements. However, unlike his contemporaries, he experimented with highly innovative middle-movement structures in which the content is of unusual profundity and in which special emphasis is placed on interesting and uncommon sonorities. Beethoven linked the slow movement directly to the final movement, without pause, in four of his later concertos—the Triple Concerto, the Violin Concerto, and Piano Concerto No. 4 and No. 5. He retained the air of the brilliant, light-hearted eighteenth-century rondo finale, but he also changed it. He expanded its size and virtuosic scope, and introduced greater contrast and an increased level of tension by placing the second episode in a minor key. Further, Beethoven treated in highly original ways the solo trills that had traditionally marked conclusions to important solo sections, including cadenzas, often using those trills as entries into striking expansions of the solo sections.

Beethoven's innovations and approach to the concerto exerted a powerful influence on his successors. The notion of beginning a concerto with explosive soloistic bravura, as in the "Emperor" Concerto, became extremely popular. Dozens of nineteenth-century concertos contain slow movements that lead directly into the fast finales. And Beethoven's experimentation with the musical interrelationships among movements became a standard practice. But in spite of Beethoven's strong influence and the interest of many of his followers in his innovations, most later nineteenth-century composers were to depart radically from the Classical tradition which informed Beethoven's genius.

Part III

THE ROMANTIC CONCERTO

THE VIRTUOSO CONCERTO

The concerto, like any other viable musical form, changed to reflect changing tastes over time. In the early decades of the nineteenth century, musical audiences seemed increasingly to seek sensational display, and composers looked for ways to satisfy their demands. This tendency was particularly noticeable in works intended for performance in the larger concert halls which were also an early nineteenth-century response to the burgeoning middle class's growing demands for concerts. The role of the composer likewise started to change in this period, as composers pursued careers as freelance composers and touring artists rather than holding appointments as court musicians. In this new situation musicians had to create works that were not only accessible but also exciting to the generally less-sophisticated middle-class listener.

An increased preoccupation with the individual and his or her emotional sensibilities was at the heart of the Romantic movement. Perhaps the concerto soloist represented this new sense of the individual's importance in society, and thus gained greater prominence. If the soloist stepped forward as an heroic figure, the orchestra slipped back to a more subordinate role. Such a basic change of approach and roles led composers to make numerous revisions in the form.

Following Beethoven's lead, composers introduced the heroic figure at the outset of the work, thereby clearly identifying the musician in charge. Many composers eventually discarded the old ritornello form entirely, relying instead on a loose sonata-allegro form for first movements in which the soloist played virtually throughout. The solo instrument both presented thematic material and played virtuoso figuration while accompanying the orchestra during its presentation of thematic material. The old tension between orchestra and soloist was replaced by a nearly continuous use of a brilliant solo part set against a generally subdued orchestra. Slow movements, inherently poorly suited as vehicles for virtuoso display, tended to be short, viewed simply as introductions to the very fast and highly virtuosic finales. Indeed, following Beethoven's example, composers often linked the slow movement to the finale without pause, thereby accentuating the view of the slow movement's function as introductory to the finale. Final movements had always been the most brilliant in a concerto, and nineteenth-century practice only heightened this tendency.

Cadenzas also underwent change. They still appeared as important vehicles for display, but instead of relying on the solo performer to improvise the cadenza as in the past, composers increasingly wrote them to maintain control over the final product and particularly to control a most virtuosic element. Since the old ritornello form had been replaced by other less carefully defined forms—or, at least, forms that did not depend upon a vigorous contrast between orchestra and soloist—a new place for the cadenza had to be found. Early nineteenth-century composers experimented with placing the cadenza in a variety of places in the movement, often integrating this traditional moment for intense virtuoso display into the work's larger form. Some composers even experimented with accompanied cadenzas.

Several composers, exploring new modes of expression, preferred to write works for solo instrument and orchestra that avoided any of the formal problems associated with the concerto. These works were concerto-like in featuring a solo instrument in an orchestral setting, but they were largely single-movement works in variation or rondo form, the latter often utilizing elements of variation technique. Both variation and rondo form commonly employed simple, often popular or at least familiar thematic material, such as well-known operatic airs. This kind of material provided the perfect foundation for the extensive use of dazzling displays of virtuoso figuration, which could be readily and meaningfully organized within the regular constraints of these forms. Variation form in particular is perfectly suited to showcase virtuosic display, as each variation could be loaded with a different pattern of virtuoso figuration. Although many of these works now seem trite, some were masterfully created and have had both lasting musical impact and a history of continuing performance. These single-movement concerto-like works were particularly popular in the 1820s, but the form has remained viable to the present day.

The concerto, of course, shared the tidal changes in general musical style and taste that marked the nineteenth century. For example, a new intensity of musical expression surfaced in a great fondness for the minor mode. Few concertos of the eighteenth century were composed in the minor mode, but a majority of nineteenth-century concertos were. Other significant stylistic changes are found in a sharper focus on thematic content and a strong predilection for the evocative effect of tone color, which gave that element new importance.

The piano was considered the queen of the instruments. Much had been done by early nineteenth-century builders to perfect the instrument; it gained a very wide range of expression, including the ability to mimic certain orchestral effects, yet all within the control of a single performer. The piano was perfectly suited to the romantic temperament. Second to this supreme solo instrument in concertos of the period was the violin, with its marvelous capacity, in the hands of a virtuoso, to produce extended, passionate melodic passages of great intensity. Well down in third place was the cello. Most works that have remained in the repertory were written by outstanding composer-performers for their own use, although a notable exception is Brahms's violin concerto composed for Joseph Joachim, friend of the composer.

Although Beethoven's fourth and fifth piano concertos clearly exerted a powerful influence on his successors, the concertos of his contemporaries are also important roots of the nineteenth-century virtuoso concerto. Particularly significant contributions were made by the violinists and pianists of Paris and London, where the better- and longer-established concert traditions encouraged interesting developments in the concerto before and shortly after the turn of the century. Contemporary pianists active in Vienna also helped to lay the groundwork for the virtuoso tradition of the nineteenth century.

PARIS

As we saw in Chapter 8, the violin had been the dominant instrument in the symphonie concertante of eighteenth-century Paris, a position the instrument retained even as the symphonie concertante gave way to the solo concerto.

G. B. Viotti (1753–1824) was another of the Italian-born composers to make his mark while living in France, which he did from 1782 to 1791. The crowning figure of the French Classical school as well as the herald of new trends in the nineteenth-century violin concerto, he composed twenty-nine concertos for violin. All are brilliant, demandingly virtuosic works that demonstrate the advance in playing technique that earned Viotti the title "Father of Modern Violin Playing."

Viotti's concertos span the stylistic changes from the *galant* to the deeply Romantic, yet all but the final two were composed before the turn of the century. The opening movements are generally in concerto-sonata form; middle movements are elaborate romances; and the final movements, rondos. The first twelve belong to an early *galant* phase, while the next seven, composed between 1788 and 1791, introduce a new style which calls for more symphonic treatment of the orchestra, especially in the opening tuttis, as well as calling for more elaborate solo parts. Several are in the minor mode, the expressive power of which is carried over into the rondo finales of Concerto No. 17, No. 18, and No. 19, an unusual practice, since the rondo is typically light-hearted. All share a quality recalling contemporary works of the young Beethoven. Mozart was especially fond of No. 16 in E Minor and provided it with an enriched orchestration for Viennese performances.

Viotti also lived in London from 1792 to 1798, during which time he was a featured soloist in Johann Peter Salomon's concert series, often sharing the limelight with Salomon's famous visitor, Haydn. Eight of Viotti's last ten concertos were written in the 1790s and the last two in the very early 1800s. All employ a more lively orchestration, possibly the result of his exposure to Haydn's symphonic music. Elements of these late works anticipate what were to become common Romantic formal devices intended to achieve greater unity in multimovement works. Some movements are linked without pause; themes first articulated in the opening movement are recalled in later movements; and sometimes a slow introduction (in itself an unusual feature of some Romantic concertos) hints strongly at thematic material in the fast movement to follow. No. 28 includes an accompanied cadenza, a feature that was to appear more frequently in the nineteenth century.

Viotti's highly idiomatic writing for the violin reveals a continuing concern to produce strong, clear sonorities. He avoided awkward leaps and double stops in the upper register, preferring to write double stops in the more secure lower register with open strings to enhance the sound. He used a variety of bowings to excellent effect.

Viotti's impact on early nineteenth-century French violin playing was great (we noted his influence on Beethoven's Violin Concerto in Chapter 11). Indeed Viotti's influence can be traced in most violin concertos of the first half of the nineteenth century and was still felt in the second half of the century in the music of Brahms. Brahms and his violinist friend, Joachim, greatly admired the music of Viotti, holding in particularly high esteem his Concerto No. 22 in A Minor, which is alluded to in both of Brahms's works for Joachim—the Violin Concerto and the Double Concerto for Violin and Cello.

Three of Viotti's leading French disciples also contributed significantly.

Pierre Rode (1774–1830), perhaps Viotti's prize student, made his Paris debut at the age of sixteen playing a concerto by Viotti. Rode traveled widely and in so doing acquainted much of Europe with Viotti's new style of violin playing. Among Rode's more important compositions are thirteen violin concertos which are technically somewhat more demanding of the soloist than those of Viotti, while displaying a thorough idiomatic understanding of the instrument.

Rodolphe Kreutzer (1766–1831) was reputed to be a more powerful and rugged performer than his elegantly polished friend, Rode. Kreutzer's nineteen concertos, completed by about 1809, require a quite different technique to perform. They make frequent use of trills, exposed arpeggios, tricky double stops, and a variety of bowings. At times his concertos are rather dry, a feature replaced at other moments by genuine melodic warmth. His last two concertos, No. 18 in E Minor and No. 19 in D Minor, represent the best of those of his generation of French violin composers.

Pierre-François Baillot (1771–1842), the third of Viotti's notable pupils, was best known for his powerful talents in interpreting the music both of contemporary composers and of the eighteenth-century masters. Baillot wrote nine concertos in the traditional form. Several follow the standard character of the French violin concerto, but several are much more intimate, stressing musical rather than virtuoso values. His finales are all cast in the usual rondo form, but often with an exotic coloring, such as the polonaise. This nationalistic coloring of the finales, with their rustic, folklike dance quality, became commonplace in the nineteenth-century concerto for violin.

LONDON

For years London had offered the outstanding professional musician, particularly the pianist, great opportunities. The city enjoyed a well-developed concert tradition into which new series were regularly introduced to serve the highly appreciative and growing audiences. For example, in 1783, two of the great pianists of this period, Muzio Clementi and Johann Baptist Cramer, together with the violinist Johann Peter Salomon, were responsible for starting a new series, Professional Concerts, to feature professional musicians in performances of new works. J. C. Bach had organized a concert series earlier (1765–81) with his friend C. F. Abel. As we saw in Chapter 8, it was during this period that the London Bach is thought to have been, in 1768, the first to play the piano in a public concert and to popularize the instrument in the following decade.

London was to become not only a major center of piano making but also a leading source of innovation, for London builders were noted for inventing and installing significant new technical features. Several firms built pianos in late eighteenth-century London, the most important of which was Broadwood, founded in the 1770s, the oldest firm of keyboard makers still in existence today. London was also a principal center of the music publishing industry.

These factors worked together to attract to London numerous musicians, particularly pianists, in search of fame and fortune. Until about the middle of the nineteenth century, most played music of their own composition. These performer-composers created a body of music that, although little known today, made major contributions to the development of an idiomatic style that was to characterize much nineteenth-century piano music. The transitional figures of this London school were particularly significant in developing a better understanding of the piano and its idiomatic potential. Some were justifiably singled out for their creation of a singing legato style impossible to realize on the harpsichord. Several made important innovations in the use of the pedals. Many contributed to the exciting new virtuoso techniques particularly well-suited to the new keyboard music. Because of the emphasis on technical display, much of the music of this period in London now seems shallow, and so only rarely is performed in concert. On the other hand, present-day teachers still use the published exercises of several of these keyboard artists to give students a firm grounding in the technique and art of piano playing. The technical innovations of these keyboard composers were ultimately incorporated into standard piano writing and playing techniques and had an obvious impact on the history of the piano concerto.

Muzio Clementi (1752–1832) was born in Rome but moved to England in 1774. Clementi, the first great piano virtuoso, knew Haydn, Mozart, and Beethoven. His music is largely cast in the Classical style, but with clear and strong premonitions of the coming Romantic style. Clementi was the first performer-composer to comprehend clearly the differences between the harpsichord and the piano. By virtue of this insight he developed a keyboard style and pianistic techniques that were to become standard in nineteenth-century virtuoso piano writing. Important techniques include octave melodies with triadic accompaniments; rapidly repeated notes; rapidly executed chains of double thirds, sixths, and octaves; fast scales; arpeggios; and rich, orchestral chords, especially in the low register. Paradoxically some of these techniques occur in the idiomatic harpsichord music of Domenico Scarlatti (1685–1750), but Clementi transformed them into a true piano style. Clementi was also involved in the business of the manufacture and sale of pianos as well as music publishing. Only one concerto by Clementi is extant, dating from 1795 or earlier, and it is in the standard classical form.

Jan Ladislav Dussek (1760–1812) spent his early life in Prague before traveling to Amsterdam and Paris. He fled Paris at the time of the French Revolution and spent the next eleven years, until 1799, in London, where he reached his compositional maturity.

Dussek was one of the first touring concert artists; numerous audiences experienced the powerful impact of his awesome piano style. In addition to the continuing display of virtuosity—such as fast figures for both hands, rapid changes of direction, large leaps, and fast arpeggios and scales over several octaves—Dussek's piano music is characterized by a fullness of sonority that probably related to the well-rounded, rich sound of the London-made pianos he used. This fullness of sound anticipates the style of the German composers Weber and Mendelssohn. Dussek was the first to play the new six-octave piano in public in 1794. He also explored the possibilities of the pedals; their use in his music predates that by most other composers. As an artist quite aware of his impact on audiences, Dussek is credited with being the first to place his right side to the audience. This was a more dramatic position than that of most keyboard artists who faced the audience from behind the instrument. Dussek composed some fifteen concertos in the conventional Classical form, although the figurative content is more elaborate. The highly decorative slow movement of the E-flat Concerto anticipates the style of Chopin.

Johann Baptist Cramer (1771–1858) came to London from Mannheim as a small child with his family in 1774. Cramer studied with Clementi, becoming a brilliant pianist noted for his legato touch and singing style, qualities of piano playing the later Romantics especially appreciated. Cramer's eighty-four technical studies, published in two sets in 1804 and 1810 as *Studio per il pianoforte*, were among the earliest publications designated specifically for the instrument. These studies, still played by pianists today, demonstrate Cramer's creative use of figuration perfectly suited to the instrument. Cramer composed nine concertos from approximately 1795 to 1822. All combine a Classical sense of form with a newly extensive exploitation of idiomatic passage work for the solo instrument.

John Field (1782–1837), an Irishman who moved to London in 1793 where he studied with Clementi, spent most of his active career in Russia after 1802. Field was renowned not only for his light, graceful touch, but also for his development of a very original style of idiomatic decoration that seems to have little connection with any previous keyboard style. He made use of the pedals to blend harmonies, and he created rich passage work. In addition to the usual sonatas and chamber music, Field also wrote nocturnes, which clearly provided models for Chopin. In these slow lyric pieces the right hand characteristically has a beautifully rich and sensuous melodic line, played over the accompanying left hand's smooth, wide-ranging, undulating arpeggios.

Field's seven concertos were published between 1814 and 1835, but we know he played one of his own composition as early as 1799. Typical of Field's approach, these concertos depend not on the virtuoso display so fashionable at the time, but rather on a deeply felt lyricism. The orchestral tuttis seem almost Classical in design, but the solo parts are Romantic in conception, the consequence of his profound understanding of the lyrical and sonorous potential of the piano. The slow movements are very much like his solo piano nocturnes, with simple orchestral accompaniments.

Field performed his Concerto No. 1 in E-flat Major, his favorite key, in London in 1799 and again in Russia in 1804. It is colored with material associated with the British Isles: The slow movement is a set of variations on an air by James Hook, "Twas within a Mile of Edinburgh Town," in which some of the variations are presented in the character of a nocturne. The finale makes use of bagpipe imitations with its long drones.

Frédéric Kalkbrenner (1785–1849), a French pianist of German extraction, spent most of his career in Paris where he was one of the early great students at the Paris Conservatory, but his ten years in London from 1814 to 1824 were central to the development of his reputation. Following his stay in London, he enjoyed one of the most successful careers of any touring virtuoso of the time. Kalkbrenner began by composing in the somewhat Classical tradition of the generation of Clementi, Dussek, and Cramer, but by the 1820s his music resembled Hummel's, with a generous helping of virtuosity. And in keeping with this predilection for the technical, he had little interest in lyric beauty. He composed four concertos for one piano, one double piano concerto, and a number of shorter works for piano and orchestra in variation or rondo forms.

Ignaz Moscheles (1794–1870), the Czech composer, made a great splash in London, filling the vacuum created by Kalkbrenner's departure. He started in London, in 1825, as a true virtuoso in the Clementi tradition, but soon developed a style later compared to that of Mendelssohn and Schumann. Moscheles wrote eight piano concertos between 1819 and 1838.

VIENNA

Carl Czerny (1791–1857), working primarily in Vienna, directly linked two giant composers of piano music: Czerny was a pupil of Beethoven and teacher of Franz Liszt. He wrote more than 1000 compositions in a variety of forms, including six piano concertos, practically all of which have faded into oblivion for want of significant musical content.

Johann Nepomuk Hummel (1778–1837) was the major figure of this transitional period. His career centered in Vienna until 1816, except for a short period in London in the early 1790s. From 1816 to 1819 he held an appointment in Stuttgart and then another from 1819 until his death in Weimar. His concert tours in the 1820s, undertaken during the three-month periods of each year when he had no responsibilities as Kapellmeister in Weimar, took him to many European musical centers. Despite generous earnings from his appointments and concert tours, his greatest source of income was his lucrative teaching career.

In his youth Hummel was a student of Mozart, with whom he lived from 1786 to 1787; later he studied with Clementi. The style that Hummel developed possesses the clarity and characteristic thinness associated with Mozart but incorporates Clementi's more virtuosic techniques, including a distinct fondness for double notes in octaves or thirds. His music also demonstrates his keen awareness of the value of counterpoint, which he must have gained in composition and counterpoint studies with Albrechtsberger and Salieri. In addition to his formal studies with Mozart and a short contact with Haydn as an organ student, Hummel could not have failed to absorb some of the piano style of his great contemporary in Vienna, Beethoven. While Beethoven was still able to perform and improvise at the piano, Hummel was regarded as his greatest rival and the second-most-gifted pianist and improvisor in this musical city.

Hummel was essentially a Classicist who employed a more romantic, elegant, highly decorative style, thanks in part to the lighter action of the Viennese piano. His inventive passage work anticipates much of what became common in Chopin's and Weber's piano writing. He particularly exploited a very active right hand, often moving into the highest, most theatrical register over a sustained bass in the left hand. Simple melodies were embellished with amazingly rich decorations, often obliterating the melodies beneath an exquisite layer of pianistic glitter. Hummel was very sensitive to the piano's resonance and insisted that the sustaining pedal should be used with any regularity only in slower movements.

His piano concertos were among those that most directly influenced early nineteenth-century composers. They possess all those qualities sought by contemporary audiences: simple, lyric themes; frequent use of the minor mode; and dazzling virtuoso displays, particularly in the codas. His concertos had become so popular by 1820 in and around Vienna that up-and-coming young pianists commonly made their public debuts playing a Hummel concerto, as did the eleven-year-old Franz Liszt. Yet the very qualities that made Hummel's works so popular probably led to their rapid disappearance from the repertory; as music intended to entertain through a titillating kind of display, these concertos were later to be viewed as showpieces devoid of meaningful content.

Hummel composed and published six piano concertos, one mandolin concerto (later transcribed by the composer for piano), one trumpet concerto, one double concerto for violin and piano, and two additional piano concertos which exist in manuscript only. Sets of variations and rondos for piano and orchestra were also published. The piano concertos are rarely performed, but the trumpet concerto enjoys a regular place in today's concerts, not just because there are so few trumpet concertos from that period, but because it is a very compelling work.

The Piano Concerto in B Minor, Op. 89 (1819), probably the best known today, is one of Hummel's stronger piano concertos. It is in the usual three movements: Allegro moderato in $\frac{3}{4}$; Larghetto in common time in G major; and Vivace in $\frac{2}{4}$ in the tonic minor, ending in major.

Hummel well understood the general outlines of the Classical concerto form of Mozart and Beethoven. He had made brilliant arrangements of a dozen of Mozart's concertos and wrote cadenzas for some. In his own concertos, he basically stayed within the traditional form.

The first movement of the B Minor Concerto is on a massive scale, opening with a huge (153-measure) ritornello for an orchestra of modest size. It was probably modeled after Beethoven's C Minor Concerto with the second theme presented in the new key, thereby placing the solo exposition in danger of a boring repetition. Such a lack of concern with the broader harmonic tensions intrinsic in the Classical style was symptomatic not only of Hummel, but also of most composers of the time. Many early nineteenth-century composers retained the old forms but focused on new concerns—thematic content and, in the case of the concerto, virtuosic passage work between the themes or even decorating the themes. Hummel's B Minor Concerto really has only two themes in the very large ritornello, one in B minor, the other in D major (Ex. 12-1). In spite of this thematic economy, the movement is very long (669 mm.) because of the extensive virtuosic passage work for the solo instrument, fully consonant with the new focus.

Ex. 12-1. Hummel, Piano Concerto in B Minor, Op. 89; I. Allegro moderato:
(a.) mm. 3–10; (b.) mm. 81–88.

The solo's first entry in m. 154 provides a pleasant surprise. First the pianist presents a left-hand, broken-chord accompaniment very softly with the sustaining pedal depressed. The harmony of this quiet passage is B major, but as the pianist's right hand introduces a new, more declamatory melody four bars later, the broken-chord accompaniment shifts to minor. The melody is repeated, each time becoming more florid and more expansive in range, while the orchestra inserts small hints of the opening theme of the ritornello. This imaginative introduction of the solo demonstrates Hummel's thorough understanding of the instrument and of its marvelous capabilities. The remainder of the exposition follows the ritornello, elaborated with much virtuoso passage work and a large concluding bravura section.

The development section focuses on the piano's new theme plus an additional idea. In the recapitulation Hummel introduces still more and different passage work, between the themes as well as at the end of the second theme. No provision is made for an improvised cadenza, as is typical in his concertos, which may seem odd in light of Hummel's reputation as a gifted improviser.

The middle Larghetto movement in G major does not employ strings. It opens with a chorale-like section for winds, which is restated by the piano in octaves in the right hand against a typical rhythmic, chordal accompaniment (Ex. 12-2). The relatively greater importance Hummel placed on the use of the pedals in slow movements is fully evident in this Larghetto. The score indicates extensive use of the sustaining pedal and the shifting pedal. The latter, as we saw in the middle movement of Beethoven's G Major Piano Concerto, caused the hammers to strike one, two, or three strings per note and could create much more diverse tone colors than on the modern piano. A middle section, shifting between D minor and major, demonstrates Hummel's florid, yet sensitive, ornamental style. A cadenza-like section leads, after a short pause, to the final spectacular Vivace. It opens with several measures of dominant harmony, before the main, Hungarian-flavored rondo tune appears in the solo instrument in the tonic key. Extensive bravura sections, featuring rapid arpeggios, alternate octaves in both hands,

Ex. 12-2. Hummel, Piano Concerto in B Minor, Op. 89; II. Larghetto, mm. 18–19.

double thirds in both hands, chromatic runs, and the repeated exploitation of the glittery upper register, expand the movement to more than 700 measures. The last 200 measures, all of which include the soloist, are in the tonic, a brilliant coda concluding this highly typical virtuoso concerto of the period.

Hummel's exciting Trumpet Concerto in E Major was written for Anton Weidinger, the Court Trumpeter at Eisenstadt who had inspired Haydn's concerto of 1796. (Modern editions of the work are often scored in E-flat to facilitate playing it on a modern trumpet.) Weidinger's keyed trumpet could play diatonic and even chromatic melodies in its lower register rather than being limited to the widely scattered lower notes of the overtone series. By 1803, the year in which Hummel composed this piece, Weidinger had made further refinements to the instrument, allowing even greater freedom of melodic movement and greater accuracy of pitch. Hummel took advantage of these refinements to write a truly engaging work that was later lost, the manuscript only reappearing in 1957. Hummel evidently did not publish the work, since Weidinger's invention had not caught on well and there was little demand for such a challenging trumpet piece.

The Trumpet Concerto was first performed on New Year's Day, 1804, as an offering of *Tafelmusik* (table or dinner music) for the Esterházy court. Trumpet music was commonly used for such festive occasions, and Hummel's brilliant music full of melodic charm greatly pleased his audience. The new-found flexibility of the instrument is thoroughly exercised in bold trills, chromatic runs, and arpeggios in keys heretofore inaccessible.

SPOHR AND WEBER

Louis Spohr (1784–1859) and Carl Maria von Weber (1786–1826), the leading Romantic composers of early nineteenth-century Germany, enjoyed surprisingly similar careers, yet their music has fared dissimilarly. Spohr's various musical accomplishments are as important as Weber's, yet the traditional assessment of Weber far overshadows that of Spohr. Much more of Weber's music is heard today; much more of Spohr's deserves to be heard.

Both men were leading composers of opera, anticipating elements of Wagner's later music dramas. But when or where do modern listeners hear Spohr's interesting experiments with leitmotives and through-composed form? These innovations heralded the demise of the traditional recitative-aria structure. Both were magnificent performers—Spohr on violin, Weber on piano. Weber's piano works are brilliant, awash with a dazzling, extroverted virtuosity that can seem to run away with the music. Spohr's violin works are full of virtuosic passages, but the works are tempered by a strong cantabile quality. The result is a more restrained musical expression and greater inward thoughtfulness. Both were excellent orchestrators, with Weber the more daring of the two in using new combinations of instruments and in giving previously overlooked instruments, such as the horns, more prominent parts. Weber's keen awareness of and interest in orchestral color seems to have carried over in his approach to the piano, yielding keyboard music at times notable for its orchestral textures. Both were among the first conductors to stand before an orchestra using a baton (Spohr may have been the first to use such a device consistently), thus providing the foundations of modern conducting technique. Both wrote outstanding pieces featuring gifted clarinetists, thereby making some of the most important contributions to the clarinet literature of the first half of the nineteenth century.

In a very general sense, Weber was a radical while Spohr was a conservative. Weber seemed to feel confined by traditional forms and modes of musical thinking, and sought ways of avoiding some forms, such as sonata-allegro form, with which he was clearly uncomfortable. He often put off writing the opening sonata-allegro form movements of his works until last. In fact, in numbers of the concertante works, he devised a new two-movement concerto-like structure in which opening slow movements serve as introductions to final rondo movements. In this way, he could leave completely aside the traditional sonata-allegro-oriented first movements. Spohr, on the other hand, was comfortable using the traditional forms of his beloved Mozart, expanding or modifying them as necessary. Both Spohr and

Weber regularly depended upon chromaticism to intensify their harmonic language, but in Spohr's work this element seems almost incidental—more melodic, in imitation of Mozart, and less shocking than Weber's.

Much about these talented and important early Romantic composers clearly invites comparison. Yet their concertos also warrant individual examination.

LOUIS SPOHR

Spohr made important contributions to the forms of opera, oratorio, chamber music, symphony, and concerto. Spohr's concertos include seventeen for violin (1802–44), of which only fifteen were published during his lifetime; four for clarinet (1808–28); a half dozen concertante works for more than one soloist (at a time when such compositions had become rare), including the very interesting Quartettkonzert for String Quartet and Orchestra; and numerous short but brilliant pieces, often called potpourri, featuring violin and orchestra, with a few for clarinet.

The Violin Concertos

Spohr's earliest musical training was on violin, an instrument he was to master to such an extent that he was favorably compared to Paganini. Spohr was not only an important violin performer and composer of violin music, but he also contributed to the development of violin technique in other ways. He was an important teacher, as documented by his *Violinschule*, published in 1831, as well as by the success of his pupils, such as Ferdinand David, for whom Mendelssohn was to write his Violin Concerto. Spohr also contributed to important physical changes made to the violin and bow by inventing the chin rest (c. 1820), which helped to free the left hand to negotiate complicated fingering with greater ease.

(Two other changes to the violin and bow, coupled with the technical achievements of the French violin school, also facilitated the extraordinary virtuosity of violinists such as Spohr and Paganini. Though not of Spohr's design, these changes are notable, for they significantly altered violin playing of the time. First, François Tourte (1747–1835) redesigned the bow about 1785, making it heavier and curving it inward toward the horsehair, thereby allowing the violinist to play with the greater power required to be heard in the ever larger concert halls, which were being built throughout Europe. The violin bow has never since that time been significantly modified. And, secondly, the fingerboard, which had previously thickened as it approached the body of the violin, was now constructed of more uniform size, making fingering much easier.)

Though Spohr was a thorough virtuoso, he tended to avoid, in his own music for the violin, the overtly showy techniques that had become commonplace. He especially avoided fancy bowings, such as *sautillé* (bounced), *spiccato* (detached), or *ricochet*, in which the bow is actively thrown or dropped at the strings, causing a bouncing action. He also disliked the use of artificial harmonics, which he felt degraded the violin, and avoided very light bowing, such as flautato (a flute-like effect produced by barely bowing the string over the fingerboard). Spohr even frowned on muting the strings. He clearly preferred a full singing tone, produced by even strokes of the bow, with careful attention to subtle variations in intensity, as can be achieved with singing. He was particularly highly regarded for his cantabile lines and beautiful tone, which was intensified by only a slight vibrato. Spohr's virtuosic interests primarily lay in a very active left hand, which is far less showy than vigorous, convoluted bow movements. The virtuoso techniques he preferred—double stops, wide-reaching tenths, trills, and very unusual chromatic scales—all require a strong and sure left hand.

The man's appearance seemed made for his calling, as described by Boris Schwarz:

> Spohr's performance and his treatment of the violin reflected his physical appearance. Tall and athletic of build, he was endowed with large arms, large hands, and strong fingers. Standing almost immobile while performing, he could produce a robust tone, well modulated in all dynamic shadings; he controlled his bow as a fine singer controlled his breath, starting a tone in pianissimo and swelling to forte while gradually adding a left-hand vibrato—a *bel canto* technique which he used in the true Italian singing style.[1]

Spohr's compositions illustrate a style with origins in early Romanticism, but strongly influenced by his deep devotion to Mozart. He used the Classical forms, but often experimented with them. The violin concertos depend upon both conservative and radical tendencies. Noteworthy modern features include:

- linking of movements—concertos Nos. 12, 15;
- serious, meditative Adagios—Nos. 2, 7, 9, 11;
- discarding of the sonata-form movement—Nos. 8, 10, 12;
- slow introductions—3, 10, 11;
- exotic dance-rhythm finales—Nos. 1, 2, 3, 6;
- written-out cadenzas—No. 8;
- absence of cadenzas—Nos. 2, 9, 12;
- free recitatives—Nos. 7, 8, 12; and
- avoidance of improvised ornamentation, writing elaborately decorated slow movements.

Spohr's harmonic language is modern, replete with chromaticism, remote modulations, enharmonic modulations, and mediant and submediant relationships (that is, key relationships by thirds, up or down). The orchestra, while important, is typically smaller than that favored by contemporaries. Slow movements are almost always written for strings alone.

Spohr's earliest concertos reveal the influence of Mozart, especially in their rich melodic content. They also have elements associated with Viotti and his French violin school. Subsequent concertos gradually move away from strong reliance on French models, although several final movements rely on exotic dances (*alla polacca* or *alla spagnola*) in the popular French tradition.

Three of Spohr's violin concertos exemplify different aspects of his style. Concerto No. 7 in E Minor (1814) is an outstanding achievement. Its opening Allegro, filled with interesting melodic content, includes an unusual opening

theme with chromatic motion in half notes (Ex. 13-1) and a captivating first theme
for the violinist, with expressive bold leaps and syncopations across the barlines
(Ex. 13-2). The soloist's entry is striking—it starts on a low sustained E, accompanied only by flutes and clarinets, and then soars upward on tasteful figuration.
The exquisite Adagio, in C major, features the solo violin in a decorative melody
against a simple orchestral background, creating a texture and mood similar to
those of a Chopin nocturne for piano. The final movement is a brilliant and challenging rondo.

Ex. 13-1. Spohr, Violin Concerto No. 7 in E Minor; I. Allegro, mm. 1–5.

Ex. 13-2. Spohr, Violin Concerto No. 7 in E Minor; I. Allegro, mm. 69–74.

Spohr's next violin concerto, No. 8 in A Minor (1816), is a true masterpiece of
highly ingenious and innovative design. It marks one of the first major departures
from the traditional concerto form in the nineteenth century, predating Weber's
unusual Konzertstück in F Minor for Piano and Orchestra by five years. Each of
these works by Spohr and Weber is performed without breaks between the movements or sections, and the movements do not follow the three-movement, fast-
slow-fast scheme that had persisted in the concerto over the past century. Weber
must have felt that his work was so removed from the concerto tradition that he
called it a concert piece, instead of a concerto.

Spohr conceived of his unique piece while preparing for a tour of Italy. Aware
of the Italians' fondness for opera, he created a work that features the solo violin in
the role of a solo singer in recitatives and arias; he called the piece a concerto in the
form of a vocal scene (Gesangsszene). It was first performed by Spohr at La Scala
in Milan on 27 September 1816, and soon became part of the standard repertory.
Today it is Spohr's only violin concerto to be played even occasionally.

The Gesangsszene is divided into movements, but they run into one another
without pause. In the Allegro molto, a powerful orchestral introduction of twenty-
seven measures in A minor sets the stage for the soloist's first appearance as a
soprano "singing" in the form of accompanied recitative. The solo part begins
simply, with vocal-style ornamentation, but ends in intense idiomatic violin figuration. The following Adagio is a brief da capo aria in the style of a cavatina or intimate song in F major. A flowing triple-meter theme, with a typical twist to A major
at the end of the first phrase, highlights the A sections (Ex. 13-3). The bold, A-flat
major B section in duple meter is characterized by expressive leaps played on the
violin's resonant G string against an accompaniment stressing the orchestral

violins' contrasting upper register. The A section returns with new ornamentation, just as in an operatic performance of such an aria.

Ex. 13-3. Spohr, Violin Concerto No. 8 in A Minor (Gesangsszene); II. Adagio, mm. 1–8.

An andante recitative, full of double stops in the solo part, serves as a transition to the final Allegro molto movement in A minor. Although this virtuoso movement may have been inspired by the increasingly popular cabaletta conclusions to solo opera scenes, with their fast tempos, short repetitive phrases, and syncopations designed to excite an audience to applause, this march-like movement is the least vocal in the work. It gives way instantaneously to the typical, virtuosic figuration of an instrumental concerto finale, culminating in a difficult, double-stop-laden cadenza supplied by Spohr. The movement feels like a rondo, but really has only one contrasting episode, beginning in the remote key of E-flat major and embracing B major in a striking enharmonic modulation.

In the many virtuosic passages of this astoundingly original piece, one can readily appreciate the work of a violinist blessed with a strong, large, left hand. Passages in Ex. 13-4 demonstrate some of the demands made on the violinist. At the same time, Spohr's emphasis on strong melodic content and clarity of form provides a solid musical foundation for these virtuoso developments. The orchestra is typically small and, during the solo parts, is unusually inactive. Spohr had learned that Italian orchestras of the time were of more limited size and ability than was the case in Germany.

Ex. 13-4. Spohr, Violin Concerto No. 8 in A Minor (Gesangsszene): (a.) I. Allegro molto, mm. 79–83; (b.) II. Adagio, mm. 158–159; (c.) III. Andante, mm. 189–191; (d.) III. Andante, mm. 197–200; (e.) IV. Allegro, mm. 233–236; (f.) IV. Allegro, mm. 267–268.

The Ninth Concerto in D Minor (1820) deserves to be returned to the concert repertory. It is technically demanding and musically satisfying. Spohr reverts, in the impassioned opening movement, to the Mozartian form, with full-scale orchestral ritornello for a substantial orchestra, including trumpets and trombones. The elegant F major Adagio makes extensive use of ornamentation, giving the effect of improvisation. The finale is a Rondo allegretto, in D major.

The Clarinet Concertos

In 1808, while Spohr was in Gotha, he received a commission from Prince Sondershausen to write a virtuoso concerto for the notable clarinetist and director of the Prince's wind band, Johann Simon Hermstedt (1778–1846). Spohr adapted his skill in writing lyrical violin concertos to create the first important concerto for that instrument since Mozart's of 1791. The compelling Adagio introduction of this C Minor Clarinet Concerto, Op. 26, begins with a timpani roll that alternates first with lyrical wind and then with string passages. The main theme of the Allegro is motivically linked to the slow introduction. The clarinet enters early and is off and running with brilliant figuration, rarely to be silent through the remainder of the work.

With this work Spohr established a deeply felt rapport with Hermstedt, who so treasured the concerto that he altered his instrument, by adding keys, in order to make the work more playable, rather than ask the composer to alter the more troublesome passages. Spohr wrote three more concertos for Hermstedt, who was especially noted for the beauty of his clarinet tone and tender interpretations.

Clarinet Concerto No. 2 in E-flat Major (1810) is a remarkably strong piece that reflects Spohr's greater understanding of the instrument. The slow movement makes very effective use of the chalumeau register, sometimes in dialogue with the flute, two octaves higher. The Third Concerto for Clarinet in F Minor (1821) is a more brilliant virtuosic work, while the Fourth in E Minor (1818), with a larger and more involved orchestra, has a more serious tone. Concertos Nos. 2 and 4 conclude with the same kind of exotic dance movements Spohr used in several violin concertos; No. 2 has a Rondo alla polacca and No. 4 has a Rondo al Espanole.

Spohr was, in many ways, the typical Romantic riddled with dualities—contrasting attitudes and approaches that on the surface, at least, seem in hopeless conflict. He looked backward to Mozart, often using concerto principles closely associated with that master; yet he embraced what was known as the "music of the future," championing Wagner's music long before most others did, by conducting outstanding performances of Wagner's dramatic works, beginning as early as 1843. On the other hand, Spohr rejected Beethoven's late works; they were probably too abstract for this early Romantic's taste. These dualities found expression in his music, which is a curious yet appealing blend of conservative and forward-looking features.

Spohr, one of the first German Romantics, was the most important German violinist and composer of violin music of the first half of the nineteenth century, filling the period between Beethoven's Violin Concerto of 1806 and Mendelssohn's Concerto in E Minor of 1844. Spohr had begun to compose violin concertos before Beethoven wrote his, almost single-handedly keeping the violin concerto alive in Germany. As we have seen, Beethoven's Violin Concerto was far from an immediate success and remained largely unplayed until Joachim resurrected it near the middle of the century. Spohr's concertos, on the other hand, were widely performed by German violinists. Ironically, if a Spohr concerto is performed today it is virtually certain to be a clarinet work, undoubtedly due in large measure to the very limited repertory available to clarinetists. Yet the violin concertos of this composer took the Romantic virtuoso concerto to new heights of expressiveness and they provide thoroughly satisfying listening.

CARL MARIA VON WEBER

Carl Maria von Weber (1786–1826) has a secure position in the history of music as a leading creator of Romantic opera. He was important as an early conductor and as an innovator in the field of orchestration. He was also an early and active music critic. But for our purposes, his brilliance as a pianist is particularly relevant.

Weber was one of the greatest piano virtuosos in the early nineteenth-century age of virtuosos. Contemporary accounts of his playing describe not only his brilliance, but also his range of tone, warm cantabile lines, and interesting special effects, often related to imitations of an orchestra. He had large hands with very long thumbs, making it easy for him to play scintillating passages, such as octave glissandos and four-part chords spanning a tenth or more in each hand. To enhance his natural gifts, he preferred the Brodmann piano, a Viennese instrument with a very light touch and narrower keys than the modern piano. In spite of his tremendous performing talents, Weber seldom concertized in public; he was too busy composing, conducting, staging operas, and writing reviews.

Like Spohr, who was only two years older, Weber spent his formative years in the late eighteenth century, becoming a youthful admirer of Mozart's music. Unlike Spohr, however, Weber left the eighteenth century behind to become one of the nineteenth century's first truly modern composers. It is shocking to recall that this thoroughly Romantic composer of strikingly new music died one year before Beethoven and two years before Schubert.

Weber's full-scale concertos were all written within the short time span of 1810 to 1812, shortly after Beethoven completed his Fifth Piano Concerto in 1809.

In addition to composing two for the piano for personal use, Weber wrote two concertos for clarinet and one for bassoon for outstanding musicians on these instruments. He also composed ten other works for solo instrument and orchestra in forms other than the concerto, including the important and frequently played Concertino in E-flat Major for Clarinet (1811) and the fascinating Konzertstück in F Minor for Piano and Orchestra (1821). These nonconcerto concertos, that is, works with concerto properties but lacking the standard three-movement concerto form, vividly illustrate Weber's distaste for sonata-allegro form. He felt it too constraining and too limiting of his desire to create a greater sense of spontaneity in his music. In several, his solution was simple: Throw out sonata-allegro form altogether by eliminating the first movement. As a result many of these works begin with a slow movement or section that serves as an introduction to a final fast movement, typically in rondo or variation form. Tellingly, Weber postponed the composition of sonata-allegro-form opening movements until the last minute. They are often the weakest movements; Weber knew his limitations. His primary interest was in writing virtuoso display music; that was followed by his passion for creating striking instrumental effects. In many cases, dramatic and formal integrity was allowed to slip into the background.

It was natural for a successful composer of opera to turn his attention to another form that pitted a soloist against orchestra, and Weber's earliest works for orchestra without voices were in the concerto vein. Weber's first several works in this genre did not feature piano, however. The very first was his short Romanza Siciliana for Flute in G Minor (1805). The effective Concertino for Horn followed in 1806; it was revised for a Munich performance in 1815. The concertino is clearly the work of an opera composer who loved the sound of the horn. Its experimental single-movement form comprises several sections approximating the soon-to-be-popular two-movement concerto-like compositions.

The Concertino for Horn opens with an Adagio-Andante introduction with a lilting tune in $\frac{6}{8}$. The next major section, Andante con moto, is a set of variations. A compelling, accompanied recitative serves as the introduction to the final scintillating Alla polacca, which contains some of the most difficult horn writing of the century. The recitative concludes with a most challenging passage in which the soloist must create chords by humming a note at a fixed interval above or below a played one, producing a third or fourth note by strengthening specific harmonics. This recitative section may date from the Munich revisions, as Weber's Bassoon Concerto and Second Clarinet Concerto, also written for Munich performers, include similar operatic passages.

Some subsequent works were the Six Variations on a Folksong for Viola (1806), the Grand Potpourri for Cello (1808), and one of the first of Weber's two-movement compositions, Andante e Rondo Ungarese for Viola, written in 1809 but arranged for bassoon in 1813–16(?). These compositions are meant to serve a virtuosic taste. Their increasingly brilliant content, often organized as simple figural variations on preexistent tunes that were familiar to audiences, was the "end," not a "means to an end." Their sole purpose was to provide virtuoso performers with bravura show pieces. Audiences seemed to enjoy these shows and liked frivolous figural variations on familiar popular tunes, such as those on the Austrian folksong "A Schüsserl und Reind'rl" in the earlier viola work or on a contemporary song by Franz Danzi (1763–1826) in the cello piece. Folk-dance movements also added to their audience appeal. For example, in the later viola piece, the two sections correspond to the *lassu* and *friss*—the slow and fast portions of the traditional Hungarian dance, the *verbunkos*.

But as might be expected, an approach so heavily dependent on the creation of virtuosic effect led to the writing of music which is, in the main, shallow in substance and lacking in any significant redeeming musical qualities. These shortcomings probably explain why these works are seldom performed today.

The Piano Concertos and Konzertstück

The Grand Concerto No. 1 for Piano in C Major, Op. 11, (1810–11) was Weber's largest piece for piano to this point in his career. Written for his personal use, it depends upon his piano technique, which was built on the foundations laid by Cramer, Hummel, and Dussek. Again, his large hands, together with the contemporary piano's slightly smaller keys, allowed him to create an impressive style turning on large leaps, widely spaced chords, rapid arpeggios over a wide range, lines doubled in thirds, quickly repeated chords, and rapid staccato passages. All was designed not only to titillate the ear, but to excite the audience's visual appreciation as well, for virtuoso performance often has an important visual dimension. The word "Grand" in the title had become a popular appellation to advise that the full power of the virtuoso was to be unleashed.

The first movement of the C Major Concerto has a martial quality, perhaps related to the popular works of the French violin school. The slow movement, as in so many of Weber's works, is perhaps the strongest. The movement is very warmly scored, especially for strings, and the delicate piano writing, in chorale style reminiscent of the piano part in the slow movement of Beethoven's Fourth Piano Concerto, contrasts nicely with the colorful orchestra. Very near the end a unique sound is heard—the piano plays a tremolando against a single held note in the violas. The finale is a rondo based on a simple arpeggiated waltz theme presented by the soloist in octaves, moving rapidly from high to low—again appealing to visual as well as musical movement.

The Grand Concerto No. 2 in E-flat (1811–12) is similar to the C Major Concerto. Points worth noting are the soloist's first blistering, arpeggiated entry and the extremely romantic sounding second movement, in which ornamental piano writing and subtle coloristic effects associated with the nineteenth-century are so abundantly present. This movement is in B major, the same key Beethoven used in the slow movement of his E-flat Concerto.

In both of these concertos, Weber wrote the first movement last, postponing what for him was the most difficult portion. He even noted after one performance of the E-flat Concerto that the slow movement and rondo made the greater effect. Perhaps as a way of avoiding the problem of the first movement with its demanding sonata-allegro form, Weber created, in his next "concerto" for piano, an altogether new form, inspired by an extramusical program. The Konzertstück (Concert Piece) for Piano and Orchestra in F Minor dates from 1821 and was completed on the morning of the first performance of one of the composer's greatest operas, *Der Freischütz*. The piano work clearly reflects the nineteenth-century composer's adaptation and manipulation of the concerto idea to fit his Romantic conception. It resembles Spohr's Gesangsszene, but goes beyond it in Romantic content and innovative organization.

The Konzertstück is in four movements without pause. Each movement relates to a literary program which, though not included with the score, has come down to us from Sir Julius Benedict, a pupil and friend of Weber who was told the program by the composer. The program is typically Romantic:

> LARGHETTO AFFETUOSO—A lady sits on her balcony alone, gazing into the distance, wondering if her knight, who has gone to the Holy Land, is alive and if she will see him again.
>
> ALLEGRO PASSIONATO—A fearful vision of her knight dying on the battlefield overcomes her. She wishes she could fly to him and die by his side. She falls back unconscious.
>
> TEMPO DI MARCIA—Distant sounds from the forest signal the return of the knights.
>
> PRESTO GIOCOSO—Love is triumphant.

In this, his last "concerto," Weber did away with concerto form entirely; the program governs the work's design, helping him through his difficulties with more abstract musical forms. In contrast with his earlier piano concertos, the Konzertstück is in minor, as was to be the case with a significant proportion of nineteenth-century concertos. The work is scored for the standard late-Classical orchestra with the addition of bass trombone.

Flutes, clarinets, and bassoons open the piece with chorale-like simplicity and a sound suggesting the organ, thus evoking a time more remote to establish the program's setting. The rests between the short phrases may reflect the loneliness of the woman (Ex. 13-5). Very soft strings and bass trombone present contrasting material, aimed at creating a sense of yearning. The rising sequences, the syncopations across the barline in the first violins' melody against the more metrically stable bass, and the chromatic harmony all contribute to this powerful mood.

Ex. 13-5. Weber, Konzertstück; mm. 1–4.

The piano enters with a brief flourish and then repeats the woodwind opening theme with a sustained melody in the outer fingers of the right hand, supported by short chords in the other fingers. The chorale texture brings to mind the slow movement of Beethoven's G Major Piano Concerto once again. Strings enter with their melody, which the piano decorates. The remainder of the slow section is given over to piano figuration with little or no orchestral support. The piano writing is thoroughly characteristic and includes rapid arpeggios and four-note chords in one hand (Ex. 13-6a), an active right hand, widely separated from throbbing chords in the left hand (Ex. 13-6b), and rapid staccato notes (Ex. 13-6c). The tremolando string parts near the end over a dominant pedal create a dramatic mood, anticipating the next scene in the program.

Ex. 13-6. Weber, Konzertstück: (a.) m. 61; (b.) m. 43; (c.) m. 48.

The Allegro passionato, also in F minor, is a simple ternary-form movement in which the agitated outer parts frame a lyrical, almost Chopinesque, A-flat major midsection. The piano is present at almost every moment, playing either the main thematic material or vibrant figurations under a sustained idea in the woodwinds. Weber intended the midsection to represent that part of the program in which the lady imagines herself going to meet her dying knight. The outer parts are frantic and full of fireworks for the soloist, including chromatic scale passages in contrary motion in which the left hand plays in alternating octaves.

The march movement, in C major, is an interlude for orchestra—the keyboard contributes only a one-measure flourish at about the midpoint. A timpani roll provides the link to the exciting piano build-up to the final Presto giocoso movement in lively $\frac{6}{8}$ time in rondo form. As is so common in the concerto's history, the final movement is the most virtuosic—here involving frequent passages in octaves in both hands—driven by the program to depict the frenetic exuberance upon the knight's return.

The Clarinet Concertos

On 11 March 1811 Weber arrived in Munich for the first performance of his one-act *Singspiel, Abu Hassan*. He remained in Munich five months, becoming a close friend of the charming clarinetist Heinrich Baermann. Weber almost immediately set out to write a new work for his friend and on 2 April 1811 completed the Concertino for Clarinet and Orchestra in E-flat Major. It debuted just three days later with several other Weber works, including one of his piano concertos. The new clarinet piece was so successful that the King commissioned two full-scale concertos for his virtuoso clarinetist, and soon everyone in the orchestra wanted one from the twenty-four-year-old composer.

Of Weber's three clarinet works, his concertino is the most spontaneous and probably the most successful, perhaps because it does not include a sonata-allegro-form movement. Weber wrote a work that not only displays the rich tone color of the clarinet, with its distinctly different registers, but also provides a showcase both for his friend's great facility and for something of Baermann's warm personality. The Clarinet Concertino consists of a slow introduction in C minor, followed by a theme in E-flat major with three variations separated by orchestral interludes. The fast final section begins as if it were another variation but soon explores new material. This kind of loose, rhapsodic structure fits Weber's Romantic style to perfection.

Less than a week after Weber's concertino was performed, he began to compose his First Clarinet Concerto, completing it about a month later. The second was finished about two months after that. The first movements, which begin with orchestral ritornellos as do the piano concertos, are again the weakest; Weber's creative impulses seem to have been defeated by the requirements of the traditional first-movement form. The slow movements are, by contrast, strikingly beautiful, and the final movements characteristically exuberant. The finale of Concerto No. 2 in E-flat Major, another of the popular *alla polacca* movements characteristic of the period, contains some of the most demanding clarinet passages in the literature.

As mentioned earlier, several members of the Munich orchestra had hoped for Weber concertos for their own instruments. He had offered to write a concerto for one of the cellists, but failed to do so. He did, however, write the Bassoon Concerto in the fall of 1811, which illustrates the depth of his understanding of wind instruments and of the widely varying coloristic effects inherent in their different registers. The bassoon's high register is used in especially effective ways, while in the clarinet works the solo instrument's low register is singled out for special treatment. Accompaniments often complement and highlight the solo instrumental colors in striking ways, especially in slower passages, as in the Clarinet Concertino where divided violas in thirds accompany the low-register clarinet part (Ex. 13-7). Other outstanding passages in both the clarinet and bassoon works involve the placement of the solo instrument against soft chorale-like chords in the horns.

Ex. 13-7. Weber, Concertino for Clarinet; mm. 125–129.

Weber could weave magical spells not only in his operas, but also in his concertos. His own virtuosity, as seen and heard in the fast movements of his piano concertos, must have been astounding. But he wished to impress through his ability to express deep feelings as well as through his technical flair. This powerful emotional rendering comes into sharp focus in a number of highly effective slow movements, in which Weber's innovative use of the orchestra and solo instruments strongly enhances the mood. Weber's single greatest contribution to the concerto, however, was the creation of a brilliant new program-driven form found in his Konzertstück. Here the dramatic genius found the perfect vehicle for combining drama and virtuosity within a flexible, yet meaningful, new design.

THE VIRTUOSO CONCERTO BROUGHT TO MATURITY

FREDERIC CHOPIN

In the Romantic view, art was a form of self-expression. Thus inspired, many Romantic composers tended to become specialists in a particular medium of performance. For example, opera fit the musical needs of Wagner, while Berlioz's musical sensibilities were intimately bound up with the orchestra. In the same way, it is impossible to think of the Polish composer Frederic Chopin (1810–1849) without also thinking of the piano. Chopin created his entire musical output with the piano at the core of his musical thought. Throughout his career he explored and mastered the resources of the piano, creating in the process some of the most wonderfully idiomatic music ever conceived for the instrument.

Chopin composed at the piano; for him there was a very close relationship between playing and composing. Many of his compositions seem so spontaneous in inspiration that improvisation must have played a powerful role in shaping them. According to contemporary accounts, he played his pieces differently each time, incorporating into his performances that all-important Romantic quality of spontaneity.

Chopin was one of the most innovative musical geniuses of the century. His style is marked by an extremely expressive, often ornately decorative, lyrical melodic approach supported by a highly original and equally expressive harmonic structure. While the basic rhythms of dance patterns, often deriving from Polish dances, permeate his music, Chopin repeatedly resorts to the use of tempo rubato, a device often associated with improvisation that was meant to introduce some flexibility into the rhythmic flow.

Chopin was an outstanding pianist from an early age and was almost self-taught in harmony and composition. He was overwhelmed by and attracted to Hummel's virtuosity when the latter played in Warsaw in 1828. Within a year, at the age of nineteen, Chopin had made highly successful appearances in Vienna. This city was still a very important artistic center, although not in the forefront of most new musical developments as were London and Paris. For these concerts he performed his own recently composed pieces for piano and orchestra in the popular virtuoso style.

These early works were in the popular variations or rondo form and were built around popular tunes and/or exotic dance rhythms. In 1827, the seventeen-year-old Chopin composed the first, Op. 2, Variations on "La ci darem la mano" (from Mozart's *Don Giovanni*, 1787). It was a great success in Vienna and spread his fame to other centers. Robert Schumann (1810–1856), at the age of twenty-one, wrote one of his first important articles in his *Neue Zeitschrift für Musik* after studying Op. 2 in published form. Schumann first explicated his distaste for the empty virtuosity of Kalkbrenner and Moscheles, but then went on to find much to admire in Chopin's display piece, which elicited his often quoted, "Hats off, gentlemen! A genius!" Clara Wieck, later to become Schumann's wife, played the work in Leipzig in 1832.

Chopin's Op. 2 is thoroughly characteristic of the nonconcerto virtuoso works for solo instrument and orchestra of the time. As we saw in Chapter 12, theme and variations form was a particularly suitable vehicle for virtuosic display. Popular tunes of the day, often from operas, regularly served as the themes for such variations to ensure widespread acceptance by audiences. The basic melody and underlying harmony were essentially given, freeing the composer to write ornamental figuration that lent itself to ready alteration from variation to variation; the composer had little else to worry about. A brief analysis of Op. 2 highlights the features typical of such an approach.

The piece begins with a long, slow introduction based on the theme's opening measure. The theme, five variations, and a final *alla polacca* section, in the style of a freer variation, follow. In characteristic fashion, each variation is more animated than its predecessor. The first variation introduces a running sixteenth-note triplet figure. The second variation is a very fast *moto perpetuo* with constant 32nd-note activity in both hands in parallel motion. Normally, in variations conceived for piano, one variation typically focuses on the left hand, a practice Chopin follows in variation three. Here an active, flowing left-hand part has some sections of rapidly repeated notes and arpeggios in Weber-like fashion. Variation four is fiery, requiring a quick, oscillating motion of the hands in contrary motion on large leaps. Short staccato notes accentuate the motion, enhancing both the aural and visual display. The final pair of variations is normally designed to serve two contrasting objectives. The penultimate variation is usually slow, in the minor mode, and designed to allow the soloist to display his or her dramatic side by playing music involving great dynamic shifts and bold accents, a pattern Chopin observed in Op. 2. The final variation or the closing section of such a piece is the most brilliant, as is the *alla polacca* finale, which, as the title implies, uses strong dance rhythms.

In a letter, Chopin reported with satisfaction that the audience applauded after each variation—a characteristic practice of the time—rather than waiting for the conclusion of the work to express appreciation. Op. 2 became so popular that Chopin often played it without orchestral accompaniment. The perfunctory orchestral part can be readily eliminated, as is often true of music in this genre. He simply had to alter the piano part in a few places to make it work as a solo piano piece.

Chopin wrote two other works of this kind. The Grand Fantasia in A Major on Polish Airs, Op. 13 (1818), builds on the virtuosity of Op. 2 but extends it. Op. 13 is truly an example of a potpourri. In it Chopin uses three themes: a pastoral folk song, a melody from an opera by Charles Kurpiński, and a *kujawiak*, a form of

Mit allerhöchster Bewilligung

w i r d

FRÉDÉRIC CHOPIN

aus Warschau,

Sonntag den 28. August

i m

Saale des philharmonischen Vereins

am Wittelsbacherplatze No. 617.

e i n

Instrumental- und Vocal-Concert

zu geben die Ehre haben.

Erster Satz eines E-moll Concertes für Piano-Forte, componirt und vorgetragen vom	Concertgeber.
Cavatine, gesungen von	Herrn Bayer.
Romanze und Rondeau aus obigem Concerte, componirt und vorgetragen vom	Concertgeber.
Vierstimmiger Gesang mit Clavierbegleitung, componirt von Herrn Stuntz.	
gesungen von	Mad. Pellegrini. Herrn Bayer. Herrn Harm, Herrn Lenz.
Phantaisie über polnische National-Lieder für Piano-Forte mit Orchester-Begleitung, componirt und vorgetragen vom	Concertgeber.

Billete à 1 fl. sind nur in den Musikhandlungen der Herrn Falter und Sohn, und Schäffer zu haben.

Anfang Mittags 12 Uhr.

The program of a Chopin concert given in Munich in 1831. In the early years of his professional life, Chopin was much under the influence of the established virtuoso pianists of the day—Hummel, Moscheles, Kalkbrenner, and Field—and tried to pursue a similar career. He wrote all of his brilliant music for piano and orchestra before moving to Paris in late 1831, at which time he gave up the life of the touring virtuoso. The program illustrated here is typical of nineteenth-century practice in that it includes a lighter work, a song, inserted between the first and second movements of his E Minor Piano Concerto.

the mazurka, thoroughly enjoyed by Chopin. The first portion is made up of unrelated variations on the first two themes. The songs are introduced in a simple lyrical fashion and then figuration patterns decorate them, an approach Chopin was to follow in his later concertos. The final portion is a blaze of virtuosity.

The second of these works is the Krakowiak: Grand Rondo in F Major for Piano and Orchestra, Op. 14 (1828). The title refers to a moderately fast Polish dance in duple meter, characterized by syncopation on the weak beat or weak part of the beat. This work seems more personal than the earlier two and is more focused, perhaps by the singular dance rhythm. The orchestra is also slightly better integrated into the texture.

Chopin's two piano concertos come from the following two years, 1829–30, the first completed when he was nineteen and the second when he was barely twenty. He wrote them under the influence of the popular virtuoso pianist-composers of the day—Hummel, Moscheles, Kalkbrenner, and Field. It is doubtful Chopin had yet heard or seen a Beethoven concerto, but he did know Hummel's Concerto in A Minor and Concerto in B Minor, Moscheles's in G Minor, and at least one by John Field. As a consequence Chopin's conception of the concerto was based on these models. None of these composers was particularly concerned with the opportunities for dramatic contrast between the piano and orchestra inherent in the form. They simply conceived of the orchestra as the means to provide a framework and unobtrusive background for their principal concern, the soloist, who played in a highly decorative and figurative style. The result, in the hands of Chopin, is a pair of concertos that may lack in great musical substance and true concerto drama, but which are eminently pianistic and contain a sufficient number of moments of melodic and pianistic magic to have kept them in the standard concerto repertory to this day.

The Piano Concerto in F Minor was the first to be completed by Chopin, but is identified as No. 2 because it was published after the E Minor Concerto. The F Minor Concerto is the stronger and more attractive, thanks to its more compact, yet more compelling, first movement. Both contain effective nocturne-style slow movements and lively finales that make use of Polish dance rhythms. The finale of the F Minor Concerto has the rhythmic quality of a mazurka and incorporates a contrasting scherzando section in the style of an *oberek*, a faster form of the mazurka. The oberek dance features rapid turns, frequent changes of direction, and lifting of the female partner. To capture the exuberant nature of this rustic dance, Chopin requires the accompanying violins and violas to play *col legno* (with the wooden part of the bow) on static pitches to imitate drums or handclapping. The finale of the E Minor Concerto is based on the *krakowiak*.

For Chopin ornamentation is not a mere addition to a melodic line; it is truly the essence of his melodic thinking. Ample evidence appears throughout the concertos. A good example is found in the Larghetto middle movement of the F Minor Concerto. The A section of this ABA form features a highly ornamented theme over a rocking eighth-note accompaniment in the manner of Chopin's and Field's nocturnes. After a dramatically declamatory midsection, the theme returns in even more decorated form. Often the ornamentation creates the feeling of spontaneity characteristic of improvisation. A particularly striking example of this effect occurs in the first movement of the F Minor Concerto after the solo instrument has presented the main theme. The piano introduces a new two-measure idea, which is then varied in an improvisatory style (Ex. 14-1).

Ex. 14-1. Chopin, Piano Concerto No. 2 in F Minor; I. Maestoso, mm. 83–86.

Both concertos suffer from problems. The orchestration is generally ineffective, although there are some very nice moments, especially when bassoon, clarinet, or horn are highlighted against the piano. Later arrangers have endeavored to enliven the orchestration, but more colorful additions in solo sections seem only to detract from the piano writing. Problems of tonal organization further mar the first movements. In the F Minor Concerto, the orchestra presents the second theme in the contrasting key of A-flat major, the key in which it also appears in the solo exposition. This creates a double exposition of the sort noted in Beethoven's Third Piano Concerto, reducing the impact of the soloist's move to the new key, while also lessening the drama of the soloist's entry. The problem is almost the reverse in the E Minor Concerto's first movement. Here the tonic key is maintained throughout the opening ritornello and the solo exposition, providing no relief or contrast for 350 measures. Curiously, when the second theme returns in the recapitulation, it appears in the relative major key, the key in which it would normally have appeared in the exposition.

One common solution to both the tonal and orchestrational weaknesses of the first movements has been to delete or significantly shorten the long and tedious opening tutti sections in modern performances. This creates no grave injustice to the music, for Chopin did, on occasion, play these concertos unaccompanied, indicating his own assessment of the orchestra's role as insignificant. Chopin had planned a third concerto which he began in 1830–31 but soon abandoned. Ten years later he used parts of the incomplete concerto in his Allegro de Concerto, Op. 46, which is structured like the first movements of his concertos, but calling only for a solo piano without accompaniment.

Chopin's last public performance in Warsaw took place on 11 October 1830, when he gave the first public performance of the E Minor Concerto. He decided to leave Poland shortly thereafter, eventually arriving in Paris in the fall of 1831. Chopin's first public appearance in Paris took place on 26 February 1832 at Pleyel's salon. The program consisted of a mixture of genres typical of the day:

Beethoven's String Quintet, Op. 29
A vocal duet
Chopin's F Minor Concerto arranged as a solo piano piece
An aria
Intermission
Kalkbrenner's Grand Polonaise with Introduction and March
An oboe solo
Chopin's Variations on "La ci darem la mano," Op. 2, arranged as a piano solo

Kalkbrenner and four other pianists joined Chopin for the performance of Kalkbrenner's piece; such an abundance of pianists and pianos was unusual.

The concert was a success and established Chopin as a formidable talent. He was soon earning an excellent income from teaching and no longer needed to pursue the career of a performer, which he found distasteful. Both his temperament and physical frailty were incompatible with the life of a performing virtuoso. As a composer, he left his large, youthful, virtuoso works behind to concentrate exclusively on writing short, lyric solo piano pieces, for which his talents were perfectly suited.

FELIX MENDELSSOHN

Felix Mendelssohn (1809–1847) was born in Hamburg and moved to Berlin with his family when he was three. He began piano studies with his mother at the age of six and composition with Carl Friedrich Zelter (1758–1832) at age eight. Zelter's enthusiasm for Mozart and Bach was passed on to his pupil, who conducted the famous revival of Bach's *St. Matthew Passion* at the Singakademie, where Zelter taught, in 1829. A meeting with Carl Maria von Weber shortly after that composer's completion of *Der Freischütz* in 1821, when Mendelssohn was only twelve, deeply affected the youth. Mendelssohn fell under the spell of Weber's pianistic virtuosity and of his orchestral effects depicting fairy elements in his opera. Two other great virtuosos of the time, Spohr, whom he met in 1813, and Moscheles, from whom Mendelssohn took piano lessons in 1824, also played a significant role in shaping the musical views of the youthful musician.

Mendelssohn, one of the most naturally gifted musicians of the nineteenth century, had been composing prolifically by age eleven and wrote some of his greatest masterpieces by the time he was seventeen; the Octet, Op. 20 (1825) and the Overture to *A Midsummer Night's Dream* (1826) are counted among the greatest works of the century. It has often been remarked that many of his later works do not match these earlier undertakings. Many have speculated that his comfortable, relatively trouble-free life led to the absence of any urgent need to communicate his deepest feelings in music, in contrast to the situation of many of his troubled Romantic contemporaries. Whether these speculations are of any substance or not, Mendelssohn was an extremely busy, restless, multitalented man, whose energies were directed toward a number of quite distinct creative outlets. In the musical field alone, Mendelssohn spent much of his time in his mature years in activities other than composition. In 1835 he became conductor of the Gewandhaus Concerts in Leipzig, presenting some of the most important concerts in Europe. He gave a series of historical concerts featuring the music of Bach and Haydn in 1837–38. He conducted the first performance of Schubert's "Great" C Major Symphony, after its discovery by Schumann in 1838. He later conducted the first performance of Schumann's Piano Concerto. In 1841 he became director of the music section of the Academy of Arts in Berlin and in the following year founded the Conservatory in Leipzig, which admitted as one of its first students the twelve-year-old violinist, Joseph Joachim. In 1845 he returned to the post of conductor of the Gewandhaus Concerts, while continuing to serve as director of the Conservatory in all but official title.

Mendelssohn's style is one of elegant, restrained Romanticism. His early fondness for Mozart's music had a profound effect on his early works, and he maintained an interest in clear Classical forms throughout his life. His interest in Bach and Handel led to a strong use of counterpoint in some works. His melodic style, on the other hand, is Romantic, although his phrasing tends to follow Classical models. He had a Romantic's interest in colorful orchestration and programmatic content. The spectacular virtuoso writing in his mature concertos is an equally obvious clue to his Romantic outlook.

Mendelssohn composed eight concertos and three shorter works for solo instrument and orchestra. Only three of the concertos are mature works; Mendelssohn completed the others between the years 1822 and 1824. Except for the two concertos for two pianos, the concertos are in the minor mode, with major mode finales in most cases. Mendelssohn's concertos in chronological order are:

Concerto for Violin in D Minor (1822)
Concerto for Piano in A Minor (1822)
Concerto for Violin and Piano in D Minor (1823)
Concerto for Two Pianos in E Major (1823)
Concerto for Two Pianos in A-Flat Major (1824)
Concerto for Piano in G Minor, Op. 25 (1831)
Concerto for Piano in D Minor, Op. 40 (1837)
Concerto for Violin in E Minor, Op. 64 (1844)

Other works for piano and orchestra are:

Capriccio brillant in B Minor, Op. 22 (1832)
Rondo brillant in E-flat Major, Op. 29 (1834)
Serenade and Allegro giojoso in B Minor, Op. 43 (1838)

Most of the early concertos were unknown until the 1950s. Several were written solely for string orchestra and in some measure convey the youthful exuberance of Mendelssohn's contemporary string symphonies, several of which are gems. These early concertos are surprisingly large. They clearly follow the Classical formal model of Mozart; each has a full-scale orchestral ritornello at the outset and proceeds in a fairly routine fashion. The orchestral writing in the solo episodes is thin, with interest clearly centered in the solo parts. Melodic content illustrates the young Mendelssohn's absorption in the practice of Mozart and Beethoven. The brilliant piano writing, however, relates more closely to Weber and Hummel; the writing for the solo violin is less demanding. Mixed with these late-eighteenth- and nineteenth-century influences are several instances of Bach-inspired fugal textures, reminiscent of the early eighteenth century. Although some passages are truly amazing, particularly in light of their creation by a mere boy, on the whole the works suffer from the young composer's inability to develop the thematic material to its potential.

The Mature Piano Concertos

Mendelssohn's first mature concerto is the Piano Concerto in G Minor, Op. 25 (1831). By this time, Mendelssohn had mastered the style which was to mark his subsequent work, as the earlier very obvious influence of Mozart receded. In this work, as well as in the Second Piano Concerto and the later Violin Concerto, a continuation of the developments explored by Weber and Spohr is evident.

Ironically, it was the conservative Mendelssohn who provided the first genuinely successful solutions to the problem Romantic composers faced when writing true concertos. His immediate predecessors—for example, Paganini—had focused intensely on the soloist and pushed the orchestra into the background, all the while relying upon the old Classical concerto-sonata form. This led to unimaginative opening orchestral ritornellos, which, in an often perfunctory way, presented the main thematic material but did not provide a dramatic opening for the soloist. Orchestral and solo sections lacked equality and were poorly integrated; composers seemed to follow reluctantly the old form, neither really understanding it nor really wishing to use it.

Mendelssohn's surprisingly simple and effective solution was to throw out the old form by jettisoning the "obligatory" opening tutti section. He organized his first movements in sonata-allegro form without reference to a ritornello structure. As a result, the solo voice was free to speak from the opening to the close of the piece and could be the first to present the main thematic material. Consequently the orchestra could be assigned a largely accompanimental role, but could, of course, play short tutti sections to provide contrast. The orchestra might also be given thematic material, to the accompaniment of the soloist performing in a virtuosic, attention-getting manner.

Mendelssohn also extended a practice begun by composers of the French violin school and used by Beethoven in his last two piano concertos: They unified the three-movement form by binding two or three movements together. The device consisted of proceeding from one movement to the next without pause or of recalling thematic material from an earlier movement in a later one, resulting in cyclical form. Mendelssohn made use of both techniques in his concertos.

In the G Minor Piano Concerto, the second theme of the first movement reappears just before the lengthy coda of the finale; furthermore, the main theme of the finale is closely related to the main theme of the first movement. Because neither of these themes is particularly memorable, Mendelssohn's cyclical treatment does not impress the listener. On the other hand, Mendelssohn effectively handles the linking of movements without pause. In the G Minor Piano Concerto a trumpet fanfare provides the transition between the first two movements and serves as the transition to the third movement, as well. This imparts a sense of the fantasia form to the G Minor Concerto and is thereby reminiscent of Weber's Konzerstück, which Mendelssohn had performed in 1829. In the Violin Concerto a single bassoon note is sustained beyond the closing chord of the first movement, providing a unique link to the second movement. This is a very Romantic gesture—the solitary note intensifies the contrast between the two movements and adds a sense of mysterious remoteness to the introduction of the slow movement.

Mendelssohn composed the G Minor Piano Concerto while he was on one of his many trips. In a letter to his father, he explained that he had tossed off the work in a great hurry. One wonders if this rush to ready a piece for performance in Munich may have motivated him to compress the first movement by eliminating the major tutti sections.

The opening of the Molto allegro con fuoco first movement sets the tone of the entire work. After a seven-measure orchestral crescendo on the G minor scale, in the style of a Mannheim crescendo, the solo piano makes a spectacular appearance. It plays a loud double-octave scale passage and display-work before presenting the main theme in true bravura style with full chords in the right hand and a rushing octave passage in the left hand (Ex. 14-2). The piano then remains the center of attention, playing in all but twenty-three of the exposition's 112 measures and in all sixty-six measures of the development. Furthermore, there is no orchestral section separating the exposition from the development, as was the case in most previous concertos. In addition to the brief orchestral opening, the orchestra's only other exposures occur at the beginning of the recapitulation and in the coda. To be sure, there are places in the movement, such as in the development and the recapitulation, where the orchestra plays the thematic component of a passage, but it is far overshadowed by the brilliant figuration in the piano.

Ex. 14-2. Mendelssohn, Piano Concerto No. 1 in G Minor; I. Molto Allegro con fuoco, mm. 20–23.

The E major Andante, in spite of its sentimental tone, is more subtle and satisfying than the outer movements. The orchestra is reduced in size and used with some sensitivity. The cellos are divided in two parts; near the beginning, the first cellos state the tune a sixth above the violas, creating an unusually warm sound. When the violins finally enter, near the end of the movement, they are divided into four parts. The middle portion of the movement is marked by extensive use of very light filigree in the solo part. The final movement, Molto Allegro e vivace, is a sort of rondo form in G major. It has a finale's usual emphasis on virtuosic display, including one passage of upper register staccato chords, modeled directly upon Weber's practice.

Mendelssohn wrote Piano Concerto No. 2 in D Minor while he was honeymooning in the Black Forest and the Rheinland in 1837. Schumann preferred this work to the first, but it is performed much less frequently today than the G Minor. The structure of the Second Concerto is similar to that of the First, although there are no cyclical thematic references and only the second and third movements are joined without pause. More than any other of his concerto movements, the finale, Presto scherzando, brings to mind the very light, elfin quality so strongly associated with the composer of the scherzo of *A Midsummer Night's Dream* music. Neither of these later piano concertos has a cadenza.

The Violin Concerto

The Violin Concerto in E Minor (1844) is among the greatest violin concertos ever composed; some musicians and listeners consider it the greatest. The extraordinarily compelling thematic content gives the work instant appeal. The violin part is outstanding for balancing effectively between display and tunefulness, yet even when the focus is on display, the musical substance penetrates. Although the violin part is clearly dominant, the composer created a more vital relationship between the performing forces than exists in his piano concertos.

The Violin Concerto was written for the violinist Ferdinand David (1810–1873) with whom the composer had had a fairly long association. David was born in Hamburg and studied violin with Spohr in Kassel from 1823 to 1825. In 1826 he took a post in Berlin where he became acquainted with Mendelssohn, often joining him to play chamber music. When Mendelssohn became conductor of the Leipzig Gewandhaus orchestra, he nominated David as concert master, a position which David held from 1836 to the end of his life. He also headed the violin department of the Conservatory, founded by Mendelssohn. David was an excellent violinist, orchestral leader, and teacher. He was instrumental in reintroducing important violin works of the seventeenth and eighteenth centuries, and he prepared the first practical edition of Bach's pieces for unaccompanied violin.

As early as 1838, in a letter to David, Mendelssohn mentioned an interest in composing a concerto for his friend, noting that ideas for it were already taking shape in E minor. Actual work on the concerto did not begin until 1839; Mendelssohn completed it in 1844. David helped with minor revisions and was largely responsible for the content of the cadenza. The concerto was first performed at the Gewandhaus on 13 March 1845, a performance the composer missed because of illness.

The Violin Concerto is built upon the formal innovations first articulated in the piano concertos. Yet here fascinating modifications give entirely new meaning to details of the music. As in the G Minor Piano Concerto, all three movements are played without pause, and the opening movement is in sonata-allegro form without the ritornello sections. The modifications to the form include an interesting sharing between soloist and orchestra in the first presentation of themes. In the opening Allegro molto appassionato, the solo violin first states the main theme softly on its highest (E) string (Ex. 14-3), while the orchestra accompanies, but the orchestra plays the theme alone shortly thereafter. Further into the movement, the orchestra first presents a transition theme (Ex. 14-4) followed by solo violin, whereupon the woodwinds introduce the second theme, accompanied only by solo violin on a sustained low note (Ex. 14-5). Finally the solo violin takes it over.

Mendelssohn modified the placement of the cadenza in the first movement by moving it from its traditional location near the end of the movement to the end of the development section. By doing so Mendelssohn gave the cadenza the important function of preparing for the recapitulation, with which the cadenza overlaps. This passage is one of the most magical in the work, but, surprisingly, the unusual placement of the cadenza was seldom imitated by subsequent composers.

Ex. 14-3. Mendelssohn, Violin Concerto in E Minor; I. Allegro molto appassionato, mm. 2–10.

Ex. 14-4. Mendelssohn, Violin Concerto in E Minor; I. Allegro molto appassionato, mm. 73–76.

Ex. 14-5. Mendelssohn, Violin Concerto in E Minor; I. Allegro molto appassionato, mm. 131–135.

Another modification places an interesting twist on traditional practice. Mendelssohn assigns to the orchestra the trills that normally appeared in the solo instrument to mark off the ends of major display sections which serve as conclusions to the exposition and recapitulation. While the orchestra plays the trills, the soloist plays snatches of thematic material that a composer would usually have given to the orchestra.

The very opening of the work is notable. The orchestra begins the piece by playing only the accompaniment, a practice Romantic composers found very effective. Such an opening, even as short as the one-and-one-half measures in the Mendelssohn concerto, establishes both a strong mood, and, of course, the musical framework of the tonal and metrical structure. By establishing a mood before presenting the main theme, the composer heightens the listener's anticipation of it, and it takes on special importance. This heightened anticipation is particularly evident in soft opening statements, as in this concerto, which suggest that the listener has just come upon a scene midway in its spinning out.

The C major Andante is in ternary form. The midsection, in A major, is more agitated, with a constantly rustling 32nd-note accompaniment. This accompaniment pattern carries on in the reprise of the main theme. A searching fourteen-measure allegretto non troppo for solo violin and strings serves as the transition to the final Allegro molto vivace.

The E major finale conjures up the fairyland world of earlier Mendelssohn. It begins with brass fanfares answered antiphonally by the soloist with flighty scherzando ascending arpeggios. The light main theme (Ex. 14-6) in the solo violin, accompanied by isolated pizzicato string chords and thin staccato woodwinds, further establishes this elfin atmosphere—Mendelssohn in one of his most ingratiating moods. Two other themes appear, both maintaining a connection with the main theme. The second theme, in B major, begins with a bouncy tutti passage, but after two bars, elements of the light main theme reappear (Ex. 14-7). The third theme, a more lyrically flowing idea first presented in G major, appears as a surprise tune in the development section (mm. 107ff.). The solo violin first sings the new theme to the accompaniment of bits of the first theme in the strings. The parts are then reversed. Eventually, at the beginning of the recapitulation, the solo violin plays a more complete version of the main theme against the third theme (Ex. 14-8). The final pages are extremely exciting, as the concerto ends with a blaze of virtuosity in which the orchestra continues to play a vital role.

Ex. 14-6. Mendelssohn, Violin Concerto in E Minor; III. Allegro molto vivace, mm. 9–11.

Ex. 14-7. Mendelssohn, Violin Concerto in E Minor; III. Allegro molto vivace, mm. 55–58.

Ex. 14-8. Mendelssohn, Violin Concerto in E Minor; III. Allegro molto vivace, mm. 133–135.

The Musical and Historical Significance of Mendelssohn's Concertos

In the case of Chopin, we found a composer whose piano concertos are of great musical interest, owing to his highly individualistic and original approach to the solo instrument and the stimulating harmonic and melodic language employed. Yet his concertos are flawed by his lack of interest in the orchestra's role and his inability to deal with issues raised by the conventional form he used. Mendelssohn, on the other hand, set forth in his piano concertos a satisfactory solution to structural problems which had bedeviled the earlier Romantic composers of virtuoso concertos. Because of this, Mendelssohn's piano concertos are historically very important. At the same time, the musical substance of Mendelssohn's piano concertos, like so many others from this period, is so slight that they may disappear from the repertory one day. Mendelssohn's last concerto, that for violin, is an altogether different matter, as it is universally ranked among the greatest violin concertos composed. It is a virtuoso concerto of great substance in which the dominant solo part is set against a lively orchestral accompaniment.

THE SUMMIT OF VIRTUOSITY: PAGANINI AND LISZT

NICOLÒ PAGANINI

Nicolò Paganini (1782–1840) and Franz Liszt (1811–1886) represent not only the pinnacle of technical virtuosity but also the culmination of Romantic composition in the virtuosic mode. Paganini, probably the most technically competent violin virtuoso of all time, exerted an enormous influence on a host of musicians, violinists and nonviolinists alike, and Liszt, a pianist and radically innovative composer, was one who came powerfully under that influence.

Paganini was first taught by his stern, indeed cruel, father, an amateur violinist, but was soon studying with some of the best violinists in Italy. Early models included the touring violin virtuosos, such as R. Kreutzer of France and August Duranowski (1770–1834) of Poland, and the publications of composers aiming to serve the virtuoso, such as Locatelli's *L'arte del violino* (publ. 1733). These twenty-four caprices for solo violin must have inspired Paganini's own, still more difficult, Twenty-four Caprices. From an early age, Paganini felt driven to develop a similar facility, so he practiced for untold hours. (Curiously, some who knew him in the prime of his later concert touring career claimed he practiced little during that period). Paganini worked hard to become a virtuoso violinist, and he was endowed with much natural musical ability and hands capable of making unusually large stretches.

Although Paganini made his first concert appearance at the age of twelve in 1794 in Genoa and played throughout much of Italy in subsequent years, he was forty-five when he began to perform in Europe's main musical centers outside Italy in 1818, catching the interest of musicians and audiences in Vienna, Berlin, Paris, and London. With his seemingly diabolical technique and intense and passionate style of performance, he took Europe by storm. His concerts were sensational successes; admission prices were double the norm, and Paganini became one of the wealthiest musicians of the century, which, among other things, allowed him to acquire a collection of the finest string instruments available in Europe.

In his early career, Paganini's concerto repertory was largely confined to works by members of the French violin school: Viotti, Kreutzer, and Rode. When he embarked on a touring career which took him to more sophisticated musical centers, he quickly sensed the public's expectation that he demonstrate not only his performance skills, but his creative abilities in composing his own music as

A caricature of Paganini. The unknown artist of this caricature has captured the fiery bravura and passion of Paganini's playing. The music sheets have caught fire, and the music stand is smoldering; although Paganini has broken all four of the violin's strings, he continues to create great music! The violinist was known to have purposefully weakened three strings that would break in performance, so that he could, in a seemingly miraculous way, continue to play on the remaining G string. Paganini took Europe by storm on his concert tours, beginning in 1818; his dazzling virtuosity had a profound effect on musicians and audiences alike.

well. Among his leading compositions are six concertos, admirably suited to serve as vehicles for his awesome gifts. While the emphasis is on virtuosity, his compositions are not vacuous. Technique and music were combined in an artistic form. Paganini was, in fact, a skilled composer with a good sense of melody and an intense awareness of drama—two sensibilities he shared with many Italian composers.

Paganini's violin prowess depended on several important technical devices, some of which were old but given a new life by him. Some are little more than tricks to make audiences and accompanying musicians stand back in awe and wonder. The most unusual devices were:

- Tuning of the strings in other than the normal way, or *scordatura* (literally, mistuning). This device had been used by earlier composers for special effects, oftentimes to facilitate unusual multiple stops or to create a different tone color on a string instrument. Paganini made use of several different tunings, but the most common was the tuning of each string one half-step above the normal pitch, the same as Mozart required of the viola in his Sinfonia Concertante. Mozart used the device to permit the solo viola to stand out more brilliantly against the orchestral violas; in a similar fashion, such tuning permitted Paganini's violin to sing out more brilliantly than the normally tuned orchestral violins, but it also permitted him to play in a flat key using the open strings. He employed this device in his Concerto No. 1, Op. 6, which was composed in E-flat major, with a solo violin part in D major for a violin with altered tuning. Paganini was one of the first musicians of the century to play from memory, so that the accompanying orchestra was never aware of his trick for this piece. They genuinely believed he was executing impossible-to-play passages. (Today this piece is usually played in D major without the use of *scordatura*.) Paganini used other tunings to produce different effects, but the overriding consideration was always the element of virtuoso display.

- Harmonics or high tones of a flute-like sonority. These are produced by touching the string very lightly, rather than fully stopping it, at the desired point, while the string is bowed or plucked. Paganini made extensive use of both natural and artificial harmonics. The former are produced on open strings, while the latter are made on stopped strings; that is, the string is first stopped to produce a string of the appropriate length and another finger touches the string lightly to create the artificial harmonic. Artificial harmonics were rare before Paganini, and he introduced double-stop harmonics, an extremely difficult and risky performance technique.

- Left-hand pizzicato. When combined with bowed passages, this effect is both startling and attractive.

- Multiple stops. The use of multiple stops was not new, but Paganini brilliantly exploited their effectiveness in all ranges of the instrument.

- Wide intervals. Paganini's unusually large hand-stretch allowed him to play extremely wide intervals easily, adding to the dramatic quality of his performance.

- Bowing. Paganini sometimes altered the normal up and down strokes in unorthodox ways, such as reversing the normal technique of downbowing on accented phrases and upbowing on upbeat phrases. He exploited other forms of bowing, particularly glittering bouncing techniques, such as his favorite, the *ricochet*, which is used extensively in the finale of Concerto No. 1.

- Extensive use of only one string. Paganini cultivated the ability to play entire pieces on the G string and still maintain a large and varied range of pitch. He could do this by making the necessary, big movements of his left hand with great speed and accuracy. There are stories of Paganini's having weakened the violin strings before a performance so that the three upper strings would easily break while he was playing, permitting him heroically to continue the performance on the remaining string. These stories are given some substance by the fact that the concertos contain many passages of extended range for the G string.

• Tone. Paganini used thinner, finer strings than did other violinists, which made some of the technical feats easier to accomplish, but it also led to a smaller tone. He was, nevertheless, noted for subtle gradations of tone and for his ability to make the violin "sing."

Paganini guarded his secrets well, publishing little music; none of the concertos was published during his lifetime. The concertos, with known premiere dates, are:

No. 1 in D/E-flat, Op. 6	1819
No. 2 in B minor, Op. 7	1827
No. 3 in E major	1828
No. 4 in D minor	1830
No. 5 in A minor (incomplete)	1830

A sixth concerto exists in a version for violin with guitar accompaniment and may represent an arrangement of a youthful work from about 1815.[1] Nos. 1 and 2 are the most frequently performed today.

Paganini used the Classical concerto-sonata form with full orchestral ritornello at the outset. This is the form Paganini knew and was comfortable using; he did not seek new forms or novel methods of organization. Instead, his innovations focused on the development of violin technique, and he gave virtuosity new musical meaning. Cadenzas usually are placed to interrupt the final ritornello. For the most part, Paganini improvised his cadenzas, so that little can be learned about their content or length.

Concerto No. 1 in D Major, originally in E-flat with *scordatura* solo violin, contains much that is typical of the composer. The Allegro maestoso first movement has a substantial orchestral introduction of ninety-four measures scored for an orchestra of fairly large size, including trombones, contrabassoon, bass drum, and cymbals. It is colorful in the Italian style, depending little on the woodwinds. The main theme has the quality of a march with its simple descending short notes (Ex. 15-1). Frequent fermatas interrupt the flow, giving the music an operatic flavor. The lyrical, contrasting second theme first appears in A major, the dominant (Ex. 15-2).

Ex. 15-1. Paganini, Violin Concerto No. 1 in D Major, Op. 6; I. Allegro maestoso, mm. 1–6.

Ex. 15-2. Paganini, Violin Concerto No. 1 in D Major, Op. 6; I. Allegro maestoso, mm. 51–54.

A commanding brilliance dominates from the very beginning of the solo section (Ex. 15-3). The march-like rhythm is retained, but clothed in grandeur. Within four bars the violin plays sweeping arpeggios linking upper and lower tones and triple and quadruple stops, all requiring careful, crisp articulation. At the close of the first phrase, the violin descends to its lowest note, G, but within three bars it has soared almost four octaves higher. A short, *dolce* statement quickly leads to a new virtuoso section with rapidly moving, staccato double thirds, great leaps, rapid scale passages, and quickly moving triple-stopped chords. The second theme retains its simple, lyrical character when repeated by the solo violin in its upper register, for Paganini knew that such a theme offered wide latitude to display many subtleties in performance. These included the use of various means of tone production, dynamics, vibrato, and even nuances of pitch. As in Mozart's concertos, this lyrical interlude is followed by a long display section, culminating in passages involving harmonics, both natural and artificial, for which Paganini was famous. In the balance of the movement, Paganini incorporates much virtuoso writing, introducing one particularly treacherous passage of fast-moving, parallel octaves and tenths. Because Paganini uses the older concerto-sonata form with its orchestral ritornellos, solo entries can be made quite dramatic, as in the almost operatic entry of the solo instrument in the development section. This B minor passage also displays the quality of improvisation.

Ex. 15-3. Paganini, Violin Concerto No. 1 in D Major, Op. 6; I. Allegro maestoso, mm. 95–98.

The slow movement, in the relative minor, stresses the violin's singing quality using melodic ideas drawn from the bel canto opera tradition. The main theme of the light but extremely demanding Rondo: Allegro spiritoso calls for the light bouncing-bow technique of Paganini (Ex. 15-4). The movement is full of double harmonics and other pyrotechnical displays.

Ex. 15-4. Paganini, Violin Concerto No. 1 in D Major, Op. 6; III. Rondo: Allegro spiritoso, mm. 3–6.

The Second Concerto in B Minor contains slightly less virtuosic writing than the D Major Concerto. Perhaps the minor key prompted Paganini to place greater emphasis on the presentation of thematic material. The rondo finale, however, is thoroughly virtuosic and is based on an old Italian melody, "La Campanella" (Ex. 15-5). Part of the movement's charm is the creation of a high-pitched, bell-like sonority in the violin and orchestra prior to each recurrence of the rondo theme and at other points. Occasionally, a gypsy flavor adds spice to the finale.

Ex. 15-5. Paganini, Violin Concerto No. 2 in B Minor, Op. 7; III. Rondo: Allegretto moderato ("La Campanella"), mm. 1–5.

In addition to composing his own works for the violin, Paganini commissioned a very interesting work for solo viola. He owned a Stradivarius viola which he wished to feature in his concerts. After hearing a rousing performance of Berlioz's *Symphonie fantastique* in late 1833, Paganini asked the young, French composer for a piece featuring solo viola. While Berlioz was flattered by the request, he initially felt incapable of writing the sort of virtuosic music the great violinist traditionally played. Paganini was insistent and the result was the unusual *Harold in Italy*, a symphony in four movements for viola and orchestra. In the end, though, Paganini was indeed dissatisfied with it for not only was the solo instrument silent for long stretches, but the part provided no real opportunity for display. He never played it, although he later heard it and liked it.

Paganini's Legacy

Paganini had a tremendous impact on contemporary and succeeding generations of violinists. He overshadowed all other European violinists for as long as he performed in public. Upon his nearly complete retirement from the concert stage in 1836, others tried to fill the void by emulating the master. Two leading contenders were Belgians who brought new life to the moribund French violin school by playing almost exclusively in France.

Charles de Bériot (1802–1870) adapted the technical display of Paganini to the elegant French style. He composed ten concertos, several of which are still used today to help students prepare for "meatier" fare. His Second Concerto (1835) was composed after hearing Paganini's playing and includes typical Paganini devices, such as harmonics, *ricochet*, left-hand pizzicato, and *scordatura*.

Henry Vieuxtemps (1820–1881), Bériot's most famous student, was one of the genuinely great violinists of the century. He was an excellent soloist and chamber musician, and an outstanding teacher. Vieuxtemps, together with Joachim (1831–1907), helped to focus younger musicians' attention both on the art of interpretation and on paying careful respect to composers' intentions. Paganini-inspired virtuoso devices appear in Vieuxtemps's seven violin concertos, which also display his masterful handling of the orchestra. These works did much to rejuvenate the French concerto. He also composed *Hommage à Paganini* (1845) for violin and orchestra and two cello concertos.

Henryk Wieniawski (1835–1880), another violinist-composer, combined Paganini's virtuosity, Romantic melodies, and colorful elements of his native Poland to good effect. He wrote two large concertos for violin, of which No. 2 in D Minor, Op. 22 (1870), is an excellent Romantic work with a colorful finale in the gypsy style.

Ole Bull (1810–1880), often referred to as the "Nordic Paganini," was a true showman whose concertos provided the vehicles for his amazing feats on the violin. He also liked to give his concertos fanciful names, such as *Farewell to Ireland* and *Concerto romantico*.

Joseph Joachim (1831–1907), one of the century's greatest performing musicians, was less touched by Paganini. Joachim composed three violin concertos, of which the *Concerto in Hungarian Style* (1861) once enjoyed popularity. It is a long and difficult work containing little dramatic display material so beloved by concert violinists, which in part explains its absence from the modern repertory. It also lacks the creative spark of many other works that can occupy a violinist's attention.

Paganini's influence clearly reached beyond the violin and violinists. Many pianists were captivated by the brilliance of his technique and attempted to translate that transcendental style to the keyboard. The mystery of his legendary performing abilities prompted many to use one or another of Paganini's short pieces as the springboard for their own compositions in this style. In particular, the theme of the Twenty-fourth Caprice found its way into many a later work, often serving as the theme for sets of extremely challenging variations in the virtuoso tradition, such as the famous works by Brahms and Rachmaninov. So excited was the nineteen-year-old Robert Schumann upon his first encounter of Paganini in 1830, that the event proved the turning point in the younger man's decision to devote himself to music. Two years later he completed his first set of studies, Op. 3, based on the Paganini Caprices. And Chopin found the Caprices an important inspiration in composing his Etudes.

Paganini dominated the European musical scene for several decades as performers and composers endeavored to deal with his nearly overwhelming impact. Many failed in their crude attempts to imitate his style and have faded from the picture, but several, as we have seen, successfully integrated aspects of Paganini's virtuosity into their music. Yet only one truly captured the essence of Paganini's virtuosity, transforming it through his own genius into an impressive keyboard idiom. This was Franz Liszt.

FRANZ LISZT

Liszt was born in Hungary in 1811 and showed an interest in music by the age of six. He moved with his family in 1821 to Vienna where he studied piano with Czerny and composition with Salieri. He gave his first public concert in 1822. In the following year the family moved to Paris where Liszt gave a series of successful concerts. He also read widely and sought out many of Europe's leading artists and writers. One of these meetings, in 1830, was with Berlioz, whose music made a great impression on the young pianist. Not long thereafter, in April 1832, he attended Paganini's second Paris concert. The twenty-year-old Liszt was overwhelmed; he determined to devote himself to creating music for the piano which would parallel the spectacular effects of Paganini's music for the violin.

Liszt established a rigorous practice routine, concentrating especially on playing parallel thirds, sixths, and octaves, tremolos, and rapid repeated notes. A very immediate compositional outcome was the *Clochette Fantasy* of 1832, based on "La Campanella," the theme Paganini used in the final movement of his B Minor Concerto. At about this time, Liszt met and formed a friendship with Chopin, to whom Liszt attributed the discovery of the poetic side of his nature. The influence of these three composers—Berlioz, Paganini, and Chopin, each from a different country—was lasting, and Liszt assimilated various aspects of their diverse approaches into his own music. But the virtuosic ideas associated with Paganini dominated.

Liszt was thoroughly devoted to the piano, coming to view it as an extension of his body, in the same way that Paganini had related to his violin. Throughout the 1830s and '40s Liszt worked relentlessly to define and solve every conceivable problem associated with piano technique. He endeavored to gain total independence for each finger, while treating his hands as a single unit of ten fingers. Like Paganini, Liszt was endowed with hands unusually well-suited to meet his goals; his hands were long and narrow with a distinct lack of "webbing" between the fingers, which allowed for wide extensions—he could reach tenths with ease. The fourth finger of each hand was abnormally long, making some otherwise difficult fingerings easy.

Additionally, Liszt exploited the damper pedal to blend harmonies and to free the hands quickly for their next movements. He used the soft pedal to achieve a greater range of expressiveness. He explored unconventional notation to record solutions to specific problems; for example, he used two different typefaces—bold and light—to depict the relative weight of different tones. He was fascinated with the problems of transcribing orchestral and vocal music to the medium of the piano, greatly expanding the repertory with his amazing transcriptions. The first version of the *Transcendental Etudes* was completed in 1838–39, establishing radically new standards of piano technique.

Liszt's most notable contributions to a new piano technique were:

- chromatic glissandi, consisting of a true glissando on the white keys played with the right hand at the same time and speed as the black keys are played with the five fingers of the left hand;
- extremely large leaps from high register to low and the reverse; and
- rapid note repetition.

Liszt's performing career spanned the years 1839–46, during which time he gave more than 1000 concerts in Europe and Asia. By 1842 he had become so popular that a kind of mass madness known as "Lisztomania" swept Europe. In the course of his performing career, he had established the concept of a piano recital, and may have even introduced the term "recital." He was the first performer to play entire programs from memory. His repertory was extraordinarily wide, ranging from Bach to Chopin, although he regularly indulged public taste by playing lighter, more dazzling pieces. By today's standards, he was probably not a good interpreter of others' music, but his performances must have been thrilling. Especially noteworthy were his frequent performances of his own transcriptions of the music of others, particularly those of excerpts from Wagner's operas. He accumulated great wealth, but was a philanthropist who gave a fortune to charity and to other artists in need.

In 1847, while concertizing in Kiev, the thirty-five-year-old Liszt met Princess Carolyne Sayn-Wittgenstein, who persuaded him to give up his concert touring to devote himself to composition. Thus at the height of his prowess he gave up performing in public. He moved to Weimar in 1848, where for the next dozen years he was musical director and conductor at the court; here he championed the

Heute Mittwoch den 18. April 1838,
um die Mittagsstunde,
wird

FRANZ LISZT

zum Besten der in Pesth und Ofen
durch Ueberschwemmung Verunglückten,
im Saale der Gesellschaft der Musikfreunde,
ein

Concert

zu geben die Ehre haben.

Vorkommende Stücke:

1. Ouverture zur Oper: Die Tage der Gefahr, von Cherubini.

2. Concertstück für Fortepiano mit Orchesterbegleitung, componirt von C. M. v. Weber, gespielt von **LISZT.**

3. Declamation von Madame Rettich, k. k. Hofschauspielerinn.

4. Reminiscences des Puritains, große Fantasie für das Fortepiano, componirt und vorgetragen von **LISZT.**

5. Adelaide, von Beethoven, gesungen von Herrn **Benedict Groß,** auf dem Claviere begleitet von **LISZT.**

6. Valse de bravour et grande étude, componirt und vorgetragen von **LISZT.**

Zur Beförderung dieses menschenfreundlichen Zweckes haben Madame Rettich und Herr Groß ihre Leistungen, so wie Herr Carl Holz die Leitung des Orchesters mit größter Bereitwilligkeit übernommen. Auch hat die löbl. Gesellschaft der Musikfreunde ihren Saal dem Concertgeber unentgeldlich zu diesem Zwecke überlassen.

• **Sperrsitze** zu 3 fl. C. M. und **Eintrittskarten** zu 1 fl. 20 Kr. C. M. sind in der k. k. Hof-Musikalienhandlung des Herrn Tob. Haslinger am Graben, und am Tage des Concertes an der Cassa zu haben.

Der Anfang ist um halb 1 Uhr.

A concert program of Franz Liszt in Vienna, 1838. Liszt, influenced by the virtuosity of Paganini, established a rigorous practice routine that enabled him to develop one of the most awesome piano techniques in history. His formidable virtuosity was combined with a highly original style of composition that led to the creation of two piano concertos of unique design, but to some extent influenced by Weber's ground-breaking Konzertstück. Liszt performed Weber's unusual work on this Vienna program and drafted Piano Concerto No. 1 in E-flat Major at this time.

operas of Wagner and Berlioz. While in Weimar Liszt not only revised many of his earlier works but also composed a significant number of new pieces, especially for orchestra. In these he explored and developed the new form known as the symphonic poem, as well as a new and unique approach to the symphony in *The Faust Symphony*.

In 1861 Liszt moved to Rome, hoping to marry the princess. Their expectations were shattered by the Pope's unwillingness to sanction her divorce. Liszt remained in Rome eight years in the course of which he took preliminary holy orders leading toward the Catholic priesthood. His compositions from this period are mostly sacred choral works and large-scale organ pieces. In 1886, his seventy-fifth year, Liszt undertook another European concert tour. He was enthusiastically received, but the illness that would lead to his death brought his astonishing and productive career to an end.

In his approach to composition Liszt proved to be one of the great innovators of the nineteenth century, together with Berlioz and Wagner. This trio of composers radically revised old forms and invented new ones in their search for the most intense musical expression. Liszt consciously discarded traditional formal structures in his quest for greater musical freedom; his concertos uniformly depend upon highly original organizational schemes. In addition to the use of unusual structures, Liszt's music greatly depends upon thematic transformation to provide interest. His sense of harmony, initially derived from the early Romantics, increasingly turned more chromatic, at times leading to the use of quite unorthodox progressions, scales, and chords. A strong rhapsodic element is present in the piano concertos and other solo piano music.

Liszt's concertos and other pieces for solo piano and orchestra were, for the most part, the products of his years as a touring virtuoso. A number of them were revised one or more times, not realizing their final shape until some years later. The earliest of these compositions was the *Grande fantaisie symphonique* (1834), on themes from Berlioz's *Lélio*. It is in two contrasting sections: the first, a meditation on "Chant du pêcheur," and the second, an Allegro on the "Chanson des brigands."

Two other shorter works for piano and orchestra—*Malédiction* and *Totentanz*—are still heard on occasion. The first, dating from c. 1840, is a quite brilliant piece for piano with string accompaniment. Its origins may date back to a lost concerto from the composer's youth. Liszt did not use the title for the complete work; it is the first of four French words with which he identified its principal themes: "Curse" (*Malédiction*), "Pride," "Tears-Anguish-Dreams," and "Raillery." The programmatic content of this work and of *Totentanz* (begun 1838 or 1839, completed in the late 1840s, revised in 1853 and 1859) strongly links Liszt with Berlioz.

The latter work is a set of free variations on the sequence *Dies irae* (Day of Wrath) from the Mass for the Dead, which Berlioz had used to stunning effect in his *Symphonie fantastique* (1830). The theme of death was one of Liszt's continuing preoccupations; tenants in his building were kept awake all night by his playing of variations on the *Dies irae* theme.[2] The *Totentanz* was inspired by frescoes attributed to Francesco Traini depicting Death as a female figure wielding a scythe. Liszt calls for a biting, percussive use of the piano and makes interesting use of canon, in variation IV, and fugato, in variation V. Variation VI, while nominally the finale, is virtually another set of variations based on a derivative of the sequence. Glissandi and rapid chromatic scales are the favored virtuosic devices. A particularly demanding presentation of chromatic scales involving alternations between hands in octaves, another of Liszt's technical innovations, is showcased in these variations (Ex. 15-6). The orchestra's role is of little consequence.

Ex. 15-6. Liszt, *Totentanz*; m. 15.

Liszt's concertos are certainly among the most unusual of the nineteenth century. While Paganini was content with the traditional form as the vehicle for displaying his technical skills, Liszt chose radically different structures. The structure of Concerto No. 1 in E-flat Major (drafted in 1838–39, completed in 1849, revised in 1853 and 1856) is related to that used by Weber in his Konzertstück and by Schubert in his *Wanderer* Fantasy, both in Liszt's repertory. Liszt's concerto has four, not three, movements, but the second and third movements are combined and linked without pause. The third movement concludes without the standard, heavy double bar, implying forward momentum directly into the fourth movement, but the latter begins with rests, causing a slight break between the final pair of movements. The concerto, in fact, approaches the one-movement structure of Liszt's tone poems, but lacks the programmatic content of those pieces. The E-flat Concerto is cyclically unified; recurring thematic statements are among the most imaginative applications of the principle of thematic transformation in the composer's entire corpus.

The first movement, Allegro maestoso, does without the tonal design of sonata-allegro form, retaining only its vaguest thematic outlines. Its structure is more rhapsodic, involving frequent changes of tempo. Tutti sections are almost nonexistent, although a four-measure orchestral opening is repeated later in slightly expanded form as a quasi-recapitulation. The opening, with its compact, martial theme (Ex. 15-7), piano passages separated by brief, but powerful orchestral chords, and very early appearance of a piano cadenza, brings to mind Beethoven's "Emperor" Concerto in the same key.

Ex. 15-7. Liszt, Piano Concerto No. 1 in E-flat Major; I. Allegro maestoso, mm. 1–4.

The very first appearance of the piano, in m. 5, introduces a bounding idea that could easily have come from Paganini's violin, except that it is played in double octaves (Ex. 15-8).

Ex. 15-8. Liszt, Piano Concerto No. 1 in E-flat Major; I. Allegro maestoso, mm. 5–7.

Liszt's characteristic method of expanding material through sequential repetition is abundantly evident in the first movement. There is also some use of thematic transformation, as, for example, when the opening idea is stated in diminished form in the bassoons and cellos (Ex. 15-9). Later the solo piano repeatedly states that version in thundering octaves that further extend the descending scale, creating one of the most brilliant piano passages in the movement.

Ex. 15-9. Liszt, Piano Concerto No. 1 in E-flat Major; I. Allegro maestoso, mm. 67–68.

The Quasi Adagio in B major, the same key used by Beethoven in his Fifth Piano Concerto, creates a pastoral mood, the result of the use of muted strings, $\frac{12}{8}$ meter, and woodwinds, which become prominent near the end of the movement. The mood is broken only by two recitative passages in the piano.

The third movement, Allegretto vivace, is a scherzo reminiscent of Mendelssohn's elfin music. A short introduction, highlighted by triangle, precedes the piano's statement of the main theme. Today it is difficult to comprehend that the delicate triangle could have aroused as much commotion as it did at the Viennese premiere. The conservative critic Eduard Hanslick wrote disparagingly of its use and dubbed the work the "Triangle Concerto;" it was not repeated in that city for years. The capriccioso scherzando theme is written in triple meter but can also give the ambiguous effect of duple meter. It is first played by the piano in staccato octaves (Ex. 15-10).

Ex. 15-10. Liszt, Piano Concerto No. 1 in E-flat Major; III. Allegretto vivace, mm. 10–12.

The third movement incorporates themes from the previous two movements. The work's compact opening theme returns, first quietly in the piano and later aggressively in trombones and strings. The diminished form of this idea, with the extended descending chromatic scale, appears in the piano, but now quietly rather than thundering as in the first movement. And after the reintroduction of the piano's original entry, woodwinds recall the pastoral theme first heard in the flute at the end of the Quasi Adagio. But in the third movement this theme is played *animato* against the rhythm of the concerto's first idea played *marcato* by the timpani (Ex. 15-11).

Ex. 15-11. Liszt, Piano Concerto No. 1 in E-flat Major; III. Allegretto vivace, mm. 144–146.

Liszt considered the Allegro marziale animato finale as a more urgent recapitulation of earlier material. Masterful use of thematic transformation gives added vitality to the recalled thematic material. The gentle opening phrase of the second movement is transformed into a vigorous march (Ex. 15-12a, b), while its second phrase rings ominously as the trombones, bassoons, and lower strings play it very loudly and *marcato* against tremolando in the upper strings (Ex. 15-13a, b). The pastoral flute theme from the end of the Adagio reappears as well in a non-legato form in triplet rhythm high in the piano's range, sounding like the ringing of distant bells. The theme of the scherzo is recalled in common time, its light triplet quality maintained but now shorn of its duple–triple meter ambiguity. And in one final thematic recollection, the piano, rushing brilliantly through the last pages of the score, offers a diminished form of the opening motive, including the appended descending chromatic scale.

Ex. 15-12. Liszt, Piano Concerto No. 1 in E-flat Major: (a.) II. Quasi Adagio, mm. 34–35; (b.) IV. Allegro marziale animato, mm. 2–3.

Ex. 15-13. Liszt, Piano Concerto No. 1 in E-flat Major: (a.) II. Quasi Adagio, mm. 36–37; (b.) IV. Allegro marziale animato, mm. 18–19.

Liszt also introduces what appears to be an exciting new theme (Ex. 15-14) in the finale, at the alla breve: più mosso section, beginning in m. 102. The theme is not entirely new, however, for it borrows its descending chromatic motion from the work's opening motive.

Ex. 15-14. Liszt, Piano Concerto No. 1 in E-flat Major; IV. Allegro marziale animato, mm. 102–104.

Weimar must have been ablaze with excitement in 1855 when Liszt first performed this concerto, his friend Berlioz conducting. The Second Concerto in A Major also premiered in Weimar, in January 1857, but by the pianist Hans von Bronsart, the dedicatee, with the composer conducting.

The A Major Concerto is less brilliant but far more original in form. Its single movement contains six main sections largely alternating between gentle and more aggressive moods. The six sections are:

    I.   Adagio sostenuto assai, starting in A major
   II.   Allegro agitato assai, starting in B-flat minor
  III.   Allegro moderato, starting in E major
  IV.   Allegro deciso, starting in D-flat major
   V.   Marciale un poco meno Allegro, starting in A major
  VI.   Allegro animato, starting in A major

The sections are strongly united thematically, the contrasting moods created by ingenious thematic transformations. In this way this concerto resembles the tone poem which Liszt created.

Five main themes (Ex. 15-15) appear in the work: Themes A and B are introduced in section I, themes C and D in section II, and theme E in section III. Themes A and D are the most important, appearing throughout the work in various forms. When first presented, theme A is in a dreamy, romantic mood with its extended note values and drifting chromaticism, while theme D is hard and aggressive with its clipped staccato notes, propulsive rhythm, and clear tonal shape.

Ex. 15-15. Liszt, Piano Concerto No. 2 in A Major: (a.) Theme A, mm. 1–4; (b.) Theme B, mm. 75–77; (c.) Theme C, mm. 116–119; (d.) Theme D, mm. 153–155; (e.) Theme E, mm. 250–252.

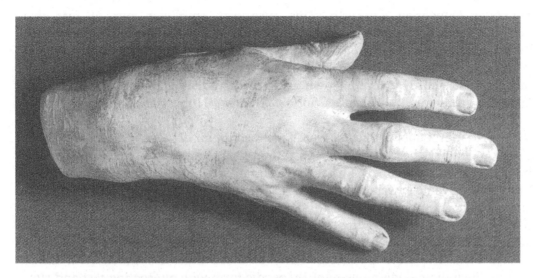

A cast of Liszt's right hand. Liszt was endowed with hands unusually well-suited to meet his goals; his hands were long and narrow with a distinct lack of "webbing" between the fingers, which allowed for wide extensions—he could reach a tenth with ease. The fourth finger of each hand was abnormally long, making otherwise difficult fingering easy.

Theme A returns as a major theme in the main slow section (section III) and as the main march theme of section V, where its initial wispy nature is completely transformed (Ex. 15-16a). Theme D is first heard in the loud Allegro agitato assai section, in $\frac{6}{8}$ time in B-flat minor. It next appears at the beginning of section III in E major in common time, *dolce espressivo* (Ex. 15-16b). Theme D also provides the "decisive" ostinato pattern (Ex. 15-16c) in the D-flat major Allegro deciso section. The march theme B, with its fanfares and growling bass line, carries forth above the D ostinato.

Ex. 15-16. Liszt, Piano Concerto No. 2 in A Major: (a.) Theme A transformed, mm. 421–424; (b.) Theme D transformed, mm. 214–215; (c.) Theme D transformed, m. 290.

Liszt may have composed one more concerto. It has an interesting history, and although no autograph manuscript has been located, there is strong evidence that the lost concerto has been found. In August 1885 Liszt wrote to his favorite and very successful female pupil, Sophie Menter (1846–1918), telling her he was writing a concerto for her. He had not orchestrated the work before his death the following year, so Menter received the work in an unusable form. The Russian composer Tchaikovsky (1840–1893) knew Menter, visiting her at her home in the Tyrol on several occasions. She asked him to orchestrate the work, identifying it as her own Hungarian Concerto. This ruse was employed out of fear that Tchaikovsky would not tackle the job because of his displeasure with some of Liszt's piano transcriptions of the Russian's orchestral music. Tchaikovsky completed the task in 1892 and conducted the work's first performance in St. Petersburg in 1893, shortly before his own death, with Menter as pianist. A few months later the score was published as Sophie Menter's Hungarian Concerto, orchestrated by Tchaikovsky.

Menter probably destroyed Liszt's manuscript for obvious reasons, so that for nearly a century the world knew only that Liszt composed a concerto that had been lost, and that Tchaikovsky had orchestrated a concerto in the Hungarian style thought to have been written by Menter. During the 1980s, however, Liszt scholars and performers came to regard the Hungarian Concerto as Liszt's.[3] There is no hard evidence supporting this hypothesis, although a close friend of Menter's allegedly overheard her confess to having presented Liszt's work to Tchaikovsky as her own. The work possesses many of those traits associated with Liszt's writing, including a one-movement rhapsodic form with alternating fast and slow sections, genuine thematic unity, and quite obvious virtuoso pianistic style.

Liszt's Legacy

Weber and Spohr had paved the way for the use of one-movement, nontraditional forms, and Paganini had provided the opening for construing virtuosity as a valid means of artistic communication. Liszt heartily adopted these innovations and molded them to serve both his sense of what the concerto should be and to shape a vehicle suitable to his awesome technical prowess. Liszt's influence on subsequent nineteenth-century composers was, however, most clearly manifested in the work of composers little interested in the concerto. His impressive piano style certainly had a broad impact and produced many imitators, but it was not until another Hungarian, Béla Bartók (1881–1945), turned to writing concertos for the piano that the model of Liszt's concertos was invoked, yet only in an attenuated fashion. Liszt's concertos remain thoroughly unique creations. They are satisfying musical works when performed with care and conviction, but in the hands of less-than-fully competent and sensitive performers slip easily into virtuosic bombast and sentimental triviality.

This chapter has dwelt on two of the century's most astounding virtuoso performers and their contributions to the virtuoso concerto. In the next chapter we will deal with two musicians whose Romantic outlook was tempered by their great reverence for the music of the past.

Chapter Sixteen

SCHUMANN AND BRAHMS

Few composers of concertos after the time of Paganini were able to escape his influence, rendering virtuosity a paramount element of the nineteenth-century concerto. We have seen that many composers, in their zeal to create great virtuoso works, downplayed the orchestra, virtually eliminating any tension between it and the soloist. To be sure, a few composers were concerned with restoring a balance between the performing forces without forfeiting the effectiveness of solo display. They realized this goal by making the concerto more symphonic—by providing the orchestra with a more prominent and vital role throughout the work. This bolstering of the orchestral role does not necessarily imply a return to the old ritornello form. Robert Schumann's Piano Concerto in A Minor is a fine example of this approach. Other composers, on the other hand, did return to the ritornello form with its inherent capacity for greater balance between the two forces. Johannes Brahms's Violin Concerto in D Major is an example of this successful revival of an older form.

Brahms, with his intense interest in earlier music, wrote four outstanding concertos that generally fall within the Classical framework, albeit with strong Romantic content. Schumann, who profoundly influenced the younger Brahms, wrote music of a more overtly Romantic nature, but in his later works he showed a strong desire to prove the current validity of Classical forms. Schumann's works for solo instrument and orchestra run the gamut from super-Romantic pieces with heroically conceived solo parts and light orchestral accompaniments to the more Classical concerto-with-ritornello form.

ROBERT SCHUMANN (1810–1856)

Early nineteenth-century piano virtuosos excited Schumann's initial interest in music, but the decisive influence was that of the violinist Paganini, first heard by Schumann in 1830 in Leipzig. Schumann was there attending law school at the request of his mother, even though his attention was increasingly drawn to music. After experiencing Paganini's performance, Schumann determined to devote his life to music, establishing a rigorous and extensive program for practicing. As part of this plan, he fashioned a device to fasten to his hands to enhance the independence of his fingers. This device was long thought to have damaged tendons, an injury believed to have dashed his hopes of pursuing a career as a virtuoso, but the deterioration of his hand coordination was more probably the result of mercury

Clara and Robert Schumann. The story of Clara and Robert's long courtship and ensuing legal battle to marry against her father's wishes is well known. It is also well known that the impending marriage in 1840 led to Robert's most intense outpouring of high-quality songs. But it is often forgotten that he began the first movement of his A Minor Piano Concerto shortly after their marriage, intending it as a performance vehicle for Clara. Clara was the foremost female piano virtuoso of the century and was well respected as an interpreter of a wide range of repertory. Although Robert originally intended the first movement of the concerto to stand alone as a fantasie, he added the second and third movements four years later. The concerto's three movements are so well integrated and thoroughly united that the listener is hard pressed to imagine that such a long interval separated the composition of the first movement from the other two.

poisoning from treatment of syphilis. When it was clear that his manual skills were inadequate for professional performance, he turned his attention both to composition and to his literary interests. He founded in 1834 and published for some years thereafter an important musical journal, the *Neue Zeitschrift für Musik*. He was not only the journal's publisher and editor, but he also wrote many of the most important articles in it.

The emotional content of Schumann's music is quintessentially Romantic, evidencing all the contradictions and tensions of the Romantic spirit with its vacillating moods—alternately passionate or dreamy, violent or capricious, humorous or serious. Three imaginary figures embodied these different facets of the Romantic spirit in Schumann's writings for the *Neue Zeitschrift für Musik*: Florestan was passionate and impulsive; Eusebius, a dreamer; and Raro, the wise leader.

Schumann's music is characterized by chordal textures, particularly in the piano music; rhythmic repetition, often involving syncopation; and warm, intimate melodic lines. The larger works are often unified thematically, with clever thematic transformations contributing to striking changes of mood.

His earliest works were largely written for the solo piano, but in forms that departed widely from the Classical sonata tradition. The best of these works are integrated cycles of short pieces, often based on programmatic themes, such as *Carnaval*, Op. 9 (1834–35). In the years before his hand ailment became severely debilitating, he initiated at least three concertos, none of which was completed. In 1840, the year of Schumann's marriage to Clara Wieck, he turned his attention to the writing of some 130 songs. He then turned to other forms of musical expression, in part to confirm that older forms were still viable. His explorations along these paths led to his important contributions in chamber music, choral music, opera, symphony, and concerto.

Schumann's completed concertos and other works for solo instrument and orchestra are:

Concerto in A Minor for Piano, Op. 54 (1841, 1845)
Concertstück in F Major for Four Horns, Op. 86 (1849)
Introduction and Allegro Appassionato (Concertstück) in G Major for
    Piano, Op. 92 (1849)
Concerto in A Minor for Cello, Op. 129 (1850)
Fantasie in C Major for Violin, Op. 131 (1853)
Introduction and Allegro in D Minor for Piano, Op. 134 (1853)
Concerto in D Minor for Violin (1853; publ. 1937)

The Piano Concerto

After the "Year of Song" in 1840, Schumann began to explore the orchestra, completing his First Symphony early in the spring of 1841. By May he completed the Fantasie in A Minor for Piano and Orchestra, which Clara Schumann, shortly before giving birth to the first of their eight children, played at a Gewandhaus Orchestra rehearsal in August. This typically Romantic work, with its thoroughly unified thematic content, then lay dormant until after the Schumanns' move to

Dresden in 1844. Schumann's conducting responsibilities in that city may have led him to compose a slow movement and rondo to follow the Fantasie, making it a traditional three-movement concerto, the Piano Concerto in A Minor. The three movements are so well integrated and thoroughly united, the listener is hard pressed to imagine that four years separate the composition of the first movement from the other two. The towering quality of the work, one of the best known and loved of nineteenth-century piano concertos, is even more astounding when one learns that Schumann suffered his first severe physical breakdowns in 1842 and 1844. The ominous symptoms of these breakdowns included terrible trembling and auditory hallucinations that made composition impossible.

In an 1839 article on piano concertos in the *Neue Zeitschrift für Musik*, Schumann wrote:

> And so we await the genius who will show us in a newer and more brilliant way, how orchestra and piano may be combined, how the soloist, dominant at the keyboard, may unfold the wealth of his instrument and his art, while the orchestra, no longer a mere spectator, may interweave its manifold facets into the scene.[1]

Schumann accomplished the task set by his 1839 article in his 1841 opening movement of the A Minor Concerto. The piano is dominant and commands our attention virtually throughout, but the orchestra is given a more active role than it had played in the virtuoso concertos of the recent past.

The Piano Concerto is a highly unified work; the first movement's opening theme (Ex. 16-1a) is the source of thematic material in every movement. The theme is highly characteristic of Schumann's writing. There is a strong contrast between the first and second four bars. The first phrase emphasizes the downbeat and clear stepwise motion, with the third and fourth bars nicely paralleling the first two. The second phrase introduces syncopations tending to obliterate the downbeat; furthermore, a dramatic, large leap preceding the first syncopation, some smaller skips, greater chromaticism in the melodic line, and more frequent changes of direction give this phrase an altogether different character. This theme may be seen as providing, on a very reduced scale, a musical illustration of Schumann's two imaginary characters, Florestan and Eusebius. The theme is first presented by the woodwind choir and then taken over by piano in a typically Schumannesque chordal texture.

Transformation of this theme is central to Schumann's compositional approach in this concerto. The main theme returns in the first movement in various forms (Ex. 16-1b–e), is the clear basis of the finale's first theme (Ex. 16-1f), and provides important motivic material in the second movement. The first transformation of the main theme serves as the opening movement's animated second theme (Ex. 16-1b), presented in the clarinet to the accompaniment of the piano. This transformation incorporates clear references to the theme's two opening motives, but its most distinctive feature is the descending octave followed immediately by the rising tenth, which is an outgrowth of motive c of the main theme (Ex. 16-1a). The development section opens in a slower tempo, andante espressivo, with a nocturne-like setting of the main theme in A-flat major in $^6_4$ time (Ex. 16-1c). A much faster, passionato, transformation of the theme, with an important leap of a sixth and a striking syncopation (Ex. 16-1d) brings the development to a close. Rising sequences bring still greater intensity to this portion of the development. The coda contains yet another transformation (Ex. 16-1e) of the main theme into an allegro molto march in $\frac{2}{4}$ time.

Ex. 16-1. Schumann, Piano Concerto in A Minor; I. Allegro affettuoso: (a.) mm. 4–11; (b.) mm. 67–70; (c.) mm. 156–158; (d.) mm. 205–208; (e.) mm. 402–407; (f.) III. Allegro vivace, mm. 1–4; (g.) II. Intermezzo. Andante grazioso, mm. 1–2.

Even though the first movement was originally identified as a fantasy, it is in sonata-allegro form. The three-measure introduction to the Allegro affettuoso first movement is powerful and attention-getting; it is another with its roots clearly in Beethoven's "Emperor" Concerto. A short, single statement of octave Es in the orchestra is followed by a forceful, rhythmically energetic chordal cascade in the piano, unaccompanied. This idea makes only one return, where it dominates the middle of the development section, bringing a sudden, shocking halt to the slower, expressive $\frac{6}{4}$ section.

The cadenza near the end of the first movement is one of the most unusual of the nineteenth century. It is carefully composed, but delivers the sense of being improvised. It lacks the extroverted bravura traditionally associated with a cadenza; it is, on the whole, more introspective. Two new motivic ideas are introduced within the cadenza, before the main theme is further explored.

The slow movement, Andantino grazioso, was given the title Intermezzo by Schumann. The title points to the movement's smaller, more intimate scope as compared with its neighboring fast movements which are larger and more dramatic. The Intermezzo is in simple ternary form. The theme of the first part uses motive b of the work's main theme in a gracious dialogue between piano and strings (Ex. 16-1g). The theme of the middle section is a more expressive idea in the cellos, making use of the upward leap of motive c; lovely piano passages fill in the joints between phrases. The delicate scoring throughout the middle movement is effective, but the most special moment occurs at the end in the transition to the third movement. The second movement's main theme gradually dies away into silence; then out of that silence arises a mysterious, remote horn-call recollection of the opening motive of the concerto's main theme in clarinets and bassoons in A major (Ex. 16-2). The horn call, a favorite sound of Romantic composers, somehow captures the essence of Romanticism with its dual connotations of remoteness and intimacy with nature. The piano responds with a gentle cascade. The horn call and cascade are repeated more quietly in minor, adding to the mystery. On the return to the major, the dynamic level picks up, other instruments are added, and the music thrusts headlong into the vivid finale.

Ex. 16-2. Schumann, Piano Concerto in A Minor; II. Intermezzo. Andante grazioso, mm. 99–100.

The most brilliant movements of a concerto are typically saved for the end. Schumann follows that practice but, avoiding the empty virtuosity that had become so common, writes a fascinating movement. The piano opens with an A major transformation of the work's main theme into a sprightly triple meter dance (Ex. 16-1f). The switch to the major with the theme starting on the raised mediant; the opening skip, omitting the B; the scalewise ascent; the following drop of a fifth and leap of an octave; and the strong dynamics measurably change the theme's character. And this version of the theme undergoes further change as it is extended in a brief fugato, beginning in m. 367, illustrating the impact of Schumann's study of Bach and counterpoint earlier in the year. The lengthy and brilliant coda introduces still another variant of a part of the main theme in which the piano decorates the theme, while the violins play only a simple outline of the theme's main notes (Ex. 16-3).

Ex. 16-3. Schumann, Piano Concerto in A Minor; III. Allegro vivace, mm. 771–774 (with part of this movement's main theme superimposed in transposed form).

The E major second theme (Ex. 16-4) of this sonata-allegro-form movement displays typical Schumannesque play with syncopation that is so consistent the listener perceives a nonsyncopated pattern of $\frac{3}{2}$ meter superimposed on the written $\frac{3}{4}$ meter. Even though the listener cannot hear the written syncopation, the notation creates a sense of urgency that is communicated to the listener.

Ex. 16-4. Schumann, Piano Concerto in A Minor; III. Allegro vivace, mm. 189–196.

Orchestral details are altered in the recapitulation, revealing Schumann as a more sensitive and imaginative orchestrator than is often acknowledged. The piano's figuration at the end of the development carries on into the recapitulation as horns and woodwinds present the theme, giving it the color of its horn-call character. The recapitulation begins in D major, opening the way for the return of the second theme in the tonic major, without adjustments to the transition section.

Clara Schumann, the greatest female pianist of the century, gave the first public performance of the complete Piano Concerto in Leipzig on New Year's Day 1846, and continued to play it throughout the balance of her long career. The concerto was one of her husband's happiest and most successful large works. It was a work of love for the woman he loved.

While the Piano Concerto is easily Schumann's greatest work in the concerto form, several of his other works for solo instrument and orchestra deserve a more prominent place in the modern repertory.

The Introduction and Allegro Appassionato for Piano and Orchestra in G Major, Op. 92, from Schumann's very fruitful year of 1849, is beautifully conceived for the piano, with rich textures and striking melodic content. Schumann pits the Eusebius-inspired expansive introduction against the fast section with its more impulsive and passionate Florestan mood. Op. 134, another coupling of an Allegro with a slow introduction, is more concise and pianistically more brilliant, with a long cadenza. Robert presented the piece to Clara on 12 September 1853 as a thirteenth-anniversary present. Later that month they met the twenty-year-old Brahms, who overwhelmed them both with performances of his own compositions. Schumann, who had not written for his journal for some time, that year wrote his still-famous article, "New Paths," praising the young Brahms, and, with the permission of his wife, changed the dedication of Op. 134 to Brahms.

Concertstück for Four Horns

Schumann wrote three other concertos, each for a different instrument. In that fruitful year of 1849, he began to explore the capabilities of wind instruments. He composed Fantasiestück (Fantasy Piece) for clarinet and piano, Op. 73; and Three Romances for oboe and piano, Op. 94. In three different works he favored the horn: Adagio and Allegro for horn and piano, Op. 70; five *Hunting Songs* for male voices and four optional horns, Op. 137; and the glorious Concertstück for four horns and large orchestra in F major, Op. 86. The last is a full-fledged, three-movement concerto. As is so typical of Schumann in his periods of intense creative activity, he completed this unusual work in a very short time, sketching it in three days in February and fully orchestrating it a few weeks later. The work communicates a tremendous sense of spontaneity and bounding energy.

Schumann's inspiration for this captivating work remains uncertain. The work of Wagner, who was then active in Dresden, could have excited Schumann with the possibilities of the valved horn. Or Schumann may have had a gifted horn section in the Dresden Opera orchestra. Whatever the reason, he created one of his most luxuriant orchestral works. The orchestra is slightly expanded to include piccolo and three trombones, while woodwinds often double the solo horn parts to add color and texture. The solo parts are both thoroughly idiomatic and quite demanding. The contrast between the sound of the horns and their accompaniment is often striking. For example, near the end of the development section in the first movement, the horns play a sustained line over hushed string tremolando.

And in the middle of the second movement, the lush horns effectively sound forth against pizzicato strings.

The Concertstück is in three connected movements, notwithstanding a brief pause between the first and second movements. It is further unified by thematic recollection: The broad theme from the middle of the second movement appears again in the finale.

It is a shame that this scintillating work is not heard more often, but the difficulty of assembling four excellent horn soloists usually stands in the way.

The Cello Concerto

In the spring of 1850 Schumann became municipal music director in Düsseldorf. The Cello Concerto in A Minor is one of his first compositions from this period. He sketched it between 10 and 16 October, completing the full score by 24 October. The composer revised it over the next two years, completing the task in February 1854, just days before his attempted suicide. There is no record of Schumann's having had a particular performer in mind for this concerto, and, as far as can be determined, the work was not performed until after the composer's death, as part of the celebrations of 1860 marking the fiftieth anniversary of his birth.

Schumann's is the first cello concerto by a major composer since Haydn's D Major Concerto of 1781. Schumann had a strong affinity for the cello and seemed to understand innately the lyrical potential of the instrument; when he first developed the problem with his right hand, he wrote to his mother that he might take up the cello. The first two movements emphasize the cello's songful quality and the third is more virtuosic, but taken as a whole the Cello Concerto is not a great display piece. At the same time, the orchestra is rarely exposed in passages without the soloist. Schumann created a solo-dominated work, but lyricism, not virtuoso display, is the primary concern.

This concerto's lyric character is already established in the engaging opening of the first movement, Nicht zu schnell (not too fast). A flute, in long notes, and first violins, pizzicato, quietly anticipate the cello's main theme, which begins in m. 4 after a measure of the murmuring accompaniment is completed. The cello's presentation of the main theme (Ex. 16-5) is accompanied by thinly scored strings only. Schumann recognized that he had to be careful to allow the cello's delicate sonority to be heard; accordingly much of the work bears this chamber-music texture. In fact, several later composers of cello concertos, including Elgar and Walton, imitated the strongly lyrical tone of the opening of Schumann's concerto.

Ex. 16-5. Schumann, Cello Concerto in A Minor; I. Nicht zu schnell, mm. 5–12.

The three movements of Schumann's Cello Concerto are joined without pause, with effective transitions linking the movements. The transition to the third movement is especially interesting. After the slow, expressive middle movement, the tempo picks up and the woodwinds play a very quiet version of the opening movement's first theme, which is continued by the solo cello. The tempo slows for three bars while the cello recalls the opening theme of the second movement. A quicker pace brings an operatic tremolo in the strings while the solo cello, in recitative, accelerates into an unaccompanied descent to the third movement's rhythmic first theme.

The short slow movement may be the strongest in the work. Evoking the quality of a lyric song, it is in simple ternary form. The accompaniment to the singing solo cello line is entirely pizzicato strings, except that a portion of the orchestral cellos plays arco, creating a kind of duet with the solo cello. In the middle section, the solo cello plays some of its rare double stops, but they are not used for display; instead they add a sonorous richness with their movement mostly in parallel sixths.

Schumann's characteristic reliance on a small repetitive rhythmic idea (Ex. 16-6) tends to mar the finale. The idea first glimmers in the opening theme and adds some sparkle in the accompaniment to the second theme, but the listener eventually loses interest as the figure repeats without gaining any real melodic definition, and fails to shine forth in the end.

Ex. 16-6. Schumann, Cello Concerto in A Minor; III. Allegro vivace, rhythmic idea.

The only cadenza in this concerto appears in the final movement. It is accompanied and very subdued, mostly remaining in the cello's lower-to-middle register. Some cellists, disappointed with the work's overall lack of brilliance, have expanded the cadenza to compensate.

Schumann's Cello Concerto is neither as challenging nor exciting as Dvořák's, but the essential lyricism of the first two movements so effectively conveys the singing quality of the cello that Schumann's concerto will always be performed by cellists wishing to display that aspect of their instrument's voice.

The Violin Concerto

Schumann first met Joseph Joachim in Leipzig when the thirteen-year-old violinist enrolled in Mendelssohn's new conservatory. Within a few years Joachim was acknowledged as one of the chief violinists of the age, spurred on by his success in reviving Beethoven's all-but-forgotten Violin Concerto. Schumann heard the twenty-two-year-old violinist play the work in May 1853 at the Lower Rhine Festival in Düsseldorf. The composer was so impressed that when the conservative Joachim approached Schumann with the request for a solid violin work, grumbling about the empty virtuosity of so much that had recently been written for the instrument, Schumann responded by composing the Fantasie in C Major, Op. 131, in early September 1853. It is a brilliant concert piece in sonata-allegro form with a slow introduction. The orchestra is clearly secondary to the showy solo part, and one wonders if Joachim was happy with the outcome.

Soon after completing the Fantasie, Schumann began the composition of a more Classically structured work for Joachim. The composer completed the Violin Concerto in D Minor on 3 October 1853, within just a few days of having begun it.

Once Joachim's suggestions were incorporated into the score, the composer and violinist hoped to play it later that fall in Düsseldorf. In the meantime, however, Schumann resigned as director, after continuing complaints of his unsatisfactory leadership. Plans for performances the next spring were also scrapped, because of the final stages of Schumann's illness.

Schumann's illness no doubt contributed to the inferior quality of one of his weakest large-scale works. The Violin Concerto is repetitive, especially in its final movement, and it is neither sufficiently idiomatic nor brilliant to satisfy most violinists—which is why it is rarely performed. These features, about which Joachim complained, must account for his never having played it in public. At the violinist's death he left the autograph score to the Prussian State Library in Berlin with instructions that it not be published until 100 years after Schumann's death, out of regard for the effects such a weak work might have on the composer's reputation.

The story of the concerto's eventual reappearance and subsequent publication and performance in 1937, well before the date stipulated by Joachim, is nothing short of bizarre. A grandniece of Joachim, the Hungarian violinist Yelly d'Aranyi, claimed to have been visited by the spirits of Joachim and Schumann, who urged her to unearth the score and bring it to the public. She further contended that she had no prior knowledge the work existed. She then persuaded officials in the library to release the score for publication and performance.

In spite of acknowledged weaknesses, the concerto does have some very intriguing features and attractive moments. It is in the standard three movements, the last two joined. The first movement brings Mozart to mind in several ways. The key of D minor, the rhythmically agitated accompaniment, and the main theme with its strong, descending, octave leaps never fail to remind of the statue of the Commendatore in *Don Giovanni*. In addition, Schumann resurrected the opening orchestral ritornello, so common in Mozart's concertos. The initial ritornello, however, shares a problem with the troublesome first movement of Beethoven's C Minor Piano Concerto: The second theme appears in the relative major key and thus anticipates the solo exposition's tonal plan, thereby creating a repetitious tonal scheme. The themes are engaging nonetheless; the first is strong with striking counterpoint in the bass line, while the second is much more gentle. Unfortunately, Schumann does little with either.

The second movement is song-like and begins with an attention-getting syncopated line in the first part of the divided cello section. The rhythmic structure clearly points to Brahms and to Brahms's very stimulating approach to rhythm. This syncopated line returns in the finale, providing the only cyclic connection in the work. The finale is a polonaise, lacking in thematic variety and in spontaneity.

Soon after he completed the Violin Concerto, Schumann's health and mental stability deteriorated rapidly. He attempted suicide in February 1854 and spent the remainder of his life in an asylum in Endenich near Bonn. A few months before his death he returned to a project he had begun three years earlier—that of providing a piano accompaniment to Paganini's caprices for solo violin. Schumann ended his career working on music by the musician who had most fired his imagination and had inspired him to devote his energies to the art of music.

Schumann's compositions for solo instrument and orchestra run the gamut from the Violin Concerto, with its Classical structure, to the brilliant and highly Romantic Concertstück for four horns, but the Piano Concerto is the most outstanding. The Piano Concerto combines brilliant solo writing and effective use of the orchestra in a Romantically conceived, highly integrated, three-movement structure replete with exciting and passionate music.

JOHANNES BRAHMS (1833–1897)

Brahms wrote four concertos, all of which remain monuments in the standard repertory. He composed the two piano concertos for his own performance, the Violin Concerto for his close friend Joachim, and the Double Concerto for Violin and Cello for Joachim and the cellist in his string quartet, Robert Hausmann (1852–1909). Brahms's concertos revive ideals and principles associated with the Classical concertos of Mozart. A crucial factor in Brahms's approach to music was his intense devotion to and study of earlier music. While Brahms's musical style is firmly in the Romantic tradition, it has a healthy mixture of stylistic ingredients associated with Classical, Baroque, and even Renaissance music.

Brahms's music is characterized by strong, clear forms, often of Classical design—this during an age when many composers had moved away from strong, formal structures, which they felt too confining. Brahms was a great contrapuntist of the nineteenth century; his music has a textural vitality deriving from the lively independence of the various parts. This, together with his fondness for the lower instrumental ranges and the doubling of lines in thirds or sixths, gives much of his music a thoroughly characteristic density and richness. While his music has a Romantic tone quality, he consciously limited the range of timbres he used. For example, he calls for an orchestra of rather limited means, relative to the standards typical of the second half of the nineteenth century. He even favored the natural horn, where other composers routinely called for the valved instrument. Brahms was as inventive as Beethoven in the art of motivic development and a master of the technique of variation, thus creating dense and intricate structures by manipulating and building small musical ideas into grand musical gestures. Brahms extended the art of rhythmic development initiated by Beethoven and Schumann, and it is Brahms's use of this fundamental musical element that marks him as one of the most progressive of the nineteenth-century composers. His music possesses an exciting rhythmic vitality that often creates tension through rhythmic and metrical conflict. Counterbalancing the strong rhythmic, motivic, and contrapuntal qualities of Brahms's music is a rich lyricism, especially evident in slow movements and in second theme areas of the sonata-allegro-form movements.

Piano Concerto in D Minor, Op. 15

Brahms began work on what was to become the D Minor Piano Concerto in early 1854 in Düsseldorf, where he had come to provide moral support and assistance to Clara Schumann, following Robert's attempted suicide in February.

Certainly this was a period of emotional upheaval—not only was he deeply affected by Robert's collapse, but he fell in love with Clara, who was fourteen years older and married to a composer Brahms revered. As happened with several other works the young Brahms began during this time, the Piano Concerto took several years to complete and underwent significant revisions.[2]

The concerto began life as a sonata for two pianos, but by the summer of 1854 Brahms was no longer happy with this medium and transformed the first of the three completed movements into a symphonic movement, sending it to his friend Joachim for comment. Brahms, at the age of twenty-one, was a gifted composer whose musical imagination had been largely formed at the piano, and he desperately needed help in writing for orchestral instruments. Joachim, though only two years older, had obtained considerable experience with orchestral instruments as a violinist and conductor, and proved a reliable and ready source of information for his friend, as revealed in the correspondence over the course of the next four years.

Joachim responded favorably to the draft of the symphony movement, requesting more. But Brahms found orchestrating a work conceived for the piano exceedingly difficult and in early 1855 thought of a new adaptation of it as a piano concerto, thus retaining some of the original pianistic qualities. The execution of this plan was delayed until late 1856. Brahms performed a number of the important piano concertos of Mozart and Beethoven in public concerts during this gestation period. In November 1855, he played the "Emperor" Concerto in his first performance with orchestra, and in January 1856, he played Beethoven's G Major Concerto. Also in January 1856, at a festival in Hamburg, celebrating the 100th anniversary of Mozart's birth, he played Mozart's D Minor Piano Concerto, K. 466. Thus, as Brahms's own concerto took shape, it appears concertos of Mozart (especially the two in minor—the D Minor, K. 466, and the C Minor, K. 491) and Beethoven (especially the Third in C Minor) may have served as models.

After much hard work and with extensive help from Joachim, particularly in matters of orchestration, Brahms completed the concerto in February 1858 for a planned performance in Hamburg, 25 March. This concert came to nothing for want of a proper piano, but Joachim arranged to lead the work in rehearsal in Hanover five days later, with Brahms playing and Clara Schumann present. The first public performance took place almost a year later on 22 January 1859 in Hanover, where it was a moderate success. The work was very poorly received in a Leipzig performance five days later. Its aggressive qualities may have proved too much for the conservative musicians and audience, who were still under the influence of Mendelssohn, while the concerto's Classical features would have found little favor with the radical elements of the Leipzig musical establishment. The Leipzig concert proved to be the greatest artistic disaster of Brahms's career. The concerto was performed again in Hamburg in March; well received this time, it gradually found its way into the standard concerto literature.

The first movements of the D Minor Concerto and the C Minor Symphony, the latter also begun close to the same time but not completed until 1876, are among Brahms's most powerful and tragic utterances. The concerto's first movement, Maestoso in unusual $\frac{6}{4}$ time, opens with what may well be the strongest orchestral statement in German music since Beethoven's Ninth Symphony.

Brahms (seated) with Joachim. There have been numerous instances of a particular performer's inspiring a composer to concerto composition; among the most outstanding results is Brahms's Violin Concerto written for his friend Joachim. Joachim provided good advice on violin matters as well as on some orchestral concerns, but his help was not as badly needed in the composition of the Violin Concerto as it was in Brahms's first work for orchestra, the D Minor Piano Concerto. Joachim figured in three of Brahms's four concertos; the Double Concerto for Violin and Cello was composed for Joachim and Hausmann, the cellist in Joachim's string quartet.

Timpani, supported by the lower-pitched instruments, open the work with a thunderous peal on the tonic note. This tone is reiterated as a lengthy pedal point underlying the bold main theme that shoots forward like a bolt of lightning (Ex. 16-7).

Ex. 16-7. Brahms, Piano Concerto No. 1 in D Minor, Op. 15; I. Maestoso, mm. 1–11.

The opening contains several notable elements. First, it begins with a lengthy orchestral introduction that harks back to the traditional orchestral ritornello of the eighteenth century. It is partly through the use of the ritornello that Brahms restored the orchestra to a position of importance equal to that of the soloist. Secondly, the use of pedal point, a characteristic Brahmsian gesture, may attest to his fascination with earlier music. Brahms routinely sent his new works to Clara Schumann for her review and comment; she rarely missed his long pedal points, often commenting with great enthusiasm about them. As in many other pieces, Brahms uses the pedal point to provide an anchor, above which harmonies may come into conflict, creating tonal or harmonic ambiguity. That is the case in this work, as the tonic pedal point, D, supports a theme beginning on B-flat which then outlines the B-flat major chord. But in the fourth measure A-flat is introduced in the melody, creating a strong pull to E-flat, a semitone away from the work's tonic. The harmonic tension, the boldness of the theme, and the thundering pedal point combine to form a powerful orchestral opening statement. And at the beginning of the recapitulation (mm. 310ff.), the harmonic conflict explodes when the piano repeats the main theme in E major against the D pedal. Before the eventual resolution to the tonic, the theme is repeated in A major against a G pedal point, bringing further conflict.

The remainder of the opening orchestral ritornello contains many features worthy of attention. Following the introduction of the main theme and the establishment of a pull to E-flat, Brahms unexpectedly shifts the pedal point down a semitone to C-sharp. Here the theme is repeated beginning in A major, and part of the orchestra splits off to play contrapuntal games with the trill from the theme. The dynamic level sinks as cellos undertake a bass ostinato pattern matching in contour the main theme's first five notes. Above this, a clarinet and first violins introduce a dark, new theme that momentarily glimmers when it reaches up to F-sharp, offering us a glimpse of the tonic major (Ex. 16-8). The F-sharp quickly dissolves into F-natural, and the passage repeats sequentially at a still lower dynamic level with violins muted. The F-sharp–A–F-sharp motive in m. 31 is thoroughly typical of Brahms. It may relate to his motto *Frei aber froh* (F–A–F: free but happy)—modeled after Joachim's *Frei aber einsam* (F–A–E: free but lonely) motto. The normal pitches for Brahms's motto (F–A–F) have been altered to add the sweet touch of the major harmony here.

Ex. 16-8. Brahms, Piano Concerto No. 1 in D Minor, Op. 15; I. Maestoso, mm. 25–34.

The closing section of the ritornello includes another theme in the still darker key of B-flat minor and a three-part canonic setting of the main theme among violins, horns in B-flat, and lower strings (mm. 67ff), from which the horns withdraw after the first phrase. The final thematic idea of the ritornello is a D major tune in high woodwinds set against the previous ostinato pattern. This pattern, drawn from the opening notes of the main theme, is now transformed to major (Ex. 16-9).

Ex. 16-9. Brahms, Piano Concerto No. 1 in D Minor, Op. 15; I. Maestoso, mm. 82–85.

Although the last complete triad of the ritornello is that of D major in m. 89, the final measure of the orchestral section sounds only the root and fifth of the chord. With this preparation the piano enters, sounding a new idea that begins on F-natural and emphasizing the minor mode (Ex. 16-10).

Ex. 16-10. Brahms, Piano Concerto No. 1 in D Minor, Op. 15; I. Maestoso, mm. 91–94.

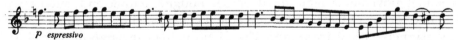

The piano's introduction with a new idea recalls both of Mozart's minor-mode concertos. Here Brahms brings in the piano almost unobtrusively, emphasizing parallel thirds and sixths, quietly and gradually advancing the piano's role. Also following Mozart's model, Brahms reserves a new lyrical theme for the solo instrument to present in the contrasting key of the solo exposition. It is a nineteen-measure, unaccompanied, chorale-style theme in F major (Ex. 16-11).

Ex. 16-11. Brahms, Piano Concerto No. 1 in D Minor, Op. 15; I. Maestoso, mm. 157–160.

The piano's outburst at the beginning of the development (mm. 226ff.) with a series of double octaves is the solo instrument's first bit of genuine virtuosic flair and one of the few conventionally virtuosic passages in the concerto. The development contains a transformation of the quiet third idea of the ritornello (Ex. 16-12a) into a more energetic and propulsive version (Ex. 16-12b). At the same time, the pizzicato violas seem to be using a transformed version of the opening theme's first four notes as filler between phrases.

Ex. 16-12. Brahms, Piano Concerto No. 1 in D Minor, Op. 15; I. Maestoso: (a.) mm. 46–47; (b.) mm. 288–289.

No cadenza is specified in the first movement, but the increased use of virtuosic double octaves near the end compensates for that traditional flourish.

The D major Adagio movement has given rise to conflicting programmatic interpretations. The manuscript Brahms presented to Joachim carries the puzzling inscription on the lower staves of the slow movement's first page: *Benedictus qui venit in nomine Domini* (Blessed is he who comes in the name of the Lord). Some believe that the inscription indicates the movement was intended as part of a Mass, noting also that the third movement of the sonata originally intended for two pianos probably found its home as the second movement of *A German Requiem*. Others, noting that Brahms sometimes addressed Schumann with "Domine," believe Brahms intended the second movement of the concerto as a kind of requiem for Robert. Confusing the issue further is Brahms's statement in a letter to Clara dated 30 December 1856, that the Adagio was a portrait of her. Whatever lies behind the movement's conception, it is an extremely intimate, highly personal statement that appears to be without model or tradition.

Like the first movement, the second is also in $\frac{6}{4}$ time, but with a lovely fluidity of motion. The conjunct structure of the melody in muted violins with the accompaniment of bassoons in double thirds in scalewise motion provides a strong contrast to the first movement's main theme, even though the tonic and meter are the same. The midportion of this ternary movement contains a new lyric idea in thirds played by clarinets in F-sharp minor. The piano writing throughout is elaborate and vintage Brahms. A brief improvisatory cadenza is placed near the end.

The finale is a seven-part rondo (ABACABA) in which the piano introduces the main theme in D minor, the polyphonic nature and syncopations of which may remind the listener of the opening of Bach's D Minor Harpsichord Concerto. The B theme is a fetching tune in F major, first stated by piano. The middle episode begins in B-flat on the theme of Ex. 16-13, which later appears as a fugue theme in minor (Ex. 16-14). The inclusion of a fugal section in the rondo may have been inspired by the final movement of Beethoven's Third Piano Concerto. The B theme returns in D minor, played more loudly and passionately than at its first appearance, ultimately transforming its original singing quality. A *Cadenza quasi Fantasia*, making use of a dominant pedal point, leads to the return of theme C in D major. The concerto closes, as do the next two, with a coda in a faster tempo built on a variation of the main theme of the movement. This D major closing section reminds some listeners of the happy ending so typical of eighteenth-century composers. Another short cadenza occurs just before the movement's end.

Ex. 16-13. Brahms, Piano Concerto No. 1 in D Minor, Op. 15; III. Rondo: Allegro non troppo, mm. 181–184.

Ex. 16-14. Brahms, Piano Concerto No. 1 in D Minor, Op. 15; III. Rondo: Allegro non troppo, mm. 238–242.

Violin Concerto in D Major, Op. 77

Brahms took up residence in Vienna in 1862. With the performance of the complete *A German Requiem* in 1868, Brahms's stature as a leading composer of his time was firmly established. But despite his growing reputation as a composer, aside from the two serenades for orchestra which were almost contemporary with the D Minor Concerto, he had not ventured into the purely orchestral medium following the stinging rejection of his concerto in Leipzig. He had obviously mastered writing for string instruments in a series of early chamber works and made use of the orchestra in the context of some large choral works. But he refused to approach a purely orchestral work until 1873 when he completed the orchestral version of the Variations on a Theme by Haydn, Op. 56A. This successful essay opened the door for the creation of several orchestral masterworks in the late 1870s and 1880s. Symphony No. 1 in C Minor was completed in 1876, and No. 2 in D Major came shortly after in 1877.

At this stage in his career, Brahms spent winters concertizing, saving his summers for composition, often in mountain resort areas away from the hot and busy city. During the summer of 1878 at Pörtschach on the Wörthersee, Brahms noted that the melodies seemed to be simply flying about as he composed his most lyrical orchestral work, the Violin Concerto in D Major, for his friend Joachim. This concerto, probably modeled to some extent on Beethoven's Violin Concerto which Joachim had saved from oblivion, is now recognized as one of the greatest violin concertos ever composed. It is a highly expressive and extremely demanding work. Brahms again called upon his friend to make suggestions for improving the work and subsequently altered some passages, typically by thinning the orchestration, to allow the soloist to stand out more comfortably. The violin part is not altogether idiomatic—the demanding double stops, wide leaps, and juxtaposition of very high with lower pitches are very taxing—nevertheless, Brahms capitalized on the instrument's singing expressiveness.

Like the B-flat Piano Concerto, which Brahms had sketched but set aside to work on this concerto, Op. 77 was originally planned to have four movements, the additional movement being a scherzo. But this idea was dropped, and a new slow movement, which Brahms referred to as a "poor Adagio," was substituted for an earlier one. The Violin Concerto is one of Brahms's richest orchestral scores, with glorious writing for wind instruments throughout, but especially in the middle movement.

The opening of the first movement, Allegro non troppo, establishes the overall lyrical mood of the work (Ex. 16-15). The gentle triple meter; the triadic nature of the opening theme, probably related to Brahms's great fondness for folk song; and simple octave doublings of bassoons, violas, and cellos, later joined by horns in octaves, all contribute to the warm, lyric mood at the outset. As in his first concerto, the orchestra plays a full ritornello, presenting all but the true second theme before the soloist enters. All the themes are lyrical, save the last which is quite rhythmic and forward-moving.

Ex. 16-15. Brahms, Violin Concerto in D Major, Op. 77; I. Allegro non troppo, mm. 1–7.

The rhythmic features of two thematic ideas deserve notice. The full orchestra presents a new idea beginning in m. 17, characterized by octaves and chromaticism, introducing hemiola, a favorite rhythmic device of Brahms in triple-meter movements. This rhythmic device has the effect of stretching three beats over two measures, creating interesting rhythmic tension (Ex. 16-16). A soft, lyrical idea (Ex. 16-17) comprising a repeated five-quarter-note figure unfolds in the first violins in mm. 53–58. The identical repetition of the five-beat figure leads to a momentary conflict with the underlying triple meter.

Ex. 16-16. Brahms, Violin Concerto in D Major, Op. 77; I. Allegro non troppo, mm. 17–26.

Ex. 16-17. Brahms, Violin Concerto in D Major, Op. 77; I. Allegro non troppo, mm. 53–57.

The soloist enters with forty-six measures of introductory display over a sustained pedal point, first on the tonic, then the dominant. The solo violin and orchestra are at first strongly juxtaposed, but they gradually join together as the woodwind instruments play a descending pattern related to the second measure of the main theme. During the solo exposition, the solo violin either plays thematic material or adds decorative material above orchestral thematic statements. Difficult triple stops amplify the strident octave theme of Ex. 16-16, which is now played *marcato* in cellos and double basses. The most extraordinary event, however, surely occurs with the solo violin's presentation of its new second theme in the dominant (Ex. 16-18). Even in so wonderfully lyrical a work, Brahms reserves a still-more-lyrical theme for the soloist. Those who treasure Brahms's lyrical second themes are forced to wait six or seven minutes for this one, but the wait is well worth it.

Ex. 16-18. Brahms, Violin Concerto in D Major, Op. 77; I. Allegro non troppo, mm. 206–210.

The development section moves through C major, as in Beethoven's Violin Concerto, to C minor, the solo violin playing the first theme of the second theme group in double stops (Ex. 16-19). The orchestra's tranquillo restatement of this theme is accompanied by the solo violin playing graceful, contrapuntal figures.

Ex. 16-19. Brahms, Violin Concerto in D Major, Op. 77; I. Allegro non troppo, mm. 304–312.

The recapitulation is based on the solo exposition. The final ritornello includes the exciting canonic treatment from mm. 27ff. of the opening ritornello. Near the movement's conclusion the ritornello serves as a perfect introduction to the cadenza, which was either improvised or prepared by Joachim. This is one of the last leading concertos in the repertory to offer the performer the space to improvise a cadenza; most of today's violinists pass over the opportunity, preferring instead to perform one written by Joachim. The coda begins with the soloist restating the opening theme, tranquillo, in its upper register, after which the movement comes to a speedy conclusion peppered with virtuosic double stops.

Brahms's tongue-in-cheek reference to the slow movement as a "poor Adagio" was his characteristic way of calling attention to one of his most beautiful slow movements. It is written in F major, the lowered mediant, with a midsection in F-sharp minor. The winds (without trumpets) play the first twenty-nine measures, featuring the oboe on the main melody. Each section of the ternary form employs the technique of variation, as the melodies become expanded and ornamentally elaborated in a highly decorative solo voice, often played in the very high register, which adds to the ethereal quality of the movement. The violin's varied expansion of the main theme's opening bars is especially intriguing (Ex. 16-20).

Ex. 16-20. Brahms, Violin Concerto in D Major, Op. 77; II. Adagio: (a.) mm. 3–6; (b.) mm. 32–37.

The finale is a rondo with strong Hungarian or gypsy elements specifically included to please Joachim who was born in Hungary. Brahms had been introduced to the music of Hungary by Reményi, and was so taken by it that he used Hungarian or gypsy elements repeatedly. But Brahms was not alone in his fascination with this exotic folklike element, for many German composers were exposed to and used it following the extensive migration of Hungarians to Germany during the 1848–49 Hungarian War of Independence. The vision of exciting gypsy dances and fiery gypsy fiddlers inspired Brahms as well as other composers of the century, so that this exotic music often found its way into violin concerto finales. Joachim, who knew the idiom intimately, was responsible for adding the qualifying terminology "but not too lively" (ma non troppo vivace) to the movement's tempo title: Allegro giocoso. This was notice for those not thoroughly familiar with Hungarian music to avoid taking it too fast, a common problem in performances of the movement.

The six-part rondo (ABACBA) begins with the rustic main theme stated by the solo instrument in double stops (Ex. 16-21), a subtle warning that this final movement, like so many in the concerto's history, will be a showcase for the soloist. A delightful example of Brahms's interest in rhythmic structures occurs in a later orchestral repeat of this theme in mm. 31–33, where stresses are shifted to different parts of the phrase. The B theme opens with an ascending scale first stated by the solo violin in double-stopped octaves, answered by the same scale inverted in the orchestra. The C theme is marvellously lyrical in triple meter (Ex. 16-22). This theme moves from G major through E major to C major. A mini-cadenza leads to the joyful, faster coda in which the rhythm of the main theme has been smoothed out. The triplet figures give the feeling of a $\frac{6}{8}$-march transformation of the main theme. The B theme also returns here, giving up its former strident quality.

Ex. 16-21. Brahms, Violin Concerto in D Major, Op. 77; III. Allegro giocoso, ma non troppo vivace, mm. 1–6.

Ex. 16-22. Brahms, Violin Concerto in D Major, Op. 77; III. Allegro giocoso, ma non troppo vivace, mm. 120–121.

Joachim gave the first performance of this concerto on New Year's Day 1879, at a Gewandhaus concert in Leipzig, after which he took it on a successful tour. He continued to play it frequently throughout the remainder of his career, but it took other violinists some time to feel comfortable with playing such a difficult, and, at times, not wholly idiomatic work. Tovey relates that the notable conductor Hans von Bülow (1830–1894) contended that Brahms had written a concerto against the violin. An answer came from the Polish violinist Bronislaw Huberman (1882–1947), who mastered the concerto and played it at the age of twelve with Brahms present. (Brahms liked the performance so much he gave the boy an autographed photograph "from his grateful listener.") Huberman later countered von Bülow's assertion by declaring the concerto was written neither against the violin nor for the violin with orchestra, "but *for* violin *against* orchestra—and the violin wins!"[3] More realistically we may say that it was written *for* violin *and* orchestra, and *both* have won.

Piano Concerto in B-flat Major, Op. 83

Brahms had begun to sketch the Second Piano Concerto on the eve of his forty-fifth birthday, 7 May 1878, following his return from his first spring trip to Italy with his friend Theodor Billroth, a physician. He then set it aside, returning to it on his forty-eighth birthday in 1881, following a second trip to his beloved Italy. The sunshine of those vacations must have flowed into the B-flat Concerto, for it is one of Brahms's warmest, yet heroic, compositions. He completed the work in July and first performed it in Budapest on 9 November 1881. Later that month he played it again in Meiningen with Hans von Bülow conducting.

Brahms playfully wrote to his friend, Elizabeth von Herzogenberg, of his completed concerto: "I have written a tiny, tiny piano concerto with a tiny, tiny wisp of a scherzo."[4] This "tiny" four-movement concerto is in fact one of the largest piano concertos ever written. In it, as in his last for violin and cello, Brahms makes some departures from the Classical tradition he had so carefully nurtured back to life in his two earlier concertos. But he does not ignore the tradition he valued so highly; rather, these departures are grafts of a few new scions onto the sturdy and reliable Classical trunk. In both of his last two concertos, he brings in the solo instruments very early, as was the practice of his contemporaries. The inclusion of an additional movement in the B-flat Piano Concerto—the scherzo—is a significant departure even from Romantic practice; in fact we know that Brahms had even considered including scherzo movements in his earlier concertos.

The magical horn-call opening of the first movement is one of those highly Romantic gestures that seems to invite the listener, as well as the rest of the orchestra and the soloist, into a performance already underway (Ex. 16-23). The soloist enters by responding with a chordal version of the horn theme. Another exchange between horn and piano leads to winds alone, followed by strings playing a complementary idea. At m. 11, the piano launches into an eighteen-measure unaccompanied passage which is the cadenza for this movement. Its scope and demands on the keyboard player foretell the magnitude of what is to follow. For the most part, Brahms writes for the piano in his very personal but demanding style, shunning the more traditional pianistic virtuosity so typical of Liszt's music. The Brahms concerto is marked by the many passages of massive chordal textures, unusually wide separation of the hands, rapid, wide-ranging movement of both hands, complicated independent rhythms, and the more traditional octaves, complemented by Brahms's fondness for doubling lines in thirds or sixths. In addition, Brahms's interest in counterpoint led to a more nearly equal use of the two hands, with many significant passages placed in the left hand.

Ex. 16-23. Brahms, Piano Concerto No. 2 in B-flat Major, Op. 83; I. Allegro non troppo, mm. 1–2.

The balance of the movement following this introduction is organized in a fairly traditional concerto-sonata format, with a compact orchestral ritornello and an expanded solo exposition. The entire movement is noteworthy for its richness of short, compact themes, which are extensively and interestingly developed.

The Allegro appassionato second movement is the scherzo in D minor, and it blends elements of the sonata-allegro form and the scherzo-trio-scherzo structure. The piano begins the movement, accompanied in its fourth bar by the lower strings with what will be an important motive (Ex. 16-24). Motives a and c from this theme are transformed and then combined to create a second theme beginning in m. 43. The largamente trio in major, which also serves as a kind of development section, begins with another transformation of these fragments; b is inverted in the upper voice and c in the lower (Ex. 16-25). These voices are reversed in a passage of invertible counterpoint. The scherzo's return is written out, with modifications, as a free recapitulation.

Ex. 16-24. Brahms, Piano Concerto No. 2 in B-flat Major, Op. 83; II. Allegro appassionato, mm. 1–6.

Ex. 16-25. Brahms, Piano Concerto No. 2 in B-flat Major, Op. 83; II. Allegro appassionato, mm. 188–189.

The $\frac{6}{4}$ Andante, in B-flat major, opens with an expressive cello solo accompanied by a lyrical counterpoint in half of the orchestral cellos while the other half and double basses play pizzicato bass notes. This lovely, warm theme was to be used again a few years later by Brahms in his deeply moving song "Immer leiser wird mein Schlummer," Op. 105, No. 2. As in the slow movement of the Violin Concerto, Brahms calls for a single instrument from the orchestra to sing the main lyrical idea for some measures before the soloist appears. In this movement, which has an ABA structure, the delicate piano sonorities contrast strongly with the piano's sound in the previous two movements. Here, in the concluding più adagio measures of the middle section, clarinets are highlighted against piano, a treatment that may have been inspired by a similar passage in the first movement of Liszt's E-flat Concerto.

The Allegretto grazioso finale, one of the composer's most light-hearted, turns again to the model of Hungarian folk music for some of its elements. A graceful dancelike character and light scoring pervade all sections of the rondo, even the brilliant, rushing coda.

The B-flat Piano Concerto, dedicated to his teacher Marxsen, is the accomplishment of an assured master. Brahms no longer shows any doubt about his work, nor did he turn to any others for assistance in the creation of this massive masterwork. Coincidently Brahms grew the beard which became a trademark, and he took on the bearing of a man fully at ease with himself and his surroundings.

Double Concerto for Violin and Cello in A Minor, Op. 102

Brahms's friend Joachim married an attractive singer, Amalie Weiss, of whom Joachim was extremely jealous. Finally in 1880 he accused her of having an affair with Fritz Simrock, Brahms's publisher and a friend of both Brahms and Joachim. Brahms was convinced Joachim's accusation was unfounded so he wrote her a long, warm, and deeply sympathetic letter, little suspecting it would later be produced in court as proof of a mutual friend's belief in her innocence. The judge was persuaded and acquitted her of adultery. Joachim, deeply wounded by what he saw as his friend's disloyalty, severed all relations with Brahms, after nearly thirty years of great and close friendship.

Even though they were not on speaking terms, Joachim continued to perform Brahms's music. Brahms tried on several occasions to break the ice, but not until 1887 when he began to write a new concerto for Joachim was the wound in the relationship healed. From the outset, Brahms conceived of the unusual Concerto in A Minor for Violin and Violoncello for Joachim and Robert Hausmann, the cellist in Joachim's quartet, and the inevitable need for consultation with Joachim helped rebuild the broken friendship.

Brahms sent the soloists their parts in the late summer of 1887 to an immediately positive reaction. Plans were made to get together, and on 21 and 22 September the three rehearsed with piano at Clara Schumann's house in Baden-Baden. The following day the work was played through with orchestra. The premiere took place a few weeks later in Cologne. The score was published with the dedication "To him for whom it was written: Joseph Joachim." Schumann noted in her diary, "This Concerto is in some degree a work of reconciliation—Joachim and Brahms have spoken to each other for the first time in years."[5]

The concerto, Brahms's last orchestral work, came on the heels of three chamber works calling for the violin and/or cello—the F Major Cello Sonata, Op. 99; the A Major Violin Sonata, Op. 100; and the C Minor Piano Trio, Op. 101. The Double Concerto is more solemn than any of his earlier concertos. Outward brilliance was largely eschewed; Joachim's written suggestions for revisions generally have to do with making the solo parts more brilliant, and Brahms subscribed only to a few of them. The quiet, introspective beauty he achieved here also appears in several of his other late works.

The Allegro first movement opens with an orchestral announcement of the opening motive and fragment of the first theme, starting on the dominant (Ex. 16-26). The dotted rhythms and triplets clearly reflect the composer's vibrant rhythmic style. The solo cellist then explores this material in a quasi-improvisatory cadenza "in the mode of a recitative." Winds tentatively introduce the more lyrical second theme, but the solo violin continues with its little introductory bit, joined quickly by the cello, and they play a composed two-part cadenza. As in the B-flat Piano Concerto, Brahms brings the solo instruments in early; in the Double Concerto he gives them the most virtuosic display material contained in the entire work.

Ex. 16-26. Brahms, Double Concerto for Violin and Cello in A Minor, Op. 102; I. Allegro, mm. 1–4.

Also as in the Second Piano Concerto, Brahms reverts to a standard concerto-sonata plan as soon as the soloists are introduced. The rhythmic main theme and lyrical second theme, presented in the solo exposition in C major, are separated by a syncopated transitional idea that later soars into the announcement of the recapitulation. The second theme is closely related rhythmically to a theme from Viotti's Concerto No. 22 in A Minor, a favorite of Joachim. Throughout this movement and indeed in most of the concerto, the cellist takes the lead, both in presenting and in exploring much thematic material.

The songful, triple-meter Andante in D major is dominated by its first theme, stated by the solo instruments in octaves, the bareness of which adds to the melancholy mood. Alternate measures are in longer notes, creating an interesting feeling of repose throughout the thematic statement. The first four notes are played slowly at the opening in the winds, almost like a distant horn call (Ex. 16-27). The movement's F-major midsection explores two other melodies, one depending upon parallel thirds, the other triplets, after which the two are contrapuntally combined.

Ex. 16-27. Brahms, Double Concerto for Violin and Cello in A Minor, Op. 102; III. Vivace non troppo, mm. 1–9.

The finale is another rondo strongly seasoned with gypsy spice. The light, dancelike, descending first theme contrasts sharply with the second episode's soaring C major theme, which calls for double stops in the solo instruments. After this theme returns in A major in both solo instruments, the work remains in tonic major to its jubilant conclusion.

This was the first significant concerto for more than one solo instrument to appear in decades. Brahms had adapted the principles of the older symphonie concertante to his conception of the Romantic concerto, resulting in a work of compelling originality. This, his last orchestral work, was completed almost four decades after his first orchestral work, the D Minor Piano Concerto. The character of each of his four concertos is unique, but they all carry the stamp of a master craftsman who was able to grasp the dramatic potential inherent in the concerto. Even though Brahms rejected the traditional nineteenth-century conception of virtuosity, he filled his solo parts with challenging and exciting music. He created concertos with deeply satisfying musical content.

Chapter Seventeen

GRIEG, DVOŘÁK, AND OTHERS

The musical contributions of several later nineteenth-century composers are commonly considered less significant than those of the giants Brahms, Wagner, and Verdi. Yet much of the music of these other composers remains of interest, and several of their concertos are prized by performers and listeners today. Furthermore, several of these concertos are quite exceptional; they are, in fact, masterpieces.

Most of the composers treated in this chapter were native to countries other than Germany. German music, especially that written for instruments, had come to dominate western European culture in the nineteenth century. As a consequence composers from elsewhere in Europe and the Americas embraced the Germanic tradition and practice, seeing it as the most legitimate of Romantic musical styles. On the other hand, a number of non-Germanic composers sought to establish an identity based on their own ethnic traditions. The most common vehicle to this end was the incorporation of native folk song and dance in their writing to give it a strong national color. This practice is evident in the music of the handful of composers, largely from Scandinavia, eastern Europe, and France, treated in this chapter.

EDVARD GRIEG

Norway's first notable composer of Romantic music was Edvard Grieg (1843–1907). He studied piano at the Leipzig Conservatory for four years, beginning in 1858 at age fifteen. His teachers included E. F. Wenzel, friend and champion of Robert Schumann, and Moscheles. He also studied composition but never felt he had received the training necessary to write for orchestra. While at Leipzig he heard much contemporary music; Clara Schumann's performance of Robert's Piano Concerto made a particularly lasting impression on him.

Despite his excellent piano training, Grieg never became a virtuoso performer, nor did he stress virtuosic elements in his compositions. Rather, he excelled in the creation of the lyric miniature, particularly songs and short lyric piano pieces. He mostly avoided the larger forms, making use of them only in his early compositions. He completed the Piano Concerto in A Minor, Op. 16 (1868), his most successful large-scale composition, when he was twenty-five. Unlike his

A Norwegian dance, the *halling*. The folk music of many regions played an ever-increasing role in music of the nineteenth and early twentieth centuries. Lively folk dances often provided inspiration for fiery concerto finales. The exuberant dance steps and vigorous motions of the Norwegian *halling* are illustrated here. Grieg made use of the quick rhythms of the *halling* in the opening theme of the finale of his A Minor Piano Concerto. Later in the movement the theme is recalled as a transformed variant, taking on the character of another folk dance, the *springdans*.

other piano compositions, the concerto does have a strong virtuoso content, particularly in the cadenza of the first movement. The latter pleased even Franz Liszt, who met Grieg in 1870 and gave a masterful performance, sight-reading the difficult work.

Grieg dedicated the concerto to Edmund Nupert (1842–1888), who first performed the work in the spring of 1869 in Copenhagen under the direction of the composer. The piece was published in 1872 with several revisions, including the second theme's first appearance in the trumpet rather than cellos, at Liszt's suggestion. But Grieg remained dissatisfied both with aspects of the orchestration and with portions of the solo part. He revised the score several times, including one major revision in 1906–07, near the end of his life. In the latter revision he restored the second theme to the cellos.

Written during the summer of 1868 at a vacation cottage near Copenhagen, this concerto was one of the first works Grieg composed after being introduced to Norwegian folk music in 1865 by the Norwegian composer Rikard Nordraak (1842–1866). Although it does not use folk tunes, the rhythms of Norwegian dances, the *halling* and the *springdans*, appear in the finale. A melodic gesture in the opening of the first movement, the descending second followed by descending third (Ex. 17-1), is a melodic cliché in Grieg's music, with folk-music roots.

Ex. 17-1. Grieg, Piano Concerto; I. Allegro molto moderato, m. 2.

The Piano Concerto is very clearly modeled upon Schumann's in the same key and shares with it a similar striking piano opening followed by a lyrical idea presented by the orchestra and then repeated by the piano. Some of the virtuosic writing seems close to Liszt's; this is especially so in the rapid octave and arpeggio passages and in the low rumbling passage of the cadenza of the first movement. Chopin's style is also evident, particularly in the nocturne-like treatment of the first movement's second theme (*tranquillo e cantabile*) in the piano. Chopin was Grieg's favorite composer, so it must have pleased him when the success of this concerto led some critics to refer to the Norwegian as "the Chopin of the North."

Grieg's concerto is in the traditional three movements, with the short, slow, second movement introducing the third to which it is connected without pause. The opening Allegro molto moderato is in sonata-allegro form. Several compact lyrical ideas emerge, but the most is made of the first theme, consisting of two parts—an initial fanfare figure in winds answered by a scale fragment in strings, and a more lyrical extension (Ex. 17-2). The second theme is first presented in C major in cellos and is immediately colored by a change to minor (Ex. 17-3). Both themes are first presented in the orchestra and then immediately varied by the solo instrument with simple orchestral accompaniment, although a bassoon counterpoint adds some interest to the piano's repeated statements of the second theme.

Ex. 17-2. Grieg, Piano Concerto; I. Allegro molto moderato, mm. 7–15.

Ex. 17-3. Grieg, Piano Concerto; I. Allegro molto moderato, mm. 49–52.

The first theme, split into its two halves, dominates the development section and the cadenza; in these places elaborate arpeggios in the piano provide decoration. The lyrical second part of the first theme provides the thematic material of the coda, where the theme's character transforms through the use of the major mode and a faster tempo.

The brief but warm triple-meter Adagio movement is in D-flat major. It fades away magically with horns repeating their descending conclusion to the main tune (first in major, than in minor) under delicate trills in the piano.

Without pause, the final movement begins with a clarinet and bassoon introduction of a lively dance rhythm, reminiscent of the beginning of the finale to Beethoven's G Major Piano Concerto. The movement is in sonata-allegro form, with a new pastoral theme substituting for the development section. Both the first theme and the pastoral theme reappear in the coda, where Grieg features the folk-dance elements mentioned earlier. The first theme, originally in the style of a Norwegian *halling* in duple meter, returns in the coda as a triple-meter *springdans*. The pastoral idea, on the other hand, loses its persistent quarter-note triplet rhythm and conforms to the natural accents of duple meter. In the final measures, the pastoral theme is repeated with its third note, the seventh degree of the scale, inflected chromatically downward, an harmonic twist much admired by Liszt.

This piano concerto is the work of a composer who had little interest in virtuosity for its own sake, and one who had little training and skill in writing larger forms or in writing for orchestra. Yet the work has strong lyrical appeal and sufficient virtuosic flair to keep it in the concerto repertory. Grieg started a second piano concerto in B minor in 1883, but never completed it.

ANTONÍN DVOŘÁK

Antonín Dvořák (1841–1904), the leading Czech composer of the nineteenth century, completed three concertos, one each for piano, violin, and cello. The earliest, for piano, is a weak composition, only rarely performed. The last, for cello, is considered one of the great masterworks in the cello concerto literature, and cellists play it frequently. The Cello Concerto overshadows the Violin Concerto, an engaging work written for Joseph Joachim. The violin piece should enjoy more recognition than it receives. Four less important one-movement works for solo instruments and orchestra—two for the violin, two for the cello—are Dvořák's arrangements of movements from some of his other compositions.

The Piano Concerto in G Minor, Op. 33 (1876), was composed more than a decade after his first stab at writing a concerto. He composed a concerto for cello in A minor in 1865, but abandoned the project before orchestrating it. The score with piano accompaniment was discovered in the 1920s and arranged for orchestra by Günther Raphael, but it is not a successful composition, which Dvořák obviously recognized.

Dvořák wrote the Piano Concerto for Karel ze Slavkovských (1845–1919), one of the few Czech pianists of the time to have taken an interest in contemporary Czech music. Although Slavkovských may have given the composer some help and although Dvořák was a pianist of considerable talent (he successfully played his own demanding Piano Quintet and Quartet), the solo part is poorly conceived with too much doubling of the hands. The Czech pianist Vilém Kurz (1872–1945) undertook a complete revision of it in an effort to make it more gratifying both to play and to hear,[1] but the concerto is not often performed today because it lacks the imaginative spirit that so characteristically fills the composer's works.

The Piano Concerto is in the traditional form, complete with a first-movement orchestral ritornello and second theme group preserved for the solo exposition. It is the only one of his concertos with the traditional cadenza in the first movement. The first movement contains hints of Beethoven and Brahms, specifically the latter's D minor Piano Concerto, while the second movement has much of Chopin about it. Only the last movement reflects the distinctive character associated with Dvořák's music. It is a vibrant, dancelike rondo with touches of the Slavonic folk elements that were soon to become prominent in his work. The contrasting lyrical theme of this movement, which first appears in B major, has an exotic quality imparted by its use of the augmented second (Ex. 17-4). The piano part of the last movement was also more satisfactorily designed; Kurz made many fewer revisions to it than to the others.

Ex. 17-4. Dvořák, Piano Concerto; I. Allegro con fuoco, mm. 104–107.

In the years immediately following the completion of his Piano Concerto, Dvořák turned his attention to the composition of pieces with a strongly Slavonic tone. The first Slavonic Dances, the Slavonic Rhapsodies, the Czech Suite, and the string sextet illustrate, through their distinctive and expressive melodies, harmonies, and rhythms, the thorough assimilation of his native folk materials. The widespread success of these works, particularly the Slavonic Dances, brought substantial critical recognition. Brahms was so enthusiastic that he assisted the Czech composer in obtaining a grant "for young, poor, and talented artists" from the Austrian government, and Joseph Joachim was so pleased with the sextet that his chamber group performed it in Berlin where it received warm welcome. In 1879 Dvořák began work on a violin concerto intended for Joachim. It, too, is enlivened by folk elements that were to remain an integral part of the composer's distinctive mature style.

In July Dvořák visited Joachim in Berlin and undoubtedly discussed aspects of the Violin Concerto. The composer sent the completed score, dedicated to Joachim, to the violinist in Berlin in November. After trying it, Joachim wrote to acknowledge the dedication but requested a thorough revision of the score. In the summer of 1880 Dvořák wrote to his publisher Simrock, whom Brahms had first encouraged to publish the Czech composer, advising that revision of the concerto had led to its complete transformation, including the introduction of new themes.

Dvořák sent the new score to Joachim, who remained silent until the summer of 1882 when he wrote to Dvořák, explaining that while the concerto had many nice features, the orchestration was too heavy and the violin part too unidiomatic.

In Berlin in the fall, Dvořák heard Joachim play through the concerto, and thereupon changed the orchestration and made cuts to the work, while Joachim further revised the solo part. Dvořák, however, refused a suggestion by one of Simrock's advisers, who had been present, to separate the first and second movements, which are linked without pause. The score was published at last in 1883 and given its first performance in Prague by František Ondříček on 14 October 1883. Strangely, Joachim never performed the work, although he offered to do so in England in 1884. But this performance fell victim to a conflict between two concert societies and the upcoming visit of Dvořák, and even this opportunity was lost. Joachim certainly had other occasions to play it, but, as Dvořák's biographer, Clapham, speculates, so extremely conservative a musician may simply have decided the work departed too far from the Classical tradition for his taste.

The Violin Concerto is intensely lyrical, bold, and filled with folk-inspired melodic ideas characterized by striking leaps and strong rhythms. The recapitulation of the first movement, Allegro ma non troppo, is cut short, which has led some to criticize the movement's truncated structure and lack of balance. The vivid movement is immediately engaging, however, and its ideas hold the listener's interest. Furthermore, Dvořák's unusual decision to link the first movement to the second with an extended slow transition is quite novel, although it may have been suggested to Dvořák by Bruch's G Minor Violin Concerto of almost a decade earlier, also dedicated to Joachim.

In contrast to his approach to the form in the earlier Piano Concerto, Dvořák followed the more common Romantic practice in the Violin Concerto, dispensing with an opening orchestral ritornello in the first movement. Instead, he wrote an abridged sonata-allegro-form movement with very few separate tutti sections, allowing the solo violinist to perform throughout most of it.

The thematic material of the first movement is of great interest. The opening A minor theme is a two-part idea shared by orchestra and soloist (Ex. 17-5). The rhythmic design of the opening orchestral fanfare establishes the feeling of Czech folk music, which is continued, in part, by the violin's dancelike motive in double stops. This last motive signals the mature style of Dvořák. A subsidiary theme in B-flat, within the first theme group (mm. 43 ff.), draws a strong Brahmsian flavor from its syncopation across the barlines, the active eighth-note counterpoint in the woodwinds, and the inflected sixth-scale degree (Ex. 17-6). Two further themes appear in the exposition, both first played by the solo violin. One, following the solo violin elaboration of the orchestral fanfare, is quite characteristic of Dvořák's style in its repetition of a short phrase incorporating rhythmic variation, perhaps in imitation of folk music (Ex. 17-7a). The other, the very beautiful theme in the second key area of C major, is again reminiscent of Brahms (Ex. 17-7b). This theme is immediately repeated in a gently decorated scherzando version in the solo violin, while the clarinets present it in original form in sixths against a pizzicato string background (mm. 162ff.). The solo violin's *fz* accents, mordants, and quick octave leaps give this passage a folklike air. Neither of these last two themes appears in the truncated recapitulation.

Ex. 17-5. Dvořák, Violin Concerto; I. Allegro ma non troppo, mm. 1–9.

Ex. 17-6. Dvořák, Violin Concerto; I. Allegro ma non troppo, mm. 43–46.

Ex. 17-7. Dvořák, Violin Concerto; I. Allegro ma non troppo: (a.) mm. 78–81;
(b.) mm. 148–152.

The unusual linking of movements I and II is accomplished by a soft, expressive transition featuring the solo violin and woodwinds on material fashioned from the second half of the main theme, which also was the primary material of the shortened recapitulation.

The Adagio ma non troppo middle movement is in ternary form, with a more active, poco più mosso middle section that at first contrasts its stormy F minor with the calmer F major opening. Brahms is again brought to mind in the early stages of the movement, where very effective woodwind writing and the long, lyrical melody in triple meter evoke the Adagio of his recently completed Violin Concerto. Dvořák's main melody is cast in clear four-bar phrases, but is far from ordinary in its impact. The very exceptional melody moves in unexpected ways and has been given a most effective accompaniment with sudden harmonic shifts and exquisite bits of contrapuntal detail, especially in the woodwinds.

Some unusual tonal features heighten the expressive quality of the Adagio. The recapitulation, signaled by a trumpet fanfare that overlaps the main theme's return, begins in A-flat major, rather than the expected F major. Later a folklike tune makes a surprising *pesante* appearance in F major in the orchestra, but it is immediately repeated by the soloist, *dolce*, in the unexpected key of A major, with a lovely bassoon counterpoint. This tune had appeared earlier, in the second half of the middle section of the movement, first in C major and then in E major, a similar tonal relationship.

A detail of orchestration deserves attention. The movement closes with a quite effective passage in which the horns enhance the main theme's folk feeling by presenting it softly in parallel thirds, while the soloist provides a delicate arpeggiated accompaniment. The folk-inspired use of horns is typical of Dvořák's colorful orchestration.

The finale, marked Allegro giocoso, ma non troppo, is a rondo with a strong, folkloric glow. The main rondo theme is a *furiant* in a form common to many simple rondo themes: aababa. The *furiant* is a fast Bohemian folk dance using alternating triple and duple meter. In the typical stylized versions of nineteenth-century composers, such as those of Dvořák, the dance is organized in triple meter. Accents regularly create pairs of beats in hemiola patterns (Ex. 17-8).

Ex. 17-8. Dvořák, Violin Concerto; I. Allegro giocoso, ma non troppo, mm. 1–10.

Three large episodes intervene between reappearances of the main theme, which is always effectively reorchestrated on its return. A charming folk-related instance of this rescoring occurs in the theme's second appearance (mm. 289ff.), where the soloist is accompanied by an imaginatively orchestrated open-fifth drone, in imitation of bagpipes.

The first episode (which also reappears as the third episode in this ABACABA rondo) offers several new themes; the first, in the woodwinds, closely resembles a folk song and is based on the *furiant* rhythm (Ex. 17-9).

Ex. 17-9. Dvořák, Violin Concerto; I. Allegro giocoso, ma non troppo, mm. 73–76.

The central episode is a *Dumka,* a kind of lament in moderate duple meter. In the hands of Bohemian composers of the nineteenth century, the *Dumka* had become an instrumental piece of melancholy quality, with interspersed livelier, more cheerful sections. Dvořák often adds figural variation to repeats of a *Dumka* theme, possibly in imitation of folk practice, and that is the case in this D minor episode. The coda begins with an A major version of the *Dumka* in double-stopped thirds in the solo instrument, bringing the Violin Concerto to an effective close.

Dvořák's Cello Concerto in B Minor, Op. 104 (1894–1895), is generally regarded by musicians and musicologists as one of the greatest works in the admittedly slim cello concerto literature. Dvořák composed this, his last major symphonic work, at the end of his three-year visit (1892–1895) to the United States, where he had served as director of the National Conservatory in New York City. Dvořák's two best-known symphonic works grew out of this American visit, but they are very different in general orientation. The E Minor "New World" Symphony, Op. 95 (1893), is inspired by the New World and its music—black spirituals, songs of Stephen Foster, and songs of Native Americans—and its impact on the Old World composer. The Cello Concerto, on the other hand, is the work of a composer looking homeward.

Dvořák's initial stimulus for a concerto for cello was an 1894 performance by Victor Herbert in New York. Herbert played his own Cello Concerto No. 2 in what must have been a very convincing performance of this work which emphasized the cello's upper range; before this Dvořák had some misgivings about the cello. He liked the instrument's middle range, but found the upper range too "nasal" and the lower range too "mumbling." Herbert's especially effective scoring for trombones with solo cello in the slow movement probably also inspired Dvořák to call for low brass in his Cello Concerto, expanding the orchestra beyond that of the Classical ensemble of his previous concertos.

Extramusical events often bear directly on musical content; in this case Dvořák had already begun work on the concerto when he learned of the serious illness of his sister-in-law, Josefina Kaunitzová. As a teenager in 1865, Josefina had studied piano with the composer, and he fell in love with her. He composed several songs with her in mind and determined to use the melody, transformed, of one of her favorites, "Leave me Alone" (published as Op. 82, No. 1), in the middle movement of the Cello Concerto. A month after his return from the United States, his former love died; the event so deeply gripped Dvořák that he revised the conclusion by adding further reference to this theme, creating a most touching requiem.

Dvořák originally conceived of the concerto as a solo vehicle for Bohemia's most respected cellist and founder of the important Bohemian String Quartet, Hanuš Wihan (1855–1920). Wihan was consulted about the solo part and suggested modifications. The composer accepted many, but he refused to incorporate Wihan's contribution of a major cadenza in the final movement, for, as in the earlier Violin Concerto, the composer sought to avoid the traditional showy cadenza. Dvořák particularly disliked Wihan's suggestion in this case, fearing that a cadenza would disturb the serious mood of the requiem-like conclusion to the work.[2] This disagreement with Wihan probably contributed to Dvořák's endorsing the first performance by another cellist, Leo Stern, in London in 1896. The work, however, bears a dedication to Wihan, who did eventually perform it.

The Cello Concerto is a major virtuoso piece of powerful, yet intimate, scope. The Czech tunesmith fashioned an abundance of melodies for cello, and the concerto's tunefulness is an immediately attractive feature. The orchestra, expanded with piccolo, triangle, three trombones, and tuba, plays a vivid role in this truly symphonic concerto. Dvořák demonstrated a strong sensitivity to the soulful quality of the solo instrument, frequently highlighting its character with extraordinarily effective and varied orchestral accompaniment. Particularly striking are those passages in which the solo cello is accompanied by the low brass choir, and when it is in duets with a clarinet, a flute, an oboe, and even once with a solo violin. Horns, as is so often the case in this composer's music, have very special passages, evoking sound images of the homeland.

Dvořák had departed significantly from the traditional forms in the Violin Concerto, but in the Cello Concerto he returned to an almost Classical structure. The opening Allegro begins with a full orchestral ritornello that includes the richly Romantic, almost dark, B minor main theme (Ex. 17-10) and the wonderfully expressive second theme (Ex. 17-11) in D major. As in Beethoven's Third Piano Concerto, the introduction of the contrasting key in the opening ritornello diminishes the effectiveness of that key when it is repeated in the solo exposition. Further it complicates the composer's attempt to provide a dramatic announcement of the soloist's entry. But the orchestral coloration, the sheer tunefulness of the themes, and their searching development more than compensate for these problems.

Ex. 17-10. Dvořák, Cello Concerto; I. Allegro, mm. 1–6.

Ex. 17-11. Dvořák, Cello Concerto; I. Allegro, mm. 57–64.

A strong mood and two important motives are established in the first few measures of the concerto. The mood is largely one of darkness created not only by B minor, but also by chromatic inflections in that key and an effective use of the orchestra. A pair of unison clarinets in their dark, low register presents the initial motive in mm. 1–2, accompanied by very soft, low strings. Subtle changes in the orchestration further intensify the dark coloration. A pair of unison bassoons enters an octave below the clarinets in mm. 3–6, and a soft timpani roll contributes to the texture in the last measure of the phrase.

The thematic material of this opening takes on a distinctive rhythmic and melodic shape. The first two measures are united by common material, as the motive of m. 1 is inverted for use in m. 2. There, the A-natural, the lowered seventh scale degree, adds a strikingly colorful, modal element, evoking a strong feeling of folk music. Some commentators see this modal element as related to Dvořák's interest in American music, but it is a sound clearly associated with eastern European folk music as well, and one much used by this composer prior to his visit to the New World.

The rhythmic structure of the opening further enhances its folkloric quality. The peculiar rhythmic design of the first motive in the clarinets is certainly of folk origin, and its accompaniment in the strings is based on a contrasting folklike rhythm. The second part of the main theme, beginning already in m. 3, brings a new rhythmic idea—a dotted-rhythm figure followed by straight quarter notes in a simple stepwise pattern. The character and shape of this second motive change as the movement progresses. The stepwise movement of the dotted-rhythm figure expands to outline a triad, and the descending scale acquires more aggressive accents. The tutti's *grandioso* restatement of the theme clearly defines this change (Ex. 17-12.)

Ex. 17-12. Dvořák, Cello Concerto; I. Allegro, mm. 23–27.

The initial idea of mm. 1–2 undergoes even more striking transformation in the hands of the solo cellist on two separate occasions. In the first instance, the transformation, involving rhythmic diminution and *spiccato* (bounced) bowing (Ex. 17-13a), serves as the soloist's first statement of the opening theme in the solo exposition. The special bowing technique and new rhythmic structure impart a strong, folk-dance quality to the theme, which previously seemed more vocal in origin. The second transformation occurs at the end of the development where a surprising shift to A-flat minor leads to a more meditative and sustained version of the main theme (Ex. 17-13b). Here a solo flute joins in to create a duet with the solo cello. Because of these varied statements of the main theme at the close of the development, Dvořák begins the recapitulation with a tutti statement of the second theme in the tonic major.

Ex. 17-13. Dvořák, Cello Concerto; I. Allegro: (a.) mm. 110–111; (b.) mm. 224–227.

The soloist's first entry echoes the initial pair of ideas in an attention-getting, operatic style. The recitative-like passage, marked *quasi improvisando*, involves intense *forzato* triple-stopped chords on the descending scale of the fourth measure, accompanied by tremolando strings. This passage signals that this is to be a virtuoso piece. The opening is made all the more dramatic by its contrast to the rustic idea (Ex. 17-14) which had been used to round off the introductory tutti. This Slavic dance figure never returns; Dvořák only required its use once, prior to the soloist's first entry.

Ex. 17-14. Dvořák, Cello Concerto; I. Allegro, mm. 75–76.

One important detail in the first movement almost goes unnoticed on its first appearance. This is a drum motive that unites the work, appearing also in the second and third movements at crucial moments. It first occurs in the solo exposition where it is played by violas under a rising trill in the solo instrument and restatements of the opening motive in woodwinds (Ex. 17-15). Later, in the recapitulation, timpani play the drum motive as an accompaniment to the solo statement of the second theme. Drum motives of this sort were often associated with death and funeral processions in nineteenth-century music; this motive powerfully underlines nostalgic moments.

Ex. 17-15. Dvořák, Cello Concerto; I. Allegro, mm. 103–104.

The middle movement, Adagio ma non troppo, in G major and triple meter, is in ternary form. The first part, thirty-eight measures long, grows in a typically Dvořákian way as new thematic ideas are subtly added to give the impression of one very long lyrical statement. Throughout the movement, Dvořák uses the orchestra masterfully. In the first section, woodwinds (especially clarinets and later flutes) are largely responsible for establishing the strong pastoral atmosphere. In one passage soft, sustained trombone chords add a peaceful note. A sigh motive, first presented in the first movement, is further elaborated in a brief passage for the solo instrument and orchestra in mm. 29–34.

The middle section of the movement opens with a stormy four-measure tutti passage in G minor, then settles into the cello's soft, tenderly expressive transformation of the "Leave me Alone" song theme (Ex. 17-16), with a very effective clarinet obbligato part. Woodwinds twice take up the song theme, each time with varied solo cello obbligato. In the final appearance of the song theme, following a return of the stormy passage in B minor, the winds are particularly sonorous as clarinets and bassoons play the theme in thirds to an arpeggiated accompaniment in the solo cello's high register. Imaginative scoring also colors the reprise of the movement's opening theme: Three horns announce the theme in harmony, accompanied by low strings offering a version of the drum motive from the first movement (see mm. 95ff.). Flutes and bassoons add colorful details to the cello's *quasi cadenza* near the movement's end. Moving new scoring contributes to the expressiveness of the coda, which focuses on elements derived from the movement's first section. The movement dies away (*morendo*) with the cello playing delicate harmonics.

Ex. 17-16. Dvořák, Cello Concerto; II. Adagio ma non troppo, mm. 43–46, and Song, "Leave Me Alone," mm. 1–4.

The finale is a rondo containing a multitude of melodic ideas. The main rondo theme, hinted at in the opening by the horns, is a march tune in B minor (Ex. 17-17). Three episodic sections separate the rondo theme statements. The first episode is short and is not used again. The second involves several ideas of a cantabile nature in a three-part aba structure. The third episode, in G major and moderate tempo, opens with a new theme in the solo instrument that has a strong, Slavic flavor with its repeated ascending fourths (Ex. 17-18). The solo instrument is again intimately coupled with the woodwinds.

Ex. 17-17. Dvořák, Cello Concerto; III. Allegro moderato, mm. 33–40.

Ex. 17-18. Dvořák, Cello Concerto; III. Allegro moderato, mm. 281–288.

The Andante coda, newly composed after the death of Josefina, includes thematic elements from all three movements. Once again Dvořák's effective use of the orchestra contributes markedly to the tender and moving quality of this music. A muted trumpet lends a distant, nostalgic air to the rondo theme at the coda's outset. Clarinets thereupon quietly recall the opening of the first movement, and a solo violin quotes the original "Leave Me Alone" song that had been used, transformed, in the second movement. As the solo cello assumes the responsibility for the theme, the timpani quietly enunciate the funeral march motive. The brass section then comes forward with a loud, augmented version of the rondo's main theme before the stormy final allegro vivo page of the score.

Brahms, in his last year, accompanied his cellist friend Robert Hausmann in an enthusiastic read-through of Dvořák's great work in Brahms's apartment. Ever Dvořák's great supporter, he expressed his admiration for the concerto by declaring, "Had I known that such a violoncello concerto as that could be written, I could have tried to compose it myself."[3]

MAX BRUCH

Max Bruch (1838–1920), a German, developed a strong interest in exotic, folk, and other nontraditional musical elements. He began composing at a very early age, producing a goodly number of works, including operas, symphonies, choral and chamber music, songs, keyboard music, and various concertos or concerto-like compositions. Today his reputation is based largely on his Violin Concerto in G Minor, Op. 26 (1866–68).

His concerto was first performed in April 1866 with Otto von Königslöw as soloist and the composer, an excellent conductor, on the podium. Bruch then revised the work and sent it to Joachim for criticism. Bruch incorporated many of Joachim's suggestions and asked if the work ought to be called a fantasy because of its unusual first movement. Joachim replied that the concerto designation was entirely appropriate, since the second and third movements were fully developed. Joachim performed the revised concerto in January 1868.

Bruch called his first movement a *Vorspiel* or prelude, perhaps referring to his interest in Wagner's preludes to his operas, but surely recognizing the unorthodox character of the movement. This seven-minute movement sounds like an introduction to the second movement. It has no introductory orchestral ritornello; the orchestra and solo violin alternate in exchanging contrasting ideas instead. The soloist at first plays improvisatory, cadenza-like passages, but eventually presents the movement's main theme, in a declamatory style. Tinges of folk song, created by the use of the lowered seventh scale degree, color the theme. The movement maintains a good balance between virtuosic flash and songful melody, for Bruch was a good melodist. The development is short, and the recapitulation is curtailed by the transition to the second movement. The first two movements are linked by a single held note in the violins, akin to the bassoon-note transition to the second movement of Mendelssohn's Violin Concerto.

The serene Adagio is built upon three lyrical themes, the second of which has a particularly yearning character; it is used in the passionate climax. The finale is a very attractive movement with an incisive, rhythmic, march-like main theme first stated by the solo violin in double-stopped thirds, anticipating the character of the opening theme of the finale of Brahms's Violin Concerto. A very appealing second theme is played on the G string of the solo violin with soft tremolando accompaniment.

Two other Bruch works for solo instrument and orchestra have remained in the repertory and are heard on occasion. Both have as their sources folk-related material. The "Scottish Fantasy," Op. 46, composed in 1879–80, was one of several of Bruch's works intended for the great Spanish virtuoso violinist Pablo de Sarasate (1844–1908). The Fantasy is an unusual five-movement work of rhapsodic character; it uses a number of Scottish folk melodies and features a harp as a second solo instrument in many sections. It is popular with violinists who enjoy mastering its idiomatic technical demands, which exceed those of the G Minor Concerto, the freer structure of the Fantasy permitting more extensive use of figuration. *Kol Nidrei* (1881) is a slow one-movement work of a devotional nature for solo cello and orchestra based on traditional Hebrew themes.

CAMILLE SAINT-SAËNS

Saint-Saëns (1835–1921) was an exceptionally talented organist and pianist as well as an amazingly prolific composer whose music epitomizes the French love of clarity and order, often elegantly expressed. In many respects he represents a return to the pre-Romantic view of the composer, by virtue of his more "objective," restrained approach. This sense was reinforced by the fact that he was a serious student and editor of earlier French music.

In 1869, with Romaine Bussine (1830–1899), Saint-Saëns founded the Société nationale de musique. Its slogan—*Ars gallica*—signaled its intention to establish French music as an alternative to the dominant Germanic musical tradition. The Society undertook the promotion of French absolute instrumental music, a type of music that had been particularly dominated by foreigners, most often German or Italian.

Nevertheless, the early stages of this "French Musical Renaissance" remained under the influence of external models, for in Paris, as elsewhere, the music of Beethoven, Schumann, and Mendelssohn found adherents, and the music of Liszt, who lived in Paris, remained a potent force. Furthermore, two of the earliest participants in the rebirth of French music were of foreign origin—César Franck (1822–1890) was born in Belgium, and Édouard Lalo (1823–1892) was of Spanish ancestry. Franck and Lalo, as well as Gabriel Fauré (1845–1924), served as committee members of the society, which sponsored premieres of their works, as well as important compositions by nonmembers.

Saint-Saëns was viewed as a leader in contemporary French music. He wrote in all the currently used musical forms, but his reputation rests most firmly on his instrumental compositions. He composed five piano concertos, three for violin, two for cello, and numerous other shorter orchestral works featuring a solo instrument. These usually featured piano or violin, but several are for flute or harp, favorite French instruments. He tended to favor the Viennese Classical forms and venerated Mozart, performing a number of the eighteenth-century composer's piano concertos in a series of concerts. Nevertheless, in his own concertos, the French composer departed from eighteenth-century traditions to experiment with a variety of formal structures, on occasion using forms other than the standard three-movement outline.

Of Saint-Saëns's piano concertos, No. 2 in G Minor, Op. 22 (1868), still is performed with some regularity. The great Russian pianist Anton Rubinstein (1829–1894) requested the work, not for his use as a soloist, but to conduct, as he wished to expand his performance horizons. Saint-Saëns completed the concerto in only seventeen days and played it with Rubinstein conducting on 13 May 1868 in Paris to a generally cool reception. Franz Liszt, however, found it worthwhile.

The G Minor Piano Concerto is in three movements, but of quite unorthodox nature. The first, the slow movement, Andante sostenuto, opens with a toccata-style piano cadenza incorporating a G pedal point which evokes the keyboard textures of J. S. Bach. A brief orchestral fanfare leads to the piano's presentation of the first theme in a declamatory style. The piano also introduces the syncopated, contrasting theme in B-flat major. As in most of Saint-Saëns's concertos, the solo instrument is called for from the beginning and introduces most of the thematic material. The solo part, as is typical in Saint-Saëns's concertos, is extremely demanding and very flashy, while the orchestra plays a clearly subordinate role. A long cadenza near the end of the movement is based on the first theme and is followed by a reprise of the piano's opening cadenza, this time with soft, sustained string support.

The second movement is a very engaging scherzo in E-flat major that may remind the listener of Mendelssohn's light and playful scherzo movements. The timpani begin, offering a jumpy dance rhythm that is often repeated, particularly in the piano. Here the dance rhythm serves from time to time, altered slightly, as an accompaniment for the lyrical second theme (Ex. 17-19). The scherzando's scintillating first theme moves rapidly, in contrast to the previous lyrical mood (Ex. 17-20).

Ex. 17-19. Saint-Saëns, Piano Concerto No. 2 in G Minor; II. Allegretto scherzando, mm. 76–80.

Ex. 17-20. Saint-Saëns, Piano Concerto No. 2 in G Minor; II. Allegretto scherzando, mm. 5–8.

The final Presto movement calls for almost constant solo bravura. It is a *tarantella*—a rapid, often wild, dance with fast triplets. An intriguing calmer section features the piano with a sequentially repeated one-measure trill motive set against sustained chorale-style chords in the orchestra.

Saint-Saëns composed several works for solo violin and orchestra for the Spanish violinist, Sarasate, the same performer for whom Bruch had written his *Scottish Fantasy*. The best known of Saint-Saëns's solo violin works is the Third Violin Concerto in B Minor, Op. 61 (1880). It is in the standard three movements, including a graceful and fluid barcarole-styled second movement. Another chorale-style passage, this one sounding much like Wagner, appears in the final movement. Unlike many of Saint-Saëns's French colleagues, he admired Wagner.

Saint-Saëns's First Cello Concerto in A Minor, Op. 33 (1872), is a more modest work. Its single-movement sectional structure and thematic relationships among sections may have been inspired by Liszt, who frequently encouraged Saint-Saëns. A fast sonata-allegro form and minuet are blended together in the first several sections. The work begins with an exposition and development in fast tempo, but before the recapitulation Saint-Saëns inserts a charming Intermezzo in the style of a minuet, which itself is also interrupted by a cadenza. A slow section, based on thematic material from both the opening section and the Intermezzo, precedes the concerto's final fast section, the only truly virtuosic portion of the piece. Cellists like the way in which the concerto focuses on the instrument's lyrical qualities, and appreciate, as well, the ease of projection above the orchestra.

Exotic strains characterize some of Saint-Saëns's works for solo instrument and orchestra. A few reveal a pronounced Spanish influence, such as the *Havanaise*, Op. 83 (1887), written for the Spanish violinist Diaz Albertini who accompanied the composer on a journey to northern France; there the crackling wood of an evening fire suggested the *habanera*, a Spanish dance. The Piano Concerto No. 5 in F Major, Op. 103 (1896), includes a theme Saint-Saëns heard on the Nile, earning this work the nickname the "Egyptian Concerto." Another short work for piano and orchestra is simply titled *Africa*, Op. 89 (1891).

OTHERS COMPOSING IN FRANCE

Édouard Lalo (1823–1892), a friend of Saint-Saëns, came by this kind of exoticism naturally. Lalo was of Spanish descent and incorporated Hispanic elements in the piece for which he is best remembered, the *Symphonie espagnole* (1875) for solo violin and orchestra. This work was also written for Sarasate, who had premiered Lalo's Violin Concerto the previous year. Sarasate was noted for his extremely delicate touch, accuracy of pitch, and rhythmic vitality, all of which come into play in the *Symphonie espagnole*. It is in five movements, the third of which is often omitted in performance. The first movement is in sonata-allegro form, with a simple but striking first theme (Ex. 17-21). The second movement, marked Scherzando: Allegro molto, is the most engaging. It is based on the Spanish *seguidilla*, a flamenco dance from southern Spain. Pizzicato strings imitate the sound of castanets accenting the exotic dance rhythm. The solo part is very light and airy. The fourth movement is an Andante in ternary form. An orchestral prelude and solo recitative lead to the cantilena of the first section; the midsection has a more florid solo part. Lively ostinato rhythmic patterns are introduced by the orchestra at the beginning of the final movement, a rondo with a joyous main theme first played by solo violin. A subsequent episode is in the style of another dance from southern Spain, the *malagueña*, a form of the fast, triple-meter *fandango*. In much of the final movement, Sarasate's dexterity and lightness of touch were exploited, especially in the staccato arpeggios and high trills.

Ex. 17-21. Lalo, *Symphonie espagnole*; mm. 42–44.

César Franck (1822–1890), organist and composer, became one of the most venerated of French musicians, although he was Belgian by birth. He relied almost exclusively upon traditional forms in his instrumental works and made some of the most distinctive contributions to nineteenth-century chamber music in France. He balanced his traditional outlook with a keen interest in the music of Liszt and Wagner, aspects of whose work can be heard in Franck's. His two compositions for solo piano and orchestra are among his later works. The first, *Les Djinns* (1884), a symphonic poem for solo piano and orchestra, is greatly overshadowed by the Symphonic Variations for Piano and Orchestra, written in 1885 and first performed by Louis Diémer at the Salle Pleyel in Paris on 1 May 1886.

The Symphonic Variations is a typical Romantic one-movement work in the form of an introduction, variations, and a finale in F-sharp minor. Franck presents two strongly contrasting ideas in the introduction that have a musical effect much like that of the contrasting ideas in the slow movement of Beethoven's Fourth Piano Concerto. Strings begin with a strongly rhythmic, compact motive (Ex. 17-22a), which is answered by a gentler, expressive idea in the piano, also built from a small motive (Ex. 17-22b).

Ex. 17-22. Franck, Symphonic Variations: (a.) mm. 1–2; (b.) mm. 5–8.

These motives are developed before the piano plays the main theme (Ex. 17-23) upon which the following six variations are built. In the final variation, molto più lento, cellos take over the main melody in major, while the piano provides a delicate arpeggiated accompaniment. Trills in both the pianist's hands introduce the final section, Allegro non troppo, the most symphonic of the work. This section is in fact a miniature sonata-allegro form with the first theme growing out of the piano's introductory motive (Ex. 17-22b) in F-sharp major in the basses, while the piano contributes the contrasting theme.

Ex. 17-23. Franck, Symphonic Variations; mm. 100–107.

Vincent d'Indy (1851–1931), one of Franck's most renowned students, composed the *Symphony on a French Mountain Air* for piano and orchestra in 1886. It is a three-movement work based on a folk tune from his native region of Cévennes. The tune appears in all three movements, sometimes cleverly transformed. The piano is ever-present, playing an important obbligato part, but it is subordinated to the orchestra, to an even greater extent than is the solo piano in Franck's Symphonic Variations. A solo harp often becomes the partner of the piano, but is largely used to play a decorative function.

Ernest Chausson (1855–1899), another of Franck's students, composed his emotionally intense one-movement *Poème* for the great Belgian violinist Eugène Ysaÿe (1858–1931) in 1896. It opens with a dark and low orchestral introduction in E-flat major, followed by the solo violin's introduction of the main theme in minor. Some passages call for double stops or other demanding violinistic techniques, but the work's emphasis is on the sincere, emotional content, as indicated by the title.

Gabriel Fauré (1845–1924) dedicated his *Ballade* (1881) for piano and orchestra to his teacher, Saint-Saëns. Like most of Fauré's music, the *Ballade* is elegant and lyric, with a somewhat ornate piano part and lightly scored orchestra.

THE CONCERTO IN RUSSIA

Peter the Great, who reigned from 1682 to 1725, was the first of Russia's czars actively to promote strong political, economic, and cultural ties with western Europe. In so doing, he encouraged many Europeans to settle in Russia. Musicians, especially from Italy or with close ties to Italy, came, laying the foundations of a Western musical tradition. Aspiring Russian musicians were, in turn, encouraged to further their education by traveling to the West. Catherine II, of German ancestry, czarina from 1762 to 1796, built upon these ties with the West yet maintained a strong interest in things Russian, even writing opera librettos based on Russian folklore and folk songs. This duality—on one hand, the desire to imitate Western models, and, on the other, a wish to establish an indigenous concert tradition firmly based on Russian models—did much to shape the history of Russian music through the nineteenth century.

Although Czar Alexander I sought early in his reign, 1801–25, to liberalize Russian life, the French invasion under Napoleon led the czar to return to the traditional autocratic policies. This return to autocracy was even more vigorously pursued by his successor, Nicholas I, who not only largely restored a despotic state, but also sought to limit foreign cultural influence during his reign, 1825–55. It was in these repressive times that Russia's first composer of any significance emerged.

Mikhail Glinka (1804–1857) received only limited formal musical training in Italy and Germany, before returning to his native Russia where he concentrated on the creation of songs and opera. Through his synthesis of Russian folk song with traditional Western art forms, he set the direction of the Russian national movement for the second half of the century.

Czar Alexander II, who ruled from 1855 to 1881, returned to a more liberal policy. His reforms helped to create an environment more conducive to artistic undertakings, and a cultural flowering occurred. This was the time during which the great writers Dostoyevsky (1821–1881) and Tolstoy (1828–1910) produced much of their work, and a number of significant figures emerged in the field of music.

Anton Rubinstein (1829–1894), the great Russian pianist, founded the Imperial Russian Music Society in 1859 to promote Russian music making, and, in 1862, Russia's first professional music school, the St. Petersburg Conservatory. Four years later his brother, Nikolay, established the Moscow Conservatory. These music schools, initially staffed largely by faculty of German origin, firmly focused on the models of traditional Western music. Anton Rubinstein, a prolific if unimaginative composer of music in the Germanic tradition, was the first Russian composer of any stature to write a concerto. The fourth of his five piano concertos, in D minor (1864), enjoyed some favor among Western pianists for a time, but has now faded from the repertory.

Mily Balakirev (1837–1910), largely a self-taught composer, developed a strong passion for using Russian folk elements in his music, inspired by a meeting with Glinka in 1855. The former, seeking to develop an alternative to the German-dominated approach of Rubinstein and his conservatory, formed the Free Music School, which was oriented toward establishing a Russian nationalistic style of music. He gathered around himself a group of composers who were generally self-trained. Dubbed by the critic Stasov as "The Mighty Handful," these men were dedicated to the encouragement of a Russian musical tradition.

These composers adopted a common working method to assist them in establishing a national idiom. Inspired by Glinka, they used folk tunes, primarily of Russian origin, to form the melodic basis of their compositions. These tunes are characteristically short and narrow in range, and Balakirev and his circle tended to rely heavily upon their repetition in order to expand the music for use in large forms, as in a symphonic movement. The Russian nationalist composers were intent upon skirting the Germanic style of motivic development, which led them to approach traditional Western musical forms in quite different ways. In place of the emphasis on motivic development, these composers preferred a mode of decorative variation that became the foundation of the Russian national style, extending all the way to the work of the twentieth-century composer Igor Stravinsky. In this style, the orchestral settings and/or accompaniments are altered as the short tunes are repeated, but the tunes themselves usually remain unchanged. Because of their interest in this approach, the Russian nationalists admired the work of Liszt, Berlioz, Chopin, and, to an extent, Schumann, over that of Brahms, Mendelssohn, and Beethoven, since the music of the first group was thought to exhibit similar tendencies toward decorative variation.

Of those making up Balakirev's group—Modest Mussorgsky (1839–1881), Nikolay Rimsky-Korsakov (1844–1908), César Cui (1835–1918), and Alexander Borodin (1833–1887)—only one, with the most extensive musical training, showed any interest in the concerto.

Rimsky-Korsakov, for many years a naval officer, composed three shorter works for wind instruments and orchestra after he was appointed inspector of bands. His later Piano Concerto in C-sharp Minor (1882–83), in a single, continuous movement, is based on a Russian folk song. The listener may well hear the inspiration of Franz Liszt in this rhapsodic work, published in 1886 and dedicated to Liszt in memoriam.

The gulf between Rubinstein's western-European-inspired music and the Russian nationalists did not last long, for those in both camps soon discovered valuable qualities in the music of their opposites. Composers in Balakirev's group were appointed to leading positions in Rubinstein's organizations, and Rubinstein recommended that Balakirev conduct the Russian Musical Society concerts in 1867. Rimsky-Korsakov, despite a musical education that could not match that of the German faculty, was appointed teacher of composition at the St. Petersburg Conservatory. Curiously, even Rubinstein eventually fell under the influence of Balakirev and wrote some works based on traditional Russian music. Borodin, of the nationalist camp, on the other hand, wrote a string quartet, a genre strongly associated with the German or the Western tradition.

PYOTR IL'YICH TCHAIKOVSKY

Pyotr Il'yich Tchaikovsky (1840–1893) in many ways blended, even united, the approaches of the Russian nationalists and of the Western or more Germanic tradition. He was trained at the St. Petersburg Conservatory and was one of its first graduates. He had a strong Western orientation, but maintained a lifelong interest in Russian folk music which colored much of what he wrote. He traveled extensively in Europe and acquired the most widespread reputation of nineteenth-century Russian composers outside his country.

Tchaikovsky's reputation in the West rests mostly on his orchestral music, although the opera *Eugene Onegin* (1877–78) has aroused much interest. The orchestra excited his imagination, and he developed a colorful, yet light—almost transparent—style of writing for the orchestra. Outstanding characteristics of his orchestration include the use of soaring, romantic melodies for the strings, supported by syncopated chords in the winds and percussion; a tendency toward bright sonorities; a striking juxtaposition of the wind and string families on small motives; and, at times, a thrilling, almost brash, use of brass and percussion.

Tchaikovsky was fully aware of his lack of mastery of sonata-allegro form. He, like his Russian colleagues, relied extensively on repetition and sequence, but his deft use of the orchestra to create marvelously varied repetitions and his wonderfully voluptuous melodic style more than compensate for this weakness. These compositional methods, combined with the stupendously dazzling virtuosity called for by his B-flat Minor Piano Concerto and Violin Concerto in D Major, have made these works two of the most popular concertos ever composed.

Tchaikovsky composed his Piano Concerto No. 1 in B-flat Minor, Op. 23, in November and December 1874, completing the orchestration 21 February 1875. He was not a concert pianist and originally intended this concerto for Nikolay Rubinstein. About three years after he played the concerto for Rubinstein on Christmas 1874, Tchaikovsky related the bitterness of that incident in a letter to his patroness, Mme. von Meck. He explained that Rubinstein figuratively tore it to shreds, declaring it vulgar, trivial, unpianistic, and utterly worthless. After the incident Tchaikovsky changed the dedication to Hans von Bülow, who happily took the work with him on an American tour, first playing it in Boston, 25 October 1875. The work was well received, and audiences called for an encore of the finale.

The B-flat Minor Concerto is in three movements, the first of which dwarfs the other two. Ukrainian folk songs are the sources of one melody in the first movement and another in the finale, while a French song provides a theme in the middle movement. Tchaikovsky relies throughout on the typical Russian style of decorative variation—thematic repetition with changes in the orchestration and accompaniment. This approach serves well in the concerto form, as the solo part is presented with the opportunity to add new decorative figures at each thematic repetition. Increased rhythmic activity and a swelling orchestration are frequently used to create climactic moments, most of which are given to the orchestra. The piano and orchestra often do not play together, as, for example, in the development portion of the first movement. The resulting sectional quality is typical of Russian music in general, and of Tchaikovsky's music in particular.

The first movement is unorthodox in its formal conception. The main movement is in B-flat minor, in common time, beginning Allegro con spirito. But before the first theme of the B-flat minor exposition is introduced, there are 107 measures of a most glorious theme in D-flat major in triple meter, marked Allegro non troppo e molto maestoso. This is the theme listeners seem to remember when leaving the concert hall, yet it is never used again. The six measures leading into the theme are as gripping as the theme itself; four horns, in unison, boldly state a four-note motive, anticipating the theme, which will first be stated in violins and cellos. Upon a repeat of the motive by horns, the rest of the orchestra joins in, coming to a sudden close on D-flat in m. 6. Here the piano enters with a series of rising, crashing chords that will form an accompaniment to the strings' thematic presentation (Ex. 18-1). This long introduction continues with a piano version of the theme in full chords, a cadenza, and a soaring, climactic repeat of the theme in the strings, in their higher register, and louder than before. The piano accompanies with forceful, rhythmically energized chords. The introduction closes quietly with distant trumpet calls, a typically Romantic gesture.

Ex. 18-1. Tchaikovsky, Piano Concerto No. 1 in B-flat Minor; I. Allegro non troppo e molto maestoso, mm. 1–11.

The true exposition begins with a rhythmically jerky piano version of a theme (Ex. 18-2) Tchaikovsky identified as a Ukrainian folk song he had heard sung by a blind beggar at a fair. (Note the altered, decorative repeat of this theme at the recapitulation, beginning in m. 451.) The lyrical second theme group contrasts strongly with the first theme. A lovely plaintive idea is first played by the clarinet (Ex. 18-3a). This tonally unstable material is followed by a more stable idea (Ex. 18-3b), which may remind listeners of the second part of the love theme from Tchaikovsky's *Romeo and Juliet*.

Ex. 18-2. Tchaikovsky, Piano Concerto No. 1 in B-flat Minor; I. Allegro non troppo e molto maestoso, mm. 114–115.

Ex. 18-3. Tchaikovsky, Piano Concerto No. 1 in B-flat Minor; I. Allegro non troppo e molto maestoso: (a.) mm. 184–187; (b.) mm. 204–208.

The long orchestral opening of the development section is characteristic of the composer. Excitement is created by quick interchanges of musical material between instrument families; the strings first play a fragment of the second idea (Ex. 18-3b) of the second theme group in alternation with woodwinds on bits of the exposition's rhythmically jerky opening theme. The tempo is then accelerated, notes shortened, the dynamic level increased, and instruments added until the climax is reached by the full orchestra. The solo instrument, which has been silent for more than fifty measures, makes an electrifying, explosive entry with double octaves on the rapid four-note descending scale motive the strings had been playing. This is an extremely demanding passage, but it is matched by others in this very difficult concerto. A very long cadenza near the movement's conclusion focuses on both elements of the second theme group.

The intimate second movement, Andantino semplice in D-flat major, combines elements of a slow movement and scherzo in its ternary form. The A part is established by quiet, muted strings playing four measures of on-the-beat chords. The flute brings in the main pastoral melody (Ex. 18-4), which is repeated by the piano against a varied background. A contrasting idea in D major is enunciated by oboes and clarinets against drone fifths in the bassoons. This new idea, still of a fluid, pastoral quality, is more energetic than the first. Two solo cellos recall the main theme against delicate staccato chords in the piano. The movement's B section is a Prestissimo in a scherzo style focusing on a waltz-like theme (Ex. 18-5) Tchaikovsky fashioned from a French song.

Ex. 18-4. Tchaikovsky, Piano Concerto No. 1 in B-flat Minor; II. Andantino semplice, mm. 5–8.

Ex. 18-5. Tchaikovsky, Piano Concerto No. 1 in B-flat Minor; II. Andantino semplice, mm. 81–84.

The Allegro con fuoco finale is an exciting movement based on the alternation of two themes. The first is a wild, rustic dance of Ukrainian origin with much rhythmic repetition and syncopation (Ex. 18-6a); the lyricism of the second is in striking contrast (Ex. 18-6b).

Ex. 18-6. Tchaikovsky, Piano Concerto No. 1 in B-flat Minor; III. Allegro con fuoco: (a.) mm. 5–8; (b.) mm. 56–60.

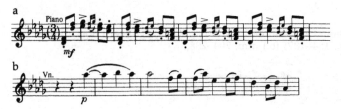

The second theme provides the material for the soaring climax (mm. 221ff.) so typical of Tchaikovsky. The first four notes of the theme are repeated sequentially higher, with a crescendo, against a dominant pedal point and high woodwinds. The winds insert a contrasting motive between the sequential repetitions. This quite romantic sequence culminates in a statement by full orchestra and piano, one of the few such united statements in the work, of the complete theme in the tonic major at the Molto meno mosso (m. 252). A fast and brilliant coda closes this compelling concerto.

N. Rubinstein in time came not only to appreciate the First Piano Concerto but to perform it successfully. This prompted Tchaikovsky to write a Second Concerto in G Major, Op. 44, in 1879–80, intended for Rubinstein, but he died before it was prepared for performance. Concert pianists are fully acquainted with Tchaikovsky's First Concerto, but many are not aware of the existence of the Second. Like the First, it is very difficult. It suffers from a very long and quite unconvincing first movement, which Tchaikovsky unsuccessfully attempted to correct. The middle movement features lovely writing for solo violin and solo cello, as well as piano; about two-thirds of the way through, some charming chamber music for this trio may remind the listener of Brahms's more delicate intermezzo-like chamber music movements.

Tchaikovsky never completed his Third Piano Concerto, although the first movement was published separately in 1893 as Op. 75. Tchaikovsky's student, Serge Ivanovich Taneyev (1856–1915), later completed the Andante and Finale, Op. 79, and glued them to the Op. 75 movement to form a concerto that is rarely played, as it does not represent the composer's intended scheme.

Tchaikovsky met the great Hungarian violinist Leopold Auer (1845–1930; teacher of Heifetz, among others) in January 1875, and was so taken with the violinist's performances that he proceeded to create several works featuring the violin. The first was the short *Sérénade mélancolique,* Op. 26 (1875), for violin and orchestra. This was followed by the *Valse-Scherzo*, Op. 34 (1877), dedicated to Josef Kotek, a young violinist to whom Tchaikovsky was physically attracted. The great Violin Concerto in D Major, Op. 35 (1878), Tchaikovsky's first major work following his disastrous marriage in 1877, was also conceived for Kotek.

Like the piano concertos, the Violin Concerto is exceedingly difficult, lying beyond Kotek's abilities. The composer approached Auer to play it, who also declined, declaring the work unplayable. Eventually, after two years of on-and-off revision by the composer, the Russian violinist Adolf Brodsky (1851–1929) played it in Vienna. There the conservative critics condemned the concerto; the leading critic, E. Hanslick, abhorred it, finding it savage. It is difficult for modern listeners to imagine such a reaction to a work of such overwhelming lyricism and beauty.

As we have seen, composers tend toward intensely lyrical writing for their violin concertos in order to take advantage of the instrument's singing tone. Tchaikovsky followed this pattern, as well as that of writing a fiery finale with a rustic, folk quality. Mendelssohn's Violin Concerto may have served as a specific model for certain details, such as the placement of the cadenza in the first movement at the end of the development and its overlap with the orchestra's start of the recapitulation.

The "very moderate" pace of the first movement is essential to establishing its graceful mood. Both themes are lyrical and are presented by the soloist, who plays throughout the entire exposition. The first theme (Ex. 18-7) was hinted at in the orchestra's Allegro moderato introduction, and is repeated in a decorative variation during which the violin shifts into a higher register via double and triple stops. The orchestral accompaniment is very light and airy throughout. A lively and very demanding transition section separates the two themes while another section of even more demanding passage work closes the exposition. The movement's climaxes, however, all belong to the orchestra. At the beginning of the development section (mm. 127ff.), for example, the strings and flute play a fortissimo version of the main theme against a martial fanfare in the winds, creating an exciting orchestral texture typical of this composer. A similar passage, extended with syncopations, leads to the culminating cadenza.

Ex. 18-7. Tchaikovsky, Violin Concerto in D Major, I. Allegro moderato, mm. 28–31.

Tchaikovsky ultimately replaced an original slow movement—using it instead as the first of three violin and piano duos, *Souvenir d'un lieu cher*—with the new Canzonetta: Andante, composed in a single day. The effective opening, employing the woodwinds, sets the mood and moves the music from D major of the first movement to G minor, the key of the Canzonetta. The muted solo violin presents the main theme over muted high strings and horns. The theme (Ex. 18-8), consisting of a short, repeated phrase, has clearly Russian roots. A second theme in E-flat major is brighter but still graceful (mm. 40ff.). The main theme returns in the solo instrument with tasteful figuration in flute and clarinet. A wonderfully romantic and mysterious link connects with the finale. The link consists of the woodwinds' repeat of the opening passage disintegrating into isolated chords passed quietly between them and the strings.

Ex. 18-8. Tchaikovsky, Violin Concerto in D Major, II. Canzonetta: Andante, mm. 13–16.

The Allegro vivacissimo finale bursts forth with a fiery orchestral introduction of a motive from the main theme in A major. The solo violin's vivacious introduction turns into a mini-cadenza, with frequent multiple stops and rapid alternation of pizzicato and arco articulation, which sets the tone of this brilliant rondo movement. The main theme is characterized by rhythmic drive and upward thrusting runs, while the secondary theme (Ex. 18-9, solo violin), juxtaposed against it in alternation, is slower (Poco meno mosso), darker, and lower. This second theme depends upon a descending motion, and it is strongly folklike with its descending fourths and rustic accompaniment of drone fifths. A curious counterpoint in the bassoon adds a meaningful coloristic element to this theme.

Ex. 18-9. Tchaikovsky, Violin Concerto in D Major, III. Allegro vivacissimo, mm. 149–152.

Of Tchaikovsky's two concerted works for cello, one, the Variations on a Rococo Theme, Op. 33 (1876), enjoys regular performances. The theme's clear, binary form, Classical phrasing, and the use of variation form all derive from Tchaikovsky's admiration for Mozart and an interest in Classical musical style. Tchaikovsky's approach to the form is,, however, not that of an eighteenth-century composer; the Russian handles the theme's structure quite freely in the decorative variations that follow. The third variation is a graceful Andante sostenuto in C major (the work is in A major); the seventh and last is a brilliant Allegro vivo featuring both soloist and orchestra.

Tchaikovsky stood head and shoulders above his Russian colleagues in his mastery of the means for blending the divergent musical traditions of the Russian national movement with those of the West. He created two enduring concertos, one for each of the solo instruments most favored by nineteenth-century composers. Russian composers of the following generations had to come to terms with Tchaikovsky's monumental influence; Stravinsky, for example, still considered Tchaikovsky the greatest composer who ever lived.

We now turn our attention to a handful of Russian composers whose musical language and points of view were forged before the 1917 Russian Revolution.

Alexander Glazunov (1865–1936) is the most important Russian composer of the generation born in the 1860s. He taught orchestration at the St. Petersburg Conservatory from 1899 on and became its director in 1906. He was one of many who sought greater freedom in the West after the Revolution, moving to Paris in 1928. Glazunov composed several concertos, both before and after his move.

The Violin Concerto (1904) was composed at about the time he was appointed director of the St. Petersburg Conservatory. Its form is similar to that of Saint-Saëns's Cello Concerto, with a short exposition, a slow section on a new theme, a development, a recapitulation, and a finale all contained within a single movement. The Piano Concerto No. 1 in F Minor (1910–11) has only two movements. The second is a set of variations and includes a coda in which thematic material from the first movement is recalled. Glazunov's Saxophone Concerto (1936) was composed in Paris. It is an attractive work with an enticing opening theme and extended fugato near the end. Glazunov's lyrical talents, akin to those of Tchaikovsky, are evident in all three works.

Alexander Scriabin (1872–1915) composed outside of the Russian national movement. He began his musical career as a concert pianist, and, like Chopin, who greatly influenced the young Scriabin, he wrote primarily for the piano. His only concerto is for the piano and was composed quite early in his career, 1896–97. It is in the traditional form: The first movement is in sonata-allegro form; the second movement is a theme with four variations; and the finale is a rondo, in which the main theme of the first movement is clearly recalled near the end. The solo instrument is present virtually throughout, often playing those delicate and fantastic decorations characteristic of Scriabin's compositional style. It is a particularly attractive piece, thanks to the effective piano writing and extensive lyrical content. Tonality is secure here; the work gives no hint of the composer's later innovative harmonic style that calls tonality into question. Nor does this concerto incorporate any of those mystical ideas which were to preoccupy Scriabin in his later years.

SERGE RACHMANINOV

Serge Rachmaninov (1873–1943) was the giant among the last generation of Russian composers fully to develop their style before the turn of the century. Rachmaninov was also the last important representative of late Russian Romanticism.

He began piano studies at a very early age, and soon enrolled at the St. Petersburg Conservatory. He later transferred to the Moscow Conservatory where he became acquainted with both Anton Rubinstein and Tchaikovsky. The latter was to exert a great influence. Rachmaninov graduated first in piano and in the following year, 1892, completed his formal studies in composition.

He was a masterful pianist with formidable technique and unusually large hands and long fingers that enabled him to reach an eleventh with ease. His playing was characterized by precision and clarity, rhythmic drive, and a smooth legato touch. His approach to performance was to identify the major climax of the

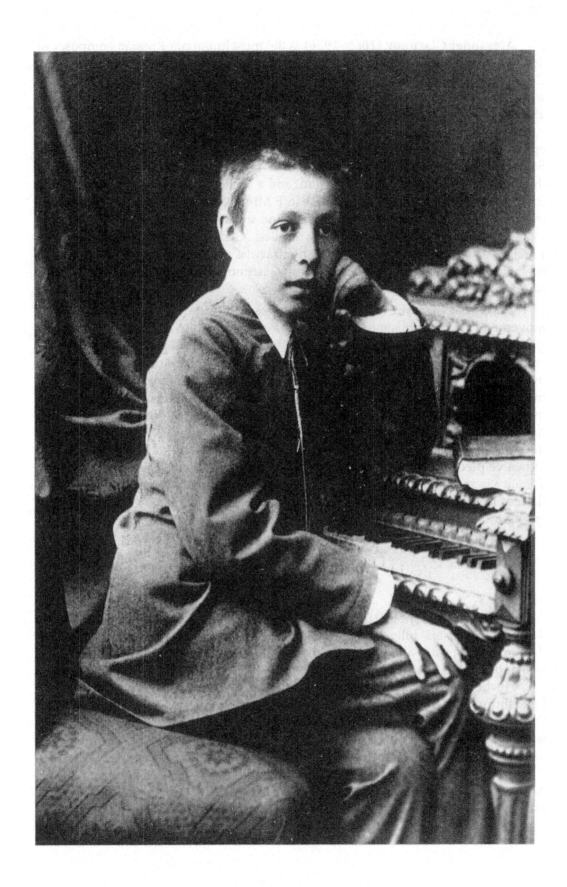

work being performed and then to gear his interpretation entirely to and from that point. His own compositions were all written with similarly carefully defined climax points.

Although Rachmaninov composed some works without piano parts—including operas, choral pieces, symphonies, and chamber music—the compositions depending upon his instrument have proved the most enduring. He was a pianist's composer, exploring the full expressive range of the keyboard instrument. His style, rooted in the music of Tchaikovsky and Rimsky-Korsakov, is passionate, characterized by intensely lyric melodies; broad, sweeping gestures; rich harmony; colorful use of the piano or other instruments; and powerful climax points. A profound predilection for the minor mode casts a strong melancholy shadow across most of his compositions. His four piano concertos and the Rhapsody on a Theme of Paganini are among the great works in the genre.

After his early, unsuccessful attempt at a concerto in C minor, Rachmaninov wrote his First Piano Concerto in F-sharp Minor, Op. 1, in 1891 while still a student in Moscow. He dedicated the work to his teacher, Alexander Siloti. Thanks to Tchaikovsky's efforts, this and several of the young composer's other works were published in 1893, but the First Concerto was rarely performed. As early as 1908 Rachmaninov was considering revisions to the work, but they were not made until the time of the October Revolution in 1917, when he worked on it relentlessly,

Rachmaninov as a boy; the mature Rachmaninov at the keyboard. The sensitive and passionate Rachmaninov had unusually large hands and very long thumbs that enabled him to reach an eleventh with ease. His playing was characterized by precision and clarity, rhythmic drive, and a smooth legato, all important qualities of his own music.

seemingly oblivious to the turmoil around him. These revisions were extensive, bringing a new clarity to the orchestration and introducing a quite daring bravura into the piano part. The work is now played in this revised form, enjoying relatively more regular performances today, after having taken a back seat to the ever-popular Second Piano Concerto and scintillating Third for years.

A large and important cadenza constitutes approximately a quarter of the length of the Vivace movement. The cadenza incorporates all the important thematic material in the movement, including the striking trumpet fanfare at the work's outset and the following, powerful, double-octave passage covering a four-octave spread in the solo instrument. This kind of stunning pianistic flourish opening a concerto is reminiscent of those of Schumann and Grieg and sets the lively mood of the F-sharp Minor Concerto. None of Rachmaninov's later concertos begins in such a dashing way.

The short slow movement, prefaced by an orchestral transition to D major, recalls a Chopin nocturne with Russian overtones. It becomes increasingly decorative as it progresses. The finale (Allegro vivace, mostly in $\frac{9}{8}$ or $\frac{12}{8}$) is in a large ternary form; the mad dash of the outer sections provides a remarkable setting for the effective, quiet central section in E-flat major. The tempo in this section drops to Andante ma non troppo, and the meter changes to $\frac{3}{4}$. The piano and orchestra engage in an intimate dialogue as the solo instrument inserts delicious, decorative echoes of the strings at the end of each little melodic unit of the theme. In the first version of the concerto, Rachmaninov brought this melody back as the culmination, but in the revised version the concerto concludes with an exciting Allegro vivace coda in F-sharp major, blazing with virtuosity.

The story of the success of Concerto No. 2 in C Minor, Op. 18 (1900–1901), and its role in restoring the composer's self-confidence following the disastrous premiere of his First Symphony in 1897, is probably as well-known as the Second Concerto itself. The poorly prepared performance of the symphony and its disappointing reception plunged Rachmaninov into a deep depression that lasted almost three years. During this time he composed nothing. Following treatment by Dr. Nikolay Dahl, who used hypnosis, the composer eventually shook off his depression and began work on the C Minor Concerto. Rachmaninov composed the second and third movements in 1900, and he performed them in Moscow in December of that year. By May 1901, he completed the entire work, performing it the following November, with the conductor Siloti.

This concerto, one of the best loved and best known of all those for piano, has a most original opening. A typical nineteenth-century concerto introduced the solo instrument by using it to present a theme, or to provide a virtuoso flourish. But here, starting in the darker subdominant region, the solo instrument plays soft, low, dark chords alternating with deep bass notes, establishing a somber, weighty mood. This opening is also one of the few places in the first movement where the piano is unaccompanied—there is no cadenza. Throughout most of the movement, the piano plays decorative figuration against thematic statements presented by the orchestra; in so doing it carries on the Russian tradition of decorative variation from the outset of the exposition. The close ensemble playing necessitated by this effective integration of piano and orchestra makes the C Minor Concerto an extremely difficult work to perform, despite the fact that it is pianistically less demanding than the concertos that bracket it. The solo piano's presentation of the grand second theme (Ex. 18-10) at the beginning of the second key area, E-flat, is one of the few places in which the piano is clearly exposed with thematic material.

Ex. 18-10. Rachmaninov, Piano Concerto No. 2 in C Minor; I. Moderato, mm. 83–89.

The intense development section, starting at the moto precedente, first focuses on the main theme as well as on a new, powerful, rhythmic figure (Ex. 18-11), of which the notes marked with a bracket are particularly important. The climax of the development builds around the lyrical second theme, which is carried upward sequentially while accelerating to Allegro, as the piano plays a powerful, chordal version of the rhythmic figure. At the Allegro this figure is transformed into *fortissimo*, quarter-note triplets, against ever-rising sequences of a portion of the second theme in the high strings. This climax, with its rising sequences and increasing volume, is engineered like those in Tchaikovsky's music.

Ex. 18-11. Rachmaninov, Piano Concerto No. 2 in C Minor; I. Moderato, mm. 162–163.

The treatment of the two central thematic ideas in the recapitulation is gripping. The orchestra transforms the main theme into a march in a maestoso tempo, while the piano accompanies with its powerful chordal version of the rhythmic motive from the development. The second theme returns first in A-flat major, augmented by horns, over pianissimo tremolando strings—emblematic of Rachmaninov in his quiet, mysterious, and introspective mood.

The Adagio sostenuto in E major opens in a manner reminiscent of the slow movements of Rachmaninov's First Concerto and Tchaikovsky's B-flat Minor Piano Concerto; that is, with a short orchestral transition from the key of the first movement to that of the second. The flute and, especially, the clarinet are given important thematic material. The more animated middle section of the ternary form centers in A major.

The Allegro scherzando finale is a type of rondo form in which the first, faster theme alternates with a more moderate, more tuneful, second theme, creating an ABABAB form, with the final B transformed into a climactic version of the theme. A tends to stay in the home key, while B occurs in other keys before finding its home in C major. A stimulating fugal exchange occurs during the second A section.

Rachmaninov completed the Third Piano Concerto in D Minor, Op. 30 (1909), nine years after the Second. It is a brilliant example of a captivating and extremely difficult piano part fully integrated with a substantial and exciting orchestral part. The sheer extent and density of the piano part—the staves of the piano score are black with notes—make the listener well aware of the importance of the solo instrument, but it does not dominate the orchestra. Rachmaninov wrote the concerto for his first American tour and practiced the extraordinarily demanding piano part on a silent keyboard on board ship to the United States. He played the concerto for the first time at a Sunday afternoon New York Symphony Society concert on 28 November 1909, with Walter Damrosch conducting. Two months later Gustav Mahler conducted a second New York performance.

A muted-string accompanimental murmur and an enticing, rocking motive in clarinets and bassoons set a dark, remote, and somewhat mysterious mood at the beginning of the first movement. The long opening theme (24 mm.) is presented in octaves by the piano in a thoroughly effective but simple fashion (Ex. 18-12). This theme has a strong Russian flavor, with its short melodic units rotating around the tonic, and, in its early measures, a narrow range—so characteristic of Russian folk melodies. The unusual placement of figures within a metric unit leads to unexpected but subtle syncopations, another characteristic of Russian folk melodies. Similar melodies also inspired some of Stravinsky's fascinating rhythmic structures. The momentary tonal shift in m. 12 is a coloristic element that probably also has its roots in Russian folk material; such shifts are a notable characteristic of Prokofiev's music, as well. When asked if this engaging theme derived from specific Russian folk-song roots, Rachmaninov contended that it did not, though the theme is close to a Russian chant he might have heard[1] and subconsciously appropriated. In typically Russian fashion, the theme is repeated in the orchestra with piano decoration.

Ex. 18-12. Rachmaninov, Piano Concerto No. 3 in D Minor; I. Allegro ma non tanto, mm. 3–11.

The expressive second theme (Ex. 18-13a) expands upon a brief, rhythmic fanfare figure (Ex. 18-13b) used in the transition. The figure gradually evolves through transformation (Ex. 18-13c). As the solo instrument repeats the second theme and takes it through higher sequences, various instruments in the orchestra engage in miniature duets with the piano.

Ex. 18-13. Rachmaninov, Piano Concerto No. 3 in D Minor; I. Allegro ma non tanto: (a.) mm. 107–110; (b.) mm. 69–70; (c.) mm. 93–94.

Both themes of this movement occur again in later movements, giving the work a strong cyclical unity, but the haunting first theme appears more frequently. The theme forms the heart of the first movement's development section, where it undergoes a syncopated rhythmic transformation (Ex. 18-14). It is recast as a waltz in the middle of the Intermezzo movement (Ex. 18-15), first having been used to accompany the piano in a scherzo-like passage. In the finale, in a brief interlude before the recapitulation, both first-movement themes appear in quick succession, only modestly altered. A fragment of the first theme serves as the basis of a macabre dance in the coda, complete with the rattling of strings struck with the wooden part of the bow—very reminiscent of a portion of the orgy dance in Berlioz's *Symphonie fantastique*.

Ex. 18-14. Rachmaninov, Piano Concerto No. 3 in D Minor; I. Allegro ma non tanto, mm. 203–207.

Ex. 18-15. Rachmaninov, Piano Concerto No. 3 in D Minor; II. Intermezzo: Adagio, mm. 137–141.

A very substantial cadenza occurs in the first movement. It is divided into two parts by an interlude involving solo woodwinds on the main theme against continuing arpeggiation by the piano. The composer provides two options for the piano in the first part of the cadenza, both built on the main theme. The longer option is the more difficult, the chords in the right hand based on the rhythmic shape depicted in Ex. 18-14.

The passionate melody on which the Adagio middle movement is based finally arrives in the remote but lush key of D-flat major in the piano after a long introduction beginning in A major. The highly chromatic and deeply expressive second movement progresses toward a cadenza-like transition to the extraordinarily virtuosic finale. The finale is one of the most exciting movements in all of the piano concerto literature: The solo part is outstandingly brilliant, and the orchestral music is just as compelling, packing a powerful punch.

In addition to quoting two themes from the first movement, Rachmaninov introduces four other themes, one after the other, in the finale. The first three (Ex. 18-16a–c) are rhythmically vital, and the last (Ex. 18-16d) passionately soaring. Succinct variations of the first fill the development section. In the recapitulation, the third idea, with its repetitious chordal syncopations and crescendo, builds to the climax of the soaring fourth theme, which shares the general contour of the

Ex. 18-16. Rachmaninov, Piano Concerto No. 3 in D Minor; III. Alla breve: (a.) mm. 3–5; (b.) mm. 39–40; (c.) mm. 74–78; (d.) mm. 103–107.

third theme. The tonal scheme of the recapitulation is unorthodox. The first theme returns in C minor, while the second begins in B-flat and moves to F, and the third remains largely centered in F. Very tricky, but optional, woodwind passages, emphasizing lightning-fast triplets, augment the tension of the mounting synco-pated chordal theme. In the consummate mastery with which Rachmaninov constructed the final climax of this ultimate virtuoso concerto, we sense this pianist-composer's overriding concern to locate points in others' works that he could carry to the utmost peak.

Some years passed before other pianists could master this extraordinarily difficult concerto; among the few who did was the Ukrainian-born Vladimir Horowitz (1904–1989), who became one of the work's principal interpreters. In the late 1920s and early 1930s, Rachmaninov made several cuts in the score he used for his own performance of the concerto, urging Horowitz to do likewise, in order to ease the demands and reduce the sheer volume of notes to be played in what is a test of endurance. Thankfully, several modern performers are now capable of performing the entire work in its original form, so it is now usually heard in that form.

Following the 1917 Russian Revolution, Rachmaninov moved to Copen-hagen, but after a short stay moved to the United States in 1918 in response to lucrative performing contracts. At the age of forty-seven, he began essentially a new career as pianist. His crowded concert schedule left him no time to compose until 1926 when he completed his fourth and last piano concerto, his first American composition. He first presented the concerto in Philadelphia under Stokowski's direction on 18 March 1927—to a cool reception. After revising it during the following year, Rachmaninov performed the concerto on several occa-sions to as little success as before. Thereupon he withdrew it until 1941, when he made significant revisions, including modifying the orchestration and cutting several long passages. This version again premiered in Philadelphia, under Eugene Ormandy, but it fared no better.

The Fourth Piano Concerto is very different from the ever-popular Second and dynamic Third. It lacks the spontaneity, warmth, and bubbling excitement found in the earlier two. Despite the cuts, it remains diffuse—there are many themes, generally less well integrated than are those in the earlier works. The themes themselves are also less compelling. The dialogue between piano and orchestra—the focus of the middle movement—lacks differentiation, as the opposing forces play very similar material. The final movement is again the climax, but it possesses little of the drive found in the finales closing the Second and Third Piano Concertos.

Two stylistic changes are important. First, obviously influenced by experi-ments with extended tonality in the early twentieth century, Rachmaninov used an expanded harmonic language, making for a noticeable chromatic quality, particu-larly in the slow movement. Second, the writing for the piano is different; a new kind of figuration focuses less on decorating the melodic material and more on creating novel and intricate textures.

In many respects Rachmaninov's last work for piano and orchestra, the Rhapsody on a Theme of Paganini, Op. 43 (1934), is his crowning achievement in this genre. This set of twenty-four variations on Paganini's popular Caprice No. 24 for solo violin is the work of a mature master, but it retains the spirited spontaneity and vivacity characterizing his more youthful works. The failure of the Fourth Concerto coupled with the success of his recently completed solo piano piece, Variations on a Theme by Corelli, Op. 42, likely prompted him to turn to the variation form for this, his last work for piano and orchestra. The theme he chose for Op. 43 is the same that inspired Liszt, Schumann, and Brahms to compose sets of variations. Rachmaninov first performed his new work at a Philadelphia Orchestra concert in Baltimore on 7 November 1934, directed by Stokowski. It was an immediate success, becoming a standard piece in the composer-pianist's repertory.

The Rhapsody on a Theme of Paganini progresses through an introduction, statement of theme, and twenty-four variations. The *Dies irae* theme from the Mass for the Dead, which we considered in connection with Liszt, makes appearances in variations 7, 10, 22, and 24. This demonic theme was probably associated in the popular mind with Paganini, whose appearance and astonishing, incomprehensible performances led some observers to imagine Paganini in a pact with the devil or somehow endowed with satanic powers. In a curious departure from the usual theme-and-variations form, the first variation, a kind of skeletal outline of the theme, occurs before the familiar theme is presented in complete form. The variations form groups, arranged by tempo, meter, tonality, and mood, that approximate the four movements of a symphony, something akin to the way in which Brahms structured his Variations on a Theme by Haydn. The following outline displays these groupings.

Rachmaninov: Rhapsody on a Theme of Paganini (1934)

I. The Introduction and variations 1–10 serve as a first movement, while variation 11 is transitional to the "second movement."

A minor. Introduction. Duple meter.
Var 1. Allegro vivace. Skeletal version, prefiguring the theme. Theme.
Var 2–6. All in same basic tempo as var. 1.
Pause.
Var 7. *Dies irae* in piano with bell-like tones.
Var 8. Theme not clearly present.
Var 9. Demonic; strings *col legno*. Triplets.
Var 10. Grotesque; *Dies irae*; starts in common time, shifts between $\frac{3}{4}$ and common time in last half.
Var 11. Moderato, triple meter. With its vague, improvisatory quality, this variation serves as both a cadenza and a transition to the next section, as it modulates away from tonic.

II. This group of variations serves as a minuet or scherzo movement.

D minor. Var 12. Tempo di Minuetto. Graceful.
Var 13. Allegro. Strings carry the theme, the piano accompanying with prominent, heavy chords.
F major. Var 14. Molto marcato. The piano is given only a modest role.
Var 15. Più vivo scherzando. The orchestra is silent in the first half. This variation is closely linked to the previous variation.

III. This group of variations serves as the slow movement.

B-flat major.	Var 16.	Allegretto. Back to duple meter. Minor key. Chamber-like texture with an emphasis on solo woodwinds.
	Var 17.	Common time, but triplets create a feeling of $\frac{12}{8}$. Modulates to the key of variation 18.
D-flat major.	Var 18.	Andante cantabile in $\frac{3}{4}$ time. This is the emotional high point of the piece. The theme (Ex. 18-17a) is inverted (Ex. 18-17b) and passionately presented, reaching a climax by means of passages of ascending sequences, accompanied by a crescendo.

IV. This group of variations serves as the finale. The variations return to the tonic key and to the work's opening duple meter and vivace tempo; each succeeding variation gains in speed.

A minor.	Var 19.	The piano part is marked quasi-pizzicato and imitates Paganini's great left-hand pizzicato technique.
	Var 20.	Characterized by rapid leaps in the piano part.
	Var 21.	Triplets are used to generate excitement.
	Var 22.	March-like. The *Dies irae* theme returns in great treble chords in the piano. A short cadenza leads to next variation.
	Var 23.	Opens in remote A-flat major, but the orchestra leads back to the tonic. Powerful octave scales are called for in the piano, played against an intense, almost explosive, orchestra. Another brief cadenza leads to the final variation.
	Var 24.	Extremely brilliant. A varied, last blast of the *Dies irae* theme is played in half-notes in brass and strings, with decorative versions in woodwinds, percussion, and the piano occurring near the end.

Ex. 18-17. Rachmaninov, Rhapsody on a Theme of Paganini: (a.) Tema, mm. 1–4; (b.) Var. 18, mm. 2–6.

This powerfully virtuosic and brilliantly orchestrated masterpiece not only marks the end of Rachmaninov's career as a composer of works for solo piano and orchestra, but it effectively marks the end of an era. It is the last great Romantic work for piano and orchestra and can be viewed as the last of the Romantic concertos. By 1934, the date of its composition when Rachmaninov was sixty-one, younger composers had pulled music in entirely different directions. Rachmaninov's Paganini Rhapsody was old-fashioned in its musical language, but it has outlived the works of many of his contemporaries because it continually sounds fresh.

Part IV

THE TWENTIETH-CENTURY CONCERTO

THE TWENTIETH CENTURY: AN INTRODUCTION

As the nineteenth century drew to a close and the twentieth opened, a fascinating array of new approaches to musical composition evolved. The domination of the Germanic style waned, and a variety of stylistic approaches, often with roots in countries outside the German-speaking nations, gave rise to a diversity of new "isms." From our vantage point nearly a century later, however, we can see that these new styles had their roots in Romanticism. Individual facets of Romanticism were fastened upon and elevated into new styles.

The very diversity of national styles had its roots in the Romantics' fascination with nationalistic or native folkloric elements. This fascination acquired a different perspective as the fledgling academic study of ethnic musics, ethnomusicology, became an increasingly important discipline. The sustained and disciplined study and documentation of ethnic music was particularly pronounced in central European countries at the turn of the century; folkloric models became widely used there, as in the music of the Hungarian composer and ethnomusicologist Béla Bartók (1881–1945). The vital rhythmic style and unusual tonal syntax of this composer are deeply rooted in the folk music of Hungary and the neighboring regions of central Europe. In England, notable for the long absence of significant native-born composers, the rebirth of classical music composition took root in the English folk-music tradition. Here the folk element was blended with stylistic ingredients associated with the last great flowering of English music during the Renaissance and early Baroque periods. This blending is well illustrated in the music of Ralph Vaughan Williams (1872–1958).

In France, whose composers have long been fascinated with sonority—the sheer beauty of sound and its coloristic potential—the new composers focused on tone color, while de-emphasizing the elements of melody and harmony. The ambiguous musical language that resulted has been called Impressionism and is particularly associated with the music of Claude Debussy (1862–1918). The interest both in sonority for its own sake and in ambiguity clearly have their roots in Romanticism.

The composers born in the 1860s in the German-speaking countries generally continued to work within the framework formulated by the earlier nineteenth-century composers, but turned to emphasizing one or another of its important features. For example, tonality was stretched to its outer limits through increased chromaticism, as composers sought to create music with greater expressive content. These composers, epitomized by Richard Strauss (1864–1949), have been called the post-Romantics.

The composers succeeding the post-Romantics extended the tonal limits to the breaking point, resulting in an atonal musical language seemingly better suited to the creation of their style of Expressionistic music. This group, led by Arnold Schoenberg (1874–1951), came to organize the twelve chromatic tones in series far removed from the tonal background of scales. Each series, row, or set of twelve tones is usually structured and used in such a way that no single pitch can assume prominence and that all are treated equally. Serial techniques will be explored further in later chapters.

Later followers of Schoenberg and his method expanded serial techniques to include additional parameters of musical composition, creating series of durations, dynamic levels, attacks, and articulations. This approach established the theoretical equality of other elements of a musical composition. Karlheinz Stockhausen (b. 1928) was an important early proponent of this thorough-going serialism, often referred to as "total serialism." It is possible to view this drive for total control as an extension of the nineteenth-century tradition in which composers continually endeavored to establish greater control over all facets of musical performance, as evidenced in their increasingly meticulous notation of every nuance.

This tendency was offset by the Romantic composers' love of spontaneity and the desire to infuse music with the quality of improvisation, or, at least, of spontaneous expressiveness. The elements of improvisation and spontaneity were also emphasized by some twentieth-century composers, especially after World War II. The creators of Indeterminate or Chance Music were led by John Cage (1912–1992). Aleatory, from the root *alea* or game of dice, is another adjective appended to this style, since the music employs chance or unpredictable elements similar to those in a game of dice.

Between the world wars, the dominant musical style was neo-Classicism, shaped largely by Igor Stravinsky (1882–1971). Neo-Classicism, based on the techniques and approaches characteristic of pre-Romantic music, offered a more objective and cooler alternative to the subjective heat of Expressionism. This revival of past traditions also shared Romanticism's fascination with the past, which eventually led to the disciplined study of music history or musicology.

We might find it fairly easy to identify the leading figures in these various schools of the first half of the century and thus select the concertos which best characterize each. But these tasks are difficult for the recent history of the form, since our perceptions are clouded by the haze of historical proximity. As we carry this account of the concerto closer to the present day, we must, therefore, focus on selected composers whose works are of interest by virtue of their exploration of new styles or techniques.

The concerto has enjoyed an important place in twentieth-century music. Modern audiences continue the time-honored tradition of hero worship, and, in turn, performers continue to dominate the musical scene. Today's symphony orchestras engage star soloists for virtually every concert. This practice is overtly designed to increase audience attendance. Virtuoso soloists continue to command exorbitant fees, and thus have the wherewithal to commission new works, typically concertos, to showcase their talents, even though the older works constitute the basis of their repertory. In a quite general sense, the virtuoso orientation of the twentieth-century concerto exceeds that of many nineteenth-century concertos. At the same time, the role of the orchestra has been revitalized as well. Thus the soloist's sizzling display is often matched by orchestral brilliance, and the two forces are integrated and opposed in an equal relationship in most twentieth-century concertos. Dramatic tension between the soloist and orchestra is a powerful creative element in these works, for most modern composers have developed new ways of exploiting such dramatic content.

We will embark on the journey into the compositional territory of the twentieth century by first discussing the significant, but somewhat isolated, contributions made by Soviet composers after the 1917 Revolution.

THE CONCERTO IN THE SOVIET UNION

The year 1917 is a critical juncture in the history of music in Russia. The revolution and the radical, new regime quickly dictated a new role for music and the other arts, just as the world lost important representatives of the older style with the deaths of Rimsky-Korsakov, Balakirev, and Scriabin. Immediately following the revolution, their most important pupils, Rachmaninov and Prokofiev, left; Stravinsky had departed a few years earlier. As a consequence a marked gap developed before the next generation of composers—those born shortly after the turn of the century—reached maturity within the epoch of the new regime.

After the revolution a rigorous discipline was imposed on the arts, which were to aid the creation of and legitimize a new society based on the precepts of Marxism-Leninism. The political alignment of the arts was placed above aesthetic considerations. This conscription of the arts was fully articulated in 1921, with the institution of Lenin's New Economic Policy. The Communist party took unto itself the total supervision of all the arts, subjecting them to the ends defined by the party. Because of the abstract nature of music, the bureaucracy experienced great difficulty in defining what was appropriate, except in the case of works with text. As a consequence, composers enjoyed somewhat greater freedom from the dictates of officialdom than did their compatriots in the other arts. The party concerned itself more with supervising the established conservatories and the business of training musicians. Interested musicians formed the Association for Contemporary Music in 1923 and were permitted to offer performances of the current new or experimental music written by modern Western composers, including Schoenberg and Berg.

With Stalin's assumption of power and the introduction of his first Five Year Plan in 1928, controls, including those on the arts, were tightened. The Association for Contemporary Music was disallowed, and the Union of Soviet Composers was established in 1932. These events marked yet another critical turning point for music in the Soviet Union. The Union of Soviet Composers was empowered to control music, all of which had to be "socialist." It was to contain socialist realism, as it was called, to portray communist truth and party spirit, and it was to do so by reaching out to the masses. This led to sanctioning the use of folk song and the exclusion of modern Western musical language. The latter was seen as too aloof and individualistic, hence decadent. The performance of modern music emerging in the West was also forbidden on the theory that it would poison the minds of both Soviet composers and the Soviet public, leading them away from Communist ideals. Not only did these rigid and arbitrary constraints isolate Soviet composers and audiences from Western developments, but they also virtually prevented Soviet music from reaching beyond its borders, because of its lack of anything approaching universal, artistic appeal.

A still more significant and thoroughly frightening blow was dealt composers in 1936, when *Pravda*, the official newspaper of the party, condemned a pair of works by Shostakovich, criticizing them for being "formalistic," that is, failing to reflect socialist realism and lacking "socially significant communication." Subsequent condemnations and censorship of other composers regularly followed over the years.

Following Stalin's death in 1953 and especially after Khrushchev became general secretary of the party in 1958, Soviet restrictions relaxed somewhat. Music from the West was occasionally performed, as were some works of previously censored Soviet composers. Composers of Russian origin who had emigrated were welcomed back; thus Stravinsky, whose music had long been banned, returned in 1962. Between 1985 and 1992, Gorbachev's policies of *Glasnost* (openness) and *Perestroika* (restructuring) opened further avenues to artistic freedom in the Soviet Union, so that younger composers became free to use once-banned modern techniques, including serialism or indeterminacy.

Four composers emerged as important representatives of the music of the former Soviet Union. Serge Prokofiev and Dmitry Shostakovich made outstanding contributions to the concerto in the twentieth century. Two composers whose work is of lesser significance are Dmitry Kabalevsky and Aram Khachaturian who largely toed the Communist party line, although the latter was criticized in 1948 for transgressing the rules.

Dmitry Kabalevsky (1904–1987) began as a poet and painter, undertaking composing to provide music for his many piano students. He subsequently entered the Moscow Conservatory to obtain greater professional training. His music is often based on Russian folk materials, and makes use of the officially approved, largely diatonic, tonal harmony, but with some spicy dissonance. He used traditional forms, energizing his music by using syncopated rhythms associated with Russian folk music. His Piano Concerto in A Minor, Op. 9 (1928), has its roots in Tchaikovsky's concertos and includes a folk song in the finale.

Aram Khachaturian (1903–1978) wrote his Piano Concerto in 1936. It continues to be one of his most popular works in the West. The composer's deep attachment to the folk music of his native Armenia and neighboring regions is reflected in the long passages of folk-inspired melodies. These are particularly prominent in the improvisatory second theme of the first movement and in the altered quotation of a true folk song in the second movement. The fresh, driving rhythms of the finale are dance-inspired, while the Maestoso coda brings the work to a fiery end in the tradition of Tchaikovsky's B-flat Minor Concerto and Rachmaninov's Third. The modest orchestral forces take on a special coloristic quality when the optional flexatone is used. The flexatone is a percussion instrument, invented in the 1920s, producing a sound similar to that of a musical saw. Khachaturian also composed a violin concerto in 1940 for David Oistrakh, and a seldom-heard cello concerto in 1946.

Of greater interest are Serge Prokofiev and Dmitry Shostakovich, who made the greatest Soviet contributions to music in this century. Both were the victims of intense criticism by Communist party officials, although both were also, on occasion, highly honored.

SERGE PROKOFIEV (1891–1953)

Prokofiev is the oldest of the composers dealt with in this chapter. He was a man of both East and West, having been in exile from the years immediately following the revolution until 1932.

As a child, Prokofiev was amazingly precocious. By the age of five he had written several piano pieces and at age eight tried his hand at an opera, after being excited by his first visit to an opera house. The composer Reinhold Glière (1875–1956), who wrote the Concerto for Coloratura Soprano and Orchestra (1942) and the brilliant Horn Concerto (1951), was invited to spend the summers of 1902 and 1904 with the Prokofievs to instruct the boy in composition. With his application for admission to the St. Petersburg Conservatory at the age of thirteen, Prokofiev submitted a substantial bundle of compositions, including four operas, two piano sonatas, a symphony, and numerous short piano pieces. He was enrolled, of course, and studied composition with Liadov and orchestration with Rimsky-Korsakov.

Prokofiev was also a marvelously gifted pianist, developing an unusually aggressive style which depended upon the instrument's percussive qualities. The works of his early maturity (1908–17) feature the piano and are notable for their driving rhythms, biting dissonances, percussive attacks, and grotesque, often dark, moods. The first two of his five piano concertos are from this period, the style of which greatly resembles that of Stravinsky and Bartók. The aggressive, rhythmic music of these composers seems to have been in reaction to the sensuous beauty of romanticism.

Prokofiev considered the First Concerto in D-flat Major, Op. 10 (1911–12), his first mature composition. It was originally conceived as a modest concertino, but grew into a sixteen- or seventeen-minute, one-movement work, with an exceedingly difficult piano part. The opening theme, which returns at several points and provides the material for the final climax, is characteristically Russian; it is narrow in range, with short, repetitive phrases that build tension through sequence. Furthermore, it is modal, as were many Russian themes and folk songs. The repeated use of motoric rhythms and the scherzo of the third section are typical of the composer's style. This concerto was dedicated to Prokofiev's conducting teacher, Nikolay Tcherepnin, and was first performed while the composer was still a student. It was regarded as the work of a shockingly rebellious modernist, but despite critics' grumbling about its raucousness, it was so well received by the audience that it was played again at Prokofiev's graduation concert in May 1914.

The Second Piano Concerto in G Minor, Op. 16, was composed not long after the first and was dedicated to the memory of Maximillian Schmidthof, a young pianist and close friend of the composer who had committed suicide in April 1913.

The work's first performance in September 1913 was met with bewilderment and hostility. Major musical institutions, including the Russian Musical Society, refused to perform it. Siloti, who had conducted several of Rachmaninov's concertos, noted to friends, "I cannot invite Prokofiev to play the Second Concerto because then I should have to conduct, and that is beyond my strength. The music of Debussy gives forth a fragrance, but this gives off a stench."[1] Yet the influential composer Miaskovsky came to Prokofiev's defense, and the work was performed in an early 1915 Russian Music Society program to more positive response. Diaghilev heard an early performance, which prompted him to invite the composer to write for his Ballets Russes; this was the beginning of a successful relationship that lasted until the ballet impresario's death in 1929. Stravinsky, who had himself just incited a riot with the first performance of *The Rite of Spring*, praised Prokofiev's dramatic and complex concerto after hearing it at a performance in Rome in early 1915.

A fire in Prokofiev's apartment at the time of the revolution destroyed the manuscript of the Second Concerto. In 1924 he reconstructed the score from memory, declaring he had so completely rewritten it that it might be considered his Fourth. The first movement of this four-movement concerto is dominated by the broad, lyrical *narrante* (narrative) theme of the opening Andantino and a massive cadenza which consumes most of the development section. The complex and extremely difficult cadenza requires three staves for much of its length, in order to accommodate the three main musical ideas the pianist must simultaneously present. The orchestra provides further material in the background of the final measures of the cadenza in preparation for the recapitulation.

The second movement is a compact, forward-driving scherzo in Prokofiev's most electrifying, motoric style, with a constant stream of sixteenth-notes in the solo instrument. The Intermezzo third movement has a gentle middle portion with suggestions of the first movement's main theme, surrounded by more primitive, atmospheric music, constructed largely over a simple bass ostinato (Ex. 20-1). The piano's delicate glissando wisps do not create a melody, only a coloristic atmosphere. The Allegro tempestoso is brilliant. The two themes are greatly contrasting; the first is rhythmic and angular with rapid leaps in the solo part, while the second is very lyrical and set to a rocking accompaniment figure.

Ex. 20-1. Prokofiev, Piano Concerto No. 2 in G Minor; III. Intermezzo: Allegro moderato, mm. 1–3.

Violin Concerto No. 1 in D Major, Op. 19 (1916–17), was one of the last works Prokofiev completed before the revolution. It is filled with that lyricism so thoroughly associated with violin concertos of the past, and reflects his contemporary preoccupation with lyrical elements; the Classical Symphony and sketches for the lyrical Third Piano Concerto are contemporary with the D Major Violin Concerto. The First Violin Concerto, like the First Piano Concerto, grew from what was originally conceived as a smaller concertino.

Prokofiev's First Violin Concerto has an unusual form that may have provided the inspiration for Walton's Viola Concerto. The order of the three movements is slow (Andantino), scherzo (Vivacissimo), and fast (Allegro moderato, with moderato introduction). The Andantino has a captivating opening: Divided violas quietly set the pastoral mood with tremolando, and the solo violin enters two bars later with a gentle and fluid theme to be played dreamily (*sognando*). The second theme, marked *narrante,* is in strong contrast, with its active leaps and numerous grace notes. The scherzo is typical of the composer; it is filled with what he might have called sarcastic humor, accented by shocking dissonance. The finale contains an effective contrapuntal combination of its opening dancelike staccato theme with the expansive lyrical theme of movement I. Trills in the solo violin's highest register embellish the lyrical theme. The first performance of this violin concerto was scheduled for November 1917, but the upheavals of the revolution resulted in its cancellation. The premiere took place five years later in Paris.

In 1918 Prokofiev left Russia and for the next fourteen years toured as a pianist, living in Paris from 1923 to 1932. His last three piano concertos come from this period. Of these, the Third has always enjoyed great popularity because of its directness and lyricism. The other two lack the melodic warmth of the Third and are played infrequently. The Fourth, in B-flat Major (1931), was written for Paul Wittgenstein (1887–1961), who had lost his right arm during World War I. It is a four-movement work of great virtuosity signalled at the outset. Here, the pianist, using only his left hand, must play extensively throughout the treble range and then execute rapid shifts of register. The Fifth Piano Concerto in G Major, Op. 55 (1932), was one of the last works Prokofiev composed before returning to the Soviet Union. It was originally to have been called Music for Piano and Orchestra, perhaps because of its five-movement, suite-like structure. Movements I, III, and V are full of wild leaps and fast passage work; movement II is like a gavotte, while movement IV is marked by bold dynamic and textural contrasts.

Piano Concerto No. 3 in C Major, Op. 26, was completed in 1921, five years after the principal themes had been sketched. Prokofiev first performed the Third Piano Concerto in Chicago on 16 December 1921 on an American tour. Although the American public did not seem to understand it, the European press reacted favorably to the premiere, and within a short time it was even accepted in the Soviet Union. The composer played it in Moscow on a tour in 1927; when he returned to the Soviet Union permanently, he played it again in a concert designed to welcome him back.

The Third Concerto opens with a sensuous and almost lyrically seductive, unaccompanied clarinet solo in an Andante tempo (Ex. 20-2). The second clarinet joins in to accompany the rising scale passage in thirds. Violins and flute repeat the idea before the main body of the Allegro movement begins. The rhythmically vital first theme, introduced by the piano after a sudden, quiet shift to the new tempo, is motivically linked in the first three notes to the clarinet theme, but instead of descending a second and rising a fifth, it descends a fifth and rises a second (Ex. 20-3). This main theme has a tremendous forward thrust, thanks to its rhythmic energy, fluctuating dynamics, and presentation typical of Prokofiev, with C pedal point and ostinato pattern in cellos. The sudden change of key at the end of the first phrase is a very charming and quite characteristic gesture of the composer. The second theme (Ex. 20-4) has a tongue-in-cheek quality. It is presented by oboe and pizzicato violins against a staccato quarter-note chordal accompaniment enhanced by castanets. A closing theme, opening with a descending chromatic scale, introduces wide-ranging triplet figuration in the piano. The short development, in the tempo of the introduction, focuses on the clarinet's introductory theme. This is treated as a canon, first between piano and bassoon in its high register, then between clarinet and piano. In the recapitulation, the Allegro introduction to the main theme greatly expands to give the soloist considerable room for bravura display. The delicate second theme is transformed into a grotesque version through Prokofiev's scoring for piano with loud chords, woodwinds, and strings *col legno*. The frequently unorthodox chord sequence creates great tension against the C pedal point.

Ex. 20-2. Prokofiev, Piano Concerto No. 3 in C Major; I. Andante; Allegro, mm. 1–7.

Ex. 20-3. Prokofiev, Piano Concerto No. 3 in C Major; I. Andante; Allegro, mm. 15–18.

Ex. 20-4. Prokofiev, Piano Concerto No. 3 in C Major; I. Andante; Allegro, mm. 68–72.

The second movement contains a theme and five variations in E minor. The aba theme resembles an eighteenth-century theme, but with the special flavor of Prokofiev. The first variation remains in the original tempo and brings in the solo instrument, which suddenly, but characteristically, veers off into a new key. The second and third variations are vigorous, with brilliant figuration in the piano and bits of the theme repeated by the orchestra. The quiet fourth variation, to be played andante meditativo, includes distant, romantic horn calls and lyrical snatches of melody for oboe, clarinet, and violins. The energetic fifth variation has a deeply Russian air about it with its manifold repetition of a simple two-measure, dancelike version of the theme (Ex. 20-5). The piano writing in this variation is brilliant. The theme is repeated at the movement's conclusion with high-register chordal filigree in the piano.

Ex. 20-5. Prokofiev, Piano Concerto No. 3 in C Major; II. Andantino, mm. 146–147.

Unison bassoons and pizzicato strings announce the first idea of the Allegro, ma non troppo, finale. Rhythmically, the theme is typically Russian; the repeated rhythmic pattern of the first eight beats defines a feeling of $\frac{4}{4}$ time, but it is placed in triple meter, leading to shifting accents or irregularities within the strict meter (Ex. 20-6). The meno mosso midsection contains some very extraordinary music. It opens with a quiet, almost spiritual theme in descending chromatic steps and expressive upward leaps (Ex. 20-7). This is followed by a grotesque idea, first in the piano, using many repeated notes and slippery, upward-moving fragments (Ex. 20-8). The first of these ideas is developed at length through many keys. The piano is radiant in the final third of the movement, which returns to the opening material.

Ex. 20-6. Prokofiev, Piano Concerto No. 3 in C Major; III. Allegro, ma non troppo, mm. 1–4.

Ex. 20-7. Prokofiev, Piano Concerto No. 3 in C Major; III. Allegro, ma non troppo, mm. 147–154.

Ex. 20-8. Prokofiev, Piano Concerto No. 3 in C Major; III. Allegro, ma non troppo, mm. 170–173.

The Third Piano Concerto's success lies in its balance of strong lyrical ideas and unusual, virtuosic, pianistic textures. Lyricism was to become an increasingly important feature of Prokofiev's music following his return to the Soviet Union in 1932, the year of the formation of the Union of Soviet Composers. He fully endorsed the Soviet notion of the social role of music, bent to the reprimands of the Central Committee and made demeaning apologies as called for, and even composed some works with openly propagandistic content.

The Violin Concerto No. 2 in G Minor (1935) was written to reconcile the devastating criticism heaped upon one of his first compositions following his return. According to the critics, this lyrical concerto is awash with "Soviet Realism" and so met the standards of the new order. The G Minor Concerto is more lyrical than the First Violin Concerto and contains none of the grotesque features found in that earlier work.

The Second Violin Concerto, like many works of his Soviet period, displays a quite Classical spirit, evident in the greater use of counterpoint and clear formal structures. This intimate concerto calls for only a modest-sized orchestra with a few exotic percussion instruments. It is in the traditional three-movement form, with two lyrical movements preceding the peasant, dancelike finale. There are many exceptional passages in this concerto, one of the truly great violin concertos.

The soloist opens the work, unaccompanied, with a simple statement of the lyrical theme. Russian roots are evident in its rhythmic structure and short, repetitive idea in the opening measures. This idea occupies five beats, but is set in $\frac{4}{4}$ time which creates that shifting of accents so common in Russian folk music and in the music of other Russian composers (Ex. 20-9). This rhythmic tension is heightened when the theme is repeated canonically between muted low strings and solo violin beginning in m. 18. The second theme is again very lyrical. It is first presented by solo violin, with Prokofiev's peculiar harmonic side-slipping from B-flat to B, E to E-flat, and C back to B-flat (Ex. 20-10). The movement is in straightforward sonata-allegro form.

Ex. 20-9. Prokofiev, Violin Concerto No. 2 in G Minor; I. Allegro moderato, mm. 1–9.

Ex. 20-10. Prokofiev, Violin Concerto No. 2 in G Minor; I. Allegro moderato, mm. 52–60.

The E-flat major Andante assai is one of Prokofiev's most glorious slow movements. It may remind some listeners of the slow movement of Mozart's Piano Concerto in C Major, K. 467. Pizzicato strings and staccato clarinet, in its lower register, establish a simple triplet accompaniment before the solo violin enters with a long-breathed melody featuring duplets against the accompaniment's triplets. The movement is in ABACA rondo form with unusual tonal relationships. There is a shift to B major in the first A section, the B section is in F, and the C section, a scherzo-like Allegretto, is in D. The final A section is exquisite, as the solo violin adds a delicate counterpoint against the orchestral violins' statement of the theme. In the final bars, clarinets, horns, and cellos restate the theme in unison in the low register—a good example of Prokofiev's creative approach to orchestration.

The violinist seems to switch to a gypsy fiddle for the finale. The solo instrument begins the finale alone on a rhythmic theme in multiple stops. Throughout the movement, the orchestra is scored thinly; the strings often serve more like a tuned percussion section. Most of the movement is in $\frac{3}{4}$, but substantial passages are in $\frac{7}{4}$ or $\frac{5}{4}$, odd time signatures associated with Russian folk music. The Second Violin Concerto had been commissioned by admirers of the French violinist Robert Soëtens, who gave the first performance of the work in Madrid, 1 December 1935. Prokofiev took pride in the fact that the Spanish, in the midst of a revolutionary upsurge, hailed him as a great Soviet artist and felt honored to have had the concerto's premiere in their country.

In 1938 Prokofiev completed his Concerto for Cello in E Minor that he had begun in 1933. It was judged a failure at its first performance, the critics dwelling on the absence of the soaring melodies that had characterized the Second Violin Concerto. Two years later he radically revised the work, and added a cadenza to the first movement. A developing collaboration with the young cellist Mstislav Rostropovich (b. 1927) inspired Prokofiev to use some of the same material in a radically altered form in his last concerto, the second one for cello. Despite the warmth of its themes, it was poorly received. The composer revised it in 1952, tightening the structure and substantially changing the orchestration. He renamed it Sinfonia Concertante in E Minor for Cello and Orchestra, Op. 125, probably because of the independent character of the orchestral part. This work was lauded but is infrequently performed. Its melodic and harmonic language is much simpler than that of his earlier works and lacks their punch.

DMITRY SHOSTAKOVICH (1906–1975)

Unlike the older Prokofiev, Shostakovich, as a mature composer, only knew of life under the control of the Communist party. Shostakovich never enjoyed the popular acclaim accorded Prokofiev, for the younger man's music lacks the melodic directness and sensuous appeal of the older's. Shostakovich's musical idiom is further removed from Romanticism and more regularly suggests a modern, twentieth-century sound. The music of both composers is rooted in their Russian heritage. Although one might expect a greater influence of contemporary non-Russian sources (such as Mahler, Berg, and Stravinsky) in the music of Prokofiev who spent so much time in the West, it is the music of Shostakovich that displays these influences in abundance.

Salient features of Shostakovich's style stem from his interest in instruments and larger instrumental forms. His melodies seem instrumentally conceived with their frequent large leaps and sudden angular turns of direction. Beneath this angularity, though, are shorter melodic fragments with the basic scalewise motion common to much Russian folk music. Frequent flatted tones give a sense of modality. Shostakovich was a master of counterpoint and handled complex instrumental forms with assurance, making extensive use of thematic development. He liked to create great contrast, as is evident in the close juxtaposition of widely disparate moods and in his masterful use of the orchestra in which the instruments are often placed in their extreme ranges, widely separated from one another. His rhythmic style is vibrant, and, in step with most Russian composers, uses rhythmic repetition as a powerfully expressive tool. He regularly employs instrumental recitative to intensify the emotional impact of certain passages. His approach to tonality is eclectic; while his music is basically tonal, he regularly inserts atonal and serial passages to realize special effects.

Shostakovich composed six concertos, two each for piano, violin, and cello. The violin concertos were written for David Oistrakh (1908–1974) and the cello concertos for Mstislav Rostropovich. The First Piano Concerto was written for the composer's personal performance, and the Second for his nineteen-year-old son, Maxim, who was later to become a conductor. Three of the concertos are in four movements. The First Cello Concerto is considered his greatest concerto; the First Piano Concerto, with its substantial solo part for trumpet, is of lasting interest as well.

The First Piano Concerto, Op. 35 (1933), is a compact, twenty-one-minute, four-movement work scored for an orchestra of strings and solo trumpet. It is Shostakovich's first composition after the opera *Lady Macbeth of Mzensk* (1930–32), which excited such severe criticism in 1936, and marks a turning toward a more popular, more tuneful, and less dissonant style. It is a lighter work with neo-Classical elements. These are especially evident in the piano's clear, crisp, transparent textures, resulting from the abundance of two-voice contrapuntal writing in the piano part. The occasional percussive use of the instrument recalls Prokofiev's approach to the piano. The opening, with descending and ascending scales in the piano accompanied only by a muted trumpet call, highlights the two featured instruments. The first movement is in sonata-allegro form. As is typical of Shostakovich, the second theme, in allegro tempo, is more rhythmic than the first, which is more lyrical in moderato tempo. The second theme clearly belongs to the trumpet. The first theme also closes the movement. The second movement is a slow waltz in ABA form with a passionate climax. The texture is quite sparse, especially in the outer parts of the form where the right and left hand of the piano part share simple material an octave apart. The very short third movement comprises a cadenza, at first unaccompanied, and then accompanied by strings, and a short middle section for strings. This movement also introduces the rambunctious finale in which the trumpet offers a sprightly little ditty reminiscent of a tune from a Haydn piano sonata.

Piano Concerto No. 2 was first performed by the composer's son on his nineteenth birthday, 10 May 1957. It is a light work full of youthful vigor. The piano writing of the outer movements is dominated by simple octave doubling between the hands. The Andante middle movement is plain yet lyrical; it is followed by a lively dance-inspired finale featuring a frequently reiterated rhythm (Ex. 20-11).

Ex. 20-11. Shostakovich, Piano Concerto No. 2; III. Allegro, m. 1.

The First Cello Concerto, Op. 107 (1959), was written for Rostropovich and fully exploits the phenomenal pitch range of the great cellist. It is another four-movement concerto marked by extremes of contrast so characteristic of the composer. The unaccompanied solo cello introduces the important, four-note motive x (Ex. 20-12) at the beginning of the Allegretto first movement. This motive forms the core of the movement and returns in the third and fourth movements. It is extensively developed in the first movement where the solo horn, the only brass instrument in the otherwise intimate orchestra, gives it special prominence by loudly punching out the motive in several places. The horn, solo cello, and woodwinds take turns playing the motive in the conclusion of the finale. The Moderato second movement is intensely quiet and lyrical. The opening solo idea returns at the end in a most ethereal setting for solo cello in glassy harmonics to which a celesta adds a heavenly accompaniment. A solo clarinet plays the melody in the middle of the movement to a countermelody in the solo instrument. The third movement, a five-minute, unaccompanied cadenza, links the second to the fourth movement. The cadenza is demanding and showy, but the listener's concentration centers on the development of thematic material. Initially, material derived from the second movement is explored, but as the tempo gradually increases to Allegro, motive x from the first movement reappears. The finale, Allegro con moto, is structured in rondo form and has a strong Russian dance flavor, with its short, repetitive rhythmic motives. From the outset, the cello reaches the extremes of its range as a short idea recurs successively in bass, tenor, alto, and soprano registers. This work, with its successful exploitation of the cello and exquisite contrasts of animation and meditation, remains a major concerto for the instrument.

Ex. 20-12. Shostakovich, Cello Concerto No. 1; I. Allegretto, mm. 1–10.

Shostakovich made towering contributions to Soviet music, and his death left a great void that required filling. One composer to occupy that space is Rodion Shchedrin.

Rodion Shchedrin (b. 1932) is likely to prove the most significant composer of the generation born in the 1930s. He was born in the year of the establishment of the Union of Soviet Composers and struggled under the artistic proscriptions of the Communist party. Shchedrin studied piano and composition at the Moscow Conservatory, marking his graduation with a performance of his lively Piano Concerto No. 1 in 1954. This concerto confirms his strong interest in the folk music of the various ethnic regions of the Soviet Union, a lifelong interest set in motion by a course involving the collection of folk songs in the field in 1951. The four-movement concerto includes the *chastushka*, a popular Russian tune, and folk melodies of Vologda. The quite conventional work has clear roots in the music of previous great Russian composers. The Molto vivo, scherzo-toccata second movement sounds Prokofiev-inspired, while the gloomy third movement, a passacaglia, seems to derive from Rachmaninov. The finale, with its clear folk idiom and striking orchestration, is reminiscent of Tchaikovsky.

Although some elements of polytonality spike the tonal language of this concerto, it is otherwise conventional. As Soviet society opened to Western culture in the 1960s, composers like Shchedrin were exposed to newer musical trends and techniques. As a consequence he and others began to incorporate the newer elements into already eclectic styles. Piano Concerto No. 2 (1966) contains atonal elements and Piano Concerto No. 3 (c. 1974) combines stylistic elements typical of several contemporary trends. While some of the work is serially organized, other parts make extensive use of aleatory techniques. Shchedrin sees aleatory techniques as a new way of entrusting a greater responsibility to the virtuoso performer. His use of atmospheric tone color seems strongly influenced by the Hungarian György Ligeti (b. 1923) and the Pole Krzysztof Penderecki (b. 1933). Shchedrin toured the West in the late 1980s as a kind of ambassador of musical glasnost. His music, previously little known in the West, was heard to some acclaim.

Soviet composers struggled under the weight of political control unknown in the West. Nevertheless, some Soviet composers succeeded in transcending the established boundaries to create concertos of universal appeal. They accomplished this feat in the usual way by writing scintillating solo parts and satisfying orchestral accompaniments. Yet there is another ingredient that is more difficult to define. The music of these fascinating composers blends elements of the East and West in ways that capture our imagination. In spite of the political gulf that existed between East and West, this music speaks directly to the hearts of listeners the world over.

THE CONCERTO IN BRITAIN

England had to wait two centuries after the brilliant composing career of Henry Purcell (1659–1695) before another native-born composer of significant stature appeared. Despite this long hiatus music remained an important factor in England's cultural life and its hub, London, remained one of Europe's great musical centers. During the eighteenth century, several great composers, including Handel and J. C. Bach, moved from the Continent to London, and throughout the nineteenth century a number of significant composers, including Mendelssohn and Dvořák, made important visits to the city, enriching its already abundant musical life. But it was not until after Edward Elgar's musical career began to flourish in the late nineteenth century that native English talent could rival that of the Continent.

EDWARD ELGAR (1857–1934)

Elgar, the son of a music shop owner, grew up in Worcester where he learned to play the piano, organ, violin, and cello, as well as several other orchestral instruments. This broad, practical, instrumental experience obviously contributed enormously to his subsequent success as an orchestrator of several important large-scale works, including two concertos. He had, however, essentially no formal theoretical or compositional training; he relied instead on the works of two of England's favorite composers, Handel and Mendelssohn, as well as those of Schumann, to serve as models for his own early compositions. Only after he and his wife, Alice, moved to London, when Elgar was in his thirties, did he hear good performances of music of the late nineteenth century. Thereupon he immediately began to incorporate stylistic elements of the music of Wagner, Brahms, and Dvořák into his own music. At about the same time other English composers, particularly Sir Charles Stanford (1852–1924) and Sir Hubert Parry (1848–1918), had determined to revitalize English musical composition by imitating the polyphony of the great English Renaissance composers. Elgar, however, remained untouched by these efforts, and continued to write in his essentially conservative, late-Romantic style to the end of his career.

Elgar's warmly attractive music is characterized by a melodic style in which wide leaps and many sequences play an important role and by luxuriant orchestral textures, resulting from his effective use of orchestral instruments. He enjoyed writing noble march themes, such as the main theme of the Violin Concerto's finale. He also made excellent use of subtle tempo changes, creating a fine sense of controlled rubato, often of an improvisatory nature. The latter feature is a particularly attractive element in his concertos, giving the impression of a rhapsodic solo improvisation. He seemed to possess an intuitively clear understanding of larger traditional forms and organized his material in convincing ways. Thematic transformation served as a fundamental element in his work within the larger forms.

In 1910, when Elgar was already in his early fifties, he wrote his first concerto. It was the first significant concerto by any native-born, English composer and was greeted with great jubilation. The wider English musical public was so anxious to hear the work that many had to be turned away when Fritz Kreisler, Elgar's friend and the dedicatee of the work, first performed it at the Queen's Hall on 10 November 1910 with the composer conducting. It has remained in the standard repertory ever since, having been played by most of the great violinists of this century. Unfortunately it has lost some of its allure in recent years.

The Violin Concerto in B Minor, Op. 61, is a large but intimate work, with a somewhat mysterious inscription in Spanish at the beginning of the score: "Aquí está encerrada el alma de. . . . ." (Herein lies enshrined the soul of . . . . .). This quotation is taken from the preface to the novel *Gil Blas* by Alain-René Lesage, but Elgar's reasons for using it are unknown. Several writers have speculated as to the identity of the person indicated by the dots, with Michael Kennedy, in his *Portrait of Elgar*,[1] providing the most convincing solution. Kennedy believes the inscription refers to Alice Stuart-Wortley (1862–1936), who was closely associated with Elgar and his music during this time. She was an excellent pianist and sensitive musician who loved Elgar's music and was sympathetic to his artistic temperament. The relationship was, according to Kennedy, not one of love, but one based on artistic understanding. Elgar was also befriended by Lord Stuart of Wortley, Alice's husband, and Elgar's wife knew them both as well. Elgar wrote more than 400 letters to Alice Stuart-Wortley during the period 1909 to 1931; in the letters that refer to the Violin Concerto, he usually writes of "our concerto." She also inspired parts of the Second Symphony, composed at the same time, which he called "your symphony." A copy, on notepaper, of the Lesage quotation in Elgar's handwriting was found in Alice's effects.[2]

In 1912, after completing the Second Symphony (1911), the choral ode *The Music Makers* (1912), and the Violin Concerto, Elgar wrote to Alice Stuart-Wortley, "I have written out my soul . . . in these three works I have *shewn* myself." And in writing to another friend about the Violin Concerto, he noted, "It's *good!* awfully emotional! too emotional but I love it. . . ." Elgar had, indeed, exposed his deepest emotions in these works, and the Violin Concerto is probably Elgar's most personal work, written to showcase an instrument he knew intimately and played very well.

The concerto is in the standard three-movement sequence of fast-slow-fast, with the dramatic weight located in the finale, the longest movement. A long orchestral tutti opens the work. Several short themes are presented therein, of which two are central. One is the initial theme, with its distinctive leaps, and short, sequentially developed, two-measure phrases so typical of Elgar (Ex. 21-1). The ideas which follow are also presented in two-measure phrases, extended through sequence.

Ex. 21-1. Elgar, Violin Concerto; I. Allegro, mm. 1–8.

Elgar referred to the second important theme (Ex. 21-2) as a "windflower" theme, further connecting the work to Alice Stuart-Wortley through a name he often called her. It is marked *pianissimo, semplice, dolce,* and stands quite apart from the previous, more active themes. The orchestra offers but a hint of the windflower theme in the opening tutti; only later does the theme assume its complete form when the violin states it with extraordinary directness in G major against a thin orchestral accompaniment. The windflower theme also appears at important places later in the movement. In the development section it accompanies rhapsodic solo work, and later its rising sequences lead to a loud, forceful climax built on the descending patterns of mm. 5–8 of the opening theme.

Ex. 21-2. Elgar, Violin Concerto; I. Allegro, mm. 134–142.

The solo instrument's first entry is quite unusual. It follows an orchestral restatement of the movement's opening two measures, and gives the opening theme a new sense of repose. The *nobilmente, molto largamente* start of the solo passage gives way to Elgar's characteristic rubato style, full of subtle nuances, including frequent changes of tempo and fluctuations in dynamic levels. A brief recitative-like passage, marked *più tranquillo,* adds to the music's expressive quality.

The Andante movement begins in the remote key of B-flat major. The orchestra sings the flowing main theme (which reminds some of the slow movement of Brahms's Violin Concerto) which again comprises short phrases developed in Elgar's characteristic manner. The solo violin never plays this theme, but joins its repeat with a sonorous counterpoint. A more passionate midsection starts in D-flat major, then moves to D major. Allusions to the two main themes of movement I occur in this section.

The Allegro molto finale is the longest movement, and its lengthy and remarkable cadenza near the end forms the emotional high point of the work. The solo instrument initiates the finale with brilliant figures that establish the tonic key of B minor, but the main rondo theme appears in D major. It is one of Elgar's typical march themes (Ex. 21-3), complete with short sequences. It is first played by the orchestra in a strong chordal setting, a setting maintained in frequent solo presentations of the theme through the effective use of triple stops on the violin. The final appearance of this theme illustrates Elgar's use of thematic transformation; the theme, in augmented form and finally in the tonic key of B major, is here marked with Elgar's characteristic term, *nobilmente.*

Ex. 21-3. Elgar, Violin Concerto; III. Allegro molto, mm. 28–32.

Along the way several new themes emerge, including a very rhythmic one at rehearsal no. 72 that is strongly reminiscent of the closing theme of the first movement of Brahms's Violin Concerto. A *nobilmente* section (at no. 94) presents the chordal theme of the slow movement's climax, transformed in fast tempo, initially in B major. The subsequent climax fizzles, and a most unusual and gripping cadenza follows.

The cadenza moves mostly in a very slow tempo, although frequent changes of tempo and expression markings, including *mesto* (sad) and *poco animato* (a little animated), suggest the passionate wanderings of a Romantic soul. The highly expressive cadenza contains references to the two important themes of movement I, namely, the tender windflower theme and the noble opening theme. For the first time in the work, the solo instrument plays the latter in its entirety, investing it with new, emotional depth. The cadenza is accompanied intermittently by the orchestral strings using a new technique formulated by Elgar. It is the *pizzicato tremolando,* a kind of dramatic strumming, or "thrumming" as Elgar put it, made by brushing the strings with the soft tips of three or four fingers. Perhaps this is meant to imitate Spanish guitar music, alluding to the Spanish inscription at the beginning of the score. It lends a dramatic air to the important cadenza.

Elgar's Violin Concerto is an historically important and thoroughly satisfying concerto that, unfortunately, is overshadowed by his Cello Concerto in E Minor, Op. 85. It is true the latter is a masterful composition, but the Violin Concerto is equally impressive and deserves more regular performances.

While the Violin Concerto is a work of love, the Cello Concerto tells deeply of the grief caused by World War I. It was composed in 1918–19 when Elgar was over sixty years old. All his works of this time share a strongly introspective element tinged with despair. Elgar was a great mood creator, and here he created a predominantly somber mood, although there is contrast from movement to movement. The Cello Concerto is full of meditative moments, enhanced by the generally subdued orchestration, partially required by the nature of the solo instrument. The solo instrument is frequently accompanied only by strings or strings and woodwinds. Even in tutti sections, the full orchestra is rarely used.

This concerto has an unusual structure. Its four movements are joined in pairs:

  I. Adagio; Moderato; (in E minor), linked to:
 II. Allegro molto (in G Major).

III. Adagio (in B-flat major); ending on the dominant, linked to:
 IV. Allegro (starting in B-flat minor); Moderato (Quasi recitative); Allegro ma non troppo (in E minor).

The Cello Concerto, like Elgar's Violin Concerto, is cyclical. The final movement recalls both the work's opening and a portion of the third movement's main theme.

The general mood of the Cello Concerto is set by the five-measure, introductory, *nobilmente* passage for solo cello (Ex. 21-4). The passage begins with multiple stops over a fairly wide range and then thins to a descending, voice-like setting with recitative-style accompaniment in the low strings of the orchestra. The final, slow crescendo descent to the low E captures a dark, lonely, almost bleak mood, to which equally somber clarinets and bassoons respond.

Ex. 21-4. Elgar, Cello Concerto; I. Adagio, mm. 1–5.

A brief, light flourish leads to the first movement proper, a seven-minute-long Moderato cast as a pastorale, involving the use of $\frac{9}{8}$ and $\frac{12}{8}$ time, lilting long-short-long-short rhythms, and parallel thirds characteristic of the traditional pastoral setting. Yet the peaceful mood is disturbed by the contrary emphasis on darker timbres and the minor mode, as, for example, when unaccompanied violas and cellos state the main theme (Ex. 21-5). Other factors contribute to the somber mood: Full orchestra appears only twice, once for six measures and once for three; there is a notable lack of virtuoso writing for the soloist; and the largely diatonic harmony is austere. The movement is not cast in the traditional sonata-allegro form. Instead, it is in ternary form, with a brighter, dolcissimo section in E major occupying the very center of the movement.

Ex. 21-5. Elgar, Cello Concerto; I. Moderato, mm. 9–14.

The tiny, scherzo-like second movement in G major is more animated than the first, yet it is still cloaked in melancholy. The cello offers the main theme, but this lacks the characteristic warmth of most cello themes. Its many short, repeated notes and frequent stress of the cello's upper ranges give it a brittle quality. But an effectively contrasting theme (Ex. 21-6), first appearing in E-flat major, brightens the environment in a most arresting, although brief, fashion. Only Elgar could have created a two-measure idea that packed such joy in its lyrical and dancelike passing.

Ex. 21-6. Elgar, Cello Concerto; II. Allegro molto, mm. 40–41.

The four score pages containing the whole of the brief Adagio in B-flat major finally let the cello sing out. A single, broad melody drawn out over sixty measures maintains the general quality of calm, although again tinged with a sense of a melancholy. This movement ends on the dominant of B-flat, and the fourth movement begins in B-flat minor with a clear hint of the Allegro ma non troppo's main rondo theme. This theme (Ex. 21-7), similar to Elgar's earlier march themes, complete with off-beat chords in the accompaniment, is based on the soloist's opening recitative gesture of movement I. The recitative itself makes a clear return before a cadenza-like flourish leads to the Rondo proper in E minor.

Ex. 21-7. Elgar, Cello Concerto; IV. Allegro, ma non troppo, mm. 20–22.

The freely constructed rondo takes on the more robust characteristics associated with prewar Elgar. The contrasting, almost playful, second theme in G major (first heard at rehearsal no. 47) provides the lightest moment in the work. At the return of the main rondo theme at no. 59, the solo cello plays in the unison company of tutti cellos (and, at times, violas, double basses, bassoons), creating a very unusual effect atypical of the Romantic use of the solo instrument. This treatment endows the theme with greater warmth.

The lighter mood of the rondo dies, giving way to a very serious and expressive Lento section with a new, chromatically descending theme (Ex. 21-8). A still more passionate theme in $\frac{3}{4}$, involving a three-fold descending sequence, follows (Ex. 21-9). As the concerto plunges into the realm of despair, the solo cello, in its high register, recalls the second portion of the Adagio's melody, but in the new lento tempo. This leads to a surprising restatement of the work's opening cello recitative, complete with its descent to its low and lonely sounding E. The dark mood is broken by the fast coda, which includes a brief appearance the rondo main theme.

Ex. 21-8. Elgar, Cello Concerto; IV. Allegro, ma non troppo, mm. 282–285.

Ex. 21-9. Elgar, Cello Concerto; IV. Allegro, ma non troppo, mm. 306–310.

Elgar described the work to a friend as "a real [sic] large work & I think *good & alive.*" It is certainly alive in the cellist's repertoire. The Cello Concerto glimpses into the heart of an aging composer racked by the grief of a war thought to end all wars. Felix Salmond was the cellist in the first performance on 27 October 1919 in Queen's Hall with Elgar conducting the London Symphony Orchestra. All in attendance agreed that inadequate rehearsal rendered a very poor performance of the work. If Pablo Casals had not rescued the concerto later, it might have enjoyed only a short life. The great British violist, Lionel Tertis (1876–1975), made an authorized transcription of the work for his instrument, but it is only infrequently performed.

Elgar, who could play the bassoon, composed the short Romance for Bassoon and Orchestra, taking advantage of the instrument's abilities to sing lyrical lines. He destroyed an earlier attempt at a violin concerto and left unfinished a piano concerto he had begun in 1909.

VAUGHAN WILLIAMS AND CONTEMPORARIES

During the first two decades of the twentieth century, British composers in general eschewed the newer musical developments occurring on the Continent. Elgar and composers of the next generation, including Gustav Holst and Ralph Vaughan Williams, carried on the Romantic tradition, albeit with an English flavor.

Vaughan Williams (1872–1958) began to collect English folk tunes in 1903 and introduced them to his friend Holst in that year. The simple directness of the folk tunes had a profound effect on both composers. Vaughan Williams's music is full of quotation or imitation of folk tunes, and Holst, who had previously depended upon Wagner-inspired chromaticism, turned to these simpler, more diatonic, modal structures. In general, these composers, particularly Vaughan Williams, evolved a musical style in which virtuosity had no place. Their concern was with flowing melodic ideas; dramatic tension played a background role. Though both composers wrote concertos, they did not have the satisfaction of seeing these enter the standard repertory, probably because of their stylistic idiosyncrasies.

Among Vaughan Williams's half-dozen works for solo instrument and orchestra are the Concerto in D Minor for Violin and String Orchestra (1925) and the Concerto for Piano (1926–31). Both works provide evidence of the composer's interests in neo-Classicism and the "Back-to-Bach" movement. The Piano Concerto is in three movements played without a break. It begins with an Allegro moderato movement in the style of a restless toccata. A cadenza leads to the intimate Romanza, which concludes with an effective passage for oboe and viola over a timpani roll. The complex, third movement is begun by trombones, which announce the angular theme of the first *fuga chromatica* (chromatic fugue) section. A difficult cadenza leads to the last section, a sinister waltz based on a transformation of the fugue theme that may remind listeners of Liszt's *Mephisto Waltzes*. The quiet ending derives from a 1946 version of the work for two pianos and orchestra; some critics had complained that the scoring of the orchestra was too thick for a single piano to cut through. While this may be true in parts of the first movement, it is generally agreed that the original version is preferable to the later. The Tuba Concerto from 1954 enjoys occasional performances; it has a very beautiful slow movement. The peaceful romance for violin and orchestra, *The Lark Ascending* (1914, revised 1920), is Vaughan Williams's most frequently performed concerto-like work.

Gustav Holst (1874–1934) wrote two concertos in the 1920s that demonstrate his fondness for contrapuntal textures and neo-Classical techniques. The earlier work, called *A Fugal Concerto* for flute, oboe, and strings, has the quality of chamber music. The Double Violin Concerto is in three connected movements.

The first is a fugal scherzo, the second is a Lament with Holst's favorite bitonal coloring using two keys at once, and the finale is a set of variations on a ground bass with much rhythmic vitality.

Frank Bridge (1879–1941), another British composer of this generation, tended to create intimate, poetic fantasies, far removed from the virtuoso world of the traditional concerto. This pacifist's requiem for the dead of World War I took the form of a colorful, single-movement *Oration, Concerto elegiaco* for cello and orchestra (1930).

Frederick Delius (1862–1934) spent much of his life in France writing Impressionistic music characterized by delicate orchestral textures, extreme chromaticism, and lyricism. Of all the English composers discussed here, his style is the least suitable for the concerto, yet he composed four. The most effective is the Violin Concerto of 1916, which uses the solo instrument in a songful but mostly decorative fashion throughout. The melodic flow grows from the opening two measures and fills the unusual continuous form in which the main sections of sonata-allegro form are separated by other movements. Delius's Double Concerto for Violin and Cello (1915) was written for May and Beatrice Harrison after Delius heard the sisters perform Brahms's Double Concerto under Sir Thomas Beecham.

WILLIAM WALTON (1902–1983)

Composers of the generation born approximately 1900 to 1905 still tended to follow in the tradition established by Elgar and Vaughan Williams, showing little inclination to experiment with newer compositional techniques. Outstanding in this group of English composers is Sir William Walton.

Although Walton's style generally joins the conservative Romantic tradition, he did admit some modern elements into his musical language. In particular, a rhythmic sense akin to that of Stravinsky enlivens his music. Some of his earlier works, such as the well-known *Façade* (1922), are infused with elements of jazz. Syncopation, frequent changes of meter, and clear percussive attacks mark his later works as well. His earlier neo-Classical path was replaced by a more Romantic approach beginning with the Viola Concerto (1929).

Walton described himself as a "classical composer with a strong feeling for lyricism." His ability to write long, poignant, lyrical melodic lines is much admired. This quality often combines with his works' strong rhythmic features. The melodies have colorful harmonic support; Walton's music is tonal but spiced with dissonance, chromaticism, and a heady mixture of major and minor modes. He preferred the larger instrumental forms and tended to use his thematic material cyclically, often coupled with thematic transformation. He used the orchestra in brilliant and imaginative ways.

Walton, knighted in 1951, was a slow and careful worker who completed a short list of highly polished works. His tendency to perfect his scores even led to a revised edition of the Viola Concerto more than thirty years after its first performance.

Walton's three concertos, one each for violin, viola, and cello, share a strong lyrical orientation and provide clear portraits of the solo instruments. The works are demanding of the soloist, but are not written in the traditional virtuoso concerto tradition. Indicative of Walton's distaste for bravura writing is the conciseness of the few cadenza passages in the concertos. Each concerto is in three movements, but not in the usual fast-slow-fast sequence. Walton tended to begin and end with slow, lyrical movements surrounding lively, scherzo-like, middle movements, much in the manner of Prokofiev's First Violin Concerto (1916–17), which may have influenced Walton.

Walton's earliest attempts in the concerto genre are two works featuring piano. The earliest, known as the Fantasia Concertante for two pianos, jazz band, and orchestra, was composed in 1923; the music is lost, possibly destroyed by the composer. The second, the Sinfonia Concertante for Piano and Orchestra (1928), includes one of his first strongly lyrical movements. Jazz-inspired rhythms dominate, and the structure is thematically linked, as is the case with his later, larger works.

The Viola Concerto, composed in 1929 at the suggestion of the conductor Sir Thomas Beecham, was written with the great English violist, Lionel Tertis, as the intended soloist. Tertis, however, refused to perform the work, so Paul Hindemith, an accomplished violist as well as composer, performed it under Walton's direction in Queen's Hall, London, on 3 October 1929. The concert was a success and led to a close friendship between the two composers. Just before Hindemith's death in 1963, Walton wrote a set of variations on a theme from Hindemith's Cello Concerto, also including references to the German composer's opera *Mathis der Maler*. Both the music and the recognition greatly pleased Hindemith.

Walton's Viola Concerto is considered one of the most outstanding works featuring that normally overlooked and somewhat ungainly, but warm, instrument. This concerto, true to the character of the instrument, has a deeply emotional appeal. The orchestra, originally scored for three of each woodwind, is handled with care so that the soloist is not overwhelmed. Almost every time the viola plays, the number of players in the string section is reduced. Later performances of the concerto inspired the composer to revise the orchestration, which he did in 1961 by reducing the woodwinds to pairs, dropping one trumpet, and adding a quite effective harp part. Some passages were significantly rescored, and in places the solo part is lowered an octave to provide greater balance.

The first of the Viola Concerto's three movements, an Andante comodo in A minor, is the slowest. It is in sonata-allegro form. The E minor second movement, marked Vivo, con molto preciso, is energized by several restless motives and a boundless rhythmic vitality. The changing meter gives it a character similar to that of Stravinsky's music. The movement is a rondo, based on a jumpy main theme introduced by the violist. Subsidiary ideas include a jazzy figure first given by muted brass (at no. 21) and a lively syncopated passage first given by the soloist (at no. 22) and later expanded in some exciting orchestral interludes. The finale, in moderate tempo, is the longest and most highly organized of the movements. Thematic material from the first movement is recalled in its important coda.

Walton makes imaginative use of thematic transformation in the Viola Concerto, applying the technique to the first movement's two principal themes on several occasions. The most dramatic example occurs in the first movement's animated developed section, where the originally calm, songlike, first theme (Ex. 21-10a), played at the movement's outset by the solo viola in $\frac{9}{8}$ time, is transformed into an urgent, orchestral statement in $\frac{3}{4}$ (Ex. 21-10b). This theme also reappears in the coda of the finale (beginning at no. 61), where the viola plays it in $\frac{9}{4}$ time over a long pedal point on E and an ostinato in the bass clarinet and harp, a pattern based on the opening part of the third movement's main theme. The second theme of the first movement receives similar treatment. First played by the solo instrument in its lower register, in $\frac{3}{2}$ time, it is repeated almost immediately in a higher register in a dreamy (*sognando*) passage in $\frac{7}{4}$ time and returns in the recapitulation in an *appassionato* setting in the instrument's highest register in $\frac{4}{4}$ time.

Ex. 21-10. Walton, Viola Concerto; I. Andante comodo: (a.) mm. 4–5; (b.) mm. 108–111.

The orchestra is often responsible for creating major climaxes in Walton's concertos. In the two outer movements of the Viola Concerto, these climaxes are followed by calming episodes featuring the solo instrument. In the first movement, the calming influence comes from a very small, softly accompanied cadenza based on the very opening of the concerto, and in the finale the viola quotes the lyrical opening theme of the first movement.

The first four measures of the Viola Concerto (Ex. 21-11) are important in setting a quiet, expressive mood and developing a leading motive of the work. These few measures are exquisite, and Walton's attention to detail is worthy of study. The sound of muted strings, joined by the clarinet in its chalumeau register, sets the stage. The all-important motive is the interval of the rising third, in both major and minor forms. First violins first play a major third (B-flat–D); this is followed immediately by a minor third (D–F), stretched chromatically to the major third (D–F-sharp) in the violas. Another major third (C–E) in the first violins in m. 2 is followed by successive minor thirds (C-sharp–E; E–G) in m. 3, also in the first violins. These repetitions prepare for the marvelously ambiguous entry of the solo viola in m. 4, where its rising minor third to C-natural is set against the major third, C-sharp, in the orchestral violas and bassoon. This major-minor conflict is an important element in the composition and is isolated in the woodwinds in m. 13 in

Ex. 21-11. Walton, Viola Concerto; I. Andante comodo, mm. 1–4.

a figure that serves as a motto (Ex. 21-12), recurring numerous times throughout the work. The solo violin sometimes plays the motto in poignant double stops, as it does at the conclusion of the final movement. Here the motto underlies the ambiguous final cadence of the work, in which both the C-natural and C-sharp sound above the A.

Ex. 21-12. Walton, Viola Concerto; I. Andante comodo, m. 13.

The Viola Concerto is often considered Walton's greatest masterpiece, but it is seldom included on concert programs simply because there are very few touring solo violists. On the other hand, because the Viola Concerto features such a frequently neglected instrument, it overshadows his Violin Concerto, a work of equal interest.

Walton completed the Violin Concerto in 1939 on commission from the violinist Jascha Heifetz. Walton's Violin Concerto shares the intimate feeling and the same key, B minor, as Elgar's Violin Concerto. Walton's Violin Concerto is even more lyrical and more Romantic in character than his Viola Concerto. Once again the slowest movement is placed first, a scherzo movement is second, and the final movement, a lively one this time, is interrupted near the end by an exquisitely stated recollection of the first movement's opening theme, providing that thematic unity so characteristic of Walton's music. Also characteristic is Walton's use of thematic transformation as a means of developing the musical material.

The quiet two-bar orchestral introduction to the Andante tranquillo sets the stage for the dreamy (*sognando*) entry of the solo violin. The soloist's octave ascent opens into a long lyric line with many opulent rising intervals, especially the powerfully expressive seventh. A countersubject in bassoon and cellos adds to the warm, expressive atmosphere of the opening (Ex. 21-13), which gives no hint of the virtuosic display to come.

Ex. 21-13. Walton, Violin Concerto; I. Andante tranquillo, mm. 1–10.

Interesting examples of Walton's technique of thematic transformation occur throughout the movement. These include a dynamic version of the main theme given to the winds (Ex. 21-14), the following syncopated version by the soloist (Ex. 21-15), and, finally, the winds' more marked transformation of the countersubject (Ex. 21-16).

Ex. 21-14. Walton, Violin Concerto; I. Andante tranquillo, mm. 76–79.

Ex. 21-15. Walton, Violin Concerto; I. Andante tranquillo, mm. 84–88.

Ex. 21-16. Walton, Violin Concerto; I. Andante tranquillo, mm. 100–103.

The orchestra's *subito vivace* climax focuses on still another significant transformation of the lyric opening theme as it moves through changing measures of compound time (Ex. 21-17). In Walton's typical fashion, the orchestral climax softens to a calmer segment featuring the soloist. The flutes highlight the return of the main theme (at no. 22), while the solo violin offers the countermelody.

Ex. 21-17. Walton, Violin Concerto; I. Andante tranquillo, mm. 204–206.

The second movement, a wild dance entitled Presto capriccioso alla napolitana, is the most overtly virtuosic of any movement in Walton's concertos. Susana Walton revealed, in her recent biography of her husband, that he had been bitten by a tarantula while working on the concerto and decided to mark the event by writing a tarantella, a fast dance of southern Italy featuring continuous runs of triplets. He seems to have been greatly pleased by this wild movement, for he wrote to his publisher, Hubert Foss, that he felt: "quite gaga, I may say, and of doubtful propriety after the Ist movement."[3]

This dance movement is in a scherzo-trio-scherzo form. The scherzo proper has three themes: the first, beginning with the orchestral first measure, sets the wild mood with triplets and augmented triads; the second features a strident unison orchestral presentation of a strongly rhythmic idea reminiscent of Bartók, and the third is a waltz for the violin in sweet, double-stopped sixths. The trio, marked *canzonetta*, features a C major tune, first in the horn, with an accompaniment in A-flat major. The violin later takes the tune in its high range and then in harmonics, perhaps in imitation of a folk singer's falsetto. Clever instrumental effects enhance the wild character of the movement.

The Vivace finale is a rondo which alternates two rigorous march-like ideas with strongly contrasting lyrical melodies, the first of which seems dimly related to the main theme of movement I. An unexpected, highly expressive moment occurs when the solo violin quotes the concerto's opening theme in double-stopped sixths; the theme sings out against a background consisting of a pedal point on E, tremolando in the upper strings, and a countermelody based on the finale's opening theme in the bassoon, clarinet, and cellos. This precedes an accompanied cadenza, most likely inspired by the very expressive cadenza at the conclusion of Elgar's Violin Concerto. And as in the Elgar concerto, the cadenza is followed by several pages of march material, based on a transformation of the final movement's first lyric theme.

So ends one of the most striking violin concertos of the twentieth century. Its success is rooted in Walton's thorough understanding of the instrument's personality and potential—its great ability to sing lyric melodies and to play fiery virtuosic passages—combined with his mastery of orchestral writing that provides an exciting contrast to the solo violin part.

Walton's Cello Concerto (1956) was commissioned by Gregor Piatigorsky (1903–1976). The delicate scoring, which allows the low, solo instrument to be heard, is enhanced by an exotic combination of vibraphone, celesta, xylophone, and harp, and extensive use of string *tremolandi* and *sul ponticello* (bowing near the bridge to produce a soft, nasal sound), giving the work an exotic quality. The Moderato first movement is lyrical and meditative, the second is a scherzo, and the third is a most unusual and intensely expressive set of variations. The third movement, also the longest, begins Lento and is characterized by slower tempos. The muted solo cello presents the theme in its upper range; four variations follow. In the first, the orchestra takes the theme while the cello adds a counterpoint in triplets. In the second, unaccompanied solo cello holds forth in a resolute and bravura style. Variation III climbs to the orchestral climax of the movement, a toccata-style section in compound meter. Unaccompanied solo cello offers the fourth variation, playing in a more rhapsodic style. The concluding solo trills continue into the last section, an epilogue that quotes a cantabile theme from the first movement.

Walton's contribution to the concerto literature for string instruments was not only quite unique but also very significant in that it depended upon such a different, yet very successful, approach to the concerto style and form.

BENJAMIN BRITTEN (1913–1976)

Benjamin Britten, the leading British composer of his generation, could set the English language to music with uncanny sensitivity. As a consequence, his principal musical contributions are in the realm of vocal music—solo songs, opera, and choral works. Britten's lyrical musical thought was best suited to shorter forms, which he often connected to form significant, larger works. His musical style was less well suited to the standard, large, instrumental forms, such as the sonata, symphony, and concerto. In his extensive body of chamber and orchestral music, he favored the forms of more limited scope, such as the suite, and developed a fondness for variation forms, especially the passacaglia, which allowed him to employ his lyrical fantasy within well-defined limitations. His concertos confirm his musical predilections.

His two earliest concerto-style compositions were given the title "Concerto" and do indeed share several of the form's classic characteristics. Yet these early works also depart from the norm in other ways. Britten was an accomplished pianist; he composed the Piano Concerto (1938, revised 1945) for himself and for display of the piano's various "voices." The suite-like structure of four movements—Toccata, Waltz, Recitative and Aria, and March—is quite atypical of the traditional, bravura concerto. The first movement, sounding as if inspired by Prokofiev, pits a percussively conceived piano part against sustained orchestral parts. In the third movement's original form, the piano first plays a recitative, but then repeatedly interrupts the efforts of solo woodwinds to play a sustained tune by inserting incongruous fragments of a polka, a blues, a waltz, and other lighter forms. This movement was replaced in a 1945 revision of the concerto with an Impromptu in passacaglia form.

Britten composed the Violin Concerto (1939) during his stay in the United States. (He was unhappy in England, finding the hostilities of war too upsetting, so emigrated first to Canada in 1939, and then to the United States, where he spent almost three years.) It is a difficult, imaginative, and passionate showpiece in the standard three movements, but performed without a break. The first movement, Moderato con moto, focuses on the solo instrument's songlike quality; its opening drum motive recalls Beethoven's Violin Concerto. The second movement is a brilliant Vivace in the form of scherzo-trio-scherzo. The outer parts demand extraordinary technical skills of the soloist, who must play the harmonics, rapid scales in thirds, sixths, octaves, and tenths, and glissandi. The scherzo is characterized by rhythmic propulsion and unusual scoring; for example, there is an effective ostinato for piccolo and tuba underlying the solo violin's harmonics at the start of the reprise. The lyrical trio provides effective contrast and makes an additional, abbreviated return following the main reprise of the scherzo. The cadenza, which serves as a link to the passacaglia finale, includes references to thematic material from both first and second movements. The passacaglia, Britten's first, is a powerfully emotive movement that concludes with a lament. The Violin Concerto was first performed by Antonio Brosa of Spain; perhaps the lament was intended for the dead of the Spanish Civil War.

The best of Britten's large-scale instrumental works is the Cello Symphony of 1963, one of six pieces he was to compose for Mstislav Rostropovich. Because the cellist was ill at the time the work was completed, Rostropovich did not perform it until the following spring in Moscow, with the composer conducting. It is a hybrid of the symphony and the concerto. The cello plays an important solo role throughout, yet the orchestra is given an equally important role. This equality is not realized through the use of the traditional ritornello form, but by an interesting distribution of responsibilities within a structure that is more like that of a symphony. It has four movements, although the last two are joined. The orchestra is fairly large, but great care is taken never to overshadow the solo instrument. For example, the composer's imaginative use of the bassoon and contrabassoon on bass lines allows the solo cello to play in its lower register without forcing it to function as the bass part. Further, the violins are limited to a minor role, allowing the lower cello notes to be more easily heard through the smaller mass of orchestral sound. As is so often the case in Britten's music, the percussion section, including bass drum, gong, cymbals, tenor drum, snare drum, tambourine, tam-tam, whip, and vibraphone, is very important. The vibraphone especially adds a striking tone color that very beautifully complements the solo cello.

While Britten usually avoided sonata-allegro form, he made extremely effective use of it in the first movement of the Cello Symphony, centered in D minor. The solo cello presents three main themes in the exposition, while the orchestra provides novel and active accompaniment. The very opening establishes the balance of the forces. Here a concise ostinato pattern is played by the double basses, tuba and contrabassoon, accompanied by timpani roll and gong; against this, the solo cello presents the chordally set main theme in multiple stops. Important motives in the theme are the quickly repeated notes (a) and the following semitone descent (b), both found in m. 3 (Ex. 21-18). These ideas are explored both sequentially and simultaneously before presentation of the second theme, a descending scale decorated with minor thirds. The third theme is a declamatory exploration of the repeated notes and semitone motive of m. 3. The development section focuses on the small motives—the thirds, the repeated notes, and the semitone—as well as on an intense contrapuntal development of the opening two-part ostinato pattern in inversion. In the recapitulation, the cello takes over the accompanimental role of the orchestra, while the orchestra presents the themes.

Ex. 21-18. Britten, Cello Symphony; I. Allegro maestoso, mm. 1–12.

The short, restless second movement, marked Presto inquieto, is a scherzo with a quieter trio or midsection. The scherzo develops from the tiny three-note scale motive x (tone plus semitone, comprising a minor third) heard at the outset in the solo instrument (Ex. 21-19).

Ex. 21-19. Britten, Cello Symphony; II. Presto inquieto, mm. 1–2.

The ternary form Adagio is the emotional center of the work. Here the cello theme explores the melodic interval of the third (major and minor), focusing on two related, long-short rhythmic patterns (Ex. 21-20). Phrases of the theme are separated by woodwind interludes. In the reprise, solo brass instruments take turns with the theme, while the solo cello plays the interludes. The quiet timpani roll on G at the movement's opening recurs repeatedly throughout the movement, but with a continually changing character. The timpani roll introduces and overlaps with the beginning of the lengthy cadenza that, as in the Violin Concerto, links this movement to the finale. In the cadenza, the solo instrument even imitates the sound of the timpani. The cadenza contains little of a traditional bravura quality; Britten instead concentrates on poetic content.

Ex. 21-20. Britten, Cello Symphony; III. Adagio, mm. 5–9.

The finale is a fascinating combination of passacaglia and theme and variations. The expert on variations, Britten here created one of his most intriguing instrumental movements. The solo cello initiates the five-measure ground (or passacaglia) bass. The bass line is repeated three more times, at different pitch levels but with quite varied endings. The ground bass accompanies the main tune in the solo trumpet, which is a transformation of the B theme from the Adagio (Ex. 21-21). Both the tune and the ground bass are altered in the following six variations. The way in which the ground's ending changes is especially captivating.

Ex. 21-21. Britten, Cello Symphony; IV. Passacaglia: Andante allegro, mm. 1–13.

Britten's Diversions for Piano and Orchestra (1941) is a set of eleven variations on a theme; the final variation is a bristling tarantella.

MICHAEL TIPPETT (B. 1905)

Sir Michael Tippett came to music relatively late in life. Although eight years Britten's senior, he did not write any music of substance until after Britten had established a significant reputation. Tippett was largely overshadowed by Britten, especially in the international community, but following Britten's death in 1976, Tippett's reputation as the greatest living English composer grew. Tippett shared many interests with Britten, and both were important composers of opera. Both were influenced by Stravinsky and Berg, but Tippett proved a much more eclectic composer, embracing musical characteristics of many eras and cultures. Elizabethan madrigals and sixteenth- and seventeenth-century harpsichord music fascinated him; he explored early polyphonic music and made counterpoint a powerfully strong element of his style. A vital rhythmic component enlivens his music and often highlights lines in the polyphonic web he weaves. He has a keen interest in the spirituals of American blacks, and has incorporated real or imitation spiritual tunes in several of his works. American jazz has also been an inspiration. He has had a lifelong admiration for Beethoven, which may account for his interest in the sonata and techniques of thematic or motivic development. He commonly juxtaposes or superimposes strongly contrasting musical ideas. Tippett is, like Britten, essentially a neo-Classicist who has embraced tonality. His later works are more dissonant and chromatic but are still tonally centered.

Tippett's earliest completed concerto is the Concerto for Double String Orchestra (1938–39), which is considered his first great work. The exclusive use of strings characterizes his early music; in later years he sought greater orchestral color to heighten the contrast of contrapuntal lines. The concerto element in this piece is not that of a virtuosic soloist pitted against the orchestra, but harks back to the original form of contrast between string orchestras—a neo-Baroque device. The extraordinary rhythmic independence of the two parts at the beginning signals Tippett's highly contrapuntal style (Ex. 21-22).

Ex. 21-22. Tippett, Concerto for Double String Orchestra; I. Allegro con brio, mm. 1–8.

The work is in the standard three movements. In the first, dancelike movement, the returns of the opening statement suggest a ritornello structure, while a development section and the feeling of a recapitulation both point to sonata-allegro form. The Adagio is based on a lyrical theme that alternates with a restless fugal section; the latter eventually emerges in the accompaniment for the repeat of the lyrical section. The songlike second movement is followed by an Allegro molto finale that alternates a dancelike rondo refrain with songlike episodes, creating an ABACABD form. In the final D episode Tippett pits a tune (Ex. 21-23) with black spiritual qualities against the dance elements of the main theme.

Ex. 21-23. Tippett, Concerto for Double String Orchestra; III. Allegro molto, mm. 7–14 after No. 40.

Tippett wrote his Fantasia Concertante on a Theme of Corelli (1953) for the Edinburgh Festival to mark the 300th anniversary of the Baroque composer's birth.

Tippett based his work on part of the second movement of Corelli's Concerto Grosso Op. 6, No. 2. This excerpt consists of a brief Adagio idea, repeated in a four-fold sequence, and a very short Vivace with quick repeated notes in the orchestra and short solo bursts from the concertino of two violins and cello. While Corelli's music occupies no more than a single score page, Tippett has searched the depths of these simple ideas to create a neo-Classical, or better, a neo-Baroque, work of close to twenty minutes' duration for a string ensemble like Corelli's, but with double string orchestra replacing Corelli's single orchestra. The work consists of seven variations on Corelli's theme, peaking in the complex fugue of the fifth variation, which relates to J. S. Bach's Fugue for Organ on a Theme of Corelli, BWV 579. (The theme is from the second movement of Corelli's Op. 3, No. 4.) The concertino instruments have but little solo space in Tippett's work, and this is concentrated near the end as in Corelli's concertos.

Tippett's Piano Concerto of 1953–55 is an extended work of more traditional scope: A single solo instrument is treated in a virtuosic manner. He once explained that his inspiration for the work was hearing Beethoven's Fourth Piano Concerto in rehearsal. He wanted to create a similarly lyrical work in which the piano would "sing." The second movement may have been directly inspired by Beethoven's unusual middle movement; the strings move in and out until silenced by the piano. The finale is a rondo in which the orchestra plays the rondo theme while the piano plays the episodes. The first episode has a jazzy feeling; the final one calls for a favorite Tippett instrument, the celesta, in duet with the piano.

Two other Tippett concertos require mention. The Concerto for Orchestra (1962–63) was dedicated "to Benjamin Britten with affection and admiration in the year of his fiftieth birthday." Here Tippett explored old meanings of the term *concerto* in new and unconventional ways. No instruments are singled out as soloists; rather the composer exploits the element of *stile concertato*, that Baroque notion of contrast among parts of the performing ensemble. Instruments are grouped into small autonomous ensembles that play strikingly different music against one another. For example, in the first movement four groups play passages of fiercely independent counterpoint:

flute	oboe	two trombones	piano
clarinet	English horn		xylophone
bass clarinet	bassoon		
	contrabasson		

The groupings change throughout the work; thus Tippett departs from the conventional fixed arrangement of families of instruments in the score in favor of a flexible system that allows him to display the changing relationships among the instruments. Because of the unusual groupings, the composer calls for a different orchestral seating arrangement to facilitate forming the various configurations throughout the work. Strings, which had been so prominent in his early works, play no part in the first movement. But they are very important in the Lento middle movement and at least present in the last movement, which depends largely on the trombones and percussion. Woodwinds and piano dominate the first movement.

The Triple Concerto for Violin, Viola, and Cello (1978–79) is a significant piece in which the lyricism that had played so prominent a role in Tippett's earlier works is brought to the fore again. The concerto's basic plan is the traditional three-movement one, but presented without interruption; interludes occur before and after the second movement. In the first movement, after the initial presentation of what Tippett calls the "birth motive," the soloists appear separately in cadenzas, then together playing the main theme. For the most part, the soloists are featured separately, but when they do appear all at once, each is given an independent and contrasting part.

OTHER COMPOSERS

Two younger British composers, Peter Maxwell Davies and Thea Musgrave, have contributed concertos of distinction.

Peter Maxwell Davies (b. 1934) is one of several important British composers born in the 1930s and trained at the Royal College of Music in Manchester. His eclectic style includes elements of chant and other aspects of early music. Among these are isorhythm, metric proportions, and varied canonic devices, as well as serial techniques, popular music, and theatrical devices, such as requiring players to move about the stage. He is especially fond of percussion instruments, often nontraditional, which he incorporates in his chamber music, a genre to which he is partial.

His powerful, dramatic Violin Concerto was commissioned by the Royal Philharmonic Orchestra to celebrate its fortieth anniversary. The work was first performed in June 1986 at the St. Magnus Festival in the twelfth-century cathedral of St. Magnus on the Orkney Islands. The setting, at the extreme north of Scotland between the Atlantic Ocean and North Sea, inspired much that characterizes the work: The sounds of the sea and sea-birds are imitated throughout; Scottish rhythms and melodic ideas appear, especially in the subdued violin melody of the slow movement based on a bagpipe tune and in the fiddler's reel of the third movement. The cathedral's natural acoustics heightened these unusual effects. Timpani play an important role in marking structural divisions and in sharing in the third movement's cadenza.[4] A challenging violin cadenza occurs near the end of the first movement. The three movements are played without pause, and the reappearance of the opening idea in the final movement further contributes to the work's unity. The concerto was written for Isaac Stern, who premiered it with André Previn conducting.

Thea Musgrave (b. 1928) first studied music in her native Scotland at the University of Edinburgh where her major composition teacher was Hans Gál. She then went to Paris to study with Nadia Boulanger (1887–1979), a remarkably influential teacher of numerous important twentieth-century composers.

Musgrave's early works are lyric and diatonic, but as she became more familiar with the serial style of Schoenberg and Webern in the late 1950s, her works took on a highly chromatic quality. She came to the United States in 1959 as a scholarship student at the Tanglewood Summer School, where she met Aaron

Copland (1900–1990) and Milton Babbitt (b. 1916). There she also gained acquaintance with the music of Charles Ives (1874–1954), which was to affect her profoundly. In 1965 she completed her first opera, *The Decision,* revealing a powerful native flair for the dramatic. She has not only composed several other successful operas, but has also incorporated this dramatic sensibility into a series of instrumental works which she characterizes as "dramatic-abstract." This term emphasizes that the works are not programmatic, having no story to tell, but that the instrumental performers can be likened to characters in a play. She has noted, "In my instrumental music, I have gradually evolved a style where at times certain instruments take on the character of a dramatic personage, and my concern is then directed toward the working out of a dramatic confrontation."[5] What better form than the concerto to work out these ideas?

The Clarinet Concerto (1968), dedicated to the great clarinetist Gervase de Peyer (b. 1926), is the first of these "dramatic-abstract" works. In this twenty-two-minute, one-movement concerto, the clarinetist both plays a traditional virtuoso role and adds a theatrical element by physically moving to four different places within the orchestra to play with various concertante groups. These groups, in turn, compete against the remainder of the orchestra. The clarinetist occasionally assumes the role of an independent conductor, leading one or another of these groups. The concertante sections are linked by tutti passages, giving the work the shape of a concerto grosso. Musgrave presents the various personalities of the clarinet, placing each against an orchestra that includes several exotic, percussion instruments and piano accordion. She first heard the accordion in Paris accompanying a Yugoslavian dance group and was intrigued by the effective blending of accordion and clarinet in that ensemble. She uses the accordion in the concerto in duet with the solo clarinet and to provide soft, background chords for free cadenza passages.

In 1971 Musgrave composed the Horn Concerto for Barry Tuckwell (b. 1931), and in 1973 she completed the Viola Concerto for her husband, Peter Mark. In both of these works she further exploited the possibilities of the "dramatic-abstract" concept by having the soloists interact with their orchestral colleagues in unusual ways. In addition, she extends the idea of spatial separation. For example, in the Horn Concerto, the orchestral horns play from different places in the hall, and, in the Viola Concerto, the orchestral violas sit in the place normally reserved for the violins, enabling greater dramatic interaction with the soloist.

In a series of three chamber concertos, Musgrave has experimented with new ways of highlighting contrast among various parts of the ensemble. Here she develops a form of asynchronized music in which the parts need not be coordinated at all times. The first Chamber Concerto (1962) was dedicated to Charles Ives, who was a master at effectively juxtaposing various layers of disparate music to create astounding effects. In her own way, Musgrave created a similar approach by successfully assimilating many different musical techniques into a highly personal and dramatic style. Hers are some of the most imaginative concertos of the twentieth century and certainly some of the most important by a British composer.

TWO SCANDINAVIANS: SIBELIUS AND NIELSEN

JEAN SIBELIUS (1865–1957)

The history of music in Finland parallels that of Russia. Early nineteenth-century Finnish composers received their training in Germany and worked in the German style. During the late nineteenth-century struggle for independence from Russia, strong feelings of nationalism arose throughout the populace. As a consequence several leading composers, including Robert Kajanus (1856–1933) and Martin Wegelius (1846–1906), turned to Finnish folklore for their inspiration. The young Sibelius, a student of Wegelius, was powerfully moved by this rising tide of nationalism, and his continuing desire was to depict musically his country's legends and geography, but without reference to folk music. Although he wrote much programmatic orchestral music in pursuit of nationalistic ends, he also composed masterful pieces of abstract orchestral music, including the most popular violin concerto written in the twentieth century.

Sibelius, the leading Finnish composer of the twentieth century, worked almost entirely within a nineteenth-century Romantic framework, virtually unaffected by the new musical approaches. His music has a dark, somber quality, relieved by majestic gestures and broad romantic themes in pieces composed generally before 1910. He had always preferred to work with small motivic ideas, developing and transforming them, and after 1910 this compositional approach dominated. Consequently his writing became more condensed and economical, verging on the austere at times, as the broad, romantic themes disappear. His only concerto precedes this turn of events, so it is a strongly romantic work of immense appeal to audiences and replete with rewarding challenges for the performer.

As a young musician, Sibelius studied violin with the intent of becoming a virtuoso performer. In the end, he abandoned these youthful plans, writing his Violin Concerto not for his own use but probably for Willy Burmester, concert master of the Helsinki Orchestra in the 1890s. However, the composer wished to have the work performed shortly after he completed it in the fall of 1903, earlier than Burmester could find time to prepare it. Thus a lesser violinist, Viktor Nováček, was engaged to give the premiere in the spring of 1904. Even though he performed it, the work proved too difficult for Nováček. Once Burmester found time to work on it, he, too, noted its extreme difficulties, and urged the composer to alter the concerto. Sibelius weeded out most of the difficult places in the 1905 revision, which was first performed in Berlin under the direction of Richard Strauss with yet another soloist, Karl Halir, who had been nominated by Sibelius's publisher.

The role assigned the soloist is very much in the Romantic tradition; the solo instrument stands out in sharp relief throughout the concerto. The soloist either plays the main thematic material or accompanies the orchestra's presentation of thematic material with highly decorative passage work. Rarely do the soloist and orchestra engage in a dialogue as equal partners, although striking tutti sections provide some contrast in this solo-dominated concerto. Throughout, the dark-toned strength of the orchestra stands in strong contrast to the lyrical tone of the solo violin.

The D Minor Violin Concerto is in the standard three movements, clearly separated by pauses and without any thematic connection. The opening of the first, and most profound, movement is one of Sibelius's most immediately appealing creations. Muted orchestral violins divided into four parts provide nothing more than a tonic murmur over which the solo violin announces a broad, lyrical melody of great beauty (Ex. 22-1). Its initial three-note motive and the drop of the fifth between the second and third notes are significant thematic elements.

Ex. 22-1. Sibelius, Violin Concerto; I. Allegro moderato, mm. 4–13.

This movement can be viewed as being cast in an unusual, but loose, sonata-allegro form. The exposition contains three distinct thematic areas. A brief cadenza and transition separate the first from the second. The transition contains references to the descending fifth interval and forecasts the shape of the second theme, which initially appears in B-flat major in bassoons, before it is given to the solo violin (Ex. 22-2). The violin presents the theme with great lyric intensity in double-stopped sixths and octaves in D-flat major, later turned to minor. The strength of the third thematic section, with its more rapid tempo (Allegro molto) and marcato orchestral violin statement of a march tune (Ex. 22-3a), makes the preceding five minutes of music sound like an introduction. This new B-flat tune actually has its roots in the solo violin's lead-in material to the second theme (Ex. 22-3b). In the latter part of the second theme—on the way to becoming the march-like, third theme—the tune was also taken up by the orchestral violins to accompany the solo violin. This transformation and varied use of a small melodic idea is thoroughly characteristic of Sibelius's style.

Ex. 22-2. Sibelius, Violin Concerto; I. Allegro moderato, mm. 93–94.

Ex. 22-3. Sibelius, Violin Concerto; I. Allegro moderato: (a.) mm. 118–121; (b.) mm. 100.

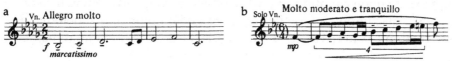

A large, virtuosic cadenza serves as the development section. The recapitulation includes several passages deserving of mention. The warm opening theme returns in G minor, first in the bassoons, next with the solo violin on its dark G string. A new tutti section, concluding with powerfully stated descending fifths in the horns, then trombones, precedes a striking, new transformation of the small lead-in material of Ex. 22-3b. Here the oboe converts it into a full-fledged lyric tune (Ex. 22-4).

Ex. 22-4. Sibelius, Violin Concerto; I. Allegro moderato, mm. 348–351.

The second movement, Adagio di molto, is in ternary form and has the character of a romanza, with its quite dramatic midsection. The midsection is based upon the lyric introduction. The cantabile main theme of the first section is given out by the soloist in its lower register, but in the reprise this theme is played by the orchestra, while the soloist provides delicate and elaborate decoration throughout most of its range.

The Allegro, ma non tanto, finale is in D major in dancelike triple meter. This virtuosic movement depends upon two themes. The first, played by the solo instrument, is an energetic and highly rhythmic one. The second, appearing first in the orchestra in B-flat major, alternates between measures with a feeling of $\frac{6}{8}$ and those in straight $\frac{3}{4}$ time. This gives the second theme a particularly effective lilt. The soloist then takes over the theme in multiple stops, adding still greater rhythmic vitality through syncopation. In the second half of the movement, the solo instrument rises to its upper register, adding a light elfin quality; and in the repeat of the second theme, a long passage in glassy harmonics adds a very effective, distant, ethereal quality.

Sibelius wrote several shorter pieces for violin and orchestra, including two serenades (1911–12) and six humoresques (1917). These make even greater technical demands on the soloist, but all are of a lighter quality than is the Violin Concerto.

CARL NIELSEN (1865–1931)

Nielsen, the foremost Danish composer at the end of the nineteenth and the beginning of the twentieth centuries, developed a unique style of composition that eludes classification. He was devoted to Mozart's music, and the influence of Mozart, as well as of Haydn and Beethoven, is clearly revealed in his early works. His quite personal style emerged from these Classical roots by 1900. He viewed melody as an element of fundamental importance, and developed his skills in manipulating melodic material through motivic development, thematic variation, and thematic transformation. With melody central in his approach, he developed a strong reliance upon counterpoint, which is increasingly evident in his later works. Rhythm was also important to Nielsen; it gives definition to his melodic ideas, and driving rhythmic patterns are common in his music. Although he remained within the tonal tradition, he developed a boldly original conception of harmony. He extended tonality through the free use of all twelve chromatic pitches, each of which he saw as directly related to the tonic. In addition to this unusual view of chromaticism, Nielsen evolved a dynamic technique in which his music seems to search for a final tonal resting place different from the beginning tonality. This final tonality often emerges only after an extended battle with an initially established tonality. The evolving conflict between tonalities frequently results in lengthy dissonant passages.

Like Sibelius, Nielsen was devoted to the larger instrumental forms and made particularly significant contributions to the symphony. His three concertos are all unconventional in form. The Violin Concerto (1911), the earliest, largest, and least interesting of the three, is in two movements, each divided into two parts—slow and fast. The tonal plan calls for moving from G minor at the work's beginning to D major at the conclusion.

The two later concertos for woodwind instruments are more intimate than the Violin Concerto and are of greater interest. Although Nielsen studied the violin at the Copenhagen Conservatory, he had played trumpet as a boy and developed a great sensitivity to wind instruments, which occupy an important place in his orchestral music. The Concerto for Flute (1926) and the Concerto for Clarinet (1928) were both inspired by a rehearsal of a symphonie concertante in E-flat for oboe, clarinet, horn, and bassoon, then thought to have been a work of Mozart. This rehearsal, which took place in 1921, involved members of the Copenhagen Wind Quintet, who were friends of Nielsen. Nielsen was fascinated by the way in which the individual character of each instrument was exploited. He wrote his Wind Quintet, Op. 43, for his friends in the following year, highlighting not only the distinct quality of each instrument, but the character of each performer as well. In addition to the quintet, he planned to write a concerto for each of the five instruments.

He did not complete the first of these projected concertos until 1926, by which time the Copenhagen Quintet had a new flautist, Holger Gilbert Jesperson. Thus the Flute Concerto was written for him. Nielsen completed it on 1 October 1926 while he was living in Italy, and it was first performed in Paris the following November. Jesperson was a good-humored man possessed of elegant taste, qualities which the Flute Concerto reflects in its overall light and appealing character. The small orchestra consists of pairs of oboes, clarinets, bassoons, and horns, a single bass trombone, timpani, and strings. The solo flute repeatedly converses with solo representatives of the wind quintet, particularly the clarinet and bassoon. These little duets and occasional trios add great charm to the piece. The several duets between the bass trombone, with its quite different timbre and character, and the flute, seem an incongruous intrusion, perhaps relating to some humorous aspect of the soloist's character.

The work is in two movements, their tempos, Allegro moderato and Allegretto, helping to establish and maintain the light quality of the concerto. A brief, darker adagio section in the second movement is the only real disruption of the work's largely sunny character. The characteristic search for a tonal center brings the piece to a close in E major (Nielsen initially had closed it in D major, but revised the ending after the first performance). This tonal resolution follows a first movement centered at first in D minor and ending in G-flat major, and a second movement opening in G major. Surprisingly, the bass trombone leads the way to the E major tonal center, reaching the low E with the second of its humorous glissandi. The flute, accompanied only by timpani, greets the E major tonality with delight, and the concerto's bright ending includes four more glissandi in the bass trombone. The last movement combines elements of scherzo and theme-and-variation forms, with an adagio episode as a substitute for the trio. The Allegretto's main theme (Ex. 22-5) is characteristic of the entire work.

Ex. 22-5. Nielsen, Flute Concerto; II. Allegretto, mm. 12–15.

Early in 1928 the clarinetist in the Copenhagen Quintet, Aage Oxenvad, reminded Nielsen of his promise to write a concerto for each of the members, whereupon Nielsen set to work on the Clarinet Concerto, completing it 15 August 1928. It was to be his last major orchestral work. It is a piece very different in character from the sunny, almost pastoral Flute Concerto, not only because it was written for a different instrument, but also because it was intended for a performer of a more temperamental disposition. Nielsen had long recognized that the clarinet could be either warm and tender or wild and tempestuous, and he employed these widely differing qualities to good effect in creating the harsh conflicts raging through the concerto. As is typical of Nielsen's mature works, conflict is also portrayed tonally, here between two keys only a semitone apart, E and F. Quite unlike Nielsen's common practice, the winning key of F is also the key opening the concerto.

The intensity of the conflict is fully apparent in the first two pages of the score. The cellos and basses present a Mahler-like theme (Ex. 22-6) in F, followed by a decorated repeat in the clarinet. The theme then rumbles forth in low strings and bassoons in E, but in a more agitated setting. From that point until the end of the work, conflict prevails. A striking example of this conflict occurs after the clarinet's aggressive, first cadenza. The cadenza ends quietly, and bassoons, cellos, and basses calmly establish the dominant of F for the recapitulation, but, led by the snare drum, the music is wrenched once more into E, after which the battle continues more intensely. The solo clarinet participates fully in the conflict, alternating between aggressive, even harsh, and calm, lyrical statements. The more tender passages, interestingly enough, tend to be associated with F or closely related keys.

Ex. 22-6. Nielsen, Clarinet Concerto; I. Allegretto un poco, mm. 1–8.

Nielsen not only liked to set keys in opposition, contending for superiority in successive musical statements, but he also cultivated the ambiguity of different keys sounding simultaneously. Witness the opening of the Poco adagio where a horn presents a new idea in C minor, accompanied by a contrapuntal line in the bassoons in E major.

The Clarinet Concerto is cast in a single continuous movement but divided into three major sections—Allegretto un poco; Poco adagio, with several changes of tempo; and Allegro vivace, with several significant returns to Poco adagio. The concerto is scored for a smaller orchestra than the Flute Concerto; in addition to strings, the only winds are pairs of bassoons and horns. The only percussion instrument, the snare drum, plays a major role throughout the work. The drum opens the way to passages of intense conflict, and its march-like rhythms and clear aggressiveness regularly accompany the solo clarinet.

This concerto, one of the most significant for clarinet since that of Mozart, is a brilliant showpiece for the instrument. The soloist is called upon to play both tenderly and aggressively to display the deep and dramatic conflict inherent in the work. At the heart of the conflict are the two cadenzas, one in the Allegretto, the other in the Poco adagio.

We now move from the more remote Scandinavia to the country whose musical influence was paramount between the world wars—France.

STRAVINSKY, RAVEL, AND NEO-CLASSICISM IN FRANCE

IGOR STRAVINSKY (1882–1971)

The term neo-Classicism refers to a style of music that developed as a general reaction against the unrestrained emotionalism of Romantic music. The new style took as its base a return to "objectivism," and the revival of pre-Romantic musical structures and other stylistic elements. Among its salient features are:

- a leaning toward compositions of more intimate dimensions and smaller scope;
- the use of less extravagant musical forces, with a preference for chamber ensembles and small orchestras;
- a greater use of counterpoint in a transparent scoring aimed at setting the contrapuntal lines clearly apart from one another;
- a renewed interest in and creative use of diatonic tonality, but in a revised twentieth-century manner;
- the use of older forms, such as the suite, toccata, and passacaglia.

Baroque music of the seventeenth and eighteenth centuries was of particular interest to the neo-Classical composers, and in many ways the new style might more appropriately be called neo-Baroque, for so many of its features were derived from that period. The concerto underwent numerous changes in the context of this new style. Perhaps the most striking was the rebirth of the concerto grosso.

Neo-Classicism was in the air by the turn of the twentieth century and was affecting numerous European composers who were attracted to its ideals and musical characteristics. But it was not until after World War I that the style first took hold in France in a significant way. Curiously, the leading proponent was the Russian émigré Igor Stravinksy, who lived in France from 1920 to 1939. At the outbreak of World War I, Stravinsky first sought refuge in Switzerland, and after learning of the realities of the Bolshevik Revolution in October 1917, he determined he would never return to his homeland. He was eventually drawn to Paris, where he had visited on earlier occasions for performances of his three early ballets by the Ballets Russes.

Stravinsky's three early masterpieces, *The Firebird* (1909), *Petrushka* (1911),

and *The Rite of Spring* (1913), are far removed from the neo-Classical world. They are ballets in which the element of rhythm is of major and growing importance from one piece to the next. The exciting, jagged, syncopated, and often unpredictable rhythmic patterns of *The Rite of Spring* have their roots in Stravinsky's Russian heritage, as do many other aspects of his style. As we saw in Chapter 18, concerning nineteenth-century Russian composers, Russian folk melodies are often characterized by both odd and frequently changing metric patterns, as well as narrow, short, repetitive melodic units. These rhythmic and melodic qualities were to remain the basic elements of Stravinsky's music, despite the later, remarkable changes in his compositional style.

Upon completion of his epochal ballet, *The Rite of Spring*, with its primitive pounding rhythms and heavy reliance on ostinato patterns, Stravinsky became increasingly interested in the use of chamber ensembles and structural and textural characteristics associated with pre-Romantic music. The dawn of twentieth-century neo-Classicism is marked by his Three Pieces for String Quartet (1914), *The Soldier's Tale* (1918), and *Pulcinella* (1919). By the time of the Octet for wind instruments (1923), Stravinsky's music displayed all the characteristics associated with neo-Classicism.

Stravinsky composed some ten concertos or concerto-like works during his neo-Classical period, which lasted up to 1951. Thereafter, he turned to the use of serial techniques. Although many elements of the neo-Classical style persisted in his later music, he wrote no further concertos.

Stravinsky's earliest work to make strong use of concertante principles is the Concertino for String Quartet of 1920. This rugged, six-minute miniature has no place for an orchestra. The concertante element is focused in the soloistic first violin part, which contains many tricky double stops and a short cadenza, accompanied by the other instruments. The work's intimate scope and use of a chamber ensemble are fully characteristic of neo-Classicism, but the percussive use of the strings, with their many successive downbows, is a holdover from Stravinsky's earlier period.

Stravinsky's next two works in the concerto genre feature his instrument, the piano. The near elimination of strings in the Concerto for Piano and Winds (1924)—only double basses are called for—provides yet another characteristic of the neo-Classical style: Stravinsky and others who had moved away from the Romantic tradition viewed the warm string instruments, particularly the violin, as closely associated with what they considered subjective emotion, which they sought to avoid. To distance himself further from Romantic practice, Stravinsky exploited the piano's percussive potential in the outer movements. Only in the Largo middle movement is a legato approach called for. Stravinsky's own performances of this concerto were particularly dry and percussive.

Several elements of the work have their roots in the music of the Baroque era. The first of the three movements has a slow introduction in the style of the opening of an eighteenth-century French overture. The majestic dotted rhythms in the brass instruments evoke the grandeur of Handel's orchestral music. The solo instrument opens the Allegro section in the spirit of Baroque harpsichord music reminiscent of Bach or Scarlatti. A new cantabile theme in the first movement remains the property of the orchestra, Stravinsky obviously denying the piano the

Igor Stravinsky and Samuel Dushkin. Stravinsky composed his most masterful concerto for the brilliant violinist Dushkin in 1931. The composer made use of an unusually widespread, triple-stopped chord as a motto in each movement, which Dushkin, at first glance, declared unplayable. But upon trying it, he found it surprisingly easy to negotiate. Stravinsky's Violin Concerto is a neo-Classical (or neo-Baroque) work in four movements, each modeled on some Baroque form.

opportunity to sing out a lyrical theme as it had in so many nineteenth-century concertos, or even in Mozart's. The middle movement is warmer and includes some fairly fluid cadenza sections in tempo rubato. The light third movement returns to a brittle harpsichord style involving many syncopations.

Stravinsky retained exclusive performance rights to the Concerto for Piano and Wind Instruments, and played it approximately forty times in the first few years after its completion. He then felt the need for a new and entirely different piano concerto. The three-movement Capriccio for Piano and Orchestra was composed in 1928–29. It seems to carry forward the graceful charm of the just-completed *The Fairy's Kiss,* which Stravinsky wrote under the influence of his compositional hero, Tchaikovsky. In the capriccio Stravinsky has written a piano part in the tradition of the brilliant virtuoso writing of the great Romantics, setting aside the strong percussive quality of his earlier concerto. The third movement, Allegro capriccioso, was written first and provided the name for the work. A full orchestra, with both concertino and ripieno string sections, accompanies the piano.

Stravinsky wrote the Violin Concerto (1931) for the young American violinist Samuel Dushkin at the request of Willy Strecker, director of Schott, Stravinsky's music publisher. Stravinsky initially hesitated to write a virtuoso violin work, feeling he lacked a sufficiently profound understanding of the instrument. But

Hindemith urged him to take on the commission, noting that Stravinsky enjoyed the advantage of not playing the instrument, so was not likely to fall into the use of violin clichés. In characteristic fashion, Stravinsky first undertook the study of major violin concertos of the past, but seems to have adopted none of them as a model for this highly original and engaging work. Stravinsky sought Dushkin's advice on violin matters, once asking the violinist if a particularly widely spaced chord (Ex. 23-1) was playable. Dushkin, having never seen a chord with such a reach, first said no, but once he tried it on the instrument, he found it surprisingly easy to play. This chord, called by Stravinsky his "passport" to the concerto, begins every movement.

Ex. 23-1. Stravinsky, Violin Concerto; Violin chord.

The Violin Concerto has four movements, all with Baroque titles: Toccata, Aria I, Aria II, and Capriccio. The outer movements are energetic, while the two cantabile arias replace the standard slow movement. The Toccata opens with the triple-stopped chord followed by three aggressive, downbowed chords that serve as a motto for the opening of the first three movements. The pair of trumpets then presents the Toccata's main theme, an idea typical of the composer with its short, narrow melodic fragments that move with a distinctively rhythmic forward momentum (Ex. 23-2). The multiple stops of the solo violin's opening motto repeatedly recur in the solo part and become particularly significant when the soloist presents the main theme in parallel thirds. Stravinsky often requires the soloist to create strong contrapuntal lines through the use of multiple stops.

Ex. 23-2. Stravinsky, Violin Concerto; I. Toccata, mm. 1–9.

The almost constant sixteenth-note motion of the first movement is in toccata style. In the Baroque period, the term *toccata* referred to a style of virtuoso keyboard composition, but in adapting the style to the violin, Stravinsky developed his own version of broken-chord figuration and a kind of *bariolage* technique characteristic of Baroque violin concertos. Toccata also referred to processional fanfares for trumpets and timpani, so that Stravinsky's main theme, presented in trumpets, may have been inspired by this form of the toccata. Both of these older forms of the toccata, the trumpet fanfare type and the virtuoso keyboard type, called for extensive improvisation, the freedom of which Stravinsky captures in this movement. The movement's form resembles sonata-allegro form in its general outlines. A contrasting second theme in the dominant is introduced at no. 20, and the main theme is repeated in the tonic at the end.

The middle aria movements emphasize a lyricism atypical of Stravinsky. Both movements are in ternary form, in which the return of the A section is decorated by the solo violin. Stravinsky perhaps had in mind the traditional Baroque da capo aria in which the solo singer embellishes the first portion of the aria upon its repeat

at the aria's conclusion. Quite effective harmonics mark the first Aria, while a delicate transformation of the motto marks the beginning of each section of the second
(Ex. 23-3).

Ex. 23-3. Stravinsky, Violin Concerto; III. Aria II, m. 1.

The final Capriccio is a scintillating showpiece with great rhythmic vitality,
especially in its final pages where the meter frequently alternates between $\frac{3}{8}$ and $\frac{2}{8}$.
A dolce, cantabile theme in a solo horn part at no. 103 provides a striking contrast
to the surrounding activity. Counterpoint is extensively used throughout the work;
the Bach-like setting of the Capriccio's second theme is entirely characteristic (Ex.
23-4).

Ex. 23-4. Stravinsky, Violin Concerto; IV. Capriccio, No. 94, mm. 1–8.

The collaboration with Dushkin and interest in the violin extended to the Duo
Concertante (1931) for violin and piano. Neither this duet nor the impressive
Concerto for Two Solo Pianos (1931, 1934–1935), composed for himself and his
son, Soulima, calls for an orchestra. In the absence of an orchestra, both works
approach the sonata, but the two instruments are treated as equals in a concertante fashion, thus suggesting the titles given them.

The Concerto in E-flat for Chamber Orchestra (1938), known as *Dumbarton
Oaks,* was commissioned by Mr. and Mrs. Robert Woods Bliss of Dumbarton Oaks,
near Washington, D.C., for their thirtieth wedding anniversary. Nadia Boulanger
conducted the first performance; Stravinsky was ill with tuberculosis in Europe.
Stravinsky described the work as "a little concerto in the style of the Brandenburg
Concertos."[1] Bach's Brandenburg Concerto No. 3 must have been the model, for,
as in that Baroque masterpiece, Stravinsky singles out no solo group, but at various
times treats each of the fifteen instruments in the chamber orchestra as a soloist.
The opening (Ex. 23-5) also recalls the beginning of the Third Brandenburg: as
Bach did, Stravinsky builds the movement by way of the continuous development, or spinning out, of this opening idea. A distinct fugal texture characterizes
both the first and last movements of this neo-Baroque work; the fugato theme of

the first movement is typical, with its short melodic units and shifting accents (Ex. 23-6). The thin middle movement is most unusual, as different instruments stand alone performing tiny motives against a nearly silent background.

Ex. 23-5. Stravinsky, *Dumbarton Oaks*; I. Tempo giusto, mm. 1–2.

Ex. 23-6. Stravinsky, *Dumbarton Oaks*; I. Tempo giusto, No. 13, mm. 1–5.

Stravinsky emigrated to the United States in 1939. In 1945, he completed his last large-scale orchestral work, the powerful Symphony in Three Movements, a testament to the end of World War II. He conceived the symphony in 1942 as a concertante work for piano and orchestra. The piano was eventually incorporated into the orchestra, as it had been in the ballet *Petrushka,* and the concertante element evolved into a series of distinct sections written for small concertino groups playing against the remainder of the orchestra.

The *Ebony Concerto* (1945), for jazz clarinetist Woody Herman and his band, is one of Stravinsky's numerous forays into the world of jazz. The composer was greatly taken by several Woody Herman Band numbers, so, when asked, agreed to write a work for the band featuring the clarinet. After listening to a number of Herman's recordings, Stravinsky concluded that a change in the band's normal orchestration was called for; a French horn was added. The clarinet is certainly featured—it presents a theme and cadenza in movement I and is given a splendid virtuoso passage in the last variation of movement III—but the other instruments are also given prominent solo roles, as could be expected in light of the jazz tradition. The first movement, Allegro moderato, is in a miniature sonata-allegro form. The Andante is a slow blues in minor, concluding in major, and the finale is a set of variations on a simple, almost monotonous, theme.

The Concerto in D for string orchestra (1946) was commissioned by Paul Sacher for the Basle Chamber Orchestra. It is a light-hearted work with so little in the way of concertante material that one wonders what prompted the composer to choose "concerto" for its title.

Movements for piano and orchestra (1958–59) is not a concerto for piano, but features the instrument in a set of changing chamber music configurations. *Movements* is a very concise interpretation of the serial technique by a seventy-six-year-old composer who had eschewed the tone row until 1951, when Arnold Schoenberg died. As in earlier phases of Stravinsky's career, when the music of other composers so stimulated his creative thought processes, he now derived great stimulus from Webern's condensed serial style. With this shift of interest, Stravinsky must have considered the concerto incompatible, so he wrote nothing more in this form. His contributions to the genre are confined to his neo-Classical period, when his attention was focused on discovering and reviving older forms. He never lost his interest in the music of earlier periods even in his serial phase, but the concerto seemed antithetical to his intentions.

Each of Stravinsky's concertos is a unique response to the concerto idea. The Violin Concerto of 1931 stands as a high point, not only among his concertos, but also among all concertos in the neo-Classical style, while the Concerto for Piano and Winds (1923–24) is surely one of the earliest concertos conceived in this new style.

MAURICE RAVEL (1875–1937)

The music of Maurice Ravel is often associated with that of his contemporary, Claude Debussy (1862–1918), the master of French Impressionism in music, but Ravel made only sparing use of Impressionistic techniques and then only for very special effects. Rather than the misty vagueness and ambiguity characteristic of Debussy's music, Ravel's is noted for its clarity and precision, rhythmic drive, colorful use of tonal harmony, and brilliant instrumental effects. Ravel's music is largely of a Classical orientation and so fits most comfortably within the stylistic realm of neo-Classicism. He was obviously influenced by Mozart and François Couperin (1668–1733), one of the great French Baroque harpsichordists. But both Spanish music, particularly that of his native Basque region, and American jazz, which influenced numerous French composers in the '20s and '30s, greatly interested him. Ravel was a composer of brilliant, highly virtuosic music for both the piano and the orchestra; it was only natural that he turned to the concerto, composing two for piano.

Ravel completed both concertos in 1931; he began the G Major Concerto in 1929 but put it aside while he completed the unusual D Major Concerto for the Left Hand, for the one-armed Viennese pianist Paul Wittgenstein. Travel stimulated Ravel's pronounced use of exotic elements in both concertos. His firsthand exposure to jazz, resulting from his 1927–28 tour of Canada and the United States, is evident in both of these remarkable works. The Piano Concerto in G Major also contains Spanish elements inspired by Ravel's first visit to Spain in 1929 and by his native Basque region, which is where he started to work on the concerto.

In an often-quoted interview published in the *Daily Telegraph,* the composer explained that he believed "a concerto can be gay and brilliant, and that there is no necessity for it to aim at profundity or big dramatic effects." He also added that the Concerto in G Major was "a concerto in the strict sense, written in the spirit of Mozart and Saint-Saëns."[2] Linking Saint-Saëns with Mozart may seem paradoxical, yet Saint-Saëns greatly admired Mozart and presented inspired performances of the Viennese master's piano concertos. Although the G Major Concerto may have been written in the spirit of these two composers, much of Stravinsky, Gershwin, jazz, and Spanish music colors the concerto, making it one of the French composer's most fascinating works.

The G Major Concerto is in three movements, with a very lyrical and quiet second movement surrounded by rhythmically vigorous outer movements. The Allegramente literally takes off at the crack of a whip in the percussion section, with bitonal arpeggios of G major and F-sharp major in the piano supporting a Basque-inspired G-major tune in the piccolo (Ex. 23-7). The bitonality, rhythmic vitality, and dry scoring bring Stravinsky to mind, especially the Stravinsky of the ballet *Petrushka*. The trumpet restates the tune after a descending series of nine major and minor chords in the piano left hand, which presages the orchestral chords that bring the movement to its sparkling conclusion. Wind instruments, particularly the solo trumpet, are given significant and effective roles throughout the concerto.

Ex. 23-7. Ravel, Piano Concerto in G Major; I. Allegramente, mm. 1–6.

Two subsidiary themes with jazz elements shape the second part of the unusual sonata-allegro form exposition, which moves through a series of descending keys—G, F-sharp, and E. A less active theme in the piano in F-sharp major introduces a blues flavor with its blue third, the flatted third degree of the scale, which clashes with the major third, as in early jazz (see circled "blue notes" in Ex. 23-8). This mood continues as the clarinet and muted trumpet, and later, the piano, develop a slightly different third theme with wood blocks and cymbals in the accompaniment. The exposition closes with a fourth theme in E major. After a brief development, focused mostly on the first theme, the recapitulation begins an ascending sequence of keys from G to A, but returns to the tonic, G, at the end. The second, jazz-inspired tune returns with unusual flutter-tonguing effects in oboe, clarinet, and trumpet, accompanied by a slide in the trombone, recalling the music of an early jazz band. At this point, the piano's arpeggios—built on A major in the left hand and A minor in the right—accentuate the conflict between the blue, or minor, third and the major third. Other special features of the recapitula-

Ex. 23-8. Ravel, Piano Concerto in G Major; I. Allegramente, No. 4, mm. 1–9.

tion include a short, Andante "quasi-cadenza" for harp (at no. 22), with glissandi in one hand and a sustained tune in harmonics in the other; later (at no. 27) the woodwinds present a challenging imitation of this harp cadenza. The piano's cadenza features a continuous series of trills in the right hand over an intricate arpeggiated left-hand part that includes the exposition's fourth theme.

The simple beauty of the expressive Adagio assai (Ex. 23-9) was based, according to the composer, on the slow movement of Mozart's Clarinet Quintet. The piano plays the first thirty-three measures unaccompanied, presenting a long, cantabile line in the right hand against a simple accompaniment that divides the $\frac{3}{4}$ bar into two groups of three eighth-notes. The piano part becomes increasingly elaborate in the right hand as the movement progresses. Upon the return to the movement's tonic, E, the piano provides a quite decorative accompaniment for the English horn's restatement of the main theme. This is one of Ravel's most delicate movements.

Ex. 23-9. Ravel, Piano Concerto in G Major; II. Adagio assai, mm. 1–5.

The finale is a festive Presto reminiscent of the circus atmosphere of *Petrushka*. The piano has much virtuosic material in a perpetuum mobile style, inspired, perhaps, by the music of another Russian, Prokofiev. The movement's first theme is presented shrilly by the tiny sopranino clarinet, a rarely used instrument. The second theme (Ex. 23-10) depends upon the repetitive small units and syncopation also found in much of Stravinsky's music, while the third theme gallops in $\frac{6}{8}$ against a simple $\frac{2}{4}$ background.

Ex. 23-10. Ravel, Piano Concerto in G Major; III. Presto, No. 4, mm. 1–8.

Ravel dedicated the G Major Concerto to Marguerite Long, who first performed it under the direction of the composer on 14 January 1932 at the Salle Pleyel as part of a Ravel Festival.

The Concerto for Left Hand is a more serious work in one continuous movement of several contrasting tempos. The piano part is even more elaborate than that of the concerto for two hands; Ravel sought to overcome the limitations of writing for only one hand, making it so complex that at most times two staves are required to notate the music. In preparation for this unusual composition, he studied Saint-Saëns's etudes for the left hand and transcriptions of Chopin's etudes, as well as the challenging exercises by Czerny and Scriabin designed to strengthen the normally weaker hand.

The shimmering Lento introduction is an example of Ravel's use of Impressionist techniques. The low strings open with an ambiguous rumble that suggests two centers of tonality, E and D. The contrabassoon presents a tentative idea in a very low range that rises in pitch and becomes brighter as other instruments join in. After the Lento's climax, the piano enters with a cadenza that reshapes the opening material into the work's main theme (Ex. 23-11). A contrasting, lyric theme is given by the piano at the più lento.

Ex. 23-11. Ravel, Concerto for the Left Hand; No. 4, mm. 5–8.

The middle portion of the work is in faster tempos and includes an Allegro march in $\frac{6}{8}$, distinguished by a series of descending triads in the piano and later by a *spiccato* dancing theme, colored by jazz syncopation and blue sevenths. Another *Petrushka*-like section in $\frac{2}{4}$ introduces a short, repetitive tune. Snare drum and wood blocks are called upon to help build the driving rhythms of this section to a climax, after which the main theme returns dramatically in the orchestra. The very difficult cadenza near the end requires the pianist to articulate three different voices—all with only one hand.

Wittgenstein performed the work, with Ravel conducting the Orchestre Symphonique de Paris, for the first time in Paris on 17 January 1933 in an all-Ravel program. In addition to Prokofiev's Fourth Concerto, discussed earlier, Wittgenstein commissioned works for piano left hand and orchestra by Strauss and Britten, but Ravel's is the most successful.

Ravel's *Tzigane* (1924), a short showpiece for violin, was originally written with piano accompaniment, but the composer almost immediately thereafter orchestrated it. The title means Gypsy, and Ravel described the work as a piece in the style of a Hungarian rhapsody. It has, at times, the quality of a *csárdás*, a fast, duple-meter Hungarian dance, although a Spanish tinge is also discernible. *Tzigane* opens with violin alone and throughout makes great technical demands upon the violinist with nearly impossible harmonics and challenging multiple stops.

FRANCIS POULENC (1899–1963)

In 1920 the critic Henri Collet published an article in which he related the work of a group of six young French composers to Erik Satie (1866–1925). Despite differences, all were united in their anti-Romantic, anti-Wagnerian, and anti-Impressionistic approach so eloquently expressed by their literary spokesman, Jean Cocteau, who wrote, "Enough of clouds, waves, aquariums, nymphs, and perfumes of the night. We need a music that is down to earth—an everyday music."[3] Les Six were not modernists but remained within the broad framework of neo-Classicism. The music of two—Germaine Tailleferre (1892–1983) and Louis Durey (1888–1979)—is seldom heard. Georges Auric (1899–1983) concentrated on film music. The remaining three—Darius Milhaud (1892–1974), Arthur Honegger (1892–1955), and Francis Poulenc—became leading French composers after World

War I. Each made important contributions to the concerto, of which Poulenc's were the closest to the spirit of neo-Classicism.

Poulenc's generally light style is marked by a range of traits: simple, tuneful melodic ideas of narrow range and short duration; lively rhythmic content often using ostinatos and a fluidity of changing meters; clear, transparent textures with little contrapuntal writing; an essentially diatonic tonal language spiced by some dissonance; and clear forms, occasionally involving cyclical recall of thematic material. He did not employ much thematic development, but built his forms by way of repetition and contrast of thematic ideas, often relying on new keys or altered scoring to enliven the succession of melodies. Many movements of his concertos are organized in a ternary form. Poulenc avoided traditional virtuoso display, preferring to involve the solo instrument in dialogue with the orchestra. Thus in numerous passages the solo instrument lightly accompanies the orchestra, and in many long passages the soloist is entirely absent. The traditional cadenza has no place in his concertos.

Poulenc, a gifted pianist, composed five concertante works, all featuring keyboard instruments—piano in three, organ and harpsichord in one each. The earliest, for the harpsichord, is probably the most obviously based upon neo-Classical models. The *Concert champêtre* (Pastoral Concerto, 1927–28) for harpsichord and orchestra was inspired by a great harpsichordist of the first part of this century, Wanda Landowska (1879–1959). Landowska had taken up residence in France in 1900 and acquired a country home in Saint-Leu, near Paris, where she often gave concerts in her studio. She devoted her career to the mastering of the great harpsichord music of the Baroque era, especially that of Bach, Scarlatti, Rameau, and François Couperin. Her performances led to a notable renewal of interest in the French clavecinists, Poulenc having remarked that it was she who fired his interest in the music of the seventeenth- and eighteenth-century French masters. This interest was clearly manifest in the *Concert champêtre* and *Aubade* (1929). Not only are Baroque practices clearly evident, but the impact of Stravinsky's parallel concerns are equally obvious.

Poulenc completed the *Concert champêtre* in October 1928 and played a piano reduction of the orchestral score to accompany Landowska in the first performance of the work the following spring at her country home. On 3 May 1929, she played the work in its first public performance at the Salle Pleyel with Pierre Monteux conducting. This concerto is not only one of the very few important works for harpsichord written in this century, but it was also one of the composer's earliest neo-Classical compositions. This spirit emerges in the use of harpsichord and in the style of writing for the instrument, with its many grace notes, ornaments, rolled chords, and accompaniment patterns. These evoke the *style galant* and the influence of Couperin and Rameau. The pastoral setting of Landowska's music room led Poulenc to investigate eighteenth-century outdoor serenades, which in turn led to the prominent role of wind instruments in this piece. Stravinsky's influence is obvious in the strong rhythmic vitality of the work, especially in the use of odd and frequently changing meters in the final movement, and in the so-called "wrong-note" technique of harmonizing a basically diatonic or clearly tonal melody with unusually dissonant tones falling outside harmonic convention. Stravinsky, or Prokofiev who had befriended Poulenc, undoubtedly influenced his prominent use of ostinato patterns.

The Pastoral Concerto is in three movements and calls for a large orchestra. The opening Allegro molto in D minor introduces numerous thematic ideas which return near the end, making for a sense of reprise. The G minor Andante is a lyric and tender Siciliana in which the harpsichord plays a largely accompanimental role. Some material from movement I is recalled in the Presto finale, which opens with a light-hearted rondo tune.

In the following year Poulenc composed *Aubade: Concerto choréographique* (1929) for piano and an orchestra of eighteen instruments. This innovative and unusual work moves even more decisively in the direction of neo-Classicism. It was conceived as a ballet to feature, simultaneously, a dancer and a pianist. Nijinsky created the original choreography to the story written by Poulenc. The work has been performed as a ballet on only a few occasions. The orchestration of the *Aubade* is one of its most marked neo-Classical elements; there are no violins and the remaining strings play a minor role, while the double woodwind quintet recalls the sound of eighteenth-century divertimento music. The piece's structure resembles that of an eighteenth-century suite with ten clear sections in a single, continuous, twenty-minute movement. Poulenc sought to reach his audience in a quite unusual way in this work; it begins and ends on a serious note, with jagged recitative sections and restless horn-call motives, while the middle portion is light, even impish, in mood. Specific reference to Stravinsky's dissonant *Petrushka* motive occurs in the final section; in the previous section, the changing meters accompanied by strong accents and harsh dissonances also bring to mind the Russian composer.

The more traditional Concerto in D Minor for Two Pianos and Orchestra (1932) is one of the composer's most widely heard compositions. It was commissioned by Princess Edmond de Polignac for performance at the annual International Society for Contemporary Music Festival held in September 1932 in Venice. Poulenc and his boyhood friend, Jacques Février, were the pianists in the first performance. The pianos play throughout the work, frequently alone, but they are rarely given truly virtuosic display material. The opening Allegro ma non troppo is in Poulenc's favored ternary form with a lush, slow middle section hinting at Prokofiev's lyricism. The coda of the first movement evokes the exotic sounds associated with Balinese music he heard at the Paris Exposition in 1931. Of the middle movement, the composer said:

> In the Larghetto of this concerto, I allowed myself, for the first theme, to return to Mozart, for I cherish the melodic line and I prefer Mozart to all other musicians. If the movement begins *alla* Mozart, it quickly veers, at the entrance of the second piano, toward a style that was standard for me at that time.[4]

The middle section of this movement's ternary form also has a more romantic quality. The lively finale, rich in thematic material, includes a lighter music-hall tune (Ex. 23-12) and near the very end contains a reference to the Balinese material of movement I.

Ex. 23-12. Poulenc, Concerto for Two Pianos; III. Finale: Allegro molto, No. 52, mm. 1–4.

After 1936, Poulenc's music begins to take on a more serious tone; the Organ Concerto in G Minor (1938) clearly demonstrates how he grafted this new approach onto his earlier neo-Classical style. Poulenc scored the work for organ, strings, and timpani, with the thought that such a modest group could more readily play the concerto in church, even though it is not, strictly speaking, one of the growing number of religious works he composed in his later years. The organ is given some fairly lengthy solo sections largely alternating with the strings, although the two perform together in some passages. Baroque organ music, especially the fantasia style of Bach, provided the basic model for this almost-twenty-minute, one-movement work, which is organized in seven main sections. Its changing moods and tempos and use of thematic transformation also resemble the tone poem. The dark, declamatory opening marks this as one of Poulenc's most serious compositions. The core of the concerto is the third section, Andante moderato, which begins with a lengthy organ solo depending heavily on an uncharacteristic use of counterpoint, but concludes with a lyric, romantic section for strings. The final Largo section effectively recalls the declamatory opening.

Poulenc's final concerto is for solo piano. The Piano Concerto was commissioned by the Boston Symphony Orchestra for Poulenc's 1949 American tour with his favorite singer, Pierre Bernac. Like the Concerto for Two Pianos, this one is in the traditional three movements. The first two fully reflect Poulenc's late serious style, with an increased reliance on strings to present the warm, fluid melodies. Yet light-hearted, thematic material, typical of his earlier style, sets off these melodies. Poulenc used his favorite ternary form for these two movements, creating strongly contrasting middle sections. In the first movement, an interesting Largo evokes his late, religious music. The generally peaceful second movement has a quite restless middle portion, and closes with striking juxtapositions of minor and major tonic chords. The last movement has been criticized for too light a character in comparison with the first two movements. This Presto giocoso Rondeau à la Française includes startling references to Stephen Foster's "Old Folks at Home," which Poulenc identified as a black American spiritual, and Offenbach's famous cancan tune, as well as frequent use of a tango-related rhythm. As in his earlier concertos, Poulenc provides but limited opportunities for virtuosic display; the piano only plays about three dozen unaccompanied measures.

DARIUS MILHAUD (1892–1974)

Milhaud, one of the most prolific twentieth-century composers, was the most adventuresome of the French neo-Classicists, invoking not only polytonality but also New World jazz and dance elements. A stay in Brazil in 1917–18 excited his interest in Latin American dance music, while a subsequent visit to New York's Harlem district in 1922 stimulated his use of jazz elements. Milhaud used jazz rhythms and blues harmonies before most European composers did.

He composed some thirty concertos for various instruments, including several for instruments seldom represented in the concerto literature, such as marimba, a battery of percussion instruments, and trombone. Among the more noteworthy of his early concertos is a four-movement Viola Concerto (1929) for

Paul Hindemith, which contains striking polytonal passages in the first two movements and jazz-influenced writing in the last. His brief two-movement Concerto for Percussion and Orchestra (1929) features a single percussionist playing four timpani and fifteen other percussion instruments. Milhaud, surprisingly, made no references to jazz in this concerto. Milhaud's most often performed concerto is the unusual Concerto for Marimba and Vibraphone (1947). The two very different sounding mallet instruments are played by one performer, who must, at times, quickly move from one to the other to obtain the exotic contrasts Milhaud desired. Five different types of mallets are specified to achieve varying sonorities, and a still different sonority is created by the use of the hands to strike the marimba.

Small-scale forms and resources are particularly characteristic of the neo-Classical style, and these aspects are central to Milhaud's four concertos titled after the seasons of the year. The *Concertino de printemps* (Spring; 1934) is a one-movement work for solo violin and chamber orchestra capitalizing on one of Milhaud's favorite Latin American dances, the *maxixe* of Brazil, which is the syncopated ancestor of the samba. A suitable pastoral mood opens the *Concertino d'été* (Summer; 1950) for solo violin and nine-instrument chamber orchestra. A dark-hued chamber orchestra, consisting of only violas, cellos, and horns, accompanies the two solo pianos in the *Concertino d'automne* (Autumn; 1950), and a solo trombone imitates the chattering and shivering of winter using special flutter-tongue passages in the *Concertino d'hiver* (Winter; 1953). The First Concerto for Cello (1934) includes a strong Latin American flavor in the last of its three movements.

OTHER COMPOSERS

Arthur Honegger (1892–1955) was the least sympathetic of Les Six to French ideals and neo-Classicism. He composed only three concertante works, of which the Cello Concerto (1934), in one movement, is probably the most interesting, thanks to its lyricism and the blues-inspired second theme.

Jacques Ibert (1890–1962), of the same generation but not associated with Les Six, also composed three concertante pieces. The earliest, Concerto for Cello and Winds (1925), is another of those short neo-Classical works in which the orchestra contains no strings; thus the composer effectively eliminates the usual problem of the string ensemble's overwhelming the sound of the solo cello. Ibert's Flute Concerto (1934) is a recognized masterpiece for the instrument, and his *Concertino da camera* (1935) is an elegant piece for solo alto saxophone and a chamber ensemble of eleven instruments.

FIVE IMPORTANT EARLY TWENTIETH-CENTURY COMPOSERS

ARNOLD SCHOENBERG (1874–1951)

The early music of the Viennese Arnold Schoenberg comes from a composer thoroughly imbued with the tradition of late German Romanticism. This highly expressive music, of which *Verklärte Nacht* (Transfigured Night, 1899) is an apt example, combined the pronounced chromaticism and dissonance of Wagner with the motivic development and dense counterpoint typical of Brahms. Seeking for still-greater expressiveness, Schoenberg stretched tonality to its outer limits, further weakening any sense of a tonal center. This disquieting ambiguity comes about through even greater use of chromaticism, nontraditional resolution of dissonances, and more frequent use of the interval of the fourth, both melodically and harmonically; the latter device calls into question the traditional system of tertial harmony—the use of chords built in thirds.

Schoenberg was largely self-taught; he took only a few counterpoint lessons with Alexander Zemlinsky (1871–1942). By 1908 Schoenberg had entirely abandoned tonality in his Expressionistic works. Compositions such as the Five Pieces for Orchestra, Op. 16 (1909), the monodrama *Erwartung,* Op. 17 (1909), and *Pierrot Lunaire,* Op. 21 (1912), are emotional and dramatic works composed with no reference to traditional rules of tonal harmony. Schoenberg's atonality grew out of his wish to create extremely expressive music, just as his friend, the painter Wassily Kandinsky (1866–1944) moved toward abstract painting in order to realize a greater degree of expressive content. Thus parallel trends in painting and music developed at exactly the same time and out of similar intentions.

Between 1908 and 1913 Schoenberg's compositions became increasingly dissonant and more difficult for the generally conservative Viennese audiences to appreciate and understand. From 1914 to 1923 he published no new music, but rather formulated the principles of his twelve-tone method, which was designed to insure that no single tone would be given a dominant role and that all twelve of the chromatic tones would be of equal value in a composition. Schoenberg referred to the equality of the pitches as pantonality. His new technique of dodecaphonic composition offered a new system of musical order as an alternative to tonality.

The method formulated by Schoenberg stipulated that the twelve chromatic pitches were to be arranged in an order such that no sense of tonality was implied. In practice, a series, set, or row of pitches was to serve as the basis of a composition. The pitches were to be used repeatedly in the same order as the first row, but could be displaced by one or more octaves. All twelve pitches were to be used before one could be repeated. The row could be used in its original form (O), or any one of three alternate forms: Inverted (I), retrograde (R), or retrograde inversion (RI). Furthermore, any one of these row forms could be transposed to start on any pitch. In a sense, the row was more readily defined as a series of intervals between pitches rather than one of pitches, while the allowable forms of the row and their transpositions could be thought of as a rigorously constrained extension of the technique of theme and variation. It was permissible to use the tone row both melodically and harmonically. The composer was free to choose any of the row forms to be used at any given point in the composition, and, of course, had total liberty to create an original row for each dodecaphonic composition. The four permissible forms of the tone row are illustrated in Schoenberg's Piano Concerto (Ex. 24-1).

Ex. 24-1. Schoenberg, Piano Concerto; Tone Row.

Schoenberg's first published work making use of the new technique is the final piece of the Five Piano Pieces, Op. 23 (1923),[1] a waltz. His use of the technique remained tentative and experimental in this piece, but within a few years he was exploiting it with considerable mastery to create large compositions, such as the Variations for Orchestra, Op. 31 (1927–28).

Berlin was much more receptive to new artistic developments in the early decades of the twentieth century than were Vienna or other European cities, so Schoenberg lived there for varying lengths of time at three different periods. He settled in that city for the last time in 1926 to take up a position at the Prussian Academy of Arts, but Hitler's rise to power and consequent persecution of Jews led Schoenberg to depart in 1933. He spent a short time in France before moving to the United States in 1934, where he held positions at two major universities in the Los Angeles area. During this final period of his long creative life he sought to reconcile tonality with his serial compositional method. This iconoclastic composer long held the view that his music was completely rooted in the history of European music and repeatedly contended that his extensive use of counterpoint derived from a tradition older than tonality. He also argued that, from its inception, the tonal system contained within itself the very elements that led to its eventual demise; yet he was never able to escape entirely the pull of tonality, and in later works tonal elements reappeared in the complex fabric of his music. Schoenberg's late embrace of tonality may also have been prompted by his realization that his music could not reach an American public largely ignorant of, or indifferent to, music outside the tonal realm. Schoenberg's two original concertos come from this late phase of his career and demonstrate this softening of his musical approach in varying degrees.

Schoenberg's earliest compositions in concerto form are adaptations of the work of eighteenth-century composers. In 1932 he wrote his three-movement Concerto for Cello after a harpsichord concerto in D minor by the early Viennese Classical composer Georg Mathias Monn. Monn must have intrigued Schoenberg for he also edited a Cello Concerto by this predecessor of Mozart for the *Denkmäler der Tonkunst in Österreich* in 1912. Schoenberg, in his adaptation of Monn's harpsichord concerto, used Monn's thematic material but expanded upon it considerably. Even though Schoenberg used harmonies more characteristic of the late nineteenth century, he never moved beyond the limits of tonality in this arrangement. Schoenberg intended the concerto for Pablo Casals, who played it only once in a private performance. A similar adaptation of Handel's Concerto Grosso in B-flat major, Op. 6, No. 7, led to the Concerto for String Quartet and Orchestra (1933). This demanding work was written for the Kolisch Quartet, which championed the new music advanced by Schoenberg and his pupils. These interesting forays into eighteenth-century music clearly reflect Schoenberg's connections with neo-Classicism, an approach which influenced him in a great variety of ways, even though the musical result is radically different from that of Stravinsky's brand of neo-Classicism. From the time he proposed the serial method of composition, Schoenberg turned to use Classical forms to introduce greater stability in his music.

Schoenberg composed two original concertos, one for violin and the other for piano. They are large, demanding works reflecting the composer's mature approach to the use of serial techniques. The Violin Concerto, Op. 36 (1934–36), was dedicated to one of Schoenberg's most devoted disciples, Anton von Webern. It was begun before Schoenberg's other principal follower, Alban Berg, undertook his better-known Violin Concerto, but Schoenberg's was not completed until months after Louis Krasner had premiered Berg's. The Violin Concerto is one of Schoenberg's first American works, composed during a period of great loneliness and dejection.

The concerto's fiendish difficulty was reluctantly acknowledged by the composer, who conceded it required a violinist with at least six fingers on his left hand. The soloist must negotiate very large intervals, triple and quadruple stops, treacherous harmonics in double stops, left-hand pizzicato, and nearly simultaneous exploitation of the instrument's extreme ranges. Although a large orchestra is called for, with triple or quadruple winds and an expanded percussion section, the orchestra is used mostly in a chamber fashion and collaborates closely with the soloist. Special effects, such as flutter-tonguing in the woodwinds and *col legno* in the strings, enliven the texture.

The Violin Concerto is in the standard three movements. The opening Poco allegro movement follows the thematic outlines of sonata-allegro form. The solo violin is the center of attention from the outset, stating all the main thematic material, while the accompaniment plays motivically derived chords using other notes of the row. As we see in Ex. 24-2, Schoenberg first states the original form of the row and then inverts it and transposes it.

Ex. 24-2. Schoenberg, Violin Concerto; I. Poco allegro: (a.) Tone row—Original and inverted (transposed) forms; (b.) mm. 1–8.

After the calm beginning, the music intensifies. A contrasting developmental section, in the character of a waltz in Vivace (ma non troppo, grazioso) tempo, occupies the middle of the movement. Later a feeling of recapitulation is created, first by a return to the initial motive in m. 162 and, secondly, by the eventual recall of the opening tempo and meter. A short but very difficult cadenza occurs near the movement's end. Overlapping stretto entries of the distinctive opening motive bring the movement to a close as it fades away in a gentle Lento.

The second movement, Andante grazioso, is in ternary form. The lyrical outer parts surround a more lively scherzando midsection. The lyrical opening theme is based on the form of the row originally established in movement I, transposed up a fifth (Ex. 24-3). The Allegro finale is in clear rondo form with a march-like main theme. Early in the movement there is a small "quasi cadenza" for solo violin, accompanied by snare drum. Near the movement's conclusion there is a huge cadenza, accompanied lightly but effectively by parts of the orchestra, with one intriguing passage using piccolo, flute, and xylophone. The main theme of the second movement is quoted in the cadenza, while the poco meno mosso conclusion to the concerto calls for fortissimo statements of the march theme together with bits of material from the first two movements.

Ex. 24-3. Schoenberg, Violin Concerto; II. Andante grazioso, mm. 266–275 [of the work].

The rarely performed Violin Concerto is one of the most formidable works in the violin repertory. It is entirely within the twelve-tone idiom with only tiny hints of tonality; nevertheless, it does possess a kind of lyricism, characteristic of violin concertos of the past, and Schoenberg's orchestration is less dense than in many of his earlier works. In addition, the phrase structure of the themes is easily comprehended and never obscured by accompanimental patterns. The concerto was first performed by the American violinist Louis Krasner with the Philadelphia Orchestra under Leopold Stokowski 6 December 1940. Schoenberg was not present for the performance and did not hear the work until a recording of it was made available to him shortly before his death. He was sufficiently moved to declare it his favorite work.

Schoenberg was sixty-eight years old when he composed the Piano Concerto, Op. 42 (1942). A significant relaxation of the serial technique is evident in its vaguely tonal atmosphere. From the beginning, the sound is closer to the tradi-tional, and, indeed, reminds some of the music of Brahms. The form of this concerto, however, departs from tradition, for it is in one continuous movement containing four distinct sections: Andante in waltz style, scherzo, adagio, and rondo. The first theme returns in the final section, creating thematic unity. A note in Schoenberg's handwriting, found among the sketches, records a programmatic sketch which he presented to Oscar Levant, who was to perform the concerto:

> Life was so easy [andante]
> suddenly hatred broke out [allegro molto]
> a grave situation was created [adagio]
> but life goes on [rondo].[2]

The Piano Concerto is an emotional work in which passages of quiet lyricism alternate with others of great agitation. It is more symphonically conceived than the Violin Concerto, with a stronger sense of contrast between the solo instrument and orchestra.

The lyric, solo piano opening of the andante creates a romantic mood; the main waltz theme, based on the tone row, is presented in clear four-bar phrases (Ex. 24-4). The repetition of notes 9, 10, and 11 is unusual; earlier in his career, Schoenberg would have judged such note repetition as a violation of the canon, but here artistic considerations somehow warranted a break from the strict rules of orthodoxy. The entire theme requires the piano to play the original form of the row, followed by the retrograde inversion, the retrograde, and the inversion (Ex. 24-1).

Ex. 24-4. Schoenberg, Piano Concerto; I. Andante, mm. 1–8.

The andante is constructed along the lines of sonata-allegro form, and, in one interesting twist, Schoenberg repeats the main theme transposed up a fifth in the violins to serve as the second "key" area (see mm. 47ff.). The clear repetition of the main theme on its original notes signals the beginning of the recapitulation in m. 134.

The molto allegro second section is in the form and character of a scherzo, with a poco tranquillo trio in slower triple meter. The outer passages are quite intense, making great use of the snare drum and xylophone, together with flutter tonguing in the winds. A sense of dialogue between winds and strings recurs repeatedly.

The adagio section, a set of five variations on a lyrical theme presented by oboe and bassoon, forms the emotional center of gravity of the work. A brief cadenza leads to the Giocoso finale in a five-part rondo form: ABACA. The rondo's main theme (Ex. 24-5) shares the buoyant, dancelike character of eighteenth-century rondo themes, and, as in so many eighteenth-century concertos, is first presented by the solo instrument. The first six notes of this theme are notes 1 through 6 of the inverted form of the row while the second six are notes 1 through 6 of the retrograde form. The second episode, C, includes brief reminiscences of the main themes of the andante and the adagio. The full andante theme returns near the end of the concerto in a triumphant transformation as a march. In the next-to-last measure the rondo theme of the piano's left hand is mirrored in the right hand, which uses the original form of the row. The final chord is a C major triad with an added major seventh. Many listeners think of C as the (ambiguous) tonal center of the concerto, with F-sharp as the conflicting tonal region. Interestingly, the final chord is approached from F-sharp.

Ex. 24-5. Schoenberg, Piano Concerto; IV. Giocoso, mm. 330–333 [of the work].

This sense of tonality helps make this one of Schoenberg's most approachable twelve-tone works. Also contributing are frequent octave doublings, which Schoenberg had formerly forbidden for fear of giving one pitch or another greater prominence; the lyrical melodic ideas; the stable textures; and the simpler rhythms. The pianistic difficulties call upon all the skills of a virtuoso performer, but, more important, the soloist is compelled to bring out the inherent lyricism of the work. No matter how virtuosic the solo part, it does not overshadow the orchestra; both are well integrated. Oscar Levant did not find the work suitable so never played it. It was first performed by Eduard Steuermann, an important champion of Schoenberg's music, on a broadcast of the NBC Symphony Orchestra conducted by Leopold Stokowski in 1944.

As early as 1904 Schoenberg solicited private composition students in Vienna, two of whom were profoundly influenced by his ideas and shaped those ideas in intensely personal ways. Anton von Webern not only adopted Schoenberg's serial technique but expanded it, in informal ways, to include other parameters of Webern's highly condensed compositions. Unlike Schoenberg, once Webern had adopted an atonal style he stuck with it, never returning to tonality. Alban Berg, on the other hand, pursued a far more eclectic approach, integrating the atonal style and serial technique with a variety of diverse musical idioms, including folk song and jazz, in his small but profoundly effective output. Both of these students of Schoenberg made important contributions to the concerto.

ANTON VON WEBERN (1883–1945)

Webern completed a Ph.D. in historical musicology at the University of Vienna in 1906 under the direction of a noted musicologist of the early part of this century, Guido Adler (1855–1941). Webern's dissertation dealt with the music of Heinrich Isaac (1450–1517), whose complex contrapuntal textures were to find modern expression in the music of the student. While at the university, Webern became a private composition student of Schoenberg.

Like Schoenberg, Webern was first attracted to the music of Wagner and Brahms, but his style evolved in ways parallel to Schoenberg's. By 1922 he had experimented with the twelve-tone method and by 1924 had adopted it as his principal system of pitch organization. He applied Schoenberg's principles with absolute strictness to create some of the most brilliantly original compositions in the history of music.

Webern's music is highly concentrated in its motivic unity so the works tend to be very short. They are also very quiet, but frequent, subtle nuances of dynamic shading occur within the generally low dynamic range. There is also extensive modification of the basic tempo of a movement, especially through the frequent use of ritardandos, and these tempo variations often help to clarify phrase beginnings and endings. He used the instruments of the orchestra to paint with musical dots of isolated sounds much like the pointillistic painters; these brief instrumental flourishes are designed to intensify and clarify motivic relationships within the transparent texture thus created. All of these features are to be found in Webern's only concerto, the Concerto for Nine Instruments, Op. 24 (1934), dedicated to Schoenberg on the occasion of his sixtieth birthday.

Op. 24 was originally planned as a piano concerto, but Webern instead integrated the keyboard instrument into a tight, chamber music texture. The work is scored for flute, oboe, clarinet, horn, trumpet, trombone, violin, viola, and piano. The instruments are used in a concertante fashion, but the piano, with its very different sound and easily produced chords, tends to stand out. It is more commonly pitted against the other eight instruments, yet at the same time the piano seems to hold the ensemble together. The work, for which Webern stipulates a time duration of about nine minutes, is in three movements.

As with several of Webern's pieces, the basic tone row is itself highly structured. The pitches are arranged in groups of three, and the groups all relate to a basic three-note cell. If the first three notes of the row are thought of as forming a mini-series of two intervals—a descending minor second and rising major third—it follows that the other three-note cells can be related by means of retrograde inversion, retrograde, and inversion of these two basic intervals (Ex. 24-6). Thus, the row embodies within it the principle of variation. Given these strong inner relationships Webern was able to create a highly unified, yet varied, work.

Ex. 24-6. Webern, Concerto for Nine Instruments; Tone Row.

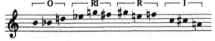

The opening three-measure phrase of the first movement (Etwas lebhaft—somewhat lively) draws the listener's attention to these three-note cells and their relationships (Ex. 24-7). Each note cell is presented by a different instrument, employing different note values and different modes of articulation. The minor second intervals have been stretched by displacing one note an octave, to create Webern's characteristic use of widely spaced, dissonant, melodic skips of minor ninths and augmented octaves. The piano responds with the retrograde inverted form of the row, making use of a still different rhythmic placement of the three-note groups. The movement continues with ever-varied permutations of the three-note groups, which the piano eventually plays as chords. The sixty-nine-measure first movement contains markings for sixteen ritardandos, subtle fluctuations of tempo which impose a larger structure on the many variations of the small, three-note motive.

Ex. 24-7. Webern, Concerto for Nine Instruments; I. Etwas lebhaft, mm. 1–5.

In the slow middle movement the music seems to move through pairs of notes, rather than groups of three. This is because Webern, in his typical pointillistic approach, isolates the first note of each cell in an orchestral instrument, while giving the remaining two notes to the piano in the form of two-note chords. The single notes in the orchestral instruments are then united to form melodic pairs of notes (Ex. 24-8).

Ex. 24-8. Webern, Concerto for Nine Instruments; II. Sehr langsam, mm. 1–4.

The finale returns to the clear presentation of three-note groups by isolated instruments in the outer parts of the movement, with pairs of notes in the middle portion. The movement begins with a canon in inversion (Ex. 24-9), but the fracturing of the lines among different instruments makes it difficult to hear it as a traditional, linear canon; rather, the listener is more aware of the intricate motivic relationships. The small chordal motive played by the piano, beginning in m. 16, is also cast in inverted canonic fashion, while the earlier canon continues. Elaborate canonic structures like these are very common in Webern's music.

Ex. 24-9. Webern, Concerto for Nine Instruments; III. Sehr rasch, mm. 1–6.

Webern's concerto is no doubt one of the most unusual in the concerto literature. The piano is the most nearly treated as a solo instrument of the nine in that it engages in more musical discussions with the other instruments; yet neither it nor any of the other instruments is treated in a traditional, virtuosic manner. The concerto quality derives from the interrelationships of the instruments, which, in turn, are used to clarify the motivic relationships making up the work.

This concerto is one of Webern's most analyzed works, for theorists and composers sought to come to a greater understanding of its patterns of motivic relationships. Traditional themes are replaced by minuscule motives, and instrumental colors, dynamics, and rhythmic patterns assume greater importance than they had in the past. Several young composers immediately following World War

II looked to this concerto and other works by Webern as models for their own music. Composers such as Pierre Boulez (b. 1925) and Karlheinz Stockhausen (b. 1928) saw in Webern's music the roots of what was to become known as Total Serialization, a musical style, or technique, in which other parameters in addition to pitch are prearranged in rigidly defined series. This group of composers saw Total Serialization as a means to insure equality of the various elements of a musical composition and to move away from thematically dominated musical textures, akin to the equality of pitches which Schoenberg had sought in formulating his twelve-tone method of composition. In spite of Webern's historical importance and the particular significance and originality of his concerto, it is seldom performed for it strikes even today's audience as strange and unapproachable.

ALBAN BERG (1885–1935)

Alban Berg, like Webern, became a student of Schoenberg in 1904, receiving solid training from his teacher in tonal harmony and counterpoint. Berg's earliest works are in a late Romantic style, characterized by chromatic harmony and a great warmth of expression. In 1909 he followed his teacher, Schoenberg, and colleague, Webern, in the path of atonality, but Berg's approach was quite different from the outset. Most important, Berg not only combined tonality with atonality but also made use of traditional forms as well. Berg discovered he could use such disparate elements for powerful dramatic effects, and did so in his few but significant completed works, including two of the most important operas of the twentieth century—*Wozzeck* (1917–22) and *Lulu* (1928–35—the orchestration of Act III was not completed before his death, but was realized in 1978 by Friedrich Cerha). Of Berg's modest number of completed works, two are concertos of very different types.

The Chamber Concerto (1923–25) for piano, violin, and thirteen wind instruments was completed almost a decade before Webern's Concerto for Nine Instruments and was belatedly dedicated to Schoenberg on the occasion of his fiftieth birthday. Berg composed it during his early assimilation of the twelve-tone technique, and it contains serial, free atonal, and tonal elements. The Adagio movement does make use of several different twelve-note series in linear fashion similar to Schoenberg's method, but the harmonies are not derived from a strict ordering of the pitches. The first movement opens with a fascinating motto statement, incorporating the musical equivalents of the names Arnold Schönberg (Schoenberg did not adopt the spelling of his name with the *e* following the *o* as a substitute for the umlaut until he moved to the United States), Anton Webern, and Alban Berg (Ex. 24-10). Berg must have been intrigued to find the eight notes required to spell the name of his teacher were sufficient to also spell the name of his fellow student and his own name. These musical cryptograms are used like small sets or series of tones. To these Berg added the four missing chromatic pitches at the beginning of Schoenberg's motto to form the twelve-tone theme that underlies the set of variations comprising the first movement.

Ex. 24-10. Berg, Chamber Concerto; I. Motto: Aller guten Dinge (Of all good things), mm. 1–5.

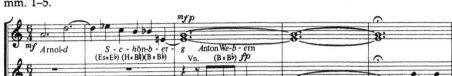

Berg's Chamber Concerto is in three movements linked without pause. The piano is the solo instrument in the first and the violin in the second, while both are used in the finale. The brilliant writing for the solo instruments culminates in the lengthy cadenza for both instruments that also introduces the third movement. The movements are intricately structured, and the recollection of thematic material in the finale brings a strong sense of unity.

The first movement, Tema scherzoso con variazioni, is a set of five variations on a theme. The variations are organized to make the general shape of sonata-allegro form. The theme is presented by the winds, while the piano, unaccompanied, presents variation I, based on the original form of the theme. Piano and winds collaborate in the remaining variations. Variations II, III, and IV serve as a development section in which the theme appears in retrograde, inverted, and retrograde inverted forms. The fifth variation serves as a recapitulation in which the theme reappears canonically.

The central Adagio movement is constructed as a palindrome, in which the second half is a retrograde version of the first half, and each half is in ternary form. Berg, a man obsessed with strict, mathematically symmetrical designs, planned the printing of the orchestral score so that the midpoint, between measures 360 and 361, is revealed in the mirror image of the facing score pages. The piano, which is otherwise silent in the Adagio, plays in the middle six measures, three on each side of the midpoint.

The finale, in which both the violin and piano play, amounts to a concurrent reprise of movements I and II, in that all the thematic material of the finale appeared in one or the other of the earlier movements. The final movement's title, Rondo ritmico con introduzione, reveals the importance the composer attached to the rhythm used in this movement. In his opera Wozzeck, Berg had introduced the concept of a "constructive rhythm," to which he attributed greater structural significance than in traditional musical practice. In that work and others, including the Chamber Concerto and Violin Concerto, Berg used a recurrent rhythmic pattern in a developmental fashion, independent of melodic or harmonic material. As in those other works, Berg identifies the main rhythmic motive of the Chamber Concerto's finale (Ex. 24-11) with the symbol Ⴙ (for Hauptrhythmus or main rhythm) at the beginning and a bracket at the ending. This rhythmic motive, which first appears as a part of a thematic idea in the second movement, is characteristic of Berg's constructive rhythms. It is compact, its striking syncopation making it stand out against the rest of the musical texture. Characteristically, it appears as an isolated rhythmic pattern repeated on one tone or one chord, extensively developed by way of augmentation, diminution, retrogression, and various other modifications. Douglas Jarman, in *The Music of Alban Berg*,[3] has identified two other rhythmic ideas in the final movement that he believes relate to Berg's description of the final movement in his dedicatory "Open Letter to Arnold Schoenberg."[4] Jarman, having discovered several relationships among these rhythmic ideas, has described the movement as a sonata-rondo form, in which one of the rhythms serves as the main rondo theme.[5]

Ex. 24-11. Berg, Chamber Concerto; III. Rondo ritmico con introduzione, m. 2. Hauptrhythmus.

Much of Berg's music is autobiographical and programmatic, although many of the programs of individual works may have remained private. The Chamber Concerto is no exception, the composer noting in his "Open Letter" to Schoenberg, "If anyone realized how much friendship, love, and a world of human-emotional associations I spirited into these three movements, the proponents of program music . . . would be delighted. . . ."[6] The opening motto on the names of Schoenberg, Webern, and Berg clearly is a "human" reference to the three Viennese composers who remain linked as a trio of composers of twentieth-century music—Berg portrays their emotional connection through the shared musical tones of their names.

Berg, like Schoenberg, was fascinated by numerology and revered certain numbers. In his "Open Letter" to Schoenberg, he revealed in detail how he gave the number *three* great significance in his concerto. There are three movements and three important musical performing forces—piano, violin, and winds, the latter made up of fifteen different instruments, just as in Schoenberg's First Chamber Symphony. Numbers divisible by three seem to pop up wherever one looks. In addition to the fifteen instruments just mentioned, all metronome markings in the work, of which there are many, are multiples of three. The first and second movements are each 240 measures long, with important structural divisions in measures 30, 120, and 150 of each of these movements. The finale is exactly as long as the first two movements combined, if all the repeat marks of the finale are observed. A silent measure, no. 630, marks the exact middle of the finale. Forms of triple meter are stressed but not used exclusively, but where duple meter is prevalent, as in the center of the middle movement's palindrome, quarter-note triplets are stressed.[7]

Brenda Dalen has discovered some fascinating "secret" program notes by Berg with titles for each of the movements: I. Friendship; II. Love; and III. World. Names of people closely associated with Schoenberg are mentioned beside the shorthand notation for each variation in movement I. For example, the pianist Steuermann's name appears beside the indication for variation I, which is for solo piano. Dalen identified the object of love in movement II by merging the mysterious designation "Ma" in the program notes with Berg's separate enigmatic description of a "high point" or "pivot point," associated with the letters:

A h d e   e d h A

The letters turn out to be the German names of the pitches used to approach and depart from the center point of movement II and reveal another musical crypto-gram for M*athilde* (*h* in German = B-natural). This is most likely a reference to Mathilde Schoenberg (1877–1923), the then-recently deceased wife of Arnold Schoenberg.[8] Surely the movement titles relate to the dedicatory letter with Berg's reference to being inspired by *"friendship, love,* and a *world* of human-emotional associations." [Italics mine.] The final movement contains a "world" of musical ele-ments from the first two movements, but in new relationships.

In 1935, while Berg was working to complete *Lulu,* he received a commission from the American violinist Louis Krasner (b. 1903) to write a violin concerto. Krasner had become fascinated with twelve-tone music, and with the help of his accompanist, the musicologist Dr. Rita Kurzman, he selected Berg as the most appropriate of the early composers of serial music to write a violin concerto. This decision was made, in part, because Berg was felt to be the one who could best exploit the lyrical potential of the violin. Berg initially balked at the idea of writing a virtuoso concerto, but eventually agreed, accepting it as a challenge. In prepara-tion, he frequented violin recitals and spent much time with Krasner to familiarize himself with both the man and his violinistic idiosyncrasies.

Just as Berg began thinking of the Violin Concerto in a specific way, he was shaken by the death on 22 April 1935 of Manon Gropius, the eighteen-year-old daughter of Gustav Mahler's widow, Alma, by her second marriage, to the architect Walter Gropius. This event triggered the idea of making the concerto into a kind of requiem for the girl, dedicated "To the memory of an angel." The work clearly has the character of a concerto, with its brilliant violin part pitted against the effec-tively scored orchestra, but it also has qualities of a tone poem. It characteristically incorporates programmatic features and, like the Chamber Concerto and other works by Berg, has its roots in autobiography—in this case, Berg's sense of loss.

The Violin Concerto is in four movements, paired to form two parts. Move-ments I and II are linked without pause, as are movements III and IV. The contrast between the two parts is exceptionally strong; part one portrays the life of a young girl, part two her suffering and death. Berg composed the concerto using the twelve-tone technique, but the series of pitches he chose as the work's basis possesses strong tonal tendencies (Ex. 24-12). The first nine pitches form a series of overlapping minor and major triads, in the relationship of tonic and dominant harmonies. Major sections of the concerto open with solidly stated triads, and part one ends with a clear G minor chord to which is added a major seventh in the solo violin. Part two concludes on a B-flat major chord with an ambiguous added sixth, G-natural, which is the same kind of chord Mahler (much admired and loved by Berg) used to conclude "Der Abschied"—The Farewell—of *Das Lied von der Erde* (1908–09), a work which also deals with suffering, death, and the realization of final peace.

Ex. 24-12. Berg, Violin Concerto; Tone Row.

Throughout Berg's concerto, sections of vague or very clear tonality repeatedly intrude upon the overall feeling of atonality. The sections of clearest tonal content involve the quotation of a folk song and a chorale tune, unusual non-dodecaphonic elements within a dodecaphonic work—but characteristic of this eclectic composer who often quoted material for emotional and dramatic effects. The tone row and the chorale tune are related: The final four notes of the tone row are the same as the opening four notes of the chorale, "Es ist genug," which begins with an unusual series of three rising whole-tone intervals, derived from the Lydian scale.

Part one opens with a ternary-form Andante, preceded by a short introduction in which the tones of the row are freely used in imitation of a violinist tuning (Ex. 24-13). The tender outer parts and *un poco grazioso* middle section of the Andante suggest the portrait of a gracious and charming girl. As is so typical of Berg, strict contrapuntal techniques play a role in even these lyrical sections; canonic entries appear in the middle section and hints of invertible counterpoint in the reprise of the first part, perhaps designed to strengthen the symmetry of the movement.

Ex. 24-13. Berg, Violin Concerto; I. Andante, mm. 2–7.

The second movement, Allegretto, is a scherzo with two trios arranged symmetrically:

Scherzo–Trio I–Trio II–Trio I–Scherzo

The scherzo portion contains three thematic elements: an opening figure marked *scherzando*, a *wienerisch* (Viennese) waltz-like motive with sweet parallel thirds and energetic skips, and a lively *rustico* theme (Ex. 24-14). The strongly lyrical central trio is flanked by a vivacious trio with many energetic triple stops and wide leaps in the solo violin. Near the end of the movement a Carinthian folk song, "A Bird on the Plumtree," is quoted *come una pastorale* (in the style of a pastorale). The geographic home of the folk song, Carinthia in southern Austria, was of considerable significance to Berg, for there his father owned a summer estate which the family visited frequently.

Ex. 24-14. Berg, Violin Concerto; II. Allegretto: (a.) mm. 105–107 [of Part One]; (b.) mm. 111–112 [of Part One]; (c.) mm. 114–115 [of Part One].

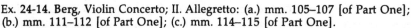

This Ländler-style yodler brings with it $\frac{3}{8}$ time and a key signature of six flats establishing G-flat major (Ex. 24-15). It is startling to encounter the folk song with its clear tonality in the midst of an otherwise serial, atonal framework. The horn first sings the tune followed by trumpets, with the solo violin adding a contrapuntal line above that. It is a direct adaptation from an 1892 published collection of Carinthian folk tunes which must have served as Berg's source.[9] The solo violin's shift to harmonics in m. 226 may be a stylized imitation of peasants singing in falsetto or yodelling. The folk song adds a sense of naiveté to the portrait of the young girl, despite a somewhat risqué text.[10]

Ex. 24-15. Berg, Violin Concerto; II. Allegretto, mm. 214–228 [of Part One].

Part two deals with suffering, death, and eventual peace through a musical language that is at first harsh and dissonant but later resolves in greater consonance and a strong sense of tonal harmony. Movement III, Allegro, is again in ternary form and the A section is also in three parts, with the first and third in two highly contrasting subsections. The first subsection employs much rubato in a cadenza style, while the second is marked *molto ritmico,* and is dominated by a brutal main rhythm (Ex. 24-16). The main rhythm is repeated twelve times in the orchestra and seven times in the violin in harsh, aggressive triple or quadruple stops, with each sequence accompanied by a gripping crescendo.

Ex. 24-16. Berg, Violin Concerto; III. Allegro, m. 23. Hauptrhythmus.

The B section of the third movement opens with the whole-tone phrase of the chorale in retrograde and continues with dreamlike recollections of material from part one, perhaps something like the brilliant flash of Marie's motives just before she dies in *Wozzeck.* The last portion of the B section is a cadenza, culminating in a four-part canon for solo violin based on the lyrical material of trio II from movement II. (Berg provides an option for this demanding canon by writing two of the parts for solo viola.) The return of A is marked by a reduction in the length of the rubato section with a compensating increase in the ritmico section leading to the *Höhepunkt,* or climax, of the Allegro. The triple *forte,* intensely dissonant, nine-note chordal setting of the rhythm is truly disturbing. The transition to the final Adagio is remarkable: The horrible chord loses its grip, as note-by-note it disintegrates, while the solo violin, note-by-note, slowly introduces the opening motive of the chorale.

The chorale, "Es ist genug," forms the basis of the Adagio final movement. The tune was composed in the seventeenth century by Johann Rudolf Ahle (1625–1673) and was used by J. S. Bach in his Cantata No. 60. Berg not only uses the tune, including a portion of the text by F. J. Burmeister under the solo violin part (Ex. 24-17a), but the harmonization by Bach as well (Ex. 24-17b). The chorale text is a prayer for deliverance from suffering on this earth and a farewell to the world in anticipation of final peace. Berg's setting is full of meaningful allusions. There is a sense of call-and-response similar to that of responsorial singing, as the violinist first presents a phrase of the tune followed by the repeated phrase in the woodwinds in Bach's harmonization, and the sound of the woodwinds evokes that of an organ. The phrases proceed much like a set of variations. Near the end of the movement the Carinthian folk song is very quietly recalled in a slow tempo, "as if from afar." Berg's use of these tonal elements and the powerfully emotional recollection of the folk song create an extremely intense yet peaceful mood, culminating in the ambiguous final chord.

Ex. 24-17. Berg, Violin Concerto; IV. Adagio: (a.) mm. 136–142 [of Part Two]; (b.) mm. 142–145 [of Part Two].

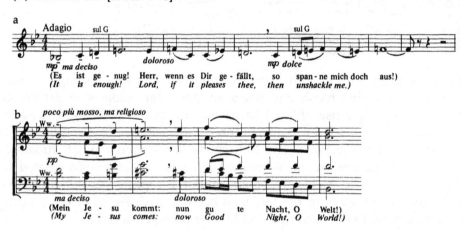

The Violin Concerto is Berg's last completed work and one of his most appealing. Berg finished the writing in August 1935, but did not live to hear Krasner play it at the International Society for Contemporary Music Festival in Barcelona on 19 March 1936. It was played thereafter on numerous occasions, becoming one of the very few twelve-tone works by composers of the second Viennese school to enter the standard repertory. It ranks among the greatest violin concertos of the nineteenth and twentieth centuries, standing alongside those by Beethoven, Mendelssohn, Brahms, and Prokofiev.

BÉLA BARTÓK (1881–1945)

Bartók, speaking of Debussy, once said the French composer

> restored a feeling for chords to all musicians. He was as important as Beethoven who revealed to us progressive form, and as Bach who introduced us to the transcendence of counterpoint. I always ask myself, could one make a synthesis of these three masters and create a vital contemporary style?[11]

Bartók not only did so, but added other ingredients mostly from his native land of Hungary.

This brilliant composer was also a great pianist and piano teacher, and he gave the piano a prominent place in many of his compositions. He began his piano studies with his mother, and at the age of eighteen enrolled at the Royal Academy of Music in Budapest, where he received a thorough education as both pianist and composer. Early influences included the music of Liszt, Strauss, and Debussy.

A strong nationalist movement emerged in Hungary around the turn of the century, as Hungarians sought to displace the dominant Austro-German culture. The young Bartók was swept up by these feelings, and in 1904 began collecting folk songs in the countryside, developing a great sensitivity to and understanding of folk music. In many respects he was one of the first important ethnomusicologists, and methods he developed to study ethnic music remain valid today.

Bartók's interest in folk music became a deep passion, a passion that came to influence much of his own compositional style. By 1908 folkloric elements permeated much of his music. Especially notable are the use of scales other than major or minor; asymmetrical metric patterns, such as $\frac{5}{8}$ or $\frac{7}{8}$; frequent changes of meter; ostinato patterns; narrow, short melodic phrases; and rhythmic patterns derived from either dance or speech, or, to use Bartók's categorizations, *tempo giusto* or *parlando rubato*. (*Tempo giusto* means a just or precise tempo, characteristic of dances, and *parlando rubato* means a flexible tempo or pulse of a speech-like quality.) Other salient features include strong, often imitative, contrapuntal textures; extreme chromaticism, but without any resort to atonality; clear forms, often in symmetrical, arch or bowlike shapes; extensive use of motivic development and thematic transformation; and colorful orchestration with a virtuosic handling of a wide variety of instruments. His use of chromaticism goes hand in hand with Bartók's favorite interval, the minor second, which is used not only melodically but also harmonically in highly pungent, dissonant tone clusters. Bartók's music is further characterized by great contrasts, especially from movement to movement within a composition.

Bartók composed a dozen concertante works, including three piano concertos, two violin concertos, an incomplete viola concerto, the Concerto for Orchestra, and several shorter works for piano or violin and orchestra. The first two are shorter works for piano very much in the mode of Franz Liszt. The Op. 1 Rhapsody for piano and orchestra (1904) follows the pattern of Liszt's Hungarian Rhapsodies, with a slow section, followed by one with a quick, dancelike quality.

Violin Concerto No. 1 (1907–08) is of a similar design but larger in scope; each section is transformed into an independent movement. Although this work was never performed in the composer's lifetime and was not even published until 1958, it has entered the repertory of a great many concert violinists. The violin's strongly lyrical nature is exploited in the warm, Strauss-like, Andante sostenuto, which opens with a long, sustained line in the unaccompanied solo instrument. The texture becomes increasingly contrapuntal as various sections of the orchestra enter, eventually creating a fugal atmosphere possessing an intensity similar to the first movement of Bartók's later *Music for Strings, Percussion, and Celesta* (1936). The robust Allegro giocoso second movement is in sonata-allegro form with sudden changes of mood. The lengthy development section focuses on the first of the three main thematic ideas.

The work is dedicated to Stefi Geyer, an Hungarian violinist with whom Bartók was then in love. Bartók's letters tell of the creation of a musical motive for her, which appears in several of Bartók's works from this time, including the First Violin Concerto. The four-note motive appears in the solo instrument at the very beginning (Ex. 24-18). The motive is recalled at the end of the work in a brief Lento in the orchestra, and last of all, tenderly, in the solo violin's very high register.

Ex. 24-18. Bartók, Violin Concerto No. 1; I. Andante sostenuto, m. 1.

Bartók's manuscript carries an enigmatic entry over a somewhat humorous and incongruous tune in A major at the beginning of the coda. Here the composer names a small town, Jászberény, east of Budapest, with the date 28 June 1907, just three days before he began to work on the concerto. No one has discovered the significance of this notation and of the strange tune it accompanies, but they perhaps had to do with Bartók's relationship with Geyer, since they had not separated until early 1908, about the time Bartók completed the concerto. This episode also probably explains why he neither published the work nor heard it performed. Instead, the composer gave the manuscript to Stefi Geyer, who bequeathed it to Paul Sacher with instructions that he conduct it in performance with the Swiss violinist Hans-Heinz Schneeberger. It was first performed in Basel on 30 May 1958.

A gap of almost twenty years separates Violin Concerto No. 1 from Bartók's next concerto, his first for piano, composed in 1926. In the meantime, Bartók not only incorporated increasing amounts of folk material in his music, but did so with ever greater mastery, eventually synthesizing a highly original style. The piano figured prominently in his compositions during this period of personal, stylistic synthesis and expansion. The year 1926 saw the creation of several important works for the piano, including the Sonata, *Out of Doors Suite,* and Nine Little Piano Pieces, as well as the First Piano Concerto. Bartók, like Prokofiev, was interested in exploring the percussive potential of the piano, which is made very obvious in the Piano Concerto No. 1. This use of the piano may account, in part, for the fact that it is the least favored of Bartók's three piano concertos. The outer movements of this three-movement work pound with savage, repeated notes and ostinato patterns that create a strong rhythmic drive, while the inner movement, Andante, has the unusually delicate, atmospheric quality associated with the "Night Music," the fourth movement of the *Out of Doors Suite*. Tone clusters, groups of closely adjacent notes sounding together to form highly dissonant chords, further augment the percussive quality of the work. Bartók said he was inspired to use these tone clusters by the music of the innovative American composer Henry Cowell (1897–1965), who called for pianists to play large clusters of tones by striking the piano keys with an entire hand or a forearm.

In 1928 Bartók composed two rhapsodies for violin and piano, one for each of his close friends, the violinists Joseph Szigeti (1892–1973) and Zoltán Székely (b. 1903). These pieces were later orchestrated, but the orchestra is largely confined to the role of accompanist, never gaining any real independence. Both pieces use Rumanian folk songs and follow the traditional dance pairing of the slow *lassú* with the fast *friss*. The orchestra for the first rhapsody includes a cimbalom, a large dulcimer-like Hungarian instrument clearly associated with gypsy music.

The Second Piano Concerto (1930–31), like the first, was written for the composer's own use. Virtuosity and percussiveness are tempered by more appealing thematic material and more brilliant orchestration than is the case with the First Piano Concerto. The result is one of the most dazzling and exciting piano concertos of the twentieth century. The Second Piano Concerto is a prime example of Bartók's capacity to assimilate successfully and integrate a wide variety of techniques and styles into a highly organized and symmetrical structure. This concerto is in three movements, with the middle movement in three sections to form an overall five-part arch form with a Presto in the center:

I. Allegro   II. Adagio-Presto-Adagio   III. Allegro molto

An unusual use of the orchestra throughout the work underlies the overall arch structure. The strings are silent in movement I, resulting in the stark juxtaposition of piano and winds, the piano often in conjunction with the percussion instruments. Strings and timpani join the piano in the Adagio portions of the middle movement, while in the central Presto the forces are gradually increased with the addition of winds as the climax is approached. The finale makes use of the full orchestra with strings prominent at times, and winds at others. Thematic relationships between the outer movements also reinforce the arch structure.

The first movement is in sonata-allegro form, with themes inverted or retrograde and inverted in the recapitulation. For example, compare the opening pair of motives in trumpet and piano with their reversed appearance in inverted form at the recapitulation (Ex. 24-19). And just before the cadenza in movement I, motive a reappears in retrograde inverted form (Ex. 24-20). Important structural junctures in the movement are marked by stretto, or overlapping imitative entries of the main theme.

Ex. 24-19. Bartók, Piano Concerto No. 2; I. Allegro: (a.) mm. 2–6; (b.) mm. 180–183.

Ex. 24-20. Bartók, Piano Concerto No. 2; I. Allegro, mm. 212–213.

In the opening adagio portion of the middle movement, the strings begin with a quietly intense chorale in parallel fifths in the upper strings, accompanied by parallel fifths in the lower strings moving in contrary motion to the upper line (Ex. 24-21). Piano and timpani intervene on two occasions, playing the extremely delicate sounds associated with Bartók's "Night Music." The presto midsection is an unconventional pianistic display of rapidly repeated notes, fragments of chromatic scales, and tone clusters (see Ex. 24-22), mostly in very hushed tones, which adds to the mysterious yet exciting mood. At the return of the adagio, the piano and timpani layer their night music atop the chorale, which is then played by the strings *sul ponticello* (close to the bridge).

Ex. 24-21. Bartók, Piano Concerto No. 2; II. Adagio, mm. 1–5.

Ex. 24-22. Bartók, Piano Concerto No. 2; II. Adagio, m. 94.

The final movement is a rondo in which the main theme at times becomes a hard-driving ostinato figure in the timpani and lower strings. The episodes in this movement contain transformed references to ideas first appearing in the first movement, such as the triplet versions of motives a and b in the first episode (Ex. 24-23). The first theme of movement I occupies a prominent place in the coda, completing the arch shape of the work.

Ex. 24-23. Bartók, Piano Concerto No. 2; III. Allegro molto: (a.) mm. 66–68; (b.) mm. 45–47.

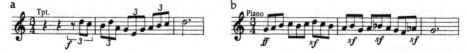

In this concerto, Bartók succeeds in synthesizing the disparate musical styles that so interested him. It incorporates the motivic and thematic development of Beethoven, the contrapuntal artistry of Bach, the impressionistic techniques of Debussy, the thematic transformation and pianistic virtuosity of Liszt, and the naiveté and some scale structures and rhythmic features of folk music. All are combined within a logical organization of the highest artistic merit to form a work of sensuous beauty and dynamic power.

Bartók's last concerto before he moved to the United States in 1940 was the

Second Violin Concerto, composed in 1937–38 for Zoltán Székely. Bartók wished to write a set of variations, but the violinist convinced the composer to write a traditional three-movement concerto. Bartók agreed, but included a theme and variations as the second movement and made the first theme of the last movement a transformed variant of the opening movement's first theme (Ex. 24-24). In addition, much of the finale is based on variants of material first presented in movement I. Folk songs are not directly quoted in the work, but their impact is always present, as in the stress on intervals of the fourth in the main theme (Ex. 24-24).

Ex. 24-24. Bartók, Violin Concerto No. 2: (a.) I. Allegro non troppo, mm. 1–4; (b.) III. Allegro molto, mm. 1–6.

The Concerto for Orchestra (1943) was written in response to a commission from the Koussevitsky Foundation for the Boston Symphony Orchestra. Bartók, who was quite ill with a form of blood cancer, polycythaemia, was unwilling to accept charity and even hesitated to accept half of the $1000 commission in advance, for fear that he might not complete the work. During a period of remission, he worked virtually day and night for seven weeks to complete what was to become his most widely performed work. Like the other compositions of his last few years, it is marked by an appealing tunefulness, warmth of expression, and generally firm sense of tonality, making it almost instantly accessible and readily accepted by audiences.

Bartók called the work symphony-like, but used the title "concerto" to point to the virtuosic orchestral writing and soloistic treatment of most instruments. In his program notes for the first performance, which took place in Boston, 1 December 1944, Bartók provided an almost programmatic interpretation. He wrote, "The general mood of the work represents, apart from the jesting second movement, a gradual transition from the sternness of the first movement and the lugubrious death-song of the third, to the life-assertion of the last one."[12]

The Concerto for Orchestra is in five movements, but not organized in his usual archlike form. The first movement, Introduzione, includes an andante opening section and allegro vivace in a twentieth-century version of sonata-allegro form. At the outset, basses present an idea loaded with melodic fourths, an interval rooted in Hungarian folk music. When used in succession, fourths weaken the sense of tonality. The introductory theme (Ex. 24-25) has the familiar arch shape associated with many of his melodies. Impressionistic writing for the strings, with Bartók's characteristic mirrored melodic lines, and a declamatory idea in imitation of the *parlando rubato* folk style Bartók had identified in his field work complete the introduction. The allegro vivace's main theme is thoroughly characteristic of the composer's pen. It again emphasizes the interval of the fourth, and opens with a quick run up to the tritone, or augmented fourth, one of Bartók's favorite intervals.

This compact idea contains several linked fourths, typical changes of meter, and a second phrase which is an inversion of the first (Ex. 24-26a). Trombones transform this theme into a new one cast in more regular triple meter (Ex. 24-26b), while later in the movement the brass instruments develop it fugally. An almost static second theme over a drone bass contrasts sharply with the vibrant first theme.

Ex. 24-25. Bartók, Concerto for Orchestra; I. Introduzione—Andante non troppo, mm. 1–6.

Ex. 24-26. Bartók, Concerto for Orchestra, I. Introduzione—Allegro vivace: (a.) mm. 76–81; (b.) mm. 316–323.

The second movement is entitled Giuoco delle coppie (Game of Pairs); Allegretto scherzando. It is a light dance movement featuring wind instruments. In the outer parts of the scherzo winds play in pairs, each pair presenting a dance figure in parallel motion at a specific interval:

- bassoons at the sixth;
- oboes at the third;
- clarinets at the seventh;
- flutes at the fifth;
- muted trumpets at the second.

The trio, or midsection, is in the style of a chorale for brass instruments. Additional instruments are added to some pairs in the reprise of the scherzo: The pair of bassoons is accompanied by a third bassoon in independent counterpoint; the pair of clarinets is joined by a pair of oboes in mirror-like inversion; and the pair of flutes is joined by a clarinet to form interlocked fourths.

The Elegia third movement is another example of Bartók's "Night Music" style, with some reference to the work's opening material at the beginning of the movement. The fourth movement, Intermezzo interrotto (Interrupted Intermezzo), is in the form ABA-Interruption-AB. The main themes are folklike, while the interruption is a quotation by the clarinet from Shostakovich's Seventh Symphony (Leningrad). Bartók happened to hear a broadcast of Shostakovich's work while at work on the Concerto for Orchestra and found the theme so ridiculous that he decided to parody it. Jeers and rude noises from the orchestra greet the tune.

The finale, the most substantial movement of the Concerto for Orchestra, begins with a perpetuum mobile, includes a complex fugue, and closes with exceptionally brilliant orchestral writing.

Bartók was permitted by his physician to attend the rehearsals and first performance in Boston. The composer reported, "It was worth while, the performance was excellent! Koussevitsky is very enthusiastic about the piece, and says it is 'the best orchestra piece of the last 25 years' (including the works of his idol Shostakovich!)."[13]

Bartók's last orchestral compositions were two concertos left in quite different unfinished states at his death. The Third Piano Concerto (1945), for his second wife, Ditta Pásztory (1902–1982), is very different from the earlier piano concertos, in which the piano's percussive quality and its association with the percussion instruments was so strongly stressed. Here lyricism is the objective. The middle movement, Adagio religioso, with its chorale-style theme and use of bird song bring to mind Beethoven's *Heiliger Dankgesang* from his A minor String Quartet, Op. 132, composed upon his recovery from a serious illness. Bartók did not recover but seemed to find peace, as expressed in this music. Bartók completed the orchestration of the Third Piano Concerto, except for the final seventeen measures, which were filled in by Tibor Serly, who knew the composer's work intimately.

The state of the Viola Concerto (1945) was less secure, for in this case Serly had only the composer's sketches.[14] It was to have been played by the great violist William Primrose (1903–1982). Although one can discover Bartók's imprint and violists would like to claim the work of this great composer for their largely neglected instrument, the Viola Concerto cannot truly be considered a work of Bartók.

PAUL HINDEMITH (1895–1963)

Paul Hindemith was an accomplished, multitalented musician, successful as a virtuoso violist, teacher, theorist, and composer. He made significant contributions in all these fields, but his compositions no longer enjoy the place in the repertory that they once did.

His early music of the 1920s is characterized by highly dissonant, linear counterpoint, often departing from traditional rules of harmony. Following his appointment as professor of composition at the Berlin Hochschule für Musik in 1927, Hindemith became increasingly aware of the practical problems faced by composers and musicians. As part of his response to these problems, he wrote a composition textbook, later published under the English title *The Craft of Musical Composition* (*Unterweisung im Tonsatz*, 2 v., 1937, 1939), and eventually *A Composer's World* (1952) in which he presented his philosophy of music.

Hindemith came to understand that the complex, dissonant quality of his early works had alienated most audiences, so in 1927 he undertook to reduce the harshness. Hindemith fully recognized the importance of reaching his audience and of communicating with his performers; indeed he even set about creating music for amateurs to play. The term *Gebrauchsmusik* (music for use) came to be associated with music written for amateur players, in spite of Hindemith's intense dislike of the label. He preferred the term *Sing-und Spielmusik* (Music to Sing and Play) to identify this simpler, more direct music. He also came to recognize the need to write music for instruments with only slim solo repertories, and made important contributions by writing sonatas and concertos for a wide variety of instruments, including the tuba, trombone, and bassoon.

Hindemith had no sympathy for twelve-tone music or atonality. His music is always tonal, although he developed some unique theories of pitch and interval relationships based on an elaborate study of the overtone series. Hindemith firmly believed that music had its roots in nature and that the role of tonality, which he found to be derived from physical laws, could not be denied. The major triad symbolized this direct link with nature so that no matter how dissonant the music may be at times, Hindemith leads it to a final cadence on a major triad.

Hindemith's mature music may be described as largely neo-Classical or, perhaps more appropriately, neo-Baroque. It is characterized by strong counterpoint, driving rhythms, the use of Baroque forms, chamber music textures, and a strong preference for wind instruments in orchestral works to counterbalance the weight given to the string section by the Romantics.

Hindemith's vast compositional output includes some twenty concertos. His earliest effort, a cello concerto of 1916, remained unpublished until after his death. Another early work for the left-handed pianist, Paul Wittgenstein, has been lost. A series of seven works, each entitled *Kammermusik* (Chamber Music) from 1924 to 1927 includes six small-scale concertos for a variety of solo instruments and chamber orchestra. No. 2, for piano and a twelve-instrument ensemble, is typical with its four-movement suite-like structure and toccata-inspired fast movements. Hindemith uses much imitative counterpoint and bustling rhythmic activity, while relying on monothematic forms, all of which lend a strong Baroque air to these works.

A less harsh, more lyrical, and simpler style is apparent in his *Konzertmusik* of 1930 (the first of three such works), dedicated to Darius and Madeleine Milhaud. This divertimento-like, five-movement work features solo viola accompanied by an orchestra comprising four cellos, four basses, woodwinds, and brass. The solo viola is not treated in a virtuoso manner. The viola, Hindemith's major instrument, is also featured in *Der Schwanendreher* (The Swan Turner, 1935), a concerto based on old folksongs. Hindemith, about this time, had become interested in the direct appeal of folk songs, using several in his contemporary opera, *Mathis der Maler* (Matthias [Grünewald], the Painter), some of which are identical to folk songs used in *Der Schwanendreher*. He also used German folk melodies as the basis for counterpoint exercises he assigned students.

The remainder of Hindemith's concertante works are true concertos in both spirit and title and most are in the standard three movements. The Violin Concerto (1939), commissioned by the Dutch conductor Willem Mengelberg, is a substantial work noted for its broad lyrical lines in the solo instrument, such as the opening theme that soars in the violin's upper register (Ex. 24-27). Hindemith's typical preference for the winds makes for strong contrasts, especially when the brass instruments are given the responsibility for major climaxes. An extensive cadenza for the violin occurs near the end of the final movement.

Ex. 24-27. Hindemith, Violin Concerto; I. Mässig bewegt Halbe, mm. 1–4.

In 1940, the year Hindemith emigrated to the United States and joined the faculty at Yale University, he completed his Cello Concerto. It was first performed by Gregor Piatigorsky with the Boston Symphony Orchestra. The second movement is of particular interest not only because William Walton used the first theme as the subject of his 1963 Variations on a Theme of Hindemith, but also because of its unusual structure. The first part quietly expands in a melodious manner, involving many solo passages for various members of the orchestra. A lively scherzo fills the middle section. These two markedly contrasting ideas appear in simultaneous layers in the final section.

In 1947 Hindemith wrote a lightweight and thoroughly lyrical concerto for Benny Goodman (1909–1986). Even though Hindemith, like several other European composers, took to jazz in the 1920s, he made no reference to the idiom in this concerto for the famous jazz clarinetist. The work's four movements feature the clarinet in a largely lyrical, not obviously virtuosic, role, well integrated into the orchestral texture.

The Concerto for Horn (1949) has a similar feel; Hindemith emphasized the lyrical qualities of the brass instrument, minimizing the virtuoso content, even though it honors one of history's most gifted horn players, Dennis Brain (1921–1957). The Horn Concerto's first movement, in the key of F major, a superb key for the horn, is in a brief sonatina form, without development. The martial character of the opening theme (Ex. 24-28) comes alive in its orchestral presentation. It undergoes fugal treatment before the horn takes it over in a more lyrical fashion. The second movement, a small scherzo, focuses on one of Hindemith's favorite intervals, the fourth, which extends to a seventh when doubled (Ex. 24-29a). The concluding horn call repeats the same interval (Ex. 24-29b).

Ex. 24-28. Hindemith, Horn Concerto; I. Moderately fast, mm. 1–3.

Ex. 24-29. Hindemith, Horn Concerto; II. Very fast: (a.) mm. 3–12; (b.) mm. 132–134.

The final movement's unusual form consists of variations on two alternating themes:

A	B	A'	recitative	B'	A''
(very slow)	(moderately fast)	(fast)	(lento)	(lively)	(very slow)

Very slow tempos begin, and, most unusually, end the finale. The central section comprises a fast tutti section and an extraordinary lento, recitando for solo horn with tremolando string accompaniment. The horn's notes declaim eight lines of poetry by Hindemith, printed in the score. The poem appears printed in standard poetic format at the top of the score page, but the placement of the German words under the horn melody clarifies the relationship (Ex. 24-30).

Ex. 24-30. Hindemith, Horn Concerto; III. Very slow, mm. 114–115.

Hindemith composed two concertos for organ. The first is the final work in his *Kammermusik* series, No. 7, from 1927, and the other is from the penultimate year of his life, 1962. The New York Philharmonic commissioned the latter for the opening season of Lincoln Center, first performing it there on 25 April 1963 with Anton Heiller as organist and the composer conducting. The Organ Concerto (1962), a quintessentially late-Hindemith work, combines strident harmony (except in the unusual third movement, "Canzonetta in Triads") with his most sensuous and subtle orchestration.

The first movement, entitled "Crescendo," is one long dynamic swell from the first pedal note in the organ, as instruments gradually join in and the volume intensifies. The fourth and final movement, "Phantasy on Veni Creator Spiritus," is a set of variations on the Latin hymn associated with Pentecost. Perhaps Hindemith included this tune as a kind of musical prayer in the hope that the Creator Spirit would come to reside in the new home for the performing arts in New York. The organ presents the theme in chorale-style phrases separated by more vigorous orchestral passages. The first variation features winds in its first half, while the organ plays the *cantus firmus* in longer note values on the pedalboard. The second variation features the organ in a siciliana-like setting. All the orchestral instruments are muted in the light third variation, during which the organ performs wide-ranging flourishes. A muted trombone plays the opening phrase of another famous old tune, "L'homme armé," from the fifteenth century, or at least the trombone phrase is strikingly like that popular Renaissance melody. An extended organ cadenza serves as the final variation.

In the Concerto for Trumpet and Bassoon (1949–1952), Hindemith joins these two disparate instruments in a most effective way, often resorting to rapid, echolike exchanges. The miniature Vivace third movement was added in 1952 to what was originally a two-movement concerto.

While Hindemith may have been the least innovative of the five composers discussed in this chapter, and much of his music may no longer sustain the interest of audiences, his Violin Concerto and Horn Concerto are fully deserving of greater attention. Not only are they direct and accessible, but they are also compelling, idiomatic concertos in which the solo instrument and orchestra are well integrated and effectively contrasted.

Chapter Twenty-Five

OTHER COMPOSERS
IN EUROPE,
LATIN AMERICA,
AND CANADA

We will travel extensively in this chapter, exploring colorful and exotic music made on three continents. Many of the composers here incorporated native folkloric elements in their work, paradoxically giving it universal appeal. Others stamped their music with highly personal qualities, often blazing new trails by introducing novel sounds and innovative techniques to the world of twentieth-century music. This music ranges from the broadly attractive concertos of the Spaniard Manuel de Falla to the esoteric, atmospheric offerings of the Hungarian György Ligeti. Whatever their stylistic stances, the composers treated here contributed significantly to the concerto in the twentieth century and some wrote works of outstanding merit.

SPAIN

Spain enjoyed the riches of such illustrious sixteenth-century composers as Tomás Luis de Victoria, Luis Milán, and Antonio de Cabezón. Yet thereafter the country had to wait until the late nineteenth century for the reemergence of significant native talent,[1] although the Spaniards did support a rich growth of folk music and serious guitar playing in the interval. Felipe Pedrell (1841–1922), composer, teacher, and musicologist, was largely responsible for the revival of Spanish music. He excited people's interest in the diverse wealth of the Spanish musical heritage by introducing them to Spanish folk music and sixteenth-century Spanish art music. He also knew about contemporary developments in other countries, and accordingly inspired young composers to create a new Spanish art music. His three leading students were Isaac Albéniz (1860–1909), Enrique Granados (1867–1916), and Manuel de Falla (1876–1946). (Granados wrote no concertante music so is not dealt with here.)

Albéniz studied piano with Franz Liszt in Paris, becoming a brilliant virtuoso. In the 1890s, at the urging of Pedrell, Albéniz began to make greater use of Spanish folk music, developing a distinctive corpus of piano music that blended folkloric and virtuosic ingredients. His solo piano music, especially the picturesque suite, *Iberia* (1906–09), remains popular. But his only two concertante works are little performed today—the Piano Concerto in A Minor (1887), his only piano concerto, and his *Rapsodia española* for piano and orchestra (1887).

Manuel de Falla, like Albéniz and Granados, spent a substantial period in Paris (1907–14), where he was profoundly influenced by the music of Debussy and Ravel. Falla especially admired the way in which Debussy evoked images of Spain without reference to actual folk music, a technique the Spanish composer mastered to good effect in much of his work up to the mid-1920s. *Nights in the Gardens of Spain: Symphonic Impressions for Piano and Orchestra* (1911–15) is a masterful example of this approach, and was probably inspired by Debussy's "Fragrances of the Night" from *Iberia* (1908) and Ravel's "Prelude to the Night" from *Rhapsodie espagnole* (1907).

Falla had begun *Nights in the Gardens of Spain* in Paris as early as 1909, bringing the incomplete manuscript with him when he returned to Spain in 1914. He completed the work in the ideal surroundings of Sitges, a coastal village. This piece was initially conceived for the solo piano, but Albéniz urged Falla to give it a larger setting. He recast it into a piece for piano and orchestra in which the piano plays an important coloristic role, but only rarely is the role comparable to that of the solo instrument in a concerto. The titles of the three movements, which are three short but related tone poems, evoke the moods and settings of Andalusia. Falla described the musical themes as based on stylistic features of the folk and popular music of Andalusia, but he did not directly quote any such tunes. Nor does Falla call for any typically Spanish instruments in the orchestra. Instead he imitates the sounds of several: the guitar by the strings, harp, and piano; castanets by short decorating grace notes in the woodwinds; a tambourine by trills in several instruments; and Basque drums by the strings.

The first movement, "At the Generalife," is marked *allegretto tranquillo et misterioso*. The Generalife was the summer palace of the thirteenth-century Moors in the Alhambra, overlooking Granada. A narrow-ranged *canto* (song) rises mysteriously from the harp and violas, *sul ponticello* (played near the bridge) and tremolo, in an Andalusian dance rhythm. Falla develops and expands this simple melody as the principal thematic material of the first movement. "Distant Dance," allegretto giusto, is the flamenco-inspired second movement with brilliant, guitar-like writing for the piano. The vivo third movement returns to a specific garden setting, this time "In the Gardens of the Mountains of Cordova." This movement, joined without pause to the second, is in the form of a *copla* and *estribillo*, which is similar to rondo form. The *estribillo*, used in refrain-like fashion, captures the gaiety of an evening party with a band of gypsy musicians. The music fades into night-time quiet at the close.

In the 1920s Falla turned to composing music in the manner of Stravinsky's neo-Classicism; the Harpsichord Concerto (1923–26) is a typical example. This work, scored for a chamber ensemble of harpsichord, flute, oboe, clarinet, violin, and cello, was written for Wanda Landowska, who requested a concerto from Falla after playing in a performance of his *El Retablo de Maese Pedro* (Master Peter's Puppet Show, 1919–22).

Falla viewed all six of the instruments as solo instruments but gave the harpsichord greater prominence. He draws surprisingly harsh sounds from the small ensemble by exploiting each instrument distinctively. The harpsichord plays in a percussive manner, with much chordal texture and frequent arpeggios. It is occasionally given rapid repeated notes and other figures recalling Spanish guitar music, but Falla avoided the kind of ornamentation so characteristic of much eighteenth-century harpsichord music. The harmonic punch and percussive drive may derive, however, from his study of the harpsichord music of Domenico Scarlatti, the great Italian Baroque composer who spent much of his active life in Spain. The flute is often scored in its shrill, highest register. The oboe and clarinet often double the flute in octaves, creating a primitive sound in the context of such a small chamber ensemble. The two solo string instruments add bold, incisive strokes, indicated by the strong bow markings in the score. Rarely do they provide the lush sounds usually associated with them.

The harmonic vocabulary of the concerto is similarly harsh, with jolting polytonal passages, such as when the fifteenth-century Castilian folk song, "De los Alamos, Vengo, Madre," appears as the main theme of the first movement. The flute and oboe play the tune in B major in octaves, while the right hand of the harpsichord part is in A minor, the left hand in B-flat minor, and the clarinet in B-flat major. These harmonic conflicts arise against equally disturbing rhythmic ones, and the impact of the whole is intensified by the unblended use of the instruments (Ex. 25-1).

The first movement is in sonata-allegro form. The second, Lento (giubiloso ed energico), is one of Falla's most profound creations. An inscription at the end of the movement indicates that it was connected in the composer's mind with Corpus Christi Day 1926. According to Falla's biographer, Suzanne Demarquez, Falla was inspired to write this movement during a lecture about the Middle Ages in a setting surrounded by illustrations of ancient instruments. The movement was to represent a Corpus Christi "procession moving slowly around the arches of a Gothic cathedral, to be suggested by the amplitude of the melodic lines and by the clashing resonances of large arpeggios written for the harpsichord."[2] The main theme of the movement closely relates to the fifteenth-century song used as the main theme in movement I. The Vivace finale (flessibile, scherzando), like the middle movement, contains some canonic writing, but the last movement is more playful.

Wanda Landowska played the concerto for the first time at a Falla Festival in Barcelona on 5 November 1926. It was not well received, possibly because of insufficient rehearsal time and poorly transcribed parts. Landowska refused thereafter to play the work, probably because it did not suit her temperament.

Joaquín Rodrigo (b. 1901), blind since age three, wrote the most popular guitar concerto ever composed, the *Concierto de Aranjuez* (1939). This attractive concerto is highly idiomatic and filled with Spanish color, especially in its dancelike, fast movements. The Adagio is a lament for those lost in the Spanish Civil War.

Ex. 25-1. Falla, Harpsichord Concerto; I. Allegro, mm. 21–25.

FRANCE AND SWITZERLAND

Ernest Bloch (1880–1959) was born in Geneva, Switzerland, but wrote much of his music in the United States. He emigrated to the United States in 1916 and held important teaching and administrative positions at the Cleveland Institute of Music (1920–1925) and the San Francisco Conservatory (1925–1930). He spent much of the 1930s in Switzerland but returned to the United States, where he took up residence in Agate Beach, Oregon, in 1941.

Bloch established his musical identity as a Jew through a series of epic works based on Biblical subjects. The most popular of these is *Schelomo: Hebrew Rhapsody for Cello and Orchestra* (1915–16). This emotional portrait of King Solomon makes no use of authentic Hebraic material but evokes it through the prominent use of melodic and rhythmic formulas. These include the augmented second and the "Scotch snap"—a grouping of two notes in a short-long relationship, with the short note occurring on the beat—reminiscent of Hebraic music. Percussion instruments and celesta also add an exotic flavor. *Schelomo* is a one-movement work in free form, in which Bloch suggested the listener could imagine the cello as representing the voice of the king, and the orchestra, the voice of his age. An opening cadenza for solo cello presents most of the important motives of the work, including the basic material of the main theme, which is first presented by violas (Ex. 25-2). The work alternates between austere or agitated moods and lush, calmer ones. The cello brings the work to a close in its lowest range, creating a sense of uneasiness, or feeling of despair, as if to intone, "Vanity, Vanity all is Vanity."

Ex. 25-2. Bloch, *Schelomo*.

In the 1920s Bloch turned to composing in the neo-Classical style, as did so many other composers of the time. His Concerto Grosso No. 1 for Strings and Piano Obbligato (1924–25) was written to demonstrate aspects of the neo-Classical approach to his students. In this four-movement work, Bloch makes use of several Baroque techniques, including a strong fugue in the final movement. The Violin Concerto (1937–38), in the standard three movements, is in Bloch's older, epic style. The opening theme was described by the composer as in a Native-American style; it is interesting that it includes his favorite "Scotch snap" rhythm. Bloch composed about a dozen other concertante works, none of which is performed frequently.

Frank Martin (1890–1974) was a Swiss composer of French descent. He was largely self-taught, although he studied briefly with Émile Jacques-Dalcroze (1865–1950) in 1926. In this case he sought to learn more about Eurhythmics, Jacques-Dalcroze's method of teaching music, especially rhythm, through gestures. Martin was an instructor at the Jacques-Dalcroze Institute in Geneva from 1928 to 1938, which may, in part, account for the vital rhythmic quality of much of his music. In 1946 he moved to the Netherlands, settling in Naarden for the remainder of his life, although from 1950 to 1957 he taught a composition class at the Hochschule für Musik in Cologne, in which Karlheinz Stockhausen (b. 1925) was one of his students.

As has proven typical of many Swiss composers, Martin avoided the musical extremes which have characterized much twentieth-century music. His style is unique and eludes categorizing. His early works are fairly conventional, showing the influence of Franck and Fauré, but exposure to the music of Debussy and Bartók in the late 1920s encouraged him to broaden his approach. He explored folk music, developing a particular interest in the unusual rhythmic patterns of eastern European music and in jazz. In the early 1930s he began to work with twelve-tone music and was one of the first composers to follow in Berg's footsteps by adopting elements of the technique without discarding tonality; tonal harmony remained important to him throughout his life. The First Piano Concerto (1934) illustrates his use of the twelve-tone technique, and its performance at the fourteenth Festival of the International Society of Contemporary Music in Barcelona in 1936 seems to have led other composers to adopt the technique in similar ways. His style also incorporates a rhythmic vitality; ostinato patterns; colorful orchestration; chromatic, elegantly ornamented, sequential melodies; free forms; and the occasional use of simple triads.

Martin worked in relative obscurity until 1945, the year of his *Petite symphonie concertante*, still his best-known work. It was commissioned by Paul Sacher, who conducted the first performance in Zurich 17 May 1946. It calls for a variety of string instruments, including bowed strings (the standard orchestral string instruments), those plucked (harp, harpsichord), and those struck by a hammer (piano). The second movement of the two-movement work begins Adagio but moves into a march section by means of Martin's characteristic rhythmic transformation of thematic material.

Martin's strong feeling for instruments and their idiomatic potential is amply illustrated in his concertos and other concertante pieces. For example, four highly diverse instruments are successfully featured in a series of four one-movement Ballades composed from 1938 to 1940—there is one each for alto saxophone, flute, piano, and trombone. The Concerto for Seven Instruments (flute, oboe, clarinet, bassoon, horn, trumpet, and trombone accompanied by strings and percussion, 1949) is of particular interest in that the solo instruments rarely share thematic material; the composer wishes each instrument to stand solidly on its unique qualities.

The Violin Concerto (1950–51), commissioned by the Pro Helvetia Foundation, dedicated to Paul Sacher, and first performed in Paris by Joseph Szigeti under the direction of Ernest Ansermet in 1952, is Martin's best-known solo concerto. Here again he avoids standard forms in preference for freer structures. In its very long Allegro tranquillo first movement the orchestra plays a substantial introduction before the solo instrument enters with a long lyrical line. The latter evolves into a more rhythmic section with double stops in the solo violin. These two ideas alternate through most of the movement, although there is a more lively scherzando section in the middle. Following an orchestral climax near the end of the movement, the violin reappears in a long, demanding cadenza. The final pages of the movement are quite calm, and conclude in E minor. The darker second movement, Andante molto moderato, is songful and features the violin in its very high register near the close against active, lower string parts. Brass and timpani play an important role in the energetic Presto finale, which follows the second movement without pause. The finale begins with a propulsive rhythmic idea in the violins and a distinctive theme of ascending fourths (Ex. 25-3). Both ideas reappear frequently in the movement to propel a strong forward momentum.

Ex. 25-3. Martin, Violin Concerto; III. Presto, mm. 1–6.

At the age of seventy-nine Martin composed his most demanding and hardest-driving concerto. The pungent Piano Concerto No. 2 (1968–69) was written for Paul Badura-Skoda (b. 1927), who gave the first performance as part of the Holland Festival in June 1970 at the Hague. Although the piano clearly dominates in the first movement after the timpani introduction, other solo instruments also appear in a long fugal passage initiated by the alto saxophone. The middle Lento movement is in the form of a passacaglia, its theme first stated by the piano and low strings. The bright, Presto finale is spectacularly difficult.

This extraordinarily productive and competent composer also wrote concertos for harpsichord (1952–53) and cello (1965–66).

André Jolivet (1905–1974), Parisian by birth, spent most of his active career in the French capital. For a short time he studied with the innovative Edgar Varèse (1883–1965). Varèse's most obvious impact on Jolivet resulted in the younger composer's fondness for percussion instruments and his interest in experimenting with new sounds. The latter is well demonstrated by the Concerto for Ondes Martenot (1948), an early electronic instrument. With one hand, the player of this instrument selects a single pitch on a keyboard (only one pitch may be sounded at a time), while the other hand controls aspects of the sound, including its timbre and dynamic level. A good player may also create a vibrato by wiggling the keys slightly from side to side. Jolivet fully exploited the instrument's great dynamic and pitch range in this concerto. The first movement is active; the second uses powerful, *Rite of Spring*–inspired rhythms; and the third provides a peaceful conclusion in D major.

Percussion instruments, which always played a major role in his music, are singled out in the Percussion Concerto (1958), and are particularly important in the Trumpet Concerto No. 2 (1954) and the Piano Concerto (1950). In the latter, the piano joins the elaborate percussion section from time to time. The Piano Concerto and the Trumpet Concerto No. 2 also depend heavily upon exotic musical elements. Jazz elements, often used by Jolivet, enliven the Trumpet Concerto, while melodic and rhythmic patterns typical of the music of different regions of the world color the Piano Concerto—Central Africa in movement I, the Far East in II, and Polynesia in III.

In 1936 Jolivet, together with Yves Baudrier (1906–1988), Daniel Lesur (b. 1908), and Olivier Messiaen (1908–1992), formed the group La Jeune France. It was dedicated to reviving and promoting French music by reintroducing values felt to be lacking in much contemporary music. At the time the group opposed the revolutionary ideas of the twentieth century, and Jolivet, in particular, eschewed "systems" or other "academic" approaches to composition. He sought to make music more human and less abstract. He viewed music as a cosmic force with magical powers capable of casting a spell. This view led him to create very rhythmic, harmonically free music for several years. But following World War II such adventurous undertakings were tempered by a return to more traditional forms. Beginning in 1948 he composed an extensive series of virtuoso concertos, concluding with the Violin Concerto of 1972.

One of the earliest was for flute (1949), accompanied by string orchestra. Jolivet perceived the flute as a particularly important instrument because of its common and central role in primitive music. The work is in an unusual form consisting of two movements, each divided into a slow introduction and fast main part. The Piano Concerto, noted above in connection with its strong dependence upon percussion instruments, is a violent and agitated work that excited audience protest at its first performance.

The Concertino for Trumpet, Piano and Strings (1948) is a much more attractive piece, and is probably his most commonly played work. The piano has only a short solo section near the end; for the rest, it substitutes for the percussion section in this rhythmically lively piece. The work is a loose set of five variations, all but the fourth in lively tempos. This intimate and immediately appealing tonal composition must have provided a strong and startling contrast to the highly theatrical dodecaphonic First Piano Concerto of Hans Werner Henze (b. 1926) when both were performed on the same International Society of Contemporary Music Festival program in Oslo, 1953.

Jolivet's Trumpet Concerto No. 2 (1954) depends heavily on the idiom of jazz. It recalls, in many respects, one of the earliest, jazz-inspired classical works—Darius Milhaud's *La Création du monde* (1923)—with its prominent use of saxophones and percussion and its polytonality. The small ensemble calls for two flutes, clarinet, English horn, two saxophones, piano, double bass, and fourteen percussion instruments. The solo trumpet sets the jazz tone using a wah-wah mute in the introduction. The following dance sounds much like Milhaud's work, with its Latin American dance rhythm and prominent saxophones and percussion. The lyrical Grave slow movement has bluesy overtones and the Giocoso finale contains earthy trombone smears and a solo percussion passage in the middle.

Jolivet's last three concertos are all for string instruments, but percussion instruments feature prominently in two of them—the energetic Cello Concerto No. 1 (1962) and the passionate Violin Concerto (1972). The quietly intense Second Cello Concerto (1966), written for Rostropovich, is scored for strings only.

Henri Dutilleux (b. 1916), like so many French composers of the past two centuries, studied at the Paris Conservatory, later assuming a teaching position there. And like most French composers of his generation, he was influenced by Debussy and Ravel. Upon that foundation he developed a style that, in his words, emphasizes the "careful avoidance of prefabricated formal scaffolding, with an evident predilection for the spirit of variation."[3] In keeping with his French heritage, he clearly treasures sonority for its own sake—beyond any meaning given it by melody or harmony. Dutilleux has not been a prolific composer, but several of his orchestral works have won considerable critical acclaim.

The Concerto for Violin, *L'Arbre des songes* (The Tree of Dreams, 1985), was commissioned by Radio France for Isaac Stern and was dedicated to the violinist. In preparation for its composition, the composer reviewed much of the virtuosic violin literature, concluding that he could not, nor did he wish to, write a typical virtuoso concerto. He endeavored to make the solo instrument and orchestra more dependent upon one another. He also turned his back on the standard division of a concerto into movements separated by pauses; his Violin Concerto is made up of four main sections linked by interludes, the latter dominated by the orchestra.

The lyricism of the violin is often set against a group of "ringing" percussion instruments, the core of which includes chimes, vibraphone, piano, and celesta, with harp and antique cymbals added from time to time. This generally concertante-like pitting of a part of the orchestra against the rest of the ensemble characterizes much of Dutilleux's work. To create specific instrumental colors, he uses the archaic oboe d'amore in the slow third part and occasionally brings in the cimbalom, that dulcimer-like instrument put into action earlier by Bartók and a few other composers. Dutilleux's exquisite sense of the unique quality of each instrument and of how to feature them leads to a sensuous musical experience. One unusual passage in the final section creatively imitates an orchestra tuning.

The composer has explained that the title of the work, *The Tree of Dreams*, was inspired by the music, not vice versa, for he has generally avoided program music. He considered the work had developed as a tree, "because trees have a lyricism whose ramifications keep multiplying and are constantly renewed."[4] The periodic return of thematic material, stated by the "ringing" percussion instruments, seems to relate to the notion of dreams.

Stern first played the piece with the Orchestre National de France under Lorin Maazel on 15 November 1985 in Paris. The work won the *Prix de la Critique musicale*. In 1970 Rostropovich commissioned a work for cello and orchestra from Dutilleux. This demanding and sensuous work is in five sections played without pause. The title, *Tout un monde lointain* . . . (All a world distant . . .), is taken from Baudelaire.

ITALY

Although the concerto had its beginnings in Italy, most Italian composers of the latter part of the eighteenth century and throughout the nineteenth paid little attention to the form, concentrating instead on opera. Interest in instrumental music faded to such an extent that the history of Italian Romantic music is largely a history of Italian Romantic opera. But in the twentieth century some Italian composers have returned to instrumental music. The roots of the revival of interest in instrumental music are found in the works of Giuseppe Martucci (1856–1909), who composed two concertos for piano (D minor, 1878; B-flat minor, 1885), neither of which is performed today.

Alfredo Casella (1883–1947), encouraged by Martucci, became the central figure of the Italian instrumental music renaissance, forming the Società Italiana di Musica Moderna in 1917 to promote modern Italian instrumental music. Casella and the three most significant members of his society—Malipiero, Castelnuovo-Tedesco, and Respighi—each made minor contributions to the concerto.

Casella ultimately developed a personal, neo-Classical style, characterized by clear linear textures and driving rhythms. He was an outstanding pianist; although he wrote no full-fledged piano concerto, he did compose several other types of concertante works for piano and orchestra, including the interesting *Scarlattiana* (1926) based on themes taken from the works of the great eighteenth-century Italian composer of harpsichord music, Domenico Scarlatti (1685–1757). Among Casella's half-dozen concertos is a Violin Concerto in A Minor (1928), composed for Joseph Szigeti, who played the work frequently.

Gian Francesco Malipiero (1882–1973) is a composer perhaps best known for his scholarship through which he helped Italians discover the diversity of their musical past. In addition to his work on Vivaldi, noted in Chapter 4, Malipiero edited Monteverdi's complete works. This musicologist also composed six piano concertos and concertos for other instruments, including a unique one for violin and baritone voice (1959–60) in six movements.

Mario Castelnuovo-Tedesco (1895–1968) wrote a number of concertos of which the tuneful Concerto for Guitar, Op. 99 (1939), composed for Segovia, is still performed.

Ottorino Respighi (1879–1936), the master composer of impressionistic tone poems, wrote several concertos, including the Concerto Gregoriano for Violin (1922), which used Gregorian melodies in the final two movements, and the Concerto in the Mixolydian Mode for Piano (1925).

Luigi Dallapiccola (1904–1975) and **Goffredo Petrassi** (b. 1904) led the next generation of Italian composers. Dallapiccola, noted for his sensitive adoption of the twelve-tone method, paid little attention to the concerto. On the other hand, from 1933 to 1972 Petrassi wrote several, including his Piano Concerto (1936–39), Flute Concerto (1960), and a series of eight intriguing works, each titled Concerto for Orchestra. These concertos for orchestra not only illustrate the wide stylistic variety of Petrassi's music, but also constitute a veritable catalog of the changing styles of the century. The earliest from 1933 and 1934, strongly influenced by Stravinsky's neo-Classicism, weaves plainsong and other early Italian musical elements into its fabric. The sixth concerto, called *Invenzione concertata* (Concerted Invention, 1956–57), is a twelve-tone work for brass, strings, and an unusually large and varied percussion section. No. 7, *Prologo e 5 invenzioni* (Prologue and Five Inventions, 1961–62, revised 1964) is a freely atonal and athematic work which focuses on the exploration of a different orchestral coloration in each of the six sections. The final Concerto for Orchestra (1970–72) returns to triadic structures and a variety of scale structures.

Bruno Maderna (1920–1973), **Luciano Berio** (b. 1925), and **Luigi Nono** (b. 1924) guided the next generation. Nono has neglected the concerto, while his colleagues have paid only moderate attention to the form. Maderna and Berio were closely associated for many years and have played a major role in shaping the music of twentieth-century Italy. Maderna attended several of the International Summer Music Courses in Darmstadt, Germany, beginning in 1951. These courses, established in 1946 when the city was still in ruins, brought together many of Europe's most promising young composers, not only to learn more about composition but also to listen to, analyze, and perform new music. The powerfully influential conductor Hermann Scherchen (1891–1966) taught there in the early 1950s; he championed the music of Webern, which he saw as the wave of the future. Many young composers who attended these summer courses ultimately adopted the pointillistic serial style of Webern, largely as a result of Scherchen's overwhelming impact. Maderna was joined in 1954 by Berio, who had already been introduced to the serial method of composition by Dallapiccola, and both followed the lead of Scherchen.

Eventually, though, Berio was one of the first of his generation to break with orthodox serialism, but paradoxically the very stimulation of serialism may have led him away from his previous path. The first divergence was evident with Berio's and Maderna's establishment of the first electronic music studio in Italy in 1955. Simultaneously they inaugurated a series of concerts devoted to new music, Incontri Musicali, and founded a journal of the same name. Next, as was the case with several other composers of the 1950s and 1960s who had adopted the serial style, they became increasingly aware of the choices they faced in establishing the various series in a composition, which in turn led to their decision to incorporate aleatory or chance elements into their work.

Maderna's earliest published concerto is his neo-Baroque Concerto for Two Pianos (1948), composed prior to his visits to Darmstadt. His Piano Concerto (1959) involves, among other unusual elements, the slamming of the piano's lid at an orchestral climax, while his three oboe concertos (1962, 1967, 1973) incorporate a number of aleatory elements along with highly expressive writing for the oboe. The Violin Concerto (1973) includes various aleatory options in the orchestral accompaniment.

Berio, although he had a predilection for the voice and was frequently inspired by literary texts, also made some interesting contributions to the instrumental concerto. His large Concerto for Two Pianos and Orchestra (1972–73) strongly contrasts with the series of smaller *Chemins* for solo instrument and small ensembles. The *Chemins* are ensemble settings of several of Berio's *Sequenzas*, which were composed for a number of unaccompanied solo instruments over the years 1957–75. For example, *Chemins* II (1967) is the same as *Sequenza* VI (1967) for solo viola, except that an ensemble of ten other instruments (flute, clarinet, trombone, electric organ, harp, marimba, vibraphone, gong, viola, and cello) accompany the viola in *Chemins* II. The work focuses on changing colors and textures.

GERMANY

Ferrucio Busoni (1866–1924) was Italian-born, of mixed Italian and German heritage. He spent his early years in Italy and, after touring and teaching in various musical centers of the world, settled in Berlin in 1894, where he spent the remainder of his life. Busoni was a master pianist with an international reputation as a virtuoso almost as great as that of Franz Liszt. And like Liszt, Busoni made piano transcriptions of the works of other composers, but, anticipating the Back-to-Bach movement and the neo-Classical interest in Baroque music, Busoni's transcriptions were largely confined to Bach's music. These transcriptions remain quite controversial for they markedly distort the textures and phrasing of the originals. Busoni also followed in Liszt's footsteps by championing the work of contemporary composers; he conducted the first performances of works by Bartók, Sibelius, and others, but, curiously, did not perform any of their piano music.

Busoni composed the one-movement Violin Concerto (1896–97) made up of several sections and a very large five-movement Piano Concerto in C major (1903–04). The latter is a late Romantic work, calling for a huge orchestra and, in the final movement, a male choir singing a German translation of a poem by the

Dane, Adam Gottlob Öhlenschläger (1779–1850). The finale also repeats themes first introduced in earlier movements. Busoni seemed to stress his Italian heritage in this work; all movement titles are Italian and the penultimate movement is an Italian dance. Busoni's last concertante work is the Concertino for Clarinet (1919). Its limited nature, both in length and resources, mark it as neo-Classical.

Richard Strauss (1864–1949), the master composer of opera and tone poems, devoted little attention to the concerto, although he composed four concertos and four other works for soloist and orchestra. He wrote the two earliest concertos before he turned twenty—the Violin Concerto (1880–82) and Horn Concerto No. 1 (1882–83). The last two, Horn Concerto No. 2 (1942) and the Oboe Concerto (1945, revised 1948) are works of his last years, when his creative powers declined and he returned to a more conservative approach. These two later works, nevertheless, still possess a sufficient measure of Strauss's melodic and instrumental genius to warrant their inclusion in the contemporary concerto repertory, although they are only occasionally performed now. Horn Concerto No. 2 is of special interest because that instrument so attracted the composer, whose father was principal hornist in the Munich Court Orchestra. The other concertante works include three for piano, two of which were written for the left-handed Paul Wittgenstein—*Parergon zur Symphonia domestica* (1924), and *Panathenäenzug* (1927), symphonic etudes in the form of a passacaglia. The former is a companion piece to Strauss's tone poem, *Symphonia domestica* (1902–03), only in that it uses a principal theme from the earlier work. The latter takes its title from a festival of ancient Athens, which climaxed in a brilliant procession. There is also the very late Duett-Concertino for clarinet and bassoon with an accompaniment of strings and harp (1947).

Max Reger (1873–1916), who adopted the highly chromatic but thoroughly tonal musical language of post-Romantic composers, wrote two large concertos, one each for violin and piano, and two romances for violin and orchestra. The concertos differ markedly from one another in mood and in the integration of the solo instrument and orchestra. The Violin Concerto in A Major, Op. 101 (1908) is longer and brighter than the stormy Piano Concerto in F Minor, Op. 114 (1910). The Violin Concerto's first movement includes a full-fledged orchestral ritornello with a multitude of themes, whereas the Piano Concerto brings in the solo instrument after only a short orchestral introduction, and the thematic development is more concentrated. Both works make great demands on the soloists, but in the Piano Concerto the solo instrument appears more frequently. Reger's characteristic keyboard style, involving many passages in double octaves and dense chords, permits the piano to dominate the sometimes heavily scored orchestra.

Boris Blacher (1903–1975) formulated a very personal style within the framework of tonality. His concertos were more adventurous than Reger's. His bright, generally cheerful music often incorporated a unique rhythmic process calling for systematic changes of meter that he dubbed "variable meters." In this approach, the meter is changed every measure, resulting in constantly shifting accents. Quite typically, as in the Second Piano Concerto, Op. 42 (1952), Blacher establishes a number of kinds of repetitive patterns. In the Moderato middle movement each metrical pattern starts with two units, and expands and contracts by single increments in continually broadening symmetrical groups, for example:

2–3–2–3–4–3–2–3–4–5–4–3–2–3–4–5–6–5–4–3–2, etc.

The solo instrument opens the movement, its phrasing making the coincidence of metrical construction and melodic construction obvious (Ex. 25-4).

Ex. 25-4. Blacher, Piano Concerto; II. Moderato, mm. 1–15.

The first movement proceeds in other intricate patterns of variable meter. The rhythmically propulsive finale, Molto vivace, is largely built around a recurring 4–3–4–5 pattern. Its more consistent rhythmic quality gives the movement a dancelike character.

Hans Werner Henze (b. 1926), one of the most gifted composers of twentieth-century Germany, is easily the most important contemporary German composer of concertos. Henze was a student of Wolfgang Fortner (b. 1907), who first introduced him to the music of Stravinsky, Bartók, and Hindemith. Fortner later introduced Henze to the Darmstadt Summer School where he was so taken by the serialism of Schoenberg and Webern that he went to Paris to study with René Leibowitz (1913–1972), who had devoted himself to the thorough analysis of many twelve-tone works.

In 1953 Henze moved to Italy, where he soon established his quite personal, eclectic style. He gave up strict serialism in favor of a freer, more expressive approach, somewhat in the manner of Alban Berg. Henze has a special proclivity for writing lyrically for the voice; when combined with his natural flair for drama, this talent yielded some of this century's most widely heralded operas. In the mid-1960s he developed a strong interest in socialist communism, which crystallized during a year-long stay in Cuba, 1969–70. As a consequence, his vocal works were increasingly based on political texts, delivered in a musical language calculated to be more accessible by referring to tonality. Henze was a pioneer of his generation in the return to a tonal basis.

Henze is one of the rare twentieth-century composers who, although associated at one time with modern approaches to composition, continued to work within traditional genres, including opera, symphony, and concerto. His strongest works depend upon elements derived from diverse sources: the rhythmic vitality of Stravinsky and Bartók, the expressiveness of Berg, the lyricism of Italian opera, and a scintillating use of the orchestral instruments that he probably acquired from French music. All these elements are used in the concertos, and like the concertos of another great musical dramatist, Mozart, Henze's reveal his dramatic genius.

Henze's earliest concertos, the Chamber Concerto for Piano, Flute, and Strings (1946), the Concertino for Piano, Winds, and Percussion (1947), and Violin Concerto No. 1 (1947), are student works in a conservative neo-Classical style, although a twelve-tone series appears tentatively in the Violin Concerto. Henze's creative attention was focused on opera and other forms of vocal music during the next twenty years, but in the late 1960s he turned to the concerto as a prime creative vehicle.

The intimate *Doppio Concerto* for oboe, harp, and strings (1966) was commissioned by Paul Sacher for the brilliant oboist, Heinz Holliger, and his talented wife Ursula Holliger, harpist. It is in a single movement, based upon a design inspired by the "doubles" found in eighteenth-century French harpsichord suites. In some of the dance movements, doubles, or variants, usually in a faster-moving series of notes, were presented after both strains of the original dance had been played. The form becomes ABA'B'. In Henze's *Doppio Concerto* this form becomes:

> Allegro
> Andante
> Reprise (variant of Allegro)
> Coda (variant of Andante)

It is a beautifully lyrical work in which the solo instruments are given the principal responsibility for presenting thematic material; the eighteen solo string instruments making up the orchestra help to develop it. It is a thoroughly modern work incorporating the then-very-new technique of multiphonics, the simultaneous sounding of more than one pitch on a wind instrument.

His Double Bass Concerto (1966) was followed by the very large Second Piano Concerto (1967), a demanding, forty-five-minute, one-movement work written for Christoph Eschenbach. In the latter, sections in strict form are placed against others in free form; some sections are clearly thematic, while others tend toward the atmospheric. The piece is in three large parts. Part I is largely in Moderato tempo in which material first presented in the piano is developed and expanded. Part II, Vivace, consists of several shorter segments arranged in the order ABCDBA. The third, with its many changes of tempo, incorporates a soulful Lento that is the emotional core of the work. The latter was inspired by a phrase from Shakespeare's Sonnet 129, "The expense of spirit in a waste of shame/ Is lust in action."

Henze's next concertos are more theatrical, and two call for the playing of prepared electric tapes coordinated with the live performance. Concerto No. 2 for Solo Violin, Electric Tape, and Thirty-Three Instruments (1971) includes the recitation of a poem by the German socialist Hans Magnus Enzensberger, which uses the image of Baron Münchhausen, a German legendary figure known as a teller of tall tales. The soloist's entry on the stage in measure 5 establishes the theatrical mood; Henze indicates in the score, "The violinist enters hastily. He is wearing a tricorn hat with feather, and a flowing red lined opera cape." The violinist is asked to perform in the spirit of Baron Münchhausen, humorously making several false starts before finally playing his first note. A few measures after entering the stage "the violinist takes off coat and hat," then "raises violin to chin," "puts bow to strings," but "lowers arm with bow" as a tape starts to play a recording of the poem, sung by a male voice in quarter tones. The violin's eventual entry provides a clear example of the integration of an element of indeterminacy, as the rhythm is only suggested with unique notational symbols (Ex. 25-5) while the pitches are precisely indicated. The soloist, while playing the violin, is also asked to recite parts of the poem through a neck microphone. If the soloist is unable to do so, a tape of the poem is played.

Ex. 25-5. Henze, Violin Concerto No. 2; II. Teorema, m. 1.

A cadenza for the solo violin accompanied by a solo trombone introduces improvisational elements used by Henze and other composers of this era. The pitches the two instruments are to play are indicated, but their duration and many other aspects of articulation are left to the performers to determine. The violinist is instructed to play his notes "very lively, excited, giving each note a different value; constant change of colour," while the trombonist is "freely accompanying solo violin, also following its dynamics."

This concerto is in many respects an excellent example of the avant-garde music of the early 1970s. The musical techniques of the period included a variety of new elements, and here we find all manner of diverse ingredients: theatrical effects, a spoken poem, prepared tape, electrical amplification of instrumental parts, an abundance of exotic percussion instruments, prepared piano (pieces of paper and rubber are inserted between specified strings to alter the sound), rhythmic indeterminacy, and graphic notation to illustrate improvisational sounds.

Tristan: Preludes for Piano, Electronic Tape, and Orchestra (1973), commissioned by the London Symphony Orchestra, is based on elements of Wagner's opera *Tristan und Isolde*. It is a six-part concerto-style work for piano, in which elements of the concerto blend with those of solo piano music, electronic tape music, the tone poem, and orchestral music. The final section, Epilogue, includes a taped heartbeat and a few lines of English text poignantly recited by a child. The text, inspired by the conclusion of Wagner's opera, reads: "She takes him in her arms and then lying out full length, she kisses his face and lips and clasps him tightly to her, Then straining body to body, mouth to mouth, she at once gives up her spirit and of sorrow for her lover dies thus at his side."

Henze has written at least one other theatrically inspired concerto-style composition for clarinet and thirteen players, entitled *Le Miracle de la Rose* (1981). He has repeatedly proved himself a leader in incorporating avant-garde techniques into the concerto, while simultaneously maintaining the integrity of the form—this by carefully preserving the dynamic balance between the solo instrument and orchestra.

CZECHOSLOVAKIA, HUNGARY, AND POLAND

Leoš Janáček (1854–1928), Dvořák's Moravian friend, assumed the role of the region's foremost composer following the death of Dvořák in 1904. Janáček, strongly influenced by Moravian folk music, developed a highly personal style relying on the repetition of succinct melodic and rhythmic ideas. His Concertino for Piano, Two Violins, Viola, Clarinet, Horn, and Bassoon (1925) is more a piece of chamber music than a true concerto, for while the piano is featured, the other instruments play leading roles in all four movements. For example, the horn reiterates a short motive in movement I, while the clarinet is given important solo passages in the second movement. The composer's letter to a friend reveals a humorous, light-hearted programmatic interpretation of the work.

Bohuslav Martinů (1890–1959), Czechoslovakia's leading and most prolific composer of the first half of the twentieth century, was taught by Dvořák's finest student, Josef Suk (1874–1935). Martinů was at first caught up in Czech folk music, but like many other composers of the period was deeply influenced by cultural developments in Paris. A small scholarship allowed him to travel to Paris in 1923, where he remained for seventeen years, despite living in relative poverty. The neo-Classical style dominated the Parisian musical scene and Martinů's music took on typical neo-Classical traits. His study of the work of Baroque composers, especially the concerti grossi of Corelli and Vivaldi, led him to adopt several Baroque stylistic elements, including a clear toccata style with its accompanying rhythmic vitality. Martinů also developed a love affair with the concerto grosso; many of his more than thirty concertos or concertante works involve more than one solo instrument.

Martinů's works in neo-Classical or neo-Baroque Parisian style include the Concerto for String Quartet and Orchestra (1931). The latter grew out of a postconcert get-together in Montparnasse, during which members of the Pro Arte Quartet encouraged the composer to undertake the work. In spite of Martinů's turn to neo-Classicism, the finale testifies to his continuing fascination with folk music. The Concerto Grosso (1937), scored for two pianos and string orchestra, is a strongly contrapuntal work in which the pianos often provide a very elaborate but modern version of a basso continuo.

The second concertino, the Concertino for Piano Trio and String Orchestra (1933), pits the classical chamber ensemble of piano, violin, and cello against an orchestra, as in Beethoven's Triple Concerto, but the effect is not reminiscent of Beethoven, for the approach is so markedly neo-Baroque. Much of the writing for the solo violin in the first movement, with its highly syncopated and rhythmic multiple stops, closely resembles passages for the solo violin in Stravinsky's *L'Histoire du Soldat* (The Soldier's Tale, 1918), an early neo-Classical masterpiece. In the second movement the piano holds forth effectively against the other solo instruments in several passages. The third movement, Adagio, opens with a series of strange harmonies in double stops on the solo string instruments. The final, fourth movement has that transparent clarity so characteristic of neo-Classical music. Sharing this same transparent quality is the composer's Sinfonietta Giocosa for piano and small orchestra (1940). Several of these concertos are in four movements, probably reflecting Martinů's interest in the early Baroque concerto grosso.

With the Nazis' occupation of France, Martinů sought quieter, safer surroundings, making his way to the United States, where he remained from 1941 to 1953. So far removed from his native background, he turned to a more Romantic style and the extensive use of Czech folk-inspired materials. A comparison of the neo-Classical Violin Concerto No. 1 (1930) with the neo-Romantic Violin Concerto No. 2 (1943) clearly reveals these differences. The effective and very demanding solo violin part of the Second Concerto, with numerous double stops, is conceived in the Romantic virtuoso tradition. The Poco Allegro finale, based on Czech dance rhythms, contrasts sharply with the songful middle Andante moderato in $\frac{6}{8}$ time. The First Concerto has a more intimate scale, bears little or no evidence of Czech folk influence, and makes extensive use of the typical, transparent, neo-Classical textures, in contrast to the lusher, more Romantic textures of the second.

Martinů returned to Europe for the last six years of his life, during which he continued to write in his favorite form, the concerto. It is a shame that so much of this very prolific composer's music has fallen out of favor. He did rely heavily on repetition and passage work, but his music has a rhythmic and instrumental vitality that maintains interest, just as does that of his favorite Baroque composers. The attractive combinations of various instruments, and, on occasion, engaging melodic material make several of these works worth exploring; many would be particularly suitable for talented university musicians.

György Ligeti (b. 1923) has become the foremost Hungarian-born composer since Bartók. Ligeti is one of those many radical composers born in the 1920s who were drawn to the music of Anton von Webern in the 1950s. He saw in Webern's fragmented lines the foundation of a new kind of texture in which the individual lines congealed to form static masses of sound. Beginning in the late 1950s Ligeti developed a style focused on musical texture, virtually eliminating any sense of individual lines or colors. This elemental material consists largely of sustained chromatic chord clusters, or figures that enliven sustained sounds, scored for a large orchestra. A limited sense of forward movement is created through the interaction of different masses of sound, as they merge, dissolve, or collide. Ligeti referred to this texture as "micropolyphony." The process is relatively simple, and the results can be effective but unnerving to the listener accustomed to a more conventional emphasis on melody and harmony. Ligeti's music can, however, elicit attention in other ways; for example, the vacillation between periods of calm and activity, or the sheer concentration on sonority for its own sake can lead to effective results. By the late 1960s the composer modified the technique to allow the separate lines to stand out slightly more clearly, but the general sense remained much the same.

His concertos are certainly far from conventional. The Chamber Concerto for Thirteen Players (1969–70) was composed for the Viennese avant-garde chamber ensemble, *Die Reihe*. According to the composer, the term *concerto* was chosen not to indicate any relationship between soloists and tutti, but to indicate that all parts are virtuosic. The twenty-one-minute work is in four movements, beginning in a gentle, flowing manner and ending in a sort of perpetuum mobile with snatches of melody seeming to emerge out of nowhere, but then disappearing. The Double Concerto for Flute and Oboe (1971–72) is a bit closer to the normal idea of a concerto, in that it calls for two true soloists who interact with an orchestra. In the first of the two movements, the soloists and woodwinds in the orchestra produce microtones by means of unconventional fingering and blowing techniques. The score calls for no violins in the orchestra; only violas, cellos, and basses make up the string section and do much to create the serene mood, thanks to the steady projection of special bowings and harmonics. The flute part in this movement is written first for an alto flute, then for bass flute. The two soloists take the lead in the gradual changes of pitch that characterize the movement, but they do not really stand apart from the orchestra. The second movement becomes much brighter, in part because the flute player discards the bass flute in favor of the standard flute, and in part because the soloists are more independent of the orchestra.

Ligeti's most radical scores were neither performed nor published in Hungary during the Stalinist period, a period marked by the Communist party's all-pervasive and oppressive grip on all aspects of society within the Eastern block. It was not until 1956, when Ligeti moved to Vienna, that he was finally able to hear performances of the newer Western music and to have his own music performed.

The situation for young composers in Hungary continued to be grim following Stalin's death in 1953, but it was quite different in Poland where a great renaissance of new music composition took place. Poland became a leading center of modern music-making in Europe.

Witold Lutoslawski (b. 1913) led the way with an amazing variety of styles. Lutoslawski's earliest works reflect the strong influence of Bartók and eastern European folkloric elements. This is particularly the case in what is probably his best-known composition, the Concerto for Orchestra (1950–54). It was written not only to pay homage to Bartók's Concerto for Orchestra but also to give the young musicians of the Warsaw Philharmonic Orchestra a chance to display their talents. The work is in three movements. The first is a symmetrical structure of seven sections, not unlike many of Bartók's movements, opening and closing over a sustained F-sharp pedal point. The Capriccio notturno ed arioso second movement places an angular arioso melody in brass in the middle section surrounded by rapidly moving, quiet figures in the outer sections, slightly reminiscent of Bartók's "Night Music." The finale is an elaborate series of variations on a theme (Ex. 25-6) first used as a basis for a Passacaglia. It also appears, transformed, in the succeeding Toccata and Chorale which close the movement. As in much of Bartók's music, an important thematic recollection occurs in the finale; here it is the second theme of the first movement.

Ex. 25-6. Lutoslawski, Concerto for Orchestra; III. Passacaglia, Toccata, and Chorale, mm. 1–8.

With the lifting of the governmental ban on atonality in the late 1950s, Lutoslawski was among the first of the Polish composers to experiment with the twelve-tone system. Shortly thereafter, a performance of John Cage's Concert for Piano (1957–58) kindled Lutoslawski's interest in indeterminacy, while at about the same time he became fascinated with athematic music somewhat along the lines of Ligeti. Blocks of sound, rhythm, and texture became dominant elements in his

"Limited Aleatory Music," in which the performer could improvise, usually rhythmically, within set limits. The pitches of all parts are precisely notated, but rhythms are improvised in what Lutoslawski called "aleatory counterpoint." The Cello Concerto (1970), for Rostropovich, includes examples of "aleatory counterpoint" and pits the cellist against the orchestra in a highly dramatic way. It is an exciting work of many varied moods.

Lutoslawski continued to refine his aleatory counterpoint, which led to such interesting results as those found in his Double Concerto for Oboe and Harp (1980), written for Heinz and Ursula Holliger, the same musicians for whom Henze wrote his similar *Doppio Concerto*. After an orchestral introduction, the two soloists play in a cadenza in which the two parts are totally independent; indeed, the score includes the instruction that they should not be coordinated. Throughout the concerto, the soloists enjoy a rhythmic freedom the orchestra does not normally share. The Double Concerto is scored for an orchestra consisting of strings and a large percussion section; the total absence of winds from the orchestra makes the solo instruments stand out nicely. The work is in three movements: Rapsodico, Dolente, and Marciale e grotesco.

Krzysztof Penderecki (b. 1933), the best known twentieth-century Polish composer, aroused great interest when he submitted three compositions under different pseudonyms to the Polish Composers' Union Competition in 1959, and all three won first prizes in their respective categories. Like other composers discussed in this chapter, his style focuses on sound and dense tone clusters, often involving mass glissandi and new techniques of producing sound on conventional instruments, perhaps inspired by the growth of electronic music. These aspects of his style were widely imitated during the 1960s. In the 1970s Penderecki gradually altered his approach, and as has been the case with many composers of his and the subsequent generation, he developed a neo-Romantic approach incorporating more conventional elements such as identifiable tunes and tonality. Many composers of the 1970s and 1980s felt the need to resort to traditional musical practices to make their music both more expressive and more accessible. For Penderecki, the search for an emotionally expressive style has been a continuing concern. The music of this deeply mystical composer has always had a profound emotional component, and his series of gripping works based on religious texts has enjoyed particular success.

Penderecki's Violin Concerto (1974–76), for Isaac Stern, is a prime example of the revival of the Romantic tradition within the late twentieth century. It is in a single, long movement of approximately forty minutes' duration, based on the broad outlines of sonata-allegro form interrupted by a short scherzando between the development and recapitulation sections. The overall mood is dark and sorrowful, maintained by repeated references to a descending sigh motive (x) found at the end of the main theme (Ex. 25-7a). This motive is immediately transformed into a slower rhythmic setting (Ex. 25-7b), taking on the qualities of a dirge or lament in its numerous repetitions. The repetitions are evocative in their own right, however, as this small motive and the opening of the theme are developed and varied throughout the work. The scherzando section, although very brief, provides some relief from this lament and the feeling of all-pervading gloom, thanks to its mixed march and Viennese waltz motive. The work is cast in the Romantic virtuoso tradition so the violin functions within those conventions, establishing its lyrical presence immediately upon entering after a short orchestral introduction. The soloist plays almost constantly and is highlighted in two cadenzas, incorporating traditional virtuosic details. Isaac Stern first played the concerto with the Basle Symphony Orchestra under Moshe Atzmon on 7 April 1977.

Ex. 25-7. Penderecki, Violin Concerto: (a.) mm. 6–7; (b.) m. 8.

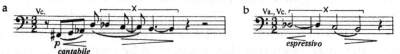

Penderecki also wrote the large one-movement Cello Concerto (1982) for Rostropovich and the smaller one-movement Viola Concerto (1983) for José Vasquez.

LATIN AMERICA

The music of the Latin American composers of the early part of the twentieth century has been quite folkloric in orientation, although some composers have adopted modern techniques often blended with folkloric elements.

Heitor Villa-Lobos (1887–1959), Brazil's foremost composer, wrote at least a thousand works of uneven quality in which the folkloric element is often intermingled with neo-Classical elements, most especially those associated with one of his favorite composers, J. S. Bach. Villa-Lobos's concertos come from the last phase of his career (1945–1959) when he turned to the writing of virtuosic works in the larger forms. His concertos are generally acknowledged to lack any lasting significance; the only one still occasionally performed is the Concerto for Guitar and Small Orchestra (1951). It was originally conceived as a one-movement fantasia, but the great Spanish guitarist Andrés Segovia (1893–1987) convinced the composer to turn it into a full-fledged concerto with a cadenza between the second and third movements. As is typical of his later works, the concerto contains no quotations of actual Brazilian tunes, but the spirit and feel of Brazilian folk music runs throughout. Villa-Lobos composed five piano concertos, all in four movements—two for his own instrument, the cello; and a concerto each for harp and harmonica.

Alberto Ginastera (1916–1983) composed works firmly based on the folk music of his native Argentina until about 1954. As his style evolved to include newer approaches, such as serialism, indeterminacy, and the use of textural masses, the folkloric element faded, although Argentinian dance rhythms remained evident. His few concertos were written during this later period. The First Piano Concerto (1961), commissioned by the Serge Koussevitsky Foundation and dedicated to Serge and Natalie Koussevitsky, was first performed in Washington, D.C. on 22 April 1961 with the National Symphony Orchestra conducted by Howard Mitchell and the pianist João Carlos Martins. It requires a large orchestra, including, as do most of his concertos, a battery of percussion instruments played by five performers. A serial approach emerges in its four unusual movements. In the first, Cadenza e varianti, the orchestra opens with a few measures in sustained chords of steadily increasing volume. The piano answers with improvisatory material virtuosically presented in octaves and full chords. These two ideas alternate, evolve, and grow into a set of ten contrasting variations. The second movement is an extremely rapid Scherzo allucinante with a mysteriously quiet mood, engendered by string harmonics and other delicate pointillistic sounds. This movement may relate to the composer's interest in magic and the supernatural. The lyrical Adagissimo third movement is in ternary form, moving to a passionate climax in the midsection. The tempo is very flexible, intensifying the mood of improvised spontaneity. The spectacular Toccata concertata finale depends for much of its effect on the characteristic and lively Latin American alternation of $\frac{3}{4}$ and $\frac{6}{8}$ time (Ex. 25-8).

Ex. 25-8. Typical Latin American dance rhythm.

Ginastera's Second Piano Concerto (1972) quotes material from the works of earlier composers, a practice common to several composers in the 1970s, as they grasped for a more accessible musical language from the past. The first movement consists of thirty-two variations on the dissonant orchestral chord Beethoven introduced in the finale of his Ninth Symphony just prior to the startling baritone recitative. The chord contains all seven tones of the D harmonic minor scale. A theme from near the end of Chopin's B-flat Minor Sonata appears in the finale. The Violin Concerto (1963) is an extremely demanding work that explores new techniques of playing the instrument. It includes quotations from Paganini's famous Caprices and features all the orchestra's principal players in solo passages in the Adagio. The work is dedicated to its first performers, violinist Ruggiero Ricci, conductor Leonard Bernstein, and the New York Philharmonic Orchestra. Ginastera also composed one concerto each for harp (1956) and cello (1961).

Carlos Chávez (1899–1978) was Mexico's best-known and most influential composer. He was also a gifted conductor who helped to found the Mexican Symphony Orchestra in 1928. In the same year he became director of the National Conservatory of Music in Mexico. Chávez gave the people of Mexico their first exposure to modern music, while he simultaneously exposed the rest of the world to the music of Mexico. He was a cosmopolitan musician, but he built his style upon the native Mexican and Spanish elements of his culture. He befriended Aaron Copland and introduced Mexican music to the American composer on a firsthand basis. Chávez's Concerto for Piano (1938–40) illustrates the composer's highly developed sense of rhythm and his effective use of the orchestra, often in hard-driving percussive ways. His writing for orchestra is as virtuosic as that for the soloist and the two interact on an equal level. It is a large and powerful work in the three standard movements; the middle movement, with its slow-moving lines and chamber music transparency, provides a sharp contrast to the outer movements. The American pianist Eugene List gave the work's premiere in New York City. The later Violin Concerto (1948–50) is in a very unusual form: one movement of approximately thirty-six-minutes' duration, made up of a number of short sections arranged in a strictly symmetrical fashion. The central portion includes nine variants of a brief scherzando theme. At the very center a huge, demanding cadenza interrupts with a constantly fluctuating tempo that creates a strong sense of spontaneity.

CANADA

Although there was much musical activity in the major cities of Canada in the early decades of the twentieth century, orchestral music was of relatively little importance until the founding of professional orchestras in Toronto (1923) and Montreal (1934). Few Canadian composers significantly contributed to orchestral music until the 1940s. The two leading composers of the first half of the century each wrote one concerto.

Healey Willan (1880–1968), an immigrant from England in 1913, brought to Canada the conservative style he had learned in his native country. His important contributions are largely in the fields of organ and sacred choral music, English Renaissance models serving for the latter. His orchestral compositions, on the other hand, are in a Romantic vein and were written later in his career. The Piano Concerto (1944) is a tuneful work in the tradition of Brahms and Elgar. Willan, often referred to as the "Dean of Canadian Composers," held important posts at the Toronto Conservatory of Music and at the University of Toronto where he strongly influenced several composition students.

Claude Champagne (1891–1965) held a similarly prominent position in French-speaking Canada. Champagne was born in Montreal and received his initial musical training there, before traveling to France for further education (1920–28). He found the music of Debussy particularly exciting and noted some similarity between the modal scales common in much French music of the time and French Canadian folk music. He integrated French Canadian folkloric material into his compositions in an effort to create a specifically Canadian music. His appealing impressionistic, programmatic works culminated in his masterwork, *Altitude* (1958–59), stimulated by his first trip to the Canadian Rocky Mountains. The Piano Concerto in D Minor (1948), in a neo-Classical mold, numbers among his very few abstract works.

For the most part, Canadians were exposed to little of the contemporary musical developments in Europe until the 1940s. About this time a group of three Canadian composers—John Weinzweig, Jean Papineau-Couture, and Barbara Pentland—took the lead in appropriating those new stylistic elements, using them to create distinctly modern-sounding works of high quality. In the 1950s several significant developments created a positive climate for the intense growth of contemporary Canadian music. In 1950 the conservative Healey Willan retired as professor of music at the University of Toronto, to be replaced by the more progressive John Weinzweig in that influential position in 1952. Shortly thereafter other young modern composers were appointed to similar positions in several universities across the country. Weinzweig also formed the Canadian League of Composers in 1951 as a support group to help foster new music. Additionally, the

CBC International Services and CBC Symphony provided important new outlets for contemporary music. The Canada Council, founded in 1957, stimulated creative activity in all the arts with supporting grants and commissions, and the Canadian Music Centre was established in 1959 to provide a library of scores, recordings, and other information concerning Canadian music and to promote Canadian music worldwide. The confluence of all these developments led to a remarkable burgeoning of new Canadian music, which, for the most part, has developed along lines parallel to those in Europe and the United States.

John Weinzweig (b. 1913), a native of Toronto, studied with Willan before continuing his studies at the Eastman School of Music in Rochester, New York, in 1937, with Bernard Rogers. There he came into contact with the music of Stravinsky, Schoenberg, Berg, and others, which led him to employ similar elements in his own work. He composed the first twelve-tone work by a Canadian in 1939. Berg's influence seems particularly strong in Weinzweig's Violin Concerto (1951–55), a major work in three movements that combines clear neo-Classical structures and serial techniques in a romantically expressive way. A different tone row occurs in each movement, and the composer confines their use largely to melodic material. Even though the work is serial, it projects a sense of tonality in the harmonic structure. Weinzweig's Piano Concerto (1965–66) is a fascinating serial work in three movements in which the solo instrument and orchestra engage in frequent very short dialogues. This departure from the more usual, lengthier passages for soloist and orchestra is held together by the taut and vigorous development of a four-note motive. Weinzweig's lively rhythmic style adds to the effectiveness of the give-and-take texture. The Concerto for Harp (1967) is in a single movement of six sections. Here the composer explores more recent techniques in which tone color and texture are emphasized over melody and harmony.

Barbara Pentland (b. 1912), like Weinzweig, discovered contemporary music during her studies in the United States in the late 1930s at the Juilliard School of Music. Her early interest in the music of Stravinsky and Hindemith is reflected in her Concerto for Violin and Small Orchestra (1942), written in a neo-Classical style. Her subsequent association with Weinzweig and Dika Newlin, a disciple of Schoenberg, stimulated her to break with tonality in 1949, while attendance at the Darmstadt Summer Course for New Music in 1955 brought her into contact with Webern's work and the music of the young European post-Webernites. Her Concerto for Piano and String Orchestra (1955–56), with its transparent textures and economy of means, is characteristic of this idiom.

Jean Papineau-Couture (b. 1916), the Montreal-born grandson of Guillaume Couture (1851–1915), one of Canada's most important nineteenth-century musical figures, also became acquainted with contemporary developments in the United States. He studied with Nadia Boulanger, who taught in the United States from 1940 to 1946. His Concerto Grosso (1943, rev., 1955) combines Impressionistic sounds with neo-Classical contrapuntal textures and methods of organization. In the 1950s he adopted serial techniques but retained a sense of tonality in much of his music. He remains fascinated with logical organization schemes, a concern well illustrated by a series of five works, titled *Pièces concertantes*, composed over the period 1951–63. No. 1 for piano and strings (1951–52), subtitled "Repliement" (meaning a folding back), splits at the precise middle whereupon the first half of the piece is played in a note-for-note retrograde manner. No. 2 for cello and chamber orchestra (1959) has the name "Eventails" (Fans), which relates to the fanlike changes in density. No. 3 (1959) is a set of variations on a twelve-tone theme and includes a concertino comprised of flute, clarinet, violin, cello, and harp. No. 4, "Additions" for oboe and string orchestra (1959), is based on a mathematical, intervallic scheme; and No. 5, "Miroirs" (Mirrors, 1963), is a concerto for orchestra involving mirror images of melodic and harmonic ideas. The slightly later Piano Concerto (1965) makes use of mirror chords in a single movement of alternating tempos.

Violet Archer (b. 1913), a native of Montreal, was a student of Claude Champagne before studying with two major European composers who had taken up residence in the United States; she was a pupil of Bartók in New York in 1942, and, for a longer period of time, of Paul Hindemith at Yale in 1949. Both composers had a powerful influence on her music, which is strongly contrapuntal, rhythmically aggressive, and exceedingly well crafted, usually within neo-Classical boundaries. Archer's Piano Concerto (1956), composed during her residence at the MacDowell Colony in New Hampshire, is a fine, compact, three-movement work scored for an orchestra of late-eighteenth-century proportions. The finale is a toccata-style scherzando. Her Violin Concerto (1959) is more modern sounding with agitated rhythms in the orchestra contrasting with long lines in the solo instrument. Evocations for Two Pianos and Orchestra (1988) depends heavily upon ethnic music of Canada, including songs of the Inuit of northern Canada and a French Canadian folk song. In the first movement, Fantasy, the composer develops the repeated notes and major and minor triads distinctive of the French Canadian song, "The Owl and the Lemming," with the pianos and other percussion instruments taking particular responsibility for exploring the repeated notes. The middle movement is a nocturne in the style of a barcarole based on an Inuit lullaby, and the frenetic final movement, Primeval Dance, uses the interval of a third and repeated notes of a dance associated with the Inuit. The composer has explained that the title, Evocations, refers to the ethnic music's having evoked these compositional responses. The Timpani Concerto (1939) by the young percussionist-composer and her intimate Clarinet Concertino (1941) are earlier works by one of Canada's foremost composers. Violet Archer has had a significant impact on the music of western Canada since her appointment in 1962 at the University of Alberta, where she has taught composition and has actively promoted contemporary Canadian music.

Norman Symonds (b. 1920) is the most prominent Canadian composer to have embraced jazz elements. Jazz strongly colors his Concerto Grosso for jazz quintet and symphony orchestra (1957) and the *Democratic Concerto* for jazz quartet and orchestra (1967). His *The Nameless Hour* is an introspective interpretation of twilight time that features the soft, warm, but dark sound of the fluegelhorn, and requires the soloist to improvise. The nine-minute piece is in four sections, involving solo improvisation in the inner two.

Jacques Hétu (b. 1938) of Quebec studied with Papineau-Couture and, for a short time, with Olivier Messiaen in France. His music frequently involves the piano, and the Piano Concerto (1969) is typical with its vigorous rhythms, often intensified by active percussion instruments. Striking changes of tempo occur in the first two movements; the third is a motoric Presto from beginning to end.

R. Murray Schafer (b. 1933) is one of Canada's best-known composers. He studied with Weinzweig and with Peter Racine Fricker (b. 1920), a British composer who taught at the University of California in Santa Barbara from 1964 to 1989. Schafer is an eclectic composer of highly diverse compositions, often incorporating avant-garde techniques. His writings about the human relationship to the acoustical environment are immensely provoking, and his music often takes one by surprise. He has composed two concertos: the youthful, neo-Classical Harpsichord Concerto (1954); and the Guitar Concerto (1989), jointly commissioned by the Toronto Symphony, the Montreal Symphony Orchestra, and the Calgary Philharmonic Orchestra for guitarist Norbert Kraft. To achieve an appropriate balance between solo guitar and orchestra, Schafer thinned the lower strings and eliminated all brass, except for one trumpet. Some unusual percussion instruments and a synthesized musical saw add to the unexpected sonorities Schafer coaxes from the ensemble. The work is in six movements played without interruption. For one who once despised the guitar, Schafer handles it effectively and idiomatically.

Immigrants have long played a major role in Canada's cultural development. The first immigrants were largely from England and France, but since World War II the population has become more diverse, with newcomers from around the world. The unprecedented growth enjoyed by Canada's universities in the 1960s and early 1970s resulted in the filling of faculty positions by immigrants from a variety of countries. Foreign-born composers joined the ranks and have made important contributions to Canada's musical life, including several who have written concertos of interest.

Otto Joachim (b. 1910, Germany) spent sixteen years in the Far East before coming to Montreal. His Concertante for Violin, Strings, and Percussion (1955–57) is a fairly strict twelve-tone work with an important role for colorful percussion instruments from the Far East.

Oskar Morawetz (b. 1917, Czechoslovakia) won a national competition sponsored by the Montreal Symphony with his romantic Piano Concerto (1962). It was first performed by Anton Kureti with Zubin Mehta conducting.

Talivaldis Kennis (b. 1919, Latvia) studied with Messiaen in France before coming to Canada. He composed his expressive one-movement Violin Concerto in 1974.

Malcolm Forsyth (b. 1936, South Africa), who came to Canada in 1968, teaches at the University of Alberta. Forsyth's Piano Concerto (1979), his first composition for the instrument, has an unusual form resulting from his initial plan for the piece as a fantasia. The concerto consists of sixteen variations on the ideas presented in the Introduction. The variations are distributed over three movements; variations 1–6 make up movement I, movement II contains variations 8–11, and the remainder are in the finale. Variation 2 was inspired by an African folk song and a native percussion instrument.

In 1992 Forsyth composed *Tre Vie*, a saxophone concerto, for his friend and colleague William Street. The title, referring to three roads leading into Rome, was prompted by knowledge that the concerto would receive its first performance in Italy as part of an International Saxophone Congress in September 1992. The work was slightly revised for a performance in Edmonton early the next year. *Tre Vie* has an unusal four-movement plan, with two rhythmically active movements flanking calmer, more lyrical ones. The first two movements are particularly contrasting; the opening movement is in a propulsive $\frac{10}{16}$ meter, while the second verges on non-metrical fluidity. This improvisatory second movement, the last of the concerto to be written, is in homage to Olivier Messiaen, whom Forsyth greatly admired. This movement includes a quotation from Thelonious Monk's melancholy jazz ballad, " 'Round Midnight," a tune enjoyed by saxophonist Street.

Chapter Twenty-Six

THE CONCERTO IN THE UNITED STATES

THE NINETEENTH CENTURY

By the early eighteenth century, concerts of music by European composers were being presented in the United States, and by the end of the century a few native-born composers were beginning to develop a concert-music tradition based on European, particularly German, models. In the first half of the nineteenth century, growing numbers of European musicians traveled to the United States to perform, and some remained, further strengthening the still-tender concert music tradition. By midcentury American composers were beginning to make important contributions to this tradition.

The pianist-composer Louis Moreau Gottschalk (1829–1869), a native of New Orleans, was America's first internationally acclaimed virtuoso, touring the United States, Canada, Europe, and Latin America with great success. As a teenager he went to Paris in 1842 to study music and remained in Europe until 1853. Chopin predicted a great future for the young American. Gottschalk composed hundreds of short piano pieces and several for piano and orchestra. Unfortunately, the only concerto he is reported to have composed for piano (1853) is lost.

Edward MacDowell (1860–1908) has the distinction of being named the composer of the first significant concerto by a native-born American composer. As a young man he studied abroad, first at the Paris Conservatory and later in Germany. He remained in Europe until 1888, when he returned to the United States as a successful composer, pianist, and teacher. He later accepted a professorship at Columbia University in 1896. His music was strongly influenced by Liszt, who met the American and convinced him to devote himself to composition. The music of Grieg and, to a lesser extent, that of Schumann were also influences. MacDowell wrote in a solidly Romantic style.

MacDowell concentrated his compositional energy on small pieces for solo piano. He also wrote songs and four symphonic tone poems, but in the main shied away from the larger standard forms. The most notable exceptions are the two piano concertos that he wrote in Germany. The First, in A minor (1882), was dedicated to Franz Liszt. The better-known Second Piano Concerto in D Minor (1888) was dedicated to his former teacher in the United States, Teresa Carreño, originally from Venezuela. Its three movements are a little unusual in that there is no slow movement. Instead, MacDowell composed a substantial slow introduction to the first movement and an interesting slow introduction to the Molto allegro finale; the middle movement is a Presto giocoso in a scherzo style with a steady stream of sixteenth notes in the piano part. The piano's cadenza entry and style of presenting the first lyrical theme in the main part of the first movement establish the work as a virtuoso concerto in the Romantic tradition. The pianist plays the main theme in octaves between the hands, while at the same time playing rippling decoration between the octaves (Ex. 26-1). MacDowell first played the Second Concerto in New York on 5 March 1889, with Theodore Thomas conducting.

Ex. 26-1. MacDowell, Piano Concerto No. 2; I. Poco più mosso, e con passione, mm. 49–50.

Mrs. H. H. A. Beach (1867–1944) was the married name of Amy Marcy Cheney. She was a musical child prodigy and mathematical genius who puzzled out music theory on her own initiative at an early age. Her gifts as a performing pianist led to her performance of Chopin's F Minor Concerto with the Boston Symphony when she was only eighteen. In the 1890s she became the most prominent of a group of female composers active in Boston, and was the first American woman to achieve success as a composer of large musical forms. She wrote the first symphony by an American woman and was the first woman to have her music performed by the New York Philharmonic Society. She was also one of the first American composers to be trained entirely in the United States. Her only concerto is the C-sharp Minor Concerto for Piano (1899), dedicated to the same piano teacher who was similarly honored by MacDowell in his D Minor Concerto, Teresa Carreño. Beach's musical horizons were much shaped by Brahms, so it is not surprising her concerto has four movements, like Brahms's second, and includes a brilliant perpetuum mobile scherzo as the second movement. The very large opening movement starts with an orchestral statement of the main theme, which the piano presents again in a more lyrical form following an introductory cadenza.

Upon the death of her husband in 1910, Mrs. Beach largely gave up composing to return to an active career as pianist, performing her concerto widely throughout Europe. She spent most summers at the MacDowell Colony, which Edward MacDowell's widow had established as a quiet place for artists, musicians, and writers to work.

Victor Herbert (1859–1924), the Irish-born composer of highly successful American operettas, including *Babes in Toyland* (1903), was another of the American composers trained in Germany, where he grew up; his stepfather was a German physician. Herbert played the cello and wrote two concertos for his own use. The first, composed in 1884, dates from before his move to the United States in 1886. The second was written in 1894 and performed during Antonin Dvořák's tenure as director of the Nationa Conservatory of Music in New York, where Herbert also served on the faculty. It was this concerto, with its songful use of the cello's upper register, that inspired Dvořák to compose his own.

Dvořák was the most important composer to have visited the United States to that date. His fascination with folk music carried over to that of the United States where he explored the music of Native Americans and Afro-Americans. The principal themes of his *Symphony from the New World* (1893) suggest similar melody types, and Dvořák urged American composers to turn likewise to the indigenous music of their own land for inspiration and identifiable thematic material. A few composers followed Dvořák's advice, incorporating Native American melodies into their works, but not until the 1920s did a clearly identifiable American sound resonate in the works of a significant number of American composers. This was largely in response to the growth of the uniquely American idiom, jazz.

JAZZ-INSPIRED CONCERTOS

Jazz originated in the United States as a result of a unique synthesis of Afro-American and European musical elements. The instruments, tonal-harmonic system, and basic melodic structures came from Europe. Variant forms of rhythm, phrasing, tone production, and some harmonic deviations derive from the Afro-American tradition. The most characteristic elements of jazz are:

- its unusual rhythmic structure, often called "swing," which results from a distinctive kind of syncopation—an uneven division of the beat and unusual stress patterns within a metrical unit or phrase;
- a freedom and spontaneity of performance in which improvisation plays a major role;
- the unusual sonorities created by a different approach to standard orchestral instruments, such as those created by the use of special mutes on the brass instruments, or by the use of instruments not commonly associated with the standard orchestra, such as the saxophone;
- the common use of "blue" notes, or slightly flatted tones, most commonly the third and seventh degrees of the major scale, which often results in conflict with the regular pitch, either stated or implied; and
- a performer- rather than composer-oriented music in which individual performers develop highly personalized styles of phrasing and tone coloration.

As we have seen in Chapter 23, the exotic, exciting sounds of jazz had captured the attention of some classical composers in Europe, especially those resident in France. Stravinsky, Ravel, and Milhaud, to name several, exploited jazz elements in some of their compositions. The first American composer successfully to incorporate jazz elements in a "serious" concert piece came from the world of popular music and the fledgling American musical theater.

George Gershwin (1898–1937), one of America's greatest song writers, integrated his understanding of the early jazz style with his incomparable ability to craft attractive, memorable tunes. The results were two concertante works featuring the piano. Gershwin composed *Rhapsody in Blue* for jazz band and piano (1924) at the request of the popular dance band leader, Paul Whiteman. Gershwin, who had at that time essentially no training in counterpoint, orchestration, or composition, was reluctant to undertake the work, for he had no confidence in his ability to write an extended piece for a larger ensemble. Whiteman countered by explaining that his arranger, Ferde Grofé (1892–1972), would orchestrate the work. Gershwin, working on the musical *Sweet Little Devil* at the time, later recalled how ideas for the Whiteman composition took shape on the train to Boston for the out-of-town opening of the comedy:

> It was on the train, with its steely rhythms, its rattlety-bang that is often so stimulating to a composer . . . I frequently hear music in the very heart of noise. And there I suddenly heard—and even saw on paper—the complete construction of the *Rhapsody*, from beginning to end. No new themes came to me, but I worked on the thematic material already in my mind and conceived the composition as a whole. I heard it as a musical kaleidoscope of America—of our vast melting pot, of our unduplicated national pep, of our blues, our metropolitan madness. By the time I reached Boston I had a definite *plot* of the piece, as distinguished from its actual substance.[1]

Gershwin completed the work in January 1924, and Grofé orchestrated it in time for the 12 February premiere at Aeolian Hall in New York. Whiteman had advertised the concert as an "Experiment in Modern Music," leading numerous well-known musicians from the world of classical music to attend, including Jascha Heifetz, Serge Rachmaninov, Leopold Stokowski, Willem Mengelberg, and Walter Damrosch. Gershwin played the piano part, which required some filling in with improvisation; Paul Whiteman's Palais Royal Orchestra, expanded with some additional musicians, accompanied.

The work is truly rhapsodic, made up of numerous sections frequently separated by pauses. Gershwin's inexperience in writing a larger work is clearly demonstrated by the absence of effective transitions between sections and by the continued reliance on repetition, rather than the development of the thematic material. But the rich melodic content, lively syncopations, and profusion of blue notes and jazz harmonies more than compensate for any technical shortcomings. Unforgettable in *Rhapsody in Blue* is the opening clarinet glissando (Ex. 26-2). Gershwin had originally written it as a seventeen-note scale passage, but during a rehearsal the clarinetist, Ross Gorman, played it as a glissando to make a joke. The composer liked the effect, so it was retained. The following thematic idea is colored by blue notes (the blue third and seventh circled in Ex. 26-2).

Ex. 26-2. Gershwin, *Rhapsody in Blue*, mm. 1–5.

Other themes are also beguiling: the theme given the saxophone, with a lowered seventh of the chord (a blue note), near the beginning (Ex. 26-3a); the bass theme, which slides into a prominent blue third, in the con moto section (Ex. 26-3b); and the lush, romantic theme of the andantino moderato, complemented by an odd jazzy figure that seems to pull the theme out of the nineteenth century into the twentieth (Ex. 26-3c). Several of these thematic ideas are transformed on later appearance, often with greater rhythmic interest. The Andantino moderato theme just noted is, for example, reshaped by one of Gershwin's favorite rhythmic devices: the grouping of even eighth-notes—or sixteenths or quarters—into patterns of three, and often coupled with triplets, creating a larger pattern of shifting accents (Ex. 26-4).

Ex. 26-3. Gershwin, *Rhapsody in Blue*: (a.) mm. 8–11; (b.) No. 14, mm. 1–2; (c.) No. 28, mm. 1–4.

Ex. 26-4. Gershwin, *Rhapsody in Blue*, No. 36, mm. 1–2.

After the first performance, Grofé reorchestrated the piece for large orchestra. For years it was generally known in this adapted version, until approximately sixty years later when it was republished in its original, expanded jazz band setting. Most who know the original are convinced of its superiority.

Although *Rhapsody in Blue* was an immediate success, Gershwin's ability to compose music for large-scale forces remained to be proved, especially since Grofé had orchestrated the work. Soon thereafter, however, Gershwin was given an opportunity to establish unquestionably his role as a composer of classical concert music. The German-born conductor, Walter Damrosch (1862–1950), who had served as artistic director of the New York Symphony Society since 1903, was among the many musicians who attended the first performance of *Rhapsody in Blue*. He persuaded the Society to commission a piano concerto by Gershwin to be played first in New York, then in Washington, D.C., Philadelphia, and Baltimore. The composer began work on it in July 1925, and completed it in September, putting off the orchestration until October and November of that year. In the meantime he studied orchestration on his own; before adding the finishing touches, he even rented a theater and engaged an orchestra and conductor-friend to read through his score so he could better judge its orchestral merit. He had originally intended to call the work *New York Concerto,* but in the end preferred the more abstract and more serious, classical title, Concerto in F for Piano and Orchestra. It was first performed in Carnegie Hall on 3 December 1925, and marked Gershwin's full acceptance as one of America's greatest composers.

The Concerto in F is in the traditional, fast-slow-fast, three-movement form. The first movement approximates sonata-allegro form with two central themes and a principal rhythmic idea, all of which are further developed. The first theme (Ex. 26-5a) is built by the bassoon around arpeggiation of a seventh chord; the second theme, really the concerto's main theme, is presented by the piano upon its first appearance (Ex. 26-5b). The central rhythmic figure (Ex. 26-5c) is similar to a rhythmic idea noted in the *Rhapsody in Blue*; here it involves the syncopated groupings of even eighth notes by threes, coupled with triplets. Later in the work, the figure occasionally includes a pair of eighth notes mixed with the groups of three notes, resulting in still greater syncopated patterns of 3+3+2 or 3+2+3.

Ex. 26-5. Gershwin, Concerto in F; I. Allegro: (a.) mm. 5–8; (b.) No. 4, mm. 1–6; (c.) No. 7, mm. 1–2.

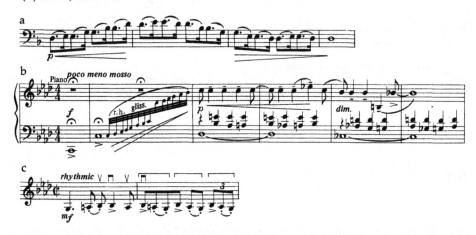

The Andante con moto second movement in D-flat major divides into two sections, separated by an intervening cadenza. The opening melody of the movement is one of Gershwin's most memorable. The Allegro agitato movement is a typically virtuosic concerto finale, characterized by great rhythmic vitality. Thematic material of the first two movements recurs in the finale; while reference to second movement material is sketchy, the memorable main theme of the opening movement forms the climax near the work's conclusion.

Even following the successful reception of the Concerto in F, Gershwin continually sought to improve his understanding of music theory and composition, taking lessons throughout his life. This devoted study culminated in the composition of the outstanding American opera, *Porgy and Bess* (1935).

Aaron Copland (1900–1990) in the 1920s led the ranks of other American composers who integrated jazz elements into their writing. Copland, like Gershwin a native of Brooklyn, was greatly taken by the new music of France in the first part of the century. Arriving there to study at Fontainebleau in 1921, he became Nadia Boulanger's first American student and at the same time fully explored the vital French musical scene of that heady decade, which then included the music of

Igor Stravinsky and Serge Prokofiev. Shortly before Copland's return to the United States in June 1924, Boulanger was invited by Walter Damrosch and Serge Koussevitsky to appear as a guest organ soloist with their orchestras in New York and Boston, respectively. Upon her acceptance she asked Copland to write something appropriate for these occasions. The resulting Organ Symphony (1924) is an aggressive work in which the organ has several solo passages, but it is not treated as a solo instrument in the concerto tradition. Jazz plays no part in this piece, for the composer was still emulating his European heroes. The work's aggressive dissonance prompted the usually taciturn Damrosch to turn to his audience at the first performance, remarking, "If a young man at the age of 23 can write a symphony like that, in five years he will be ready to commit murder."[2]

Upon returning to the United States, Copland increasingly devoted himself to creating music that could readily be recognized as American. As a consequence, he turned to popular music and jazz, or what he thought of as jazz, for his inspiration. The "Dance" movement of his *Music for the Theatre* (1925) is among his first explicit ventures into the jazz idiom. The Piano Concerto (1926), which followed soon after, is built upon a thorough synthesis of several jazz elements with the modern neo-Classical style.

The concerto, scored for a large orchestra with alto and soprano saxophones and extra percussion, including tam-tam, Chinese drums, woodblock, and xylophone, is in two contrasting but linked movements. The first movement, Andante sostenuto, opens with a short orchestral introduction of a three-note motive played sixteen times in the first eight measures, giving the listener an unequivocal sense of its central importance (Ex. 26-6). The piano enters in a quite improvisatory style, after which the movement develops the feeling of a slow blues, replete with blue notes and a main theme built around the minor third in a syncopated setting (Ex. 26-7). The theme recurs in the piano, against which canonic imitations are played by the alto saxophone, bassoon, and horn. Later the strings take up the theme in an effective threefold canonic statement, leading to a great climax.

Ex. 26-6. Copland, Piano Concerto; I. Andante sostenuto, mm. 1–2.

Ex. 26-7. Copland, Piano Concerto; I. Andante sostenuto, No. 4, mm. 1–3.

The second movement begins with an elaborate piano cadenza of great rhythmic energy, based on Copland's creative reworking of the jazz-piano stride style, which evolved from ragtime. In this jazz-piano style, the left hand provides an anchor by striding between a low bass note and upper chord in a fairly consistent rhythmic pattern, while the right hand moves more freely and actively, presenting the melody against this simple background. The molto rubato notation is probably Copland's way of indicating that his rhythmic notation can only be construed as an approximation of the swing element so characteristic of jazz and inadequately stated in standard music notation. The piano works with this material extensively before the soprano saxophone introduces a contrasting syncopated idea developed by a small jazz ensemble that Copland forms from within the large orchestra. The piano provides a vamp-like, repetitive accompaniment in this section. Jazz elements dominate the final large cadenza as well, as the pianist's left hand repeats a steady quarter-note ostinato pattern while the right hand plays syncopated chords above. The work's opening three-note motive is worked in near the concerto's end.

Koussevitsky had urged Copland to write this jazz-inspired work, and he conducted the first performance with Copland as pianist with the Boston Symphony Orchestra on 28 January 1927. Its pungent, dissonant atmosphere coupled with its unorthodox and constantly changing meters lacked the appeal of Gershwin's gracious melodic style. As a consequence neither the critics nor the audience responded favorably. We, today, can look back at it as an early masterpiece from the "jazz age." Copland's Piano Concerto is the most impressive large-scale work of any kind by any composer at that time in which the idiom of jazz played a central role.

In the early 1930s composers in Europe and the United States moved away from the overt use of jazz elements as the fad faded. Copland himself concluded that he should leave the jazz style to those who could improvise.[3] Although Copland largely abandoned elements of jazz, the rhythmic vitality associated with it remained an important ingredient in his later music.

He turned at first to an abstract, austere, and even acerbic style as demonstrated in the demanding Piano Variations (1930), an uncompromising work based on a four-note motive. But as the years passed and the Depression deepened, Copland together with many other composers turned in yet another direction. Writing about the impact of the Depression, Copland noted how it "aroused a wave of sympathy for and identification with the plight of the common man."[4] A visit to Mexico at the invitation of composer and conductor Carlos Chávez intensified Copland's identification with "the people." Copland came to understand that his earlier works were too demanding for the average listener and sought to create a simpler and more direct music. He found the key to this departure in the simple, traditional tunes of various ethnic groups, which he then incorporated into an extraordinary series of orchestral ballets and other works, beginning with *El Salon Mexico* (1933–36).

In 1947 the jazz clarinetist Benny Goodman commissioned concertos from both Copland and Paul Hindemith. The latter was previously discussed. Copland's Concerto for Clarinet (1948) calls for a small orchestra of strings, harp, and piano. Like the earlier Piano Concerto, this one is in two movements of similar design. The expressive first movement is slow and fluidly lyrical, akin to his expansive ballet scores; the second is lively, filled with jazzy rhythms and melodic turns of phrase. A cadenza, linking the two movements, hints at thematic material of the second. The piano appears only in the second movement, serving as a percussion section. The second movement was designed to exploit Goodman's mastery of the instrument's high register. The rhythmic main theme (Ex. 26-8) of the rondo finally emerges in the clarinet against a rhythmically complicated background.

Ex. 26-8. Copland, Clarinet Concerto; II. Rather fast, No. 155, mm. 155–162.

Copland's approach to musical composition continued to shift during the postwar years, but the concerto no longer played a role in his work.

Although interest in assimilating jazz elements into classical music faded in the 1930s, it returned in a slightly different guise in the late 1940s and 1950s. In its new incarnation the objective was to amalgamate the two traditions into what Gunther Schuller termed the "Third Stream." Interest in this approach came from both jazz and classical musicians.

Jazz musicians' early experiments in this direction include the work of blind pianist Lennie Tristano (1919–1978), who had his saxophonists Warne Marsh and Lee Konitz play Bach two-part Inventions without modification at the beginning of a set to advise his audience of the musical roots of what was to follow. Claude Thornhill (1909–1965), composer and band leader, formed a big band, adding instruments then more closely associated with the world of classical music, such as horn, tuba, and bass clarinet. He was fascinated by the music of Debussy and had his principal arranger, the Canadian Gil Evans (1912–1988), incorporate Impressionistic techniques into the arrangements for the band. Evans and other members of the Thornhill band, Gerry Mulligan and Lee Konitz, independently joined with the young Miles Davis (1926–1991) in 1949 to chart the development of a new approach to jazz in the early 1950s. This approach came to be known as the cool style, which established closer ties with classical music. The cool style called for a new appreciation and cultivation of counterpoint; a greater variety of tone colors; and the use of more complex forms. The hornist Gunther Schuller and pianist John Lewis, the two musicians who came to be most closely associated with and representative of Third Stream music, played in the influential Miles Davis Nonet recordings of 1949, collectively known as the "Birth of the Cool" sessions. Schuller approached the amalgamation from the classical stream and Lewis from the jazz stream, and both made contributions to the concerto literature.

Gunther Schuller (b. 1925) is a multitalented man of music. He became a professional musician at the age of eighteen, playing principal horn for the Cincinnati Symphony Orchestra from 1943 to 1945 and for the Metropolitan Opera Orchestra from 1945 to 1959. In 1959 he gradually withdrew from performance to devote himself to composition. He has been a respected teacher and administrator, serving as president of the New England Conservatory, 1967–77. He is an articulate writer whose scholarly interest in jazz has culminated in widely respected books on the history of jazz;[5] he has also written a book on horn technique. He founded a music publishing company as well as a recording company to disseminate the music he champions. Schuller is a prolific composer who has shown an interest in using not only jazz elements, but also many avant-garde techniques. One of his earliest works is a concerto for his own instrument, the horn (1944).

Schuller coined the term Third Stream music in a lecture at Brandeis University in 1957. From his close association with jazz and classical music, Schuller developed the strongly held belief that both streams could only benefit from an artistic cross-fertilization. Jazz could offer classical music a sense of rhythmic vitality and spontaneity, while classical music could provide jazz with a greater breadth of dynamic range and diversity of forms. Among his earliest compositions to arrive at this fusion is the Concertino for Jazz Quartet and Orchestra (1959). It was written for John Lewis's group, The Modern Jazz Quartet, and includes sections for the quartet and its individual members to improvise. Schuller's later Concerto for Orchestra No. 1 (1965–66) is also in a jazz style.

Schuller has a remarkable sensitivity to orchestral instruments, and since the late 1960s has written concertos for double bass, contrabassoon, alto saxophone, violin, trumpet, horn, cello, a quadruple concerto for violin, flute, oboe, and trumpet, and the *Concerto Festo* for brass quintet and orchestra. In these later works he has depended less on overt jazz elements, as, for example, in the recent *Eine kleine Posaunenmusik* (A Little Trombone Music, 1980) composed for John Swallow. This five-movement concerto-like piece for trombone and wind ensemble, plus harp, piano, celesta, and double bass, is not a Third Stream piece, but Schuller does make reference to jazz in the variety of jazz mutes used by the solo instrument; in a passing tribute in the second movement to jazz trombonist Lawrence Brown, for whom Schuller has special admiration; and in some rapid jazz episodes in the finale.

John Lewis (b. 1920), pianist and music director of the Modern Jazz Quartet from the midtwentieth century onward, represents the jazz musician who appropriates elements from the world of classical music to enrich his own music. The members of the quartet—Milt Jackson, vibraphone; John Lewis, piano; Percy Heath, bass; and Connie Kay, drums (the original drummer, Kenny Clarke, was replaced by Kay in 1955)—created an intimate, contrapuntally interactive style of improvisation in their interpretation of both jazz standards and original Lewis compositions. Both Lewis and Jackson are strong blues players, and Jackson is an ebullient and fluent improviser whose flamboyance is balanced by Lewis's restrained manner. The general tone of an MJQ performance typically matches their appearance, as they usually wear formal concert attire and approach their music in much the same manner as a classical string quartet.

They have repeatedly performed with symphony orchestras, playing works written for them by Lewis or others. Lewis, who completed a Master's degree in composition at the Manhattan School of Music in 1953, usually tries to leave room for quartet and solo improvisation in his concerto-like works for the group. The composition *In Memoriam* (1972–73) is an example of his Third Stream approach. It is a two-movement work for the MJQ and orchestra. The first movement was composed in memory of Walter Keller, Lewis's piano teacher in his undergraduate days at the University of New Mexico. The more lively second movement was added later as a tribute to other musicians admired by Lewis. These include jazz performers Louis Armstrong, Lester Young, Coleman Hawkins, Charlie Parker, Eric Dolphy, Scott LaFaro, Ben Webster, and Johnny Hodges, and composers Igor Stravinsky, Béla Bartók, and Arnold Schoenberg, although their music is not evident in this movement.

Larry Austin (b. 1930) applied his strong interest and background in jazz to further explorations of improvisation in his classical compositions. Aleatory, or chance, elements are important in his Improvisations for Symphony Orchestra and Jazz Soloists (1961), in which the soloists are free to determine the rhythmic articulation of notated pitches in many sections.

Jorge Calandrelli (b. 1939) successfully blended jazz and classical elements in his Concerto for Jazz Clarinet and Orchestra (1984, revised 1989). Calandrelli, who moved to the United States in 1978 from his native Argentina, has both classical and jazz background. He studied harmony, counterpoint, and composition privately in Buenos Aires and has led his own jazz trio as a pianist. He is currently a successful composer and orchestrator of major television and motion picture productions, having received numerous honors for his work in these media, including an Oscar nomination for the film score, *The Color Purple*. These popular honors are not to be taken lightly, for Calandrelli is a gifted composer with a profound understanding of orchestral instruments and a strong rhythmic sense, which has its origins in three sources: American jazz, Latin American dance music, and the asymmetrical rhythmic patterns of Stravinsky and Bartók, whose music he has long admired. Added to these elements is a lyrical, melodic approach, which gives his music great appeal. All these features come together in the Concerto for Jazz Clarinet and Orchestra, written on commission for the jazz clarinetist Eddie Daniels (b. 1941).

The work, in the standard three movements, effectively integrates solo improvisation into its scintillating orchestral textures and tight formal structures. For example, the middle of the first movement is given over to clarinet improvisation in a jazz style, accompanied by orchestral chords quite reminiscent of the syncopated chords in the "Dance of the Adolescents" from Stravinsky's 1913 ballet, *The Rite of Spring*. Similarly, in the middle of the second movement, which is in the style of a bluesy jazz ballad, jazz improvisation plays a significant role. In Daniels's recorded performance of the work, the second half of this extended improvisation is accompanied by only a rhythm section of piano, bass, and drums, thereby exposing a jazz quartet without orchestral accompaniment. The finale, in rondo form, incorporates not only solo improvisation but also a striking orchestral "improvisation" leading up to the cadenza. This passage is not in a jazz style, but rather in an instrumental-performance style similar to that of Penderecki and others in the 1960s: The performers are given note patterns, but are not expected to play them precisely coordinated with the other members of the orchestra. This passage also makes use of unusual instrumental techniques, such as the string players' tapping of the soundboard with fingernails and their bowing of the strings between the bridge and the tailpiece. This is the only nontraditional passage in this otherwise traditional, but highly unusual, and impressive work.

The score calls for a large orchestra, including a large percussion section, but Calandrelli uses these resources sparingly, often creating an intimate chamber music atmosphere entirely appropriate for the clarinet. The additional resources, however, have enabled him to compose an unusually effective and sensuous score. The concerto was commissioned by conductor Jack Elliott and the Foundation for New American Music and was first performed in Los Angeles in March 1985 with Daniels as soloist.

THE MAINSTREAM TRADITION

In contrast to the strongly jazz-influenced and therefore overtly American concerto style, the mainstream European tradition also flourished in the United States, especially in the work of four composers. These men, all born in the 1890s, were recognized as ranking among America's leading composers in the 1930s and 1940s, even though they had no particular interest in using obvious American elements in their works. Most were students of Nadia Boulanger in Paris, and most came to hold leading academic positions in America's great universities, where they influenced the careers of a number of younger composers.

Walter Piston (1894–1976) taught at Harvard University for forty years. His textbook on harmony was the standard on the subject for many years, and his textbooks on counterpoint and orchestration were also valued. As might be expected, his work as a composer focused on the large formal patterns and harmonic principles that governed the music of the eighteenth and nineteenth centuries. His early Concerto for Orchestra (1933) confirms his interest in Baroque practices, especially in the strong contrapuntal textures and driving rhythms of the first movement, and the passacaglia and fugue of the finale. Piston's Viola Concerto (1958) is a substantial work for this often-neglected string instrument. In it he solved the recurring problem of balancing the instrument's characteristically intimate, warm, alto tone and the power of the orchestra. Further, he took full advantage of the viola's warmth in the romantic-sounding slow movement, Adagio con fantasia, which has a strong improvisational quality. Piston's music enjoyed more frequent performances than did that of most American composers. This distinction derived not only from the generally accessible musical language he used, but also from the strong local support of Serge Koussevitsky, conductor of the Boston Symphony Orchestra (1924–49) and champion of contemporary music.

Howard Hanson (1896–1981) markedly influenced the course of music education in the United States during his forty-year term as director of the Eastman School of Music in Rochester, New York. He promoted American music by means of an annual festival, which also aimed to nurture the careers of young musicians. His Organ Concerto (1926) and Piano Concerto (1948) are quite conservative works.

Virgil Thomson (1896–1989), the only composer of this group who did not hold an important teaching position, is best known for his operas and his collaborations with Gertrude Stein. He was also among America's most astute music critics. His musical style is clear, simple, and essentially diatonic. As in the Cello Concerto (1950), he frequently quoted Baptist hymn tunes, familiar from his youth.

Roger Sessions (1896–1985) held teaching positions at Princeton University, the University of California at Berkeley, and the Juilliard School of Music. He studied at Harvard and Yale, under Horatio Parker, and privately with Bloch. From a fairly early stage Sessions developed a strongly contrapuntal style in which the various lines are markedly independent of one another, as in the opening of the third movement of his Violin Concerto (1935) where a basset horn provides a linear accompaniment to the solo instrument (Ex. 26-9). This dense polyphony remained a constant characteristic of Sessions's style, though it evolved from his neo-Classical beginnings to one embracing serialism and a greater expressiveness. Interest in serialism spread widely in Europe and the United States in the 1950s, and Sessions was among the few mature composers to modify his style to assimilate the new technique. His music became increasingly dissonant and rhythmically more complex as he grew older.

Ex. 26-9. Sessions, Violin Concerto; III. Romanza: Andante, mm. 1–5.

Sessions's twelve-tone Concerto for Violin and Cello (1971) was commissioned by the Juilliard School of Music. It was first performed in Alice Tully Hall in New York by the gifted violinist Paul Zukofsky (b. 1943), whose repertory is heavily oriented to twentieth-century music, and by the composer's son John on cello. The Double Concerto is in three connected movements and concludes with an exposed statement of the twelve-tone series in the unaccompanied cello. The continual contrapuntal interaction and dialogue between the two solo instruments hold the listener's attention. A year later Sessions completed the Concertino for Chamber Orchestra (1972), composed for the Contemporary Chamber Players of the University of Chicago, where he was a visiting professor. The work provides multiple opportunities for solo performances by all members of the ensemble, making particularly good use of the woodwind players' abilities to double on other instruments. The flute player also plays piccolo, the oboist doubles on English horn, the clarinetist plays three kinds of clarinets, and the bassoonist doubles on contrabassoon, making extensive use of this deep woodwind sound in the expressive slow movement.

Sessions won the Pulitzer Prize for his Concerto for Orchestra (1979–81), a work commissioned by the Boston Symphony Orchestra for its centennial and completed when the composer was age eighty-five. It is quite unlike Bartók's Concerto for Orchestra (1943) composed for the same orchestra. Bartók's concerto is in five distinct movements; Sessions's is in three linked sections—Allegro, Largo, and Allegro maestoso. Furthermore, Sessions does not so explicitly feature members of the orchestra in solo roles, although different portions of the piece highlight sections of the orchestra. Woodwinds predominate in the first section; brass come forth in the second, with contrasting high woodwinds in the center of the second section; and in the final section beginning with a trumpet call, a broader orchestral spectrum is evident. The strings have relatively little exposure but take on greater importance in the work's quiet, hymnlike conclusion.

American composers born in the second decade of the century and later enjoyed the good fortune of receiving a solid musical education without leaving the country. And not surprisingly, their styles were largely shaped by their teachers. The contributions of two traditionally oriented composers who reached early maturity in the 1930s are particularly noteworthy.

William Schuman (1910–1992), who had studied with Roy Harris and benefited from a background in jazz, developed a rigorous, economical, and highly rhythmic style of instrumental composition. He produced a large number of works for orchestra and band in which his use of brass and percussion instruments contributes a great sense of brilliance. His Violin Concerto (1949) was commissioned by Samuel Dushkin, for whom Stravinsky composed his Violin Concerto. Schuman, unhappy with the score, revised it twice (1956 and 1959), finally settling on an unusual two-movement form with several shifts of mood in each movement. The development of the violin's lyrical opening and the rhythmic orchestral accompaniment provide a continuing thread throughout the work. The contrast between the violin's lyricism and the orchestra's percussive vigor is quite striking and is made even more so by the occasional reversal of these roles. The propulsive, syncopated rhythms so characteristic of Schuman's style are more evident in the earlier Piano Concerto (1942) in three movements. His *Concerto on Old English Rounds* for viola, women's chorus, and orchestra (1974) is among the most unusual concertos in the history of the form. It is in five movements, played without pause; the fifth movement is a reprise of the first. An unaccompanied viola opens the work by playing the melody of an old English round for which Schuman provides the text underneath the music "to enable the performer to project the melody with the clarity of a singer."

Schuman held two very important administrative positions; he was president of the Juilliard School of Music (1945–62) during its period of greatest growth, and president of the Lincoln Center for the Performing Arts in New York City (1962–69).

Samuel Barber (1910–1981) was a child prodigy who was composing at the age of seven. He entered the Curtis Institute in Philadelphia at fourteen, and became one of the few composers of the last three centuries to be trained in voice. A strong interest in song probably helped to shape his lyrical approach to composition, for he developed a refined, yet dramatic, style readily intelligible to a broad audience. This, in turn, has led to Barber's status as a most-frequently performed American composer, along with Aaron Copland. Barber was a romantic who wrote from his heart, relying upon the tried-and-true classical forms, which he filled with romantic feeling and colorful scoring. Barber's early works, prior to his Violin Concerto (1939), are conservative; later works are more dissonant and more complex, but they retain a firm sense of tonality. He flirted with serial techniques only in the Piano Sonata (1949).

Barber composed three significant solo concertos and one in the concerto grosso idiom. The earliest is the Violin Concerto, which is a watershed between his earlier, conservative style and his later, less conservative approach. He completed the first two movements while he was living in a small Swiss village, from which he moved to Paris where he intended to complete the work. But this plan was frustrated when American citizens were ordered out of the city in advance of the Nazi invasion. The war, which interrupted his work, may have led to the change of style so clearly evident between the first two movements and the last. Another reason for this difference could be Barber's response to the request of the violinist for whom he was writing the concerto. The performer, having played through the first two movements, found them too simple and asked for a more complex finale. But in the end, the finale proved too difficult and the violinist relinquished his claim to perform the work. It was eventually premiered by Albert Spalding with the Philadelphia Orchestra, conducted by Eugene Ormandy, 7 February 1941.

The supple rhythms of the long, expressive opening theme of the first movement are clearly the work of a sensitive songwriter (Ex. 26-10). The second theme (Ex. 26-11), introduced by the clarinet, is in a light scherzando mood and employs Scotch-snap rhythm, a favorite Barber device. The first movement is in sonata-allegro form. The second movement is still more songful with the oboe presenting the first melodic idea over sustained muted strings and pizzicato bass. The solo violin leads the theme to an intense climax over tremolando strings after a brief contrasting midsection. The Presto in moto perpetuo finale stresses a repeated triplet pattern introduced in the first measure by muffled timpani.

Ex. 26-10. Barber, Violin Concerto; I. Allegro, mm. 1–4.

Ex. 26-11. Barber, Violin Concerto; I. Allegro, No. 2, mm. 2–3.

The Cello Concerto (1945), which is at last gaining a wider following, is a supremely lyrical work marking Barber's return to an earlier style after writing a number of less lyrical compositions. The first movement opens with a lively orchestral introduction, the second features the cello in a lilting siciliano theme, and the finale begins with an effective orchestral fanfare in which the duration of notes is successively reduced (Ex. 26-12).

Ex. 26-12. Barber, Cello Concerto; III. Molto allegro e appassionato, mm. 1–5.

Barber's Piano Concerto (1962) entered the standard repertory with its first performance by John Browning and the Boston Symphony Orchestra, conducted by Erich Leinsdorf for the opening of the Lincoln Center for the Performing Arts. It was commissioned by the music publisher G. Schirmer to commemorate its 100th anniversary. The brilliant work is begun by the unaccompanied piano in a quasi-recitative style in a simple octave statement (Ex. 26-13a) of what will become a dominant theme of the movement. Other leading ideas are a lyrical theme introduced by the orchestra (Ex. 26-13b) and an "arrogant," to use the composer's word, rhythm first in the piano (Ex. 26-13c). The cadenza, which prepares the way for the recapitulation, is formed around the arrogant rhythm and the lyrical theme. Barber titled the second movement Canzone (song), an apt means of conveying its delicate texture, based on brief woodwind solos played against muted, tremolando strings. The Allegro molto finale is hard driving, in $\frac{5}{8}$ meter all the way, with a central idea built on a bass ostinato figure first played by the piano (Ex. 26-14). Occasional episodes, including one presented initially by the clarinet over a xylophone ostinato, provide some lyrical relief.

Ex. 26-13. Barber, Piano Concerto; I. Allegro appassionato: (a.) mm. 1–3; (b.) No. 2, mm. 1–5; (c.) No. 5, mm. 9.

Ex. 26-14. Barber, Piano Concerto, III. Allegro molto, mm. 6–7.

Paul Creston (1906–1985), a lesser-known composer, wrote music in a conservative vein, largely of interest because of its attractive melodic and rhythmic content. Creston, self-taught as a composer, was an effective orchestrator who maintained a continuing fascination for unusual instruments. His concertos include one for marimba (1940), another for accordion (1958), and yet another for saxophone (1941). The latter is a particularly effective piece.

RADICAL INNOVATORS

The 1910s also witnessed the birth of several composers who were to become some of America's most daring musical innovators. The most revolutionary of all was John Cage from Los Angeles. This influential iconoclast grew up knowing little of traditional music. But in 1933 he was introduced to non-Western music, as well as folk and contemporary music in the classes of an older California innovator, Henry Cowell.

Cowell (1897–1965), an early explorer of diverse music traditions ranging from Eastern cultures to conventional Western music, was an experimenter who wanted "to live in the whole world of music."[6] In his teens, Cowell began to experiment with the piano, inventing new ways to play it. A new technique involved the playing of blocks of white or black keys with the forearm, the palm of the hand, or the fist to create dense concentrations of dissonant tones called "tone clusters." Cowell incorporated tone clusters in his Piano Concerto (1928–29), which he first performed in Havana, with a guard of Cuban policemen on hand to protect him and to prevent disturbances from the audience. (Shortly thereafter, Bartók used similar tone clusters in his Second Piano Concerto, first seeking the explicit permission of Cowell.) Cowell's other experiments with the piano involved playing the strings inside the instrument to produce harp-like effects and other novel sounds.

Cowell's interest in unusual sounds and rhythms drew him to the electronic instrument inventor Leon Theremin. Together they developed the rhythmicon, an instrument designed to produce a variety of complex combinations of beat patterns. Cowell's *Rhythmicana* (1931) was written for this device and orchestra. His twin concerns for rhythm and Eastern music inspired the creation of two other concertos, the Percussion Concerto (1963) and the Concerto for Koto and Chamber Orchestra (1962). The latter, first performed by the blind koto player Kimio Eto with the Philadelphia Orchestra and conductor Leopold Stokowski, is in three movements. The first movement reflects Eastern influences; the second, Western; and the third, a combination of the two.

John Cage (1912–1992) proved a true follower of Cowell in several ways. He pursued the use of percussion instruments and complex rhythmic structures. He further explored the piano, creating the "prepared piano," in which the usual sound of the instrument is altered by placing objects, such as screws, paper clips, bolts, and rubber erasers, in the strings. About 1950 Cage was captivated by the exoticism of the Orient and Zen Buddhism, eventually devising a variety of aleatory or chance procedures presumably based upon the Chinese *I-Ching* (Book of Change). Cage's view of music, which embraced everything from traditional tonal music to environmental acoustical phenomena including incidental noises and chance sounds and rhythms, powerfully influenced followers in the 1950s and 1960s.

Cage composed two concertos. The Concerto for Prepared Piano and Chamber Orchestra (1951) is an early work to call for a random selection of pitches, although the rhythmic elements remain carefully predetermined. A table

John Cage's prepared piano. John Cage requires that various objects be inserted between the strings of the piano in order to prepare it for a performance of his Concerto for Prepared Piano and Orchestra (1951). The altered sounds often emphasize the percussive nature of the instrument, an effect of interest to both Cage and his tutor, Henry Cowell.

printed at the beginning of the score provides precise instructions for the preparation of the piano. Those instructions dictate the placement of a variety of objects in the strings, affecting fifty-three of the instrument's eighty-eight notes. As a consequence some normal piano sounds can be played among altered sounds; many of the latter resemble the percussion sounds associated with gamelan music.

Throughout the 1950s Cage endeavored to increase the element of chance in his music and to involve the performer more actively in the process of creation, not simply the re-creation of what the composer had written. The Concert [not Concerto] for Piano and Orchestra (1957–58) is an important monument in the history of aleatory music. Chance elements affect every detail of the composition. The very pitches to be played were determined by imperfections found in the music manuscript paper. There is no master score since the piece will take a radically different shape in every new performance. Only the instrumental parts are notated, and they contain a combination of conventional musical symbols and quite unconventional symbols. The printed parts contain a number of short musical gestures or fragments that may be played in any sequence. The greater or lesser space between printed gestures may, but need not, be used as a relative timing guide. For example, the piano part consists of eighty-four gestures, which may be played in whole or part, in any sequence and any time. The soloist may or may not be joined by any orchestral players who may choose to play. Referring to the role of performer choices, Cage regarded "this work as one 'in progress' which I intend never to consider as in a final state, although I find each performance definitive."[7]

Lukas Foss (b. 1922 in Berlin) followed in Cage's footsteps. Also greatly taken by jazz improvisation, Foss organized the Improvisation Chamber Ensemble in Los Angeles in 1957 to inject improvisation into serious concert music. Although his indeterminate music contains many ideas similar to Cage's, Foss preferred to retain greater control over the improvisation by establishing clear thematic elements, formal designs, and coordinated timing constraints. His Cello Concerto (1967) for Rostropovich illustrates this approach.

POST-WEBERN SERIALISTS

While Cage and his disciples were exploring indeterminacy, another group of composers was creating works in which most of the musical components were carefully and precisely defined—the scores for which the performers were expected to follow rigorously. As we saw in the previous chapter, total serialism builds upon Schoenberg's twelve-tone method and Webern's pointillistic extension of the technique. The new serialists established several series in which not only pitch but also the other parameters of the musical environment—including dynamics, duration, articulation, and timbre—are fully and precisely defined and ordered.

Milton Babbitt (b. 1916) was among the earliest composers in Europe or the United States to experiment with and adopt the total serial approach. The Philadelphia-born Babbitt, trained in math as well as music, studied with Roger Sessions, whose style moved toward serialism. Eventually he joined Sessions on the faculty at Princeton University.

Babbitt, like others devoted to total serialism or other related systems that approach music mathematically, prefers to compose chamber, rather than orchestral, music. This is so for the practical reason that the coordination of the many parts making up the characteristically complex textures and rhythms of orchestral music in this style requires financially unsustainable amounts of rehearsal time. This, at least in part, explains the small number of concertos in this style. Babbitt completed his Piano Concerto in 1985.

Charles Wuorinen (b. 1928), Babbitt's composition student and a brilliant pianist, composed his Piano Concerto (1965) in a highly pointillistic style.

Ben Weber (1916–1980) endeavored to combine traditional lyricism with serial techniques. Several of his works, including the Piano Concerto (1961) commissioned by the Ford Foundation, have been well received by a broader public, and he has won several prestigious awards.

David Martino (b. 1931), another serialist student of Babbitt and Sessions, composed the Triple Concerto for Clarinet, Bass Clarinet, and Contrabass Clarinet (1977), in which the three clarinets are frequently used in a special sequence creating the illusion of a single "superclarinet" possessing a six-octave range.

ELLIOTT CARTER

Elliott Carter (b. 1908) is among America's most respected composers, even though his music is not particularly familiar to the general public. He studied with Walter Piston at Harvard, was a student of Nadia Boulanger for three years in Paris, and explored great quantities of music on his own to which his teachers had not exposed him. His musical style evolved from one dependent upon a fairly simple, diatonic language to one that is complex, dissonant, and chromatic. He has adapted aspects of serialism and other contemporary techniques to suit his personal style. Time is probably the most important element in Carter's musical approach. He is a great rhythmic innovator, having developed a sophisticated system of "metric modulation," involving gradual changes of meter and tempo. Carter is a fine contrapuntist regularly superimposing markedly independent lines on one another. He also employs spatial separation of the independent parts to suggest the coexistence of two entirely different musical entities within the same performance space. Most of Carter's quite demanding works were written for small performing forces until the late 1950s, when he witnessed, at Darmstadt, what an orchestra could accomplish if given sufficient rehearsal time. His first important work for orchestra is the highly significant Double Concerto for Harpsichord and Piano, which he composed between 1956 and 1961.

In 1956 the harpsichordist Ralph Kirkpatrick requested Carter to compose a piece for harpsichord and piano. When Carter turned to the task he had to contend with the fundamental differences between the two keyboard instruments. To avoid submerging the sound of the harpsichord in that of the piano, Carter called for them to play antiphonally most of the time. When they play together he places them in widely separated registers to make both clearly audible. Additionally, he wrote rapid filigree for the piano, rather than asking it to play dense, heavy sounds. To further distinguish between the instruments, Carter requires that the harpsichord be equipped with several stops, for he specifies changes in the harpsichord registration throughout, and especially in the harpsichord's cadenza. Finally, each instrument is associated with a unique orchestral group. Of the nonpercussion instruments, only the horn is found in both ensembles; otherwise the wind and string instruments of one ensemble are entirely different from those of the other. A chamber orchestra with a Baroque-like sound is associated with the harpsichord, while a large ensemble provides a more Romantic accompaniment for the piano. An enormous collection of percussion instruments, requiring four percussionists, is fully integrated into the score. Wooden and metallic instruments complement the harpsichord, while drums of various kinds are associated with the piano. The players are situated on the stage according to the plan shown here, with as much space as possible between the two groups. The four percussion players back the other performers.

Percussion I		Percussion II			Percussion III		Percussion IV
	Trombone					Bassoon	
Horn I	Trumpet		Flute		Oboe	Clarinet	Horn II
	Contrabass		Viola		Violin		Cello
	Harpsichord					Piano	

Conductor

Each group is given distinctive material, involving preferred sets of intervals, metronome speeds, and complex rhythmic schemes.

The Double Concerto for Harpsichord and Piano with Two Chamber Orchestras is in seven linked movements arranged symmetrically:

Introduction
Cadenza for harpsichord
Allegro scherzando (features piano group with harpsichord
    interruptions)
Adagio
Presto (features harpsichord group with piano interruptions)
Two Cadenzas for piano
Coda

As in many of Carter's other works, the sections do not remain autonomous, for material from one section overlaps or is superimposed on another.

This is the ultimate concerto, in many respects. Solo instruments are pitted against each other and against an ensemble, and the two ensembles in turn are pitted against one another; yet all are integrated into a complex whole.

Carter composed three more concertos. The Piano Concerto (1963–65) was dedicated to Igor Stravinsky on his eighty-fifth birthday—Stravinsky and Carter much admired each other's music. It combines aspects of a solo concerto and concerto grosso, and Carter emphasizes the romantic, expressive qualities of the solo instrument as it struggles against a massive, monolithic, impersonal orchestra. The sensitive piano part is often supported by a group of seven instruments, a concertino consisting of flute, English horn, bass clarinet, violin, viola, cello, and bass. The music of the concertino is always lyrical, in contrast to the almost coarse sounds of the orchestra. The piano part is treated with great imagination and variability; the orchestra tends to repeat its music, unchanged. Carter created a dramatic instrumental work in which the conflict, as he described it, was like that "between an individual of many changing moods and thoughts and an orchestra treated more or less monolithically."[8]

The Concerto for Orchestra (1970) was commissioned by the New York Philharmonic Society for its 125th anniversary. Its general character was suggested to the composer by Vents ("Winds"), a Nobel-prize winning poem by St. John Perse, which speaks of winds sweeping the United States, constantly transforming the past into something new. The orchestra is divided into four groups, largely according to range:

SOPRANO	ALTO	TENOR	BASS
violins	violas	cellos	basses
flutes	oboes	bassoons	trombones
clarinets	trumpets	piano	tuba
metallic percussion	horns	marimba	timpani
	snare drums	harp	
		wooden percussion	

The music of each group is differentiated harmonically, rhythmically, and expressively. A different group dominates each of the four movements, which are linked without pause. The opening Allegro non troppo is dominated by the tenor group in phrases characterized by a repeated slowing of the pace in rubato style. The second movement, Presto volando, features the soprano group in fast, steady phrases. The phrases in the Maestoso third movement repeatedly increase in speed in the bass group, and the final Allegro agitato is dominated by the alto group in swelling phrases. Characteristically, the different groups and movements are thoroughly integrated throughout the work. It is truly a concerto for orchestra in that not only are different groups of the orchestra pitted against one another, but each instrument is cast in a solo role at one time or another.

Carter's Oboe Concerto (1986–87), composed for Heinz Holliger, is structured much like the Piano Concerto. The oboe is embedded in a concertino of four violas and percussion. The concertino in turn plays against a large orchestra that sounds forth with highly contrasting musical material.

NEO-ROMANTICS AND ECLECTICISM

During the 1950s, the Serialists tended to dominate musical composition in the United States and abroad, yet by the mid-1960s serialism had been rejected by many composers as too confining. In Europe composers moved to indeterminacy (Stockhausen) or to a style emphasizing textures and sonorities while de-emphasizing melody and harmony (Penderecki, Ligeti). Some United States composers followed the same trends, but others turned to an entirely different approach, initially stimulated by the sudden acquaintance with the music of an almost-unknown fellow American, Charles Ives (1874–1954). His music received a flurry of attention in the few years leading up to the 100th anniversary of his birth. These composers identified with Ives and the many sources of his eccentric brand of eclectic music and were stimulated to pursue a broad range of eclectic approaches to musical composition. They made use of a great diversity of styles, often integrating or juxtaposing them within the same piece. This eclectic approach typically refers to earlier styles, often accompanied by quotations from the works of previous composers, as in the music of Ives.

George Rochberg (b. 1918) wrote music that reflects these changed postures and approaches to composition. His thorough training in theory and composition supported the typically neo-Classical style of his earliest works from the 1940s. These works illustrate his assimilation of musical elements from Stravinsky, Hindemith, and Bartók. In 1950 he traveled to Italy to study the dodecaphonic technique with Luigi Dallapiccola and proceeded to write twelve-tone pieces in an expressionistic vein similar to Schoenberg's. As was typical of so many other young composers in the 1950s, he then turned to Webern's pointillistic, fragmented style as in Rochberg's *Cheltenham Concerto* for small orchestra (1958).

He became increasingly frustrated with the serial techniques that he had once viewed as liberating, and by the mid-1960s he had utterly rejected serialism. He found it too limiting in its "range of gestures that always seemed to channel the music into some form or other of expressionism." He further complained about "the over-intense manner of serialism and its tendency to inhibit physical pulse and rhythm;" this he felt made it "virtually impossible to express serenity, tranquillity, grace, wit, energy."[9] In his search for a new way to write music he turned to the music of other composers. With parody and "collage" techniques, he strung together bits and pieces of music written by others or bits of his own to make a new piece. The quite different music of Bach, Berio, Boulez, Ives, Mahler, Mozart, and Varèse could be juxtaposed and combined in the same piece. In the 1970s he carried this approach further to forge what he called a "multi-gestural" style in which different sections of a piece are based on different earlier styles, most notably those of the Classical, Romantic, and post-Romantic eras. In choosing to incorporate the musical language of the past in his own music, he recognized the central importance of tonality to his work. He discovered that tonality provided a flexible, comprehensible, and satisfying means of making music, and so by the mid-1970s had moved into a neo-Romantic style in the company of numerous other composers. This neo-Romanticism marked a return not only to tonality, but also to the forms, genres, and musical gestures of Romanticism, including its preoccupation with lyrical melody. Rochberg's Violin Concerto (1975) epitomizes this late-twentieth-century style.

Rochberg's Violin Concerto is thoroughly romantic in content, but of unusual form. It is in five movements symmetrically arranged around a central Fantasia— an adagio conceived as a memorial for a close friend. The Fantasia movement makes use of material from the first movement, which is the Introduction, and the fifth movement, the Epilogue. The second and fourth movements, immediately adjacent to the Fantasia, are called Intermezzo (A) and Intermezzo (B), and they share thematic material and contain cadenzas, the major one of which appears in Intermezzo (B). The concerto is scored for a large orchestra, which plays an important role in creating the various lush, lyrical, tender, and melancholy moods. The technical requirements of the solo part fall within the traditional use of the instrument, involving frequent multiple stops, for example. The piece ends quietly in D major, the traditionally strong violin key, used by Beethoven and Brahms for their violin concertos.

Rochberg's Violin Concerto was commissioned by the Pittsburgh Symphony in memory of Donald Steinfirst and was written for Isaac Stern. Stern first performed the work on 5 April 1975 with André Previn conducting.

John Corigliano (b. 1938) is one of the younger neo-Romantics whose eclectic music sounds modern, yet is readily accessible. Corigliano, a native of New York City, was trained at Columbia College and the Manhattan School of Music. He includes numerous and highly disparate elements in his musical scores; passages range from those containing simple triads, clear tonal progressions, and regular metrical organization to those embracing twelve-tone rows, tone clusters, wild metrical shifts, dissonant textures, and unusual sonorities. Some passages sound as though they have come out of the seventeenth century while others are clearly twentieth-century fare. Corigliano developed a profound sensitivity to the sounds and textures of the orchestra and its instruments during his father's twenty-three-year term as concertmaster of the New York Philharmonic. As a result, Corigliano is partial to the orchestra, which he uses quite effectively. His Oboe Concerto (1975) and Clarinet Concerto (1977) show this understanding of the orchestra and its members.

Corigliano's Clarinet Concerto was commissioned by the New York Philharmonic in the series of concertos written for its principal players, thanks to a gift from Francis Goelet. Stanley Drucker was the clarinetist and Leonard Bernstein the conductor in the first performance on 6 December 1977. The composer was well acquainted with Drucker's command of his instrument and with the strengths of other players in the orchestra, and successfully premised his piece on this intimate knowledge.

The Clarinet Concerto is in three movements. The first movement, "Cadenzas," features the clarinet in two cadenzas separated by an interlude. The clarinet gradually appears, playing as fast as possible in the first cadenza, subtitled "Will-o'-the-wisp," then gradually disappears. The thematic and harmonic materials of the movement are introduced in this cadenza. The second cadenza, subtitled "Corona solis" (the crown or corona of the sun), transforms the opening cadenza into bursts of energetic sound. The consistently quiet and introspective second movement is "Elegy" in memory of the composer's father who had recently died. A solo violin partakes of an effective dialogue with the clarinet in this movement, which is marked by long melodic lines. The third movement, "Antiphonal Toccata," brings in several instruments not used in the previous two movements: five horns, two trumpets, and two clarinets, which are dispersed to different locations in the auditorium. Corigliano, recognizing the problem of precise coordination of players dispersed in a large concert hall, wrote passages for these players that do not require precise synchronization. In contrast to these loose sections, he devised tight, regular, motoric rhythms characteristic of the toccata style. The often lyrical solo clarinet engages in discussion with various parts of the orchestra. An intriguing passage involves a dialogue between the solo clarinet and the two orchestral clarinets; the latter are to occupy places above the orchestra, thus adding a spatial dimension to the element of contrast.

EPILOGUE: THE ENDURING FORM

Important melodic material near the beginning and again near the end of the third movement of Corigliano's Clarinet Concerto is quoted from Giovanni Gabrieli's *Sonata Pian e Forte*. This takes us back to the roots of the concerto in the hands of the late sixteenth-century Venetian composers who first exploited the new concertante style. Nearly 400 years later the concerto is thriving in the hands of creative composers who remain fascinated with the possibilities for juxtaposing a solo instrument or group of solo instruments against an orchestra. Virtuosity, too, remains a vital element in our contemporary musical world, and its place in the music of the future seems assured. After all, gifted performers still wish to display their talents in new works composed for them. Audiences will continue to be thrilled by virtuosic display, and the best composers will continue to work such passages into their concertos in musically meaningful ways. And as composers discover new ways to write concertos, the fundamental duality of opposition and cooperation between soloist and orchestra will continue to lie at the heart of the form.

The concerto has flourished during its first three centuries, developing a sumptuously rich and amazingly varied history. It has continued to prove its vitality in the twentieth century and indications are that it will continue to do so in the future.

NOTES

Chapter One
THE CONCERTO PRINCIPLE

1. Modern editions of Gabrieli's Magnificat and "In ecclesiis," discussed next, are found in *Corpus Mensurabilis Musicae*, series 12, vols. 2 and 5, respectively. See music portion of Bibliography for details concerning music cited in the text that is not readily available in single editions.

2. The basso continuo (literally, continuous bass) was an invention of the early Baroque period, developed to form a simple chordal accompaniment for speech-like monody. Typically the basso continuo part is notated as bass line with numerical figures (hence, also known as figured bass) indicating in a well-understood abbreviation system the required harmony of the upper parts. Thus, the basso continuo performed two important functions: it provided both a strong independent bass line and the basic harmony. Normally two performers are required: one to play the bass on a single-line bass instrument and the other to play harmony as well as to reinforce the bass line on a keyboard or other chord-producing instrument. Intrinsic to the basso continuo idea was the concertato principle, involving the opposition of high versus low—a polarity of the outer voices that remained characteristic throughout the Baroque era. The basso continuo appears in most Baroque ensemble music and is unique to that period. Its function was gradually replaced by other means in the Classical era.

Chapter Two
THE EARLY CONCERTO GROSSO

1. The use of the term *tutti* has been modified during the concerto's long history, creating some confusion and inconsistency in current discussions of the concerto. Tutti initially referred to the united performance of solo and orchestral forces of the same musical material. Gradually, around 1800, tutti came to denote only the orchestra in some scores, and later in the nineteenth century this was almost consistently the case. Some writers on the concerto have adopted this later use and equated tutti with orchestra throughout the concerto's history. This is misleading, however, since most Baroque and Classical composers used *tutti* to indicate the combined forces. Mozart, in his violin concertos, for example, has the solo violin play along with orchestral first violins in tutti sections. Even in Mozart's piano concertos, where the piano is not given the main melodic material of the orchestra in the tutti sections, strong evidence suggests the keyboard artist functioned as continuo player when not playing solo material.

2. McCrickard 1971.

3. Jean Baptiste Lully (1632–1687) had also experimented with episodes for a trio of instruments, usually woodwind, in the orchestral dance music of some of his operas. Obviously the concept of a concerto grosso style of instrumentation was consistent with

Baroque style and was being developed by various composers in various centers at the same time. It was the Italian composers, however, who first fully developed the idea.

4. Newman 1983a, p. 157.

5. Hansell 1966, p. 401.

6. Corelli's use of the phrase *ad libitum* in Op. 6, No. 8, has been interpreted in various ways. For example, some contend it was used to inform the performers that improvised ornamentation is permitted in this movement, in contrast with the earlier Grave that is marked *come sta* (as it stands), indicating that this slow movement should not be decorated. Deas (1953) argues that the tied note linking the preceding Allegro to the pastorale is an indication that the latter is not optional. I conclude that Corelli marked the pastorale, a traditional Christmas Eve movement, as optional in the printed version so that the concerto could be played without the pastorale on occasions other than Christmas Eve.

7. Bukofzer 1947, p. 221.

Chapter Three
THE EARLY SOLO CONCERTO

1. Bukofzer 1947, p. 227.

2. Giazotto 1945.

3. Quantz 1985, p. 323.

Chapter Four
ANTONIO VIVALDI AND THE MATURE BAROQUE CONCERTO

1. The RV numbers identify specific works by Vivaldi as tabulated in Peter Ryom's authoritative catalog of the composer's music (see Bibliography entry, Ryom 1986). This catalog includes all of Vivaldi's music and provides a thematic incipit of all opening acts or movements of approximately 750 extant, or previously known and since lost, compositions. Valuable tables provide quick identification of Vivaldi's published works and concordances, coordinating Ryom's catalog numbers with those of previous catalogs by Rinaldi, Pincherle, and Fanna, as well as the work's volume number in the complete edition of Vivaldi's music published by Edizioni Ricordi. The work list in the *New Grove Dictionary of Music and Musicians* was prepared by Ryom and contains similar information in a condensed format, without the Fanna catalog numbers.

2. Quantz 1985, p. 179.

3. Kolneder 1970, p. 123.

4. One of the most interesting is found in the final movement of the D major Violin Concerto *fatto per la solennità della S. Lingua di S. Antonio in Padua 1712* (composed for the feast of the Holy Tongue of St. Antonio in Padua 1712, RV 212). This and one other are printed in their entirety in Kolneder 1979, pp. 52ff.

5. Some have asserted that the collections named by the composer and appearing in the earlier portion of each publication period contain the superior concertos. In support of this view, nine of the ten Vivaldi concertos transcribed by J. S. Bach were from the collections with fanciful titles. Op. 3 must have greatly interested the German composer, who arranged half of them for his own use. The following table lists the Vivaldi concertos and corresponding arrangements by Bach. No orchestra is called for in those indicated for organ. The keys in which Vivaldi and Bach scored each are indicated as the last statement within the parentheses; lower case indicates the minor mode.

Vivaldi Concertos		Corresponding Arrangement by Bach
Op. 3, No. 3, RV 310 (vln., G)	=	BWV 978 (hpsd., F)
Op. 3, No. 8, RV 522 (2 vlns., a)	=	BWV 593 (organ, a)
Op. 3, No. 9, RV 230 (vln., D)	=	BWV 972 (hpsd., D)
Op. 3, No. 10, RV 580 (4 vlns., b)	=	BWV 1065 (4 hpsd, a)
Op. 3, No. 11, RV 565 (2 vlns., d)	=	BWV 596 (organ, d)
Op. 3, No. 12, RV 265 (vln., E)	=	BWV 976 (hpsd., C)
Op. 4, No. 1, RV 383a (vln., B-flat)	=	BWV 980 (hpsd., G)
Op. 4, No .6, RV 316a (vln., g)	=	BWV 975 (hpsd., g)
Op. 7, No. 5, RV 285a (vln., F)	=	BWV 594 (organ, C)
Op. 8, No. 8, RV 332 (vln., g)	=	BWV 973 (hpsd., G)

Chapter Seven
JOHANN SEBASTIAN BACH

1. At the same time, Walther also made keyboard transcriptions of a number of concertos by diverse composers, including Albinoni, Vivaldi, and Torelli, among others.

2. Geiringer 1966, p. 318.

3. Besseler 1955. A slightly earlier version of Brandenburg Concerto No. 5 was edited later by A. Dürr in the *Neue Bach Ausgabe*, series 7, vol. 2 (supplement).

4. The *Stadtpfeifer* tradition was common in Germany from the fourteenth century. The *Stadtpfeifer*, or town piper, was one of a group of musicians who usually played wind instruments, employed by municipalities on various public occasions.

5. Krey 1961.

6. Brandenburg Concerto No. 1 is the only one of the six that calls for resources not immediately available at Cöthen. For this reason it may not have been performed there until September 1721, when, according to court records, the necessary pair of hornists was hired for a special performance. Cf. Smend 1951.

7. An example of such an extemporized movement is given in Krapf 1983, pp. 77–78.

8. The complete recapitulation of the closing of part 1 (mm. 5–12) as the closing of part 2, but transposed (mm. 41–48), recalls in a small way the early development of sonata form.

9. Bach referred to these instruments as "Fiauti [or Flauti] d'Echo," probably because of their echolike use in movement II. The term has caused some puzzlement as to the exact instrument intended. Most believe recorders were meant, but some feel Bach intended the transverse flute. Cf. Higbee 1962.

10. The term for the keyboard instrument in these works is the generic term *clavier*—meaning any keyboard instrument, but usually confined to those with strings, thus excluding the organ. It is generally assumed that a large two-manual harpsichord was the solo instrument intended in these works. Bach does, however, use the term *cembalo* or harpsichord in the concertos for more than one keyboard instrument.

11. W. Fischer's reconstructions are found in the *Neue Bach Ausgabe*, series 7, vol. 7 (supplement).

12. The lost violin concerto has been reconstructed by W. Fischer in the *Neue Bach Ausgabe*, series 7, vol. 7 (supplement). Some scholars believe too many elements in this concerto are foreign to Bach's style and so argue the original is not by Bach. Curiously though, opinion varies as to the identity of the original author. Some, for example, think it may have been by Vivaldi (cf. P. Hirsch 1929), while others see in it evidence of an early Classical style and so assign its present form to an arrangement by Carl Philipp Emanuel Bach (cf. Aber 1913). Bachian elements do occur, however, such as the characteristic use of pedal points, the cantilenas of the slow movements over a quasi-ostinato bass, and the driving ♪♫

rhythm with its associated motivic development of the finale. Counterbalancing these Bachian traits are a reliance on a less contrapuntal texture than the master usually employed and a more rigidly conceived bass line. I believe this is an original work by Bach.

13. The outer movements have been reconstructed as an oboe concerto by W. Fischer in the *Neue Bach Ausgabe,* series 7, vol. 7 (supplement).

Chapter Eight
THE EMERGENCE OF THE CLASSICAL CONCERTO

1. Green 1970.

2. Dounias 1935.

3. Simon 1954, pp. 45–48.

4. Boccherini's works are customarily identified by G numbers, which are assigned each work in Y. Gérard's comprehensive *Thematic, Bibliographical, and Critical Catalogue of the Works of Luigi Boccherini,* 1969.

5. Wolf 1981, p. 14.

6. White 1980, vol. 7, p. 397.

7. I have adopted the French term, *symphonie concertante,* for this form, because the form's history is so closely associated with France and the French term was more widely used than the Italian counterpart, *sinfonia concertante.* An exception will occur later when we discuss the most famous of all such works, that by Mozart for violin and viola, K. 364, since it is so well known under the Italian term. This may have come about because of the strong Italian influence in Salzburg, where Mozart wrote the piece, but Mozart's manuscript does not survive and there is no mention of this work in his letters, so that we do not know which term he applied to K. 364. Curiously, in Mozart's mention of other works in this form, he normally used the French term.

8. Brook 1980, vol. 18, p. 433.

9. A modern edition of C. P. E. Bach's Harpsichord Concerto in D Minor appears in *Denkmäler deutscher Tonkunst,* vol. 29–30, pp. 62–102.

10. Stevens 1965, pp. 97–101.

11. Crickmore 1958, p. 233.

12. Stevens 1965, pp. 109–110.

13. Stevens 1965, pp. 119–120.

14. See Simon 1957, pp. 114–115, for a discussion of this movement.

15. Newman 1983b, p. 707, notes that approximately eighty percent of Christian Bach's sonatas are in two movements and call for no key change between movements.

16. J. C. Bach may have even been the first to perform a solo piano concert in public anywhere in the world, although conclusive supporting evidence is not available.

17. The score of the first movement of J. C. Bach's Op. 7, No. 5, is readily accessible in the *Norton Anthology of Western Music,* No. 119.

18. Anderson 1989, p. 800.

Chapter Nine
WOLFGANG AMADEUS MOZART

1. Evidence, in the form of manuscript scores and solo parts, suggests the solo keyboard performer in a late eighteenth-century keyboard concerto followed an older tradition by playing along with the tutti sections in the style of a basso continuo realization. The tradition persisted even though the harmonic necessity of continuo instruments had already faded as composers filled in the vital harmonies in the orchestral parts. The autograph score of a work as late as Mozart's Piano Concerto in C Major, K. 503 (1786), includes the direction *col Basso* (with bass) in the piano part during the ritornellos. Such directions are rarely followed in modern performances, because the continuo part is not essential for the harmonic foundation and because the impact of the solo entry would be diminished by the earlier appearance of the keyboard instrument.

2. My understanding of Mozart's concerto-rondo form is much influenced by Green 1979, pp. 250–253.

3. Einstein 1945, p. 290.

4. The original sources of Mozart's early pasticcio-concertos (patchwork-concertos) are:

K. 7 in F:	I. Raupach, Op. 1, No. 5, I.
	II. Unknown—perhaps Mozart's own.
	III. Honauer, Op. 2, No. 3, I.
K. 39 in B-Flat:	I. Raupach, Op. 1, No. 1, I.
	II. Schobert, Op. 17, No. 2, I.
	III. Raupach, Op. 1, No. 1, III.
K. 40 in D:	I. Honauer, Op. 2, No. 1, I.
	II. Eckard, Op. 1, No. 4, single movement.
	III. C. P. E. Bach, *La Boehmer*, W. 117.
K. 41 in G:	I. Honauer, Op. 1, No. 1, I.
	II. Raupach, Op. 1, No. 1, II.
	III. Honauer, Op. 1, No. 1, III.

5. The numbering of Mozart's works used here follows the current convention. Most are identified by the numbers Köchel assigned them in his thematic catalog of Mozart's music. A few are identified by two numbers: In these cases the first number is Köchel's original, while the second is the revised number appearing in the 6th ed. of Köchel's chronology.

6. It is generally assumed that Mozart's earliest keyboard concertos were intended for the harpsichord and the later ones for the piano. Keyboard concertos of the transition period were probably suitable for either instrument, but the borderlines between periods are necessarily fuzzy. To reflect present-day practice in which audiences are apt to hear any of Mozart's concertos played on the piano and to simplify discussion, I shall refer to the piano as the solo instrument in all of Mozart's keyboard concertos. For further information relative to Mozart's keyboard instrument uses, see Broder 1941.

7. The date was stricken through on the autograph manuscript, but it had been thought to have read 3 May 1773, leading many earlier scholars to take this as Mozart's first original concerto-style composition. Modern technology has shown the date to be 31 May 1774. The Concertone was composed after the Piano Concerto K. 175.

8. Einstein 1945, p. 294.

9. The term *aperto* literally means open, and was usually used by musicians to refer to the open horn or, occasionally, the open strings of a stringed instrument. It was very unusual for a composer to use the term as part of a tempo and expression marking at the head of a movement; Mozart's uses of the term here, in the early Piano Concerto in B-flat Major, K. 238, and in the A Major Violin Concerto, K. 219, are some of the very few such occasions. Another meaning of the term is "broad," and *aperto* used in conjunction with the term *allegro* seems to denote a fast tempo with some feeling of expansiveness.

10. A symphonie concertante in E-flat for oboe, clarinet, horn, and bassoon, K. Anh. C14.01/297b, is in print and recorded under Mozart's name. It was once thought to be a reworking of the Parisian composition with oboe and clarinet replacing flute and oboe, respectively. But its authenticity is now in doubt, the only source being a mid-nineteenth-century manuscript.

11. Einstein 1945, p. 277.

12. In most modern performances violists retain normal tuning but play the part as though it were written in E-flat, largely out of the fear that the extra tension on the tuning pegs will lead them to slip during the performance.

13. A fragment of this work, K. Anh. 104/320e, containing 134 measures, fifty-seven fully scored, survives. Nothing is known about the circumstances surrounding its composition.

14. Landon 1956, p. 256.

15. Quoted by Reginald Morely-Pegge 1980, p. 699.

16. The dating of three of these works is certain because the dated autograph manuscripts survive: K. 371 (21 March 1781), K. 417 (27 May 1783), and K. 495 (26 June 1786). The dates of the other three are less certain and even confused. The autograph of K. 447 was not dated by Mozart, but its call for clarinets and bassoons in the orchestra suggests a late date, perhaps 1786 or later. However, the work is not entered in Mozart's thematic catalog, which he began to keep in February 1784, and no other work of comparable importance is omitted, suggesting K. 447 was composed prior to February 1784, and probably after the summer of 1783. Further confusing the issue is the fact that Mozart used two sequences of page numbers in the score: one for movement I and the other for movements II and III, suggesting separate dates of composition. (See King 1978, p. 62.)

The history of K. 412/386b is even more confused. The autograph, possibly from 1782, provides a completely scored first movement and a draft score for strings only of the rondo. A more complete version of the rondo (formerly identified as K. 514) is dated 6 April 1797 and includes oboes, but not bassoons, which appear in movement I. This manuscript was previously taken as an autograph simply misdated by Mozart for 1787, but it is now known to be in a handwriting other than Mozart's; the original autograph disappeared in World War II, leaving us with the printed text of the non-Mozart manuscript. (See King 1978, pp. 58–59 and Köchel, 6th ed., p. 428.) In complete contradiction of an early date of composition, Sadie, in his Mozart article in NG (XII, 707), contends the date can firmly be set as 1791. The E major fragment, K. 494a, is difficult to date; the 6th ed. of Köchel's catalog places it "perhaps in July 1786."

17. Quoted from Italian in Köchel 6th ed., p. 428. King 1978, p. 58, quotes a bit more in addition to identifying the location of some remarks.

18. Anderson 1989, p. 833.

19. Anderson 1989, p. 877.

20. A bassoon might well have doubled the bass line in the earlier concertos, but in K. 450 the bassoons are given meaningful independent parts.

Chapter Ten
FRANZ JOSEPH HAYDN

1. The score of Hob. XIV:C2 is published as No. 325 in the series *Diletto musicale*.

2. The score of Hob. XIV:12 is published as No. 323 in the series *Diletto musicale*.

3. Geiringer 1982, p. 217.

4. Landon 1976–1980, vol. 2, p. 344, notes that Haydn made two entries, of which one was later canceled, for the G Major Concerto in his draft catalog "slightly before 1770." Hoboken writes "before 1782" as the date of composition in his thematic catalog.

5. Landon 1976–1980, vol. 2, p. 344.

6. Landon 1976–1980, vol. 2, p. 509.

7. Geiringer 1982, p. 295; Ripin 1981, p. 306; Landon 1976–1980, vol. 2, p. 572.

8. The scores of the violin concertos may be found in *Joseph Haydn: Werke*, series 3, vol. 1.

9. The functional need for the basso continuo faded long before the convention of scoring for it and using it in performance came to an end. The phasing out of the basso continuo was particularly marked in the early 1770s, as melody instruments playing in the inner texture were increasingly called upon to fill out the harmony. Inclusion of the basso continuo in the performance of most works from this time period is desirable if not clearly contraindicated.

10. Landon believes that after completing the Trumpet Concerto, Haydn may have composed a concerto for two horns and one for bassoon, which are now lost. Landon 1976–1980, vol. 4, p. 226.

11. Landon 1976–1980, vol. 4, p. 235.

Chapter Eleven
LUDWIG VAN BEETHOVEN

1. WoO is the abbreviation for *Werk ohne Opuszahl*, meaning a work without opus number. Beethoven's surviving works in this category are assigned identifying numbers in Kinsky 1955.

2. These themes are given in Thayer 1967, pp. 126–127.

3. WoO5 is contained in the Supplement to the *Beethoven Gesamtausgabe*, vol. 3, pp. 44–69. The fragment was first published in the supplement to Schiedermair, *Der Junge Beethoven*, pp. 427–478.

4. Kinsky 1955, p. 92.

5. Thayer 1967, pp. 329–330.

6. Wade 1977, p. 271.

7. Tovey 1936, p. 80.

8. Jander 1985, pp. 195–212.

9. Solomon 1977, p. 361.

10. See Lockwood 1970, Cook 1989, and Lockwood 1990 for discussions of the manuscript sources of Beethoven's unfinished piano concerto.

11. Schwarz 1958.

12. Schwarz 1958, p. 442.

Chapter Thirteen
SPOHR AND WEBER

1. Schwarz 1983, p. 243.

Chapter Fifteen
THE SUMMIT OF VIRTUOSITY: PAGANINI AND LISZT

1. Schwarz 1983, p. 195.

2. Walker 1983, p. 151.

3. Hinson 1983 is the principal source of information concerning Liszt's Hungarian Concerto.

Chapter Sixteen
SCHUMANN AND BRAHMS

1. Schumann 1965, pp. 146–147.

2. Two other works begun about the same time had even longer gestation periods. The Symphony No. 1 in C Minor, begun in 1855, was not completed until 1876, while the Piano Quartet in C Minor, Op. 60, also begun in 1855, was completed in 1875. The Piano Quintet in F Minor, Op. 34, begun in 1861 and completed in 1865, went through changes similar to those of the D Minor Concerto. The Piano Quintet began as a string quintet, becoming a sonata for two pianos, before finding its form as a quintet for piano and strings. In an unusual move, Brahms published the Piano Quintet version as Op. 34a and the Sonata for Two Pianos as Op. 34b.

3. Tovey 1936, p. 126.

4. Kalbeck 1909, p. 134.

5. Litzman 1913, vol. 2, p. 392.

Chapter Seventeen
GRIEG, DVOŘÁK, AND OTHERS

1. Kurz's revised piano part is included directly beneath Dvořák's in the score of the *Antonín Dvořák Gesamtausgabe*.

2. Clapham 1966, p. 104.

3. May [1948], vol. 2, p. 663.

Chapter Eighteen
THE CONCERTO IN RUSSIA

1. Piggott 1974, pp. 49–50.

Chapter Twenty
THE CONCERTO IN THE SOVIET UNION

1. Nestyev 1960, p. 83.

Chapter Twenty-One
THE CONCERTO IN BRITAIN

1. Kennedy 1987, pp. 160–162.

2. De-la-Noy 1983, pp. 157–158.

3. Walton 1988, p. 90.

4. I wonder if the prominent use of timpani in the Violin Concerto of Peter Maxwell Davies was prompted by their important role in Beethoven's Violin Concerto. Beethoven also incorporated timpani in the cadenza he wrote for the arrangement he made of that work as a piano concerto.

5. "Defining" 1976.

Chapter Twenty-Three
STRAVINSKY, RAVEL, AND NEO-CLASSICISM IN FRANCE

1. White 1979, p. 401.

2. Downes 1981, p. 735.

3. Machlis 1979, p. 202.

4. Daniel 1982, p. 149.

Chapter Twenty-Four
FIVE IMPORTANT EARLY TWENTIETH-CENTURY COMPOSERS

1. The opus number and publication year of Schoenberg's compositions frequently have parallel numeric sequences, e.g., Op. 23 and 1923. Schoenberg, an extremely superstitious man, often withheld publication of a composition until its opus number matched the year. He believed that by doing so he would magically insure its success. Thus, for example, much of Op. 23 was completed by 1920.

2. Stephan 1972, p. 9.

3. Jarman 1985, p. 153.

4. Berg's "Open Letter" appears in English translation in Brand et al. 1987, pp. 334–337, and Reich 1965, pp. 143–148.

5. Jarman 1985, pp. 153–155.

6. Brand et al. 1987, p. 337.

7. Berg details these references to the number *three* in his "Open Letter." See Brand et al. 1987, pp. 334–337, and Reich 1965, pp. 143–148.

8. Dalen 1989. See also Floros 1987.

9. Liebleitner 1892.

10. Knaus 1976.

11.. Hansen 1978, p. 230.

12. Stevens 1964, p. 280.

13. Stevens 1964, p. 102.

14. Serly 1975.

Chapter Twenty-Five
OTHER COMPOSERS IN EUROPE, LATIN AMERICA, AND CANADA

1. There is one notable exception in the eighteenth-century composer Antonio Soler (1729–1783) who wrote six concertos for two organs without orchestra. These are light works, five of which are in the common *galant* form of two movements; Soler favored a fast first movement followed by a minuet with variations. These concertos were intended for performance by Soler and his royal pupil, Prince Gabriel.

2. Demarquez 1968, p. 163.

3. Bayer 1980, p. 760.

4. Dutilleux 1987.

Chapter Twenty-Six
THE CONCERTO IN THE UNITED STATES

1. Downes 1981, p. 352.

2. Butterworth 1985, p. 30.

3. Duke Ellington (1899–1974), surely the most significant jazz composer in the history of the genre, wrote a number of short, concerto-like works for his band. Ellington was particularly noted for his ability to shape his music according to the peculiar talents of the members of his band, and it is not surprising that he created specific pieces to showcase the talents of specific players. Pieces such as "Concerto for Cootie" (for Cootie Williams, trumpet, 1940); "Clarinet Lament" (for Barney Bigard, clarinet, 1936); "Cotton Tail" (for Ben Webster, tenor saxophone, 1940); and "Jeep's Blues" (for Johnny Hodges, alto saxophone, 1939) are really mini-concertos in which the music is tailor-made for the featured soloist, who interacts with the band in animated ways. Improvisation, of course, played a major role in the performance of these pieces.

4. Copland 1968, p. 153.

5. Schuller 1968; Schuller 1989.

6. Saylor 1980.

7. Cage 1959.

8. Schiff 1983, p. 228.

9. Rochberg 1973.

BIBLIOGRAPHY

BOOKS AND ARTICLES

Abbreviations

JAMS   *Journal of the American Musicological Society, 1948–*.
M&L   *Music and Letters, 1920–*.
MQ   *The Musical Quarterly, 1915–*.
NG   *The New Grove Dictionary of Music and Musicians,* ed. Stanley Sadie (London: Macmillan, 1980).

Aber, Adolf. 1913. "Studien zu J. S. Bachs Klavierkonzerten." *Bach-Jahrbuch* 10:5–30.

Abraham, Gerald, ed. 1982. *The New Oxford History of Music.* Vol. 7, *The Age of Beethoven: 1790–1830.* London: Oxford University Press.

Anderson, Emily, ed. and trans. 1989. *The Letters of Mozart and His Family.* New York: W. W. Norton.

Bayer, Francis. 1980. "Dutilleux, Henri." NG 5:760–761.

Besseler, Heinrich. 1955. "Zur Chronologie der Konzerte Joh. Seb. Bachs." *Festschrift Max Schneider zum achtzigsten Geburtstag.* Ed. Walther Vetter. Leipzig.

Boyden, David D. 1957. "When is a Concerto not a Concerto?" MQ 43:220–232.

Brand, Juliane, Christopher Hailey, and Donald Harris. 1987. *The Berg-Schoenberg Correspondence: Selected Letters.* New York: W. W. Norton.

Broder, Nathan. 1941. "Mozart and the 'Clavier.' " MQ 27:422. Reprinted in Lang, ed. *The Creative World of Mozart,* 1963.

Brook, Barry S. 1980. "Symphonie concertante." NG 18:433–438.

Brown, Clive. 1984. *Louis Spohr: A Critical Biography.* Cambridge: Cambridge University Press.

Bukofzer, Manfred. 1947. *Music in the Baroque Era.* New York: W. W. Norton.

Burney, Charles. 1776–1789. *A General History of Music from Earliest Ages to the Present.* 4 vols. London: Printed for the author. Reprinted with critical and historical notes by Frank Mercer. London: Foulis; New York: Harcourt, 1935. 4 vols. in 2. Reprint of the Mercer ed. New York: Dover, 1965.

Butterworth, Neil. 1985. *The Music of Aaron Copland.* [Gloucester]: Toccata Press.

Cage, John. 1959. Notes for "The 25-Year Retrospective Concert of the Music of John Cage." Album produced by George Avakian. N.p.

Carner, Mosco. 1983. *Alban Berg: The Man and the Work.* 2nd ed. New York: Holmes & Meier Publishers.

Chase, Gilbert. 1966. *America's Music: From the Pilgrims to the Present.* 2nd ed. New York: McGraw-Hill Book Co.

Chissell, Joan. 1952. "The Concertos." *Benjamin Britten: A Commentary on His Works from a Group of Specialists.* Ed. Donald Mitchell and Hans Keller. Westport, Conn.: Greenwood Press.

Clapham, John. 1966. *Antonín Dvořák: Musician and Craftsman.* London: Faber & Faber.

Cook, Nicholas. 1989. "Beethoven's Unfinished Piano Concerto: A Case of Double Vision?" JAMS 42:338–374.

Cooper, Martin, ed. 1974. *The New Oxford History of Music*. Vol. 10, *The Modern Age: 1890–1960*. London: Oxford University Press.

Copland, Aaron. 1968. *The New Music: 1900–1960*. New York: W. W. Norton.

Crickmore, Leon. 1958. "C. P. E. Bach's Harpsichord Concertos." M&L 39:227–241.

Dalen, Brenda. 1989. "'Freundschaft, Liebe, und Welt': The Secret Programme of the Chamber Concerto." *The Berg Companion*. Ed. Douglas Jarman. London: Macmillan Press.

Daniel, Keith W. 1982. *Francis Poulenc: His Artistic Development and Musical Style*. Ann Arbor: UMI Research Press.

Davies, Richard. 1965. "The Music of J. N. Hummel: Its Derivations and Developments." *The Music Review* 26:169–191.

Deas, Stewart. 1953. "Arcangelo Corelli." M&L 34:1–11.

"Defining their Roles." 1976. *Opera News* 40 (14 February 1977), 16. Unsigned article.

De-la-Noy, Michael. 1983. *Elgar: The Man*. London: Allen Lane.

Demarquez, Suzanne. 1968. *Manuel de Falla*. Translated from the Spanish by Salvato Attanasio. Philadelphia: Chilton Book Co.

Desautels, Andrée. 1969. "The History of Canadian Composition 1610–1967." *Aspects of Music in Canada*. Ed. Arnold Walker. Toronto: University of Toronto Press.

Dounias, Minos. 1935. *Die Violinkonzerte Giuseppe Tartinis*. Wolfenbüttel, Berlin: Kallmeyer.

Downes, Edward. 1981. *Guide to Symphonic Music*. New York: Walker and Co.

Drummond, Pippa. 1980. *The German Concerto: Five Eighteenth-Century Studies*. Oxford: Clarendon Press.

Dutilleux, Henri. 1987. Notes for recording of Violin Concerto, Columbia CBS MK 42449.

Einstein, Alfred. 1945. *Mozart: His Character, His Work*. New York: Oxford University Press.

Emery, Frederick Barclay. 1969. *The Violin Concerto*. New York: Da Capo Press.

Engel, Hans. 1970. *Die Entwicklung des deutschen Klavierkonzerts von Mozart bis Liszt*. Hildesheim: Olms. Reprint of Leipzig ed. of 1927.

_____ . 1971. *Das Instrumentalkonzert*. Wiesbaden: Breitkopf & Härtel.

Evans, Peter. 1979. *The Music of Benjamin Britten*. London: J. M. Dent & Sons, Ltd.

Fiske, Roger. 1971. *Beethoven Concertos and Overtures*. Seattle: University of Washington Press.

Floros, Constanin. 1987. "Das verschwiegene Programm des Kammerkonzerts von Alban Berg: Eine semantische Analyse." NZ: Neue Zeitschrift für Musik 110:11–22.

Forman, Denis. 1971. *Mozart's Concerto Form: The First Movements of the Piano Concertos*. London: Rupert Hart-Davis.

Geiringer, Karl, with Irene Geiringer. 1954. *The Bach Family: Seven Generations of Creative Genius*. London: George Allen & Unwin, Ltd.

_____ . 1966. *Johann Sebastian Bach: The Culmination of an Era*. New York: Oxford University Press.

_____ . 1982. *Haydn: A Creative Life in Music*. 3rd ed. Berkeley: University of California Press.

Giazotto, Remo. 1945. *Tomaso Albinoni*. Milan: Fratelli Bocca.

Girdlestone, Cuthbert. 1964. *Mozart and His Piano Concertos*. New York: Dover. Unabridged and corrected reprint of the 2nd edition first published by Cassell & Co., Ltd., London as *Mozart's Piano Concertos*.

Green, Douglass M. 1970. "Progressive and Conservative Tendencies in the Violoncello Concertos of Leonardo Leo." *Studies in Eighteenth-Century Music*. Ed. H. C. Robbins Landon and Roger Chapman. New York: Oxford University Press.

_____ . 1979. *Form in Tonal Music*. 2nd ed. New York: Holt, Rinehart and Winston.

Hamm, Charles. 1983. *Music in the New World*. New York: W. W. Norton.

Hansell, Sven Hostrop. 1966. "Orchestral Practice at the Court of Cardinal Pietro Ottoboni." JAMS 19:398–403.

Hansen, Peter S. 1978. *An Introduction to Twentieth Century Music*. 4th ed. Boston: Allyn and Bacon, Inc.

Higbee, Dale. 1962. "Bach's 'fiauti d'echo.' " M&L 43:192–193.

Hindemith, Paul. 1952. *A Composer's World: Horizons and Limitations*. Garden City, N.Y.: Doubleday & Co., Inc.

_____. 1941–45. *The Craft of Musical Composition*. 2 vols. Translated from the German by Arthur Mendel. New York: Associated Music Publishers, Inc.

Hinson, Maurice. 1983. "The Long Lost Liszt Concerto." *Clavier* 22:21–23.

Hirsch, Paul. 1929. "Über die Vorlage zum Klavierkonzert in d-moll." *Bach-Jahrbuch* 26:153–174.

Hitchcock, H. Wiley. 1974. *Music in the United States: A Historical Introduction*. 2nd ed. Englewood Cliffs, N.J.: Prentice-Hall.

Hoboken, Anthony van. 1957. *Joseph Haydn: Thematisch-bibliographisches Werkverzeichnis*. Vol. 1. *Instrumentalwerke*. Mainz: B. Schott's Söhne.

Hutchings, Arthur. 1950. *A Companion to Mozart's Piano Concertos*. 2nd ed. London: Oxford University Press.

_____. 1973. *The Baroque Concerto*. 3rd ed. London: Faber & Faber.

Jander, Owen. 1985. "Beethoven's 'Orpheus in Hades': The *Andante con moto* of the Fourth Piano Concerto." *19th Century Music* 8:195–212.

_____. 1965. "Concerto Grosso Instrumentation in Rome in the 1660's and 1670's." JAMS 21:168–180.

Jarman, Douglas. 1985. *The Music of Alban Berg*. Berkeley: University of California Press.

Kalbeck, Max, ed. 1909. *Johannes Brahms: The Herzogenberg Correspondence*. Translated from the German by Hannah Bryant. London: John Murray. Reprint. New York: Vienna House, 1971.

Kemp, Ian. 1970. *Hindemith*. London: Oxford University Press.

Kennedy, Michael. 1987. *Portrait of Elgar*. New ed. Oxford: Oxford University Press.

King, A. Hyatt. 1978. *Mozart Wind and String Concertos*. Seattle: University of Washington Press.

Kinsky, Georg, and Hans Halm. 1955. *Das Werk Beethovens: Thematisch-Bibliographisches Verzeichnis. . . .* Munich: Henle.

Knaus, Herwig. 1976. "Berg's Carinthian Folk Tune." *Musical Times* 117:487.

Kolneder, Walter. 1968. *Anton Webern: An Introduction to His Works*. Translated from the German by Humphrey Searle. Berkeley: University of California Press.

_____. 1970. *Antonio Vivaldi: His Life and Work*. Translated from the German by Bill Hopkins. London: Faber & Faber.

_____. 1979. *Performance Practices in Vivaldi*. Translated from German by Anne de Dadelsen. Winterthur, Switzerland: Amadeus Verlag.

Köchel, Ludwig von. 1862. *Chronologisch-thematisches Verzeichnis sämtlicher Tonwerke Wolfgang Amadeus Mozarts*. Leipzig: Breitkopf & Härtel. 6th ed. Ed. F. Giegling, A. Weinmann, and G. Sievers. Wiesbaden: Breitkopf & Härtel, 1964.

Krapf, Gerhard. 1983. *Bach: Improvised Ornamentation and Keyboard Cadenzas: An Approach to Creative Performance*. Dayton, Ohio: The Sacred Music Press.

Krey, Johannes. 1961. "Zur Entstehungsgeschichte des ersten Brandenburgischen Konzerts." *Festschrift Heinrich Besseler zum sechzigsten Geburtstag*. Leipzig. Deutscher Verlag für Musik.

Landon, H. C. Robbins. 1956. "The Concertos: (2) Their Musical Origin and Development." *The Mozart Companion*. New York: W. W. Norton.

_____. 1976–1980. *Haydn: Chronicle and Works*. Vol. 1, *The Early Years, 1732–1765*. Vol. 2, *Haydn at Esterháza, 1766–1790*. Vol. 3, *Haydn in England, 1791–1795*. Vol. 4, *Haydn: The Years of "The Creation," 1796–1800*. Vol. 5, *Haydn: The Late Years, 1801–1809*. Bloomington: University of Indiana Press.

Lang, Paul Henry, ed. 1963. *The Creative World of Mozart*. New York: W. W. Norton.

Layton, Robert, ed. 1988. *A Companion to the Concerto*. London: Christopher Helm.

Liebleitner, Karl. 1892. *Wulfenia—Blüten: Einige fünfzig Lieder und Jodler aus Kärnten*. Vienna: Universal Edition.

Litzman, Bertold. 1913. *Clara Schumann: An Artist's Life Based on Material Found in Diaries and*

Letters. Translated and abridged from the 4th German ed. by Grace E. Hadow. 2 vols. London, Macmillan and Co., Ltd. Reprint. New York: Vienna House, 1972.

Lockwood, Lewis. 1970. "Beethoven's Unfinished Piano Concerto of 1815: Sources and Problems." MQ 56:624–646. Reprinted in Paul Henry Lang, ed. *The Creative World of Beethoven*. New York: W. W. Norton, 1971.

———. 1990. "Communications." JAMS 43:376–382.

MacDonald, Malcolm. 1987. *Schoenberg*. London: J. M. Dent & Sons, Ltd.

Machlis, Joseph. 1979. *Introduction to Contemporary Music*. 2nd ed. New York: W. W. Norton.

May, Florence. [1948]. *The Life of Brahms*. 2nd ed. 2 vols. London: William Reeves.

McCrickard, Eleanor Fowler. 1971. *Alessandro Stradella's Instrumental Music: A Critical Edition with Historical and Analytical Commentary*. Unpublished Ph.D. dissertation, University of North Carolina.

McGee, Timothy J. 1985. *The Music of Canada*. New York: W. W. Norton.

Mekota, Beth Anna. 1969. *The Solo and Ensemble Keyboard Works of Johann Christian Bach*. Unpublished Ph.D. dissertation, University of Michigan.

Morely-Pegge, Reginald. 1980. "Leutgeb, Joseph." NG 10:699.

Münster, Robert. 1980. "Toeschi." NG 19:24–25.

Nestyev, Israel V. 1960. *Prokofiev*. Translated from the Russian by Florence Jonas. Stanford: Stanford University Press.

Newman, William S. 1983a. *The Sonata in the Baroque Era*. 4th ed. New York: W. W. Norton.

———. 1983b. *The Sonata in the Classic Era*. 3rd ed. New York: W. W. Norton.

Orenstein, Arbie. 1975. *Ravel: Man and Musician*. New York: Columbia University Press.

Piggott, Patrick. 1974. *Rachmaninov Orchestral Music*. London: BBC.

Plantinga, Leon. 1984. *Romantic Music*. New York: W. W. Norton.

Proctor, George A. 1980. *Canadian Music of the Twentieth Century*. Toronto: University of Toronto Press.

Quantz, Johann Joachim. 1985. *On Playing the Flute*. 2nd ed. Translated with notes and an introduction by Edward R. Reilly. London: Faber and Faber.

Radcliffe, Philip. 1978. *Mozart Piano Concertos*. Seattle: University of Washington Press.

Randel, Don Michael. 1986. *The New Harvard Dictionary of Music*. Cambridge, Mass.: The Belknap Press of Harvard University Press.

Reich, Willi. 1965. *Alban Berg*. Translated from the German by Cornelius Cardew. New York: Vienna House.

Ripin, Edwin M. 1981. "Haydn and the Keyboard Instruments of His Time." *Haydn Studies*. Ed. Jens Peter Larsen, Howard Serwer, and James Webster. New York: W. W. Norton.

Rochberg, George. 1973. Liner notes for Nonesuch Recording H 71283. G. Rochberg, *String Quartet No. 3*.

Ryom, Peter. 1986. *Répertoire des Oeuvres d'Antonio Vivaldi*. Copenhagen: Engstrom & Sødring.

Sadie, Stanley, ed. 1980. *The New Grove Dictionary of Music and Musicians*. 20 vols. [NG] London: MacMillan.

Saylor, Bruce. 1980. "Cowell, Henry." NG 5:8–12.

Schiff, David. 1983. *The Music of Elliott Carter*. London: Eulenburg Books.

Schuller, Gunther. 1968. *Early Jazz: Its Roots and Musical Development*. New York: Oxford University Press.

———. 1989. *The Swing Era: The Development of Jazz 1930–1945*. New York: Oxford University Press.

Schumann, Robert. 1965. *Schumann on Music: A Selection from the Writings*. Translated from the German and ed. by Henry Pleasants. New York: Dover. 1988 reprint, with corrections. Originally published as *The Musical World of Robert Schumann: A Selection from His Own Writings*. London: Gollancnz, 1965.

Schwarz, Boris. 1958. "Beethoven and the French Violin School." MQ 44:431–447.

———. 1983. *Great Masters of the Violin*. New York: Simon and Schuster.

Schwinger, Wolfram. 1979. *Krzysztof Penderecki: His Life and Work*. London: Schott.

Serly, Tibor. 1975. "A Belated Account of the Reconstruction of a 20th Century Master-piece." *College Music Symposium* 15:7–25.

Simon, Edwin Julien. 1954. *The Double Exposition in Classical Concerto Form*. Unpublished Ph.D. dissertation, University of California, Berkeley.

———. 1957. "The Double Exposition in the Classic Concerto." JAMS 10:111–118.

Simpson, Robert. 1979. *Carl Nielsen: Symphonist*. New York: Taplinger Publishing Company.

Smend, Friedrich. 1951. *Bach in Köthen*. Berlin: Christlicher Zeitschriftenverlag.

Solomon, Maynard. 1977. *Beethoven*. New York: Schirmer Books.

Stephan, Rudolf. 1972. Preface to Arnold Schoenberg, *Klavierkonzert*, Op. 42. Vienna: Universal Edition (Philharmonia Scores).

Stevens, Halsey. 1964. *The Life and Music of Béla Bartók*. Rev. ed. London: Oxford University Press.

Stevens, Jane R. 1965. *The Keyboard Concertos of Carl Philipp Emanuel Bach*. Unpublished Ph.D. dissertation, Yale University.

Swalin, Benjamin F. 1941. *The Violin Concerto*. Chapel Hill, N.C.: University of North Carolina Press. Reprint. New York: Da Capo Press, 1973.

Tawaststjerna, Erik. 1976. *Sibelius*. Vol. 1, *1865–1905*. Translated from the Finnish by Robert Layton. Berkeley, University of California Press.

Thayer, Alexander Wheelock. 1967. *Thayer's Life of Beethoven*. Rev. and ed. by Elliott Forbes. Princeton, N.J.: Princeton University Press.

Tovey, Donald Francis. 1936. *Essays in Musical Analysis*. Vol. 3, *Concertos*. London: Oxford University Press.

Veinus, Abraham. 1964. *The Concerto*. New York: Dover Publications, Inc.

Wade, Rachel. 1977. "Beethoven's Eroica Sketchbook." *Fontes Artis Musicae*, 24:254–289.

Warrack, John. 1976. *Carl Maria von Weber*. 2nd ed. Cambridge: Cambridge University Press.

Walker, Alan. 1983. *Franz Liszt*. Vol. 1, *The Virtuoso Years: 1811–1847*. New York: Alfred A. Knopf.

———, ed. 1972. *Robert Schumann: The Man and His Music*. London: Barrie & Jenkins, Ltd.

Walton, Susana. 1988. *William Walton: Behind the Facade*. Oxford: Oxford University Press.

White, Chappell. 1980. "Giornovichi, Giovanni Manne." NG 7:397–398.

White, Eric Walter. 1979. *Stravinsky: The Composer and His Works*. 2nd ed. Berkeley: University of California Press.

Wolf, Eugene K. 1981. *The Symphonies of Johann Stamitz: A Study in the Formation of the Classic Style*. Utrecht: Bohn, Scheltema & Holkema.

MUSIC

Most of the musical works referred to in this book are readily available in single editions. The few that are not are listed below by composer and are largely contained within the collected editions of the relevant composer or selected monuments of music.

Bach, C. P. E. Concerto for Harpsichord in D Minor, W. 23. *Denkmäler deutscher Tonkunst*, vol. 29–30, pp. 62–102. *Instrumentalkonzerte Deutscher Meister*. Ed. by Arnold Schering. Leipzig: Breitkopf & Härtel, 1906; New ed. by Hans Joachim Moser, Wiesbaden, 1958.

Bach, J. C. Concerto for Keyboard Instrument in E-Flat Major, Op. 7, No. 5. *Norton Anthology of Western Music*, ed. Claude V. Palisca. No. 119. New York: Norton, 1988.

Bach, J. S. Brandenburg Concerto No. 5 in D Major, Early Version. *Neue Bach Ausgabe*, series 7, vol. 2 (Supplement). Ed. Alfred Dürr. Kassel and Basel: Bärenreiter, 1975.

Bach, J. S. Lost Solo Concertos in Reconstruction. *Neue Bach Ausgabe*, series 7, vol. 7 (Supplement). Ed. Wilfried Fischer. Kassel and Basel: Bärenreiter, 1970.

Beethoven, Ludwig van. Concerto for Violin in C Major, WoO5, fragment. *Beethoven*

Gesamtausgabe, Supplement, vol. 3, pp. 44–69. Ed. Willy Hess. Wiesbaden: Breitkopf & Härtel. 1960. Previously published in Schiedermair, Ludwig. *Der junge Beethoven.* Leipzig: Quelle & Meyer, (1925).

Dvořák, Antonín. Concerto for Piano in G Major, Op. 33. *Antońn Dvořák Gesamtausgabe,* series 3, vol. 10. Ed. Otakar Šourek, with both Dvořák's original piano part and the revised piano part by Vilém Kurz. Prague: Supraphon, 1965.

Gabrieli, Giovanni. "Magnificat," from *Sacrae Symphoniae,* Part I. *Corpus Mensurabilis Musicae,* series 12, vol. 2, pp. 44–69. Ed. Denis Arnold. Rome: American Institute of Musicology, 1959.

Gabrieli, Giovanni. *In ecclesiis* from *Sacrae Symphoniae,* Part II. *Corpus Mensurabilis Musicae,* series 12, vol. 5, pp. 32–55. Ed. Denis Arnold. Rome: American Institute of Musicology, 1969.

Haydn, Joseph. Concerto for Harpsichord in C Major, Hob. XIV:12. *Diletto Musicale,* No. 323. Ed. H. C. Robbins Landon. Vienna: Doblinger, 1969.

Haydn, Joseph. Concertos for Violin, Hob. VIIa:1, 3, 4*. *Joseph Haydn Werke,* series 3, vol 1. Ed. Heinz Lohmann and Günter Thomas. Munich: G. Henle, 1969.

Haydn, Joseph. Divertimento for Harpsichord in C Major, Hob. XIV:C2. *Diletto Musicale,* No. 325. Ed. H. C. Robbins Landon. Vienna: Doblinger, 1969.

INDEX

Page numbers in **boldface** type indicate the more important references; *italic* numbers indicate illustrations or their captions.

CPSIA information can be obtained
at www.ICGtesting.com
Printed in the USA
LVOW03s1433170117

521252LV00001B/41/P